Western

CW01262035

A rock climbing guidebook
to selected routes
on the western edges
and quarries
of the Peak District,
south Lancashire
and Cheshire

Text, topos, photo-topos, maps
Chris Craggs and Alan James
Additional editing Jack Geldard

Photos by Chris Craggs
unless otherwise credited

All maps by ROCKFAX
Some maps based on source maps kindly supplied by
Collins Maps (www.collins.co.uk)

Printed by John Browns Printers, Nottingham
Distributed by Cordee
(Tel: (+int) 44 (0) 145 561 1185)

Published by ROCKFAX Ltd. April 2009
© ROCKFAX Ltd. 2009

All rights reserved. No part of this publication may be reproduced, stored in a retrieval system, or transmitted in any form or by any means, electronic, mechanical, photocopying or otherwise without prior written permission of the copyright owner.
A CIP catalogue record is available from the British Library

All Rockfax books are printed in the UK.
We only use paper made from wood fibre from sustainable forests and produced according to ISO 14001 environmental standard

ISBN 978-1-873341-22-3

www.rockfax.com

This page: Ramshaw's jagged ridge catching the evening light.
Photo: Jon Read

Western Grit 2003
Winner of the Outdoor Writers Guild Guidebook of the Year Award 2004
"A virtually flawless climbing guide - an admirable and practical book - extraordinary clarity"
OWG Judges, November 2004

Cover: Meiiee Raffe climbing *Commander Energy* (E2)
- page 81 - on the Lower Tier at the Roaches.
Photo: Nick Smith

ROCK ON

Find our shops at:

Redpoint Climbing Centre
77 Cecil Street,
Birmingham,
B19 3SU.
Tel: 0121 359 8709

Mile End Climbing Wall
Haverfield Road,
Bow, London,
E3 5BE.
Tel: 0208 981 5066

Craggy Island
9 Cobbett Park,
Slyfield Estate,
Guildford,
GU1 1RU.
Tel: 01483 565635

www.rockonclimbing.co.uk

Bulging with Climbing Gear!!

Many shops claim to be climbing specialists.
At **Rock On** we sell climbing/ mountaineering equipment
and books, and absolutely NOTHING ELSE.
Now thats specialist.

Dominic Sutcliffe slaps for Sly Stallone, Newstones.

Contents

Introduction 4
    Access 8
    Acknowledgments 10
    Advertiser Directory 12

Western Grit Logistics 14
    Accommodation 19
    Shops and Pubs 20
    Climbing Walls 22

Western Grit Climbing 24
    Gear and Ethics 26
    Grades 28
    Guidebooks 30
    Graded List 32
    Crag Tables 38

Staffordshire 42
    Back Forest 44
    Roaches Skyline 46
    The Five Clouds 58
    Roaches Lower 64
    Roaches Upper 82
    Hen Cloud 92
    Ramshaw 104
    Newstones and Baldstones 118

Windgather Area 126
    Windgather 128
    Castle Naze 136
    New Mills Tor 144

Kinder 150
    Kinder South 152
    Kinder North 166
    Kinder Downfall 178

Bleaklow and Longdendale 190
    Shining Clough 192
    Laddow 204
    Tintwistle 212
    Hobson Moor Quarry 218

Chew Valley 224
    Wimberry 226
    Upper Wilderness Valley 236
    Dovestones Edge 240
    Ravenstones 252
    Standing Stones 259
    Upperwood Quarry 266
    Alderman 270
    Running Hill Pits 272
    Den Lane Quarry 284

Lancashire 288
    Hoghton Quarry 290
    Denham 292
    Anglezarke 298
    Wilton 1 304
    Wilton 2 and 3 316
    Brownstones 327
    Egerton 332
    Cadshaw Castle 336
    Littleborough Area 338

Cheshire 344
    Helsby 346
    Frodsham 358
    Pex Hill 366

Route Index 376
General Index and Map 384

Henry Tyce climbing *Golden Tower* (E2) - *page 302* - at Anglezarke. Photo: Laurence King

Western Grit — Introduction

Jon Barton on the classic *Upper Tor Wall* (HS) - *page 160* - on Upper Tor, Kinder South. Photo: Keith Sharples

Introduction — Western Grit

Western Grit covers an extensive sweep of gritstone and sandstone from the Staffordshire cliffs, through the wild outcrops of Kinder and Bleaklow, the quiet gems of the Chew Valley, the quarries of south-east Lancashire, and the best of the Cheshire sandstone outcrops. The success of the original volume published back in 2003 vindicated both the concept and the effort required in bringing it to fruition. To further that success, all the cliffs have been rephotographed and revisited for this new edition, and the guide has been illustrated with resplendent full-page crag photographs and superb action shots that really capture the soul of the climbing.

Staffordshire remains far and away the most popular of the main areas covered in Western Grit with the celebrated trio of the Roaches, Hen Cloud and Ramshaw Rocks always being busy. The smaller crags of Windgather and Castle Naze are also popular, sat in glorious surroundings with many fine lower grade climbs.

The moors of Kinder Scout and Bleaklow feature rugged grit that is often an hour or so from the road. Meeting another team on these wild and lofty cliffs is unusual and they are perfect summer venues for when you need to get away from it all. The Chew Valley has an array of fine cliffs high above the reservoirs with superb settings, good rock and no crowds. Sadly the choice venue of Wimberry faces north and is often green, however the sunnier outcrops such as Alderman or Standing Stones offer more reliable conditions with the same appealing moorland vista.

Lancashire has some good climbing but visitors from afar remain rare. The quarries have a rogue reputation but they are home to some first-rate routes, it is just a matter of choosing your time and venue to match the weather. We have added a few extra cliffs to broaden the appeal of the area - give them a try, you might be pleasantly surprised.

The Cheshire sandstone outcrops have a rich history with Helsby being climbed on since the start of the 1900s. Frodsham and Pex Hill both give excellent bouldering on attractive sandstone, perfect for an evening or weekend workout.

Whilst some crags saw a resurgence in popularity following the release of the first Western Grit, other cliffs such as Laddow, and the southern edges of Kinder still remain slightly out of vogue. With its lavish and inspiring coverage, we hope this new edition will encourage more people to visit some of these great and tranquil venues.

Guidebook Footnote

The inclusion of a climbing area in this guidebook does not mean that you have a right of access or the right to climb upon it. The descriptions of routes within this guide are recorded for historical reasons only and no reliance should be placed on the accuracy of the description. The grades set in this guide are a fair assessment of the difficulty of the climbs. Climbers who attempt a route of a particular standard should use their own judgment as to whether they are proficient enough to tackle that route. This book is not a substitute for experience and proper judgment. The authors, publisher and distributors of this book do not recognise any liability for injury or damage caused to, or by, climbers, third parties, or property arising from such persons seeking reliance on this guidebook as an assurance for their own safety.

Western Grit   Introduction

Mike Hutton topping out on Martin's Traverse (V1) - page 120 - at Newstones. One of the crags with plenty of interest for boulderers. Photo: Self-portrait

Bouldering

Western Grit has much to offer the boulderer and we have covered some of the most popular venues like Brownstones, Denham, Frodsham and Pex Hill in detail. Other areas are marked on the relevant maps throughout the book, with brief details to get you going, but without the more in-depth approach provided by a dedicated bouldering guide (see page 30 for more on other guidebooks). Where boulder problems occur at the crags that are fully covered, they are indicated on the topos and given a boulder grade (see page 28).

Web Site

The ROCKFAX web site www.rockfax.com contains extra information relating to this book. If there are major new developments then we will post pdf updates and also occasional free pdf downloads of other crags. There is also a database of every route in the book where you can vote on grades and star rating, as well as lodging comments about the routes. Please use this database to tell us about inaccuracies, grade opinions and new developments so that we can improve future editions of the guidebook.

The Book

It has only been 6 years since the award-winning first edition of Western Grit. During this time there hasn't been a huge amount of new route development, or new crags discovered, but our production technique has moved forward in leaps and bounds. During 2008 every crag was re-photographed using a bigger and better camera with more mega pixels, a wider angle lens and more know-how. The result is bigger and better photo-topos than ever, giving the most inspiring visual coverage you will find in any rock climbing guidebook. We have loosened up the pages to make them appear less cluttered but have also managed to add another five crags and around 300 more routes. Hopefully the end result is a guidebook that makes locating and choosing your chosen climb easier than ever, whilst inspiring you to visit new crags and try different routes.

Chris Craggs and Alan James, March 2009

Dan O'Brien taking a big tumble off *San Melas* (E3) - *page 50* - on Alpha Buttress on the Skyline. Photo: Graham Haslehurst

Western Grit Access

We climbers are very fortunate these days to be able to benefit from the years of patient work that has gone on behind the scenes to secure unrestricted access to the crags on the Western Grit area. This work is usually carried out by the BMC and its many volunteers who spend countless hours attending meetings, writing letters and generally presenting the case on behalf of all climbers. Special thanks need to be made to Dave Bishop, Henry Folkard, Rick Gibbon and Les Ainsworth amongst others who have all put many years of effort into negotiating access for the areas covered in this book.

Many of the crags in this guidebook are on open access land defined under the Countryside and Rights of Way Act 2000 (CRoW). This includes the Staffordshire crags, Kinder, Longdendale, Bleaklow and the Chew. The only restrictions likely on these crags will be temporary fire restrictions in times of extreme dry weather, and occasional restrictions for nesting birds. In both these eventualities notices will be placed at the crags.

Other crags in Lancashire and Merseyside are not on CRoW land but have few access problems. Detailed notes are provided with the crag introductions and on the crag pages where there are special requirements or restricted times - for example, at Hoghton Quarry and Wilton 2 and 3.

Parking at the Roaches.
Photo: Jon Read

Parking
Please use the designated parking areas whenever possible and be aware of the increased incidence of car crime. The tell-tale sign of broken glass in any car park means it is a good idea to leave nothing of value in the car. If you park away from the recognised areas the car needs to be right off the road or you stand a good chance of getting ticketed.

Access **Western Grit** 9

BMC
If in doubt check the BMC Access database - www.thebmc.co.uk/bmccrag/. If you do encounter access problems contact the BMC. Tel. 08700 104 878   access@thebmc.co.uk

General Behaviour
A little Country Code sense is all that is required, no fires, leave no litter, close gates after you, park sensibly, avoid disturbing farm animals and leave your dog at home. Make sure you check the access situation at the crags you are visiting and, if confronted, then be polite and leave if requested. Climbers have a very good reputation when it comes to access, especially with regard to nesting birds, however all the good work of the past could easily be lost by one thoughtless action. Don't forget that there are many alternative routes in this book if you unexpectedly can't get on your chosen target route.

Hen Cloud, one of the crags now on Open Access Land. Photo: Jon Read

Western Grit — Acknowledgements

Working on the rewrite of the original Western Grit turned out to be less of a toil than the first time round, with longer to get the required crag shots (I started a couple of years early) it felt a less pressured experience. I did make the rather basic mistake of leaving much of Kinder to the end, always expecting the weather to improve, though the long damp summer of 2008 almost spoiled things. In the end it was down to the old team of myself and the ever-patient Sherri to head up into the hills on a regular basis. The occasional late evening or crack of dawn trip was also necessary to catch the light - Wimberry at 5:30am was especially memorable! I even treated Sherri to a three day break in Lancashire, visiting a whole host of delightful quarries, whilst the rest of the team were scattered far and wide from California, to Lofoten, to the Dolomites!

Thanks to friends old and new who helped with advice, company and photography; Dave Spencer, Steve Cunnington, Colin Binks, Mark Binney, Graham and Dan Parkes, Dave Vincent, Brian Rossiter, Steve Warwick and Dave Gregory.

This book brings together information from 5 separate areas all of which have long climbing and guidebook histories. The documenting of the information in these areas has been carried out by many people over the years and we would like to thank all of those that have made a contribution. We would also like to acknowledge the role of the BMC in coordinating the work of the Guidebook Committee since 1971.

We have received hundreds of comments and votes via the Rockfax Route Database as well as masses of other feedback. I would like to thank all those who have taken an interest in the Internet side of this guidebook and hope that you will continue to let us know what you think in the future.

Most of my stock photographs were used in the first edition of Western Grit so it was great this time to receive contributions from more people than any previous Rockfax guidebook, many of whom were contacted via the UKClimbing.com photo database. Chris Tan deserves a special mention, trekking up to Kinder Downfall on three occasions to get the crags shots, after I had given up and gone abroad in search of some sun! He also supplied an excellent array of action shots. Thanks also to John Read for his many beautiful photos; and to Alex Messenger, Chris Sims, Dave Bond, David Williams, Ashly Fusiarski, Ian Parnell, John Coefield, Mark Sharrat, Keith Sharples, Laurence King, Mark Glaister, Mike Hutton, Nick Smith, Nick Verney, Paul Smith, Philip Ashton, Sean Kelly, Chris Hannah, Tristan Peers, Will Hunt, Graham Haslehurst, Matt Thompson, Col Allot, Alexandra Sturrock, Jack Finney and others who sent photos which we haven't got room for.

The book builds significantly on the foundations of the first edition and we are very grateful to the following who helped first time round: Carl Dawson, Graham Hoey, Ben Tye, Martin Kocsis, Kevin Thaw, Ian Fenton, Gaz Parry, Phil Kelly, Pete Chadwick, Dave Ranby, Andy Farrell and Mark Hounslea. Jordan Buys, Sam Whittaker and Ben Bransby have also offered some helpful comments for this new edition on some of the harder routes.

Thanks also to Jack Geldard, who is now an integral part of the Rockfax team, for his contributions to layout and proofing.

Alan James has been a constant cyber-side-kick in our search for perfection - eight years on we are still getting better. We doubted we could improve on the magnificent award-wining tome that was Lofoten Rock - but just maybe…….

Chris Craggs, March 2009

Sherri Davy on one of the many trips to the remote crags covered in Western Grit. This time it was Kinder Downfall in the fog.

Craggsy taking his first steps on the *The Catwalk (HS) - page 248* - at Dovestones. Photo: Craggs collection.

Western Grit — Advertiser Directory

Guiding Services

AMI Guides - *page 21*
www.ami.org.uk

James Thacker - *page 31*
www.jamesthacker.co.uk   Sheffield. Tel: 0114 2659722

Alternative Adventures - *page 27*
www.altadv.co.uk   Seddons Farm House, Bury. Tel: 0161 764 3612

Gear Shops

Alpenstock - *Back flap*
www.alpenstock.co.uk   35 St. Petersgate, Stockport. Tel: 0161 480 3660

Mountain Intelligence - *Inside back cover*
www.mountain-intelligence.co.uk   70 North Street, Leeds.

Rock On - *page 2*
www.rockonclimbing.co.uk
Redpoint Climbing Centre, Birmingham. Tel: 0121 3598709
Mile End Climbing Wall, London. Tel: 0208 9815066
Craggy Island, Guildford. Tel: 01483 565635

Climbing Walls

Awesome Walls - *page 23 and 29*
www.awesomewalls.co.uk
St. Alban's Church, Liverpool. Tel: 0151 298 2422
The Engine House, Stockport. . Tel: 0161 494 9949

Entre-Prise - *opposite*
www.ep-uk.com   Kelbrook. Tel: 01282 444800

Manchester Climbing Centre - *page 31*
www.manchesterclimbingcentre.com
St. Benedict's Church, Manchester. Tel: 0161 230 7006

The Leeds Wall - *page 27*
www.theleedswall.co.uk   Gelderd Road, Leeds. Tel: 0113 234 1554

Other Advertisers

Berghaus - *Inside front cover*
www.berghaus.com   Extreme Centre, Sunderland. Tel: 0191 516 5700

Black Diamond - *Outside back cover*
www.blackdiamondequipment.com   Tel: 0162 958 0484

Plas y Brenin - *page 17*
www.pyb.co.uk   Capel Curig, North Wales. Tel: 01690 720214

Finishing *Solid Geometry* (E1) - *page 99* - at Hen Cloud. Photo: Jon Read

Photo: Craggy Island 2 Bouldering & Caving Centre

ENTRE PRISES
Climbing Walls

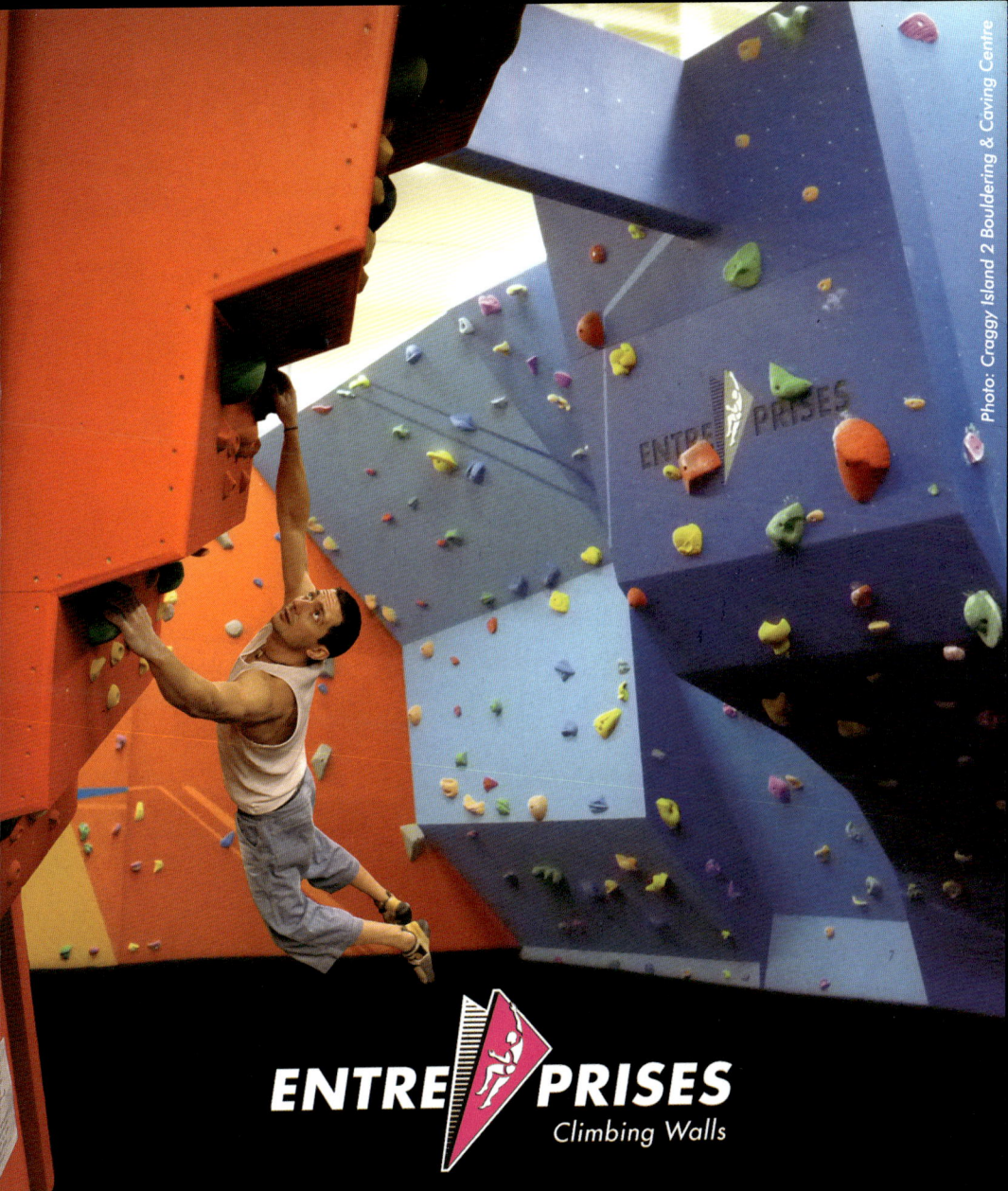

Bolt-on holds   Training boards   Bouldering Walls

Leading Walls   Mobile Towers   Ice Walls

Artificial caves

Entre-Prises (UK) Ltd
T: 01282 444800   F: 01282 444801
info@ep-uk.com   www.ep-uk.com

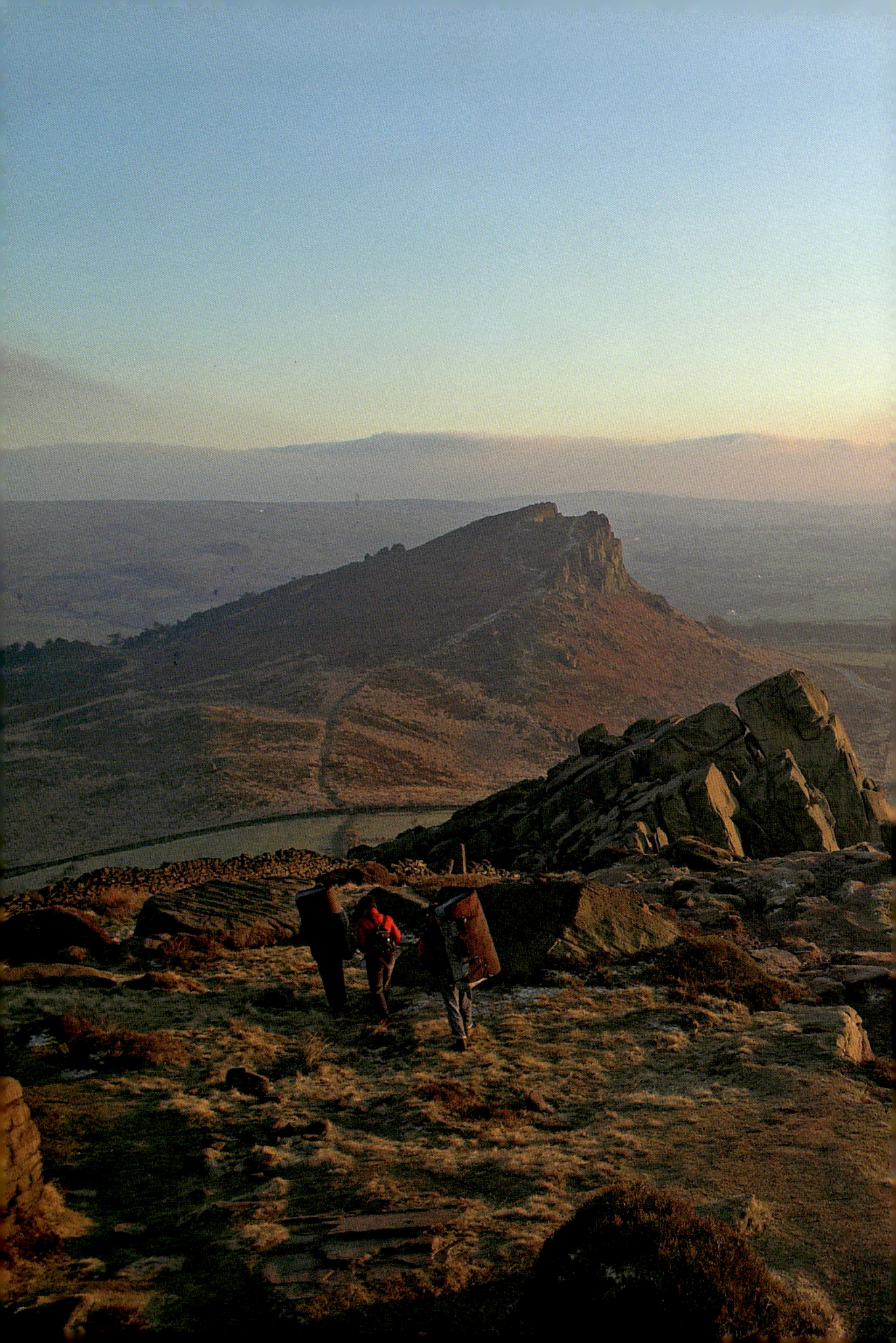

Western Grit Logistics

Heading for home from the Roaches. Photo: Jon Read

Western Grit Logistics

Mountain Rescue
In the event of an accident requiring the assistance of Mountain Rescue:

Dial 999 and ask for 'POLICE - MOUNTAIN RESCUE'

All mountain rescue incidents in the Peak District area fall under the responsibility of Derbyshire Constabulary. If in any doubt request Derbyshire Police Operations Room.

Edale Mountain Rescue Team - www.edalemountainrescue.co.uk
Peak District Mountain Rescue Organisation - www.pdmro.org.uk

British Mountaineering Council
British Mountaineering Council, 177-179 Burton Road, Manchester, M20 2BB.
Tel: 0870 010 4878 Fax: 0161 445 4300. **Web:** www.thebmc.co.uk **Email:** office@thebmc.co.uk
The BMC is the official body representing climbers in Britain. If you have problems regarding access to any of the areas in this book, then get in touch with the BMC Access Officer at the address above.

Tourist Information Offices
If you are visiting the areas in this book and need some accommodation, or just fancy doing something other than climbing, then take a look at the **Tourist Information Offices**. They contain much more useful information than is possible to include on these pages.
Buxton - Tel: 01298 25106   www.highpeak.gov.uk
Leek - Tel: 01538 483741   www.staffsmoorlands.gov.uk
Manchester - Tel: 0161 234 3157   www.manchester.gov.uk
Macclesfield - Tel: 01625 504114   www.macclesfield.gov.uk
Saddleworth - Tel: 01457 870336   www.oldham.gov.uk
Bolton - Tel: 01204 334200   www.bolton.gov.uk
Preston - Tel: 01772 253731   www.preston.gov.uk
Runcorn - Tel: 01928 576776   www.halton-borough.gov.uk
Warrington - Tel: 01925 632571   www.warrington.gov.uk
St Helens - Tel: 01744 755150   www.visitsthelens.com
More information and other travel tips are at www.travelengland.org.uk

Looking up the Fair Brook Valley towards Kinder North.

Get Better Soon.

Are you suffering from an acute lack of development in your climbing? Maybe we can help. Come to Plas y Brenin and spend a few days with our expert climbing instructors and we guarantee you'll improve, no matter what standard or grade you climb at.

Whether you climb for fun or you would like to forge a career as an outdoor instructor you won't find a better place to learn.

We run courses for all levels from total beginner right up to the most experienced climber. And as our instructors love to climb just as much as you, they'll make especially sure you get as much time as possible out on the rock, because that's where you learn the most.

If you're showing no sign of improvement call 01690 720214 or e-mail brochure@pyb.co.uk and we'll send you our brochure.

THE NATIONAL MOUNTAIN CENTRE
PLAS Y BRENIN

National Mountain Centre   Canolfan Fynydd Genedlaethol
Capel Curig Conwy LL24 0ET   Tel: 01690 720214   Fax: 01690 720394   www.pyb.co.uk   Email: info@pyb.co.uk

Western Grit Logistics — Accommodation and Getting Around

Rockhall Cottage
The quaint little house just below the cliff is built into the boulders and for some years was the home of Doug, self-styled Lord of the Roaches. After he moved out, the place was bought by the BMC and named the Whillans' Memorial Hut in memory of one of the greatest gritstone pioneers. The climber in the background is on the wide classic of *Kestrel Crack* (VS) - *page 77*.

Accommodation and Getting Around **Western Grit Logistics** 19

Accommodation

For short stays the following camp sites are well-positioned for the climbing in some of the areas. More campsites and huts can be found on the following web sites -
www.ukclimbing.com/listings
www.visitderbyshire.co.uk
camping.uk-directory.com
www.ukcampsite.co.uk
www.find-a-campsite.co.uk
www.stilwell.co.uk
www.thebmc.co.uk

Staffordshire Area
Don Whillans Memorial Hut (left) Rockhall Cottage, The Roaches. Bookings - Tel/Fax: 01433 639 368
Web: **www.mountain-house.co.uk/hut.html**
Email: **mike@mountain-house.co.uk**
Hen Cloud Campsite - Small site on the right, just before Hen Cloud.

Kinder Area
Edale - Newfold Farm, Grindsbrook, Edale, Hope Valley, S33 7ZD. Tel: 01433 670372
There are many other camp sites near Edale.

Bleaklow and Longdendale Area
Crowden Campsite - Hadfield, Glossop, Derbyshire. Tel: 01457 866057

Youth Hostels - There are YHAs in Buxton, Edale, Gradbach Mill (near Staffs crags) and Crowden.
www.yha.org.uk

Getting Around

The easiest way to get to most of the areas covered in this book is by car and the approach descriptions are written assuming you have access to a car. However if you are trying to get to the crags by public transport here is a list of useful contacts which may help.
Trains - There is a regular service from Sheffield and Manchester to Edale from where the Kinder crags are within walking distance. Trains also stop at New Mills.
Buses - There is no one location to go for reliable information about buses, however most of the operators have reasonably efficient web sites.
National sites - www.pti.org.uk - www.firstgroup.com
Staffordshire - www.firstgroup.com/firstpmt
Derbyshire - www.derbysbus.net
South Yorkshire - www.sypte.co.uk
Merseyside - www.merseytravel.gov.uk
Manchester - www.stagecoachmanchester.co.uk

Western Grit Logistics Shops and Pubs

Climbing Shops
The main cities of Manchester and Liverpool have big city centre outdoor shops.
More shops listed at - www.ukclimbing.com/listings/

Alpenstock (*cover flap*) - Stockport. Tel: 0161 480 3660   www.alpenstock.co.uk
Mountain Intelligence (*inside back cover*) - Leeds.   Tel: 0113 246 9843   www.mountain-intelligence.co.uk
The Leeds Wall (*page 27*) - Leeds. Tel: 0113 234 1554   www.theleedswallshop.co.uk
Outside (*page 31*) - Manchester Climbing Centre.   www.outside.co.uk
Rock On (*page 2*) - Redpoint CC, Birmingham. Tel: 0121 359 8709   www.rockonclimbing.co.uk

Hitch 'n' Hike - Hope Valley. Tel: 01433 651013   www.hitchnhike.co.uk
Paul Braithwaite - Oldham. Tel: 0161 620 3900   www.mountainfeet.co.uk
Fell and Mountain - Accrington. Tel: 01254 390986   www.fellandmountain.co.uk
Outdoor Action - Blackburn. Tel: 01254 671 945   www.outdooraction.co.uk
Adapt Outdoors - Liverpool. Tel: 0151 709 6498   www.adaptoutdoors.com
Campfour - Macclesfield. Tel: 01625 619 204   www.campfour.co.uk

Pubs
There are many pubs in the areas covered by this book. The following is a selection of the favourite après-climb pubs contributed by readers of **UKClimbing.com**.
More pubs at - **www.pub-explorer.com**

Photo: Alex Messenger

Staffordshire Area
The Lazy Trout - In Meerbrook, which is the little village by the Tittesworth Reservoir Visitor Centre.
The Wilkes' Head - In Leek on St. Edward Street - first left after Market Square towards Macclesfield.
The Rock - Upper Hulme. Not as popular with climbers as one might expect.

Whaley Bridge Area
The Bee Hive - In Coombes below Castle Naze and Windgather.
The Navigation - In Whaley Bridge just by the Canal Basin.
The Walzing Weasel - In Hayfield (on the road between the main junction in Hayfield and New Mills). Excellent food and drink.

Kinder and Bleaklow Areas
The Nag's Head - In the centre of Edale (*map page 159*). Good beer but ordinary food.
The Globe - High Street in Glossop. Live music.

Chew Area
The Church - Above Uppermill and near Running Hill Pits (*map page 224*). Wide selection of ales.
The King William - On the main road through Greenfield and has a good variety of real ales.

Lancashire Area
The Black Dog (photo above) - Drive north up the A675 from Wilton 1 to Belmont. Turn left in the middle of the village at the signpost for Horwich.
Bob's Smithy - Continue past Brownstones from Wilton to the next junction.
The Dresser's Arms - In Wheelton (near Anglezarke and Denham) on the east side of the A674 between Chorley and Blackburn. Good range of guest beers.

Cheshire Area
The Unicorn - Just past the lights in Cronton village (*map page 366*). Good beer but no decent real ales.

For the best in Instruction

ASSOCIATION OF MOUNTAINEERING INSTRUCTORS — AMI

LEARN FROM EXPERIENCE

www.ami.org.uk

Western Grit Logistics Climbing Walls

Birmingham
Creation Climbing Centre
582 Moseley Road, Birmingham.
Tel: 0121 449 8000
www.creationwall.co.uk

Redpoint Climbing Centre
77 Cecil Street, Birmingham. Tel 0121 359 1777
www.redpointclimbingcentre.co.uk

Blackburn
Boulderuk.com
10 Heaton Street, Blackburn. Tel: 01254 693056
www.boulderuk.com

Glossop
Glossop Leisure Centre
High Street East, Glossop. Tel: 01457 863223

Huddersfield
Huddersfield Sports Centre
Southgate, Huddersfield. Tel: 01484 223630

Leeds
The Leeds Wall - *page 27*
100a Gelderd Road, Leeds.
Tel: 0113 234 1554
www.theleedswall.co.uk

City Bloc
Airedale Industrial Estate, Kitson Road, Leeds.
Tel: 0113 391 2652
www.citybloc.co.uk

Liverpool
Awesome Walls CC - *page 29*
St. Albans Church, Athol Street, Liverpool.
Tel: 0151 2982422
www.awesomewalls.co.uk

Manchester
Manchester Climbing Centre - *page 31*
St Benedicts Church, Bennett Street,
Manchester. Tel: 0161 230 7006
www.manchesterclimbingcentre.com

Newport
Shropshire Climbing Centre
Springfield Industrial Estate, Newport.
Tel: 01952 814566
www.newportrock.com

Preston
West View Leisure Centre
Ribbleton, Preston. Tel: 01772 796788

Salford
Broughton RC
Camp Street, Broughton. Tel: 0161 792 2375

Stockport
Awesome Walls CC - *opposite*
The Engine House, Stockport Road West,
Stockport. Tel 0161 494 9949
www.awesomewalls.co.uk

Marple
Rope Race
Goyt Mill, Upper Hibbert Lane, Marple.
Tel: 0161 426 0226
www.roperace.co.uk

Warrington
The North West Face
St. Anns Church, Winwick Road, Warrington.
Tel: 01925 650022
www.northwestface.com

A frosty day on the Staffordshire moors - a good day for the wall? Photo: John Read

AWESOME WALLS CLIMBING CENTRE

STOCKPORT

23.5m lead walls, 400sqm bouldering
no membership fees, loyalty card

Awesome (adjective) - *so impressive or overwhelming as to inspire a strong feeling of admiration or fear.*
(Encarta Dictionary U.K.)

The Engine House, Pear Mill Ind Est, Lower Bredbury
Stockport, SK6 2BP. TEL 0161 494 9949
www.awesomewalls.co.uk

Photo: David Simmonite

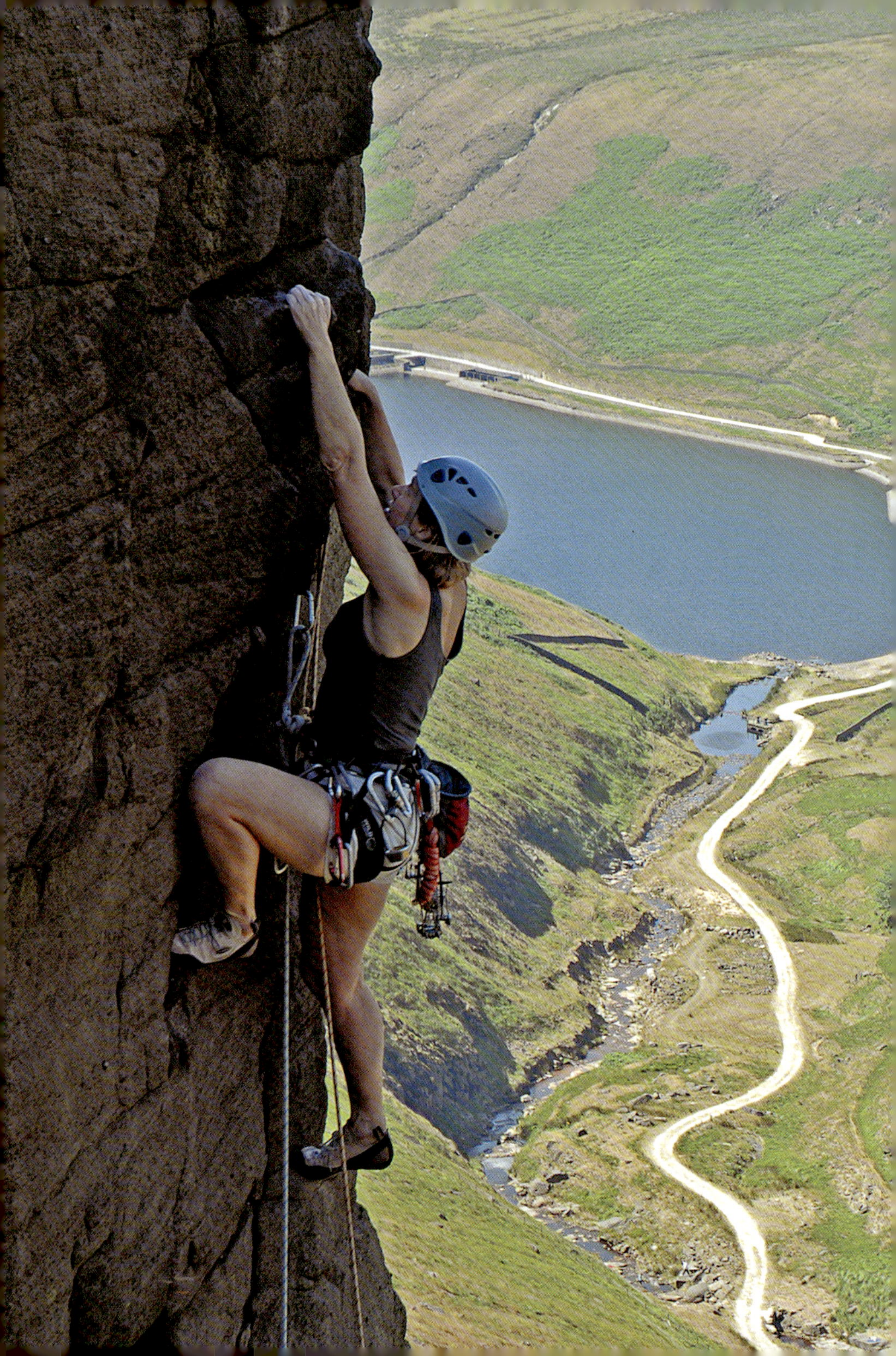

Western Grit Climbing

A climber on the fine *Trinnacle East* (HVS) - *page 257* - at Ravenstones in the Chew Valley.

Gear

The flared breaks and cracks make gritstone an ideal place for camming devices. Many old routes which were bold and unprotected leads in their day are now relatively safe with the modern protection devices available. A typical gritstone rack consists of a single set of wires, a few hexes and a full range of cams. One or two slings will also be found useful on some routes and often on the cliff-top belays. For harder routes, micro-wires and more-advanced camming devices may be found essential. Most grit routes are short enough to be climbed on a single 10mm or 11mm rope. The only exceptions to this are routes which wander around, in which case you may need to consider 2 x 9mm ropes. Other useful items are; tape for bandaging your hands before, or after, they are wrecked by some savage crack, a toothbrush for cleaning the smaller holds on the harder routes and a bouldering mat for those unprotected starts. The only other thing you need is this book!

Ethics

Climbing is an anarchic pastime and one of its great attractions is the lack of rules and structure. Despite this there is a long history of ethical purity; the way individuals climb a piece of rock is up to them, although the way they report the ascent is a more public affair. The best form of ascent is a ground-up lead, placing the gear as you go, in a single push. Resting on gear and pre-placing gear are widely regarded as forms of cheating. On the harder and more serious routes, the individual moves are often practiced extensively and then the route led or soloed in what has become known as a *headpoint*. In reality nobody really cares how you do the route as long as the rock doesn't suffer.

Rock damage at Newstones.

There is no reason for adding fixed protection (pegs or bolts) or attempting to improve holds on any of the routes in this guide and if you think otherwise then you are wrong. Brushing on the harder routes needs to be done with great care as even iron-hard gritstone can be damaged by over-zealous cleaning, and wire brushes should never be used. Most modern damage to the crags in this book has occurred when climbers have attempted to retrieve stuck gear. Equipment that gets stuck is invariably gear that is badly placed, so think before you place it. If it does get well and truly jammed it may be better leaving it for someone who can get it out without damaging the route.

Top Roping/Groups

Indoor walls have introduced a new generation to climbing who enjoy it for the physical aspects and do not feel the urge to seek the adrenaline high generated when leading climbs. Sometimes this leads to the monopolisation of certain (usually very accessible) routes at busy times as a line of unfortunate souls are introduced to outdoor climbing on a bow-taught top rope. Please be aware of the needs of others, remove ropes that are not in use and avoid popular climbs at busy times. Consider leading easier routes rather than top-roping harder ones, this will spread the load and ultimately is much more rewarding.
If you do visit the cliffs in a large group, please consider other climbers. What feels like good-natured banter and horseplay can seem like yobbish behaviour to others on the cliff who are there for a bit of peace and quiet. Keep your kit in one area and try to avoid monopolising classic climbs for extended periods of time.

www.theleedswallshop.co.uk

The Leeds Wall
100a Gelderd Road, Leeds, LS12 6BY
0113 2341554 Open 7 days a week

Alternative Adventure

Rock Climbing and Mountaineering
Courses for all abilities in Lancashire

Learn to Lead
Self Rescue for Climbers
MTLE Climbing Wall Award, Single Pitch Award,
Walking Group Leader *, Summer Mountain Leader *
First Aid 16hr
NNAS Bronze/Silver/Gold
British Orienteering – Teaching Orienteering/coaching awards

Stuart Igoe
Outdoor Activities Service,
Seddons Farm House, Newington Drive,
Bury, Lancs. BL8 2EG
Tel 0161 764 3612
E-mail oas@altadv.co.uk

AMI
nnas
MLTE

Western Grit Climbing — Grades

The British Trad grade is probably never more appropriately used than it is on outcrop routes. Here the subtleties and versatility of the Trad Grade can be appreciated to their maximum.

Bold Routes - Some gritstone routes have limited protection and you can easily find yourself in very serious situations, especially on the harder climbs. This possibility should be clear from the route descriptions but please make sure you use your own skill and judgment as to whether you will be able to safely complete a chosen climb. A bold E2 may only feel like an indoor grade 6a on a top-rope but it is a very different proposition as a lead or solo.

British Trad Grade

1) Adjectival grade (Diff, VDiff, HVD, Severe, Hard Severe (HS), Very Severe (VS), Hard Very Severe (HVS), E1, E2, E3, E4 and upwards).
An overall picture of the route including how well protected it is, how sustained and a general indication of the level of difficulty of the whole route.

2) Technical grade (4a, 4b, 4c, 5a, ...).
The difficulty of the hardest single move, or short section.

Colour Coding

The routes and boulder problems are all given a colour-coded dot corresponding to a grade band and approximate difficulty level. This colour code is designed to indicate routes and problems that a particular climber might be happy attempting. Since most people are happier bouldering at a harder level than they lead, the boulder problems tend to have harder individual moves on them for the same colour-code.

Green Routes - Severe and under and V0 and under. Good for beginners and those looking for an easy life.

Orange Routes - Hard Severe to HVS and V0+ to V2. General ticking routes for those with more experience including a lot of excellent routes and problems.

Red Routes - E1 to E3 and V3 to V6. Routes and problems for the experienced and keen climber including many of the areas' great classics.

Black Routes - E4 and V7 and above. A grade band for the talented.

ROUTE GRADES

British Trad Grade (See note on bold routes)	Sport Grade	UIAA	USA
Mod (Moderate)	1	I	5.1
Diff (Difficult)	2	II	5.2
VDiff (Very Difficult)	2+	III	5.3
HVD (Hard Very Difficult)	3-	III+	5.4
	3	IV-	5.5
Sev (Severe) 3c	3+	IV+	5.6
HS (Hard Severe) 4a/4b	4	V-	5.7
VS (Very Severe) 4b/5a	4+	V	5.8
HVS (Hard Very Severe) 5a/5b	5	V+	5.9
E1 5a/5c	5+	VI-	5.10a
E2 5a/6a	6a	VI	5.10b
E3 5b/6a	6a+	VI+	5.10c
E4 5c/6a	6b	VII-	5.10d
E5 6a/6c	6b+	VII	5.11a
E6 6b/6c	6c	VII+	5.11b
E7 6c/7a	6c+	VIII-	5.11c
E8 7a	7a	VIII	5.11d
E9 7a/7b	7a+	VIII+	5.12a
E10 7b	7b	IX-	5.12b
	7b+	IX	5.12c
	7c	IX+	5.12d
	7c+	X-	5.13a
	8a	X	5.13b
	8a+	X+	5.13c
	8b	XI-	5.13d
	8b+	XI	5.14a
	8c	XI+	5.14b
	8c+		5.14c
	9a		5.14d
	9a+		5.15a

Bouldering Grade	VB	V0-	V0	V0+	V1	V2	V3	V4	V5	V6	V7	V8	V9	V10	V11	V12	V13	V14
UK Tech Grade	4c or easier		5a	5c		EASY	6b	HARD		6c or harder								
Font Grade	4		4+	5	5+	6a	6a+	6b	6c	6c+	7a	7a+	7b	7b+	7c	8a	8b	8b+	8c

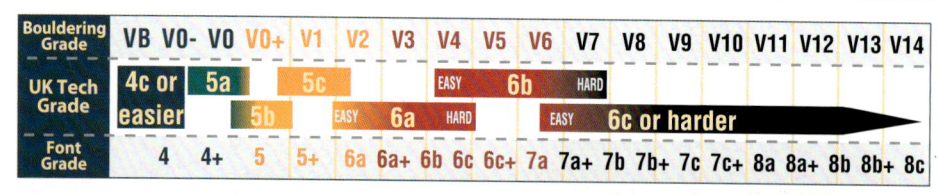

AWESOME WALLS CLIMBING CENTRE LIVERPOOL

0151 298 2422

60 Lines,
7 Bouldering Areas,
Over 1,500m² of Climbing Surface,
No Membership Fees,
Loyalty Card Scheme

www.awesomewalls.co.uk

AWCC LIVERPOOL & STOCKPORT
www.awesomewalls.co.uk

Awesome Walls Climbing Centre, St Albans Church, Athol St, off Great Howard St, Liverpool. L5 9XT

Western Grit Climbing — Guidebooks

Guidebooks old and new.

This book is a selective guidebook which means that it only covers the major buttresses, on the major crags, on the western side of the Peak District, up into Lancashire and across as far as Cheshire. A more complete list of routes on many of these crags, and other smaller venues, is provided by the BMC with their series of guidebooks. For any frequent visitor to the area, these books will be found to be indispensable and will compliment the coverage given here.

Staffordshire Grit (BMC, 2003)
The Staffordshire crags. The Roaches, Hen Cloud, Ramshaw, Newstones, Baldstones, Windgather, Castle Naze and The Churnet Valley, plus many other minor venues.

Over the Moors (BMC, 2009/10)
Covers, all the crags around the Kinder plateau and the Bleaklow and Longdendale areas, plus all the Chew valley Crags. At the time of writing these areas are served by two older guidebooks: **Kinder** (BMC 1991), and **Moorland Gritstone** (BMC 1988).

Lancashire Rock (BMC, 1999 reprinted 2006)
Covers Wilton, Brownstones, Anglezarke, Denham and Littleborough crags in greater detail than in this book, plus many more cliffs across Lancashire and Cumbria.

On Peak Rock (BMC, 1995 reprinted 2002)
An attractive selected climb book covering the whole of the Peak District. Nothing from Lancashire and Cheshire.

Peak District : Bouldering
(Vertebrate Graphics, 2004)
A book dedicated to the bouldering across the Peak District, covering Staffordshire and Wimberry.

Web Sites
There are a couple of great web sites which give extra coverage of the Lancashire bouldering.
brownstones.wetpaint.com
www.southlancsbouldering.tk

The North West's Premier Indoor Climbing Venue

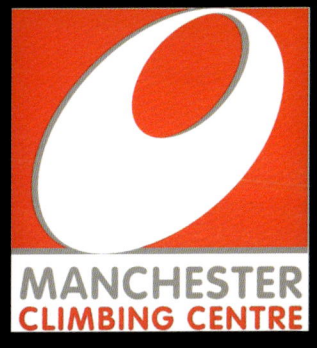

MANCHESTER CLIMBING CENTRE

Outside

Britain's best mountain shop at MCC. Opening April 2009.

Manchester Climbing Centre, St. Benedict's Church, Bennett Street, West Gorton, Manchester, M12 5ND
www.manchesterclimbingcentre.com   0161 2307006

Intro to Rock
Resin to Rock
Learn to lead..

james thacker Mountaineering

Climbing instruction and guiding in the Peak District and UK wide..

T: 0114 2659722 M: 07887 992745
E: enquiries@jamesthacker.co.uk
www.jamesthacker.co.uk

HAGLÖFS

ASSOCIATION OF MOUNTAINEERING INSTRUCTORS AMI

Western Grit Climbing — Graded List

This graded list was compiled by careful analysis of the grade voting on the Rockfax Route Database. This enabled us to, not only see how hard people thought routes were, but also to find out which routes people did the most. The 450 routes in this list are almost certainly not the best 450, but they are the 450 routes that have received the most voting opinions over the last 6 years indicating a level of popularity. As ever, the upper end of the list is more open to conjecture though we have sought a consensus wherever possible. If you think there are errors in the graded list, or you disagree strongly with it, then please let us know via the Route Database on the web site - www.rockfax.com

E9
			Page
***	☐	Appointment with Death	232

E8
*	☐	Toxic Bilberrys	307
**	☐	Ultimate Sculpture	107
**	☐	Gigantic	313
**	☐	Vortex	335
**	☐	MaDMAn	230
**	☐	Doug	69
***	☐	Obsession Fatale	81

E7
Top 50	☐	Appointment with Fear	232
***	☐	The S-Groove	319
***	☐	B4 XS	98
***	☐	Clippity Clop, Clippity Clop, ...	111
**	☐	Ray's Roof	124
**	☐	Chocolate Girl	313
***	☐	Paralogism	90
Top 50	☐	Dangerous Crocodile Snogging	111

E6
***	☐	Thing on a Spring	74
Top 50	☐	Wristcutter's Lullaby	230
***	☐	King of Kings	302
***	☐	Master of Reality	94
**	☐	Bloodspeed	75
***	☐	Art Nouveau	49
***	☐	A Fist Full of Crystals	69
**	☐	Ou est le Spit?	91
***	☐	Piece of Mind	81
***	☐	Neptune's Tool	230
Top 50	☐	Painted Rumour	88
Top 50	☐	Barriers in Time	68

E5
***	☐	Black Magic	369
***	☐	Consolation Prize	233
**	☐	Apache Dawn	66
***	☐	Constable's Overhang	324
***	☐	Thin Air	81
***	☐	Entropy's Jaw	49
***	☐	Catastrophe Internationale	66
**	☐	Over the Moors	254
Top 50	☐	Track of the Cat	48
***	☐	Daytona Wall	342
***	☐	Nobody Wept for Alec Trench	335
**	☐	Clive Coolhead	76
***	☐	Tierdrop	110
**	☐	Mirror, Mirror	59
***	☐	Gable End	221
***	☐	Gates of Perception	302

E4
**	☐	Scale the Dragon	223
**	☐	Phaestus	278
**	☐	Bullworker	294
***	☐	Chameleon	103
Top 50	☐	Bob Hope	250
***	☐	Adrenaline	313
***	☐	Calamity Crack	274
***	☐	Caesarean	97
Top 50	☐	Ramshaw Crack	113
***	☐	Hart's Arete	373
**	☐	Acid Drop	52
***	☐	The Brush Off	353
Top 50	☐	Master Spy Direct	314
**	☐	Willow Farm	48
***	☐	Borstal Breakout	98
**	☐	Isle of White	312
***	☐	Kicking Bird	75
***	☐	Master Spy	314
***	☐	Fingertip Control (Anglezarke)	301
***	☐	Death Knell	78
***	☐	Lazy Friday	308
Top 50	☐	Wings of Unreason	48
***	☐	Traveller in Time	106

E3
*	☐	The Les Dawson Show	173
**	☐	Northern Ballet	235
**	☐	Chalkstorm	80
***	☐	The Grader	324
***	☐	Hunky Dory	80
***	☐	Corinthian	100
***	☐	Rhododendron Arete	291
***	☐	White Slabs Bunt	312
***	☐	Ascent of Man	66
***	☐	The Big Wall	200
***	☐	Comedian	100
***	☐	The Swan	74
***	☐	Great Expectations	221
***	☐	Appaloosa Sunset	60
***	☐	San Melas	50
***	☐	The Swine	320
***	☐	Wilton Wall	320
***	☐	Supercrack	312
***	☐	Max	307
***	☐	Cheat	310
***	☐	Smear Test	75
Top 50	☐	True Grit	257
**	☐	Charm	233
**	☐	Electric Circus	147
*	☐	Leucocyte Left-hand	306
***	☐	Dateline	369
Top 50	☐	Arabia	158
**	☐	Weaver's Wall	280
**	☐	Sickbay Shuffle	231

John Camateras grabbing conditions when most people are happy at home sitting in front of the tele. *Wings of Unreason* (E4) - *page 48* - the Skyline area. Photo: Jamie Moss

Western Grit Climbing — Graded List

E2

		Page
**	Warlock	374
**	Drizzle	223
*	Dragon's Route	223
	Mandarin	291
***	Spanner Wall	276
**	Ruby Tuesday	87
	Rhododendron Buttress	291
	Elegy	76
***	Boadicea	291
**	End of Time	297
***	Big Brother	172
**	Heavy Duty	149
	Blasphemy	231
**	Flower Power Arete	61
**	Paradox	306
	Hanging Crack	248
***	Commander Energy	81
*	Canine Crucifixion	325
***	Falling Crack	320
***	Wipe Out	314
**	Windbreaker	278
***	Gumshoe	108
**	Prolapse	264
	Wombat	83
**	Brown's Crack	110
*	Viaduct Wall	148
	The Arete (Tintwistle)	215
**	Chalk Lightning Crack	335
	The Golden Tower	302
**	Topaz	55
*	Something Better Change	70
**	Enigma Variation	52
**	Mather Crack	146
**	Wombat Chimney	307
**	Hartley's Route	155
**	Belladonna	143
***	Foord's Folly	117
**	Hanging Slab	220
**	Wafer Wall	348

E1

**	Pinball Wizard	228
**	Chromium Crack	352
**	Cobweb Crack	374
**	Crack of Gloom	71
**	Turtle	268
**	King of the Swingers	149
**	Galileo	199
**	Shortcomings	55
**	Solid Geometry	99
**	The Untouchable	108
***	Encouragement	98
***	Hawkwing	77
**	Time	297
**	Humdinger	86
**	The Disappearing Chip Buttie Traverse	335
***	Fallen Heroes	262
*	Private Display	59
**	Sneeze	107
**	Blue Light's Crack	231
***	Grave's End	339
	Ocean Wall	265
**	Cave Arete Indirect	211
**	Chicken	94
*	Choka	78
**	Bulwark	94

**	Central Route (Wilton 1)	307
**	Ann	310
***	Safety Net	55
***	Shivers Arete	326
**	Gomorrah (Running Hill Pits)	279
**	The Bee	319
**	The Trouble with Women is	263
**	Triple Point	49
**	Slowhand	94
***	Dorothy's Dilemma	70
**	Intestate	172
*	Louie Groove	106
	Eliminate 1 (Helsby)	357
**	Crack and Up	373
*	Babbacombe Lee	90
***	First Finale	301
**	Tighe's Arete	223
**	The Web	374
**	Lady Jane	372
*	Moonshine	120
***	Cameo (Wilton 1)	308
	The Trident	230
*	Scoop Face Direct	141
***	The Ivory Tower	161
*	Sodom (Running Hill Pits)	279
***	Mantis	50

HVS

	Freddie's Finale	228
***	Hen Cloud Eliminate	100
*	Many Happy Returns	301
**	Don's Crack	110
**	Golden Pillar	352
**	Hypothesis	70
*	Roscoe's Wall	90
**	Virgin's Dilemma	315
**	Dawn	310
	Twisted Smile	175
*	Matinee	72
**	Second's Advance	100
*	Yellow Crack	247
	Bachelor's Left-hand	101
***	Priscilla Ridge	208
**	Wild Thing	49
***	Saul's Crack	86
**	Viaduct Crack	148
**	Valkyrie Direct	72
**	The Mincer	75
	The Sloth	89
	Delstree	97
*	Obyoyo	263
**	Zarke	301
**	Herringbone Slab	233
***	Prostration	110
**	Alcove Crack	146
***	Terror Cotta	301
*	Crabbie's Crack	61
**	Rhodren	78
	Rubberneck	60
**	Gallows Pole	335
	Central Crack (Wilton 3)	325
***	East Rib	195
**	Canopy	326
	Pisa Super Direct	199
*	Mad Karoo	297
**	Magic Roundabout Direct	115
**	Wallaby Direct	83
**	Wood's Climb	354

Graded List Western Grit Climbing

HVS Continued...
- *** Herford's Route 155
- * Gideonite. 222
- ** Scoop Direct 141
- ** Prelude to Space 48
- ** Route 2 (Cows Mouth) . . 342
- Top 50 Parker's Eliminate 222
- ** Pagan's Direct 337
- ** Pebbledash 74
- * Portfolio 131
- ** Bengal Buttress 70
- *** Jester Cracks 175
- Top 50 Scoop Face 141
- Top 50 Legacy (Kinder North) . . . 172
- *** Baldstones Arete 124
- * Libra 84
- * Diamond Wednesday 87
- ** Bachelor's Buttress 86
- * Wheeze 56
- ** Mammoth Slab 245
- ** Gideon. 222
- * Karabiner Slab 52
- * The Vixen 123
- * Calcutta Buttress 91
- ** Pigeonhole Wall 348

VS
- * Route 1.5 134
- ** Thrug 54
- * Main Crack 97
- * Pagan's Progress 337
- * Transformation (Anglezarke) . 300
- ** Central Climb Direct 98
- *** Moneylender's Crack 163
- *** Fairy Nuff 263
- * Pincer 75
- ** Rainbow Crack 103
- * West's Wallaby 83
- ** Mohammed the Medieval Melancholic 295
- * Rotunda Buttress 86
- Top 50 Flash Wall 164
- * Mantelshelf Slab 52
- * Piggy's Crack 146
- *** Samarkand 302
- *** Bachelor's Climb 101
- * The Bulger 76
- *** Cherry Bomb 334
- *** Womanless Wall 263
- ** Reunion Crack 97
- ** Z Crack 343
- Top 50 Valkyrie 72
- ** Communist Crack 63
- ** Leucocyte Right-hand . . . 306
- ** Christeena 310
- Top 50 Phoenix Climb 195
- ** Storm 303
- Top 50 Eureka 170

- * Spare Rib 54
- Top 50 Tower Face (Laddow) . . . 209
- *** Complete Streaker 297
- ** North Buttress Arete Direct 130
- ** Crooked Crack 326
- ** Blackout 314
- ** The Crank 107
- ** Pocked Wall 264
- *** Route II (Wimberry) 232
- ** Cornflake (Tintwistle) . . . 216
- ** Dunsinane 173
- * Monkey Puzzle 195
- Top 50 Nozag 142
- * Flingle Bunt 308
- ** Niche Arete 140
- ** Battle of the Bulge 108
- *** Crew's Route 222
- *** Metamorphosis 300
- Top 50 Plumb Line 279
- ** Hedgehog Crack 100
- Top 50 Flake Crack (Helsby) 356
- ** Forked Cracks 323
- * Kay 326
- Top 50 Misty Wall 168
- *** Ornithologist's Corner . . . 228
- * Black Pig 54
- ** Coffin Crack 229
- * Contrary Mary 84
- ** Throsher 319
- ** Eliminate (Wilton 1) 310
- Top 50 Mohammed the Mad Monk . . 295
- * Great Slab 315
- * Pinnacle Arete (Skyline) . . 52
- Top 50 Twin Crack Corner 262
- ** Flywalk 311
- ** Condor Slab 56
- ** Left Embrasure 244
- ** Jelly Roll 90
- ** The Crack 142
- ** Flaky Wall Direct 114
- ** Hollybush Crack 87
- ** Keep Arete 141
- ** Kestrel Crack 77
- ** Central Route (Roaches U) 89
- Top 50 Via Dolorosa 71
- ** Stable Cracks 199
- *** Grooved Slab 353
- Top 50 Central Climb (Hen Cloud) 98
- * Foghorn Groove 223
- ** Atropine 143
- * Roof Climb 98
- * Director 132
- * Noddy's Wall 244
- * The Comedian 111
- *** The Mermaid's Ridge . . . 182
- ** Modern 98
- ** Fingernail 308
- ** Little by Little 354

Brian Rossiter on the magnificent Bachelor's Left-hand (HVS) - page 101 - at Hen Cloud.

Western Grit Climbing — Graded List

HS
		Page
*	Epitaph Corner	222
*	The Nose (Castle Naze)	139
**	Cascade	238
**	Pilgrim's Progress	140
*	Sifta's Quid	81
Top 50	Upper Tor Wall	160
	Route 1 (Cows Mouth)	342
*	Artillery Chimney	161
***	Nasal Buttress	243
	Traditional	133
**	Right-hand Route (Roaches Upper)	90
*	Fledgling's Climb	77
Top 50	Route I (Wimberry)	232
***	Technical Slab	88
**	Studio	140
***	Pillar Ridge	206
**	Wedge	300
***	Jeffcoat's Buttress	86
**	Calcutta Crack	91
Top 50	The Left Monolith	257
***	Layback Crack (Dovestones)	246
**	Damascus Crack	84
Top 50	999	315
**	Central Wall	337
*	The Arete (Castle Naze)	138
**	Whittaker's Original	300
**	Mo	326
**	Runner Route	84
**	Twin Caves Crack	356
*	Ogden Arete	54
***	Crack and Corner	90

S
*	The Medicine	131
**	Left-hand Route (Roaches Upper)	90
**	Twin Cracks (Wimberry)	233
*	Tealeaf Crack	84
	The Flywalk	140
**	Cooper's Crack	242
**	Glister Wall	302
**	The Niche	140
*	Green Slab	130
**	Hiker's Crack	160
**	K2	98
**	Parallel Cracks	323
**	Slab and Arete	52
Top 50	Great Chimney (Hen Cloud)	103
***	Bertie's Bugbear	231
*	Keep Corner	141
*	Bird Chimney	311
*	The Nithin	139
***	Via Principia	195
**	Magic Roundabout	115
Top 50	Black and Tans	87
*	Kelly's Shelf	89
**	Green Crack (Windgather)	130
*	Heather Slab	83
*	Yong Arete	70
**	Fern Crack	82
*	Aged Crack	133
Top 50	Long Climb (Laddow)	208
*	Mississippi Crack	131
*	Black Slab	130
***	Black Velvet	87
*	Wall and Groove (Ramshaw)	106

HVD
*	Beckermet Slab	83
***	Phallic Crack	108
Top 50	Pedestal Route	88
***	Maud's Garden	83
**	Nose Direct	132
Top 50	Answer Crack	246
**	Yong	70
*	Chicken Run	82
*	Centre	133
*	Prow Corner Twin Cracks	80
*	Rooster	82
*	Slime Chimney	324

VDiff
*	Middle Buttress Arete	131
*	The Groove (Wilton 3)	323
**	The Arete (Hen Cloud)	98
*	Orange Groove	322
*	Ancient	98
**	Jeffcoat's Chimney	86
***	Splash Arete	297
**	Rappel Wall	326
**	Central Tower (Dovestones)	244
**	Perched Block Arete	54
*	Footprint	132
Top 50	Zig-zag	185
**	Rambling Route	311
*	Toe Nail	132
*	Oak Leaf Crack	323
*	Prow Corner	80
*	Pocket Wall (Hobson Moor)	223
*	Corner Crack (Windgather)	133
Top 50	Boomerang (Ramshaw)	112
***	Right Route (Roaches Upper)	89
**	Prow Cracks	80
**	Ogden	54
*	Sheltered Crack	138
*	Zig-a-Zag-a	142

Diff
*	Double Crack	138
Top 50	Inverted Staircase	82
*	The Rainbow	202
Top 50	High Buttress Arete	132
*	Chockstone Chimney (Windgather)	131
**	Raven Rock Gully	71

Mod
*	South Buttress Crack	135
*	The Staircase (Windgather)	130
**	Downfall Climb	187

> **Top 50** The Top 50 routes is a carefully picked selection of the best routes, across the grades, from each of the areas. There are plenty of really good routes that don't get Top 50 status - *Hen Cloud Eliminate* for example - but you can be sure that any route with the Top 50 symbol is a great route and a worthy tick. Work you way through this list and it will take you to some wonderful remote and diverse locations.

Matt Thompson climbing the excellent unsung gem of *The Left Monolith* (HS) - *page 257* - at Ravenstones. Photo: Mike Hutton

Western Grit

	Area	Routes	up to Sev	HS to HVS	E1 to E3	E4 and up
Staffordshire	Back Forest	25	14 ✓	10 ✓	1 ✓	- ✗
	Roaches Skyline	80	30 ✓✓	24 ✓✓	14 ✓✓	12 ✓✓✓
	The Five Clouds	43	9 ✓	13 ✓✓	13 ✓✓	10 ✓✓
	Roaches Lower	104	18 ✓✓	22 ✓✓✓	28 ✓✓✓	36 ✓✓✓
	Roaches Upper	76	20 ✓✓✓	31 ✓✓✓	13 ✓✓	12 ✓✓
	Hen Cloud	98	13 ✓✓	33 ✓✓✓	22 ✓✓	30 ✓✓✓
	Ramshaw	126	29 ✓✓	37 ✓✓	31 ✓✓	29 ✓✓✓
	Newstones/Baldstones	70	16 ✓	26 ✓✓	18 ✓✓	10 ✓✓
Windgather	Windgather	60	45 ✓✓✓	14 ✓✓	1 ✗	- ✗
	Castle Naze	60	31 ✓✓	25 ✓✓✓	4 ✓	- ✗
	New Mills Tor	34	2 ✓	16 ✓✓	12 ✓✓	4 ✓
Kinder	Kinder South	113	26 ✓✓	32 ✓✓✓	39 ✓✓	16 ✓✓
	Kinder North	104	24 ✓	39 ✓✓✓	28 ✓✓✓	13 ✓✓
	Kinder Downfall	81	21 ✓✓	39 ✓✓	20 ✓✓	1 ✓
Bleaklow/Longdendale	Shining Clough	69	23 ✓✓	30 ✓✓✓	11 ✓✓	5 ✓✓
	Laddow	37	21 ✓✓	11 ✓✓✓	5 ✓	- ✗
	Tintwistle Knarr	25	- ✗	10 ✓✓	10 ✓✓	5 ✓
	Hobson Moor Quarry	41	4 ✗	13 ✓✓	14 ✓✓	10 ✓

Approach	Sun	Green	Shelter	Windy	Access	Summary	Page
30 min	From mid morning					The western extension of the Skyline crags offers a small set of buttresses in a quiet setting.	44
15 to 20	Afternoon					The continuation of the Roaches Upper Tier. Some superb compact buttresses dotted along the ridge. Usually quiet and secluded.	46
10 min	Afternoon				Bird restriction	A small set of crags in front of the main areas. Quiet with some good routes and good bouldering. Occasional bird restriction.	58
10 min	From mid morning	Green				The lower half of the area's best crag. Brilliant routes and buttresses set in the trees. Always busy but plenty of classics to go at.	64
10 min	From mid morning	Green			Bird restriction	The upper half is exposed, popular, and has rock and routes of similar high quality to those below. Occasional bird restriction on central section.	82
10 min	From mid morning	Green				Towering battlements, high on the hill and with a great selection of crack and arete climbs. Often looks greener than it actually is.	92
3 to 10 min	Morning	Green				East facing and easy of access with plenty of wide cracks and rounded exits. Good bouldering and reasonable routes across the grades.	104
5 to 12 min	Morning	Green				A couple of idyllic east facing venues, more famous for bouldering than climbing but worth a look whatever you are into. Good in hot weather.	118
3 min	Afternoon					A delightful little outcrop, the most popular in the book. It faces west and is a great spot for a little gentle after-work action.	128
5 min	Afternoon					A quiet crag with a nice set of crack climbs and plenty in the green and orange zone. A good place for pushing your grade.	136
5 min	Sun and shade		Sheltered			The Peak's attempt at an outdoor climbing wall and a great place for a workout. It has some ever-dry bouldering but is a little urban.	144
60 min	Lots of sun			Windy		The sunny side of Kinder, big blobby outcrops of coarse rock in a lovely setting. It is possible to link several cliffs in one day by a walk along the rim.	152
50 min	Not much sun	Green		Windy		The dark side of Kinder, as remote as any in the area, with an hour's approach and a good chance of having the place to yourself.	166
70 min	Sun and shade	Green		Windy		Wild and windy, a place enjoyed by the pioneers and still well worth a visit especially if the Downfall is frozen!	178
40 min	Not much sun	Green		Windy		Bleaklow's finest, a set of tall buttress a long way from the road and facing north. A great hot weather retreat.	192
40 min	Morning			Windy		Lofty and neglected buttresses, once at the cutting edge but now seeing little traffic. It has some good low to mid grade routes.	204
20 min	Lots of sun					A neglected quarry with a good selection of climbs, most of which are hard, and all of which need more traffic.	212
1 min	Sun and shade		Sheltered			Western Grit's roadside cliff, catching the afternoon sun, it is great for a quick fix.	218

Staffordshire | Windgather | Kinder | Bleaklow | Chew | Lancashire | Cheshire

Western Grit

	Routes	up to Sev	HS to HVS	E1 to E3	E4 and up
Chew Valley					
Wimberry	78	13 ✓✓✓	19 ✓✓✓	21 ✓✓✓	25 ✓✓✓
Wilderness Valley	32	13 ✓	12 ✓	4 ✓	3 ✓
Dovestones Edge	87	35 ✓✓	33 ✓✓	14 ✓✓	5 ✓✓
Ravenstones	61	19 ✓✓	22 ✓✓	15 ✓✓	5 ✓✓
Standing Stones	52	9 ✓	20 ✓✓	19 ✓✓	4 ✗
Upperwood Quarry	33	1 ✗	11 ✓	13 ✓✓	8 ✓✓
Alderman	13	6 ✓	4 ✓	3 ✗	- ✗
Running Hill Pits	90	9 ✗	37 ✓	30 ✓✓	14 ✓✓
Den Lane	25	2 ✗	17 ✓	5 ✓	1 ✗
Lancashire					
Hoghton	7	- ✗	3 ✓	4 ✓✓✓	- ✗
Denham	42	11 ✓	11 ✓✓	13 ✓	7 ✓✓
Anglezarke	46	3 ✗	23 ✓✓	9 ✓✓	11 ✓✓
Wilton 1	61	3 ✓	22 ✓✓	14 ✓✓✓	22 ✓✓✓
Wilton 2 and 3	82	28 ✓✓	22 ✓✓	25 ✓✓	7 ✓✓
Brownstones	47	24 ✓✓	15 ✓✓	7 ✓✓	1 ✓
Egerton	18	- ✗	10 ✓✓	4 ✓	4 ✓✓
Cadshaw Castle	28	19 ✓✓	7 ✓✓	2 ✗	- ✗
Littleborough Area	71	10 ✓	35 ✓✓	18 ✓✓	8 ✓
Cheshire					
Helsby	94	11 ✓	24 ✓✓✓	30 ✓✓✓	29 ✓✓✓
Frodsham	67	25 ✓	22 ✓✓	15 ✓✓	5 ✓
Pex Hill	125	13 ✓✓	25 ✓✓	49 ✓✓✓	38 ✓✓✓

Quality and range of routes in different grade bands: ✓✓✓ - Excellent ✓✓ - Good ✓ - Okay ✗ - Not worth a visit

Approach	Sun	Green	Shelter	Windy	Access	Summary	Page
30 min	Not much sun	Green		Windy		A superb cliff with soaring cracks and grooves as well as some intimidating blank faces. Excellent across the grades but it needs good conditions.	226
30 min	Afternoon			Windy		Three small outcrops in a remote setting. Always quiet but worth the effort if the weather is on your side.	236
30 min	Evening			Windy		A bit of a hike but a fine set of lower and middle grade climbs that catch the evening sun. Gritty after rain.	240
25 min	Not much sun	Green		Windy		North-facing, green and miles from the road! The good side? A cracking set of climbs in a majestic moorland setting.	252
15 min	Lots of sun			Windy		Sunny of aspect and relatively easy of access compared to other Chew crags, yet strangely neglected.	259
3 min	Morning					An east-facing quarry, high and cool and best used as a retreat on hot days. The climbs are generally hard but worthwhile.	266
15 min	Lots of sun			Windy		A very pleasant outcrop set above a massively steep slope. Multi-pitch routes possible.	270
10 to 15 min	Sun and shade	Green	Sheltered			A small series of quarries with some great rock. Unfortunately the aspect means that the place is often green. Best on warm summer evenings.	272
2 min	Morning		Sheltered			Only minutes from the road, an east facing quarry, with some steep jamming cracks and tough grades.	284
4 min	Not much sun	Green	Sheltered		Restrictions	A magnificent but neglected quarry with 3 of the best E2s around. Limited and very strict access requirements hence neglected and green.	290
4 min	Afternoon		Sheltered			A west-facing quarry, seconds from the road and with some pleasant climbs and good bouldering.	292
2 to 5 min	Sun and shade		Sheltered			An easy accessible quarry with rock of variable quality. Popular with groups but with good climbing if you seek it out.	298
5 min	Morning	Green	Sheltered			An impressive and imposing quarry with climbs to match. Good cracks and walls but can be green. Now owned by the BMC.	304
3 min	Sun and shade		Sheltered		Restrictions	The friendly side of Lancashire quarries with many lower-grade climbs. Restricted access times and one bird restriction.	316
3 min	Afternoon		Sheltered			Roadside bouldering, short and sunny and on excellent rock.	327
10 min	Sun and shade		Sheltered			A large quarry with a few good buttresses. A number of top notch climbs and good in hot weather.	332
20 min	Lots of sun		Sheltered			A very popular little crag with a good set of easy and mid grade routes in a pleasant location.	336
15 to 20 min	Afternoon					Three venues, which are close enough together to be visited in the same day.	338
10 min	Evening	Green	Sheltered		Restrictions	Cheshire's finest, an excellent sandstone cliff with quality routes. Often stared at but seldom visited. Occasional bird restriction on one section.	346
10 min	Evening	Green	Sheltered			Strenuous bouldering in a wooded setting, a great place for a full body work out (reaches the parts that Pex Hill doesn't).	358
5 min	Sun and shade		Sheltered			Merseyside's own outdoor climbing wall, and a cracker it is too. A place designed to hone technique and sharpen finger strengthen.	366

Staffordshire

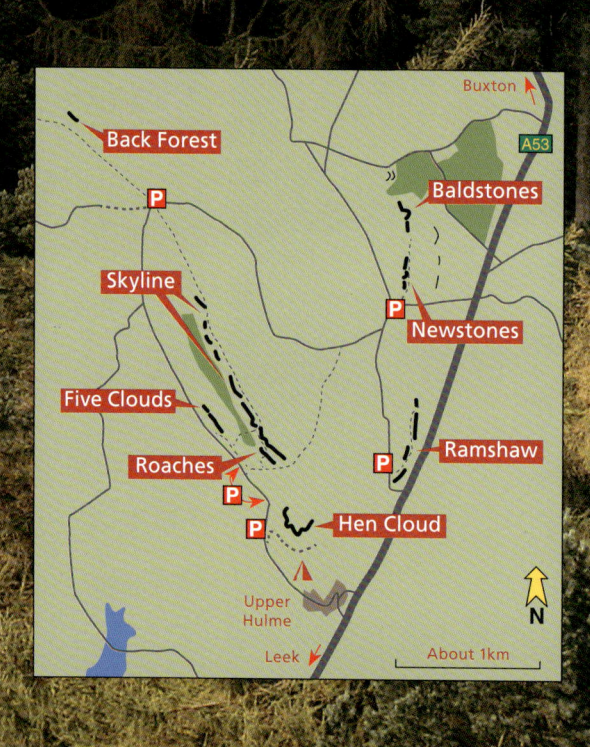

Glorious light on the magnificent *Valkyrie* (VS) - *page 72* - on the Lower Tier of the Roaches. Photo: Jon Read

44 Back Forest

Back Forest is the western extension of the Skyline section of the Roaches and it consists of several pleasant bits of rock scattered along the ridge, only a couple are mentioned here. The area is very tranquil when compared to nearby honey-pots, the lack of major classics and the slightly awkward parking situation tend to keep the crowds away. It is not a good venue for large groups and this is actively discouraged by The Peak Park.

	No star	★	★★	★★★
Mod to S	9	4	1	-
HS to HVS	3	6	1	-
E1 to E3	-	-	1	-
E4 and up	-	-	-	-

Approach   See map on page 42
There is limited parking either side of the cattle grid at Roach End where the minor road that runs under The Roaches and the Five Clouds crosses over to the east of the ridge. **Please park sensibly.** Cross the style and follow the wall northwest-wards for 800m until the path splits. The Main Crag is another 300m along the track and is easily reached from the upper (ridge-crest) path.

Conditions
The various buttresses face pretty much south and so get all the sun that is going, though they are exposed to southwesterlies. The crag dries rapidly after rain and is generally clean and lichen-free.

Beyond the Back Forest cliffs the solitary buttress of the Hanging Stone can be seen standing in the field behind Hanging Stone Farm. There are less than half a dozen routes here and although the best of these is excellent, climbing on the rock is discouraged by the Peak Park and by the farmer who owns the rock.

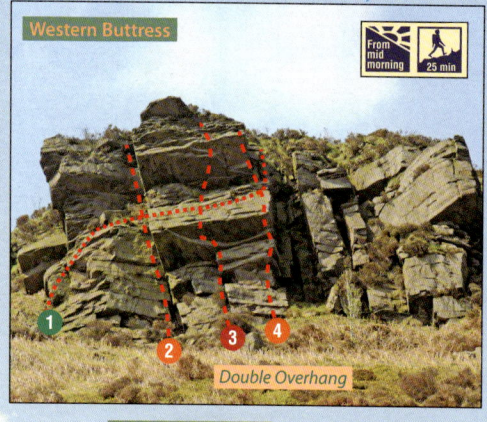

Western Buttress
This small outcrop is around 900m further on from the main crag, past a small buttress known as the Rostrum (not described).

① The Gaping Void . . . . . . ★   **VDiff**
14m. A mild but exciting crossing of the buttress via the mid-height line which is easier for shorties.
FA. Dave Salt 1971

② Burnham Crack . . . .   **VS 4b**
10m. Pleasant bridging up the steep groove on the left.
FA. Dave Salt 1971

③ Double Overhang . . ★★   **E1 5b**
10m. A midget gem and worth the walk. Attack the double overhangs phlegmatically. A long reach and some power help too.
FA. Dave Salt (one nut) 1971. FFA. Tony Barley 1974

④ Mr Creosote . . . .   **HVS 5b**
10m. The steep right arete of the buttress.
FA. Roger Nichols 1991

Back Forest

Main Crag
The rest of the routes are on the Main Crag, which is the first section of rock reached from the road.

5 Twin Thin .... ☐ **S 4a**
8m. The left-hand side-wall of the buttress is pleasant enough.

6 Eye of Japetus .... ☐ **HVS 5a**
8m. Nice moves up the wall just to the left of the arete.

7 Holly Tree Niche Left ... ☐ **S 4a**
8m. Climb just right of the arete to the niche (wot - no holly?) then finish up the flakes in the bulge to the left.

8 Holly Tree Niche .... ☐ **Diff**
8m. The niche is entered and exited direct.

9 The Keeper .... ☐ **HVS 5a**
8m. Pull over the roof to gain the fingery side-wall and climb it rightwards to exit.

10 Portcullis Crack .... ☐ **S 4a**
8m. The steep central crack has good moves. Finish leftwards on the well-positioned arete.

The next routes are either side of a deep and wide rift.

11 Keep Face .... ☐ **S 4a**
8m. Hop onto the jutting ledge using a convenient block then climb leftwards to easy ground. The arete of the previous route gives the best finale.

12 The Saucer .... ☐ **VDiff**
8m. Follow the slanting slab round the arete to gain the crack in the side-wall of the chimney.

13 Capstone Chimney ...... ☐ **S 4a**
8m. The narrowing is blocked by some blocky blocks!

14 Bollard Edge .... ☐ **VS 4b**
8m. The left edge of the jutting buttress is climbed past a roof early on an the jutting (and loose?) block of the bollard. Finish up the left-hand side of the final overhang. Steep!

15 Toe Rail .... ☐ **HVS 5a**
8m. Tackle the right-hand side of the arete as direct as the holds allow. Another short but shocking one! A **Direct Start** over the initial bulge is a stretchy **5c**.

16 Pseudo Crack .... ☐ **HVD**
8m. The open groove has some nice holds and moves.

17 Bastion Corner .... ☐ **VDiff**
8m. Balance up the right wall of the corner to reach the arete.

The next buttress has twinned triangular overhangs near the top.

18 Green Shaker .... ☐ **VDiff**
8m. Climb onto the block/ledge then loop out onto the left-hand face, finishing rightwards.

19 Central Route .... ☐ **HS 4b**
8m. From the block/ledge climb to the capping roofs and squeeze between them for an awkward exit.

20 No So Central Route ...... ☐ **S 4a**
8m. From the block/ledge move right to outflank the roof then finish up the side-wall.

21 Thin Crack .... ☐ **HS 4a**
8m. The cracks in the right wall are reached from the right then sprinted to the top. A **Direct Start** is **5b**.

The next short buttress has the final set of worthwhile routes.

22 Requiem for Tired Fingers ☐ **HVS 5b**
6m. The left-hand side of the wall is quite pushy.

23 Grasper .... ☐ **HS 4a**
6m. Climb up the centre of the wall to testing exit via the diagonal crack.

24 Mustard .... ☐ **S 4c**
6m. A sharp pull gains the easier wall left of the arete.

25 Rocking Stone Ridge ...... ☐ **VDiff**
6m. Pull right to gain the crest then amble up it.

To the right are a series of short walls that give some pleasant bouldering.

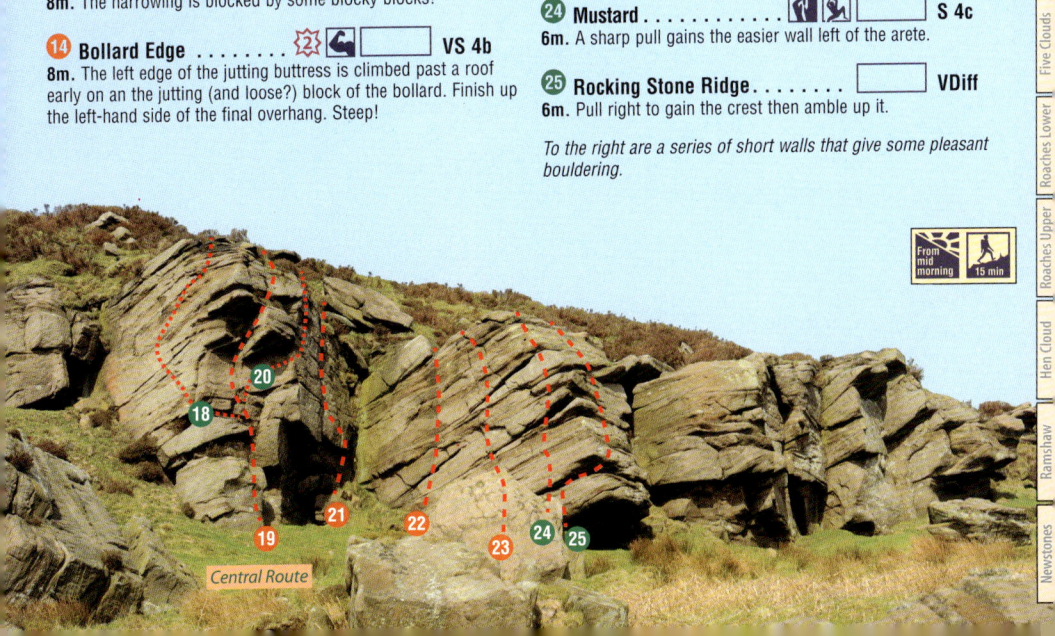

Roaches Skyline

	No star	★	★★	★★★
Mod to S	14	11	5	-
HS to HVS	6	14	4	-
E1 to E3	3	5	3	3
E4 and up	1	5	3	3

Although close to the busy Upper and Lower Tiers at the Roaches, the Skyline area offers climbing in much quieter and more remote setting. The Skyline edge presents a series of small buttresses dotted along the ridge, often rising out of a tree-covered base. The main path runs along the top of the ridge meaning that there is little passing traffic and the only other people you are likely to meet are other climbers who have put in the effort to walk that bit further. Once under the crag you will find rock and routes as good as on the main Roaches crags with some real gems hidden away.

Approach
The Skyline can be approached from either end and it is best to pick out which buttress you want to head for before you make your decision. The most common approach is via the Roaches Main Crag along the popular path which leads up under the Upper Tier and onto the crag top. From there it follows the cliff-top edge path past the Doxey Pool all the way to Roach End. For a slightly shorter walk if you are intending on Far Skyline or Hard Very Far Skyline, you can approach from the limited parking on the minor road from Roach Grange to Hazel Barrow, it is about 10 mins along the ridge to the Hard Very Far Skyline buttress.

Conditions
The Skyline is exposed to bad weather and there is little shelter from the wind but it dries quickly following any rain and can be a great venue on a crisp winter's day.

Roaches Skyline

47

Andy Turner claiming his wings as he leaps for the top hold of *Wings of Unreason* (E4) - *page 48* - on the Skyline. Photo: Jon Read

Roaches Skyline — Hard Very Far Skyline

Hard Very Far Skyline

❶ Willow Farm **E4 6a**
10m. The elegant slab on the left edge of the buttress is gained steeply and climbed precariously. As good and as unprotected as it appears from below.
FA. Chris Hamper 1977

❷ Track of the Cat Top 50 .... **E5 6a**
12m. A powerful start and a technical groove (pull out right as soon as you can) culminate in an insecure and smeary reach for the top. On the final crucial section, the gear is a little too far away for comfort. Low in the grade though harder for the short.
FA. Jonny Woodward 1977

❸ Nature Trail **E5 6b**
10m. Make a hard pull onto the slab (cams in low pocket to avoid gear in *Wings*) and blast up the slab to a final smeary move.
FA. Simon Nadin 1985

❹ Wings of Unreason .... Top 50 .... **E4 6a**
10m. The tough start gains the centre of the slab and a runner slot. Mantel then stretch/leap for the top. The tall have an unfair advantage (**E2 5c-ish**) and the short will struggle (**E5 6b**).
Photo on pages 33 and 46.
FA. Jonny Woodward 1977

❺ Counterstroke of Equity
.... **E5 6c**
10m. A delicate combination of intense smearing and frantic scratching topped off with a dynamic finish. Use the *Wings of Unreason* pocket for much-needed protection. A **Direct Start** and no runners make it more like **E7 6c**.
FA. Richard Davies 1985. FA. (Direct) Julian Lines (solo) 2003

❻ Prelude to Space .... **HVS 4c**
10m. The delicate right-hand arete forms a pleasant contrast to the tough offerings further left. As expected, it is unprotected.
FA. Andrew Woodward 1977

Very Far Skyline **Roaches Skyline** 49

Very Far Skyline

7 Triple Point E1 5c
8m. Slap and flap over the flat roof as for *Wild Thing*. Step up to a good wire slot, then head left to the arete and sprint up this. A **Direct Start** up the undercut arete is **6b**.
FA. Jonny Woodward 1982

8 Wild Thing.......... HVS 5c
6m. Enter the groove by frustrating moves and balance up it delicately. Pretty much all over after the first couple of moves, though oddly the starting moves would get 6a were they at the top!
FA. Andrew Woodward 1977

9 Entropy's Jaw .. E5 6b
8m. Start up *Wild Thing* but follow the impossibly-thin seam up the smooth slab to the right. Good but hard-earned small wires protect; they have been tested but this definitely isn't to be recommended.
FA. Andrew Woodward 1982

10 Script for a Tier ... E6 6c
8m. Step out from the flake of *Mild Thing* to gain the face left of the undercut arete and sketch up this.
FA. Simon Nadin 1985

Hard Very and Very Far Skyline

A remote series of small buttresses with a collection of great climbs on some of the best rock around.
Approach - From the left-hand end of the Upper Tier, follow the cliff-top path past the Doxey Pool and on for about 500m (30mins from the main parking.)
Or, from the limited parking on the minor road from Roach Grange to Hazel Barrow, it is about 10 mins along the ridge to the Hard Very Far Skyline buttress.

11 Mild Thing .... Diff
6m. Use the flake to gain the floral cracks. Well-named.
FA. Andrew Woodward 1977

100m right is a solitary block below the path.

12 Art Nouveau ... E6 6c
6m. A brilliant undercutting exercise "the best sequence on grit" up the rising diagonal overlap. The main small wire placement has gone west so it is solo only now, although the landing can be padded but it is still E6!
FA. Simon Nadin 1985

Roaches Skyline — Alpha Buttress

Alpha Buttress
A pleasant slabby buttress situated in the middle of nowhere - almost always quiet and a good place to escape the crowds that populate the Main Crag.
Approach - From the left-hand end of the Upper Tier, follow the main path on the top of the crag. Head left until you reach a muddy pond - The Doxey Pool. Skyline Buttress is below here and Alpha Buttress is a little further along. The best descent is beyond the buttress.

1 Melaleucion............ HVS 5a
8m. The butch front of the first buttress has a steep start and a bevy of shelving overlaps above.
FA. Steve Dale 1976

2 Devotoed............ VS 5a
8m. Tackle the crack in the right wall to a rounded exit.
FA. Gary Gibson 1979

3 Alpha............ VDiff
8m. The shallow groove is awkward but the gear is good.

4 Alpha Arete............ S 4a
8m. The acute arete by some pleasantly mild laybacking.

5 Breakfast Corner............ Mod
6m. The main groove is about as easy as they come.

6 Formative Years............ E3 6a
8m. The narrow technical slab needs blinkers really.
FA. Howard Tingle 1982

7 Breakfast Problem............ VDiff
8m. A pair of cracks in the left-hand edge of the slab fuse as they rise. Avoiding the right-hand crack is tricky.

8 Days Gone By............ S 4a
8m. The right-hand crack has nice moves but is squeezed.
FA. Gary Gibson 1978

9 San Melas............ E3 5c
8m. The centre of the slab to a move right at half height and a delicate finish. The start is bold but the smeary upper slab is protected by large cams in the break.
Photos opposite and on page 7.
FA. Andrew Woodward 1977

10 Hallow to our Men............ E4 6b
8m. A direct-ish start to San Melas up the shallow groove. A right-hand finish is also possible, but not very independent.
FA. Gary Gibson 1981

11 Mantis............ E1 5b
8m. The elegant arete on its right then left with a bold start to large cams in the break - a breather - then an airy finish.
FA. Andrew Woodward 1974

12 Sennapod............ VDiff
8m. The corner named is after its famous Welsh counterpart. It is better that it looks with good bridging moves.
FA. Gary Gibson 1978

13 Sennapod Crack............ VDiff
8m. The crack just right of the corner.

14 39th Step............ E2 6a
8m. The groove right of the corner and the slab above. An easily-placed side runner is normal at the grade.
FA. Gary Gibson 1979

15 Wallaby Wall............ HS 4b
10m. The wide awkward crack in the centre of the slab leads to ledges. Excellent moves (or the inferior grassy flakes just left - **S**) and a short tricky traverse to the left-hand flake on the upper wall and a sweet layback completes the fun.

16 Definitive Gaze............ E1 5c
10m. Artificial but with some good moves and decent protection and quite popular for an eliminate. Climb through a scoop and up the indefinite flaky crack directly above.
FA. Gary Gibson 1979

17 Right-hand Route............ S 4a
12m. Worth seeking out. Climb the jamming crack into the chimney then step out left - choice of levels - to reach a well-positioned flake. Finish up this.

18 Looking for Today............ HVS 5b
8m. The thin crack and short face.

Alpha Buttress **Roaches Skyline** 51

John Read and Mark Sharrat imitating each other on *San Melas* (E3) - *opposite*. Photos: Sharrat and Read

11 *Mantis*
12
13
14
15
16
17
18

Roaches Skyline — Skyline Buttress

Skyline Buttress

Rather remote but with a good selection of lower grade climbs. There is usually a team or two here although the crowds of the Upper and Lower Tier will not be present.

Approach - From the left-hand end of the Upper Tier, follow the main path up to the top of the crag. Head left until you reach the pond of The Doxey Pool. Skyline Buttress is below the edge here.

The first three routes are on an isolated slab down and left.

1 Pinnacle Crack . . . . **Diff**
6m. The crack is over far too soon.

2 Split Personality **E1 5b**
6m. The centre of the face of the block, starting up the right-hand arete and finishing up a thin crack-line.
FA. Gary Gibson 1979

3 Pinnacle Arete . . . . **VS 4c**
6m. The arete of the block is a bold little number.
FA. R.Desmond-Stevens 1945

Back on the main edge.

4 Mantelshelf Slab . . **VS 4b**
12m. From the arete, trend left and climb the slab, using the eponymous move at least once. Bold in the middle then easing.

5 Enigma Variation **E2 5b**
12m. The arete is followed past the overlap, then trend left up the slab. Delicate and not too well-protected though low in the grade.
FA. Andrew Woodward 1976

6 Karabiner Chimney . . . **HVD**
10m. The right-facing cleft is a mini-classic of its type.
FA. R.Desmond-Stevens 1945

7 Karabiner Slab . . . . **HVS 4c**
10m. The slab just right is climbed direct on rounded breaks.

8 Karabiner Cracks . . . . **Diff**
12m. The scruffy crack system to fields and a chimney finish.
FA. A.Simpson 1947

9 Slab and Arete . . . . **S 4a**
18m. Reach the ascending traverse from the left (awkward) using the scruffy crack as little as possible. Originally the pocketed slab just right was the start, but this is a polished 5b now. Follow the break out to the right arete and a nicely exposed finish. The direct start up the right-hand arete is **Slips, E3 6a**.
FA. G.Stoneley 1945. FA. (Slips) Gary Gibson 1982

10 Drop Acid **E4 6a**
14m. Climb the left-hand side of the slab and difficult overhang - a runner on the left is sensible to protect the roof. Contrived.
FA. John Allen 1987

11 Acid Drop **E4 5c**
16m. Delicate dancing, then a butch and bold finale. Trend rightwards up the slab following an undercut flake. Pull over this then tackle the centre of the overhang. Poorly protected and reachy.
FA. Jonny Woodward 1987

12 Skytrain **E2 5b**
14m. Climb the left-trending crack (hard) then the delicate (and avoidable) slab left of the easy upper section of *Slab and Arete*.
FA. John Peel 1977

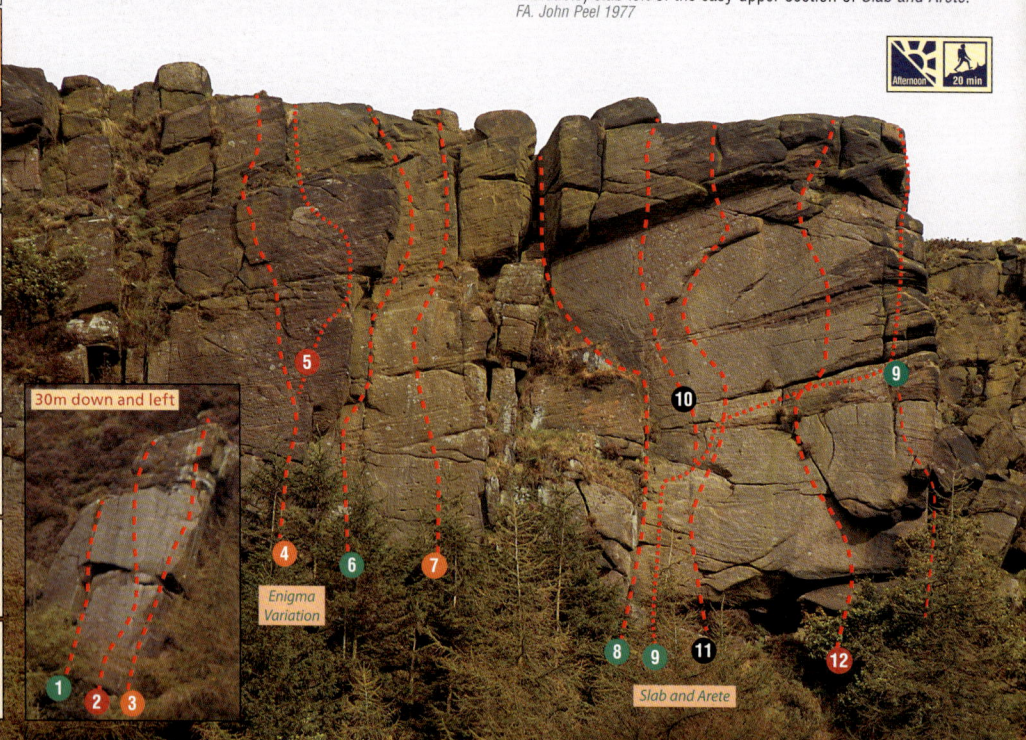

Andy Turner nearing the top of *Topaz* (E2) - *page 55* - on Tower Buttress on the Skyline. Photo: Jon Read

Roaches Skyline — Tower Buttress

Tower Buttress

An interesting set of walls and towers with a good mix of climbs, including a number of short lower grade offerings, and a smaller collection of bigger beefier routes.

Approach - From the left-hand end of the Upper Tier follow the small path along the crag base leftwards and uphill passing under Condor Buttress.

The rather green side-wall is home to **Sorcerer's Apprentice, E1 5b**. *The lower face leads to a hanging crack which features a grim exit.*

1 Tower Eliminate .... HVS 5b
14m. In the left-hand face of the tower, steep cracks lead past a poor rest in a niche. It is also possible to finish up the arete.
FA. Colin Foord 1967

2 Tower Face E2 5b
14m. Climb an initial groove and follow tenuous cracks until forced right for a steep finale on the front. Scary and rounded.
FA. Al Simpson 1977

3 Tower Chimney .... Diff
16m. The chimney splitting the buttress is very traditional.

4 Perched Block Arete .... VDiff
16m. Climb the right arete of the buttress on its right-hand side, passing over the perched block to the final wall where spooky moves left into the chimney become imperative. A **Direct Finish** is **VS 4b** and a bold **Right-hand Finish**, via a flake, is **HVS 4c**.

5 Thrug .... VS 5a
8m. The th(r)uggish crack splitting the steep wall. Short-lived.

6 Bad Poynt .... Diff
10m. The slab and crack above a boulder was a late find. Beware the odd wobbly hold.
FA. Gary Gibson 1978

7 Oversite .... HVD
10m. The slabby and (mildly bold) arete was also over-looked.

8 Ogden .... VDiff
8m. The pleasant left-trending crack on polished footholds.

9 Ogden Arete .... HS 4c
8m. The neat arete with a powerful start and pleasant above.

10 Ogden Recess .... VDiff
8m. Grunt up the wider fissure then finish direct.

11 Black Pig .... VS 4c
8m. The thin crack in the right wall of the chimney deserves its name (and 5c) if you don't use the footholds behind you!

12 Spare Rib .... VS 4c
8m. The right arete of the wall is serious but well worth doing.
FA. Jonny Woodward 1977

13 Bad Sneakers E2 5c
8m. This attempt to climb the smooth slab almost gets forced into the gully before looping back right to finish. Direct is **E3**.
FA. Dave Jones 1977

14 Spectrum .... HVS 4c
8m. The right-hand side of the slab to a short crack.
FA. Jonny Woodward 1977

15 Middleton's Motion .... VS 4b
10m. Climb straight to, and through, a short roof crack. Not quite as stiff a problem as you might be expecting.

SAFETY NET **Roaches Skyline** 55

16 Topaz E2 5b
10m. The slanting crack on the right-hand side of the overhang is approached via the rib and has a moment or two of interest up the final exposed rib. *Photo on page 53*.
FA. Gary Gibson 1979

17 Strain Station E4 5c
12m. From the top of the rib, attack the roof leftwards to a finish up the bold hanging arete above the lip. May still be unrepeated.
FA. Gary Gibson 1981

18 Letter Box Gully .... Mod
10m. The slabby left-hand side of the recess leads to a cave recess where you can post yourself to make a subterranean exit. Not recommended for the chunky!

19 Letter Box Cracks ..... VS 4c
10m. Twin cracks above deep recess are separated by a huge keyed-in block. Approach via the corner below then climb one (jamming) or both (bridging) to the top.

20 Safety Net E1 5b
10m. The centre of the buttress leads over an overhang to another that caps the wall, and is cleaved by an excellent flake. Finish up this with gusto. A classic E1 experience. *Photo page 57*.
FA. John Allen 1975

21 Shortcomings E1 5c
10m. The flake that runs up the right edge of the buttress is the substance of the route. Reach it with difficulty (hard for everybody and especially so for the short - **E2**) and sprint up it by quality barn-door layback moves.
FA. Gary Gibson 1978

Safety Net
The start of the main section of the Skyline Area is a wide set of buttresses, wall and grooves. On the right is a rounded and undercut buttress split by an overhang at half-height. It is home to a couple of popular test-pieces.
Approach - From the left-hand end of the Upper Tier follow the small path at the crag base leftwards and uphill under Condor Buttress via vague tracks.

22 Left Twin Crack .... HS 4b
10m. The twin cracks in the left wall of the recess via a groove. The route starts as for *Square Chimney* and improves with height.

23 Square Chimney .... Diff
8m. The mild angle in the left-hand corner of the recess.

24 Trio Chimney .... VDiff
8m. The right-hand angle is better than it looks. Start inside.

25 Substance .... VS 4c
8m. Despite the name, the left-hand arete of the next buttress is of no great substance.
FA. Gary Gibson 1978

26 Lighthouse .... VDiff
10m. The centre of the face has a polished and perplexing start. It is pleasant above though the gear does not inspire.

27 Ralph's Mantelshelves ..... S 4a
8m. From the right toe of the buttress mantel-a-way up the face heading leftwards. A more direct version is the same grade.

Roaches Skyline — Condor Buttress

Condor Buttress

Being home to several worthwhile lower and middle grade routes makes this the most popular destination on the Skyline.

Approach - From the left end of the Upper Tier, follow the small path under the crag leftwards and uphill, above the fence. Where this path heads up towards the crest of the moor walk leftwards for a couple of minutes.

1 Condor Slab .... VS 4c
14m. The centre of the slab is climbed passing a hole to a ledge then a finish up the face above and slightly right. Good climbing that is poorly-protected. A large cam is useful near the top.

2 A.M. Anaesthetic ..... HVS 4c
14m. The right arete of the buttress is precarious, and although low in the grade, protection is somewhat lacking.
FA. Gary Gibson 1978

3 Cracked Arete .... HVD
14m. Climb the well-travelled slab (tricky to start) to a ledge then tackle the well protected crack left of the final chimney.

4 Condor Chimney .... VDiff
8m. The chimney at the back of the ledge is pleasant enough and is easiest if you don't get in too deep. Finish on the right.

5 Nosepicker E1 5a
8m. Climb the acute arete throughout, carefully following the left-hand side of the jutting nose of rock to a finish on the right.
FA. Jonny Woodward 1976

6 Time to be Had .... HVD
8m. The thin twisting cracks in the wall to the right are pleasant and well-protected. There is a choice of finishes.
FA. Gary Gibson 1978

7 Tobacco Road .... VS 4c
8m. The centre of the wall on improving holds. The initial bulge (5b direct) might have you puffing a little.

8 Wheeze .... HVS 4c
14m. Climb the easy lower rib to the break (large gear) then the poorly-protected upper arete, stepping right above the bulge for the maximum exposure.
FA. Jonny Woodward 1976

9 Bruno Flake .... VS 4b
8m. The steep groove just round to the right is awkward; especially passing the overhang. You may arrive at the top ready rubbed and big gear may help.

10 Navy Cut .... VDiff
8m. The twisting groove/niche in the slab to the right leads to a position below the roof and has an unlikely exit.

11 Chicane .... S 4a
6m. The blunt central rib from a block. Head right then left.
FA. Gary Gibson 1978

12 Lung Cancer .... S 3c
6m. The right edge of the wall, zigzagging through the bulges. Typically the climbing eases as soon as the runners arrive!
FA. Jonny Woodward 1977

Paul Evans on the superb *Saftey Net* (E1) - *page 55* - on Tower Buttress on the Skyline. Photo: Nick Smith

The Five Clouds

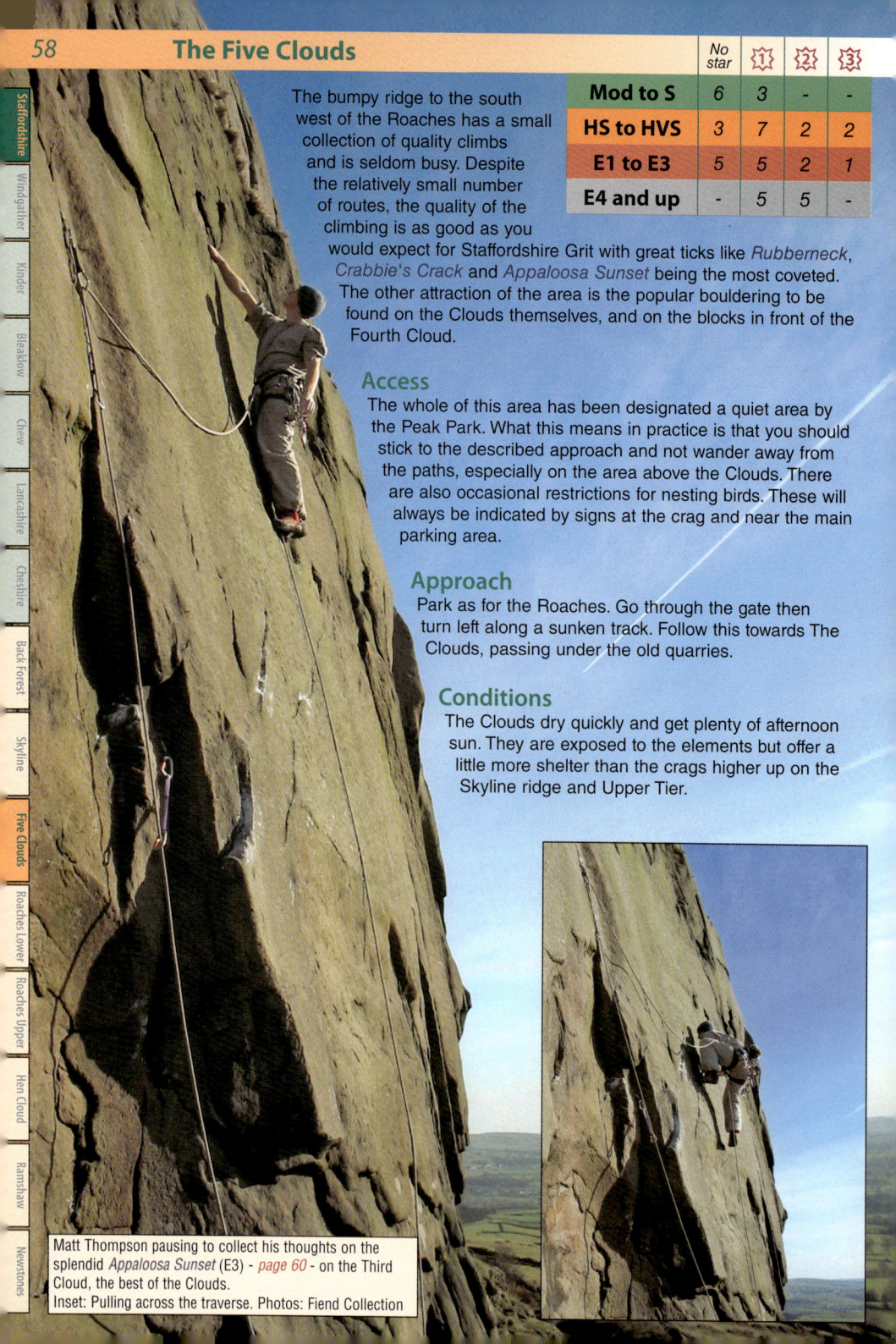

	No star	★	★★	★★★
Mod to S	6	3	-	-
HS to HVS	3	7	2	2
E1 to E3	5	5	2	1
E4 and up	-	5	5	-

The bumpy ridge to the south west of the Roaches has a small collection of quality climbs and is seldom busy. Despite the relatively small number of routes, the quality of the climbing is as good as you would expect for Staffordshire Grit with great ticks like *Rubberneck*, *Crabbie's Crack* and *Appaloosa Sunset* being the most coveted. The other attraction of the area is the popular bouldering to be found on the Clouds themselves, and on the blocks in front of the Fourth Cloud.

Access

The whole of this area has been designated a quiet area by the Peak Park. What this means in practice is that you should stick to the described approach and not wander away from the paths, especially on the area above the Clouds. There are also occasional restrictions for nesting birds. These will always be indicated by signs at the crag and near the main parking area.

Approach

Park as for the Roaches. Go through the gate then turn left along a sunken track. Follow this towards The Clouds, passing under the old quarries.

Conditions

The Clouds dry quickly and get plenty of afternoon sun. They are exposed to the elements but offer a little more shelter than the crags higher up on the Skyline ridge and Upper Tier.

Matt Thompson pausing to collect his thoughts on the splendid *Appaloosa Sunset* (E3) - *page 60* - on the Third Cloud, the best of the Clouds.
Inset: Pulling across the traverse. Photos: Fiend Collection

The Fourth Cloud **The Five Clouds** 59

The Fourth Cloud

The Fourth Cloud is not as good as its bigger neighbour number Three but still has a few short problems of interest that are worth calling in for.
Access - Birds have nested on the ledge above *Boysen's Delight* and access has been restricted in the past. If the birds return, signs will be posted.

1 Meander .... VDiff
8m. The centre of the slab, trending left once past the overlap.

2 Meander Variation E1 5b
10m. Climb the short layback flake, meander left then climb the steep sidewall.
FA. Chris Hamper 1977

3 Stranglehold E1 5b
10m. Undercut up the right edge of the wall then go!

4 Smun .... VS 4c
8m. Smun indeed! Spring up the wall to a diagonal flake and follow this strenuously rightwards until the crack on the right can be reached for an easier finish.

5 Left-hand Block Crack .... S 4a
6m. Climb the roof and take the left-hand groove in the recess.

6 Right-hand Block Crack .... S 4a
6m. It's all in the name.

7 Winter in Combat E1 5c
6m. The slab and arete on the side-wall are quite technical.

8 The Shining Path .. E7 6c
10m. A hard pull over the roof leads to a horizontal break (cams) then smear up the centre of the impossibly bald slab.
FA. Mark Katz 1996

9 Private Display E1 5b
10m. Start from a boulder then climb the arete and thin crack. Pleasantly technical climbing with good small wire protection.
FA. John Yates (in ripped trews) 1970

10 Boysen's Delight .... HVS 5c
10m. A thin crack leads with difficulty (and good runners) into the easier twisting fissure above and often via some bird plop.
FA. Martin Boysen 1968

11 Milky Buttons V8
The blank bubbly scoop as far as the break

12 Mirror, Mirror E5 6b
10m. A little beauty. Climb the centre of the wall with difficult moves left and a crucial section past the curving overlap (small wire up and right). A right-hand exit is somewhat easier.
FA. Andrew Woodward 1977

13 Mantelshelf Route .... Diff
10m. Mantel up the ledges and finish up the groove.

14 Chockstone Corner .... Diff
6m. The groove with the expected jammed stone.

15 Roman Candle .... HVS 5b
6m. From the block shoot hard left into the short crack.
FA. John Henry Bull 2002

16 Roman Nose E2 5b
6m. Start on the right and stride out onto the beak which is followed delicately via sketchy finger flakes and neat moves. Low in the grade as long as the creaky flakes stay where they are.
FA. Dave Jones 1977

The Five Clouds — The Third Cloud

The Third Cloud

The juiciest climbing on the Clouds is on the third and largest lump, *Rubberneck* and *Appaloosa Sunset* are the best but *Crabbie's Crack* and *Flower Power Arete* are also well worthwhile. If you are into gritstone at its most technical then the well-named *Who Needs Ready Brek?* should offer food for thought - just make sure you have that extra Weetabix!

1 Glass Back .... **VDiff**
6m. The awkward left-hand fissure in the main buttress.

2 Elastic Arm **E1 5b**
6m. The wide crack in the upper half of the face can be gained from the left and is a nightmare of a thrash. A Curbar refugee.
FA. Dave Salt 1960s

3 Persistence .... **V3 (6a)**
Finesse up the thin flakes above the lip of the overlap. Escape left or get some gear thrown up and have a go at .....

4 Sands of Time **E4 6a**
6m. Climb *Persistence* to the break and step right. The blunt nose above gives a (much) more serious continuation.
FA. (Sands of Time) Richard Pickford 1993

5 Who Needs Ready Brek?
.... **V10**
8m. The grade has been the cause of some controversy. Start up *Persistence* and follow the unbelievably-thin break rightwards with concentrated desperation. Pull up to the main break then bale out.
FA. Simon Nadin 1986. Rarely repeated over 20 years later.

6 Cloudbusting **E4 6b**
8m. A technical test-piece, although less so than *Ready Brek*. Start left of *Rubberneck* and climb the wall diagonally leftwards (a little lower than you might expect) by a mega-stretch (6c for shorties?). Escape off left.
FA. Simon Nadin 1986

7 Rubberneck .... Top 50 **HVS 5a**
14m. Follow the superb central crack with good gear and fine sustained climbing - the start is rather perplexing. At the top of the crack, climb the wall up and right for the most fitting finale.
FA. Robin Barley 1967

8 Appaloosa Sunset **E3 5c**
16m. Quality face climbing with a bold central section. Climb the right arete of *Rubberneck* (a highish runner is permissible) then trend right by high-stepping/rockovers and tricky mantelshelves before following holds straight up the wall, which eases gradually with height. *Photos on page 58*.
FA. Dave Jones 1977. They graded it E1 5b as they thought that was as hard as they could climb. Protection included a 'big hook like one off a ladder' weighted down with steel krabs.

9 Eclipsed Peach **E4 6a**
16m. The direct start to *Appaloosa* is technical and bold until holds on the regular route are reached.
FA. Alan Williams 1983

10 Laguna Sunrise **E6 6c**
14m. Climb to the right of the overlap then head up and left with great difficulty (bold and tricky to read with only marginal protection down and right) to join *Appaloosa*. Finish up this. Originally done with a distant side-runner at E4 and since done without.
FA. Simon Nadin (with side-runner) 1984. FA. Andi Turner (without) 2008

The Third Cloud **The Five Clouds** 61

⑪ **Crabbies Left-hand** . . . . **HVS 4c**
16m. The flakes to the left of the fine crack are sustained and awkward to access. A more direct start is **Bakewell Tart, E2 5c**.
FA. John Yates 1968. FA. (Bakewell Tart) John Hudson 1991

⑫ **Crabbie's Crack** . . . . **HVS 5a**
16m. A classic jamming crack. Gain the fissure awkwardly and follow it to its end. Finish up the exposed arete on the right - **Flaky Wall Finish** - or (more in keeping but less exciting) the thin crack on the left.
FA. Bob Downes early 1950s

⑬ **Flower Power Arete.** **E2 5c**
14m. Unbalanced but the lower section has some excellent climbing and the upper section is not without interest. Climb the rib to a crusty hollow then stretch right to access the hanging flake with difficulty, continue up a tricky groove to ledges. An easier but rather wide corner crack is all that remains.
FA. Martin Boysen 1968

⑭ **Icarus Allsorts** **E4 6a**
14m. Struggle with the roof crack if you must (or walk round) then from the block balance out left then climb the slab to the base of the wide crack/groove of *Flower Power Arete*. Move out left again and carefully climb the exposed arete. Not well-protected so care is required.
FA. Al Simpson 1977

The next routes are in the gully that cuts behind the buttress.

⑮ **The Bender** . . . . **VS 4b**
6m. The short thin crack in the back right-hand corner of the bay.

⑯ **Tim Benzadrino** **E3 5c**
6m. Climb the short intense wall above a poor landing.
FA. Dave Jones 1979

⑰ **The Little Flake** . . . . **HVS 5a**
8m. The little flake on the right is inclined to be luminous and is an awkward tussle. Not one for your new mountain wear.
FA. Dave Salt 1960s

⑱ **Geordie Girl** **E3 5b**
8m. The front face of *The Big Flake* is climbed by precarious laybacking and delicate smearing. Hard and scary.
FA. Geoff Hornby 1990s

⑲ **The Big Flake** . . . . **HS 4b**
8m. The flake is really more of a groove-cum-chimney thing. and excellent (if you like that kind of thing) but exhausting.
FA. Simon Nadin 1983

The Five Clouds   The Second Cloud

The Second Cloud

The first significant rock reached from the parking is on the Second Cloud. The routes here are often considered as extended boulder problems although there are also a few good cracks to have a go at using ropes and runners.

1 Jimmy Carter .... S 3c
6m. Amble up the bubbly wall to a spooky last move.

2 Stalin .... S 4a
8m. The crack gives good jamming at the grade.

3 Legends of Lost Leaders ... E3 5c
8m. The centre of the wall has a tricky mantelshelf and layback flake, unless you sneak off left into the last route.
FA. Gary Gibson 1979

4 Lenin .... VDiff
8m. The widening and right-trending crack has a tricky start.

5 Yankee Jam .... HS 5a
8m. Climb the awkward leaning fissure - good practice for "Yoosimideee" - well, kind of. Finish up the crack or the delicate ramp on the right for a bit of a contrast.

6 Nadin's Secret Finger .. V9
The desperate left-hand side of the face aiming for the crack.
FA. Simon Nadin 1985

7 Finger of Fate V4 (6a)
8m. The left-hand side of the sharp arete is precarious. The landing is worse than it appears at first. *Photo this page*.

8 KGB .... HVS 4c
6m. Start on the other side of the arete and finish on the crest.
FA. Ian Johnson 1977

Andy Healey finishing off the high boulder problem *Finger of Fate* (V4) - *above* - on the Second Cloud. Photo: Dave Bond

The Second Cloud **The Five Clouds** 63

9 The Outdoor Pursuits Cooperative
.... E1 5a
8m. Step right from the block and make fingery moves to pass the shield-shaped flake. Starting from the direct below is harder.
FA. Peter Buswell 1998

10 Communist Crack VS 5a
8m. The right-leaning crack is best climbed by awkward laybacking, just plug in a unit and go! Easy for the bold.

11 Marxist Undertones.. V2 (5c)
8m. From just right of the crack, under-cling up and right via flakes to reach easy ground. From the pocket is harder and there are other variations too.

The First Cloud away to the right is a bit of a nonentity.

The Roaches

	No star	★	★★	★★★
Mod to S	11	15	5	6
HS to HVS	7	25	16	8
E1 to E3	5	21	9	7
E4 and up	4	13	18	15

Peak guru Paul Nunn once suggested that the best climbing in Derbyshire was actually in Staffordshire. Although you could question his geography, his sentiment wasn't too far wide of the mark. The Roaches remains the most popular of all of the Western Edges and with good reason; there are hundreds of routes on offer of every imaginable style, from the most amiable of ambles through to some of the hardest routes around.

The cliff splits easily into two sections. The Lower Tier is partly sheltered by a stand of ancient pine trees and is home to some great crack climbs and a superb set of pebble-dashed walls and slabs. Up the ancient steps lurks the Upper Tier; tall and imposing, throwing down a challenge that is hard to resist, with a host of fine climbs, many of a very reasonable grade - plus plenty of harder ones too.

Individual recommendations at the Roaches are largely a matter of choice; at a mild grade try linking *Raven Rock Gully* (Diff) on the Lower Tier with *Pedestal Route* (HVD) and *Inverted Staircase* (Diff) on the Upper or if you are after the classic Orange Spot introduction simply do *Valkyrie* (VS) on the Lower Tier, followed by *Saul's Crack* (HVS) and *The Sloth* (HVS) on the Upper one. You should go away well satisfied and with just a little idea of the quality of the climbing available on this superb cliff.

Both Tiers at the Roaches.

The Roaches 65

Approach Also see map on page 42

There is parking for about 80 cars on the roadside lay-by under the cliff. If this is full (it happens very early on fine summer weekends) there are two alternatives. The first option is to leave the car at the Park and Ride scheme based on the extensive parking at Tittesworth Reservoir (drive towards Leek and keep an eye out for the signs). The other option is some limited parking below the towers of Hen Cloud where there is usually space (about 25 cars in two spots) and take the 15 minute walk to the cliff, either via the road or following the track across the fields.

WARNING - If you can't park in the designated spots below the Roaches, and you attempt to squeeze the car onto a grass verge, then you will be ticketed.

Conditions

The Lower Tier tends to be green after rain or in the winter partly because of the trees, and partly because of it being at a lower altitude than the rest of the cliff. By the same logic, it is sheltered from the worst of the weather and offers shade (at least at the base of the wall) in high summer. The Upper Tier is cleaner and drys more quickly but can get a bit blowy when the weather is wild.

Roaches Lower — Slippery Jim

> **Slippery Jim**
> To the left of the steps is a series of short undercut walls with good (and popular) bouldering and some worthwhile though hard climbs. The left-hand section is split centrally by the open groove of *Slippery Jim* with half a dozen good pebble-pulling offerings to either side.

❶ Apache Dawn **E5 6c**
8m. The pebbly wall gives desperately thin climbing on pebbles and gets worryingly high before the heather cornice is reached. Completely independent of *Catastrophe Internationale*.
FA. Julian Lines 1993

❷ Catastrophe Internationale
. . . .   **E5 6c**
8m. From the right-hand end of the long slot, climb straight up the steep wall by hard pulls on pebbles and desperate friction. The top-out is a hard mantel or heather-wrestling! *Apache Internationale* is probably the easiest method of getting up the wall and *Catastrophe Dawn* the hardest!
FA. Nick Dixon 1985

❸ Slippery Jim . . . .   **HVS 5a**
8m. The awkward and oft-green groove is squirmed to a rounded exit. The route is not popular though, if you happen to find it dry, then jump aboard.
FA. Don Whillans 1958

❹ Bareback Rider **E4 6b**
8m. Climb the rounded arete on its right-hand side by technical laying away to a tenuous exit. Despite the name, an 'a cheval' approach is not a good idea, though a cavalier one helps!
Photo opposite.
FA. Dave Jones 1980

❺ K.P. Nuts **E7 7a**
10m. A desperate bouldery Nadin route. Safe with a good spotting team and there is some gear in the break for the upper moves. Start left of *Ascent of Man* and climb to the break (pre-placed wires on first ascent). Undercut up and pull over, using whatever pebbles you can find, to the finish of *Ascent of Man*.
FA. Simon Nadin 1989

❻ Ascent of Man **E3 6a**
10m. A mini-classic, intense and varied, packing a lot of climbing into a short distance. Gain the undercut flake with difficulty and follow it to its end where scary friction and pebble moves lead leftwards up a ramp to easy ground. Best climbed when the boggy area below the route is in prime condition, making falling off even less desirable (but safer) than normal.
FA. Andrew Woodward 1974

❼ Ascent of Woman **E3 6a**
10m. The right-hand start and direct finish to *Ascent of Man* goes at about the same grade although it isn't as good.

❽ Days of Future Passed . .   **E3 6b**
10m. Climb the rounded arete by laybacking to good gear and a though-provoking mantelshelf finish.
FA. Andrew Woodward 1974

❾ The Aspirant **E3 5c**
8m. Climb the centre of the left-hand side-wall of the gully, passing a useful flake to an exit on the left.
FA. Gary Gibson 1978

Jordan Buys soloing *Bareback Rider* (E4) - *opposite* - on the Lower Tier at the Roaches. Photo: John Coefield

Roaches Lower — Teck Crack

① Ackit .... **HVS 5b**
14m. Follow the right-trending flake by awkward laybacking (good gear is available but it is tricky to place) to bulges, which are crossed by a steep pull and a delicate exit out left. A fine line.
FA. Don Whillans 1958. FA. (Direct Finish) Tony Barley 1967

② Just for Today **E6 7a**
16m. The wall and slab. The crucial huge stretch for a sloper is protected by a side runner in *Ackit*, placed on route. Finish direct.
FA. Paul Clark 1994

③ Barriers in Time Top 50 .... **E6 6b**
16m. The elegant arete is superb but slightly harder for shorties. Make a tricky start to reach the first break then tackle the arete above by some hard laybacking. Cams in the second break may permit a long scraping fall to be taken. The last reach will remain in your memory for a long time! Said to be low in the grade.
FA. Simon Nadin 1983

④ Inertia Reel Traverse
.... **V12**
The well-chalked low-level traverse is a classic and about as pumpy and as rounded as they come.
FA. Jerry Moffatt 1980s

⑤ Ant Lives .... **V6 (6b)**
8m. Start by a fun mantelshelf then make a powerful move to the ledge before galloping off rightwards.
FA. Nick Dixon 1987

⑥ Sunday at Chapel **E6 6c**
10m. The steep right-hand side of the arete above *Ant Lives* is bold and slappy to the final crack. A distant side runner in *Ackit* was used on the first ascent. Finish up *Barriers in Time* if you want an even more intense experience.
FA. Nick Dixon 1988

⑦ Inertia Reel **V8**
Attain a small flake and the rounded ledges above from a minute undercut in the low break. Escape right or jump off!
FA. Johnny Dawes 1986

⑧ Teck Crack Direct .. **V4 (6b)**
Reach the thin crack from the left by hard moves and then a rapid hand-traverse.

⑨ Teck Crack Super Direct **V9**
Gain the thin crack from directly below making a hideous pull on a poor crack and pebbles.

⑩ The Dignity of Labour .. **V6 (6b)**
From the right-hand arete, move left to holds and yet another fearsome mantelshelf finish which may be dirty. Virtually a route.
FA. Nick Dixon 1983

⑪ Teck Crack **E1 5c**
A classic and one of the hardest HVSs in the Peak for years!
1) 4a, 10m. Climb the grotty gully and cross the slab leftwards to a stance at the foot of the steep crack.
2) 5c, 14m. Jam and layback the crack to a pleasant, seated stance by a plaque that explains the route's name, which surprisingly is nothing to do with it being technical!
FA. Joe Brown 1958

Teck Crack
The tallest buttress left of the steps has a couple of reasonably graded routes (as long as you like awkward cracks) but is mostly desperate bouldering and a few harder routes on slopers and pebbles.

Crystal Grazer — Roaches Lower — 69

12 Joe's Hanging Crack E3 6a
10m. The hanging crack splitting the nose is a mini *Ray's Roof* and leads, in the unlikely event of success, into the clutches of the substantial holly.
FA. Joe Brown 1950s. Described as the hardest off-width he had ever done!

13 Lightning Crack .... HVS 5b
1) **5b, 10m.** Quickly gain the thin hanging crack with difficulty and follow it to ledges and a belay.
2) **4c, 15m.** The wall on the left is climbed via a rounded mantelshelf. The pitch can be improved by hand-traversing the rounded pod that runs out towards the arete just below the top.
FA. Don Whillans 1958

14 Mushin'. V10
The direct start to *Pindles Numb* is one for the obscenely strong. Pull up on these into the groove above to finish (**E4**) or jump off.
FA. Ben Moon 1990s

15 The Boozy Traverse. V8
Stagger left-wards along the grossly rounded shelf until you have had enough for one session.

16 Pindles Numb E4 6b
10m. Finger traverse left from the with increasing difficulty (**V5** to here) and pull into the leaning corner with great difficulty. Once established, finish easily.
FA. Nick Dixon 1984

17 Crystal Grazer E5 6a
10m. Gain the lip of the roof from the diagonal crack on the right then foot traverse left to a shallow groove. Climb the left-hand side of this to finish. Thought by some to be 6b.
FA. Phil Burke 1982

18 A Fist Full of Crystals E6 6b
12m. Follow *Crystal Grazer* to the groove and balance up this with some trepidation and nothing in the way of gear. Very blind.
FA. Nick Dixon 1983

19 Doug E8 6c
12m. Start as for the last two routes but climb the right-hand edge of the buttress to a delicate finale up a shallow scoop. Popping pebbles haven't helped. Named after cottage's most famous resident.
FA. Nick Dixon 1986

20 Fred's Cafe .... VS 5a
10m. The right-slanting crack leads awkwardly to an easy slab. Well-protected but a thrash and often choked with pine needles.
FA. Gary Gibson 1978

Crystal Grazer
An impressive hanging slab which has one of the hardest and blankest routes in the area. With the buttress being so close to the steps, you might expect the routes to be popular - well they aren't! Unfortunately the shrouding tree keeps things rather green.

From mid morning | 10 min | Green

Roaches Lower — Dorothy's Dilemma

Dorothy's Dilemma
To the right of the stone steps the Lower Tier thrusts forward with one of the finest buttresses on grit. The big names are further right, but the left-hand area is home to many routes which are only marginally less classic.

1 Yong Arete .... S 3c
8m. The scooped arete just to the right of the steps is climbed on well-scratched holds after a precarious start. Delicate and without too much protection.

2 Poisonous Python .... HVS 5b
8m. Although short-lived, the thin snaking-crack on the front of the buttress has good moves and good runners.
FA. Gary Gibson 1978

3 Yong .... HVD 4a
10m. The mild jamming crack has good hidden layaway holds. Western Grit's answer to Froggatt's renowned *Heather Wall*.

4 Something Better Change .... E2 5b.
10m. The centre of the delicate slab on small but improved holds. The exit is very rounded and avoiding the crack to the left requires will-power especially near the top. A (sensible?) side runner in *Yong* lowers the grade a couple of notches.
FA. Gary Gibson 1978

5 Wisecrack .... VS 4b
8m. The steep diagonal crack in the face.

6 Hypothesis .... HVS 5b
10m. Small wires protect the delicate left-hand arete.
FA. Colin Foord 1968

7 Destination Earth E7 6b
12m. The slab is bold and precarious. A side-runner (placed on route) may stop you repeating the first ascensionist's bouncing trick but then the route is only really worth **E4**.
FA. Simon Nadin 1984

8 Cannonball Crack .... S 4b
12m. The wide crack is awkward to start and leads to a leftwards exit over a chockstone.

9 Graffiti E1 5b
16m. Start up the arete and move left to a groove and crack which used to be the **Direct Finish** to *Cannonball Crack* before it was usurped.
FA. Gary Gibson 1978

10 Dorothy's Dilemma E1 5a
18m. The fine delicate arete is not over endowed with gear and requires commitment and neat footwork. Start on the left, move onto the front face (wires) then press on and stay cool.
FA. Joe Brown, Slim Sorrell, Dorothy Sorrell 1951

11 Bengal Buttress .... HVS 4c
28m. Climb the left arete of the buttress past holes to a ledge then trend right via a grassy ledge to the right-hand arete. Up this delicately (poor protection) then step left to finish up a short flake crack. Mild at the grade but with a serious section that requires a careful approach.
FA. Ivan Waller 1930

Raven Rock Gully **Roaches Lower** 71

Raven Rock Gully

The deep dark rift that splits the buttress has some worthwhile if gloomy climbs from the constricted struggles of the *Raven Rock Gully* routes to the glorious jamming of *Crack of Gloom*. From here on, we have grit on a grand scale.

12 Schoolies E3 5c
20m. Good bold climbing though escapable. Climb the bulges (reachy) then straight up the centre of the face to the final crack of *Bengal Buttress*.
FA. Phil Burke 1978

13 Crack of Gloom E1 5b
20m. The ever-leaning crack in the left-hand side of the gully would be a mega-classic in a more open setting. Here it is well-named, moody and magnificent. Jam the never-ending series of overhangs to the great boulder blocking the rift then make a tricky traverse left to a difficult exit where big fists sure help.
FA. Joe Brown 1958

14 Raven Rock Gully Left-hand VS 4b
20m. The back of the great rift has a crack/groove in each angle. The long steep groove on the left leads by sustained climbing to an exit through the small gap.
FA. Dave Salt 1969

15 Raven Rock Gully . . . . Diff
20m. The deep and gloomy rift to a tight and scruffy exit through the manhole. A worthwhile and atmospheric route that is a lot easier than it looks from below.
FA. J.W.Puttrell 1901

16 Swinger . . . . VS 4c
20m. The steep and neglected crack in the right wall of the gully leads to the upper section of *Via Dolorosa*.

17 Sidewinder E5 6a
24m. A devious oddity that grapples with the left-hand edge of the great roof. From the base of the crack of *Swinger*, ape right and climb a groove to a possible stance under the giant overhang. A flake on the left leads past the lip then stretch right, passing a flake, to climb the arete.
FA. Phil Burke 1980

18 Via Dolorosa . . . . Top 50 VS 4c
32m. A long and wandering trip up the huge buttress, which can be split into two or three pitches if required to ease rope drag problems. Start below a battered holly on the right-hand side of the buttress and climb glazed rock to the roof (**4c**). Escape out left passing the holly to ledges (possible stance) then climb to the left-hand corner of the huge roof by a choice of ways (**4a** - possible stance). Continue to runners then reach a flake on the right wall of the gully with difficulty. Once established, finish out right on the front of the buttress (**4c**). It is also possible to start on the left-hand edge of the buttress where a short pumpy traverse right leads to the regular route - a lot less polished but, historically, a rather dubious approach.
FA. Morley Wood early 1920s

Roaches Lower — Valkyrie

1 Valkyrie Direct .... HVS 5b
28m. A long and elegant pitch up the steep jamming cracks in the arete. Climb the crack and the bulges to a rest at the base of the flake on the regular climb. Finish as for the normal route, or via the tricky bulging short-cut crack just right of the arete.
FA. Joe Brown, Don Whillans (The Dream Team) 1951

2 Matinee .... HVS 5b
24m. The lower crack is almost always damp and usually smelly. Ignore this fact and jam up it to a (possible) stance on the giant flake. The continuation is awkward, especially the fist-grinding belly-flop into the wider finishing section. *Photo opposite.*
FA. Brown and Whillans 1951. Named after the astounded audience.

3 Valkyrie .... Top 50 VS 4c
A wandering climb of great quality - perhaps the archetypical grit classic and thought by many to be worth HVS. *Photo page 42.*
1) 4b, 15m. Climb the slabby groove to its top then traverse left to a stance on giant jammed blocks with a variety of belays.
2) 4c, 25m. Climb on to the flake (a big sling on it stops the rope jamming down the back) and descend its edge until a hidden foothold gives respite. Gain a crease on the left and teeter along this and all the way round onto the front face. One tricky move leads to the well positioned slabby finish. Great care is needed to avoid the rope jamming and to protect the second.
FA. Peter Harding 1946

4 Northern Comfort .. E6 6c
14m. From the tip of the *Valkyrie* flake, climb the wall past some useful flakes to a finish up the left arete. Wild and very reachy.
FA. Niall Grimes 1996

5 Licence to Run E4 6a
12m. The right-trending flakes in the wall above the *Valkyrie* stance are pumpy though good gear is available if you can stop!
FA. Gary Gibson (1 rest) 1980. FFA. Pete O'Donovan 1980

6 Licence to Lust E4 6a
12m. A counter-diagonal across the wall, utilising the same holds and runners in the central section at *License to Run*.
FA. John Allen 1987

Valkyrie
A huge Easter Island statue of a buttress, perhaps the single most imposing bit of grit in the country, with routes to match. *Valkyrie* may just be the best VS on grit, the *Direct* is only marginally inferior and the sustained jamming on *Matinee* is glorious, especially for the uninitiated who usually get mauled.

Andi Turner on the glorious *Matinee* (HVS) - *opposite*. Photo: John Read

Roaches Lower — The Mincer

1 Eugene's Axe — E2 5c
20m. Climb the rounded arete to reach the steeper rock then take the wall above, left then right, then finally left again.
FA. John Codling 1979

2 Pebbledash — HVS 5a
1) 5a, 10m. Head up the groove to steep rock then pad left at the limit of HVS friction and move left to a stance in the corner.
2) 4b, 8m. Finish up the main groove or the flake to its left.
FA. Dave Salt 1969

3 Secrets of Dance — E4 6a
20m. Follow the groove of *Pebbledash* then climb the disappearing crack in the steep wall until a right-trending ramp can be followed rapidly to easy ground.
FA. Simon Nadin 1984

4 Against the Grain — E6 7a
20m. Intense. Climb the easy flake and thin curving crack to where it withers then move left and climb the wall on tiny holds (each move is a touch harder then the last) to finish, grasping just a little, up the ramp of *Secrets of Dance*. E5 for gurus.
FA. Simon Nadin 1986

5 Thing on a Spring — E6 7a
20m. Another desperate route up the wall above the traverse of *The Swan* with a safe fall-out zone beneath very hard wall climbing up a slight ramp. From the thin crack, teeter across the wall diagonally rightwards using a crucial pebble (which did come off but has been glued back on) and a ramp for the feet to desperately rounded ledges and a final easy crack.
FA. Simon Nadin 1986

6 The Swan — E3 5c
26m. An elegant pitch requiring commitment on the traverse. Climb thin cracks to where they fade, place a high runner, then tiptoe round the bulge and traverse right until a stiff pull is needed to reach the continuation crack. A runner on the tree to the right can be used to shorten the pendulum if you muff the traverse.
Up the Swanee, E4 5c. As for *The Swan* but make the traverse with your feet in the higher break instead of your hands. Twice as gripping as *The Swan* and especially so for the toppling tall.
FA. John Gosling (one peg) 1969. He should have called it The Goose. FFA. Ron Fawcett 1977. FA. (Up the Swanee) John Yates 1970

7 Swan Bank — E4 5c
20m. Links *The Mincer* with the end of the traverse of *The Swan* via some bold and reachy climbing. Finish rapidly up this.
FA. Gary Gibson 1981

The Mincer and Smear Test
To the right of the huge prow of *Valkyrie* is this area named after the classic (and awkward) undercut crack climb, and the superbly blank slab round to its right. The area is best known for its superb collection of tenuous slab climbs - technical in all cases and bold in most.

Smear Test **Roaches Lower** 75

8 The Mincer .... HVS 5b
24m. Boulder up into the hanging groove then mince rightwards awkwardly (especially if you're long-legged) to pass the nose and climb the excellent gradually-widening cracks above.
FA. Joe Brown, Don Whillans 1981

9 Smear Test E3 6a
12m. Approach via the roofed in hanging groove to join *The Mincer*. Follow this through the bulge then from a large chockstone runner (or use it as a belay) sketch right across the slight weakness in the slab, to reach the finger crack and a short sprint to safety. Modern boot rubber is a big help, though it was five years before it was first used on this one!
Photo on page 79.
FA. Gabe Regan 1977

10 Pincer .... VS 5a
20m. Climb the short steep wall (bouldery) to a rest below the bulges then move rightwards to the shrubby gully. Up this to a traverse out left leading to a short finger and hand crack. Sadly, despite some nice moves after the start, the rest of the route is only about Severe and the line leaves a lot to desired.

11 Kicking Bird E4 6a
20m. Good but devious, and hard. Pull through the bulge then cross the overhang by baffling moves to gain the base of the slab. Climb *The Mincer* a short distance, step back onto the slab as for *Smear Test* but climb up and right (almost as far as the crack - side runner) then finish back leftwards to finish.
FA. Al Simpson, Dave Jones (alts) 1978

12 Bloodstone E5 6b
18m. Avoid the loop on the previous climb by a direct ascent of the desperate slab which eases with height. Kit under the overlap and a large cam low in *The Mincer* is all you are going to get.
FA. Simon Nadin 1983

13 Bloodspeed ... E6 6b
18m. Start as for *Kicking Bird*, pull through the overlap but then climb the slab to the right to the base of the thin crack on *Smear Test*. Gear under the overlap, and low in *The Mincer*, are all that protect you as you shuffle rightwards on poor smears and minimal handholds, trying not to think of your rope sawing on the lip in the event of a fall. A bit easier for the tall, but still 6b.
FA. Simon Nadin 1984

14 Guano Gully .... S 4b
14m. The narrowing crack leading to an open groove up and right is a less smelly experience than you might be expecting. Once past the crucial overhang, things ease dramatically.

Roaches Lower — Elegy

1 Mousey's Mistake — E2 5b
14m. Climb the right-hand side of the gully to the roof then step out above the overhang and climb the delicate left-hand side of the *Elegy* slab. Side runners lower the stress factor.
FA. Dave Jones 1978

2 A Little Peculiar — E6 7b
14m. The direct over the imposing roof features the hardest mantelshelf in the world - a free hanging one-armed flip, with no footholds! Good holds lead to the lip but above there is precious little with which to make progress. If you manage the desperate gymnastics, casually saunter up *Elegy* to finish. Protected by side-runners (a chockstone in the crack) and RPs low down.
FA. Paul Higginson 1990s

From mid morning | 10 min | Green

3 Elegy — Top 50 — E2 5c
16m. Perhaps the best slab route in Western Grit! Climb the awkward overhanging corner to the base of the upper crack and large cams. Balance left to the tantalising flake and if you are completely baffled, try a bit of lateral thinking. Follow the creaky flake to its end (slightly dubious runners) then weave a way up the final bald slab connecting a set of small blisters by brilliantly intense climbing.
FA. Mike Simpkins (tension to start) 1960. FFA. John Yates 1969

4 Clive Coolhead Realises the Excitement of Knowing You May be the Author of Your Own Death is More Intense Than Orgasm — E5 6b
14m. Strange name, good route! The right side of the *Elegy* slab is at the limit of friction and the grade varies from E4 to E6 depending on how high you put the side runner in *The Bulger*. A wire in *Elegy* can also be used to reduce the swing potential.
FA. Nick Dixon 1983

5 The Bulger — VS 4c
14m. The leaning corner (as for *Elegy*), and the awkward wide crack above, give an unsatisfying struggle. Bridge the lower section and swim up the final bit. Very graunchy.
FA. Joe Brown, Don Whillans 1951

Elegy
A magnificent slab route or two to get the heart pounding and a selection of awkward and arduous crack climbs. Also worthy of note are two tough offerings, one with the longest name on gritstone and one with the hardest mantelshelf anywhere on the planet - allegedly!

Hawkwing **Roaches Lower** 77

6 Fledgling's Climb — HS 4a
14m. Starting in the gully, traverse left above the overhang then climb the wall and the well-positioned rib. Not well-protected, rather polished, and can be green.

7 Little Chimney — Mod
10m. The little chimney in the back left-hand corner of the bay is quite unremarkable but offers a blocky quick tick.

8 Battery Crack — VS 4b
10m. Climb the awkward crack rising from the recess and head into the groove above. A successful ascent will leave you beached and battered below the final section of *Lucas Chimney*. A great route for masochists!

9 Lucas Chimney — S 4a
10m. The narrow rift in the main angle is a well-protected struggle and the leftward exit is a pig; the best advice is to try staying high. Often green early in the season or after rain, in which case it is worthy of a manky **HS 4c**.

10 Hawkwing — E1 5b
22m. An fine route up an elegant buttress. Start at the left arete then spiral up and right following cracks to the opposite arete. Place small wires before following the parallel diagonal cracks to an exposed and awkward finale back on the left-hand arete. Excellent throughout and very varied climbing.
FA. Gary Gibson 1978

11 Carrion — E3 5c
18m. Climb the centre of the front face direct, starting over the butch overhang, crossing the diagonal cracks and finishing with a flourish at a notch in the final narrow wall. A bit of a non-line but with some fine climbing if you are strict.
FA. Gary Gibson 1980

Hawkwing
Another fine jutting buttress, with a couple of classics and some rather tricky crack climbs. *Hawkwing* is the real gem here, though the awkward fissure of *Kestrel Cracks* sees (many) more ascents. *Fledgling's Climb* is a popular beginners' route but requires care.

12 Kestrel Crack — VS 4b
20m. A well-rounded classic though too much of a struggle to be a real three star outing. The striking hanging fissure has a brace of awkward starts (easiest on the left) and a wide awkward exit. A couple of tricky-to-thread chockstones help protect the main difficulties of the route. *Photo on page 18*.

13 Headless Horseman — E1 5b
20m. Climb *Kestrel Cracks* to the first thread then traverse out to the arete and teeter up this, heart in mouth.
FA. Jonny Woodward 1978

Roaches Lower — Death Knell

Death Knell

One of the less popular sectors of the Lower Tier, though the superb and harrowing *Death Knell* is worth seeking out if you are up to the scary challenge. *Flake Chimney* gives a memorable beginners' route that requires consideration to protect your second on the rope if you want them to climb again!

❶ Logical Progression — E7 6c
20m. The hanging lower arete just right of the *Headless Horseman* traverse (see previous page) is reached via a very hard traverse from the right to the enticing pockets and a lovely balancy move to stand up in them. The arete above is much easier. Good cams under the roof protect (back-rope useful) and a very poor cam in the right-hand pocket just about serves for the rest.
FA. Sam Whittaker 1998

❷ Flimney — S 4a
18m. The flake and chimney/groove passing to the left of the rhododendrons is approached via the gymnastic bulge or flake just right. Plough through the vegetation to the final dirty groove.

❸ Amaranth — E4 5c
12m. Climb the blunt arete (as for *Death Knell*) and step left onto the slab and balance carefully up this, avoiding the shrubs.
FA. Gary Gibson 1979

❹ Death Knell — E4 5c
14m. A classic frightener with sustained balance climbing. Climb the blunt rib above the rhododendrons delicately to the bulges and make committing moves up and right to reach a crack, runners and easy ground - phew!
FA. John Yates 1970

❺ Rhodren — HVS 5b
12m. A mini-*Mincer* and quite popular, though this one is easier for the tall. From the foot of the odd perched flake, climb the grungy groove to the overhang and layback rapidly rightwards round this to easy ground.
FA. Joe Brown 1958

❻ Flake Chimney — Diff
14m. Traverse the crest of the huge perched flake (walk across or ride it - the choice is yours) to reach an easy groove. Awkward to protect so be wary of scaring beginners!

❼ Straight Crack — HS 4a
10m. Bridge the leaning corner (without pushing too hard on the flake) and then step left to reach the rectilinear fissure, thankfully above the wide and potentially awkward lower section.

❽ Punch — E3 6b
14m. Force a way into the hanging groove with great difficulty (and with overhead gear) then finish more easily through the shrubbery above.
FFA. Jonny Woodward 1978

❾ Choka — E1 5c
12m. Pull through the roof further to the right using the thin crack and continue up its wider extension.
FA. Joe Brown (1 point of aid) 1958

Chris Sims making the delicate traverse on *Smear Test* (E3) - *page 75* - on the Lower Tier at the Roaches. Photo: Pippa Froggatt

Roaches Lower — Chalkstorm

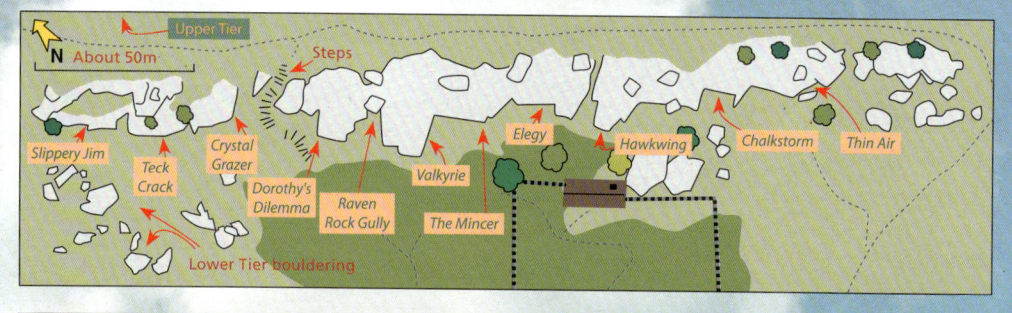

Chalkstorm

Chalkstorm, the route after which the area is named, has generated more hot air on the issue of grading than probably any other in the country (apart from *Three Pebble Slab*). Sadly the very popular easy routes here have been rather ground to death by never-ending top-roping sessions, often using inappropriate footwear. Of the harder offerings, both *Commander Energy* and *Hunky Dory* are well worthwhile and you have the added extra of baffled school kids saying "Sir, sir, sir, can we do that one next, can we, can we, please?"

1 Circuit Breaker — E3 6a
10m. Climb the fingery, bulging arete then the flake above to the final delicate slab perched on the front of the buttress.
FA. Gary Gibson 1980

2 Hunky Dory — E3 6a
10m. The thin twisting cracks in the side-wall give a technical and sustained pitch to a good rest which gives you time to psych up for the tricky mantelshelf finale.
FA. Gabe Regan 1975

3 Prow Corner — VDiff
12m. The awkward corner in the left-hand edge of the recess is worthwhile. Avoid stepping right if you want the full tick.

4 Prow Corner Twin Cracks — HVD 4a
12m. The twin cracks just right are trickiest at the overlap. Surprisingly popular.

The very narrow slab between Prow Corner Twin Cracks and Chalkstorm is **Microstorm, E1 5c**. *It offers interesting moves and zero independence.*

5 Chalkstorm — E3 5c
14m. The slab has thin unprotected moves to pass the overlap. It is often climbed with a side runner (**E1** to **HVS** depending where you put it). Arguments about the grade rage on - just to clarify, it is worth E3 for an onsight ascent without a side runner. Often dirty from the top-roping/abseiling hordes' muddy boots.
FA. Ian Johnson 1977

6 Prow Cracks — VDiff
10m. Climb the left-hand crack then transfer right at the level of the bulges. An excellent introduction to jamming.

7 Prow Cracks Variations — HVD
10m. The counter-diagonal is also well worth doing and is just a touch harder, especially the final wide section.

Thin Air Roaches Lower 81

Thin Air
The final section of the Lower Tier doesn't see too much traffic, mainly because the tough trio of three star routes don't have a single runner between them. The collection of easier climbs here makes for a decent venue when things are too busy just to the left - or head 'upstairs'. On the far right, *The Roaches Ridge* makes a good scrambling approach to the Upper Tier.

8 Commander Energy.... E2 5c
12m. The flying fin is approached up the bulging arete. Hand-traverse a flange out left then rock onto it and layback smartly, heart in mouth, up the impressive arete. *Photo on cover.*
FA. John Allen 1975

9 Sumo Cellulite E4 6a
12m. The right-hand face of the flying fin is precarious and scary.
FA. John Allen (he can't stay away!) 1989

10 Rocking Stone Gully .... HVD
8m. The grassy groove with wobbly chockstones is short-lived. If you are feeling technical, elegant semi-laybacking can avoid the worst of the grovelling. The rocking stone has been vandalised and is now only a shadow of its former self.

11 Captain Lethargy .... HVD
8m. The crack in the slab, trending left where it finishes. Packs a punch for its diminutive size and requires confident foot-work.

12 Sifta's Quid Inside Route ... S 3a
10m. Interesting! This variation avoids the hard section of the regular route by some speleological lunacy. Climb towards the slot beneath the boulders then get squirming. Helmet, harness and runners will all impede your progress.

13 Sifta's Quid .... HS 4b
10m. The tricky bulging crack-line was named after a bet that the crag was worked out; well it wasn't forty years ago and it probably isn't now!
FA. John Amies 1968

14 Obsession Fatale .. E8 6c
10m. The ultra-sketchy slab left of *Piece of Mind* is easy (ish) on a top-rope, but a mighty-bold solo. Some say it is only E7 6b but only those who are interviewed while balancing precariously at the top of the slab are really allowed to comment.
FA. Julian Lines 1992. Julian fell off it but escaped unharmed before he made the first ascent.

15 Piece of Mind..... E6 6b
12m. The unprotected blunt rib was an astounding ascent before sticky rubber and remains a bold and infrequently climbed pitch. Sadly top-roping is polishing the crucial holds just below the top.
FA. Jonny Woodward 1977

16 Thin Air........... E5 6a
10m. Heart-stoppingly precarious! The crescent-shaped ramp is gained by a hard rock-over. Once established pad carefully up and right to glory. The route is as unprotected as it looks, the finish is very fluffable and the landing truly awful.
FA. Gary Gibson 1980

17 Final Destination E8 6c
10m. Continue direct up the bald slab above the start of *Thin Air* to a finish just right of *Piece of Mind*.
FA. Ben Heason 2003

18 The Roaches Ridge....... Diff 3a
70m. Popular with outdoor groups - the long rambling ridge at the right-hand end of the cliff gives a pleasant scramble with multifarious variations. It is low in the grade and offers a good intro to rock-hopping, though the many more direct variations increase the grade and the quality.

Roaches Upper — Simpkins' Overhang

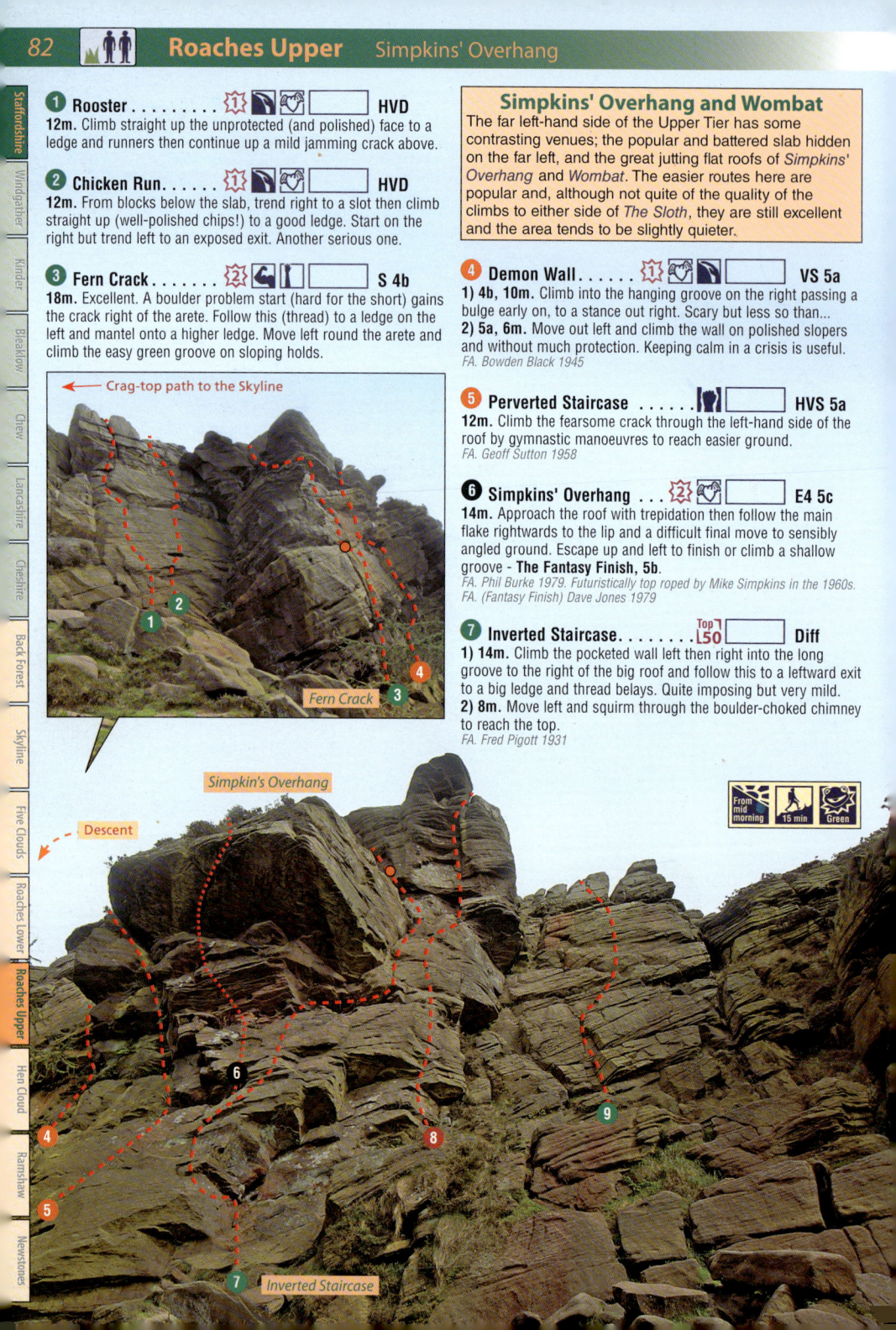

① Rooster .... HVD
12m. Climb straight up the unprotected (and polished) face to a ledge and runners then continue up a mild jamming crack above.

② Chicken Run ...... HVD
12m. From blocks below the slab, trend right to a slot then climb straight up (well-polished chips!) to a good ledge. Start on the right but trend left to an exposed exit. Another serious one.

③ Fern Crack .... S 4b
18m. Excellent. A boulder problem start (hard for the short) gains the crack right of the arete. Follow this (thread) to a ledge on the left and mantel onto a higher ledge. Move left round the arete and climb the easy green groove on sloping holds.

Simpkins' Overhang and Wombat

The far left-hand side of the Upper Tier has some contrasting venues; the popular and battered slab hidden on the far left, and the great jutting flat roofs of *Simpkins' Overhang* and *Wombat*. The easier routes here are popular and, although not quite of the quality of the climbs to either side of *The Sloth*, they are still excellent and the area tends to be slightly quieter.

④ Demon Wall ...... VS 5a
1) 4b, 10m. Climb into the hanging groove on the right passing a bulge early on, to a stance out right. Scary but less so than...
2) 5a, 6m. Move out left and climb the wall on polished slopers and without much protection. Keeping calm in a crisis is useful.
FA. Bowden Black 1945

⑤ Perverted Staircase ...... HVS 5a
12m. Climb the fearsome crack through the left-hand side of the roof by gymnastic manoeuvres to reach easier ground.
FA. Geoff Sutton 1958

⑥ Simpkins' Overhang ... E4 5c
14m. Approach the roof with trepidation then follow the main flake rightwards to the lip and a difficult final move to sensibly angled ground. Escape up and left to finish or climb a shallow groove - **The Fantasy Finish, 5b**.
FA. Phil Burke 1979. Futuristically top roped by Mike Simpkins in the 1960s.
FA. (Fantasy Finish) Dave Jones 1979

⑦ Inverted Staircase .... Diff
1) 14m. Climb the pocketed wall left then right into the long groove to the right of the big roof and follow this to a leftward exit to a big ledge and thread belays. Quite imposing but very mild.
2) 8m. Move left and squirm through the boulder-choked chimney to reach the top.
FA. Fred Pigott 1931

Wombat — Roaches Upper

8 The Tower of Bizarre Delights — E3 5c
10m. Steep and imposing. Climb directly to the ledge above the first pitch of *Inverted Staircase* then continue boldly up to the hanging crack and finish more easily out right.
FA. Dave Jones 1978

9 Heather Slab — S 3c
16m. The once heathery slab that forms the back of the recess is followed directly and is worryingly difficult to protect, especially on the upper wall. The groove on the left is **Diff**.

10 Capitol Climb — HS 4b
20m. Worthwhile. Get into the hanging groove and exit right below the overhang to reach a short crack that leads to ledges. Climb the face above without much gear, or escape off left.
FA. R.Handley 1954

11 Wombat — E2 5b *Top 50*
20m. A classic piece of roof climbing, pumpy and bold though only a bit harder than *The Sloth* if you are strong. Climb the wall to a thread then traverse the flake to its end and make a couple of strenuous pulls on less generous holds to reach easy ground. Cams behind the creaky flakes in the roof are a bad idea.
FA. Mike Simpkins 1960

12 Live Bait — E4 5c
20m. Climb the wall using a small flake, skip right to the block then cross the roof leftwards with hard moves to pass the lip. Finish much more easily up the heathery face above.
FA. Gary Gibson 1981

13 West's Wallaby — VS 4c
24m. Climb the awkward diagonal crack to the huge block tucked under the roof, then hand-traverse this and continue round the arete to a rest. Climb up then back leftwards to access the front face and finish easily. Devious and high in the grade.
FA. Graham West 1960

14 Walleroo — E2 5c
20m. Start up *West's Wallaby* then from the right-hand edge of the jammed block climb leftwards on small flakes to difficult moves around the lip and easy terrain.
FA. Mike Simpkins 1960

15 Wallaby Direct — HVS 5a
20m. Neat. Follow *West's Wallaby* to the middle of its traverse then climb steeply to an improving crack and easier ground.
FA. Mike Simpkins 1960

16 Late Night Final — HS 4a
20m. The undercut chimney that bounds the buttress on the right (thread) can be a tortuous struggle - how good is your gritstone udging? The upper section is an herbaceous amble.

17 The Valve — E4 5c
16m. Bold climbing up the right side of the arete finishing back left on the crest. Exposed and poorly-protected.
FA. Gary Gibson 1978

18 Beckermet Slab — HVD 4a
14m. Mild but bold. Bridge up the gully then hand-traverse out left (very hard for the short) to gain the front face which is climbed leftwards to a finish up the delicate slabby groove (poorly-protected) then the arete on the right.

19 Maud's Garden — HVD 3c
1) 4a, 14m. Balance up the slab then follow the crack to a stance below the bulges. A left-hand start is a grade easier.
2) 8m. Move right and squirm up the groove to outflank the overhangs then finish direct up the arete or the face to its left.
FA. Bowden Black 1945

Roaches Upper — Damascus Crack

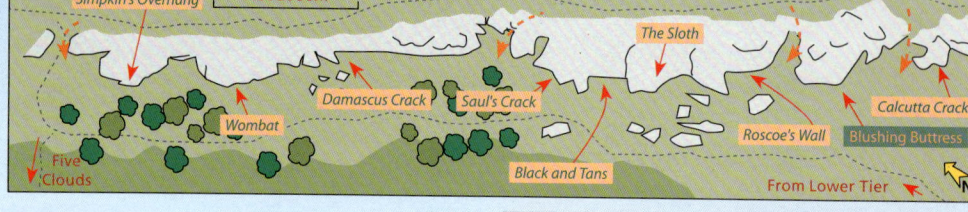

① Contrary Mary — VS 4b
16m. Climb through a notch in the overhang then continue up the heathery front of the buttress to a ledge. Above this the climbing is steeper, harder and bolder.

② Reset Portion of Galley 37 — HS 4b
12m. The steep corner and bulges above until forced out right.
FA. Geoff Sutton 1958. Named after some printers instructions that became incorporated in the text. The original name isn't known.

③ Broken Slab — HS 4b
12m. Climb the steep slab then move boldly right and pull into a crack awkwardly. Follow this to the top, or exit via the arete.
FA. A.Bowden Black 1945

④ Dawn Piper — HVS 5b
10m. The sharp arete eases with height.
FA. John Codling 1985

⑤ Runner Route — HS 4b
14m. Bold and delicate. Climb the slab rightwards to the break then crimp back left to find a finish up the flaky crack above.
FA. Nat Allen 1955

⑥ Damascus Crack — HS 4b
12m. Sustained but well-protected climbing up the crack, with a flaky exit to the right. Alternatively climb the steep and juggy (if illogical!) finish up the tower above and left (**VS 4b**).
FA. Geoff Pigott 1955

⑦ Third Degree Burn — E2 5b
10m. Climb the left-hand side of the wall - bold but at least with a heathery landing. Artificial but with some good moves.
FA. Gary Gibson 1978

Damascus Crack
Between the jutting roof of *Wombat*, and the descent at the left-hand side of the Upper Tier, is a rather nondescript section of cliffs, hidden behind the pine trees. There are no outstanding climbs here, but there are a few interesting bits and pieces and the area is rarely busy.

⑧ Libra — HVS 4c
10/14m. The well-scoured crack left of the sharp arete is sustained and precarious. Escape at the top or belay, then move left and climb the juggy tower.

⑨ Aqua — VS 4b
12m. Climb the roof crack strenuously then amble to the top.
FA. Joe Brown 1954

⑩ Tealeaf Crack — S 4a
12m. Pass the roof on the right then trend back left to gain the front arete, which gives a pleasant finale.

Ben Heason soloing *Paralogism* (E7) - *page 90* - on the Upper Tier at the Roaches. Photo: Ian Parnell

Roaches Upper — Saul's Crack

1 Rotunda Buttress — VS 4c
18m. Climb the wide crack then trend left to a ledge. From here, climb right and then left again following the best holds to an airy and bold finish up the final section.
FA. Bowden Black 1945

2 Rotunda Gully — Mod
14m. The open gully provides an awkward descent route for the competent and a suitably mild outing for timid beginners.

3 Bachelor's Buttress — HVS 4c
18m. Low in the grade but serious and with a bold finale. Once thought to be, "only suitable for married men and others accustomed to taking risks". Climb the slab to the left edge of the overhang. Move up then trend back right crossing the side-wall on polished holds to the airy arete and a finish up a short crack. It is also possible to climb the side-wall direct until an awkward move reaches holds and gear, at a more normal **HVS**.
FA. Fred Pigott 1913

4 Gypfast — E4 5c
16m. The large triangular overhang is a bit of a one-move-wonder. Fix runners to left and right (or better - don't bother) then cross the flakes rightwards to hard moves round the lip and an anticlimactic finish. Low in both grades.
FA. Phil Gibson 1979

Saul's Crack

Beyond the easy descent the cliff becomes ever more impressive and is home to a great series of climbs, long and involving, but often of a very reasonable grade. The major classic of *Saul's Crack* is a bit harder and will seek out any weaknesses in your jamming ability.

Access - Occasional restriction due to nesting birds - signs will be posted at the crag.

---

5 Saul's Crack — HVS 5a
18m. A Roaches' classic and a good test of your jamming technique. Climb into the groove then thug up the polished corner crack to the overhang and exit rapidly rightwards to easier ground.
The crack is renown for eating poorly placed gear, care required lest you lose your prized possession.
FA. Joe Brown 1947

6 Humdinger — E1 5b
18m. Climb the narrow buttress to the roofs and pull through these powerfully, hard for the short who really have to s-t-r-e-t-c-h and might want a 5c tick. Trend right to finish on *Jeffcoat's*.
FA. Mick Guilliard 1969

7 Jeffcoat's Chimney — VDiff
A classic of considerable antiquity.
1) 18m. Climb the well-scratched chimney passing an overhang on the left (polished and awkward to protect) then continue rightwards past the holly to a good stance. The wide bit is avoidable to the right at a lower grade.
2) 6m. Move left then right to outflank the overhangs, or for something harder finish up the steep corner (**VS 4c**).
FA. Stanley Jeffcoat 1913

8 Jeffcoat's Buttress — HS 5a
A classic route though with an arduous (but avoidable) start. Using the chimney start lowers the route to an amenable **HS 4b**.
1) 5a, 18m. Climb the fingery polished scoop by a long reach, or avoid it by the chimney on the left. Weave up towards the overhangs, pulling over a bulge with difficulty to enter a groove. Trend right below the huge roofs to the Pipe stance.
2) 3c, 10m. The pleasant jamming cracks on the right are awkward to enter and soon lead to the cliff top.
FA. Stanley Jeffcoat 1913

Black and Tans   **Roaches Upper**   87

9 Hanging Around ......   HVS 5b
16m. A direct pitch to the pipe stance tackles the large and strenuous bulges on a right-trending line. Finish much more easily up *Jeffcoat's Buttress*.
FA. Gary Gibson 1978

10 Ruby Tuesday E2 5b
30m. A mini-expedition, devious with some excellent climbing.
1) 5b, 12m. Climb to the block overhang and pull over to the base of a short ramp. Exit rightwards from the top of this to join *Black and Tans* which is followed to its stance.
2) 5b, 18m. Climb out left then up the short rib to a possible small stance (4b to here). Pull onto the right edge of the wall above and traverse left (gripping - tiny wires) to the exposed rounded rib.
FA. Mick Guilliard, John Yates (alts) 1970

11 Black and Tans .... Top 50   S 4a
A classic trip weaving its way up the impressive buttress.
1) 4a, 14m. Climb the left-hands side of *Hollybush Gully* and move out left and climb a groove to its top, step left across the side-wall then mantelshelf onto a small stance.
2) 4a, 16m. Continue up the groove then step left and tackle the bulges by a trio of awkward, and poorly-protected semi-mantelshelves, mild but bold. It is also possible to start up *Jeffcoat's Chimney* then follow ledges rightwards via a long traverse to the base of the groove, at about the same grade.
FA. Fred Pigott 1922

Black and Tans
Home to *Black and Tans* - regarded as one of the very best Severes anywhere on grit though *Black Velvet* is almost as good. There is also a host of routes up to E2 that are well worthy of attention. The impressive stature of these climbs makes them especially worthwhile.
Access - Occasional restriction due to besting birds - signs will be posted at the crag.

12 Black Velvet ....   S 4a
24m. Another fine climb, less popular than its near neighbour but not really much less worthy. Follow *Black and Tans* to its first groove. Climb this to its top, move left then back right to outflank the overhangs then finish up the well-positioned crack above. A big pitch at the grade.

13 Diamond Wednesday .....   HVS 5a
24m. A bit of an eliminate though with good positions, some interesting moves and low in the grade. Start up *Hollybush Crack* until above the prickly beast then climb the arete on the left passing a tricky overhang to gain the final exposed rib.
FA. Gary Gibson 1978

14 Hollybush Crack ....   VS 4b
26m. Bridge up the wide and prickly lower section of the gully until it is possible to transfer into the crack above. Continue up this, passing a possible constricted stance, to the left-hand end of the great roof. Pull over the bulge then either finish easily.
The Neb Finish, 4b - Climb as far as a thread, descend a couple of moves, shuffle rightwards on rounded holds out into space to the final exposed (and thankfully easy) rib.

Descent

Roaches Upper — The Sloth

① Technical Slab .... HS 4a
24m. Despite the name, not very technical but bold in its central section. Climb straight up the slab (harder for the short and unprotected where it matters) until you join the traverse of *Pedestal Route*. Finish as for *Pedestal Route*, or more in keeping, out right as for the *Neb Finish* to *Hollybush Crack*.

② Gilted E5 6a
28m. An odd and wild outing based on the left edge of the roof which is high in the grade and seldom repeated. From *Hollybush Crack*, hand-traverse the lip wildly to swing round the arete to a poor rest in the shallow cave in the middle of nowhere. Head up and right for one more impending move. Some ascents have escaped left on to the arete from the cave.
FA. Phil Burke 1979

③ Painted Rumour E6 6a
24m. Probably the biggest roof pitch on grit and truly magnificent. From directly above *Technical Slab*, place loads of gear at the back of the roof then attack it at its widest point, using the fragile glued flake with care. From the hole (spike runner and hands-off rest possible), pull back to the vertical using tiny rugosities and climb the wall more easily.
FA. Simon Nadin 1985

④ Pedestal Route .... Top 50   HVD 4a
28m. A great outing through some impressive territory.
1) 4a, 12m. Climb the flake-crack up the right-hand side of the huge flake of The Pedestal to a sitting stance (low belays) on its top. Starting up the left-hand side of the flake ups the overall grade to **S 4a**.
2) 3c, 16m. Reverse off the end of the ledge then traverse left and up to the left-hand corner of the great roof. To stop the rope jamming, try fixing a runner out left to direct it away from the crack, then pull over the bulge and finish up the deep groove.
FA. Morley Wood 1922

The Sloth
The overhang is the single most recognisable feature of the whole cliff. It looks huge from the car-park and even bigger up close! Of course *The Sloth* is one of the best know grit routes anywhere, though the roof is home to some much harder offerings. For more normal mortals, the slabs here have some great lower-grade routes.

Access - Occasional restriction due to nesting birds - signs will be posted at the crag.

The Sloth Roaches Upper

⑤ The Sloth   Top 50   HVS 5a
24m. The crack that splits the enormous roof is a total gripper; though like the school bully (and unlike Whillans!) it isn't as 'ard as it looks once you take it on! The climbing is straightforward though mighty harassing and the route feels like E1. Climb to a sitting position on The Pedestal then step right and climb the short tricky wall to the roof and a big sling on the massive spike of the Cheeseblock. Lean right to get the first of the creaking juggy flakes then launch across these to the lip where solid jamming helps the pull over into the final easy crack. The old roof climbing adage of "keep your feet on the rock at all costs" is worth bearing in mind.
FA. Don "It's OK if you use yer loaf" Whillans 1954

⑥ Loculus Lie   E5 6a
28m. Another arduous and devious roof pitch that visits some highly hairy situations. From the lip of *The Sloth* yard leftwards until a long stretch reaches the tiny cave under the roof. Finish direct as for *Painted Rumour*. Originally the route leapt left from the Cheeseblock runner then used fragile flakes to reach back to the lip. The less devious version has become the norm.
FA. Simon Nadin 1983

⑦ New Fi'nial   E6 6b
28m. Another bizarre and outrageous gripper that traverses right from the lip of *The Sloth* until upward escape is possible. Said to give as good climbing as *Painted Rumour*.
FA. Simon Nadin 1985

⑧ Central Route   VS 4a
16m. The centre of the poorly-protected (cams in the highest break) slab has delicate and unprotected moves at 10m (harder for the short) before it eases off. Traverse right to a stance on the crest of the buttress and walk off, or finish as for the next route.

⑨ Right Route   VDiff
24m. A classic up the slanting flake that bounds the right edge of the main slab; mild at the grade. Reach the flake via polished pockets then keep left (more polish) until is possible to outflank the roof and reach a stance on the right. Trend left above the big overhang (awkward to start) and finish up the airy crack.
FA. Morley Wood 1922

⑩ Right Route Right   VS 4c
14m. Follow *Right Route* to the overhang then pull over this to gain the hanging groove just above and follow this to the top.

⑪ Kelly's Direct   E1 5b
14m. From the shelf (see below) climb the crack on the left to a flake then move up and stretch right to rounded pockets. Continue up the crest - exciting stuff.

⑫ Kelly's Shelf   S 4b
16m. The bulging face has a narrow ramp cutting through it from left to right. Climb on to this (an ungainly struggle for most) and follow it to the base of a crack. Finish up this, or the similar, but more exposed, face just to the left (**HS 4b**).

⑬ Skin and Wishbones   E8 7a
16m. The left-hand side of the huge roof taken by *Paralologism*.
FA. Ben Bransby 2007

Roaches Upper — Crack and Corner

1 Paralogism — E7 6c
14m. The large roof under the right-hand side of the buttress is taxing. Climb leftwards across the overhang to the lip then trend back right and pull onto slabby rock. Pre-placed wires to the left and right protected the first ascent though it has been done without. There is small gear in the roof if you can hang on to place it. *Photo on page 85.*
FA. Simon Nadin 1987

2 Antithesis — E5 6b
14m. The right-hand edge of the scooped wall to the right is traversed leftwards with considerable difficulty to a finish up the airy arete. A side-runner to the right is normal, without this it would be a grade or two harder.
FA. Jonny Woodward 1980

3 Bed of Nails — E3 5b
12m. From the gully, head left across the wall to a diagonal crack (often green). From the top of this move left to finish. The name and grade tell you something about the gear and the landing!
FA. Gary Gibson 1978

4 Easy Gully Wall — HVD 4a
20m. Climb to a block to the right of the gully then continue leftwards to a ledge. Move up and left to a higher one then take the flake to the overhangs and escape leftwards under these.

5 Jelly Roll — VS 4c
22m. Follow the strenuous thin crack in the wall to a possible stance - block belay. Pull boldly over a bulge and climb the wide crack/groove (big gear) to the capping roof, which is climbed on the left (as for *Crack and Corner*) on surprising holds.

The next two routes make an excellent and varied two star combination with a mid-height stance.

6 Roscoe's Wall — HVS 5b
10m. Climb the centre of the wall (poor gear) to a flake, step right and take the steep face to ledges and a stance. Popular.
FA. Don Roscoe 1955

Crack and Corner
The best offering here is the desperate roof climb of *Paralogism*. At a lower grade *Crack and Corner* is especially worth seeking out and proves to be a bit of a shocker for 1922!

7 Round Table — E1 5b
10m. Climb the wall leftwards (bold) to the wide crack. Climb this to its top and a poor rest then exit out rightwards. Not so popular.
FA. John Allen 1974

8 Crack and Corner — HS 4c
An exciting expedition up an unlikely line at the grade.
1) 4c, 20m. Climb into the crack with difficulty (might even be 5a) then follow it to a ledge, before moving left to a block belay.
2) 4a, 18m. Take the wall to a good ledge then the groove to the final imposing overhang. Fortunately this has massive jugs.
FA. Morley Wood 1922

9 Babbacombe Lee — E1 5b
10m. From the foot of the crack, climb the buttress rightwards to a good rest and a finish up a crack and awkward rounded bulge.
FA. Dave Jones 1978. Named after a notorious murderer, at his execution the trap-door failed to open three times. He spent 23 years in jail.

10 Hangman's Crack — S 4a
10m. Start on the right and trend left to below the wide flake crack that splits the roof. Finish awkwardly up this.

Blushing Buttress
Blushing Buttress is clearly visible straight ahead from the point where the steps arrive at the Upper Tier.

11 Scarlet Wall — HS 4a
12m. Pull though the bulge and climb the crack to its end then move right to a ledge. Climb up right to the capping bulge (bold and delicate) and cross the left-hand side of this to finish.

12 War Wound — E1 6a
12m. Climb the tough wall (especially hard to start) to a ledge and gear then finish up the rounded arete on the left. Nearer **HVS 5b** for the seriously tall!
FA. Gary Gibson 1978

13 Left-hand Route — S 4b
14m. Layback strenuously through the left edge of the roof using the juggy flake then head delicately up then right to the wider crack which splits the final overhang.
FA. Lindlay Henshaw 1924

Blushing and Calcutta Buttresses — Roaches Upper 91

14 Right-hand Route ..... HS 4c
14m. Climb the desperately slippery layback crack to a ledge, step right and pull through the overhang by the crack. An easier right-hand start is a cop-out.
FA. Lindlay Henshaw 1924

15 Gully Wall .... VS 4b
10m. Follow the line of steep left-trending flakes in the right wall.

16 Grilled Fingers E1 5a
8m. A filler. From the blocky gully climb straight up the centre of the side-wall by a couple of long stretches to a gurning mantel.
FA. Dave Jones 1979

17 The Rib .... Diff
8m. The right-hand edge of the gully is pleasant enough. Starting up the gully to avoid the initial bulges is quite a bit easier.

18 Rib Wall .... S 4a
8m. The hard wall (4c direct) to a ledge, trend left then direct.

The flaky right-hand side of the wall is climbed by the bold and rather unsatisfying *Sparkle*, VS 4c (Gary Gibson 1978)

19 Sign of the Times E1 6a
6m. From the foot of *Calcutta Crack*, pull the wall to reach and climb the thin flake. Finish direct.
FA. Dave Jones 1979

20 Calcutta Crack ..... HS 4c
6m. The twisting crack is very tricky, especially for the short.

21 Mistral E2 6a
6m. Climb the wall to a break where steep and fingery moves are needed to finish.
FA. Gary Cooper 1987

22 Calcutta Buttress ..... HVS 5b
10m. Climb left of the arete the buttress, step left and make precarious moves to stand in the break. Trend rightwards to reach the overhang and finish by scuttling off left.

23 Genetix E3 6a
10m. Cross the roof with difficulty and climb the right-hand side of the arete to a grasping finish.
FA. Gary Gibson 1979

The next route is about 90m down the slope from the steps, on a lone boulder facing towards Hen Cloud.

24 Ou est le Spit? E6 6b
A gem of a route up the front of the boulder. Great moves, terrible landing and insecure throughout. It is worth brushing the nightmare sloping top before you try the on-sight.

Blushing and Calcutta Buttresses
Rather diminutive when compared to the rest of the Roaches, these smaller buttresses do offer some easier climbs; the well-polished *Left-hand* and *Right-hand Routes* are popular test-pieces. There are a few harder offerings too. The place is rarely busy.

Hen Cloud

	No star	★	★★	★★★
Mod to S	6	3	3	1
HS to HVS	8	13	7	5
E1 to E3	1	10	8	3
E4 and up	-	17	7	6

The superb castellated buttresses of Hen Cloud offer some of grit's finest crack climbs, and these include routes which are amongst the longest anywhere on grit. There are even some genuine multi-pitch climbs to savour. Perched above a steep bank, the positions are superb as is the outlook but, despite all these positives, the crag is rarely crowded. The climbs cover the grade spectrum and like the nearby crag of the Roaches, there is an excellent selection of lower grade climbs.
Basically the cliff is split in two by a diagonal grassy ramp which provides an easy descent. To the left of this are the longest routes on the cliff and, to the right, a fine wall gradually increasing in height from left to right, which swings round to face east. Both facets are split by a fine set of cracks and grooves. Over on the far left are some shorter walls and a trio of fine towers.

Accesss
In recent years there have been occasional voluntary restrictions due to nesting birds. These are indicated by signs. As soon as it is clear that the birds (ring ouzels) are not going to nest, as has happened in recent years, the signs will be removed.

Approach   Also see map on page 42
There is limited but free roadside parking on the main road to either side of the gravel road that loops round below the cliff - park sensibly here. Follow the track until it heads away to the right then tackle the steep slope direct keeping to either of the stone-flagged paths to help avoid any further erosion.

Conditions
Despite facing south the crag is inclined to be green and lichenous, especially on the left (because of the grass ledges) and as such is not a good destination after damp weather. Some routes, again particularly on the left-hand side, take seepage for the same reason. The right-hand part of the cliff tends to be cleaner and faster drying, and it also gets the sun earlier in the day, making it a viable venue on an improving day. The crag is very exposed to the wind, and will catch any precipitation carried in on Westerlies.

Hen Cloud

Andy Turner tackling *Reunion Crack* (VS) - *page 97* - at Hen Cloud. Photo: Jon Read

Hen Cloud — Far left

Hen Cloud - Far Left

The left-hand side of the cliff is dominated by three tall towers. To the right are steep walls above a green lower tier which is split by a long horizontal roof. There are some worthwhile routes here that are always quieter than the main section of the cliff. *Bulwark* is a particularly fine E1, bold and exhilarating, and *Slowhand* is only marginally less magnificent. The steep walls above the lower tier have some worthwhile but neglected climbs in the upper grades but few real gems; bald aretes and bold faces are the name of the game.

1 Nutted by Reality E1 6a
8m. The middle of the pale wall on the far left is precarious and technical (= hard) especially in the lower section.
FA. Simon Horrox 1978

2 Slipstreams .... HVS 5a
8m. Twinned shallow cracks lead to a flake on the left.
FA. Dave Jones 1979

3 Little Pinnacle Climb. .... VDiff
8m. The stepped groove at the right edge of the terrace leads past ledges to a finish over the eponymous pinnacle.

4 November Cracks ..... HS 4b
12m. Climb the near-parallel cracks up the left-hand side of the first tower to the easier groove above.
FA. Arthur Burns 1927

5 Bulwark......... E1 5b
12m. Bold and satisfying though sometimes a bit dirty. From the ledge on the right traverse out left to reach the airy arete and balance up this to a juggy finish.
FA. Probably Joe Brown, late 1950s

6 Slowhand E1 5b
12m. The right-hand side of the face past a crack and a pocket. The delicate finale is most easily overcome by a long stretch.
FA. Dave Jones 1978

7 Mindbridge ... E7 6c
12m. The right wall of the chimney is fierce and bold with low gear where you need it most but not for the finish on the fluting. Bridging on the opposite wall is not allowed. Usually very dirty.
FA. Simon Nadin 1984

8 Master of Reality E6 6c
12m. A leaning tufa provides one of the finest hard routes around. Spaced gear on the lower wall protects the hard moves to the break (or a dyno). Superb and powerful moves lead up the vein and usefully the whole route doesn't get too green in winter.
FA. Simon Nadin 1983

9 Master of Puppets.. E5 6b
12m. The right arete has a scary start to reach the break and a tough upper section on spaced monos and poor slopers.
FA. Mark Sharratt 2003

10 The Notch .... VS 4c
12m. The narrow groove between the right-hand towers. Start up the left-hand crack to a block then climb a shallow groove before moving out left to a crack near the arete.

11 Chicken............ E1 5b
12m. Climb the finger-crack in the third tower to its end then move right before stepping back left and teetering up the left-trending groove for a mildy bold finish. **The Direct** is E4 6b and not especially direct!
FA. Tony Nicholls early 1960. FA. (Direct) Gary Gibson 1981

Far Left **Hen Cloud** 95

12 Pullet E1 5b
12m. Climb the wall on the right to the ledge on *Chicken* and finish up its final scoop. A climb with the potential for many (poor?) word games and groan-worthy puns!
FA. Simon Horrox 1978

13 Piston Groove. .... VS 5a
12m. The arduous groove on the right-hand side of the tower. Bridging is the most elegant way of climbing it - on the blunt end! There is a joke in the name somewhere!

14 The Mandrake E5 6a
10m. Pull left out of *Victory Crack* to holds on the lip of the roof then thug left to the arete. Continue to a dirty rounded break, poor gear, and a bold finish. A side-runner in *Victory* protects the start but not the upper section.
FA. Jonny Woodward 1979

15 Mandrill .. E5 6b
10m. The wall to the right of *The Mandrake* has good but difficult-to-place micro-wires just over the lip of the roof, and the whole affair proves to be very exhausting.
FA. Andy Cave 2000

16 Victory .... VS 5a
10m. The angular groove which curves over leftwards at the top is an awkward thrash for most of its length. High in the grade.

17 Green Corner .... S 4a
8m. A luminous groove is one of the few lower-grade routes in the vicinity; pity it is often an unpleasant struggle.

18 Blood Blisters. . E4 6b
10m. Gain the thin crack right of the arete with difficulty then slap up the arete to a gruesome rounded exit. It may be worth getting a kindly soul to brush the finish if you are on-sighting?
FA. Gary Gibson 1981

19 Electric Chair E2 5c
10m. Devious but worthwhile. Climb just left of the arete to reach a narrow ledge then trend way left to a crack and runners before heading back right to finish up a precarious scoop.
FA. Jim Moran 1978

20 Bad Joke E4 5c
8m. From the ledge of the previous route, climb the wall direct-ish. Good climbing but bald, bold and serious! Gear is pretty much absent and the route usually needs a brushing.
FA. Gary Gibson 1979

21 Gallows. E2 5b
8m. Swing up the right-hand arete of the square wall, starting on the left and change sides to finish. Harder variations are possible.
FA. Jim Moran 1978

Hen Cloud — Black Wall

1 Recess Chimney .... HVD
8m. Reach the wide chimney by climbing the left-hand side of the large block then choose an exit; the right-hand side is technically a little easier, the left is less of a physical struggle.

2 Black Eyed Dog E6 6b
8m. A serious undertaking requiring a technical stretch for slopers and a finish that is the stuff of nightmares. The pockets are all worse than they look, with one (just) taking a small cam. Start from a block in the gully, or direct via a bouldery move.
FA. Andy Popp 1987

3 The Sorcerer E3 6a
8m. Climb the thin seam right of the arete with a taxing initial sequence then gradually improving holds. Wicked hard work.
FA. Jim Moran 1978

4 High Tensile Crack .... HVS 5b
8m. Steel yourself - the thin crack right again is tougher than it looks, proving to be a trying, tiring struggle for most.
FA. Colin Foord 1968

5 Just in Time E5 6c
8m. Twin runnels, climbed via a technical sequence and with no gear until after the difficulties.
FA. Jon Read 2006

The next routes are on the lower tier. These mostly follow cracks, though sadly the wall is often green with drainage from the grassy ledges just above.

6 Buster the Cat .... HVS 5b
8m. The thin crack and continuation groove on the far left left give awkward and usually somewhat dirty jamming.
FA. Dave Jones 1979

7 Pug .... VS 4c
8m. The better-defined jamming crack just right soon terminates in a grass-filled recess. Finish up this!

8 A Flabby Crack E6 6c
12m. Technical and excellent when dry, despite the grass on the ledge and the ugly finish. Tackle the thin crack with tricky final moves to gain the break and a gruesome exit up the wide crack.
FA. Neil Travers 1992

9 The Stone Loach E5 6b
10m. An extended boulder problem leads up the thin crack, past a niche, to the break. Finish up the evil wide crack above (*Anthrax*). NO sneaking off left - as if you would!
FA. Gary Gibson 1982

10 Myxi E6 6c
10m. Boulder up the thin crack to holds and place small nuts as high as possible. Head up the wall on crimps to just below the ledge and rock-over to glory.
FA. Andi Turner 2008

11 Anthrax E3 6a
14m. Multi-pitch pleasure. The tasty thin (and usually green) crack in the arete of the chimney to the break (possible belay) then crawl left to finish up the evil wide crack. Tough.
FA. Steve Bancroft, John Allen (alts) 1975

12 The Lum .... HVS 4c
8m. The coffin-shaped chimney is grunted direct. Finish up the hanging flake on the left or just walk off right.

13 Bantam Crack .... VS 4c
8m. The diminutive hand-crack on the right is pleasant enough.

Black Wall
The short wall below the ledge that runs across the face has some interesting crack climbs, though because of the grass above they are rather slow to dry and inclined to be dirty. Under the right conditions there are some worthwhile offerings here.

Delstree **Hen Cloud** 97

14 Chockstone Crack .... HVD
12m. A short corner leads to the chimney with its expected boulder stuck in the recess on the left side of the face.

15 The Better End E3 6a
12m. The steep crack left of a tree is a battle, especially the upper part which gives unlikely feeling laybacking. Originally called *The Bitter End* because of an aid point.
FA. Dave Salt (one nut) 1968. FFA. John Allen 1975

16 The Raid E4 6a
12m. Climb into the precarious groove in the arete to reach a ledge then take the hard crack to a finish up runnels.
FA. Jim Moran 1978

17 En Rappel .... HVS 5a
16m. Mantel up the left-hand side of the front face, linking ledges, move right up to a slabby groove and climb this to a bigger ledge. The normal finish above the groove is the best finale though the original escape up the chimney away on the right (**Blizzard Buttress**) is not without interest and was a good effort for its day.
FA. (Blizzard Buttress) Arthur Burns 1927. FA. (as described) Joe Brown 1961

18 Caesarean. E4 6b
16m. A superb line cutting up the thin cracks in the face. Well protected throughout but fingery, technical and sustained. Key holds can be gritty early in the season or after rain.
FA. Jonny Woodward 1980

19 Catharsis. E7 7a
16m. A boulder problem leads to the first break and gear. Continue to the next non-break and gear on the arete. A trio of pockets lead up and left to join *Caesarian* at the top of its flake.
FA. Andi Turner 2006

20 Main Crack .... VS 4c
16m. The left-hand of the trio of cracks is of an awkward width throughout and the exit is tricky too just to add to the fun.
FA. Joe Brown 1950s

21 Delstree .... HVS 5a
18m. The magnificent central crack set in a shallow groove is approached from a cave recess. It is delicate up the ramp and strenuous up the groove - hence the name. A rounded exit completes the job. According to an acquaintance who has been to Thailand, it is nothing like an elephant's arse!
FA. Joe Brown late 1950s

22 Levitation E5 6a
18m. Start up *Reunion Crack* then tackle the soaring arete on its right-hand side, aiming for the final flake. Often protected by a very high side-runner on the right at about E3.
FA. Phil Burke 1979. FA. (without side-runner) Simon Nadin 1990s

23 Reunion Crack ... VS 5a
18m. Bridge through the slot as for *Delstree* and then follow the slab and the curving corner by mild laybacking to a juggy exit.
Photo on page 92.
FA. Joe Brown late 1950s

24 The Pinch E1 5c
20m. From the gully, climb the right-hand face of the tower to the last horizontal then step left and improvise those last couple of metres using a pinch-grip if you want!
FA. John Holt 1978

Delstree
Now you are talking - three soaring grooves in the orange spot zone make this section of the cliff ever-popular. Add in the technical *Better End*, the fine exposed *En Rappel* and the searing *Caesarean* and you have a prime destination. Approach the starting ledge by scrambling up from the left.

Hen Cloud — Central Climb

Central Climb
The tallest part of the cliff, home to some great multi-pitch routes and the site of the only benightment on grit, on *Central Climb*, where John Laycock was rescued from above by his climbing partner and their chauffeur.

❶ Press on Regardless **E2 5b**
10m. The smart soaring arete on the right-hand side of the gully (approach via the gully) gives bold moves up the gully face, gained from the left along the first break. Wild positions.
FA. Dave Jones 1978

❷ Roof Climb. .... **VS 4b**
The first route up both tiers. Pitch 1 has some good bridging.
1) 4b, 20m. A crack leads to a step right into a groove then move back left again up another groove leading to the terrace.
2) 3b, 10m. Finish up the deep crack and easy chimney above.

❸ The Long and Short. **E1 5b**
1) 5b, 15m. Climb the luminous groove in the wall and, at its top, pull out left and climb up to the terrace.
2) 5b, 10m. The wide fissure above is hard work. At its closure exit right and finish up the wall.
FA. Tony Nicholls early 1960s

❹ Anaconda **E4 6b**
A devious climb which could do with more attention.
1) 6a, 15m. Climb the shallow groove to an overlap and move leftwards. Then trend right to a small flake and tricky moves to the ledge and belay.
2) 6b, 10m. Climb the centre of the wall (hard but a good wire protects) then move left to the boot flake. Pull up then join *The Long and Short* for a finish.
FA. John Gosling 1976

❺ Borstal Breakout **E4 6b**
A better route than *Anaconda* though it can suffer from being a bit dirty. Pitch 1 is an excellent **E4 6a**.
1) 6a, 20m. A short crack leads to a ledge (possible belay). Continue up the crack to its termination then head right up another thinner crack. Hard moves above gain a pocket and then the ledge - a great pitch.
2) 6b, 10m. Climb straight up as for *Anaconda* but move right up a crack to easier ground. Finishing direct is harder again.
FA. (Pitch 1) Jim Moran. FA. (Pitch 2) Dave Jones (1 nut) 1978

❻ Anaconda Breakout **E3 5c**
20m. Starting up *Anaconda* and finishing up *Borstal Breakout* gives a fine logical pitch, and the easiest way up the wall.

❼ Central Climb Direct ...... **VS 5a**
Not much more direct than the original and at the upper end of the grade due to the battle that is the first pitch!
1) 5a, 14m. Climb the wide crack that splits the right-hand side of the huge face awkwardly to a good stance on the regular route.
2) 4c, 14m. The flared groove, then the flake on the left, lead to a ledge. Originally the wall on the right was climbed, deviously.
3) 4a, 10m. Finish up the widening and easing crack just left.

❽ B4, XS. **E7 6b**
24m. The soaring arete is a fearsome challenge; a western *End of the Affair* perhaps? From the first stance on *Central Climb* move out to the arete and climb it firing on all cylinders. There is gear low down but a speedy belayer may still be needed. Very balancy, very scary and very, very good!
FA. Simon Nadin 1986

❾ Central Climb .... Top 50 **VS 4c**
An old classic finding a sneaky way up the crag's tallest face. The route is relatively easy for VS but oddly it is hard work all the way!
1) 4b, 14m. Shin up the wide crack with difficulty and hidden holds to a hard exit and a stance at the base of the main corner.
2) 4c, 14m. Climb the tough wide groove (okay, it may be 5a) past a ledge (stance?) to a bigger picnic-style ledge on the left.
3) 3c, 10m. The groove above the ledge to a rightwards exit (direct is harder), or the one out to the right (**4b**).
FA. John Laycock 1909

❿ Encouragement **E1 5b**
A fine climb, varied and interesting. The first pitch is sweet though it is the second one that carries the full weight of the grade!
1) 5b, 14m. Climb the wall on crisp crimps (spaced gear) to the base of an elegant groove. Bridge up this to a good stance.
2) 5b, 14m. The solid jamming crack leads all too soon (unless you are pumped senseless) to easy ground. Exit boldly left up the wall or escape out right to easy ground.
FA. Tony Nicholls early 1960s

⓫ K2. .... **S 4b**
A daunting Himalayan peak - or a worthwhile Hen Cloud outing?
1) 4a, 12m. Climb the short steep groove to a stance.
2) 4b, 18m. Starting the steep and slippery crack behind the ledge is tricky, it leads to the easy upper ridge of *The Arete*.
FA. Arthur Burns 1927

⓬ The Arete. .... **VDiff**
A rambling classic up the ridge which has a mini-Alpine feel. It is a bit of a one-move-wonder, but well worthwhile despite that.
1) 6m. Climb to a belay on the ledge below a step.
2) 20m. Tricky and exposed moves above the left edge of the ledge then relatively easy ground leads all the way to the top.

Modern Area

⓭ Arete Wall .... **VS 4b**
16m. The short but steep crack in the shady north wall.

⓮ Modern .... **VS 4b**
20m. Climb the long curving flake to a good sit-down ledge. Finish up the steep and pumpy crack in the right arete.

⓯ Ancient .... **VDiff**
16m. The right arete of the face, passing a niche, to the ledge of *Modern*. Step left to a short steep jamming crack in the head-wall.

Across to the right, and just left of the diagonal break that splits the cliff is a small jutting buttress with a collection of climbs.

⓰ Small Buttress .... **HVS 5a**
6m. The short rounded arete at the top of the gully.
FA. Dave Jones 1979

⓱ Bitching. **E1 5b**
8m. The thin crack in the left-hand side of the final buttress.
FA. Gary Gibson 1978

⓲ The Driven Bow ... **E7 6c**
8m. Harrowing climbing direct up the scary rippled wall above the short crack. The gear is very distant where it really matters.
FA. Jon Read 2002

Modern Area — Hen Cloud

Modern Area
The next routes are arranged around the walls and buttresses in the open gully between Central Climb Area and Hen Cloud Eliminate Area. They are at right-angles to the routes already described and so get the morning sun. The first two are on the tower behind The Arete and provide popular lower-grade challenges.

19 Solid Geometry E1 5b
8m. The smart jutting arete has some delightful moves to an absorbing top-out. The route is high in both the grade and in the quality stakes. *Photo on page 12.*
FA. Dave Jones 1980

20 Bow Buttress .... VDiff
10m. Follow a diagonal crack out to the arete then climb the battered flake on the adjacent face to a leftwards exit.

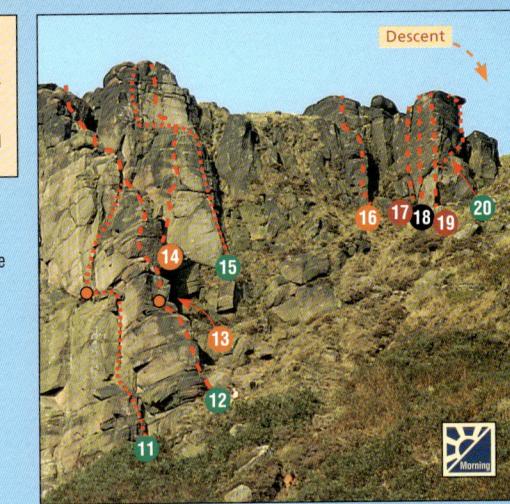

Hen Cloud — Hen Cloud Eliminate

1 Problem 1 . . . . **V2 (5c)**
A magic little problem up the right-hand vein. The left-hand vein is **V0 (5a)** as is the ramp to the left again.

2 Stokes' Line . . . . . . **V3 (6b)**
6m. Perplexing initial moves gain the crack - sometimes.
FA. Mark Stokes 1977

3 This Poison **E3 6b**
8m. The narrow wall also has a fiercely technical start. If successful, finish leftwards through the bulge above.
FA. Gary Gibson 1989

4 Slimline **E1 5b**
8m. The slim seam and crack are precarious throughout.

5 Peter and the Wolf . **E6 6b**
10m. The blank wall gives a harrowing solo. Nice pocket work leads to the final hard move, undercutting to reach the break.
FA. Andy Popp 1990s

6 Fast Piping **E4 6b**
10m. Climb the wall just left of the first long fissure. Technical and sustained until the beckoning crack above is reached.
FA. Gary Gibson 1981

7 Hedgehog Crack . . . **VS 4c**
10m. The crack widens gradually from finger locks to good hand-jams to plain awkward. So where is the hedgehog then?

8 Comedian **E3 6a**
12m. The bulging groove is approached via a steep wall and deep break. Lean left to gain the groove and follow it with sustained interest.
FA. Steve Bancroft 1976

9 Frayed Nerve **E5 6b**
12m. Climb the scooped wall just right to the break and then the steeper wall to enter a tiny but technical groove.
FA. Gary Gibson 1982

10 Second's Retreat . . . . **HVS 4c**
14m. The groove is always an awkward battle and is often lurid.
FA. Joe Brown 1952

11 Second's Advance . . . . . **HVS 5a**
14m. The wall (with tricky mantelshelf) and the hanging crack above and right are followed until an escape left into the chimney becomes imperative and rather spoils the whole affair. The green and gritty scoop of the **Direct Finish** is a spooky **E2 5c** that is rarely climbed.
FA. Bob Hassall 1962

12 Corinthian **E3 5c**
16m. The long and bulging crack is gained from the left, has a whole bunch of sloping holds, and is superb. An old peg remains but it should be backed-up.
FA. Steve Bancroft 1976

13 Hen Cloud Eliminate . . . **HVS 5b**
18m. The steep cracks give a steep and superb pitch, it is solid Hen Cloud HVS value too! Layaways and jugs lead to a tricky entry into a narrow groove/chimney which requires a bit of udgery before things ease. Well protected throughout.
FA. Joe Brown, late 1950s

14 Cool Fool **E6 6b**
18m. The long bulging arete. Climb to a block on the right then tackle the arete, sadly with a deviation at half-height to place runners in the crack on the right. Rarely repeated.
FA. Gary Gibson 1982

Hen Cloud Eliminate

The long tapering wall that forms the right-hand side of Hen Cloud has many superb routes across a spread of grades, and tends to be less green than the rock further left. The place is worth a day or two of your time. The right-hand end of the crag has more great routes including the superb Bachelor routes and yet more desperates beginning with the letter 'C'.

Hen Cloud Eliminate **Hen Cloud** 101

15 Rib Crack. VS 4c
18m. Climb into the chimney and then head up the hanging crack in its left wall by steep moves. High in the grade - the bulging section of the crack is especially tricky.
FA. Bob Hassall 1962

16 Rib Chimney S 4a
18m. The long chimney is approached by a crack to pass blocks and then gives classic bridging, as well as back and footing, if you don't get too involved with its dark and gungy depths.

17 Caricature E5 6b
20m. The upper half of the face to the right of the chimney is classy and intense. Runners in the gully and a second belayer away to the right should reduce the danger on the nasty sequence to gain the front face. From a good flake (runners) make one hard move using a mono and you're almost there - just go! Using the arete start of *Chiaroscuro* (from the gully) ups the grade to E6.
FA. John Allen 1976

18 Chiaroscuro E7 6b
24m. A hard, bold and devious route that plugs the gap in the centre of the wall. Follow *Bachelor's Left-hand* to the top of its crack then move left and teeter up the vague rib to good holds on *Caricature*. Move over to the right then climb the head-wall from right to left (runner on the right) aiming for a final thin seam.
FA. Gary Gibson 1985

19 Bachelor's Left-hand Top 50 HVS 5b
24m. A major classic up the tallest buttress here and one of the very best routes on Western Grit. Climb a tricky crack, a bulge then steeper cracks to a long move on a pocket to reach a huge flake (long tape runner). Reach the slab and ledges then step left and finish up the fine jamming crack to an awkward bulging exit.
Photo on page 35.
FA. Don Whillans late 1950s

20 Parallel Lines. E6 6c
14m. The blank wall via a thin seam and tenuous moves to reach a left-trending ramp. Finish up or down *Bachelor's Climb*. A side-runner plus some unreliable gear at mid-height give little in the way of reassurance for the crucial crimpy moves.
FA. Simon Nadin 1985

21 Bachelor's Climb VS 4c
28m. Another great route - sustained and high in the grade. Head up the steep bulging crack left of the arete on jams to a ledge, then continue by more jamming (possible stance on The Pulpit). Step back down, traverse left to the bulging crack and storm this by more glorious jamming.
FA. (pitch 2) Joe Brown 1952. Before this it finished up Great Chimney.

22 Space Probe E4 6a
1) 6a, 10m. Start on the left and make hard moves past poor gear until you can sprint up the arete to the Pedestal.
2) 5c, 8m (**The Helter Skelter Finish**). Take the continuation arete until a couple of gripping moves left enter a short groove. Continuing up the arete is *Night Prowler, E6 6a*.
FA. (Pitch 1) Jonny Woodward 1979. FA. (Pitch 2) Steve Bancroft 1977
FA. (Night Prowler) Mark Sharrat 2006

102 Hen Cloud — Great Chimney

Patricia Novelli on *Great Chimney* (S) - *opposite*. Photo: Mark Glaister

Great Chimney **Hen Cloud** 103

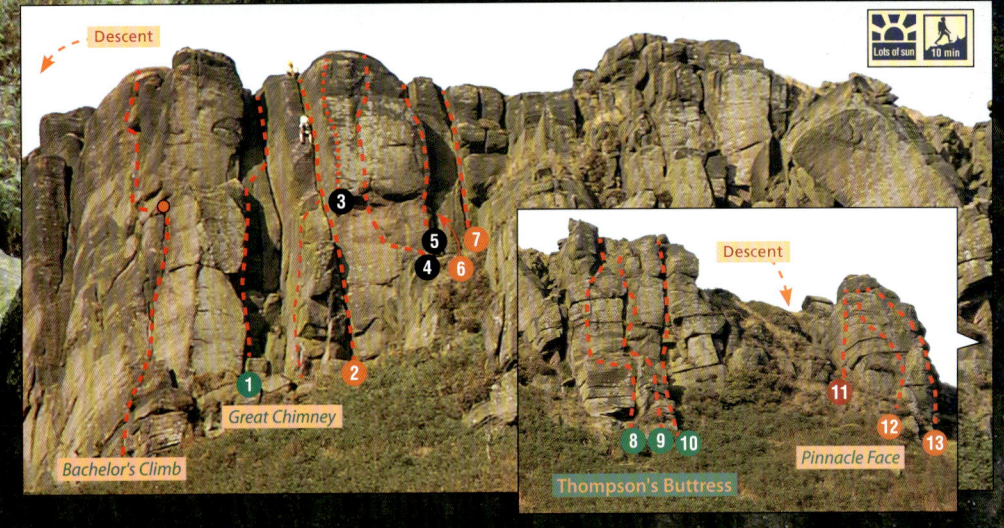

Great Chimney

The last section of wall, just around the corner from the tall Batchelor's Area, has the classics of *Great Chimney* and *Rainbow Crack* and a few top-notch hard routes like *Chameleon*. Further right the occasional worthwhile line is to be found scattered across the various secluded buttresses.

1 Great Chimney . . . . S 4a
18m. The classical wide fissure is climbed by the left-hand corner with a step left onto The Pulpit if a rest is needed. Gain the right-hand crack a little higher. The right-hand crack can be followed throughout at **HS** but the really gangly can bridge the whole affair. Well-protected throughout. *Photo this page.*
FA. Siegfried Herford 1913

2 Rainbow Crack . . . . . VS 5a
18m. The long crack and flake in the right-hand wall of the chimney give a fine jamming and laybacking pitch. It can be gained from the left (or direct which is nearer **HVS**).

3 Aretenaphobia E6 6b
18m. The soaring blunt rib left of *Chameleon*, with much-needed runners placed in that route, whilst on the lead.
FA. Seb Grieve 1995

4 Chameleon E4 6a
12m. Gain the beckoning flake in the front of the buttress from the right by strenuous undercutting to good holds above the roof. Pass this with difficulty then get motoring up the layback flakes on the head-wall. Pumpy and at the top end of the grade.
FA. Steve Bancroft 1977

5 Sauria E5 6a
10m. The right-hand arete of the *Chameleon* face.
FA. Martin Boysen 1986. An old sandbag at E3!

6 Left Twin Crack . . . . HS 4b
10m. The right-angle groove in the green recess is awkward, especially the start.

7 Right Twin Crack . . . . VS 4b
10m. The opposite corner is similar but just a gnat's harder.

To the right is a massive tilted block and beyond this a pair of buttresses separated by a grassy descent gully.

8 Thompson's Buttress Route 1 . . . HVD 4a
16m. Climb the central groove to a green exit onto a large ledge. The left side of the face behind gives a pleasant and well-protected continuation. The obvious leftward descent isn't one!
FA. Archer Thompson c1910

9 Thompson's Buttress Route 2 . . HVD
16m. Scale the awkward giant's staircase to the right of the groove to reach the big ledge then follow the wide central crack above to a tricky exit.
FA. Archer Thompson c1910

10 Tree Chimney . . . . VDiff
14m. The tree has long gone but the imposing rift remains. It is tough where it is at its shallowest and is steep throughout.

11 Cold Sweat E1 5b
8m. The side wall is climbed rightwards to a finish up a short crack. The possibility of escape rightwards is best ignored.
FA. Gary Gibson 1979

12 Pinnacle Face . . . . . . HVS 4c
12m. The best route hereabouts. The left-hand side of the face is climbed starting up a short crack and tending slightly left on holds that are mostly disappointing. Finish up the flake in the left arete. Escape from the top is rather problematical.

13 Pinnacle Rib . . . . . . HVS 5a
14m. The crack right of the arete of the block leads to its crest. The continuation arete is steeper and well positioned though at least there is some gear to be had.

Ramshaw

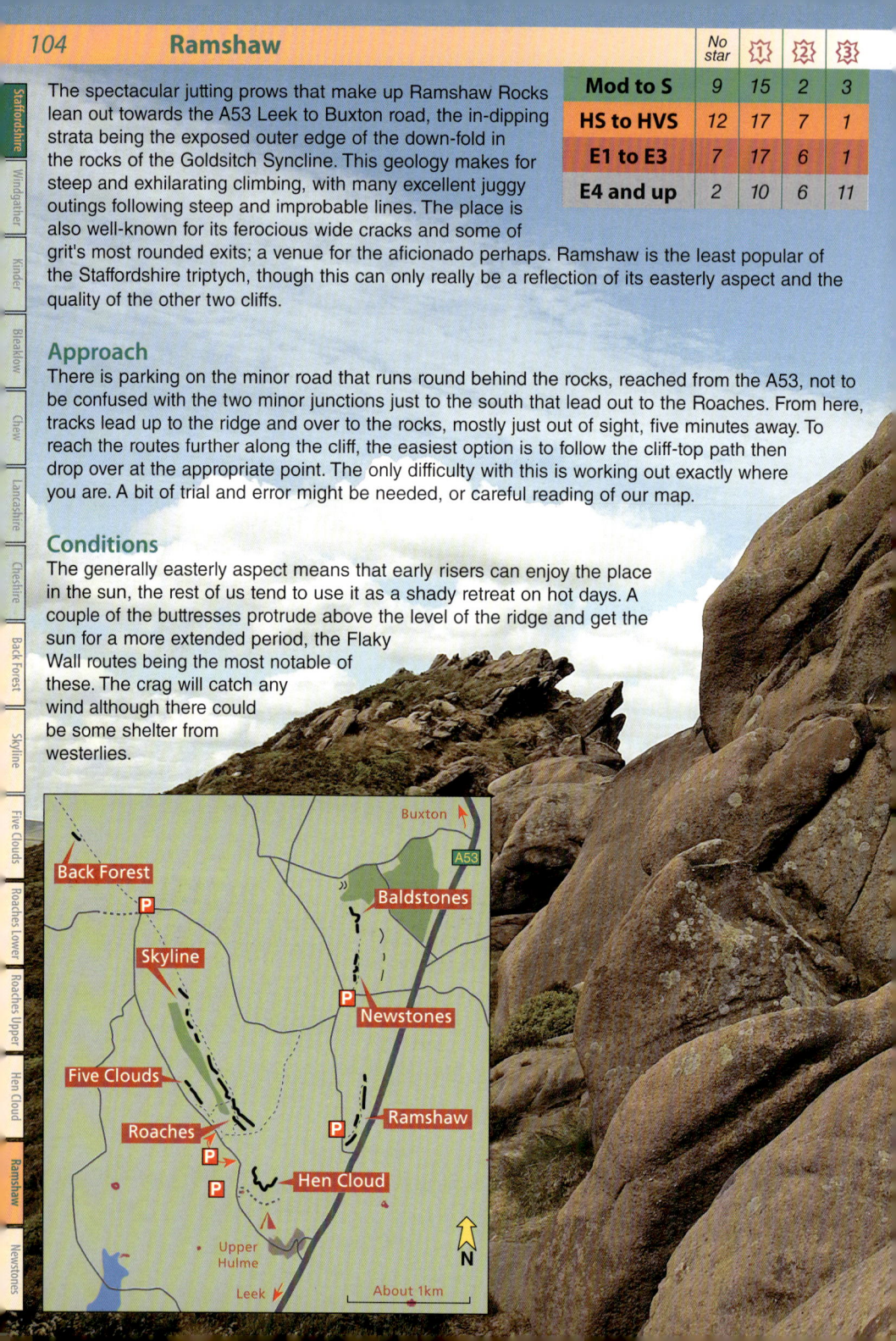

	No star	⭐1	⭐2	⭐3
Mod to S	9	15	2	3
HS to HVS	12	17	7	1
E1 to E3	7	17	6	1
E4 and up	2	10	6	11

The spectacular jutting prows that make up Ramshaw Rocks lean out towards the A53 Leek to Buxton road, the in-dipping strata being the exposed outer edge of the down-fold in the rocks of the Goldsitch Syncline. This geology makes for steep and exhilarating climbing, with many excellent juggy outings following steep and improbable lines. The place is also well-known for its ferocious wide cracks and some of grit's most rounded exits; a venue for the aficionado perhaps. Ramshaw is the least popular of the Staffordshire triptych, though this can only really be a reflection of its easterly aspect and the quality of the other two cliffs.

Approach

There is parking on the minor road that runs round behind the rocks, reached from the A53, not to be confused with the two minor junctions just to the south that lead out to the Roaches. From here, tracks lead up to the ridge and over to the rocks, mostly just out of sight, five minutes away. To reach the routes further along the cliff, the easiest option is to follow the cliff-top path then drop over at the appropriate point. The only difficulty with this is working out exactly where you are. A bit of trial and error might be needed, or careful reading of our map.

Conditions

The generally easterly aspect means that early risers can enjoy the place in the sun, the rest of us tend to use it as a shady retreat on hot days. A couple of the buttresses protrude above the level of the ridge and get the sun for a more extended period, the Flaky Wall routes being the most notable of these. The crag will catch any wind although there could be some shelter from westerlies.

Ramshaw

105

Dan Parkes checking out the loose flake on *Flaky Wall Direct* (VS) - *page 114* - at Ramshaw.

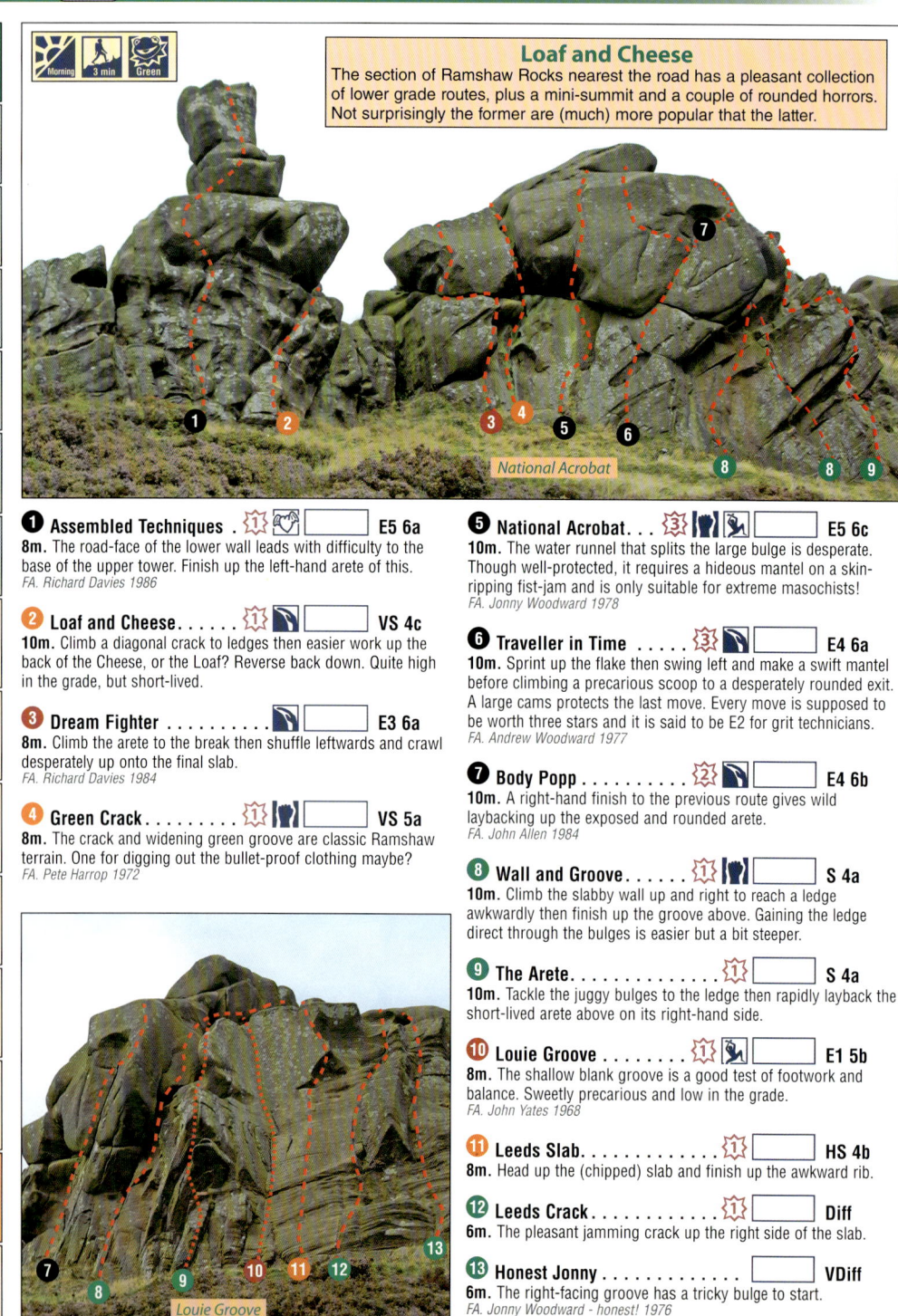

Ramshaw Rocks — Loaf and Cheese

Loaf and Cheese
The section of Ramshaw Rocks nearest the road has a pleasant collection of lower grade routes, plus a mini-summit and a couple of rounded horrors. Not surprisingly the former are (much) more popular that the latter.

① Assembled Techniques.   **E5 6a**
8m. The road-face of the lower wall leads with difficulty to the base of the upper tower. Finish up the left-hand arete of this.
FA. Richard Davies 1986

② Loaf and Cheese......   **VS 4c**
10m. Climb a diagonal crack to ledges then easier work up the back of the Cheese, or the Loaf? Reverse back down. Quite high in the grade, but short-lived.

③ Dream Fighter..........   **E3 6a**
8m. Climb the arete to the break then shuffle leftwards and crawl desperately up onto the final slab.
FA. Richard Davies 1984

④ Green Crack.........   **VS 5a**
8m. The crack and widening green groove are classic Ramshaw terrain. One for digging out the bullet-proof clothing maybe?
FA. Pete Harrop 1972

⑤ National Acrobat...   **E5 6c**
10m. The water runnel that splits the large bulge is desperate. Though well-protected, it requires a hideous mantel on a skin-ripping fist-jam and is only suitable for extreme masochists!
FA. Jonny Woodward 1978

⑥ Traveller in Time **E4 6a**
10m. Sprint up the flake then swing left and make a swift mantel before climbing a precarious scoop to a desperately rounded exit. A large cams protects the last move. Every move is supposed to be worth three stars and it is said to be E2 for grit technicians.
FA. Andrew Woodward 1977

⑦ Body Popp..........   **E4 6b**
10m. A right-hand finish to the previous route gives wild laybacking up the exposed and rounded arete.
FA. John Allen 1984

⑧ Wall and Groove......   **S 4a**
10m. Climb the slabby wall up and right to reach a ledge awkwardly then finish up the groove above. Gaining the ledge direct through the bulges is easier but a bit steeper.

⑨ The Arete...............   **S 4a**
10m. Tackle the juggy bulges to the ledge then rapidly layback the short-lived arete above on its right-hand side.

⑩ Louie Groove **E1 5b**
8m. The shallow blank groove is a good test of footwork and balance. Sweetly precarious and low in the grade.
FA. John Yates 1968

⑪ Leeds Slab.............   **HS 4b**
8m. Head up the (chipped) slab and finish up the awkward rib.

⑫ Leeds Crack............   **Diff**
6m. The pleasant jamming crack up the right side of the slab.

⑬ Honest Jonny ....   **VDiff**
6m. The right-facing groove has a tricky bulge to start.
FA. Jonny Woodward - honest! 1976

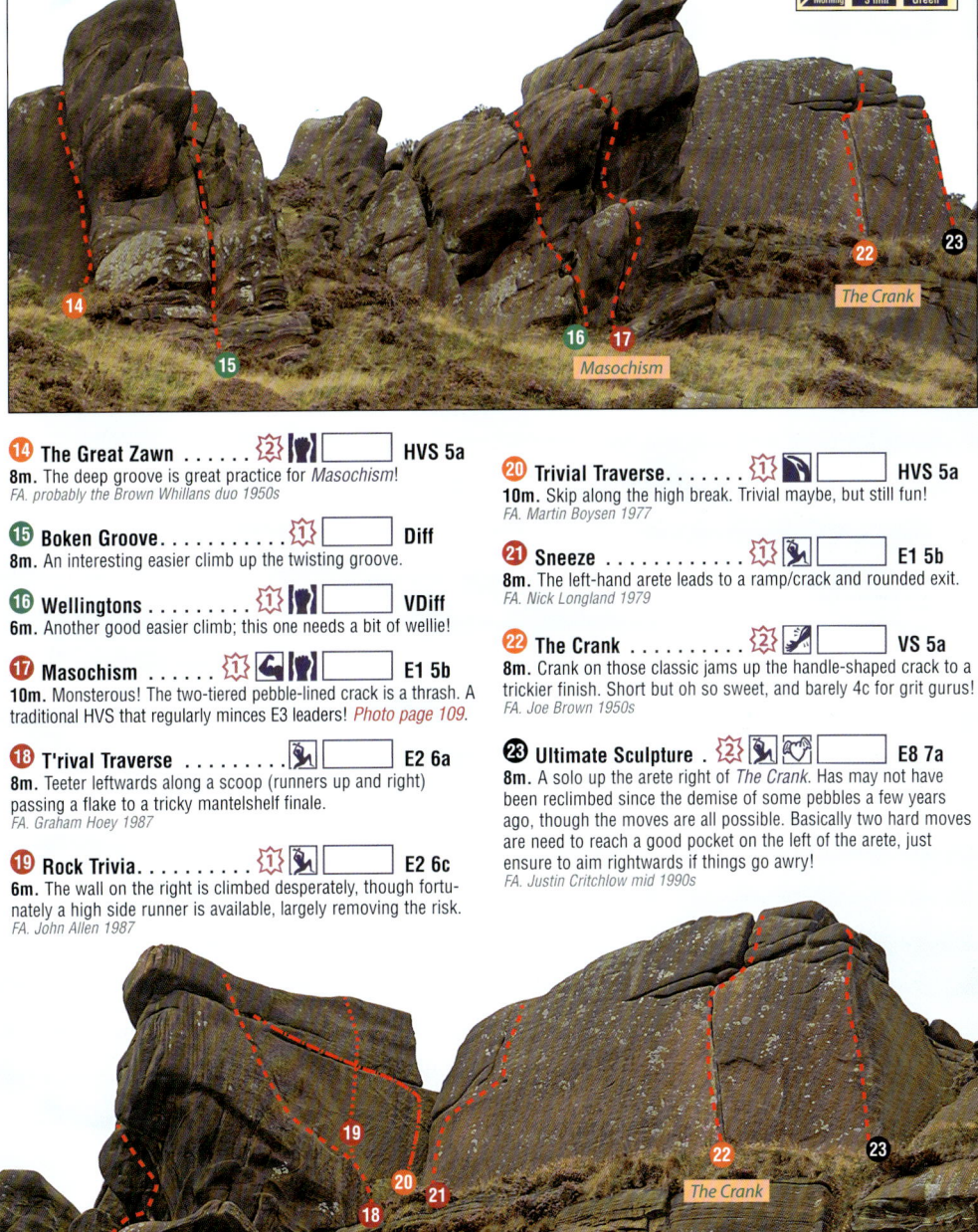

The Crank Ramshaw Rocks 107

14 The Great Zawn ...... HVS 5a
8m. The deep groove is great practice for *Masochism*!
FA. probably the Brown Whillans duo 1950s

15 Boken Groove .... Diff
8m. An interesting easier climb up the twisting groove.

16 Wellingtons .... VDiff
6m. Another good easier climb; this one needs a bit of wellie!

17 Masochism E1 5b
10m. Monsterous! The two-tiered pebble-lined crack is a thrash. A traditional HVS that regularly minces E3 leaders! *Photo page 109*.

18 T'rival Traverse E2 6a
8m. Teeter leftwards along a scoop (runners up and right) passing a flake to a tricky mantelshelf finale.
FA. Graham Hoey 1987

19 Rock Trivia. E2 6c
6m. The wall on the right is climbed desperately, though fortunately a high side runner is available, largely removing the risk.
FA. John Allen 1987

20 Trivial Traverse. ...... HVS 5a
10m. Skip along the high break. Trivial maybe, but still fun!
FA. Martin Boysen 1977

21 Sneeze E1 5b
8m. The left-hand arete leads to a ramp/crack and rounded exit.
FA. Nick Longland 1979

22 The Crank .... VS 5a
8m. Crank on those classic jams up the handle-shaped crack to a trickier finish. Short but oh so sweet, and barely 4c for grit gurus!
FA. Joe Brown 1950s

23 Ultimate Sculpture E8 7a
8m. A solo up the arete right of *The Crank*. Has may not have been reclimbed since the demise of some pebbles a few years ago, though the moves are all possible. Basically two hard moves are need to reach a good pocket on the left of the arete, just ensure to aim rightwards if things go awry!
FA. Justin Critchlow mid 1990s

The Crank
The obvious crank-handle shaped crack is the main attraction here, a glorious piece of jamming. It is graded anywhere between 4b and 5c depending how good you are at the mystic art!

Ramshaw Rocks — Gumshoe

1 Chockstone Chimney .... VDiff
8m. The tricky rift has the expected eponymous feature.

2 Maximum Hype E3 5c
10m. From the chimney, gain the tilted rib that hangs over it and climb it on the right then left, usually at speed.
FA. John Allen 1987

3 Gumshoe E2 5c
14m. Excellent climbing up the middle of the face, steep and stretchy and with plenty of buckets to swing about on. The finish feels a bit bolder and a long way off the ground and sadly the crucial runner placement is now very worn.
FA. Martin Boysen 1977

4 Wine Gums E4 6a
14m. Climb most of *Gumshoe* then move boldly rightwards up the leaning wall with considerable difficulty.

5 Tally Not .... HVS 5c
14m. Climb a series of steep grooves up the right-hand side of the steepest part of the face, and don't hang about.
FFA. Martin Boysen 1972

6 Battle of the Bulge .... VS 4b
10m. The fine bulging crack is jammed, battled and bridged.

7 The Cannon .... VS 4c
12m. A steep pushy start gains a groove and this leads to the projecting snout of the 'Cannon' which is passed with difficulty.

8 Torture E4 5c
12m. Direct through the stacked roofs. Strenuous and reachy.
FA. Gary Gibson 1981

9 Whilly's Whopper .... VS 4c
12m. Enter a shallow groove from the right and trend left up the slab, passing a bell-shaped flake near the top.

10 Phallic Crack .... HVD 4a
12m. Classic. The steep central crack-line is climbed passing the phallus early on then continue up the widening crack.

11 Alcatraz E1 5b
12m. Climb the groove to a roof, pull over then balance up to enter and climb the crack to a wide finale. Low in the grade.
FA. Dave Salt 1968

12 Juan Cur E5 6a
14m. The leaning prow is bold and strenuous although there is protection from cams and a large Hex in the slot. Originally the line traversed left to join *Alcatraz*, but it is better to swing into the finish of *The Untouchable*.
FA. Seb Grieve 1990s. Named after persons unknown who stole part of the belay whilst the route was being worked!

13 The Untouchable E1 5b
12m. The steep crack in the left wall of the angular groove is a fine and fulsome outing. It is reached via a short awkward traverse past flakes, and gives quality hand and then fist jamming. The route is always in the shade and isn't too far from three stars.
FA. Colin Foord 1968

14 Corner Crack .... S 4a
8m. The groove on the right is awkward but nice enough.

15 The Rippler .... HVS 5a
8m. Teeter up the crinkly wall to a ledge and use a couple of chipadedoodahs to finish. A **Direct Start** is 6a.

Gumshoe
This is probably the most popular section of the cliff; close to the parking, a classic jamming crack and some lower-grade juggy fare just a little further to the right.

Mark Sharrat trying to avoid the clutches of the wide upper section of *Masochism* (E1) - *page 107.*
Photo: Jon Read

Ramshaw Rocks — The Lower Tier

The Lower Tier

This section has a trio of memorable roof cracks and some more modern desperates up the walls in between. It also features some excellent bouldering above soft grassy landings. Seldom too busy, in a lovely situation, the verdant base can be very pleasant on a sunny morning, which is more than can be said for the roof cracks, any time of the day or night.

1 Crab Walk Direct .... VS 5b
10m. Pull powerfully over the roof at the crack and saunter up the grassy groove above to the top.

2 Sketching Wildly... E6 6c
14m. Tackle the tiered roofs head on. Undercut past the first overhang, to where poor cams just about protect hard moves rightwards over the next roof to better gear and, surprise surprise, a nasty sloping finish.
FA. Rob Mirfin 1994

3 Crab Walk .... S 4a
16m. Pull over the centre of the roof at a scoop then traverse crabwise leftwards (choice of levels) between the overlaps to escape up the grassy groove at the left-hand end of the face.

4 Abdomen .... S 4a
18m. A bizarre route. Start as for *Crab Walk* but climb to the roof then hand-traverse and/or crawl rightwards along the break until the welcome relief of upward escape becomes possible.

5 Brown's Crack E2 5c
14m. The central crack leads awkwardly to the capping overhang which provides the main meat of the route. An accursed struggle for most, prepare to be mauled!
FA. Joe Brown 1950s. "Technically by far the most difficult route here" - 1973 guidebook.

6 Prostration .... HVS 5b
14m. Climb rightwards to the central roof-crack, have a snooze in the slot, then pull smartly onto the wall to finish.
FA. Joe Brown 1950s

7 Hem Line V3 (6a)
An interesting boulder traverse along the lip of the lowest overhang, with crucial moves to pass the rib of *Tierdrop*, before eventually being forced back to the ground.

8 Tit Grip V10
Squeeze, crimp and leap up the leaning wall.
FA. Paul Higginson 1990s

9 Colly Wobble E4 6b
12m. The pink hanging wall is gained via a pull over the overhang past four ancient drilled holes. A tri-cam or inverted wire in one of the holes just about protects the wobbly and massive stretch to reach easy ground above.
FA. Simon Nadin 1987

10 Don's Crack .... HVS 5b
10m. Not unexpectedly, the right-hand crack is thuggish. Fortunately it is well-protected and the difficulties are soon over - a two-move wonder. Thought by many to be a harder proposition than Brown's but really it isn't!
FA. Don Whillans 1950s

11 Tierdrop E5 6b
8m. A classic micro-route which is short on length but big on impact. Just a bit too big to be considered a boulder problem, although it is usually climbed with mats and spotters at highball V7. Climb up from the right and use the ancient carved runnels before committing or wimping out.
FA. Nick Longland 1980

12 Tier's End .... VS 5a
8m. Pull over the right-hand end of the overlap (feels like 5b!) to enter and climb the hanging groove which is over all too soon.

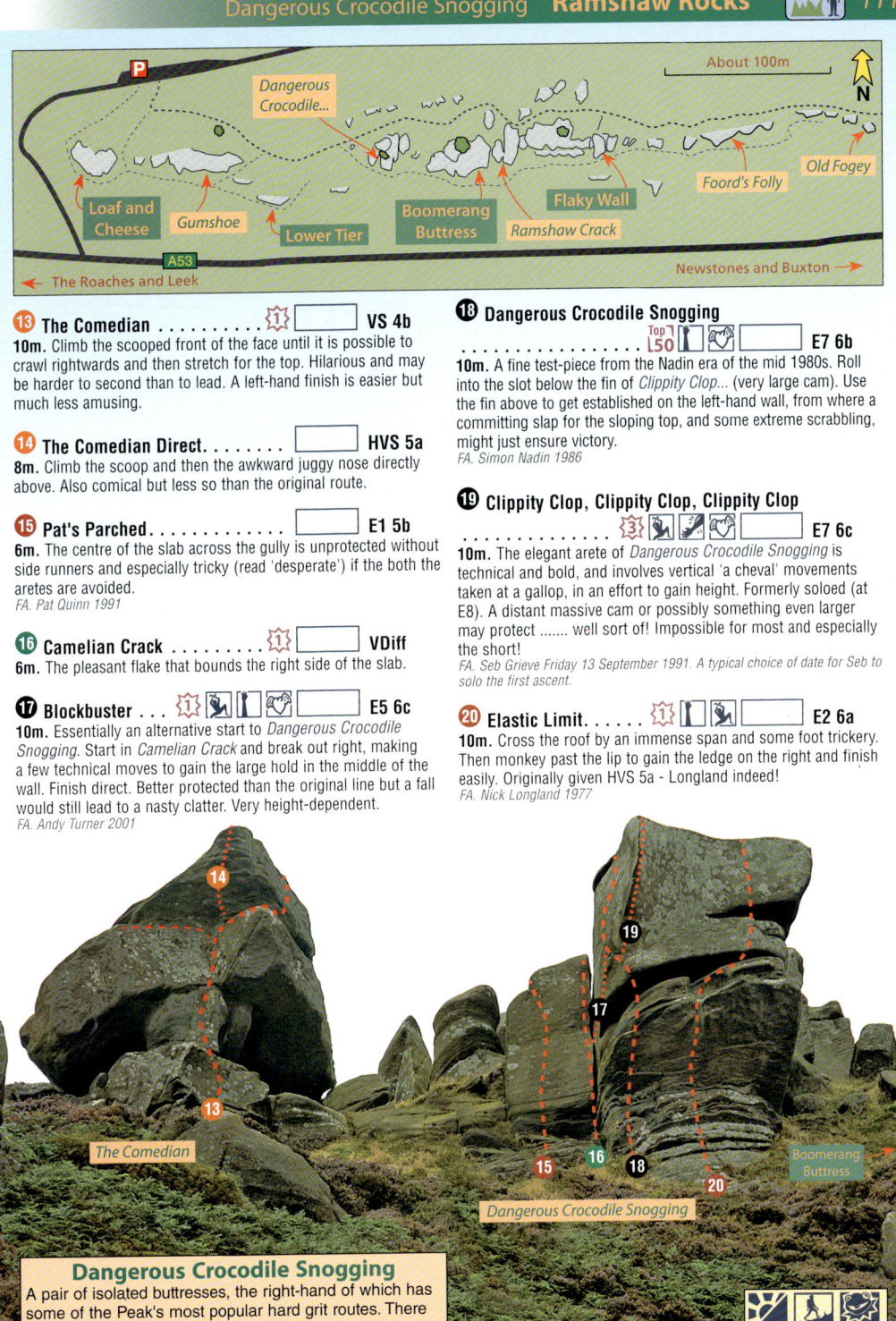

Dangerous Crocodile Snogging — Ramshaw Rocks 111

⑬ The Comedian .... VS 4b
10m. Climb the scooped front of the face until it is possible to crawl rightwards and then stretch for the top. Hilarious and may be harder to second than to lead. A left-hand finish is easier but much less amusing.

⑭ The Comedian Direct .... HVS 5a
8m. Climb the scoop and then the awkward juggy nose directly above. Also comical but less so than the original route.

⑮ Pat's Parched E1 5b
6m. The centre of the slab across the gully is unprotected without side runners and especially tricky (read 'desperate') if the both the aretes are avoided.
FA. Pat Quinn 1991

⑯ Camelian Crack .... VDiff
6m. The pleasant flake that bounds the right side of the slab.

⑰ Blockbuster ... E5 6c
10m. Essentially an alternative start to *Dangerous Crocodile Snogging*. Start in *Camelian Crack* and break out right, making a few technical moves to gain the large hold in the middle of the wall. Finish direct. Better protected than the original line but a fall would still lead to a nasty clatter. Very height-dependent.
FA. Andy Turner 2001

⑱ Dangerous Crocodile Snogging
.... Top 50 .... E7 6b
10m. A fine test-piece from the Nadin era of the mid 1980s. Roll into the slot below the fin of *Clippity Clop...* (very large cam). Use the fin above to get established on the left-hand wall, from where a committing slap for the sloping top, and some extreme scrabbling, might just ensure victory.
FA. Simon Nadin 1986

⑲ Clippity Clop, Clippity Clop, Clippity Clop
.... E7 6c
10m. The elegant arete of *Dangerous Crocodile Snogging* is technical and bold, and involves vertical 'a cheval' movements taken at a gallop, in an effort to gain height. Formerly soloed (at E8). A distant massive cam or possibly something even larger may protect .... well sort of! Impossible for most and especially the short!
FA. Seb Grieve Friday 13 September 1991. A typical choice of date for Seb to solo the first ascent.

⑳ Elastic Limit E2 6a
10m. Cross the roof by an immense span and some foot trickery. Then monkey past the lip to gain the ledge on the right and finish easily. Originally given HVS 5a - Longland indeed!
FA. Nick Longland 1977

Dangerous Crocodile Snogging
A pair of isolated buttresses, the right-hand of which has some of the Peak's most popular hard grit routes. There are a couple of things of lesser stature here too.

Ramshaw Rocks — Boomerang

1 Creep, Leap, Creep, Creep **E4 6b**
6m. The blunt arete is climbed on its right-hand side and has runners at two-thirds height. The final section can be leapt up or crept up depending on your style, or total lack of!
FA. Nick Dixon 2001. Apparently Rob Mirfin climbed the same line in 1997 as Hey Jude E1 5c!

2 The Wriggler . . . . **HS 4b**
6m. The twisting crack in the left-hand side of the buttress is as awkward as it looks, and the name tells a tale.

3 Arete and Crack . . . . . . **VDiff**
12m. Climb the pleasant arete and the crack just to the left, to a chimney. Bridge this and exit right for the easiest descent.

4 Handrail **E2 5c**
14m. Follow *Arete and Crack* to the break on the right. Swing wildly along this below the overhang to a finish through the beckoning notch.
FA. Martin Boysen 1977

5 Handrail Direct **E4 6a**
12m. A precarious and unprotected scoop leads to the start of the handrail - scary stuff! Rumoured to be only E1 with a courageous spotter, but it looks like a hell of a tumble.
FA. Simon Nadin 1984

6 Cedez le Passage **E6 6b**
12m. Climb the steepening slab until forced left into *Handrail Direct*. Apparently the direct finish is "impossible"!
FA. Nik Jennings 2000

7 Assegai . . . . **VS 5a**
12m. The groove gives awkward climbing especially at the overhang. Best enjoyed on the sharp end.

8 Bowrosin . . . . **VS 4c**
16m. Reach the crack via the slab. The bulge just above is tricky and the crack beyond that, more pleasant.

9 English Towns **E3 5c**
16m. A route that makes the most of the rock to the right of *Bowrosin*. For the harassed, side-runners can be placed from the route, lowering the grade a notch or two.
FA. Gary Gibson 1979

10 Boomerang . . . . Top 50 **VDiff**
16m. The elegant slanting groove is a classic with a steep start then a fine flake forming a mild uphill hand-traverse. The initial wide section is awkward (thread runner), after that get shimmying. The perfect place to start your comeback maybe.

11 Wick Slip **E5 6b**
14m. The aesthetic curving arete above the start of *Boomerang* is precarious and bold. Side-runners in the crack on the left only marginally reduce the grip factor.
FA. Nick Dixon 1987

12 Monty **E4 6b**
14m. Climb the slab on good pebbles to a crack. Traverse this to its end and finish up the arete. Could do with a direct finish to give the Full Monty!
FA. Mike Cluer (named after his dog) 1990s

13 Watercourse . . . . **HS 4b**
14m. The long groove is rarely travelled but is just about worthwhile when dry. Follow the groove past a grass field then take its leftward continuation before escaping out left and finishing up a good exposed crack.

Boomerang
A classic VDiff and some worthwhile routes in the 'orange zone' make this area worth a visit. Those who like their sport delicate and bold are also catered for with the memorable outings of *Wickslip* and *Handrail Direct* and for bigger challenges, just head right.

Ramshaw Crack — Ramshaw Rocks 113

Ramshaw's rocky ridge seen from the Roaches.

14 Dan's Dare . . . . **VS 4c**
10m. Climb the green groove and then the arete on the right.
FA. Pete Ruddle 1969

15 Gully Wall . . . . **HVS 5a**
10m. From a block, climb the side-wall and the prow above.

16 Little Nasty **E1 5b**
10m. Pull into the crack and climb to a ledge (traditional belay but not necessary). Finish up the wall via a shallow groove. There is a clue is in the name.

17 Electric Savage . . . **E3 5c**
12m. A short but impressive outing up the left edge of the giant roof. From above the bulge on *Little Nasty*, move right along a flange and pull over onto the terrace (possible belay). Gain the beckoning flake and, from its end, make committing moves to finish.
FA. Jonny Woodward (pitch 2) 1978. Nick Longland (pitch 1) 1979

18 Ramshaw Crack . . . **E4 6a**
12m. Climb a crack on the right (**Four Purists, VS 5a**) to the shelf (possible belay). From a lying-down position, attack the awesome roof crack which widens from hands to useless in a very short distance; holds out left help bridge the gap. Western roll into the final section and hoot for glory at having tamed the man-eater. A giant cam slammed into the crack makes it more like E3.
FA. Joe Brown 1964 (one sling). FFA. Gabe Regan 1977

19 Never, Never Land . **E7 6b**
12m. The north-facing wall is arduous and bold. From the top of the crack leap out right to a crappy, creaking flake. Stuff some gear behind this if you want, but it has been tested and it doesn't hold! When prepared, climb the centre of the wall direct to a finishing mantel guaranteed to focus the mind.
FA. Simon Nadin 1986

20 Green Corner . . . . **S 4a**
6m. The bounding groove gives pleasant climbing when it isn't too green, though sadly it usually is.

Ramshaw Crack
This is real Ramshaw territory; short routes but savagely steep walls and cracks which will repel all but the most determined of attempts. The classic *Ramshaw Crack* is a real old-style route for which grades are inadequate and training is inappropriate.

Ramshaw Rocks — Flaky Wall

Iron Horse Crack

A less popular section of the crag with its most impressive feature being the striking prow of Boom Bip.

❶ Roller Coaster **E6 6c**
10m. The prow has been climbed, but only a couple of times. Climb the arete to the break, head left then ride it!
FA. Simon Nadin 1990s

❷ Boom Bip **E7 7a**
10m. The direct line up the buttress requires a BIG dyno to the top of the crag! Gear at half-height protects (sort of).
FA. Tom Briggs 2002

❸ Imposition **E2 5b**
8m. The leaning crack to the right of the prow is an uphill struggle all the way. Big fists and a positive approach will help.

❹ Iron Horse Crack .... **Diff**
6m. Steam up the short curving, cracked groove in the wall.

❺ Scooped Surprise **E3 6a**
6m. A short diagonal crack gives access to the scoop. Interesting but barely independent.
FA. Simon Nadin 1984

❻ Tricouni Crack .... **HS 4b**
6m. The diagonal crack gives solid jamming though the nail-like pebbles in the crack are not kind to fingers.

❼ Rubber Crack .... **VS 4c**
6m. Pull into the flake system and finish up the groove above.
FA. Steve Dale 1973

❽ Darkness .... **HS 4b**
12m. Climb the slab to the steep groove on the left. Bridge this then finish up the wide crack on the right.

Flaky Wall

Across the gully to the right is the steep incisor of Flaky Wall.

❾ Flake Gully .... **Mod**
6m. The gully on the left is a grassy scramble. Continuing to the top of the tower increases the grade (**Diff**) and quality.

❿ Flaky Wall Direct .... **VS 4b**
14m. Take the juggy green streak to a rest then pull left past a rock tooth (which will come off one day - get your belayer to stand aside) into the final steep groove on solid finger jams.
Photo on page 104.

⓫ Flaky Wall Indirect .... **VS 4c**
16m. From the ledge on *Flaky Wall Direct*, follow flakes out right then swing round the arete and finish up the exposed face.

⓬ Flaky Wall Super Direct **E1 5b**
16m. A fine and pumpy start tacking the lower arete on its left.
FA. Paul Harrison 1996

⓭ Cracked Gully .... **Diff**
12m. The right-trending break that splits the face right of centre is fairly straightforward.

⓮ Cracked Arete .... **VDiff**
12m. The juggy arete just right is awkward to start then pleasant.

⓯ Arete Wall .... **VDiff**
10m. The groove bounding the buttress is approached via tricky slab. An easier start round to the right is inferior.

⓰ Crystal Tipps **E1 5c**
8m. Stride onto the slab from the left or pull on direct. Climb to and up the elegant curving flake that hangs above its left edge.
FA. Andrew Woodward 1976

⓱ The Ultra Direct **E2 6b**
8m. Scratch and power a way onto the slab then climb rightwards to a finish over the narrowing overlap that caps the wall.
FA. John Allen 1984

Flaky Wall **Ramshaw Rocks** 115

18 Magic Roundabout Super Direct
.... E1 5c
8m. Layback up the flake that splits the overhang then step right to climb the slab, finishing to the right of *Magic Roundabout*.
FA. Jonny Woodward 1975

19 Magic Roundabout Direct... HVS 4c
8m. Climb the delicate scoop then move right and follow the green streak boldly to reach a crack and easier ground.

Flaky Wall
Descent by awkward down-climb

20 Magic Roundabout .... S 4a
10m. Start at an alcove then balance precariously up the thin ramp to reach the black flake above the centre of the face.

21 The Delectable Deviation VS 4c
10m. Foot traverse the handholds of the regular *Magic Roundabout* to reach the same finish.

22 Perched Flake .... Diff
8m. Climb onto the flake on the right and finish up the rib.

23 Be Calmed E1 6c
6m. The highly technical scoop on the back of the tower.
FA. Graham Hoey 1986

24 Force Nine E4 6c
8m. The pebbly slab direct is harrowing even on a calm day.
FA. Simon Nadin 1985

The slab below Flaky Wall has three pleasant routes.

25 Port Crack .... S 4a
8m. Enter the crack by bridging an awkward groove, or by a traverse from the left, then follow it pleasantly. Sharp!

26 Time Out E2 5c
8m. The central seam is hard where it fades. Stretch up and right to finish up a second shorter crack.
FA. Gary Gibson 1979

27 Starboard Crack E1 5b
8m. The right-hand crack is short, sharp and 'ard, with difficulties concentrated in passing the bulge at one third height.

The Crippler - 80m →

Magic Roundabout

Flaky Wall
The juggy routes on the well-named Flaky Wall have always been popular. The Flaky Wall routes finish on top of a tower. Belaying is a bit awkward and getting off the summit requires exposed down-climbing or even a simul-ab!
Round to the right is the pleasant and popular slab of Magic Roundabout and below it a short face with three neglected but worthwhile crack climbs.

Port Crack

Ramshaw Rocks — Foord's Folly

Descent

④ **Escape** **E1 5b**
10m. Swing onto the wall and climb it with increasing difficulty.
FA. Martin Boysen 1977

⑤ **Mantrap.** .... **HVD**
8m. The awkward chimney is hard and often dirty work.

⑥ **Great Scene Baby** .... **S 4a**
10m. Traverse left or right to reach the crack (or do it direct at **V0+ (5b)**) which leads to a good steep finish over the nose.

⑦ **Groovy Baby.** .... **HS 4b**
10m. The next groove is technical (for that read awkward) to access but much easier and more pleasant above.

⑧ **Pile Driver** .... **HVS 5a**
16m. Start as for *Groovy Baby* but move right to climb a groove then move right again and scale the left-hand side of the prow via a good jamming crack. A bouldery **Direct Start, V4 (6b)** is also possible for the suitably talented.

1 — The Crippler
2, 3
4
5 — Foord's - 20m

① **Big Richard** .... **S 4a**
10m. Climb onto the rhino's horn (sling runner) then continue up a wide crack and the juggy wall on the right.

② **The Proboscid** **E1 5b**
10m. Join *Big Richard* to the ledge then move right and boldly layback the flying nose on rounded holds.
FA. Nick Longland 1980

③ **The Crippler.** .... **HVS 5a**
12m. Excellent juggy climbing. Follow the diagonal overlap leftward strenuously then pull over and sprint up a short flake.
FA. John Yates 1969

Foord's Folly
The final few buttresses appear to offer little more than steep bouldering until you stand underneath them. *The Crippler* gives an excellent steep HVS while *Foord's Folly* is a classic thin finger-jamming exercise, and there are other quality outings.
Approach - Use the crag-top path and keep walking to just beyond the highest point of the ridge to where the crags appear on the right.

Old Fogey - 120m

6
7 — The Press
8
9
10
11 — Foord's Folly
12
13
14

Old Fogey   **Ramshaw Rocks**   117

9 The Press E1 5b
16m. An exciting expedition. Climb *Pile Driver* but stay low until it is possible to gain the steep crack running up the right-hand side of the prow. Press on up this rapidly before you get too pumped and finish up the green wall. There are runners up there, honest!
FA. Bob Hassall 1971

10 Night of Lust E4 6b
14m. Climb the bulge (great boulder problem - **V5**) then continue up the bulging scoops to eventually join *The Press*. A left-hand start along the crimpy finger-rail is **V7**.
FA. John Allen 1984

11 Curfew .... HVS 5b
12m. The leaning groove is best entered by a swift barn-door layback. Once established, it eases with height.

12 Foord's Folly E2 6a
10m. The superb crack and groove are usually soloed as stopping to place gear is such hard work. Worth scary **V4** above a mat.
FA. Colin Foord late 1960s. FFA. John Allen 1973. Originally it was climbed on a wet day using nuts to an in-situ peg and called The Big Frig (VS and A1). The name was changed just before the 1973 guide went to print. Chris Craggs took the peg out in the late 70s.

13 The Swinger........... VS 4c
12m. Swing up and left using the diagonal breaks to a good rest before finishing up the steep and exposed arete.
FA. Martin Boysen 1972

Back on the crag top, about 40m right of the last routes, is a leaning roof.

14 Shark's Fin V0 (5a)
6m. The flake that crosses the overhang is great training for the bigger Ramshaw routes, and one or two at the Roaches! The shortest three star route in the guide? From its top, try and spot the huge frog.

Continuing along the crag-top path for another 50m, past half-a-dozen short and indifferent routes, reaches the tiered buttress of Ceiling Zero just below the cliff edge. Down and right is the more impressive Old Fogey buttress.

15 Ceiling Zero......... HVS 4c
6m. Climb through the centre of the bulges via a jug-fest.
FA. Gary Gibson 1980

16 Pocket Wall .... HS 4a
6m. Climb the steep pocketed wall behind the lower buttress.

17 Curver................ HVD
8m. The curving line below the bulges, just down the slope, finishing up a flake crack on the right-hand wall. A bit grassy.

Down and right is the last major buttress.

18 Old Fogey E3 5c
12m. From the gully on the left cross a ramp to the arete, move round this and follow the steep, flaky crack. Good sport, though inclined to be dirty early in the year.
FA. Martin Boysen 1977

19 Old Fogey Direct...... E5 6b
16m. The steep wall used to have some pebbles on its left-hand side. These have gone but you can still climb the slab on its right at about the same grade. The flake crack above gives sanctuary. Short-lived but both absorbing and gripping.
FA. Jonny Woodward 1980

20 King Harold .... S 4a
10m. The wide rift on the right-hand side of the buttress.

21 Little Giraffe Man .... HS 4a
16m. Climb the rib until it is possible to cross the chimney past the poop to climb the thin crack that splits the roof.
FA. John Yates 1969

Old Fogey
The final small buttresses are 120m from *Shark's Fin* and 160m from *The Swinger*. The first has a large roof and the second is home to the superb *Old Fogey*.

Newstones and Baldstones

	No star	★	★★	★★★
Mod to S	12	2	2	-
HS to HVS	9	14	1	2
E1 to E3	3	11	3	1
E4 and up	3	5	1	1

The elation of success! Tom Randall celebrates a very rare ascent of *Ray's Roof* (E7) - *page 124* - at the Baldstones. This mighty test-piece from 1977 by American crack expert Ray Jardine, has stood the test of time like almost no other. Inset: Tom embroiled in the crack.
Photos: Nick Smith

Newstones and Baldstones

119

A pair of secluded and quiet outcrops that can easily be combined in a single visit. Although well-known as a bouldering venue, there are also some worthwhile roped climbs here, with the added attraction of a mini-summit or two, so it is worth bringing the rope and runners along.

Approach   Also see map on page 42

There is parking for half a dozen plus cars on the roadside by the cottage. Take the track to the right of the cottages to arrive at the obvious nose of *Charlie's Overhang*, the first buttress of the Newstones, in about five minutes. To reach the Baldstones continue along the base of the crag to its end and a stile. Cross this then follow the ridge downhill along the line of the collapsed drystone wall to reach the cliff which remains hidden until one is quite close.

Conditions

The cliffs take the form of two sets of rounded buttresses separated by 800m of grassland. The cliffs generally face east and so are in the sun in the morning, like nearby Ramshaw. On hot summer days, the cliffs make an ideal venue, with the rock in the shade but the sun easily available a couple of steps away. The cliffs are the most tranquil in the area, a great place to chill, and maybe do the odd route!

Newstones — Charlie's Overhang

Charlie's Overhang
The first buttress encountered has an impressive nose which sets the heart racing of many a boulderer. The routes here tend to be a little high to be given V-grades but they are usually soloed anyway.

1 S & M V7
The flake-crack in the side wall leads to a grim exit. Heading left is around **V5**.

2 Leather Joy Boys .. E4 6c
Climb steeply to the break then traverse along it rightwards on baggy jams and slopers. Jeans help! Highball **V8**.
FA. Mark Stokes 1984

3 Little Traverse V2 (5c)
The bumpy left-to-right traverse is a popular pump.

4 Charlie's Overhang E2 5c
6m. A brilliant little mini-route. The climbing is very straightforward until it isn't. **V3** if you are confident.
FA. Tony Barley 1970s

5 Newstones Chimney .... Diff
6m. The awkward chimney. Starting up the jamming crack of *Charlie's Overhang* is worth **VDiff**.

6 Moonshine E1 5c
6m. Climb the middle of the wall through a bevy of bulges to an exit that will surprise and delight,.... or shock and depress!

7 Praying Mantle .... HVS 5b
6m. Swarm on to the nose and finish warily through the sloping scoop above. A sit-start is a worthwhile **V2 (5c)**.

8 Wraparound Arete V5 (6b)
The right arete of the wall has a bulging start.

Hazel Barn
Past some smaller buttresses is a fine wall with an unmistakable seductive line of diagonal ripples.

9 Ripple V3 (6a)
The super line of finger-holds is longer and harder than it looks.
FA. Dave Jones 1977

10 Martin's Traverse V1 (5b)
The lower line is quite a bit easier. Direct up the wall from halfway across the traverse is a good **V3 (6a)**. *Photo on page 6*.

11 Crack and Arete V3 (6a)
The leaning crack leads to a hard exit then easy ground.

12 Short Wall V1 (5b)
Climb the right wall of the short jutting buttress on crusties.

13 Short Chimney .... Diff
8m. Meander up the wide and easy rift.

14 Hazel Barrow Crack .... S 4a
8m. Climb the juggy groove to bulges which are passed by moving leftwards.

15 Hazel Barn .... VDiff
8m. The shallow groove (quality holds) leads to a steeper exit.

16 Hazel Groove V4 (6b)
Gain the short groove in the side-wall.

Hazel Barn **Newstones** 121

⓱ **Nutmeg** . . . . ☐ HS 4b
8m. Climb past the solid flake onto the wall above.

⓲ **Nutmeg Groove** . . . . ☐ V2 (5c)
Entry to the shallow groove is perplexing.

Round to the right is a short wall that has a small selection of popular boulder problems distinguishable by their names:

⓳ **Square Cut Face** . . . . ☐ V2 (6a)

⓴ **Left Arete** . . . . ☐ V2 (5c)

㉑ **Wall and Mono** . . . . ☐ V3 (6a)

㉒ **Varicose** . . . . ☐ V3 (6a)

㉓ **Varicose Traverse** . . . . . ☐ V3 (6a)
From the *Grinding Sloper* drop down onto the sloping shelf and traverse it leftwards to finish up *Square Cut Face*.

㉔ **The Grinding Sloper** . . . ☐ V3 (6a)

㉕ **Easy Slab** . . . . ☐ V0 (5a)

㉖ **Easy Slab Right-hand** . . . . ☐ VB (4a)

㉗ **Right Arete** . . . . ☐ V2 (6a)

Hazel Barn
The jutting buttress has the classic fingery traverse of *Ripple* and beyond this is the pleasant *Hazel Barn*. The short wall behind *Hazel Barn* has some of the best micro-problems hereabouts.

Newstones — Sly Buttress

> **Sly Buttress**
> The final buttresses at the Newstones are very pleasantly situated. They offer less for the boulderer but there is still plenty there; just follow the chalk and your imagination. For roped teams, the cracks on Sly Buttress are of considerable interest.

1 Scratch Crack .... HS 5b
4m. The undercut crack requires determined jamming to enter. The sit-down start is a **V3 (6a)** problem.

The side-wall has some popular problems. The holds have suffered badly through overuse - please clean your boots.

2 Itchy Groove V4 (6a)
The shallow scoop is taxing to enter.

3 Itchy Fingers V2 (6a)
Climb the small wall on crimpy edges, starting on the right.

4 Bridget V0- (4c)
The slabby corner is pleasant, try bridge-ting it.

5 Puffed Up E4 6b
8m. Powerful moves up the sidewall lead to a harrowing exit.
FA. Martin Boysen 1986

6 Rhynose .... VS 4c
8m. Climb the easy crack in the sidewall then make exposed and awkward moves in to the final groove that cuts the roof.

7 Hippo .... VDiff
8m. Follow the groove and the shallow chimney through the bulges and wallow on up the front face.

8 Rosehip .... S 4b
8m. Climb rightwards through the lower bulges then continue up the easier flaky wall above.

9 The Witch .... Diff
8m. Climb the groove left of the flakes (thread) then step left and wander up the mild face watching for crusty rock.

10 Candy Man .... S 4a
8m. Climb rightwards up the front of the buttress over a series of bulges on the large perched flakes.

11 Trepidation E4 6a
10m. One for cold weather only. Climb to the left-to-right break. Take this into the centre of the wall and finish with..... well you guess!

12 Stallone Arete V6 (6b)
The left is as rounded as a very round thing.

13 Sly Stallone V4 (6b)
From a small edge, leap for the lip.

14 The Snake .... HS 4b
12m. Access the ramp with difficulty, sneak left then crawl back along the break to reach relief in the easy chimney. Inelegant fun.

15 The Fox E2 5b
10m. Use cunning to tackle the wide crack. The chockstone had gone but is back again, its rotation compounds the already considerable difficulties. At least a grade harder for shorties.

Sly Buttress **Newstones** 123

⑯ The Vixen . . . . HVS 5a
10m. The right-hand crack gives excellent though short-lived jamming. Step left into the easy chimney to finish.

⑰ The Sly Mantelshelf . . . . . . HVS 5b
10m. Reach the left-hand edge of the elegant vein then crimp right and mantel onto its centre. Finish more easily up green rock.

⑱ Valley of Ultravixens . . . E3 5c
10m. From the vein, step left onto the slab and balance up warily.
FA. John Allen 1989

⑲ Sly Super Direct V1 (5c)
Gain the centre of the vein from directly below.

⑳ Captain Quark V6 (6b)
A fierce problem aiming for the apex of the vein.

㉑ Sly Direct V0 (5a)
Finger traverse in from the right. **VS** if you finish up the slab.

㉒ Sly Corner . . . . VS 4c
Start around to the right and rock up onto the arete. Tiptoe along to the centre of the vein then up.

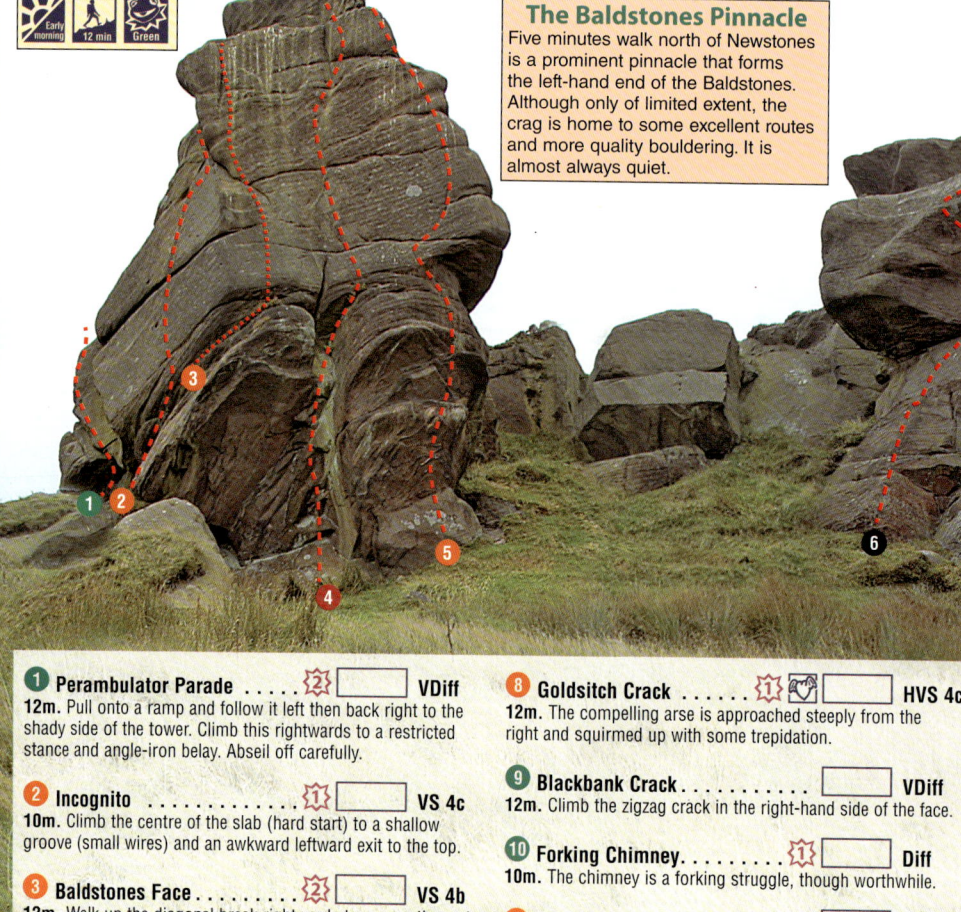

Baldstones — The Baldstones Pinnacle

The Baldstones Pinnacle
Five minutes walk north of Newstones is a prominent pinnacle that forms the left-hand end of the Baldstones. Although only of limited extent, the crag is home to some excellent routes and more quality bouldering. It is almost always quiet.

① Perambulator Parade .... VDiff
12m. Pull onto a ramp and follow it left then back right to the shady side of the tower. Climb this rightwards to a restricted stance and angle-iron belay. Abseil off carefully.

② Incognito .... VS 4c
10m. Climb the centre of the slab (hard start) to a shallow groove (small wires) and an awkward leftward exit to the top.

③ Baldstones Face .... VS 4b
12m. Walk up the diagonal break rightwards to access the arete and finish up this in a fine position.

④ Original Route E2 6a
12m. The central groove is problematical until the first decent finger-jam is reached (a **V2** problem). Teeter up the scoop above (no gear after the start) to an easier finish.
FA. Martin Boysen 1960s

⑤ Baldstones Arete .... HVS 4c
12m. Climb the leaning wall on the right to ledges then balance out to the arete and climb this, first right then left. Superb.

To the right is a wide bulging wall.

⑥ Gold Rush E4 5c
10m. An impressive line but usually dirty and seldom climbed. Traverse out right to enter the inverted scoop in the overhangs and exit rapidly up a short crack. Unprotected and harrowing.
FA. Jim Campbell 1976

⑦ Baldstones Traverse V7
The line of sloping holds gives a pumpy traverse.

⑧ Goldsitch Crack .... HVS 4c
12m. The compelling arse is approached steeply from the right and squirmed up with some trepidation.

⑨ Blackbank Crack .... VDiff
12m. Climb the zigzag crack in the right-hand side of the face.

⑩ Forking Chimney .... Diff
10m. The chimney is a forking struggle, though worthwhile.

⑪ Bareleg Wall .... VS 4b
10m. Climb the groove then make an awkward move rightwards towards a better finish up the wide crack.

⑫ Morridge Top .... VS 5a
8m. The pleasantly technical wall on the far right.

The next routes are across the gully to the right.

⑬ Minipin Crack .... VDiff
6m. The kinked fissure gives a couple of awkward moves.

⑭ All-star's Wall .... HVS 5a
6m. The right-hand side of the wall utilises a useful pocket and a horizontal break though it is all over far too soon.
FA. Martin Boysen 1970s

⑮ Ray's Roof E7 6c
8m. The widening hanging fissure is the hardest of its sort in the Peak. Getting a foot jammed near the lip is just the start of your difficulties! A total body pump. *Photos on page 118.*
FA. Ray Jardine 1977

Ray's Roof **Baldstones** 125

Ray's Roof
The penultimate buttress is home to one of the most infamous routes on grit - *Ray's Roof* - a legendary ascent from 1977 by visiting American Ray Jardine. It has only seen handful of repeats since despite many attempts. Apart from this there are a few other routes and some superb bouldering.

16 Johnny's Indirect Rear Entry E5 6b
6m. The three dimensional slug-trail on the wall round right.
FA. The Johnnys (Woodward and Dawes) one summer in the 90s.

Right of Ray's Roof is a small wall with some near-perfect bouldering and excellent landings.

17 Ganderhole Crack . . . . S 4a
4m. The crack starting behind a block.

18 Fielder's Indirect V1 (5b)
Spiral round the rib from left to right, then climb the slab.

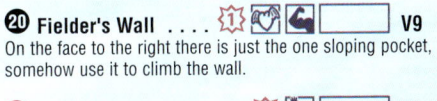

19 Fielder's Corner V5 (6b)
Accessing the beckoning hanging groove requires the strenuous use of a mono.

20 Fielder's Wall V9
On the face to the right there is just the one sloping pocket, somehow use it to climb the wall.

21 Elephant's Eye V4 (6a)
From the flake, span left to a pocket, and then go.

22 Elephant's Ear V0 (5a)
The elegant curving flake gives quality laybacking moves.

23 Clever Skin V7
The tiny arete provides this skin-trashing number which is now so painful that it really isn't much fun anymore.
FA. Martin Boysen

Windgather Area

Sarah Clough nipping up *Keep Arete* (VS) - *page 141* - at Castle Naze just as the drizzle starts.

128 Windgather

	No star	★1	★2	★3
Mod to S	16	25	4	-
HS to HVS	5	8	1	-
E1 to E3	1	-	-	-
E4 and up	-	-	-	-

Sarah Clough enjoying a swift solo of Chockstone Chimney (Diff) - page 131 - Windgather.

Windgather

Windgather is one of the friendliest and most popular crags in the Peak Distirct. The tasty grades and abundance of holds on most routes mean that most people will be able to climb something here no matter how tall, short, young, old or unfit they are. Curiously though the crag designer didn't cover the place with lots of solid runner placements and some of the routes can feel a little run out. This is also the case on the crag top where solid belays are often hard to find. Cunning searching around will usually reveal a secret runner placement or two but often an extra length of rope may be need to extend back far enough.

Despite this, Windgather is one of the best places to go for beginners of any age and ability which of course means the place can get busy with outdoor groups. Luckily though there are plenty of routes to go round and it is usually possible to find an empty route at the right grade, especially if you avoid the two central buttresses.

Considering that the cliff has been popular for a hundred years, it is in remarkable condition, please do your bit and see if we can get another hundred years out of the place.

Conditions

Looking out toward the west the cliff is inclined to catch any weather that is going, though this exposed aspect keeps the cliff free from lichen, and also helps it to dry immediately after rain. Windgather is at its most delightful on warm summer evenings when the setting can be enjoyed to the full.

Approach   Also see map on page 126

Windgather is situated above the minor road that leads south from the B5470 on the western edge of Kettleshulme. There is parking by the road below the cliff for a dozen or so cars, and from here access takes a couple of minutes via the fenced track. If the parking is full, park back up the road by the old quarry or consider a visit to Castle Naze.

Windgather North Buttress

① The Rib .... VS 5a
8m. From a block, climb the centre of the protruding rib, passing just to the left of the nose by a couple of strenuous pulls on crimpy holds, to reach much easier ground.

② The Rib Right-hand .... HVD 4a
8m. From the block, a short flake gives access to the rib and this is followed on its right-hand side apart from the last couple of moves back on the front face.

③ The Staircase .... Mod
8m. The pleasant stepped groove is as good a beginner's climb as any of the cliff, and is less polished than most hereabouts.

④ Green Slab .... S 4b
8m. Climb the flake, or the slab just left, and make a tricky move to pass the overhang and gain the wall above. Finish more easily up the face. The gear is rather spaced - care required.

North Buttress
The tall blocky buttress 120m left of the gate, recognised by the widening upper section of *Green Crack* splitting its tallest section. There are several good climbs here and they are less busy than those nearer the car park.

⑤ Black Slab .... S 4a
8m. Pull through an awkward bulge and then climb the flake above to the steep final wall. The upper section is quite awkward to protect.

⑥ Green Crack .... S 4a
10m. Climb the groove, and a polished scoop, then bridge up to enter the steep crack that splits the final wall. The wide upper section is awkward to protect, so make a point of getting a good safety net before you go for it.

⑦ North Buttress Arete Direct . VS 5a
10m. A great route though with a bold start. Pull onto the arete and climb its bulging left-hand side throughout. Thought by some to be the best route on the cliff.

⑧ North Buttress Arete ...... S 4a
10m. Climb an awkward groove and crack on the right side of the arete to a ledge then move left via a niche to the arete and continue on its pleasantly exposed left-hand side.

⑨ Chimney and Crack .... VDiff
10m. Climb onto the recessed edge then step left into the chimney and follow this and then the crack above to a taxing finish, which fortunately can be well-protected.

Middle Buttress **Windgather** *131*

⑩ Heather Buttress............ ☐ **Diff**
8m. The crinkly arete is climbed to a ledge below the roof. Make an awkward pull through then tackle the short steep wall above. Not too well-protected.

⑪ Taller Overhang......... ☐ **VS 5a**
8m. The low roof is a short-lived struggle. A beefy pull gains a rest then more of the same, or scuttle off left.

⑫ Small Wall............. ☐ **S 4b**
6m. After the short technical wall is a ledge and easy ground. Quite polished and substantially harder for the short.

⑬ The Corner.............. ☐ **Mod**
8m. The corner groove is polished as its lower part is much used as a descent route. Climb it direct.

⑭ Portfolio........ ☆1 ☐ **HVS 5a**
8m. Tricky and rumoured to be a Joe Brown offering. Climb to the bulges and pull through these (a well-protected one-move-wonder and 5b for the puny) onto the short headwall.

⑮ Wall Climb............ ☆1 ☐ **HVD**
10m. The parallel cracks and short chimney above would appear to be misnamed. Worthwhile.

⑯ Centre Route.......... ☆1 ☐ **S 4a**
10m. Climb the awkward wall past an overlap to a finish up a thin crack. Not well-protected until the upper section.

⑰ The Slant Start......... ☆1 ☐ **HVD**
10m. From the chimney on the right, trend left to the upper section of *Centre Route* using polished holds.

⑱ Chockstone Chimney...... ☆1 ☐ **Diff**
10m. Tackle the widening crack that never gets wide enough to be really worthy of the title chimney. The upper section is awkward but safe and, as expected, well-glossed. *Photo on page 128*.

⑲ Mississippi Crack..... ☆2 ☐ **S 4a**
10m. Climb into the good hanging crack in the face and finish up the groove above. Low in the grade and the gear is good throughout. Once known as *Straight Crack*.

⑳ The Medicine........ ☆1 ☐ **S 4a**
10m. Scale the stacked overhangs to the left of the arete.

㉑ Middle Buttress Arete..... ☆1 ☐ **VDiff**
10m. Start just left of the arete and climb up to and into a groove which leads to a ledge. Move left and follow the arete to finish.

Middle Buttress
This attractive buttress towards the middle of the cliff is split by a series of cracks and has a fine jutting right-hand arete. The classic is the mini-desperate *Portfolio* and there are some much pleasanter easier routes.

Windgather High Buttress

High Buttress

The most popular buttress on the cliff and with good reasons. It is the tallest piece of rock here and the majority of the climbs are well worth doing. *High Buttress Arete* is one of the Peak's better Diffs and a great introduction to the cliff on whichever end of the rope. The routes around the geological curio of the Footprint are also well worth seeking out.

1 Bulging Arete .... S 4a
10m. Tackle the small overhang by its right-hand edge. Short and just a bit sharp, at least until you find the hidden hold.

2 The Corner .... Mod
10m. The polished groove is followed throughout and makes a nice first lead with solid gear placements throughout.

Roughly halfway up the face is an orange sandy depression that has a passing resemblance to an oversized footprint.

3 Toe Nail .... VDiff
10m. Climb straight up the wall to reach the 'Toe' then continue in the same line to finish. Good climbing but the protection is somewhat lacking where most needed.

4 Zigzag .... Diff
14m. A pleasant (and misnamed) diagonal on which the protection is rather spaced. Best avoided on busy days! Start as for *Toe Nail* and trend right to finish above the ledge on *Footprint* or better still continue all the way out to the arete.

5 Footprint .... VDiff
10m. Start just to the right of the 'heel' and climb directly up the face passing a bevy of small overhangs. Good climbing but with only mediocre protection.

6 Nose Direct .... HVD
12m. Begin left of the arete at a niche and climb to the Nose. Pass this by moving left before finishing direct. Well-protected though with a steep and perplexing moves.

7 Director .... VS 4b
12m. The wall and bulges just to the left of the arete are tackled super-direct. If you get involved with any weaving about you don't really earn the tick.

8 High Buttress Arete .... Top 50 .... Diff
12m. Follow the crack up the pleasant right-hand side of the arete to a ledge then finish direct or step left, both are nicely exposed. Good gear and great positions make this one of the best climbs on the cliff - a little more length and it would get the three stars.

9 Heather Face .... HVD
10m. The south-facing wall direct via a variety of useful (and heathery) cracks. The start is on rounded holds and not well-protected, though at least the sting in the tail has good runners.

Buttress Two **Windgather** 133

⑩ Rib and Slab .... Mod
8m. The clean, narrow rib is climbed via a perched flake. Pleasantly mild.

⑪ Buttress Two Gully .... Mod
8m. Pleasant bridging up the open gully - another great first lead. Awkward belays above.

⑫ Leg Stump .... Diff
8m. Climb via a shallow groove, or the bubbly rib to its left, and then finish direct. Good moves but rather sparse gear.

⑬ Middle and Leg .... Diff
8m. The fissure has a wide middle section and a juggy finish.

⑭ Centre .... HVD 3c
8m. Pull over a nose to start and pass the overlap. There is not much gear until just below the top - so some care is required.

⑮ Squashed Finger ...... HVD
8m. Hopefully the awkward leaning crack is misnamed. Quite hard work but well-protected where it matters.

⑯ Struggle .... VS 4c
8m. Battle up the well-protected crack splitting the overhanging nose. Low in the grade but it does just what it says on the tin!

Buttress Two
A close-packed set of worthwhile routes ensures the popularity of this buttress. Although none of the climbs are outstanding, they are all worthy of attention if you can find an unoccupied line!

⑰ Corner Crack .... VDiff
8m. The leaning groove with a crack in the back is pleasant and has good gear throughout.

⑱ Aged Crack .... S 4a
8m. From a boulder, climb the bulges into the crack on the left (awkward to protect) and follow it more easily.

⑲ Traditional .... HS 4a
8m. From the boulder, swing right and climb straight up the face passing a flake. Good climbing and small cams could well be found useful.

⑳ Broken Groove .... Diff
8m. The short left-slanting groove is pleasant and well-protected.

㉑ Cheek .... VS 5a
8m. Climb leftwards to the arete from a block on the right (opposite the path to the cliff). A steep little number with good but fiddly protection.

Windgather Buttress One

Buttress One
A small set of worthwhile routes but that means it tends to be quieter than elsewhere.

1 Face Route 2 . . . . **Diff**
8m. The cracks are followed slightly rightwards to a shallow groove. Finish past the left-hand side of a small overhang.

2 Face Route 1 . . . . **HVD**
8m. Pull over a bulge then plod on up the striated face to a ledge and an interesting finish in the same direct line. Poorly-protected unless you put runners in *Face Route 2*.

3 First's Arete . . . . **VDiff**
8m. Climb into a grassy niche then exit right from this and take the crack on the right of the arete before moving back around to the left for a pleasant finish.

4 Side Face . . . . **HVD 3c**
8m. The centre of the south-facing wall is climbed using a set of unhelpful holds to a finish via a small niche.

South Buttress

5 Overhanging Arete . . . . **VDiff**
10m. From the gully, trend right across the wall to the arete.

6 Leg Up . . . . **VS 5a**
10m. From a block under the roof, pull onto the undercut arete with difficulty, then finish easily. If all else fails use a ....?

7 Route 2 . . . . **VS 4b**
10m. From the block under the roof, move right to pass the bulge then follow the good crack to a finish on the right. Beefy!

8 Route 1.5 . . . . **VS 4c**
10m. The centre of the face is steep and strenuous.

9 Editor's Note . . . . **VS 5a**
10m. From the recess, pull left and climb the right-hand side of the face. A pumpy little number and high in the grade.

The gateway to Earthly delights - welcome to wonderful Windgather.

South Buttress **Windgather** *135*

South Buttress
The most southerly buttress is a large square block of rock with a cave/recess at its bottom right-hand corner. The routes here tend to be harder than elsewhere on the cliff so hence it is often quiet.

10 South Buttress Arete Direct E1 5b
10m. From the recess, pull right onto the steep arete and sprint smartly up this. The grade is for lanky gymnasts who can actually reach the holds and manage the initial moves!

11 Route 1 . . . . HS 4a
12m. Start up the groove on the right then make a tricky traverse past the arete to a ledge. Finish up and left past blocks.

12 South Buttress Crack . . . . Mod
10m. The groove that bounds the buttress on its right.

13 Left Triplet Crack . . . . Mod
6m. The baby of the trio.

14 Middle Triplet Crack . . . . S 3c
6m. Steep but with a choice of biffos and good runners.

15 Right Triplet Crack . . . . S 4a
6m. Quite strenuous but can be well-protected

16 Overlapping Wall . . . . S 4a
6m. The short steep face that is almost the cliff's last gasp.

17 Groove . . . . Mod
6m. The shallow green groove completes things.

Castle Naze

	No star	✪	✪✪	✪✪✪
Mod to S	20	10	1	-
HS to HVS	9	5	9	2
E1 to E3	3	-	1	-
E4 and up	-	-	-	-

An excellent though not very extensive outcrop which can be considered as Wingather's bigger brother, with taller, steeper routes and more climbs in the orange zone. Many of the routes follow steep cracks and grooves and on most the protection is excellent.

Castle Naze has seen the attention of climbers for a century or so now. It is not as popular as nearby Windgather, the lack of really easy routes and the fact that fixing belays above the cliff is awkward tends to reduce the number of teams interested in top-roping. Also the style of climbing, often involving steep jamming, requires a bit of technique and gritstone savvy. If you have learnt the basics indoors or at Windgather, a session or two here should hone your technique before moving on to even bigger things.

Col Allot soloing the classic *Scoop Face* (HVS) - page 141 - in crisp winter conditions. Photo: Alexandra Sturrock

Castle Naze 137

Approach *Also see map on page 126*
The crag is situated high above the village of Coombs, to the south of Chapel-en-le-Frith. There is parking for 3 cars in a muddy layby on the minor road that runs between Dove Holes and Combs. Walk up the road for 30m and then follow the steep track that slants rightwards up the cliff passing a steep wooden fence (4b?) to the left-hand end of the cliff.

Conditions
The cliff faces west into the afternoon sun but is exposed to the west wind because of its situation close to the ridge of the hill - great for keeping the midges away in high summer but too bracing for most on drafty spring and autumn days. The crag dries quickly except for the north-facing area of rock to the left of *The Crack*.

Castle Naze — The Pinnacle Area

The first route is mentioned for its historical significance.

Herford's Girdle Traverse ..... VS 4b
90m. The route that spawned a thousand imitations from Scafell to El Cap. Left to right is usual, from the start of the cliff to *Deep Chimney* and an hour was thought a good time in the 1920s. Crossing *Keep Corner* is probably the hardest bit. The precise line and the stances are left for the adventurer to rediscover.
FA. Seigfried Herford c.1910

The Pinnacle Area
The left-hand side of the cliff has a good set of lower-grade climbs on quality rock. There is the occasional loose block and belaying at the top of the cliff requires care.

On the far left-hand end of the crag is a clean slab.

1 Double Crack .... Diff
4m. The wide fissure becomes parallel cracks and has interesting moves passing the small beak.

2 The Arete.......... HS 4b
4m. The slabby arete is short and sweet. A side-runner may help the timid and a small cam is useful just below the top.
FA. Jim Rubery 1984

The bay to the right has three short routes, not previously recorded though they have been climbed for years.

3 Easy Corner .... Diff
4m. The left-hand angle of the bay.

4 Easy Crack .... Diff
4m. The cluster of cracks to a niche and rightward exit.

5 Right-hand Crack .... VDiff
5m. The narrowing right-hand crack and short groove above.

6 Pinnacle Crack .... VDiff
6m. Climb the left-hand wall and the wide crack (awkward to reach) then step left to the crack in the wall.

7 Pinnacle Arete .... VDiff
6m. The outside edge of the pinnacle has a bold-feeling start. Be warned, the top block moves. Step left or right to finish.

8 Sheltered Crack .... VDiff
6m. The crack tucked behind the pinnacle is not sheltered from the west wind, though it is steep and well-protected.

9 Bow Crack .... HVD 3c
6m. Take the thin right-hand branch to gain a block and a steep finish. Avoiding the bridging start (and perhaps wearing blinkers) gives a more consistent pitch.
FA. Jim Rubery 1984

10 Slanting Crack .... HVD 4a
6m. Climb the crack to a groove, with tricky moves to get past the big triangular chockstone, and up the steep final corner.

11 Overhanging Chockstone Crack
.... VDiff
8m. Climb past the right-hand side of the huge chockstone using holds on the right to gain the upper crack. Easier than it looks. A dirty through-route avoids all the good climbing.

12 The Fifth Horseman.... HVS 5a
8m. Teeter up the left edge of the wall with a bold move or two.
FA. Jim Rubery 1984

13 Icebreaker E2 5b
8m. The bold slab with a semi-crucial pebble. Hard for the short.
FA. Paul Fitzsimmons 2002

Descent

The Pinnacle Area

The Nose — The Niche — Pilgrim's Progress — Scoop Face

Cliff-top Belays - Much of the cliff top is a steep loose bank and belays can be awkward to find - some care and ingenuity may be required. There are a few stakes in place and a selection of long slings might be helpful for using blocks and flakes.

The Pinnacle Area Castle Naze   139

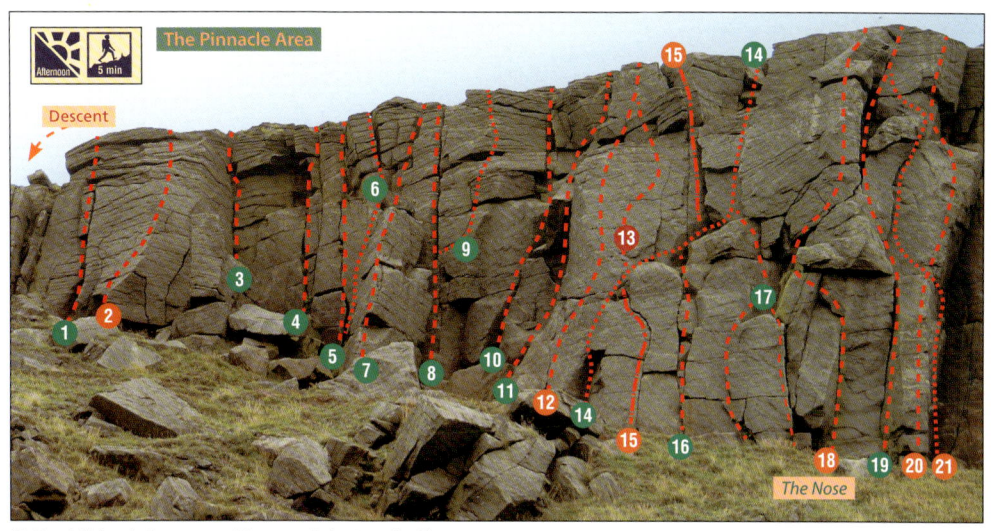

The Pinnacle Area

The Nose

To the right is a ledge accessed by several short cracks. The two interchangeable finishes are left; (Thin Cracks) a poorly protected **HS 4b**; and on the right (V-Corner) is **S 4a**.

14 V-Corner . . . . S 4b
8m. An awkward thrutch or left-facing layback leads to the ledge and a finish up the easier right-hand crack.

15 Thin Cracks . . . . VS 5a
8m. The thin crack to the ledge (hard until the footholds start to arrive) and then climb the left-hand crack to finish.

16 Muscle Crack . . . . S 4a
8m. The wider central crack (**HVD**) to the right-hand finish.

17 Bloody/Block Cracks . . . . S 4a
8m. Either fissure to the recess and the flake crack above.

18 The Nose . . . . HS 4b
12m. Climb leftwards out of the recess (wide bridging?) to a slot, then step back right onto the top of the overhang and climb the crucial upper arete which is not well-protected.

19 The Nithin . . . . S 4a
12m. The right-hand crack in the recess (awkward) to a ledge and the wide crack on the left. The arete direct is **HS 4a**.

20 Nursery Arete . . . . HVS 5b
12m. The square arete and its broader continuation has its moments.
FA. Paul Messenger 2003

21 Flake Crack . . . . HS 4a
12m. Climb a flaky crack in the gully wall to the ledge on the left and continue up the flake with care to a tricky exit.

Descent

The Crack

Central Tower

Castle Naze — Pilgrim's Progress

Pilgrim's Progress

This fine series of cracks and grooves is an excellent place for honing your jamming skills. Some of the routes are quite technical for their grade but protection is usually plentiful and easy to place A good venue for learning the art - *The Niche*, *Studio* and *Pilgrim's Progress* should do for starters.

1 Main Corner .... S 4a
10m. The groove direct. Avoiding the cracks of *The Flywalk* is practically impossible, but who cares?

2 The Flywalk .... S 4a
10m. The battered cracks in the right wall are worth doing to ledges (not bridging to the opposite wall of the groove is probably worth **VS 4b**), then finish out right.

3 The Niche .... S 4a
12m. The niched-crack gives good steep climbing on solid jams. Passing the niche is a little awkward but the gear is good.

4 Niche Arete .... VS 5a
12m. Climb the delicate arete with stretchy moves. Protection at the level of the niche feels distant and it is serious for the short.

5 Orm and Cheep E1 6a
12m. The shallow slanting groove in the side-wall leads to the pocketed face (side-runner) and sprint. No deviations allowed.
FA. Al Evans 1989

6 Studio .... HS 4b
12m. Climb the good crack then mantelshelf rightwards (hard but safe) or layback (easier but bolder) then follow the cracks only. Following the left-hand crack is harder.

7 A.P. Chimney .... HS 4a
12m. The wide crack in the groove is absolutely perpendicular and also quite steep. Classic bridging or technical thrutching are the usual forms of progress. The upper part is easier.

8 Pod Crack E1 6a
10m. Climb the fierce thin cracks past the pod to a final groove.
FA. Jim Rubery 1984

9 Pitoned Crack .... HVS 5b
12m. The thin crack is gained from the next route. Once aided and still managing to feel a little artificial.

10 Pilgrim's Progress .... HS 4b
12m. The steep crack will test your jamming technique and is very close to VS. The groove above has a tricky exit.

11 Little Pillar .... VS 4b
12m. A tough start up twin cracks and an wide awkward finish.

12 Ledgeway .... HVS 5a
12m. Climb the curving crack to a good ledge then climb the wall on the right passing a slanting crack. The arete to the left of the start is **Short and Sweet, V3 (6a)**.

13 No Name .... S 4b
12m. Climb the tough groove to the right end of the ledge and the easier continuation directly above.

14 Keep Buttress .... HVS 5b
12m. Climb thin parallel cracks to the protruding square arete and tackle this by the steep groove on the right.

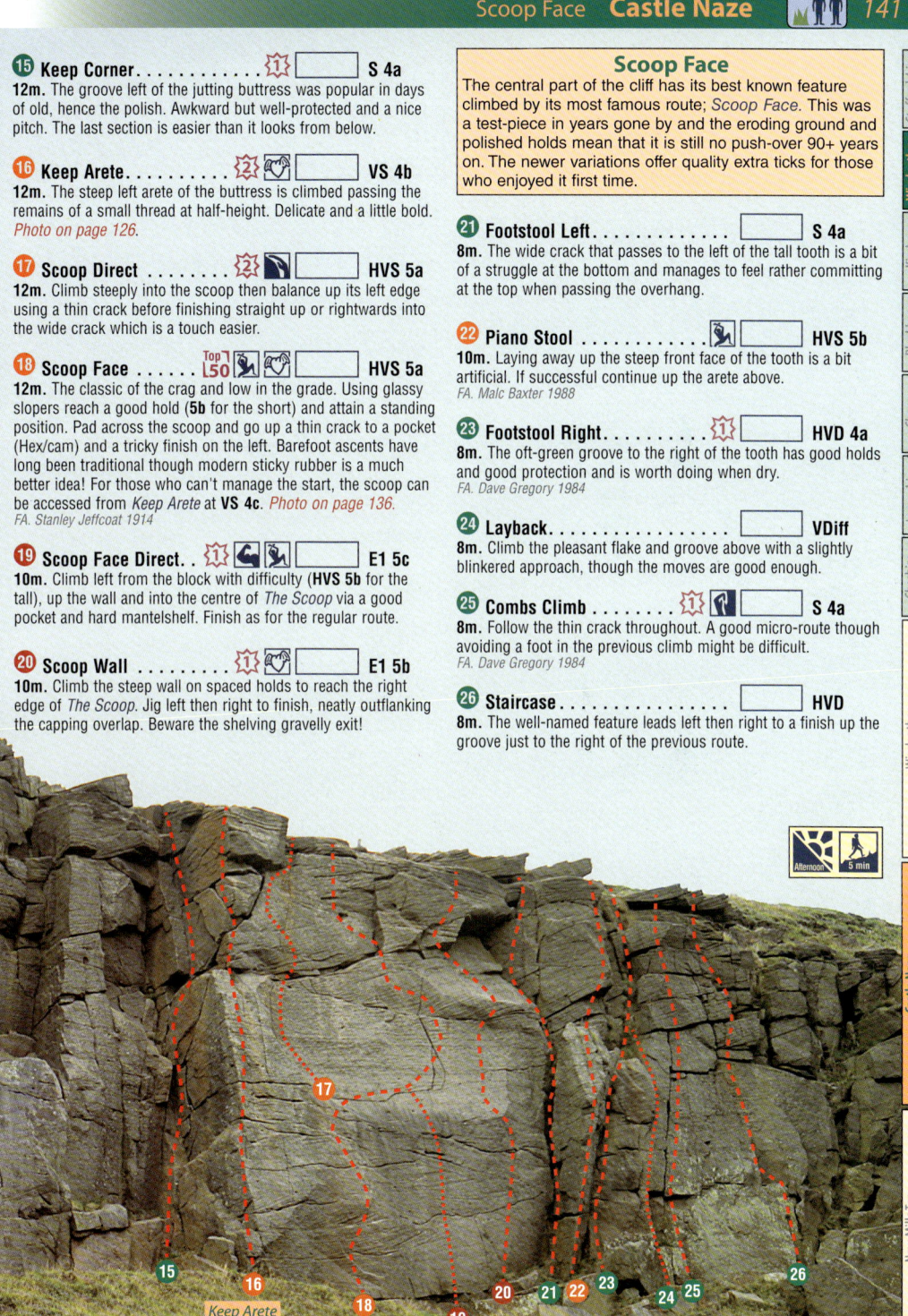

Scoop Face **Castle Naze** 141

15 Keep Corner............. S 4a
12m. The groove left of the jutting buttress was popular in days of old, hence the polish. Awkward but well-protected and a nice pitch. The last section is easier than it looks from below.

16 Keep Arete........... VS 4b
12m. The steep left arete of the buttress is climbed passing the remains of a small thread at half-height. Delicate and a little bold.
Photo on page 126.

17 Scoop Direct .... HVS 5a
12m. Climb steeply into the scoop then balance up its left edge using a thin crack before finishing straight up or rightwards into the wide crack which is a touch easier.

18 Scoop Face ...... HVS 5a
12m. The classic of the crag and low in the grade. Using glassy slopers reach a good hold (**5b** for the short) and attain a standing position. Pad across the scoop and go up a thin crack to a pocket (Hex/cam) and a tricky finish on the left. Barefoot ascents have long been traditional though modern sticky rubber is a much better idea! For those who can't manage the start, the scoop can be accessed from *Keep Arete* at **VS 4c**. *Photo on page 136.*
FA. Stanley Jeffcoat 1914

19 Scoop Face Direct.. E1 5c
10m. Climb left from the block with difficulty (**HVS 5b** for the tall), up the wall and into the centre of *The Scoop* via a good pocket and hard mantelshelf. Finish as for the regular route.

20 Scoop Wall E1 5b
10m. Climb the steep wall on spaced holds to reach the right edge of *The Scoop*. Jig left then right to finish, neatly outflanking the capping overlap. Beware the shelving gravelly exit!

Scoop Face
The central part of the cliff has its best known feature climbed by its most famous route; *Scoop Face*. This was a test-piece in years gone by and the eroding ground and polished holds mean that it is still no push-over 90+ years on. The newer variations offer quality extra ticks for those who enjoyed it first time.

21 Footstool Left.............. S 4a
8m. The wide crack that passes to the left of the tall tooth is a bit of a struggle at the bottom and manages to feel rather committing at the top when passing the overhang.

22 Piano Stool .... HVS 5b
10m. Laying away up the steep front face of the tooth is a bit artificial. If successful continue up the arete above.
FA. Malc Baxter 1988

23 Footstool Right........... HVD 4a
8m. The oft-green groove to the right of the tooth has good holds and good protection and is worth doing when dry.
FA. Dave Gregory 1984

24 Layback................. VDiff
8m. Climb the pleasant flake and groove above with a slightly blinkered approach, though the moves are good enough.

25 Combs Climb .... S 4a
8m. Follow the thin crack throughout. A good micro-route though avoiding a foot in the previous climb might be difficult.
FA. Dave Gregory 1984

26 Staircase................ HVD
8m. The well-named feature leads left then right to a finish up the groove just to the right of the previous route.

Castle Naze — The Crack

1. The Two-step .... HVD
10m. Follow the short arete on its left edge. It proves to be a bit lichenous and not too well-protected in the lower part.

2. Fat Man's Chimney .... Mod
8m. The deep rift is an outing for the gravitationally challenged. Careful use of outside footholds can ease things a lot.

3. Plankton E4 6a
8m. A poorly-protected and technical smooth wall climb. It feels like it is on the wrong cliff.
FA. Al Evans 1977

4. Deep Crack .... VDiff
8m. Obvious from the name. Pleasant moves lead up the crack, starting from the base of the chimney and keeping left.
FA. Dave Gregory 1984

5. Deep Chimney .... HVD
8m. This dark fissure cuts deep behind the buttress, severing it from the hillside behind. Get stuck in for maximum pleasure. Poorly protected but then again falling out of it would be tough!

6. Birthday Climb .... HVS 5b
14m. Start as for The Crack. Step left from this to reach a hidden flake set in the left arete and follow this strenuously to the top. Fine exposed climbing but rarely done.

7. The Crack .... VS 4b
14m. Climb the crack to a recess (a bit of a boulder problem) and follow the excellent steep fissure through the overhang and up the face above, on solid jams throughout. Mild at the grade.

8. Nozag .... VS 4c
14m. Climb a crack to the arete of the buttress. Where it starts to slant away right, pull onto the face and follow a thin crack directly and with some difficulty in the upper part (big cam). Superb climbing, as good as anything of its grade in the Peak.

9. Zigzag Crack .... HS 4b
12m. Follow the previous route but stay with the diagonal crack all the way to reach the wide fissure and an easy finish.

10. Zig-a-Zag-a .... VDiff
12m. Climb the groove to a ledge then the wall immediately right of the chimney. Beware of an unexpected loose block that lurks a short distance below the top.
FA. Dave Gregory 1984

The Crack
The tallest buttress on the cliff, home to some of the very best outings here. Routes such as *The Crack* and *Nozag* would be immensely popular were they over on the Eastern Edges; here they don't see too much traffic at all. Hopefully you won't need to queue for them.

Central Tower   Castle Naze   143

11 Long Climb .... VDiff
14m. Climb the blocky groove to a ledge then select a finish. The main angle is the easiest and there are trickier options to either side. Long but not especially satisfying.

12 Central Tower .... VDiff
12m. A green groove leads to a ledge on the right, step out left to another ledge and finish by the groove on the right. Disjointed but worth the effort and excitingly exposed towards the top.

13 Atropine .... VS 4b
14m. Excellent and exposed. Climb over a flake to a ledge (tricky) then take the slabby ramp and thin crack to more ledges. Tackle the strenuous layaway flake-crack to yet more ledges then choose a finishing crack, the right-hand one being harder and better.
FA. Lew Hardy 1977

14 Primadonna E4 6a
12m. From the top of the ramp, climb the arete on its right-hand side throughout. Difficulties are short but serious and very much height dependent, prepare for a torrid time if you are short.
FA. Joe Bawden 1997

15 Belladonna E2 5c
12m. Devious though with some good moves and a certain logic to the line. Follow *Primadonna* up the right-hand side of the arete until forced out right below an overlap. Pull over this to reach a second overlap then trend back left (beware of a loose flake) to the upper arete and an exposed finish.
FA. Al Evans 1977

16 The Ugly Bloke E3 6a
12m. Fierce and serious with only so-so gear. The wall above *Belladonna* is climbed on tiny holds to a poor pocket. From here finish with care. Said to be E5 if the runners rip!
FA. Joe Bawden 1997

17 Green Crack .... S 4a
14m. From the ledge at the start of the previous three routes, follow the groove trending right to a steep final section. It is best to belay just below the top to avoid getting too involved with the loose slope above.

Central Tower
The second most impressive part of the cliff has a small selection of worthwhile and quite long climbs in a setting that is far from central.

Down and right of the Central Tower is a quarry with a set of unremarkable routes, refugees from the one of the grottier bays at Millstone perhaps? They are not described here.

New Mills Tor

	No star	★	★★	★★★
Mod to S	-	1	-	1
HS to HVS	10	5	-	1
E1 to E3	1	6	5	-
E4 and up	-	3	1	-

New Mills Tor is a well hidden crag, set in a deep gloomy gorge right bang in the centre of New Mills. The cliff is witheringly steep, surprisingly tall for grit and composed of a rather soft and sandy gritstone, not the well-weathered stone you might be used to. These various factors all add up make the routes here intimidating and pumpy propositions. Although some of the routes are esoteric the best of the climbs here are very good and the oddness of the setting adds to the whole experience of the place - if you are passing by, call in and sample the unique experience that is New Mills Tor.

Approach   Also see map on page 126

There is limited (pay and display - time limits apply) parking on the small loop road behind the bus turning-circle in the centre of New Mills. If this is full, or you fancy climbing for longer than a hour or two, there are various quiet side-streets nearby where parking is possible. From behind the bus turning-circle a steep path leads down to the left-hand end of the cliff, five minutes away. If you have come for a big session it is worth saving enough strength for the steep walk back out!

Conditions

The crag is steep enough to stay dry in light rain and the tree canopy in summer adds to this shelter. The steepest part of the cliff is right under the viaduct, and this stays dry even in monsoon conditions, so next time the summer weather is poor it might be worth considering trying a session here - its cheaper than the wall and it will doubtless do you more good!

Bouldering

The angle of the rock, the tree and birdge canopy and the easy access make the crag a viable venue for a bouldering work-out.
The girdle of the viaduct pillar gives a good pump. The traverse from *Overlooked Groove* to *Deception* is **V3 (5c)** and the extension is **V5 (6b)**.
The low crossing of the *Electric Circus* wall is also **V5 (6b)**.
The *Honcho* start is a good **V4 (6b)** and there are worthwhile problems just left.
The area under the ramp (*Bionics Wall*) has problems from **V1 (5b)** upwards.

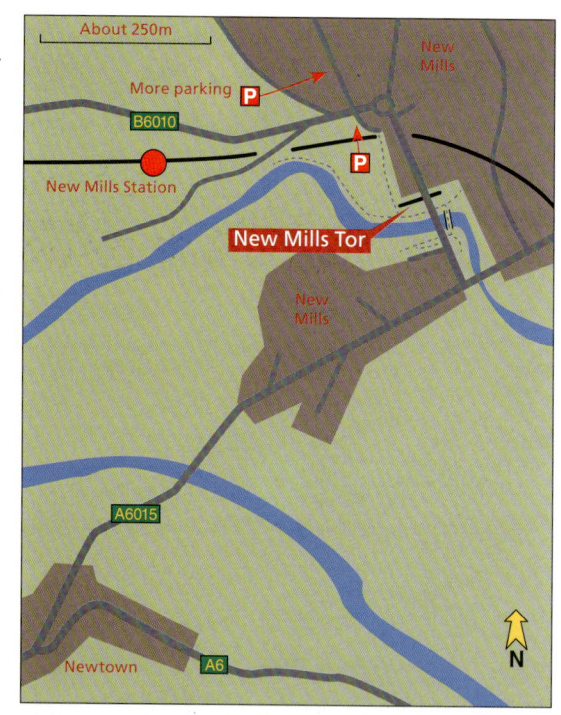

Ashly Fusiarski bouldering out the start of *Bionic's Wall* (V3) - *page 149.* Photo: David Williams

New Mills Tor   The Alcove

The Alcove and Electric Circus

From the foot of the steps the first rock encountered is a shady bay with the central classic line of *Alcove Crack*. Just beyond this is the soaring jutting edge of *The Arete*. The angle of the rock and the tree canopy means that routes here often stay dry during light summer rain.

1 Basic Arete E1 5b
8m. Climb the left arete of the alcove until an escape into the groove on the right becomes essential. Descend down here.
FA. Paul Cropper 1979

2 Alcove Crack . . . . HVS 5a
20m. The dramatic fissure in the back wall of The Alcove gives a steep (as in overhanging) and well-protected tussle.
FA. Dennis Carr 1977

3 The Sandman E1 5b
20m. The scruffy corner leads to the big ledge. Step left and follow the steep seam until the sandy hole on the right can be reached. Finish up the wider fissure. A good line but a bit grotty.
FA. Al Evans 1977

The next four routes end up on the shrubby ledge, escape from which is best effected by the groove on the left.

4 Porky's Wall . . . . HVS 5c
8m. The fingery centre of the wall on the jutting buttress on the right-hand side of the alcove.
FA. Jim Burton 1979

5 Piggy's Crack . . . . VS 4c
8m. The short crack in the wall. Beware, bees in the summer.
FA. Al Evans 1977

6 The Steeple . . . . HVS 5a
8m. The steep arete on the right of The Alcove.
FA. Loz Francomb 1977

7 Clotted Cream . . . . VS 4c
8m. The short right arete of the squat buttress is pleasant enough.
FA. Al Evans 1977

8 The Arete E2 5b
22m. A long and impressive arete with steep and intimidating climbing that is high in the grade. Some of the rock is a bit soft. Avoid the initial bulge on the left then pull back right to a ledge. Continue up the scary upper section to an easier finish. The route is often started from the gully to the left which is a little easier.
FA. (in two bits) Al Evans 1976, Jim Burton (in one push) 1977, although Gabe Regan may have soloed(!) it at an earlier date.

9 Mather Crack E2 5b
22m. The long steep crack gives a good pumpy pitch. The quality of the runners makes up just a little for the angle and the occasional disposable holds. Low in the grade but it keeps coming.
FA. Terry Wyatt 1971. FFA. Dennis Carr 1977

Electirc Circus **New Mills Tor** 147

10 Electric Circus . E3 5c
26m. A big scary pitch weaving its way up the wall - low in the grade but quite harrowing. Climb to the top of the flake then traverse right (old peg) to a crack which leads to a rattly traverse back left to reach the upper crack. The direct link is **Short Circuit** - E3 5c, high in the grade and it is even more terrifying.
FA. Dennis Carr 1977. FA. (Short Circuit) Al Evans 1977

11 Oak Tree Wall E3 5c
22m. Plugs the gap in the centre of the wall. Climb *Electric Circus* for 5m then traverse right and climb up to the overhang, then pull through (2 pegs). Finish up the steep right-hand crack in the final wall. High in the grade and hard work too.
FA. Al Evans (1 rest) 1979. FFA. Nick Colton 1979

12 The Grim Reaper E5 6b
22m. An arduous outing up the right-hand side of the wall - bold and fierce. Climb the wall - **Enigma Variation** a **V7** dyno - to a peg (or sneak in from left or right) then head right to a flake under the overhang. Pull leftwards over this (peg) and head left to a resting ledge. Finish steeply on better holds.
FA. Nick Colton 1979

Descents - Many of the routes finish in the trees at the top of the crag. An abseil from here is the best way down.

13 Transformation . . . . HVS 4c
20m. Tackle the crack and thrutchy groove past the useful shrub.
FA. Al Evans 1977

14 Stonewall Crack . . . . HVS 4c
20m. The blocky groove above the walling.

The central section of the cliff is rather overgrown and loose. The best plan is to make for the rock under the impressive arch of the road bridge away to the right where things improve somewhat.

New Mills Tor — The Bridge

⑮ The Poise — E2 5c
18m. The steep face above the right-hand bit of walling is climbed left then back right, finishing though a grotty grotto.

⑯ The Flake — VS 4b
14m. Climb the flake then move right to a crack to finish.

⑰ The Overlooked Groove — HS 4b
14m. From the strange reddish-brown orifice, climb the stepped right-facing groove throughout. The entry into the upper groove is well-protected and care is required with the exit.
FA. Al Evans 1976

⑱ The Inbetweenie — VS 4c
14m. The clue is in the name!
FA. Al Evans 1989

⑲ Original Route — VD 3c
16m. Follow the giant's staircase up and left to a mighty tree, by awkward moves between good resting ledges. Never quite as easy as it looks, but always on good holds.
FA. Terry Wyatt early 1970s

⑳ Cracked Corner — HS 4b
14m. Start up *Original Route* but continue directly up the steep crack to the continuation groove above. Leaving the good ledge and requires a bit of a stretch - harder than it looks.
FA. Al Evans 1977

㉑ Viaduct Crack — HVS 5b
14m. Start at a ledge (or more easily from the left) and climb the steep vague crack-line until it is possible to trend right to resting ledges. Escape off left, or better, continue up the short, steep and strenny wall above. High in the grade and pumptastic.
FA. Dennis Carr 1977. FA. (Direct Finish) Al Evans 1989

㉒ Haze — E1 5c
14m. A direct start to the previous climb up the blunt rib.
Microchasm, V7 is an eliminate between *Haze* and *Viaduct Wall* avoiding holds on adjacent routes. Graded for use of mats.
FA. (Microchasm) Nick Colton 1994

㉓ Viaduct Wall — E2 5c
14m. The ever-dry wall under the arches gives a steep and pumpy pitch (aren't they all) with a couple of reachy moves (**5b** for the tall) and a precarious mantelshelf to reach easier ground.
FA. Al Evans 1977

㉔ Honcho — E4 6b
14m. Begin left of *Deception's* cracks and gain a peg runner with difficulty - **V4**. Use the improving side-pull to continue direct, passing a break, to ledges and an escape. Apparently it was originally graded HVS and is now low in the (E4) grade.
FA. Nick Colton 1979

The Bridge New Mills Tor 149

The Bridge
The right-hand side of the cliff has a fair collection of steep routes on reasonable rock. The arch of the road bridge far above makes this the Peak's best wet-weather grit venue, and the angle of the routes ensures a good work-out session. The easier routes here suffer from a lack of traffic.

25 Deception . . . . HVS 5a
14m. The twin bending cracks are a bit crusty and are good practice for South Stack at Gogarth!
FA. Al Evans 1977

26 Deception to Original Route . . . V1 (5b)
The pleasant low-level traverse.

The Ramp is the ledge feature in the centre of the wall. The next routes take lines above this. The Ramp is usually gained from the right or left although the Direct Start to Bionic's Wall is the best method.

27 The Redemption of a Grit Pegging Antichrist
. . . . E3 5c
18m. Climb to the tip of the Ramp then head directly up the wall by sustained strenuous moves to a finish up a shallow corner.
FA. John Gosling 1985

28 Bionic's Wall E4 6a
18m. Sustained and strenuous but good honest fun and low in the grade! From the middle of the Ramp blast straight up the wall on flat holds and the odd jam, passing 2 peg runners. Trend right to finish. **The Direct Start** is **V3** (or **V5** from sitting). The very tall may find it considerably easier. *Photo on page 145.*
FA. Dave Beaver 1979

29 Hallelujah Chorus . . E5 6b
18m. From the tip of the Ramp, attack the wall to reach a juggy break, then take the continuation leftwards to a hard exit. A **Direct Start** is possible at the same grade,
FA. Mike Warwick 1985. FA. (Direct Start) Al Evans 1986

30 Heavy Duty E2 5b
18m. Climb into the hanging groove (peg). At its top swing up and right before trending back left by sustained climbing.
FA. Al Evans 1977

31 The Low Girdle V6
Traverse the whole crag from *Heavy Duty* to beyond *Alcove Crack*. Use the Ramp to cross the first wall (going low here is **V7**) then reverse and repeat until pooped.

32 King of the Swingers . . . E1 5b
26m. A pumpy traverse that is the easiest way up the wall but keeps on coming! Climb *Heavy Duty* to the peg then follow the break across the wall before climbing diagonally on good holds to a finish up the final shallow corner of *Redemption*......
FA. Al Evans 1989. Named after the second 'man' Andrea Evans who ended up in a nearby tree!

33 Un-natural Act . . . . . . VS-ish
18m. The half-natural, half-man made block-filled rift is included for its novelty value. Go on, you know you are tempted, and before you ask, no the author hasn't done it!
FA. Nobody dare own up to this one! 1970s

Chris Sims climbing the superb *Ivory Tower* (E1) - *page 161* - on Upper Tor, Kinder South. Nether Tor is visible in the middle distance - as you have made the effort to get this far you might as well sample it as well.
Photo: Jon Pearson

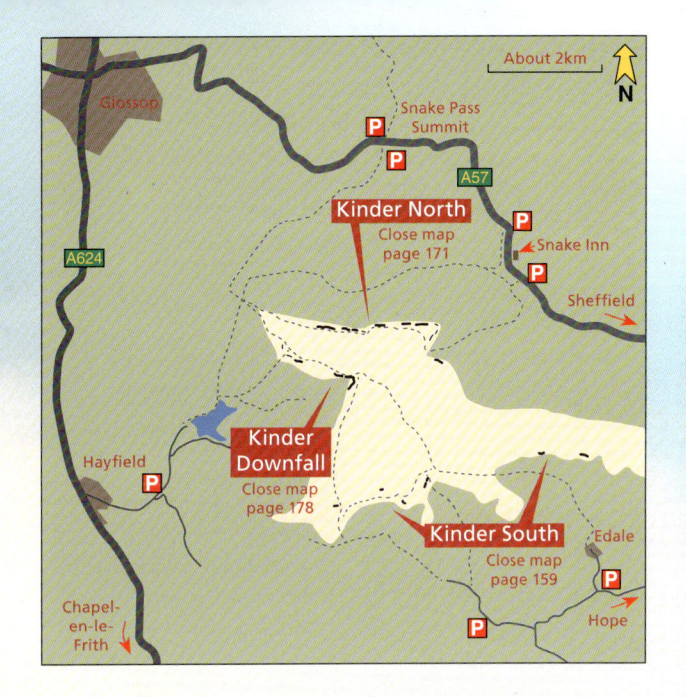

Kinder

Kinder South

	No star	✪	✪✪	✪✪✪
Mod to S	17	8	1	-
HS to HVS	15	10	3	4
E1 to E3	9	21	7	2
E4 and up	1	6	7	2

Kinder South consists of a scattering of cliffs that overlook the tranquil Edale valley, and reflect the friendlier side of Kinder - big bulbous outcrops of coarse but clean rock that get all the sun that is going. If you have never climbed on Kinder, and want to escape the crowds of the Eastern Edges, then this is probably the best place to start. The discontinuous line of crags along the rim of the moor are easily connected using the cliff-top path which means it is possible to do routes on several cliffs on a single visit. Add this to the fine views and good routes and you have the classic ingredients for a great mountain day out.

Approach   See map on pages 151 and 159

There is an extensive Pay and Display car park at the entrance to Edale village which is ideal for the steep ascents to Upper Tor and Nether Tor either directly up Grindsbook, or the path leading out right onto The Nab and up towards Ringing Roger, then back left to the cliffs.
A little further up the dead-end road, running up the main valley, is parking on the left in a large lay-by, or just before this under the railway viaduct, room in total for about 20 cars. From here a good track leads through Upper Booth and on up the steep path of Jacob's Ladder on the ancient pack-horse route over to Hayfield. A right turn at the top of the steepest section leads to the small but high quality outcrop of Upper Edale Rocks and from here the rim-path runs right past The Pagoda and then Crowden Towers which are reached by a detour out to the south. The path continues eastwards onto Crowden Clough Face then beyond this is Upper Tor and finally Nether Tor, from which point the path descends rapidly back to Edale. It is worth noting that, on some maps, Crowden Clough Face is marked incorrectly as Crowden Tower.

Jodie Cuff bouldering on the Crowden boulders of Kinder. Photo: Tristan Peers

Kinder South 153

Conditions
A set of sunny cliffs that are in condition a lot more often than might be expected from their lofty situation. They take little drainage and are rapid drying but are a little higher than the classic Eastern Edges, and so the temperature is likely to be a couple of notches lower.

Crowden Bouldering (Whipsnade)
The moors above Crowden Towers contain one of the best boulder fields in The Peak. If it was situated anywhere near a road it would be popular and well developed but its setting at the top of a steep 1 hour slog means that you are unlikely to have to queue for the problems. Don't forget the mat! Be aware of bouldering alone in remote locations!

Kinder South — Upper Edale Rocks

❶ Gather Ye Gritbudds E1 5c
8m. The roof at the left-hand end of the cliff is short but technical, and also has a hard exit.
FA. Paul Mitchell 1990s

❷ Outlook. .... Diff
10m. The open twisting groove on the left-hand side of the cliff is climbed over sloping rock.

❸ Rock Bottom .... VS 4c
10m. Follow cracks in the wall.
FA. Dave Banks 1977

❹ Pencil Slim .... VS 4c
10m. Climb the steep awkward crack to a hard exit.

❺ Avatar E1 5b
10m. The precarious wall right again to a tricky sloping exit.
FA. Jonny Woodward 1980

❻ Traverse and Crack .... HVD
10m. Mantel onto the collapsed block (originally it was hand-traversed) to reach the pleasant hanging corner crack that rises above its right edge.

❼ Jacob's Bladder E1 5c
10m. From the block, hop up the bulging arete past a useful pocket.
FA. Neil McAdie 2002

❽ Well Suited E3 5c
10m. The steep face past a pocket, to a hard exit.
FA. Steve Bancroft 1987

❾ Bending Crack .... VDiff
8m. The curving crack leads around onto the east face then into the easy finishing groove.

Upper Edale Rocks
A small outcrop of quality rock that would be very popular were it an hour nearer the road. There is an impressive collection of bold hard routes here; a suitable destination for grit gurus with big legs!
Approach - Slog up Jacob's Ladder and follow the Pennine Way northwards. Upper Edale Rocks are on the left, before Kinder Low summit, just below the plateau.

❿ Straight Crack .... Diff
8m. Climb the angular groove past a niche.

⓫ Winter's Block E2 5b
10m. The steep arete on the right reached from the groove that *Bending Crack* finishes up. The more direct start is **5c**.
FA. Mark Clark 1987

⓬ Hand of the Medici E4 6a
6m. Climb the blunt arete on its right-hand side. Short but sharp.
FA. Julian Lines 1993

⓭ Creme Eggs E5 6c
6m. Highly technical climbing up the east-facing wall using a ladder of curly crimps.
FA. Thomas de Gay 2000

⓮ Layback Crack .... S 4a
6m. The flake-crack to the left of the giant overhang.

⓯ Our Doorstep .... VS 4c
6m. The groove on the immediate left of the big roof is more awkward than it looks. Gritty laybacking may be the best way.
FA. B.Barrett 1977

⓰ Trivial Pursuits .... VS 4c
16m. From the top of *Our Doorstep*, move around the arete, descend a little then traverse above the great overhang all the way to a short crack just before the far arete.
FA. Chris Hardy 1986

⓱ Stigmata E5 6b
6m. The fine left arete of the roof is reached by some wild jumping and slapping, then gibber carefully up it.
FA. Andy Barker 1994

⓲ The Mentalist's Cupboard ... E7 6c
8m. The enticing crack that splits the lip of the roof is gained from the right by a huge swing. It gives a titanic struggle.
FA. Thomas de Gay 2001

⓳ Dari's Bedroom Pursuits E3 5c
6m. Take the line out to the arete. A direct version up the bold wall above, via the useful slot is *Help Meeee!* **E5 6b**.
FA. Julian Lines 1993. FA. Andy Barker (Help Meeee!) 1994

The Pagoda Kinder South   155

Lots of sun | 60 min | Windy

Descent

Herford's Route

20 Morrison's Route . . . . **S 4a**
18m. Start in the large groove on the left and climb this to an exit on the right to a shelving ledge. Finish up the short wall behind on slopers.
FA. Don Morrison 1956

21 Hartley's Route **E2 5c**
20m. A bulging crack is awkward then move out right to a projecting flange and pull onto a shelf with difficulty. The wall and groove lead to another harder rightward exit to another ledge - possible belay. Finish out left. Upgraded by popular demand!
FA. Herbert Hartley 1949

22 Herford's Route . . . . . . **HVS 5a**
18m. Classic grit roundedness. Climb the centre of the face (nail-scratched!) passing a slot to reach a mantel onto a ledge. Follow the rounded cracks above to an awkward grasping exit. After completing the route double check the first ascent date!
FA. Siegfried Herford 1910

23 Dewsbury's Route **E1 5b**
20m. More rounded wierdness! Climb the chimney on the right which leads to a groove and a difficult finale on slopers.
FA. Mick Dewsbury 1977

The Pagoda
A huge blob of gritstone which has four routes all named after their pioneers. The routes are well-rounded, difficult to protect and traditional sandbags. The routes are hard enough in sticky rubber, they must have been desperate in nailed boots! Maybe the old guys were good at poorly protected squirming up flared cracks and sloping ledges; obviously it's pretty much a lost art these days.
Approach - The Pagoda can be approached from either Crowden Clough or Jacob's Ladder. The latter is preferable if only because you can see the crag while walking. There is little to choose between them distance-wise.

Kinder South Crowden Towers

1 Five o'clock Shadows E1 5b
8m. The rounded left-hand arete of the buttress.
FA. Keith Ashton 1999

2 Bristly Chimney .... S 4b
8m. Climb the rough, tough and bristly chimney.

3 Flake and Chimney .... VS 5a
12m. Reach and pass the flake in the wall with difficulty then romp up the widening rift above.
FA. Keith Ashton 1989

4 Short Chimney .... S 4a
10m. The central chimney is the same height as the other two!

5 Pear Chimney. .... VS 4c
10m. The right-hand rift has a useful pear-drop (or molar!) shaped chock just before the angle eases. Finish to the left.
FA. Eric Byne 1933

The next routes are on the more impressive Eastern Tower.

6 Kensington Left Crack .... VS 4a
12m. Climb the wide crack to its end then squirm left to the tricky leaning finishing fissure. Precarious and gripping.

7 Suture. E2 5b
10m. Escape the clutches of the crack onto the bold wall above.
FA. Greg Cunningham 2001

8 Violent Outburst E2 5b
12m. The narrow face leads to a deep break and tricky pocketed wall above. Finish with a longer than average stretch.
FA. Keith Ashton 1989

9 Kensington Right Crack ...... VDiff
12m. The wide right-hand crack to an awkward finish.

10 Alpine Sports .... S 4a
18m. Climb the groove to the roof then move right round the arete and trend right to a good ledge. Finish up the final corner.
FA. Dave Banks 1976

Crowden Towers

Two isolated, contrasting rough and tough crags. The East Tower may be a good destination for the hard-core whereas the West is more suited to the tweed brigade. The leap between the towers is purported to have been done in 1952 by one of the Pigott clan, but as they are c.100m apart this appears unlikely!

Approach - Take the Crowden Clough approach from Upper Booth to the moor edge. Follow the vague summit path south west, towards the extensive boulder field. The towers are just below the rim.

Crowden Towers Kinder South

⑪ Kensington High Street ...... VDiff
12m. The left-hand chimney in the alcove is a stroll for most.
FA. Dave Banks 1976

⑫ Snow + Rock .... VDiff
12m. The crack leads to a move right to enter the ever-widening right-hand chimney. Saunter up this in casual style.
FA. Dave Banks 1976

⑬ Fashion Statement . E5 6a
14m. Start just left of the roof and climb a bold runnel to the break. Then tackle the wall on big pockets to another break (good gear at last - large cams) and then the final technical tier on smaller pockets. The crusty rock adds a touch of spice.
FA. Dave Turnbull 1990s

⑭ Bethan E5 6c
14m. Take the thin crack to a break then tackle the roof and technical groove left of the arete with extreme difficulty.
FA. Simon Nadin 2000

⑮ Privilege and Pleasure . E3 5b
12m. Climb into a recess then extend-a-way up and onto the hanging flake in the wall above. Climb this to its apex and then finish rightwards across the final wall.
FA. Keith Ashton 1989

⑯ Club Class E5 6b
12m. The thin crack and imposing pocketed wall up the right-hand side of the face give a sustained and powerful pitch.
FA. Andy Cave 1999

⑰ Kindergarten E1 5b
12m. The left-hand side of the buttress is climbed with increasing difficulty. It is more of a challenge than expected.
FA. Con Carey (in bare feet!) 1988

⑱ Piggy and the Duke .... VS 4c
12m. Climb the finger-crack then traverse out right on to the arete to a neat mantelshelf. Finish more easily. High in the grade.
FA. Dave Banks 1976

⑲ Bags That .... HS 4b
10m. The short east-facing wall passing a good ledge.
FA. Keith Ashton 1989

The next routes are on the far right-hand end of the buttress.

⑳ Dour Power E2 5b
8m. Climb the arete and wall using long reaches on good hidden pockets which lead to a final groove.
FA. Andy Barker 1994

㉑ Pocket Battle E1 6a
8m. The wall and arete right moving left to join it.
FA. Paul Mitchell

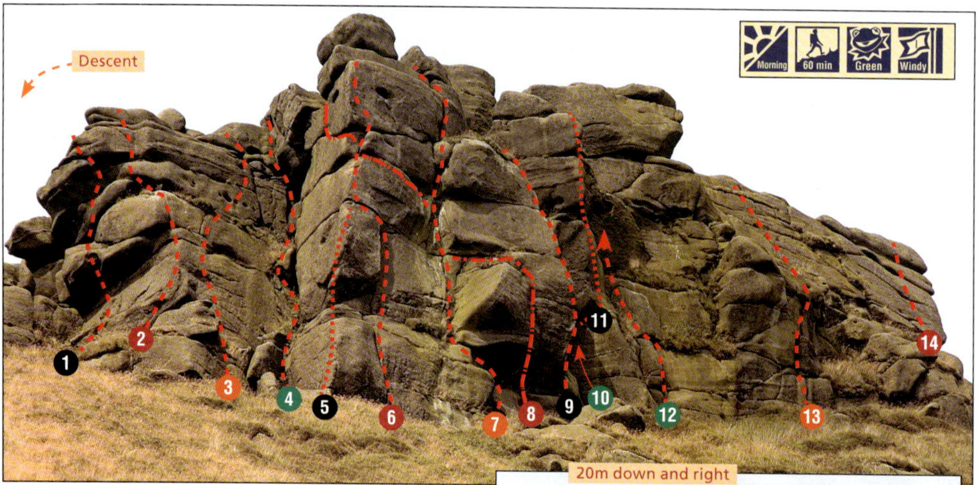

Kinder South — Crowden Clough Face

Crowden Clough Face
This fine piece of rock has a good set of routes, overlooking the upper reaches of Crowden Clough.
Approach - Use the Crowden Clough Approach from Upper Booth. Crowden Clough Face is the significant piece of rock at the top of the clough on the left. The approach takes about an hour.

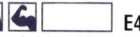

1 Nightflight **E4 6b**
12m. The arduous bulges at the left-hand side of the cliff.
FA. Neil McAdie 2000

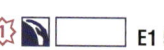

2 Olympus Explorer **E1 5b**
14m. Easy climbing leads to an overhanging crack, climb this then balance up the contrasting (and crucial) scoop above.
FA. Con Carey 1988

3 Indianapolis Slab . . . . **VS 4c**
16m. Broken ground leads to the centre of the slab which is climbed rightwards on a useful array of pockets.
FA. Dave Banks 1988

4 Grassy Chimney . . . . **Diff**
16m. The easy rift that cuts in behind the buttress to a choice of finishes including a through route. It is as about as grassy as you might expect.
FA. Arthur Birtwhistle 1936

5 Sons of the Desert **E7 6b**
20m. The direct start to *Arabia*. Layback the impressive left-hand side of the arete to the upper breaks and a choice of finishes. An even harder alternative is to climb the arete initially á cheval and then on its right (**Grooverider, E7 6c**).
FA. Andy Popp 1990s. FA. (Grooverider) Neil Gresham 1998

6 Arabia **E3 5c**
20m. The imposing rounded arete is low in the grade (which is nice) and quite superb - a moorland classic. A crack and groove leads out to the arete at half-height. This gives sustained climbing (big cams) to an exciting finish up the pocketed headwall that might leave you gasping and grasping.
FA. Mark Clark 1989

Crowden Clough Face Kinder South

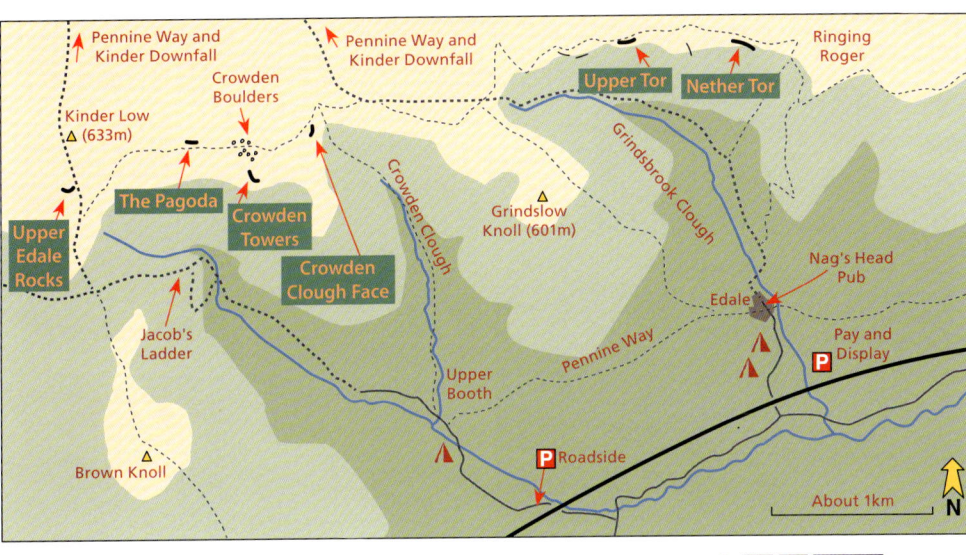

7 Central Route — VS 4c
20m. The steep crack splitting the face has an awkward start and hard finger-jamming moves around the overhang. It may well have in-situ jackdaws early in the year.
FA. Eric Byne 1933

8 Asparagus — E1 5b
24m. A wandering trip with some good climbing. Climb the leaning crack to a junction with *Central Route*. Pull through the bulge then head left round the arete on poor jams to a crack (possible stance) and then a steep finish (**5a**).
FA. Don Morrison 1956

9 Andromeda — E4 6b
14m. The blunt arete. Climb the leaning crack to the first grassy ledge (belly-flop landing) with difficulty, then continue in the same line by bold and balancy climbing to ledges and an easier finish.
FA. Harry Venables 1989

10 Middle Chimney — Diff
14m. The deepening groove starting over a block is worthwhile.
FA. Arthur Birtwhistle 1936

11 Windy Miller — E5 6a
14m. Start up *Middle Chimney* and traverse the first break to the arete. Climb the left-hand side of this to a break then move right and finish via a vague groove line.
FA. Airlie Anderson 1990s

12 Chimney and Slab Variations — VDiff
14m. Climb a crack into the deepening groove. The rift above is the line though it can be avoided by a loop out right.
FA. Arthur Birtwhistle, Geoff Pigott (alts) 1936

13 Playground Twist — HVS 5a
10m. Climb a wide rack to a troublesome bulge with a big pocket up and right. Pull over to easy ground.
FA. Keith Ashton 1988

14 Liquid Skin — E2 6a
8m. The overhang up and right via a useful (vital) flake.
FA. Olly Allen 1999

About 20m down and right is a short outcrop.

15 Book at Bedtime — E1 5b
8m. The crack is a wide little monkey.
FA. Neil McAdie 2000

16 Tall Stories — E2 6a
8m. The centre of the slab keeps going all the way to the top.
FA. Andy Cave 1999

Kinder South — Upper Tor

Upper Tor
A fine south-facing outcrop overlooking Edale. The rock is clean and rough and there are many excellent climbs. If you have never climbed on Kinder you could do worse than start your apprenticeship here since the walk-in is marginally less crippling than that to many of the other crags on the moor.

Approach (see map on page 159) - Use the Edale approach up Grindsbrook Clough. Upper Tor overlooks the upper section of the Clough and can be reached by a steep grind from directly below, or by continuing to the rim and turning right.

4 Half a Friend/High Life **E3 5c**
16m. Climb direct to *Upper Tor Wall* up the face left of its groove (HVS 5a) joining it at half height. From here tackle the well-positioned bulging upper arete out on the right.
FA. Michael Howlett 1997. FA. (High Life) Dave Simmonite 1998

5 Upper Tor Wall . . . . Top 50 **HS 4b**
18m. A classic moorland jug-fest. Climb the awkward groove then step out left and tackle the superb flaky wall to ledges and a possible stance. From the ledge, step out right to a glorious finish up the widening crack. *Photo on page 4*.
FA. Arthur Birtwhistle 1936

6 Hiker's Chimney . . . . **HS 4b**
16m. A differnt kind of classic! Follow *Upper Tor Wall* to the first roof then step right and climb the crack as it widens to chimney to find a hard exit over the huge chockstone.
FA. Arthur Birtwhistle 1936

7 Hitching a Ride **E1 5c**
16m. The crack, passing an arse-shaped overhang with difficulty.
FA. Keith Ashton 1989

8 Hiker's Crack . . . . **S 4a**
16m. Climb left of a slumped pinnacle and follow cracks up and then leftwards to an exit as for *Hiker's Chimney*.

1 Diamond Arete **E2 5c**
12m. Take the wall and arete to the left of *Chockstone Chimney* to a reachy and rounded finish.
FA. Chris Hardy 1989

2 Chockstone Chimney . . . . **Diff**
12m. The chimney is bridged past the large jammed boulder that provides its name to a right-hand exits. The **Direct Finish** is a **VS 4c-ish** graunch.

3 Plumbertime **E4 6b**
18m. The steep wall to the tricky bulge then tackle the imposing final tower on a variety of pockets.
FA. Sam Whittaker 1998

Upper Tor **Kinder South** 161

9 Hiker's Gully Left . . . . HVD
12m. Follow *Hiker's Crack* until it heads left, then climb the crack in the continuation wall into the wide upper gully.
FA. Geoff Pigott 1936

10 Hiker's Gully Right . . . . S 4a
12m. To the right of the tilted pinnacle follow the gully direct.
FA. Geoff Pigott 1936

11 Hitch Hiker. . . . . VS 4c
14m. From *Hiker's Gully Right* follow the awkward slanting flake crack and ramp up the buttress just to the right.
FA. Alan Austin 1958

12 Three Flakes of Man . . . E1 5c
14m. Climb the wall right of the arete using a series of three flakes, each bigger than the last, from finger-tip to full body.
FA. Malc Baxter 1988

13 Grunter . . . . VS 4b
16m. Climb the right-hand crack (left of a free-standing tower) then trend left to the final grunty section of the previous route. The removal of the grass moustache on the ledge has made things easier.
FA. Don Morrison 1965/Andy Bailey 1986

14 The Punter. E1 5b
14m. From the converging cracks on *Grunter*, climb the delightful but short-lived pocketed wall directly above.
FA. Pete Robins 2000

15 Snorter . . . . VS 4c
12m. The crack left of the tower is reached by bridging, then tackle its extension directly above.
FA. John Loy 1965

16 Pinnacle Gully . . . . Diff
14m. Start up *Snorter* but take the narrow gully behind.

17 Scalped Flat Top. E2 5c
10m. Sprint up the layback flakes in the right-hand face of the tower until the crack in its front face can be gained by a harrowing swing left.
FA. Mark Clark 1987

18 Brain Drain . . . E1 5b
10m. Bridge up into the gully to pass the narrowing, then hop onto the right wall and climb this on rounded holds to the top.
FA. Malc Baxter 1989

19 The Ivory Tower E1 5b
22m. Another moorland classic - varied, devious and interesting. Climb the steep wall to a ledge then the crack and bulges above. Step left to a thin crack, climb this and finish up the scary scooped wall above on sloping holds. *Photo on page 150*.
FA. John Loy 1966

20 Artillery Chimney . . . . . HS 4b
12m. Tackle the crack to the projecting spike of the 'gun'. Climb the right-hand side of this and the overhangs above.

21 Promontory Groove . . . . VDiff
12m. Climb the groove and pass to the right of the large jutting nose of the Promontory to reach easier ground.
FA. JW Puttrell 1890

22 Cave Rib . . . . HVS 5a
12m. The technical left arete of the recess leads to a finish up the milder layback flake directly above.
FA. Keith Ashton 1989

23 Cave Gully . . . . S 4a
12m. Head up to the roof of the cave then traverse out left and climb the arete and flke crack above as for *Cave Rib*.

24 Brutality E1 5b
16m. Climb the steep cracks to the bulges then move out right and reach the roof before traversing left and battling a way into the final widening fissure. A beautifully brutal beast.
FA. John Loy 1965

Kinder South — Upper Tor

Upper Tor - Right
The right-hand side of Nether Tor is dominated by a bulky buttress with a large roof.

㉕ Greenfinger .... VS 4c
12m. Climb the slabby groove to enter a green crack, then graze away up this. Almost always a little grungy.
FA. Don Morrison 1966

㉖ Robot E2 5c
12m. Climb the slab, step right and climb the hollow-sounding flake through the bulges trending right. Usually luminous!
FA. Steve Bancroft 1987

㉗ Do the Rocksteady . E7 6c
14m. The roof and wall left of *Robert*. From gear at the back of the roof reach round the lip to a poor pocket. Move left to large rounded pocket, then on to better holds above.
FA. Sam Whittaker 2001

㉘ Robert E2 5c
16m. The beckoning roof crack is a bobby dazzler of gritstone jamming and is reached by the easy groove on the right, or better, and substantially harder the front of the rib to its left. Slam in the lockers and go! Only E1 5b for hoary hardmen.
FA. Don Morrison (1 sling) 1966. FFA. Graham Hoey 1976

㉙ Pedestal Wall .... S 4b
16m. Climb the groove rightwards below the overhangs. Hand traverse right and access the pedestal by a fun move or two. Stand up awkwardly and finish up the final wall.
FA. Arthur Birtwhistle 1948

㉚ Young Turks E4 6b
16m. The leaning ramp/groove above the roof is technical and strenuous. Follow it until an easy escape out right is reached.
FA. Andy Bailey 1984

㉛ The Cheesemonger . E6 6b
12m. The roof above the ramp of *Young Turks* has hard moves on poor pockets to reach a rounded flake and a hard exit.
FA. Ben Bransby 2000

㉜ Earth Plumbit E1 5b
14m. Climb the bulging slab to access the sharp arete right of the V-groove of *Pedestal Wall*. Layback this on its left-hand side.
FA. Keith Ashton 1998

㉝ Plumber's Passage .... HVD
14m. Climbs the flake crack and corner on the right of the crag.
FA. David Simmonite 1998

Nether Tor **Kinder South** 163

Nether Tor
The impressive face at the eastern end of the moor was formed by a landslip, hence the angular unweathered nature of much of the cliff. Although quite extensive there are only two areas of real interest to the visiting climber. On the far left is a tall natural buttress split by the jagged wide crack of *Moneylender's*.

Approach (see map on page 159) - Use the Edale approach and walk up Grindsbrook Clough branching right on the path towards Ringing Roger. Some distance below the plateau a small path runs leftwards through the bracken to the terraces below the crag.

The left-hand side of the crag is more natural looking and presents a fine tall wall shot-blasted with hundreds of pockets and split by an appealing crack-line.

❶ **Loan Arranger** . . . . **VS 4c**
18m. Climb the chimney crack to a ledge, follow a flake on the left to a second ledge and an easy finish up an open groove.
FA. Al Parker (the masked stranger?) 1976

❷ **Beautiful Losers** . . . **E3 6a**
22m. Climb to the first ledge on *Loan Arranger* then swing right to a flake and climb this to a roof, which is passed with difficulty to a taxing mantelshelf. Finish out left more easily.
FA. Con Carey 1978

❸ **Moneylender's Crack** . . . **VS 5a**
18m. The wide and steep zigzag fissure is much better than it looks. Climb direct, or cop out and swing into the crack from the right, and climb the crack steeply, usually passing an in-situ nest.
FA. Arthur Birtwhistle 1950

❹ **Mortgage Wall** . . . . **HVS 5b**
20m. Climb the cracks on the right to a heathery ledge then head across the steep wall on the left for a pumpy finish.
FA. John Gosling 1976

❺ **Usurer** . . . . **HS 4b**
14m. The chimney and shallow groove that bound the buttress on the right are okay with a confident approach.

Kinder South — Nether Tor

There is a gap of about 50m between the two main sections of Nether Tor. The right-hand side appears green and broken but does have one or two flashy routes.

6 Broken Chimney .... VDiff
12m. The flake is climbed leftwards to a block-filled cleft which leads to an awkward exit

7 Edale Bobby E5 6a
16m. The imposing arete is approached via a block and climbed on an array of odd pockets to the difficult leaning upper section which gives technical and bold laybacking.
FA. Steve Bancroft 1987

8 Square Cut .... VDiff
16m. The well-named and turfy rift is tricky just before it widens. Climb the short face above or escape off left.

9 Kelvin's Corner .... HS 4b
14m. The crack leads to a hanging groove in the upper part of the wall. Finish up this or escape left across ledges.
FA. Kelvin

10 Black Seven E1 5c
22m. From a groove climb rightwards across the wall and enter a short corner with difficulty. From the top of the corner traverse left to ledges and finish directly over the narrow roof.

The slotted wall above the starting groove of Black Seven is climbed by a taxing route with the wild name of **The Incarcerated Sock Juggler vs The Mushroom Kid, E4 6a**.

11 Crimson Wall E2 5c
24m. A right-hand finish extends the experience and cranks up the grade one notch. Follow *Black Seven* to the end of its traverse then reach the next break and follow it back right to another ledge. Pass the detached block to a taxing finish up a thin crack.
FA. Jonny Woodward 1980

12 Snooker Route .... VS 5a
28m. The well-pocketed wall leads to a substantial holly that is a bloody nuisance. Skirt this to reach a ledge, then a detached block, before moving way out left to a finish up a groove. The route is rather spoilt by the holly, and also the long traverse left to finish. Using the finish of *Black Seven* improves the climb considerably but ups the grade a touch.
FA. Arthur Birtwhistle 1950

13 Hot Flush Crack ... HVS 5c
26m. Start left of the arete and climb a technical scoop and a crack to the holly bush, or the wall to the right (the original way). Step right and climb the wider crack (thread) through the capping overhang to a testing finish.

14 Flash Wall .... VS 5a
22m. Climb a slippery crack in the orange-tinted side-wall then its right-trending continuation to the final wide section. A photogenic and well-protected classic.
FA. Arthur Birtwhistle 1950

Nether Tor **Kinder South** 165

15 Bertie Meets Flash Gordon on his Way to Nether Edge E1 5b
22m. Climb the crack in the right side of the wall on finger breaks until it is possible to traverse left to the finish of *Flash Wall*, or head up and right at a pumpy **E2 5c**.
FA. Jon Blenkharn 1990s

16 Recoil Rib E2 5c
20m. Climb the arete on the right to a possible stance then the bolder upper continuation that is sustained and precarious.
FA. Al Parker 1974

The next routes start from a terrace up and right - belay advised at their base.

17 Edale Flyer .... VS 4c
8m. The groove on the left-hand side of the upper buttress.
FA. Dave Banks 1989

18 T' Big Surrey E5 6b
10m. Approach the impressive arete from the left with some difficulty and climb it with sustained interest. Needs a direct start.
FA. Gabe Regan 1989

19 Rejoyce .... HS 4b
8m. The groove just right of the arete of *T' Big Surrey* has a tricky overhang before it eases.
FA. Keith Ashton 1989

20 The Steamer E1 5c
8m. The wall on the right with hard moves to enter the thin groove and then easier climbing above.
FA. Harry Venables 1989

Lower down, to the right is a further last route.

21 Steamboat .... HVS 4c
10m. Climb the knife-edged arete below *The Steamer*.
FA. Keith Ashton 1992

Lots of sun | 60 min | Windy | Green

Nether Tor - Right
The tallest buttress on the cliff has some worthwhile routes most notably the jagged cracks up the smooth wall formed by the ancient landslip.
Many of the climbs are both long and devious, double ropes are good idea despite the pain of carrying them up here.
Descents - Descents from the cliff top are steep and awkward, best head well to the left or the right of the cliff. Beware loose blocks and flakes.

Kinder North

	No star	★	★★	★★★
Mod to S	15	8	1	-
HS to HVS	14	18	2	5
E1 to E3	4	14	7	3
E4 and up	2	8	2	1

There is much good climbing on the high and wild edges that ring the Kinder and Bleaklow plateau, and the very best of this is to be found along the north-facing escarpment of Ashop Edge. It is perhaps to be expected that the climbing along this line of cliffs is both difficult of access and out of condition for much of the year, though this adds a certain cachet to days up here - the harder won, all the more memorable.

The cliffs are not the crisp and clean Eastern Edges, but a sterner set of venues. Come prepared for a bit of a battle, wearing your old clothes and in the knowledge that you will go home grubby, battered and tired but hopefully well-satisfied. The best area for a first visit is the Brothers' Buttress, though there is enough up here to keep most climbers busy for years - and then there are all those new routes to go at!

Approach   See map on pages 151 and 171

There is roadside parking for about 30 vehicles below the Snake Inn, and more further uphill from the pub.

Fair Brook Approach - From the parking paths lead down through the trees, over the footbridge. A left turn followed shortly by a right leads to a steady climb up the Fair Brook Valley all the way to the plateau (about 50 mins). Here, a left turn leads to Chinese Wall and a right out to Misty Wall and the main section of Ashop Edge.

Ashop Clough Approach - A shorter approach (though with a slog of a final section) turns right over the footbridge, then follows a narrow path (wet in places) up onto the moor by the ruins of an old shooting cabin. From here you can select your buttress and attack the final slopes!

Snake Summit Approach - Far and away the easiest approach is to walk in from roadside parking by the summit of the Snake Pass and follow the flagged path to Mill Hill from where the rest of the route is obvious. With a willing co-driver it is possible to be dropped off here and picked up back at the Snake Inn in good time for last orders - how very civilised!

Rock sculpture on Ashop Edge, Kinder North.

Kinder North 167

Conditions
The northern edges of Kinder are only a viable venue in fine conditions; the cliffs are set as high as any in the Peak, face due north and are a respectable distance from the road. Some of the buttresses are slow to dry and become green and gritty after rain, though many jut proudly away from the moor and come into condition as soon as the weather starts to improve. It is always worth remembering, if you trek up here and things are not in prime condition, it is only 20 minutes around the rim to Upper Western Buttress or forty minutes bog-trotting through the heart of the moor to the Southern Edges.

Other Rock
Described here are about 100 of the 250+ climbs available on the northern edges of Kinder Scout. If you enjoy these there are plenty of other good routes up here to go at - consult the BMC Over the Moors Guidebook for full details.

Kinder North — Chinese Wall

Chinese Wall
A long wall of rock that faces Misty Wall across the upper reaches of Fair Brook. In general the cliff is north-facing and neglected despite having some fine climbs, however the left-hand end of the cliff swings round to form a neat east-facing wall with a small set of routes that early risers can enjoy in the sun.

Approach (see map on page 171) - Walk to the head of Fair Brook then turn left and skirt the edge of the moor - the crag is down and left and about 10 minutes from the stream.

❶ Socialist's Arete . . . . S 4a
8m. The left arete of the wall on rounded holds with a tricky bulging section providing the fun.
FA. Keith Ashton 1983

❷ Communist Route . . . . . VDiff
8m. Nice climbing up the inverted sickle-shaped crack.
FA. Arthur Birtwhisle 1938

❸ Nationalist Route . . . . . HS 4b
10m. The central fissure is followed to its end then move right awkwardly to the wide continuation and a fist-jamming finale.
FA. Arthur Birtwhisle 1938

❹ The Terrorist . . E3 5c
10m. The centre of the clean wall gives a good committing pitch on quality rock. Climb the wall on poor pockets with a jig right at mid-height and an extended reach to finish.
FA. (escaping right) Con Carey 1980. FA. (Direct) Chris Hardy 1986

❺ Rickshaw Ridge . . . . VS 4b
8m. The right-hand rib of the face.
FA. Arthur Birtwhistle 1938

❻ Mandarin's Arete . . . . . S 4a
10m. The right arete of the chimney is pleasant enough.
FA. Arthur Birtwhistle 1938

Misty Wall
A fine collection of buttresses and walls almost opposite Chinese Wall. The crag is in a sunny setting and the rock is generally rough, solid and clean. The buttress to the left of the ones covered here has a handful of routes in the S to VS range.

❼ Pieces of Eight . . . . S 4a
12m. Climb the left side of the jutting rib steeply to a big ledge (possible belay). Pull over the awkward overhang behind at a narrow crack to a crouched rest and finish leftwards, up a groove.
FA. Malc Baxter 1960

❽ Doubloon . . . . VS 4b
12m. Climb to the roof and pass this with difficulty to reach right-hand side to the large ledge where *Pieces of Eight* is joined. Finish as for this.
FA. Malc Baxter 1960

❾ Stampede E2 5b
14m. Climb the left-hand side of the steep wall through a couple of bulges then shuffle right to finish up a short crack.
FA. Chris Craggs 1992

❿ Round Up E1 5b
14m. Take the centre of the wall passing the bulges using rounded holds, and a bit of a stretch, to reach and finish up the blind crack of *Stampede*.
FA. Colin Binks 1982

⓫ Misty Wall . . . . VS 4b
14m. A Kinder classic up the rough and rugged crack just left of the arete and the wider fissures above. Gain the crack steeply from the right and follow it through bulges until it is possible to escape out right in an exposed position.
FA. Alf Bridge 1929

Descent

Misty Wall — Kinder North

⑫ Wind Wall — VS 4c
14m. Follow *Misty Wall* until it is possible to swing onto the north wall and climb the centre of this passing a deep horizontal slot.
FA. Al Parker 1977

⑬ Zyphyr — E2 6a
14m. Breeze up the thin flake in the side-wall to join *Wind Wall*.
FA. Jonny Woodward 1981

⑭ Deviation — HVD
14m. Climb the front of the separate squat buttress right of the gully. At its top step left to a deeply recessed chimney which has a tricky exit past a crusty chockstone.
FA. Malc Baxter 1964

⑮ Fixation — Diff
14m. Climb the chimney to ledges and a finish up the awkward restricted groove at the back of the bay.
FA. Malc Baxter 1961

⑯ Cassandra — E2 5c
16m. Launch up the wall to the left edge of the great roof. Pass this moving left up the wall with difficulty to a deep break and a steep finish still trending slightly leftwards.
FA. Nick Colton 1979

⑰ Trojan — E1 5b
16m. The imposing roof crack is the battle the name suggests. Approach via a huge perched block and an awkward rest then set about the chockstoned-crack (spinners!) with conviction.
FA. Paul Nunn early 1960s

⑱ Meander Arete — HVS 5a
16m. A hard groove leads to the ledge atop the prominent block. From here meander out to the well-positioned arete on the left and finish up this - reachy rounded and bold. Sadly it is also often rather dirty.
FA. Con Carey 1979

Misty Wall

The rocks overlooking the upper section of Fair Brook have a good collection of climbs in a superb sunny setting. *Misty Wall* is the classic VS although the routes just to the right are worth a look. The less popular routes are inclined to be gritty; a little regular traffic would help keep them clean.

Approach (see map on page 171) - From the parking below the Snake Inn use the Fair Brook approach. As you near the top of the valley, Misty Walls are above and right. Continuing to the plateau then turning right is far and away the easiest approach, though those after Alpine training can attack the final lung-busting slope direct.

⑲ Meander — HS 5a
16m. Follow the groove of *Meander Arete* to the platform then move right to another ledge and finish up the crack splitting the left wall. The initial groove can be avoided by walking round to the right, though that is a bit pointless.
FA. Malc Baxter 1961

⑳ Dependence Wall — HS 4b
10m. Climb the centre of the wall then outflank the roof on the left using some creaky flakes before heading back right up easier ground to finish.
A. Malc Baxter 1960

㉑ Dependence Arete — VS 4c
10m. Climb out to the arete from the left then follow it on the left-hand side passing a couple of overhangs with difficulty and finishing via a short crack.
FA. Malc Baxter 1960

Kinder North — Eureka Buttress

Eureka Buttress
Rumoured to have been named by Archimedes who was overjoyed at discovering this gritstone classic. A couple of excellent cracks and the eponymous route around the edge of the great roof make the buttress well worth a visit by climbers operating in the VS grade (when the conditions are right).

Approach - Use the Fair Brook approach and follow the cliff-top path around until you are above the wall. Alternatively the shorter Ashop Clough approach can be used but be prepared for the tough final slog up the hill. Approach is also possible from the Snake Summit parking roadside spot - long but flat-ish and flagstoned for the most part. The path loops right to Mill Hill, drops down to Ashop Head before climbing steeply to the plateau. Hang a left here to the climbing.

❶ Ashop Corner Climb . . . . HS 4b
12m. The impressive-but-scruffy groove is initially climbed direct. Move out to its right wall to finish up the flakes with a crucial final section in a great position.
FA. Geoff Pigott 1948

❷ Roman Roads. . . . . . . VS 5a
14m. Climb the corner then cross the right wall above the huge overhang to reach the front face. Climb up then sneak off left (**4c**) or, much better, continue just right of the arete to an exposed finale (**The Road's Finish**) on a useful batch of pockets.
FA. Nick Colton 1982. FA. (The Road's Finish) Malc Baxter 1987

❸ Ashop Crack. E2 5b
18m. Climb the crack (or the flaky wall to its left, which is more in keeping but a less logical line) and then enter the awkward continuation that splits the overhangs above with considerable difficulty. Long undergraded - maybe chockstones have gone or maybe the old guys were good at wriggling. We were going to give it E3 5c, but surely they weren't THAT good?
FA. Eric Byne 1932

❹ Ashop Climb . . . . HVD
18m. Start up the wide lower fissure of *Ashop Crack* but move right at the roof and awkwardly enter the wide right-hand fissure which gives classical squirming, then gradually eases to a sudden cliff-top exit. Much better than it looks.
FA. James Puttrell 1901

❺ Orgasmo E2 5b
18m. Climb the face to reach ledges, pull through the roof then step left and climb the delicate face to a bold finale a long way above everything.
FA. Rich Thomas 1984

❻ Eureka. . . . . VS 4c
18m. The classic of the wall and spectacular with it though inclined to be dirty. Climb the wall and groove to the huge overhang then traverse left in an exposed position to outflank it. Tackle the 'jump and swim' crack then weave through the bulges above to finish.
FA. Malc Baxter 1960

❼ Ure . . . . VS 4b
12m. Scramble to the short slanting crack, and climb it. Normally over in a flash ...... or two.
FA. Nick Colton 1982

Eureka Buttress Kinder North 171

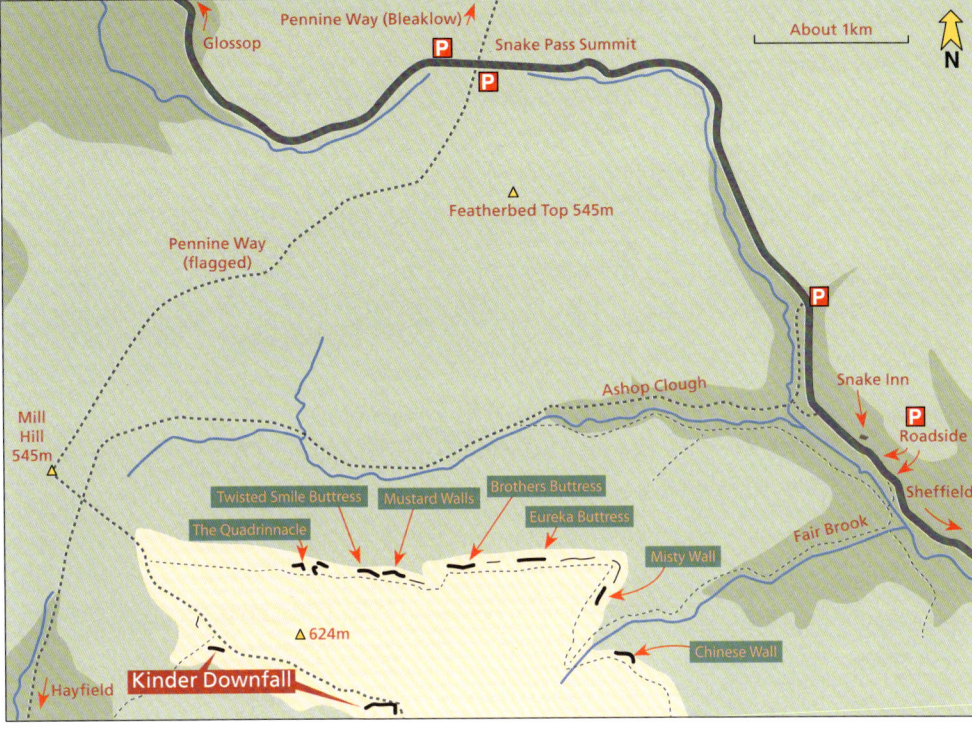

Up and right from Eureka Buttress is another buttress, with big juggy bulges, most easily reached by a short scramble up a ramp, or by a short descent from the cliff top.

8 Twister HVD
10m. Climb the crack that twists away to pass the left edge of the overhangs - short-lived but in a fine position.
FA. Ernie Jones 1961

9 Britt's Cleavage E1 5b
12m. Climb steep rock to a ledge then take the break in the roof to a hairy finish out on the left.
FA. Jonny Woodward 1982

10 Trial Balance HVS 5b
12m. The original attempt at the overhangs, Follow *Britt* to the ledge then avoid the roof on the right by a thin crack that leads to a tough sloping exit.
FA. Malc Baxter (some tension) 1965. FFA. Jonny Woodward 1982

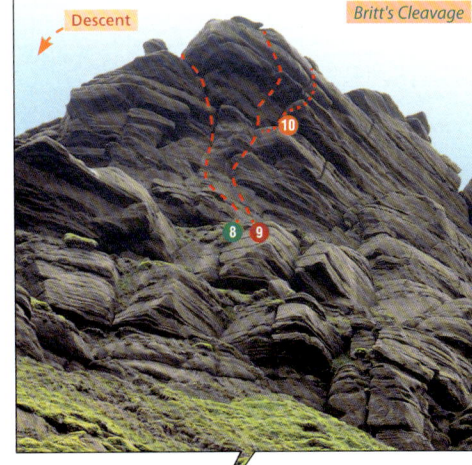

Kinder North — Big Brother Buttress

① Tin Tin Wall .... HS 4b
12m. Start up the chimney then climb the flakes on the right.
FA. Njal Parker 1961

② Barbara .... VDiff
10m. A worthwhile flaky crack started from the grubby groove.
FA. Ernie Jones 1961

③ Jelly Baby Slab .... VS 4c
12m. Wobble-a-way up the usually dirty slab.
FA. Malc Baxter 1961

④ Sliding Chimney .... S 4a
12m. Slide up (or down) the chockstoned rift.
FA. Barry Roberts 1961

⑤ Legacy .... Top 50 HVS 5a
20m. The long rising diagonal gives a fine pitch. Well-protected (cams) and with excellent romping moves in a wonderful setting. It is low in the grade.
FA. Paul Nunn 1962

⑥ Spacerunner E4 6a
18m. The left-hand side of the main face is difficult in its lower section with hard climbing on tiny holds. It eases above.
FA. Andy Bailey 1984

⑦ Intestate E1 5b
18m. Excellent and reachy. Follow *Legacy* (or better *Big Brother*) to the middle of its traverse then cruise up the centre of the wall to finish up a short crack. The **Direct Start** is a stretchy **E1 6a** protected by small opposition wires. Remember, where there's a will, there's a way.
FA. Paul Nunn (1 sling) 1967. FA. (Direct Start) Chris Craggs 1992

⑧ Big Brother E2 5c
18m. A reachy number that is as height dependant as the name suggests. Climb the steep left-hand edge of the recess and the short crack above to *Legacy*. Continue up the wall (long stretch and small holds) to the final easy section. Superb.
FA. Jonny Woodward 1981

Big Brother Buttress

The 'Brothers' are probably the best bits of rock on Kinder North; on the left is Big Brother Buttress - a fine steep wall riven by cracks and home to an excellent set of routes. Almost all the climbs here are well worth doing.
Approach (see map on page 171) - All the main Kinder North approaches are possible and all have their merits (and drawbacks). The Fair Brook approach is long and takes you to the crag top. The Ashop Clough approach is shorter but hard work on the final slope. The Snake Summit approach is the easiest, long and undulating but flagged for the most part.

⑨ Kinsman E4 6b
18m. Start up *Big Brother* but swing right and climb the difficult blunt arete to the easier upper section of *Legacy*.
FA. Al Rouse 1984

⑩ Brother's Eliminate E1 5b
18m. Climb out of the cave via the slanting crack and follow it right to a niche. Step out left and climb the wall and crack.
FA. Graham West 1960

⑪ Squatter's Rights/Blue Jade E4 6b
16m. The wall on the right is climbed desperately to the break. Recover then attack the marginally easier wall above.
FA. Paul Mitchell 1991

⑫ Little Boy Blue E1 6a
16m. Climb left of the blunt arete to reach a ledge with difficulty. Move left to the diagonal crack and, once past this, finish up the wall on the left via a perched block.
FA. Graham West 1960

⑬ Dirty Trick .... S 4b
10m. Approach the steep groove via a wall and shelf.
FA. Malc Baxter 1961

⑭ The Big Traverse ...... VS 4b
34m. Excellent but best avoided on the rare days that the crag is busy. Climb the short wall to ledges then traverse left round the rib of *Legacy* and along the upper break to the far arete.
FA. Jonny Woodward 1982

Little Brother Buttress — Kinder North — 173

Little Brother Buttress

Overshadowed by its larger sibling and often neglected, the right-hand buttress has some excellent climbs. *Dunsinane* in particular is worth a look and lovers of sloping holds should enjoy palming a way up the wrinkled bulges of *Pot Belly*.

15 Round Chimney .... VDiff
12m. The chimney on the left of the buttress is typical of its sort, Naughty but nice.
FA. Graham West 1960

16 Razor Crack .... S 4a
12m. The narrow straight slash in the right-hand wall of the chimney is worth the effort when dry. At the top of the crack trend right across the wall to finish.
FA. Graham West 1960

17 The Les Dawson Show E3 5c
12m. Ribald fun up the right-hand side of the rounded arete, with good runners at half-height. Graded for when it is clean which isn't very often.
FA. Steve Bancroft 1989

18 Growth Centre E4 6b
12m. The steep wall leads with difficulty to a desperate finale.
FA. Al Rouse 1984

19 Dunsinane .... VS 4c
16m. Take the crack to its end then move right a couple of metres to a flake. At its top trend right again to a well-positioned finish on the arete. Almost a three star outing, but sadly not quite as good as the classics just over the way!
FA. Malc Baxter 1964

20 The Savage Breast E1 5b
14m. Climb right of the crack to the break and runners then take the upper wall to a tricky finale up a shallow groove and blind crack to a rounded exit. This is the old **Direct Finish** to *Dunsinane*.
FA. Gary Gibson 1983

21 Motherless Children E1 5c
14m. The central arete of the face on its left-hand side, passing the bulges with difficulty to reach the easier upper part of *Dunsinane*. Worthwhile and not as lonely as you might expect.
FA. Chris Hardy 1988

22 Pot Belly E2 5c
14m. Climb right of the arete to a jammed block below the bulging gut (thread) and pull over it with difficulty using a shallow crack and a poor set of slopers. Once established, finish much more easily. Desperate for the short.
FA. Graham West 1960

23 Tum Tum .... HVS 5b
10m. The wide fissure is approached direct, or from the *Pot Belly*. Entering it is difficult; gravelly jams enable a boss to be reached then an awkward move reaches easier ground. Especially hard for those with a beer belly.
FA. Malc Baxter 1960

Kinder North — Mustard Walls

Mustard Walls

One of the best sections of rock on Kinder North is around Mustard Walls; a great set of routes in as remote a setting as you could want. The relatively easy walk in makes this a viable venue for summer evenings.

Approach (see map on page 171) - It is possible to use any of the three main approaches to Kinder North although by far the easiest and quickest is from the Snake Summit via Mill Hill or straight across the moor (steep final approach) if it has been dry.

1 Banjo Crack .... S 4a
6m. The flake crack left of the main bulk of the buttress.
FA. Graham West 1960

2 Daddy Crack .... HVS 5a
8m. The steep central crack is climbed on mostly solid jams.
FA. Graham West 1960

3 Mummy Crack E1 5b
8m. The right-hand crack is difficult to enter, then smack in the jams. You might need bandaging after a tussle with this one!
FA. Malc Baxter 1964

4 Wicked Uncle Ernie. E4 6a
10m. The left-hand side of the square arete saves its fun for the final tough section.
FA. Chris Hardy 1987

5 Campus Chimney .... VDiff
14m. Climb the lower crack to a deep and wider chimney.
FA. Peter Bamfield 1959

6 Mustard Walls E2 5c
16m. Traverse to the right edge of the roof and gain a ledge up and left with difficulty. Finish up the precarious steep slab.
FA. Malc Baxter 1964

7 Machine Gun .... VDiff
8m. The twisting groove up the left-hand side of the buttress.
FA. Graham West 1960

8 Glock Over. E4 6c
12m. Climb the bulge then move left where a desperate move allows a standing position on a jug to be gained. Finish more easily. Sadly using the left arete lowers the grade to **5c**!
FA. Andy Barker 1994

9 The Scratcher. .... VS 4c
8m. Scratch and scrawm up the awkward wide crack.
FA. Jim Campbell 1976

10 Two Twist Chimney .... S 4b
8m. The wide fissure requires some contortions.
FA. Jim Campbell 1976

11 Wire Brush Slab E2 5b
12m. Climb the lower arete to gain the hanging slab at a prominent pocket. Shuffle left and sprint up the excellent hanging upper arete. As wire brushes are taboo nowadays, you might want to try a toothbrush to clean the holds!
FA. Jim Campbell 1976

12 Tweeter and the Monkey Man E3 6a
12m. Trend right up the lower wall (possible stance) then step back left, above the overlap, and climb the precarious and bold upper slab on pebbles and scary friction.
FA. Harry Venables 1989

13 Knapp Hand .... HS 4b
18m. A long rambling pitch with a good finale up the scoop high on the right-hand side of the buttress.
FA. Peter Knapp 1954

14 Penniless Crack .... S 4b
8m. The steepening-crack to the left of the grassy gully.
FA. Malc Baxter 1962

15 The Slice. .... HS 4b
12m. Climb the wall to the clean-cut diagonal crack.
FA. Malc Baxter 1962

16 Exodus .... VS 4c
18m. Trend left to pass the large overhang and gain the hanging arete. Climb the crack splitting the left edge of the second roof and finish up the slab. High in the grade.
FA. Peter Bamfield (2 points) 1959. FFA. Malc Baxter 1960

The small cave here is (or was) known as the Baxter Crilly Bivouac after Malc Baxter and Dave Crilley who spent some time living up here in the early 1960s in a period of poor weather, venturing out to grab new routes when things perked up!

Twisted Smile

The penultimate buttress described is just right of Mustard Walls and features a prominent jutting prow, the jaunty jester's cap.

17 Jester Cracks .... HVS 5a
16m. Climb the side-wall and then the slab on the right to a rest (poor thread) below the big roof. Swing left with difficulty then storm the superb jamming-crack that splits the peaked cap.
FA. Richard McHardy 1959

18 Monkey Madness .. E6 6c
16m. Wild. The front of the buttress between *Jester* and *Lobster Cracks*. Pull over the bulge then stretch upwards in a position of some danger. Continue over the next bulge then attack the steep final prow. It has big holds but limited gear.
FA. Andy Barker 1995

19 Lobster Crack .... VS 5a
14m. The left-hand parallel fissure is a steep struggle.
FA. Malc Baxter 1961

20 Crab Crack .... HVS 5b
14m. The right-hand fissure is hard to enter. If all else fails try sideways shuffling.
FA. Graham West 1961

21 Candle in the Wind E3 5c
16m. The fine soaring arete is approached from the right. Slant right to pass the initial overhang, shuffle left then pull up the arete itself. This is taken by easier climbing but the gear is poor unless some VERY large cams are to hand.
FA. Chris Hardy 1988

22 Twisted Smile .... HVS 5a
16m. One of the very best HVS routes in the Peak, its remoteness adding to its cachet. Climb the centre of the front of the buttress passing a vertical crack to a fine and lonely finish.
FA. John Gosling 1972

23 Count Dracula E1 5b
16m. Climb the slab to a position below the roof, traverse out left (exposed) and gain the upper wall awkwardly. Finish direct.
FA. Andy Bailey 1984

24 Woe is Me .... S 4a
12m. The crack past an awkward narrowing.
FA. Eric Byne 1954

25 Harlequin E3 6a
14m. Steep and wild. Climb *Woe is Me* then traverse out left above the big overhang and take the right-hand side of the arete via a final bulge. The grade might need treating with respect!
FA. Johnny Dawes 1985

Three more routes are on a buttress 50m right.

26 Bow Wall E1 5b
12m. The short crack leads to a break and hard moves to easier ground and the meadows.
FA. Jim Campbell 1976

27 Tramline Cracks ...... VS 4c
14m. Slant up to the base of the crack then climb passing the large loose tooth/flake with care. From the grassy ledge amble up the slabby arete above.
FA. Graham West 1961

28 Depot Chimney .... VDiff
14m. The deepening rift has a fair bit of grass in its upper section though much of it is avoidable by a bit of bridging.
FA. Graham West 1960

Kinder North — The Quadrinnicle

① Act of Faith — **E4 6b**
8m. The rounded left arete of the buttress is technical - don't fall, you might roll for the rest of your life!
FA. Al Rouse 1985

② Pan Crack — **E1 5b**
10m. Approach the hanging crack from the chimney on the right then sprint up it to wider exit. An old VS!
FA. Malc Baxter 1961

③ The Corinthians — **HS 4c**
10m. Do battle with the chimney/flake.
FA. Rimmon Club members 1963

④ Eve — **HVS 5b**
10m. The hair-line crack is tricky, the groove above, much easier.

⑤ Adam's Apple — **S 4b**
10m. The right-facing flake-crack has some good moves.
FA. Rimmon Club members 1963

⑥ Pulpit Chimney — **Diff**
10m. The slanting groove/chimney leads to a bridging finish.

⑦ Noah's Pair — **Diff**
12m. A choice of starts leads to the easier upper chimney.
FA. Rimmon Club members 1963

⑧ Apostles' Wall — **HVS 5b**
10m. Zip up the slabby lower wall then use the solitary pocket to solve the upper section. Sidling off into the chimney (the original way) reduces the grade to **S 4a**.
FA. Tony Jones 1963. FA. (Direct Finish) Keith Ashton 1991

⑨ Mark's Slab — **VS 4c**
10m. The slabby arete leads to the ledge. Finish up the crack or wall above (both **HVS**) or escape left into the chimney.

⑩ Matthew — **HVS 5a**
10m. The desperate (5b?) corner crack to the ledge then the superb but short-lived crack in the upper wall. Varied!
FA. Graham West 1961

Dead Chimney Buttress **Kinder North** 177

The Quadrinacle and Dead Chimney Buttress
The first section of rock passed on the Snake Pass approach is the gloomy Dead Chimney Buttress. Just across the gully is the cleaner towers of the Quadrinacle. Its right-hand face is the sunniest bit of rock on this side of the moor, though it sees little action.

Approach - The shortest approach is from roadside parking at the Snake Summit. The flagged path loops right to Mill Hill, drops down to Ashop Head before climbing steeply to the plateau. Hang a left here and continue horizontally for 1km to the start of the climbing.

The side wall of the gully is split by a series of cracks. Unusual for Ashop Edge it gets plenty of sunshine, making it cleaner than most of the rest of the cliff.

⓫ Zebra E5 6b
10m. The arete is climbed with difficulty and a quick trip into the previous route for runners before embarking on the gripping rounded finale.
FA. Johnny Dawes 1985

⓬ Mark . . . . HS 4b
10m. The first chimney crack is more awkward and steeper than it looks from below - a classic graunch.
FA. Graham West 1961

⓭ Luke E1 5b
10m. Climb the dog-legged crack with hard and bold moves to enter the upper section.
FA. Graham West 1961

⓮ Seven Deadly Skins . . . E4 6c
10m. The runnel above the start of *Luke* has excellent protection.
FA. Sam Whittaker 2001

⓯ John . . . . VS 5a
10m. The right-hand fissure is another tricky one.
FA. Graham West 1961

⓰ Deborah E4 6a
8m. Across the gully the short slanting crack in the arete leads strenuously to a harrowing exit on rounded holds. Hard work considering its diminutive size.
FA. Al Rouse 1985

Dead Chimney Buttress
This sombre buttress is rarely in condition. The hard routes especially will certainly need cleaning before an attempt.

⓱ Honeymoon Route . . . . HVD
15m. The easy grassy groove leads to ledges, finish up the rift. The flake gives a hard start **Socialist's Variation, VS 5a**.

⓲ Fast Hands E3 5c
16m. From the ledge balance up the shallow groove in the slab.
FA. Jim Moran 1991

⓳ Parliamentary Climb . . . HVS 5a
18m. A classic (caveat - of its genre!) up the tall right-hand flake and the continuation crack above - scrwamtastic.
FA. R.Fryer 1959

⓴ Dead Chimney . . . . VS
16m. The imposing flake chimney has always been graded VS .... nothing else. If successful with the battle escape right.
FA. Tony Howard 1963

㉑ Natural Born Chillers . . . E6 6a
16m. Climb the arete right of *Dead Chimney*.
FA. Sam Whittaker 2000

㉒ The Grey Slayer E4 5c
10m. The crack and wall lead to a harrowing exit.
FA. Con Carey 1987

Kinder Downfall

	No star	★	★★	★★★
Mod to S	6	10	4	1
HS to HVS	14	17	6	2
E1 to E3	5	11	2	2
E4 and up	-	-	1	-

The cliffs around the famous cascade of the Kinder Downfall are amongst the most dramatic on the moor, mainly because of the superb setting but also because it is the location of a fine set of routes, across a spread of grades, with many good offerings across the lower end of the grade spectrum. The outcrops here tend to face between south and west and so get plenty of afternoon and evening sunshine. The shape of the valley tends to funnel westerly winds up towards the rim of the moor making climbing here a wild experience under these conditions and also turning the Kinder Downfall into the Kinder Upfall and showering unsuspecting passers-by on the moor behind.

Approach   Also see map on pages 151

Access from any direction is a little arduous! If approaching from the east, you have a couple of choices. From parking below the Snake Inn follow the path up Fair Brook then take the short crossing (260 degrees, 0.9 km) which will pick up the sandy bed of the Kinder River and lead you down to the top of the Downfall. Alternatively, from the top of the Snake Pass, take the flagged path to the top of William Clough via Mill Hill then continue up onto the plateau to reach the top of Upper Western Buttress. Follow the plateau edge to the Downfall. If approaching from the west, park below the Kinder Reservoir, 1km east of Hayfield, which is 8km south of Glossop. Before starting the approach check out the plaque celebrating the 1926 mass trespass and thank your lucky stars. Walk up the side of the reservoir towards William Clough then the poor track beside the River Kinder direct (marshy and not really recommended) to the Downfall or, better and drier, hang a left up William Clough. Either follow it all the way to Ashop Head and join the Snake Summit route along the moor crest, or turn right just after the bridge across the stream and attack the slope direct - shorter but harder work.

Conditions

The cliffs are arranged along the rim to the west of the cascade of the Downfall and look out south and west, so get plenty of afternoon and evening sun. Some of the rock is inclined to be gritty after rain though many of the better climbs stay clean enough throughout the year. In poor conditions some of the easier routes from 100 years ago make for a good challenging day out.

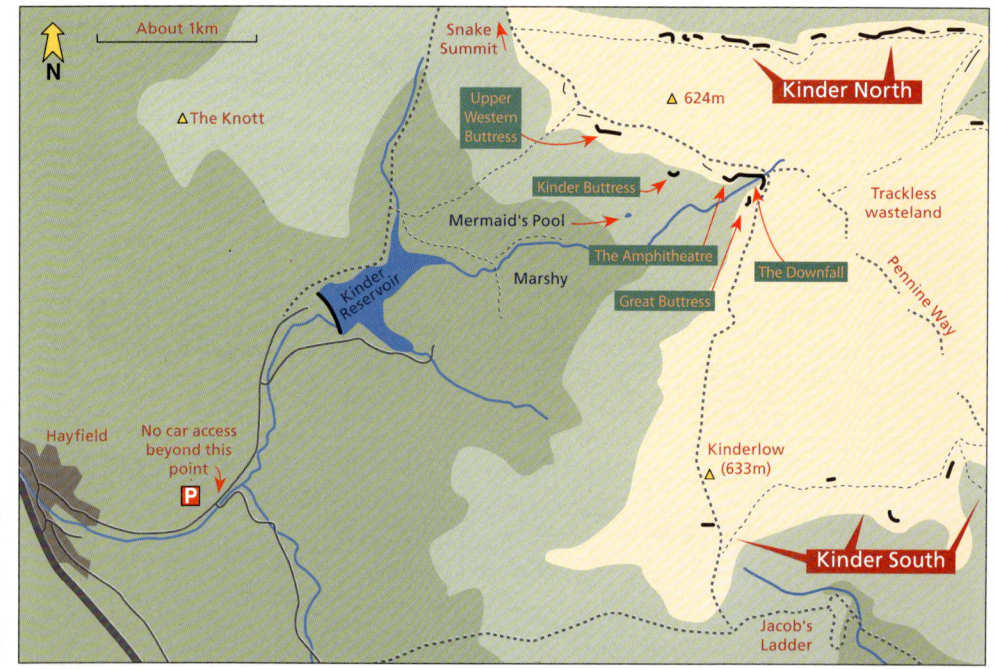

Kinder Downfall

Kinder Downfall in Winter

Under the right (rare!) conditions the Downfall forms the Peak's premier ice-park. Arrive early, or very late, or be prepared to queue! Grades and stars are condition dependent.

❶ The Direct .... ⭐2 ▢ **IV**
30m. In good winters the central ice pillar forms which gives a fine steep and serious pitch. Finish up the short steep icicle above the ledge.

❷ Central Direct. .... ⭐1 ▢ **III/IV**
40m. A small pillar that forms inbetween the *Downfall Climb* and the *Direct*.

❸ Downfall Climb. .... ⭐2 ▢ **II/III**
40m. Climb up the stepped ledges on the right to a large platform. Traverse leftwards, normally past a large icicle runner, then up a short vertical ice wall or corner to finish.

Kinder Downfall in good conditions in January 2009. Photo: Jack Finney

Kinder Downfall — Upper Western Buttress

Upper Western Buttress

The western-most decent cliff hereabouts has a sunny aspect and some good routes on the Upper Tier. The Lower Tier is dirty and best avoided and the left-hand side of the upper face is a bit crusty. Despite this, the upper right-hand area has some good routes in as fine a setting as any on the moor.

Approach (see map on page 178) - Either walk in from the Snake Summit, or take the Hayfield approach past Kinder Reservoir. Cross a footbridge over William Clough and continue up to the col or attack the slope direct. Follow the moor crest path rightwards (southeast) for about 200m until you are above the crag.

1 Yellow Brick Road E2 6a
10m. The wall just left of the hanging arete is approached by a short traverse from the left and has one extended reach.
FA. Pete Robins 1999

2 The Jolsen Finish . . . . VS 4b
12m. Gain the right-hand side of the arete from the easy corner to the right.
FA. Paul Nunn 1964

3 Spike Chimney . . . . Diff
16m. The deep rift on the left is worth seeking out and is climbed, passing the huge ringing flake of the spike.
FA. Geoff Pigott 1950

4 Once in a Blue Moon E3 6a
22m. The left arete of the buttress has taxing and reachy moves at mid-height with interesting gear. Above this things ease.
FA. Graham Parkes 1999

5 The Dark Side of the Moon E3 5c
18m. The right arete of the buttress is approached through bulges (big thread) and climbed with a brief excursion onto its right-hand side and a finish up the front. Easier for the tall. There is only a short hard section but that requires the ability to go for it!
FA. Dennis Carr 1976

6 Extinguisher Chimney . . . . VS 4c
18m. A classic narrowing-chimney which is less of a battle than it looks. Face right and squirm into the narrows to reach a ledge then finish with a restricted exit amongst the symbols. Don't disturb the symbols.
FA. Vin Dillon 1949

7 Candle Buttress . . . . HVS 5a
18m. The buttress right of *Extinguisher Chimney* is gained awkwardly from the right and climbed delicately (useful flake round left) to easier ground. High in the grade.
FA. R.Williams 1957

Photos: Chris Tan

Upper Western Buttress — Kinder Downfall

⑧ The Atrocity Exhibition E1 5b
18m. A direct variation on *Candle Buttress*.
FA. Martin Kocsis 1997

⑨ Intermediate Route .... HS 4b
12m. Climb the striated wall slightly leftwards then finish back right up the rib that forms the edge of the previous route

⑩ South Wall .... VDiff
12m. A little gem of a layback up the left-trending flakes. Western Grit's version of Stanage's *Heaven Crack*.
FA. Eric Byne 1932

⑪ Pedestal Climb .... Diff
8m. The front face of the squat pedestal leads to a groove.
FA. Eric Byne 1932

⑫ 45 Degrees .... HVS 5b
6m. The short and sketchy slab is a good test of technique and is much steeper than the name suggests.
FA. Malc Baxter 1986

⑬ Curving Crack .... S 4b
6m. The obviously-named groove is tricky to enter then eases.
FA. Geoff Pigott 1948

⑭ Rock Reptile .... HVS 5b
6m. Slink up the right wall of the open recess using a fingery flake to make progress.
FA. Con Carey 1987

⑮ Singer Corner .... S 4b
8m. Enter the hanging layback with difficulty though on biffos.

⑯ M.G. Route .... HS 4a
8m. The steep and juggy crack is quite a gripper.

⑰ Monkey Magic .... HVS 5b
8m. The steep wall to the right of the arete has a useful flake hold and provides good technical moves.
FA. Harry Venables 1986

⑱ Esgee Crack .... S 4b
6m. The steep and widening crack is uphill!

⑲ The Funnel .... HS 4b
6m. The obviously-named feature is fine for double jointed dwarfs, and a battle for the rest of us.

⑳ Eastern Promise .... HVS 5b
8m. Climb the wall, starting on the right up a thin crack, and continuing with care.
FA. Con Carey 1987

㉑ Eastern Crack .... S 4a
8m. The short-lived crack on glorious jams.
FA. Geoff Pigott 1948

㉒ Eastern Arete .... HVS 5b
8m. Pull leftwards onto the hanging arete and then sprint.
FA. Con Carey 1986

㉓ End Wall .... VS 4c
8m. The final short but unprotected wall on sloping holds.
FA. Geoff Pigott 1948

Photos: Chris Tan

Kinder Downfall — Kinder Buttress

1 Foreigner — E3 5c
16m. The steep wall high on the left side of the cliff gives a bold pitch (around left on the topo). Climb the wall to the break (gear) then continue up above moving left into a shallow scoop below an overhang before heading back out right to finish.
FA. Con Carey 1986

2 The Mermaid's Ridge — VS 4c
A Kinder classic - a fine climb, two varied and interesting pitches and of considerable historical interest.
1) 4b, 12m. Climb the bubbly ridge over a bulge (thread) to a stance on a good ledge.
2) 4c, 18m. Start around on the left of the ledge (move the belay?) and traverse right delicately onto the ridge. From here move right into a groove and climb this to the top.
FA. Siegfried Herford 1910

3 Glory Boys — VS 4c
12m. The narrowing-crack in the right wall is short and sweet.
FA. Keith Ashton 1986

4 Left Twin Chimney — VS 4c
30m. The left-hand corner of the recess leads with increasing difficulty to the midway ledge and a stance. Use *Mermaid's Ridge* to approach the groove above the roof but continue rightwards to a crack in a steep groove for an exciting finish.
FA. Siegfried Herford 1910

5 Pumping Irony — E3 5c
12m. The evil grovel of what is really *Left Twin Chimney Direct*. Start on the mid-height ledge, or by doing one of the lower pitches. Described in the old Kinder guide as VS!
FA. Con Carey 1987

6 Right Twin Chimney — HVS 5a
30m. Follow the right-hand corner of the recess easily to an awkward shallow chimney. Squirm up this to the terrace (4c - possible belay). The leaning fissure above is hard to enter, and leads to a good grass ledge. Finish up the groove behind.
FA. Siegfried Herford 1910

7 Final Judgement — E3 5c
20m. Disjointed but exciting. Climb the square right arete of the buttress by bold laying away to reach the grass ledge. Move out left (exposed) then swarm up the rounded arete to a wild finish.
FA. Con Carey 1987

8 Boulevard Traverse — HS 4a
12m. Climb the boot-shaped flake to its tip then traverse left into an awkward crack that leads to the grassy ledge. Finish up the wide chimney-crack behind.

9 Atone — E1 5b
10m. Get up onto the tip of the flake as for the previous route then pull over the roof directly above and climb the awkward, wide and steep crack to a tricky exit.
FA. Paul Nunn 1964

Kinder Buttress

A fine and remote gritstone buttress with one of Kinder's most famous outings in the shape of *Mermaid's Ridge*. The *Left* and *Right Twin Chimneys* are classics of another era whereas *Foreigner* and *Final Judgment* have a much more modern feel about them.

Approach (see map on page 178) - As for Upper Western Buttress until the slog up the ridge. At this point either continue along the path to reach Kinder Brook. Make your way up the side of the brook until the characteristic Kinder Buttress appears above you - usually damp. Alternatively follow the route to Upper Western Buttress and continue along the crest past the crag until Kinder Buttress can be seen down and right.

The Amphitheatre Kinder Downfall 183

① Domino Wall E1 5b
16m. Start left of the crusty rock and climb a bulge before shuffling right to a ledge. Continue carefully up the wall to the big shelf (stance) then finish rightwards up the short wall behind.
FA. R.Williams 1957

② The Ledge Shufflers E6 6c
14m. One of Kinder's more blatant last great problems fell! Climb crusty rock to the bulges then head left through these, then up the arete aiming for the big flake in the roof. Finish phlegmatically. Several ropes were used on the first ascent to protect the start and the moves left. Gear included RPs and huge cams!
FA. Dave Turnbull 1999

③ Raggald's Wall E1 5a
18m. Start up the groove in the right edge of the wall to its apex then move left around the arete (care with the rope work!) and climb the delicate groove to a reachy move for the ledge. Finish up the wall behind.
FA. Paul Nunn 1964

④ Great Chimney Left-hand ... VS 4c
18m. Climb the groove as for *Raggald's Wall* but continue steeply in a direct line to a good ledge (possible stance). Finish up the arete on the left.

⑤ The Great Chimney .... HS 4b
18m. Classic! The deep rift is approached via wide bridging to reach a scratched slab. From the small ledge above the left end of this slab, mantel into the chimney and follow it throughout. The exit is tricky. Originally split at a belay on the small ledge.
FA. J.W.Puttrell 1903

The Amphitheatre - Left
A fine set of routes in a wild setting, including several old classics. The area tends to funnel winds and so can be a blowy place to climb.
Approach (see map on page 178) - From the east (Snake Inn parking) take the Fair Brook path to the plateau then the 'short crossing' - (260 degrees, 0.9km) arriving above the Downfall. The easiest descent is down a gully just to the left (looking in) of the Amphitheatre - see 184. From the west follow either of the approaches as used to reach Kinder Buttress then continue to the Downfall. The moor edge path is quicker and drier than that in the valley bottom.

⑥ The Ensemble Exit .... HVS 5a
18m. From the small ledge part-way up *Great Chimney*, climb the groove on the right then take a steep crack to an undercut ledge out right. Pull over the capping block to a tricky mantelshelf finish, or nesh out right. Dirty but worthwhile.
FA. Paul Nunn 1964

The prow is an impressive Last Great Problem which has been top-roped by many but awaits a lead.

⑦ Professor's Chimney ...... Diff
14m. Weaves up the wide, shallow, chimney. Start on the right and cross over to finish up the left-hand groove.
FA. J.W.Puttrell 1903

⑧ Professor's Chimney Direct . VDiff
14m. Follow the right-hand branch direct by interesting moves.

Kinder Downfall — The Amphitheatre

Professor's Chimney

The Amphitheatre - Right

The central section of the Amphitheatre is not particularly outstanding, but around the corner are the steep cracks and walls facing the Downfall where there are some great traditional battles and the superb historical *Zig-zag*.
Approach - see previous page.

① Pegasus Left-hand **E1 5b**
14m. A short tough crack splits the overhang. Climb through this then continue up the crack above until forced left. Normally dirty.
FA. R.Williams (one peg) 1957. FFA. Con Carey 1987

② Pegasus Right-hand . . . **VS 4c**
16m. A thin slanting crack and its continuation. Pleasant but dirty.
FA. Al Parker (in mistake for the Left-hand) 1962

③ Left Fork Chimney . . . . **Diff**
16m. Climb into the chimney then follow the left-branch,
FA. J.W.Puttrell early 1900s

④ Right Fork Chimney . . . . . . **S 4a**
16m. The right-hand branch is better and harder than its neighbour and is accessed across a short glacis (a kind of easy slab) from the previous climb. Finish more steeply.
FA. J.W.Puttrell early 1900s

⑤ Embarkation Parade . . . . . . **VS 4c**
22m. This one-time classic needs a spruce up. Climb right then left to gain the steep groove which gives sustained climbing. From the big grassy ledge finish up the corner at the back.
FA. Arthur Birtwhislte 1939

⑥ Final Frontier **E2 5b**
12m. Climb to an area of oddly sculptured rock under the overhang then use the flake above to start the sprint for the big ledge above. Finish up the easy groove behind.
FA. Chris Hardy 1986

The Amphitheatre Kinder Downfall   185

7 Crooked Overhang .... **VS 4c**
18m. Climb rightwards and then up into a cave (stance?). Pull through the juggy roof carefully to a ledge and choice of exits.

8 Rodeo .... **VS 4c**
24m. A direct route up the right-hand side of the arete which supersedes the old more wandering line of *Crooked Arete*, which looped out left to the cave of *Crooked Overhang*.
FA. Rebekah Smith 1998

9 Zig-zag .... **VDiff**
18m. A fine climb in a dramatic setting. Trend left up the face to a position on the tip of a flake. Step up and right delicately on a small polished foothold to the final widening crack.
FA. J.W.Puttrell c1900

10 Zig-zag Crack .... **S 4a**
12m. The long narrowing-crack to the right of *Zigzag* leads via steepening groove to a tough exit round a bulge.
FA. Eric Byne 1929

11 Spin-up **E1 5b**
12m. Climb into the shallow left-facing groove in the steep wall then make fingery moves to easier ground and a crack. Serious.
FA. Con Carey 1987

12 Toss up .... **HVS 5a**
12m. Climb steeply into, and up, the right-hand groove. At its top, step left to join the *Spin-up*.
FA. Con Carey 1987

13 Chockstone Chimney .... **VDiff**
12m. The steep rift has a series of (well?) jammed blocks. A well-protected tussle with an awkward finish.
FA. W.J.Watson c1900

14 The Last Fling **E2 5b**
12m. Take the steep wall to the central roof then gain the ledge above this precariously. More balancy climbing gains the top.
FA. Con Carey 1987

15 Amphitheatre Crack .... **S 4b**
10m. Bridge the wide crack to where it narrows then try to get established above the overhang - hard work!
FA. possibly J.W.Puttrell c1910

16 Amphitheatre Face Climb .... **HS 4b**
12m. Oddly named! Climb the groove to the roof then shuffle out left to a rest on the arete (thread). Finish awkwardly
FA. possibly J.W.Puttrell c1910

17 Five Ten .... **HS 4a**
10m. Climb the slotted face on the right to a ledge, then continue up the tricky wall above.
FA. John Porter 1956

18 Square Chimney .... **Mod**
8m. The square rift to the right offers a very easy route or a useful way down for the competent.
FA. possibly J.W.Puttrell c1910

Photo: Chris Tan

Kinder Downfall   The Downfall

Kinder Downfall

The rock climbing here is not the best but the setting is special and some of the routes are well worth doing. The main attraction of the crag is on the rare occasions that it freezes up - see page 179 for more on this.

Approach (see map on page 178) - From the east (Snake Inn) take the Fair Brook path to the plateau then the 'short crossing' - (260°, 0.9km) to arrive above the Downfall. From the west follow either of the approaches as used to reach Kinder Buttress. The moor-edge path is quicker and drier than that in the valley bottom. If you are approaching from above (via Fair Brook or Upper Western Buttress) the scramble descent is down a gully just to the left (looking in) of the Amphitheatre a couple of hundred metres beyond the Downfall, or, in the dry make your way carefully down *Downfall Climb*.

❶ **North Tier Climb** . . . . **VS 4c**
1) 4c, 8m. Climb the strenuous jamming crack awkwardly to the wide grassy ledge that crosses the face.
2) 4b, 10m. Tackle the short-lived juggy wall above and then finish up a short groove.
FA. Paul Nunn 1964

The poised slab that used to provide **Slip Sliding Away**, E3 5c slipped and slid away and now lies at the base of the face.

❷ **Dud Chimney** **E1 5a**
14m. The shallow groove gives steep moves on rather unfriendly rock to a final difficult move.
FA. R.Williams 1957

❸ **The Glorious Twelfth** **E2 5b**
22m. Climb the juggy leaning groove (creak, creak) to a good breather on a ledge on the right. Step back left and finish up the wide crack with difficulty.
FA. Alan McHardy 1973

❹ **The Hunter** **E3 5b**
22m. Steep and serious. Climb the wall to a big jutting flake then traverse left to a second crusty horror of a flake. Layback (!) up this and press on through the bulges above to ledge. Climb the short bulging wall on the left to finish.
FA. Dennis Carr 1976

❺ **The Beast** **E2 5b**
24m. Devious. Start as for *The Hunter* but continue straight up to the roof then traverse right to the Dovecote Cave, Belay here or on the higher ledge. Move out left to finish easily.
FA. Dennis Carr 1966

Descent - reverse *Downfall Climb*, or use the gully beyond the amphitheatre

The Downfall Kinder Downfall 187

6 The Bloody Thirteenth — E1 5b
24m. Climb the left-hand side of the sharp arete starting up a flake on the left then taking the groove directly to the cave. Finish as for the previous climb, or more easily out right.
FA. Paul Nunn 1973

7 Shotgun Grooves — HVS 5b
24m. The shallow grooves running up the right-hand side of the arete give a worthwhile and awkward pitch. There is a choice of finishes the same as for the previous climbs.
FA. Al Parker 1976

8 Poacher's Crack — HVS 5a
22m. The sustained and steep cracks in the right-hand side of the wall give well-protected and steep climbing.
FA. Ted Rodgers 1976

9 Downfall Groove — HVS 5a
18m. The crack in the back of the big angular corner is hard work. The lower section can be bridged but the upper part is best jammed and proves sustained and awkward. The corner is just a shadow of one of Puttrell's earlier exploits which collapsed some years back. It now rests in pieces.
FA. J.W.Puttrell (of the original route) c1900

10 Independence Crack — E2 5c
18m. The fierce finger crack a couple of metres right of the corner gives a sustained pitch with good but hard-won gear.
FA. Dennis Carr (1 point of aid) 1976. FFA. Con Carey 1987

11 Hard Times — E2 5c
14m. Awkwardly cross the narrow ramp rightwards then climb the leaning shallow groove past a couple of unhelpful sloping ledges to reach easier ground. Finish up the buttress on the left.
FA. Al Parker 1979

12 Downfall Climb — Mod
60m. An aquatic amble across the series of sloping ledges. It is great as a winter route (see page 179) and okay as a rock climb in the dry but way too exciting if there has been much rain. Start on the right and climb up the groove or the ledges just to its left. Then follow the ramps up and left, passing the main flow, to a choice of finishing grooves. If already well-soaked, it is probably worth exiting easily rightwards.

13 Downfall South Corner — VDiff
40m. Grubby but worth doing. Start as for *Downfall Climb* but continue to a good stance in a sandy cave on the right. Pull out of the cave and take the shallow chimney to ledges then pass another bulge to a wide crack which leads to a choice of exits.
FA. J.W.Puttrell 1900

14 Harvest — HVS 5a
22m. Start from the sandy ledge part way up *Downfall South Corner* and trend left up the steep rock into a crack and onto a cave recess. Exit rightwards from this and continue steeply.
FA. Mick Dewsbury 1977

Kinder Downfall — Great Buttress

Great Buttress

Well to the right of the Downfall is the daunting bastion of Great Buttress, home to several worthwhile climbs. The old guides show the cliff as surprisingly clean (thanks to the Industrial Revolution) sadly it has become increasingly green, gritty and turf-ridden over the years and now sees little traffic. A small selection of the best of the routes are briefly described here - treat the grades with care! The routes start from a narrow ledge that cuts across the lower part of the face, though it is possible to extend the fun and start up one of several lines on the Lower Tier - multi-pitch on grit there for the asking!

Approach (see map on page 178) - The crag is best approached by descending the gully to the right (looking in) - steep - and skirting across and back up to the crag.

❶ Central Chimney .... Diff
30m. Climb the off-centre chimney-groove until it steepens then trend left to a sandy bay - possible stance. Finish up the flaky groove behind.

❷ Central Chimney Direct .... VS 4c
26m. The ascent of the intimidation and grubby upper groove requires some conviction.
FA. Herbert Hartley 1949

❸ Don't Look Back .... HVS 5a
26m. Climb the front of the buttress to the bulges then continue up the crack skirting the left-hand side of the roof to reach the top of the pillar - possible stance. Trend right to finish out on the exposed nose.
FA. Al Parker 1986. The first new route here for a generation and a bit.

❹ Gomorrah .... VS 4c
26m. Steep and thrilling climbing in a spectacular setting. Start as for *Don't Look Back* and trend right to tackle the crack splitting the right-hand side of the flat roof. Mantel into the base of the hanging groove and finish awkwardly up this.
FA. Arthur Birtwhistle 1950. On an earlier attempt he had to be rescued a judicious use of a top-rope!

❺ Sodom .... VDiff
24m. Climb the grungy gully then move right to the right-trending crack/groove. Up this to a right-trending exit across grassy ledges and up a short crack.
FA. Richard (RA) Brown 1945

❻ Trio Wall .... VS 4c
24m. Climb the lower wall to ledges then sidestep the roof by a short leftwards traverse, moving back right onto the arete. Climb up and right by a tricky mantelshelf then finish up the cracks.
FA. Herbert Hartley 1949

❼ Pigeon Corner .... VS 4c
24m. The hanging right-trending groove is approached steeply to get past the roof and then exited rightwards at the top.
FA. Herbert Hartley 1949

❽ Pocket Wall .... VS 4c
24m. Climb to the ledge then follow the trail of large holes rightwards to reach the base of a stepped groove. Finish up this.
Photo opposite.
FA. Arthur Birtwhistle 1950

❾ Great Slab .... S 4a
24m. The slab facing the Downfall is climb centrally to a good ledge and finish up the crack in the steeper wall above.

Climbers dwarfed by *Pocket Wall* (VS) - *opposite* - Great Buttress. Photo: Chris Tan

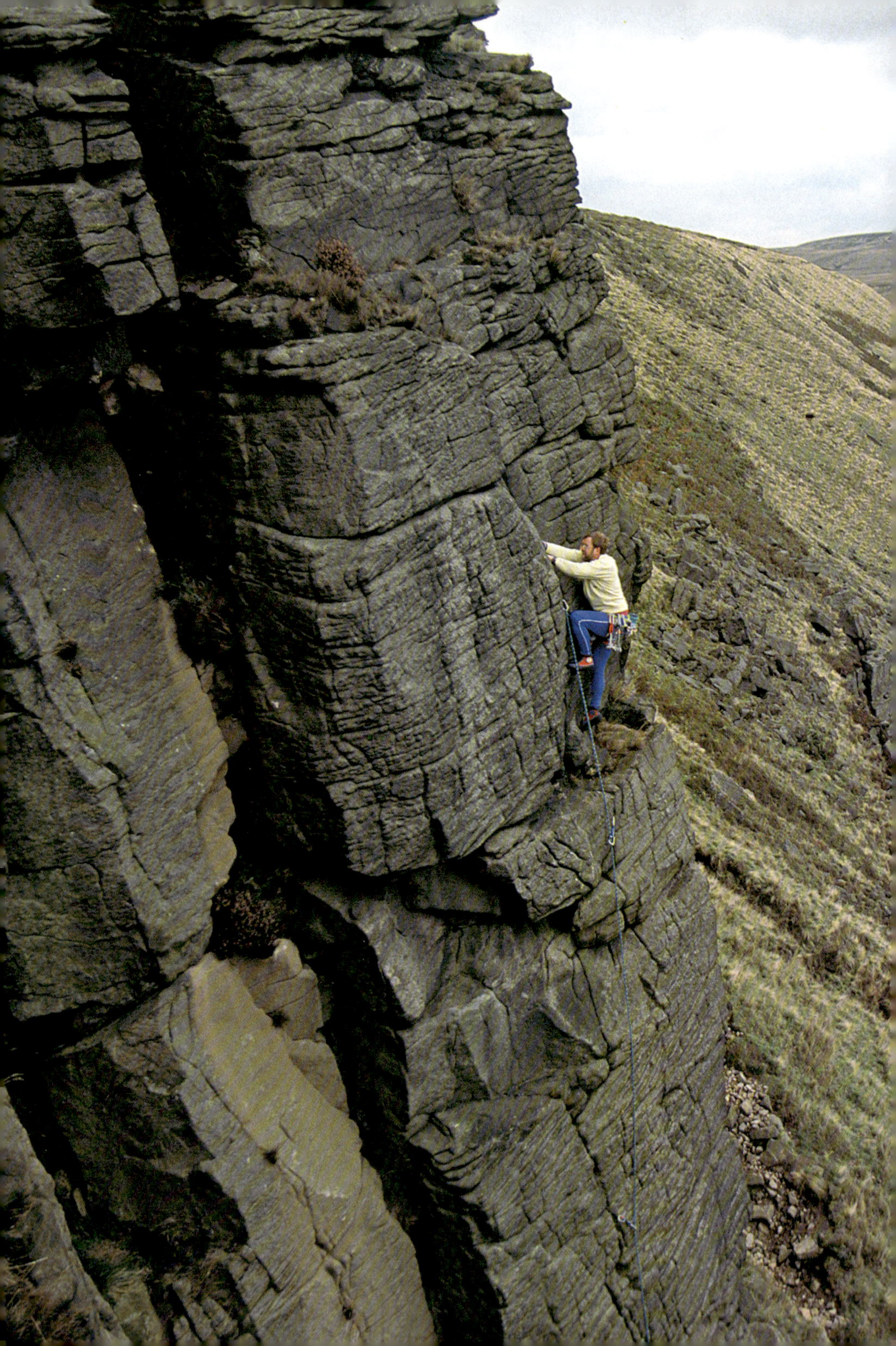

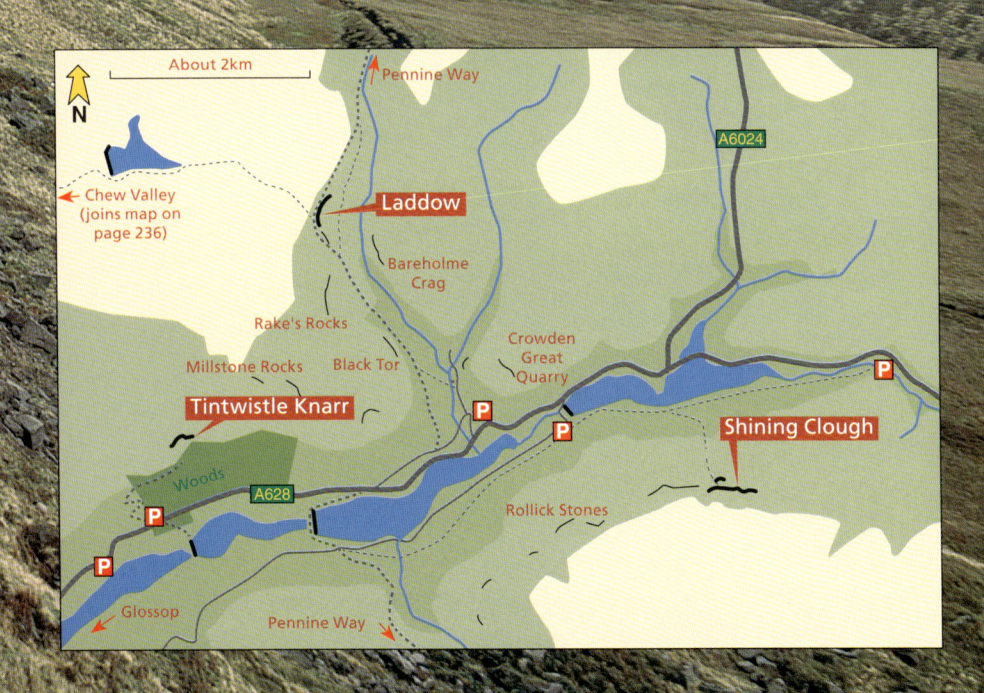

Bleaklow and Longdendale

Steve Warwick on Laddow's finest - *Tower Face* (VS) - *page 209.*

Shining Clough

	No star	★	★★	★★★
Mod to S	15	7	-	1
HS to HVS	8	17	2	3
E1 to E3	4	5	2	-
E4 and up	-	2	1	2

Shining Clough is the finest of the cliffs that fall under the banner of the Bleaklow area; it is a tall, sombre and very remote edge that is at its best on warm summer days when the cotton grass is high, the curlews mew over the plateau and the moors shimmer in the heat haze. Many of the climbs follow steep cracks, and therefore require a fair degree of proficiency in jamming. They tend to be green and gritty at the start of the season or after wet weather; in such conditions there are many better destinations in this guide.
On the far left are some short routes and then there is the collapsed buttress that was once home to the classics of Orestes and Chalkman, which fell down in the early 1980s. This is a sure-fire pointer to the fact that the whole cliff is the site of an ancient landslip and the other classics may one day head the same way. On the left-hand side of the main part of the cliff is the fine jutting arete of *East Rib* (HV) that gets the morning sun and is very photogenic.
Historically there are few details from before the 1950s, though many of the climbs put up before this date were the work of The Manchester University Mountaineering Club (Arthur Birtwistle and Co.) and later, members of the Karabiner Club along with the three Lowe Brothers.

Approach   Also see map on page 191
There is normally adequate parking by the southern end of the dam across the Longdendale reservoir. Go through the gate and follow the undulating track eastwards for just of a kilometre to a sign on the right pointing to Open Country just short of the house hidden in the trees. Head up to the top corner of the field then, as the path bends round to the left to another fence continue in the same line. Cross the second fence leftwards to reach the stream and follow its right-hand (looking up) bank until forced to the other side. Head steeply up the hillside via vague paths to the highest tree (a nice oak) then just a little higher move right to find the continuation path that leads steeply to the flat terrace below the cliff; about fifty minutes from the parking. Alternatively walk from the parking at the eastern end of the Longdendale Trail via a vague path above Near Black Clough until you can cut across the moor to the crag - this takes about the same time.

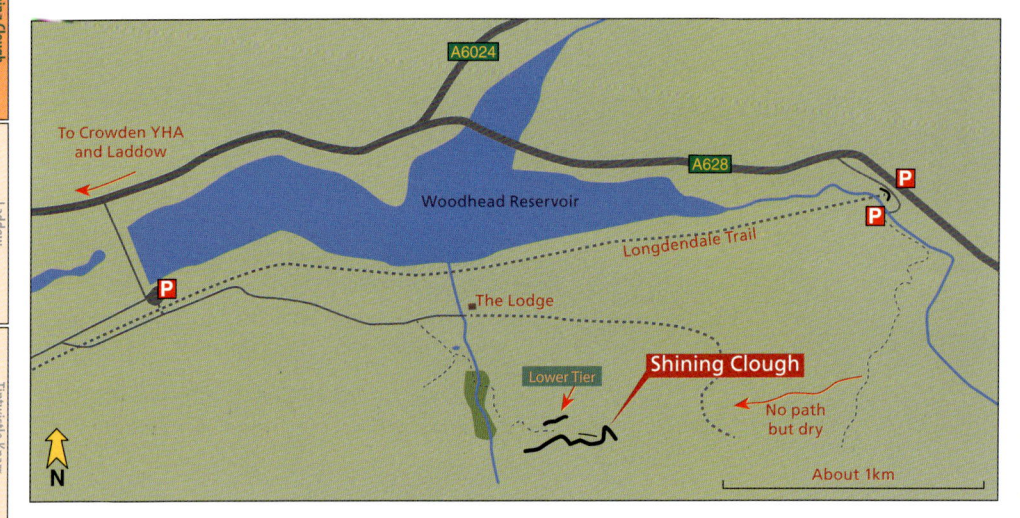

Conditions
Shining Clough is a fine venue but it is not recommended after poor weather as it is slow to dry and sees little in the way of sun. Ideal conditions are warm summer days after a dry spell, when the place can be enjoyed to the full. On late summer evenings the cliff gets its annual dose of sunshine and climbing up here under these rare conditions is magical.

Geraldine Taylor cruising *Phoenix Climb* (VS) - *page 195* - Shining Clough.

Shining Clough — Phoenix Buttress

194

Not much sun · 40 min · Green · Windy

Descent

East Rib

Phoenix Buttress
One of natural grit's more impressive buttresses and home to several worthwhile routes including the superb *Phoenix Climb*, one of Harding's very best. At a slightly lower grade *Via Principia* and *Atherton Brothers* are excellent and, a notch higher, the short but exposed and hyper-photogenic *East Rib* is a 'must-do'.

Phoenix Climb

Phoenix Buttress **Shining Clough** 195

1 Orang Arete .... VS 4b
10m. Take the crack in the centre of the south-facing side wall to the deep break then move left and climb the short arete.
FA. Martin Whittaker 1986

2 Grape Escape E3 6a
10m. Follow *Orang Arete* to where it heads left then climb the thin crack in the wall above and finish with difficulty and a monster stretch (or cop out right at a lower grade). Small wires needed.
FA. Ivan Green 1995

3 Monkey Puzzle .... VS 4c
10m. Follow the previous routes to the break but then move right (thread) to a block and a second wider crack. Finish awkwardly up this. A pumpy little number at the grade.
FA. Don Whillans late 1940s. The great man's first new route

4 East Rib .... HVS 5a
14m. Good climbing in a superb setting with good rests and protection. From the base of the crack of *Monkey Puzzle* trend right to climb a flat overhang on the right (juggy but steep) and then the airy arete above. *Photo on page 203.*
FA. John Gosling 1960s

5 East Rib Direct . E5 6a
16m. Climb the steep lower section of the arete to join the regular route. A poorly-protected lead, sometimes dirty, always bold.
FA. Loz Francomb 1979

6 Icon .... HVS 5a
16m. Climb the wide crack (huge cam or wobbly chockstone) to its end, then climb the final green wall following the easiest line.
FA. Tom Stevenson 1979

7 Green Crack .... HS 4b
14m. A poor start leads to a better finale. Climb the crack in the left wall of the deep gloomy chimney (reached by a grotty, grassy scramble) then bridge the exposed groove above.

To the right is the enclosed and unsavoury rift of East Chimney then the finest buttress on the cliff, home to Phoenix.

8 Atherton Brothers ..... S 4a
20m. Climb up to and then tackle the steep flake (not easy to protect) by sustained climbing until it is possible to mantelshelf onto a good ledge. Finish up the groove behind and wonder where the left wall of the one-time chimney went to!
FA. Arthur Birtwistle 1940s

9 Phoenix Climb .... VS 4c
26m. Vintage Harding and well-worth the walk up. The superb straight crack gives classic jamming past a useful hole to reach easier but still-steep ground. A wider section of crack gains a ledge; climb the groove on the left then finish direct or move out right for a superb airy exit. *Photo on page 193.*
FA. Peter Harding 1947

10 Via Principia .... S 4a
24m. The wide chimney crack in the nose of the buttress leads past a bulge to a gritty ledge (possible stance). Step left into the jamming crack in the exposed arete and climb this until the crack on the right can be reached. Continue up this then finish up the wall on the left. An excellent route at the grade.

11 Subsidiary Chimney ...... S 4a
24m. From the ledge of *Via Principia* squirm up the narrow chimney with some difficulty especially at the narrows.

12 Ave .... VS 4c
24m. From the ledge of *Via Principia* climb the steep flake just right of the chimney by committing layback moves to reach the wider continuation. Finish awkwardly up this. Big gear.

13 Powerplay E2 6a
8m. The centre of the short face gives a fingery pitch. Climb left then right to ledges and an escape.
FA. Con Carey 1988

14 Little Red Pig .... HVS 5b
18m. The crack and groove lead to the pillar above. Tackle the steep slab, right then left, to a series of thin cracks linked by a big shallow pocket.
FA. Chris Wright 1986

15 Vanishing Groove .... S 4a
18m. Follow the previous climb but step right to tackle the continuation of the lower groove 'til it vanishes. Finish up the face.
FA. Keith Ashton 1988

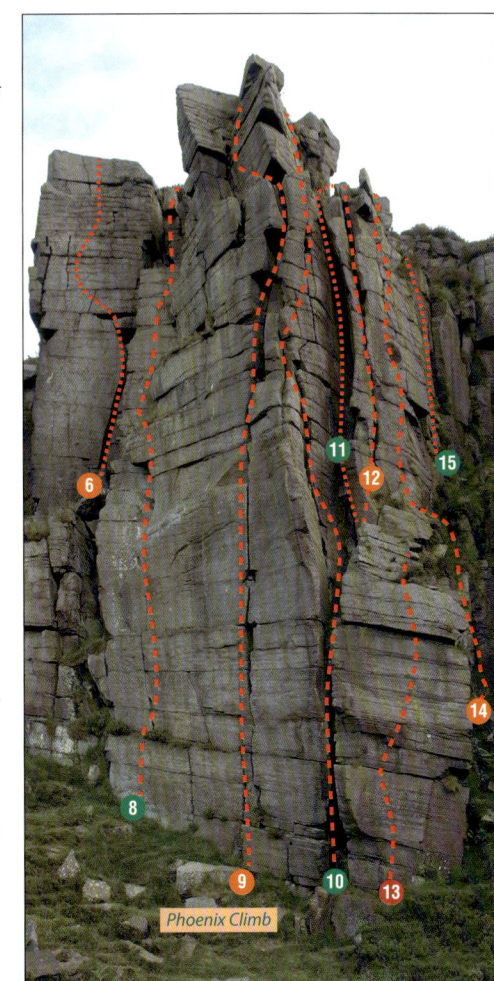

Phoenix Climb

Shining Clough — The Rainbow Flake

❶ Satyr — E4 5c
10m. The shallow ramp on the central buttress provides a delicate and harrowing lead, on which protection is lacking.
FA. Al Parker 1974

❷ Solstice — HVS 5a
8m. The zigzag crack and arete of the right-hand buttress.
FA. Al Parker 1974

❸ Some Product — E2 5c
8m. The thin crack in the north face of the fin leads out to the arete and a rapid sprint for the top.
FA. Loz Francomb 1979

❹ Bloodrush — E6 6b
16m. Climb the bold front face of the fin by an increasingly harrowing series of monkey-up-a-stick moves. A great and gripping outing which is well-named.
FA. Andy Cave 1990s

❺ Saucius Digitalis — E4 6a
12m. The thin crack in the south face is a bit of a finger wrecker though protection is good. At its end, improvise a way left out to the arete, and finish more boldly up this.
FA. Loz Francomb 1979

The Rainbow Flake **Shining Clough** 197

Powering through the bulges on *Yerth* (E2) - *below* - the astounding pillar of *Bloodrush* (E6) is difficult to ignore.

6 Nagger's Delight. . . . . **HVS 5a**
12m. The steep green groove gives good bridging and laybacking to a tricky exit out left. The final moves are often gritty.
FA. Pete Crew 1959

7 Naaden **E1 5b**
12m. Jam the fine crack in the right wall of the groove until it ends then climb the wall with a fierce fingery pull to start (5c for the short) and a stretchy final move rightwards at the top.
FA. Mike Simpkins late 1960s

8 Yerth **E2 5c**
14m. Climb through the stacked roof and follow cracks left of the arete until they end on a huge flake. Traverse round the arete, climb a short crack and make a crucial and scary mantelshelf to reach an easier finish. *Photo on this page*.
FA. Mike Simpkins late 1960s

9 Cistern Groove . . . . **VDiff**
12m. The steep groove is approached over broken ground, a successful ascent may leave you flushed with success!
FA. Eddie Birch 1960s

The Rainbow Flake
To the right the cliff is split into two tiers, with a grassy terrace between them. The lower tier is scrappy but the upper one is a little better with three short buttresses. They are most easily reached by a zig-zagging scramble from below. Right again is the striking fin of rock known as The Rainbow Flake, whose narrow front face is tackled by the dramatic *Bloodrush*. Beyond this is the deep groove of *Nagger's Delight* and the rib of *Yerth*.

Shining Clough — Pisa Buttress

198

Pisa Buttress
The finest piece of rock on the cliff, a tall barrel of a buttress with an especially fine set of climbs. *Pisa Super Direct* is the one to aspire to; check out the photo opposite. The finger cracking *Galileo* is also much sought after - and usually turns out to be harder than you were expecting!

Pisa Buttress **Shining Clough** 199

① Pisa .... VS 5a
18m. An indifferent start leads to an exciting finish. Start up the grassy gully on the left then follow cracks up the wall just left of the arete until they peter out. Move right round the arete with difficulty to reach a small exposed ledge then finish up the steep crack splitting the bulges above.
FA. Karabiner Club members 1948

② Galileo E1 5c
18m. A strenuous and sustained pitch though with good protection throughout. High in the grade. Climb the steep finger-cracks to the small ledge on *Pisa*. Finish up the easier cracks above. The lower crack is hard for for the strong and the central crack is hard for the weak.
FA. John Gosling late 1960s

③ Pisa Direct .... HVS 5a
24m. Devious but long and involving. From the lowest point of the buttress climb the crack just left of the arete, then the excellent right-slanting crack to just below the Leaning Tower. Head left for 4m to a ledge then climb the arete to a better ledge on the right. The leaning crack above leads to easier ground. Care with the rope work needed.
FA. Arthur Birtwhistle 1949

④ Pisa Super Direct ..... HVS 5a
20m. Super direct and a super route. Start direct up thin cracks in the slab just right of the arete to join the parent route which is then followed to the Leaning Tower. Then climb the bulging crack and well-positioned crest of the buttress. One of the very best routes on Bleaklow. *Photo this page.*
FA. John Gosling late 1960s

⑤ Stable Cracks .... VS 4b
20m. The continuous crack-line up the right-hand side of the face is just a touch wide for comfort. It gives a poorly-protected pitch without some really large gear. Low in the grade.
FA. Peter Harding 1947

⑥ Plastic Saddle E1 5c
18m. The narrow slab just to the right is climbed centrally and gives a bit of a rough ride. Some gardening might be needed.
FA. Tom Valentine 1988

⑦ Typists' Chimney .... Diff
16m. The deep chimney groove that bounds the right-hand side of the slab. A grubby and gloomy affair.

⑧ Unicorn Cracks. .... HS 4b
16m. Climb the diagonal crack in the right wall of the groove to its end then the cracks and a groove up and right to the top. Another route that sees no sun and few ascents.

⑨ Trungel Crack. .... HVS 5a
18m. Climb the crack just left of the arete, passing a recess, to a sloping shelf on the right. A continuation crack leads through an overhang to a finish up the crack in the left wall of *Unicorn Cracks'* final groove.
FA. Eddie Birch 1960s

High on the mega-classic of *Pisa Super Direct* (HVS) - *this page*. The pillar that gives the route its name is clearly visible.

Shining Clough — The Big Wall

① The Big Wall — E3 6a
20m. A classic with hard climbing, good runners and some lo-o-ong reaches. Climb a crack to a flat roof then stretch left to a thin crack and climb this (hard) to a ledge on the arete. A large Friend might be found of use hereabouts. Make difficult moves into a cave (often dirty) and then easier - at least for the tall - moves out of it. The short may have to avoid this last section on the left.
FA. Mike Simpkins 1960s. FFA. John Allen 1975

② Holme Moss — E1 5c
16m. Climb the cracks in the right-hand side of the face through a bulge and head up the final tricky wall. High in the grade and sadly escapable.
FA. John Hart 1979

③ Gremlin Groove — VS 4c
14m. The long groove up the right-hand side of the smooth wall gives a good pitch. The overhang just below the final groove is stubborn.
FA. Peter Harding 1947

④ Gremlin Wall — HVS 5a
14m. Climb the steep wall to a ledge then trend left and pull through a small overhang with difficulty to reach another ledge. Finish up the wall behind.

⑤ Artifact — VS 4c
14m. Follow a thin crack out to the arete and climb this until a short traverse can be made back left under an overhang and finish up the wall. High in the grade.
FA. John Gosling late 1960s

To the right is Deep Chimney, a dirty scrambling descent route.

⑥ Flake Groove — VDiff
10m. Climb the groove to the big roof (fancy a direct finish?) and escape out right using the big flake.

⑦ Flake Crack — S 4a
10m. Back-and-foot up behind the big flake to its top then about face and finish as for the last route.

⑧ Toadstool Crack — VS 4c
10m. The triple overhangs are passed with difficulty.

The Easter Island pinnacle has four climbs, the two best are:

⑨ Ordinary Route — Mod
4m. The cliff face of the pinnacle is the easiest way up - and of course, down.

Not much sun · 40 min · Green · Windy

Descent

Pisa Super Direct

The Big Wall

The Big Wall
The smooth north-facing wall towards the right-hand side of the cliff is home to one hard classic and some easier offerings. Although inclined to be a bit scruffy at the start of the season *The Big Wall* is worthy of your attention if you climb at that grade and are tall enough!

Right-hand Buttresses — Shining Clough

10 Pinnacle Face .... VS 4c
10m. The valley face is the best way to the top and climbed by a thin crack, a poorly protected slab and then the left-hand arete.

11 Pinnacle Crack .... VS 4c
14m. The crack in the wall behind the pinnacle is awkward. Trend right up the crack to the arete and an airy exit. Often very scruffy.

12 Phantom E3 6a
14m. A spooky and precarious eliminate up the left-hand side of the face right of the pinnacle. The crucial slab is protected by side-runners and avoiding the next climb is not easy.
FA. Con Carey 1988

13 Nimrod .... S 4a
14m. Climb the flake and groove in tandem to a block. From a standing position on this, climb discontinuous cracks to the top, finishing with an awkward-feeling layback.
FA. Peter Harding 1947

14 Free Fall E3 5c
12m. Climb the middle of the wall to a leftward finger-traverse then swing boldly around the arete to jugs. Climb up until it is possible to transfer back to the front face to finish.
FA. Con Carey 1988

15 Stag Party .... VDiff
14m. A riotous affair which staggers up the wide crack in the left wall of the groove and finishes up the chimney on the right.

16 Ladies' Day .... S 4a
14m. An altogether more sedate affair. Climb a crack until a traverse leads to the chimney on the left. Climb this and hand-traverse back right to a ledge below a hanging groove. Pull into this and finish steeply on good holds.

17 Ladies' Day Direct .... HVS 5a
14m. The arete direct by pleasant climbing with some long stretches to the ledge. Finish as for *Middleton Groove*.
FA. John Gosling 1960s

18 Middleton Groove .... HS 4b
14m. The steep crack just right leads to the platform. Follow the curving fissure in the back of the groove to finish.

19 Valhalla Crack .... VS 4c
14m. A steep groove is jammed to a grassy platform. The steep continuation requires more jamming, or an intimidating layback.

20 Sampson E4 6b
14m. The impressive arete is followed throughout and is highly technical. Layback and heel-hook until forced left at two thirds height then pull rightwards to pass the final roof.
FA. Rob Weston 1989. Con Carey also claimed it a couple of days later.

21 Original Route .... S 4b
14m. The long groove gives a pleasant pitch. Climb initially on the right then left of a flake and finally exit direct.

22 West Ridge .... HVS 5a
14m. The right-hand arete of the groove is another worthwhile outing and is climbed on its right-hand side by laying-away.

23 West Wall Route 1 .... S 4b
18m. Follow thin cracks up the steep slab to easier ground then finish up the steep tower directly above.

Right-hand Buttresses
The right-hand side of the cliff is the least popular section. Despite this fact there are some worthwhile lower grade routes though really the whole area could do with a bit more traffic to get spruced up.

Shining Clough — The Lower Tier

The Lower Tier

Down the slope from the main cliff, and passed on the approach, is the band of slumped rock that forms the Lower Tier. There are a dozen short offerings here that are especially suitable for those who find the main cliff rather too steep and intimidating. None of the climbs are brilliant but the smattering of stars should point out the best of this particular bunch.

1 Shandy .... VDiff
10m. The north-facing scoop on the far left.

2 Lager Lout .... HVS 5a
10m. The left-hand arete of the face is followed on its right-hand side to a finish over a small protruding beak.
FA. Keith Ashton 1989

3 Pint of Beer .... VS 5a
10m. The wide, kinked crack is a bit of a struggle - off-width or harrowing layback. Long rumoured to only have had two ascents!

4 Omelette Crack .... Diff
8m. The chimney to the right is okay.

5 The Egg Bowl .... S 4b
8m. Climb the centre of the concave face to the right, following a thin crack, to a heathery exit.

6 The Vice .... VDiff
10m. The steep crack in the left-hand side wall; get stuck into it. Above this, wander up easy ground.

7 Main Wall Climb .... VDiff
12m. Climb to a cracked recess at 6m. Exit from this and finish up a groove containing a thin flake.

8 Captain Zep .... HVS 5a
10m. Follow a thin seam in the wall to the break below the roof and cross this on the left on a good jug.
FA. Mark Leach 1983

9 Dirtier Groove .... Diff
10m. The incised groove on the right is partly filled with turf at the moment. The upper half is marginally better.

10 The Rainbow .... Diff
10m. The sharp (and clean) arete is followed on good holds and is grades easier than the routes on the feature of the same name up on the Main Cliff.

11 Dirty Groove .... Diff
10m. The next groove can be a bit of a grubby affair though as the name suggests it is cleaner than its near neighbour.

12 Left Route .... S 4a
10m. The cracks just right of the arete provide a sustained and delicate pitch.

13 Central Route .... HVS 5a
8m. The centre of the wall isn't too well-endowed with either gear or holds. Sustained but quite low in the grade.

14 Right Route .... VDiff
6m. The crack just before the boulder slope with a tricky move left at mid-height.

Andy Roberts hanging around on *East Rib* (HVS) - *page 194* - one of the great classic routes at Shining Clough. Photo: Sean Kelly

Laddow

In the early days of our sport, Laddow Rocks were one of the prime venues visited by climbers operating at the cutting edge. Today the place is very much out of fashion, haunted by ghosts and almost always quiet. It is perhaps Western Grit's equivalent of Wharncliffe Crags; in both cases the nearness of the railway line gave (relatively) easy access, and both places were immensely popular 100 years ago. Since the production of Peak Gritstone East, Wharncliffe has undergone a bit of a renaissance; it would be nice to think we can do the same for Laddow's lofty and lonely buttresses.

The main bulk of the cliff is away on the far right just below the crest of the moor, and from here the rocks straggle leftwards, gradually descending the hillside until they fizzle out close to the point where the approach path climbs onto the plateau.

Approach *Also see map on page 191*

There is extensive parking by Crowden Youth Hostel in Longdendale. The approach path follows the Pennine Way (signed) towards the distant cliff, rising in a series of steps until, having passed by the edge of The Southern Group it reaches the crest of the moor. From here it is usual to head straight to the right-hand side of the cliff, descending past the famous bivvy-cave to then work through the guide backwards! The approach takes about 50 to 60 minutes depending on how many photo-stops you have on the way. The old Pennine Way track runs out onto the flat area below the cliff and although it gives great views it is nearly always unpleasantly boggy - the ridge crest path is a much better bet.

Conditions

A fine but sadly neglected cliff that has become increasingly grassy over the years. Old photographs show extensive nail scratching and little in the way of vegetation, though those days have long since gone. The outlook from the cliff has changed little in the past 100 years and it is easy to see what the pioneers found so attractive about these tall buttresses and their lonely aspect. The cliff faces east and gets the morning sun. The grass tends to slow the drying of the place after rain, though fortunately the great classics of *Long Climb*, *Tower Face* and also the routes around the bivvy-cave are clean enough to dry quickly.

Looking up the valley towards Laddow.

Charlie Wheeler starting *Easter Bunny* (E2) - *page 206* - at Laddow. Photo: Mike Hutton

Laddow — Left-hand Buttresses

Laddow's buttresses seen from the approach path.

Labels on photo: Southern Group, Easter Ridge, Gallic Buttress, Pillar Ridge, Priscilla Ridge, Long Climb, Tower Face

The Southern Group
The first crag reached is a short series of buttresses - a Bleaklow Burbage North perhaps. These routes have never been popular (better things further up the hill) so they are not described here.

Easter Ridge
Up and right, a further five minutes walk, is the start of the Main Cliff, a series of isolated towers left of the stream-bed. All of the rest of the routes are most easily reached from the path along the crest of the ridge - The Pennine Way.

❶ Southern Arete . . . . VDiff
12m. The pleasant right arete of the left-hand buttress of the main cliff is steep, juggy and enjoyable.

❷ Easter Ridge E2 5b
12m. From the grass ledge, climb a thin crack to the bulge, cross this left, then right, and teeter up steep rock to easy ground.

❸ Easter Bunny E2 5b
12m. Climb the vertical arete on its left-hand side to the final break, then transfer to the opposite side for the final moves.
Photo on page 205.
FA. Steve Bancroft 1984

Gallic Buttress

❹ Route 4 . . . . S 4a
12m. The left-hand arete of the face, skirting the bulge rightwards. Step back left onto the final exposed arete.

❺ 2nd Holiday . . . . Mod
12m. The left-hand chimney is awkward to start. As it widens, it also eases.

❻ Route 3 . . . . VDiff
14m. Climb the slabby wall past a useful blob.

❼ Tuppence Ha'penny . . . . VDiff
14m. The kinked crack midway between the two chimneys.

❽ Route 2 . . . . HVD
14m. The narrow wall trending right.

❾ 1st Holiday . . . . VDiff
12m. The peapod-shaped chimney is climbed in classical fashion, passing the outside of the jammed boulder.

❿ Route 1 . . . . VDiff
12m. The thin crack left of the arete is good.

⓫ Route Minus One E1 5c
10m. The right arete of the buttress on its left-hand side. A one-time VS with the suggestion of jumping rightwards if it was all proving too much!

Left-hand Buttresses **Laddow** 207

Gallic Buttress
This short and relatively insignificant buttress is situated midway between Easter Ridge and Pillar Ridge. It does have plenty for the green spot climber though, and all the routes are worth a look, though they currently see minimal traffic

Pillar Ridge
100m across the hillside to the right the rocks increase in size and several good buttresses protrude from the heathery hill-side - as ever at Laddow the routes are sadly neglected.

12 A Chimney .... ☐ **Diff**
6m. The left-hand (and wider) crack to the top of the pillar.

13 A Crack .... ☐ **S 4a**
8m. The narrower right-hand crack is tricky towards the top.

14 Omicron Buttress .... ⓛ ☐ **HVD**
14m. Climb crusty cracks until it is possible to move left to a large flake. Finish up the left-hand side of this.

15 Staircase .... ② ☐ **Mod**
24m. An excellent route for beginners. Scratched holds lead up the slab to a possible stance on the left. The ridge on the right completes the outing. If in doubt, follow the polish!

16 Pillar Ridge .... ③ ☐ **HS 4b**
20m. A classic from way back (the beginning of the 20th century). Climb the crack in the front of the buttress to a possible stance, then step out right and climb the thinner crack that leads to a groove and then the final arete.
FA. Possibly A.E.Baker c.1900

Pillar Ridge
To the right is the start of the main section of the cliff. This initial area has a few easier offerings of a decent length in a great setting.

Laddow Long Climb

1 Siren's Rock. . . . . S 4a
20m. Start on the right and climb the arete to an alarming widening. Thrash up this, or better climb the exposed face to the right to reach the easy pastoral ramblings above.
FA. Unknown but pre 1907

2 Priscilla Ridge . . . . HVS 5a
20m. The fine arete is still a lonely lead and was a great effort for its day. Climb the lower arete to a ledge, pull over the overhang and follow the arete (thread) throughout. Watch for a loose block.
FA. Arthur Birtwhistle (of Diagonal fame) 1938

3 Priscilla. . . . . HVS 5a
20m. From the ledge pull over the bulge then climb rightwards up the wall to a rest (one-time stance) on the right. Traverse back left to a delicate finish which has a long reach for the final crack.
FA. Morley Wood, Fred Pigott (alts) 1921

4 Long Climb . . . . Top 50 S 4a
A classic which has crept up in grade owing to the polish!
1) 3c, 15m. Climb the slabby buttress on polished holds (a gripper in the wet) trending left then right to a good stance.
2) 4a, 20m. Climb the slippery crack/scoop into the groove above then step left and follow a series of corners to a grand finale up the crack on the right. *Photo on page 211.*
FA. One or more of the Puttrell/Baker mob, early 1900s

5 Leaf Buttress . . . . VS 4c
1) 4a, 15m. As for *Long Climb*.
2) 4c, 25m. Follow the awkward shallow groove then move out right and climb the delicate front face of the huge flake - *The Leaf*. Tackle the final wall leftwards. Bold today but bolder in 1916!
FA. Ivar Berg 1916

6 Leaf Crack . . . . HS 4b
1) 4a, 15m. As for *Long Climb*.
2) 4c, 25m. Traverse out right and follow the long crack up the right-hand side of *The Leaf* passing a tricky bulge. Climb rightwards up the final wall to finish. High in the grade.

7 Little Crowberry . . . . S 4a
18m. Climb right of the arete then monkey left to gain its front face. Continue up the left-hand flank apart from a couple of moves on the right a short distance below the top. A **Direct Start** is a less satisfying **VS 4c**. There is a possible stance in the shallow recess of the Pulpit if needed.

8 Long Chimney Ridge . . . . . . S 4a
18m. Climb the right-trending groove right of the crest of the arete until the ledge of *The Pulpit* on the right can be reached. Climb into the twin cracks above with difficulty and finish easily passing a wobbling block with care. Pity about the shrubbery.

Tower Face **Laddow** 209

Up and right is a clean wall above meadows. There are a few short routes here, though the approach means they don't see much attention. They could be used as easy multi-pitch training. The walls to either side of Straight Crack are The Blacksmith Climb and Little Innominate. Both are VS 4c, use the same side runner and were the work of Herbert Hartley in 1928.

9 Straight Crack . . . . S 4a
10m. The obviously-named crack doesn't have many holds.

10 Straight Chimney . . . . Mod
10m. The deep groove is better than the approach!

11 Garden Wall. . . . . S 4a
10m. The right-hand groove in the wall. Approaching from *Left Twin Chimney* improves the whole experience.

Long Climb and Tower Face
The right-hand section of the cliff is the show-piece of the place with an excellent collection of tall climbs on good clean rock. Arrive early for the best conditions, or use the famous bivi-cave for a sleep-over. The usual approach is along the cliff top and down the slope on the right, past the cave.

12 Left Twin Chimney . . . . Diff
16m. The left-hand chimney has some grass, a collection of jammed blocks and a grubby finish - but at least it's a good line.

13 Right Twin Chimney . . . . HVD
16m. The gradually widening and rather scruffy right-hand chimney is included out of historical interest - 1902!
FA. E.A.Baker 1902

To the right is the fine tall buttress of Tower Face, and the best route on the cliff.

14 Tower Face . . . . . . Top 50 VS 5a
18m. A great pitch, long interesting and very photogenic - the walk is worth it just to do this route. From the cave, pull onto the face (massive thread) then climb the centre of the face trending slightly left until it is possible to step back right to the well-positioned final crack. *Photo on page 190.*
FA. Harry Kelly 1916

Laddow Cave Crack

15 Modern Times E3 5c
18m. An interesting eliminate. Climb the steep right-hand side of the lower wall to mid-height then move left to climb through the overhangs and finish up the left-hand arete in a fine position.
FA. Steve Bancroft 1986

16 Tower Arete .... HVS 5a
18m. The exciting right-hand side of the arete is followed in its entirety and is more strenuous than you might expect.
FA. Albert Hargreaves 1927

17 North Climb .... VDiff
16m. Take the big groove over easy ground to a possible stance. From a thread in the chimney, shuffle left to reach and finish up the other chimney. Traversing further left is the wild **Pongo Finish**. This is better, a little harder and more exposed.

18 North Wall .... HS 4b
16m. Climb the right edge of *North Climb's* groove to the capping overhang and pass this via the steep crack and a beefy move. A stance is available on the left below the roof if the leader needs it.

19 Cave Arete .... VS 4b
16m. Follow the scoop delicately out right to the arete and climb to a ledge (possible belay). Take the hugely-exposed top pitch of *Cave Crack* to finish, or creep out right at the roof as for the *Indirect*.

On the far right-hand end of the cliff is a shallow cave much used as a bivouac by the ancients. There are several venerable outings based around this uncomfortable grotto.

Tower Face

Descent

Bivi-cave

Cave Crack **Laddow** 211

Steve Warwick and Russ Clare on the 2nd pitch of the very long *Long Climb* (S) - *page 208* - Laddow.

20 Cave Arete Indirect . E1 5b
18m. Climb the left wall of the cave to a good spike, swing round the arete and climb to ledges and a stance (5a). Head up the corner to the roof, step left and pull over rapidly to access the easier head wall - wild!
FA. Ivar Berg 1916. The first E1 ever climbed.

21 Cave Crack. . . . . . . HVS 5a
18m. Climb into the top of the cave and pull onto the face (the spinning chock can be jammed with crafty use of a sling) then climb to a ledge (possible belay). Climb the corner to the huge roof then skip left and pull over its edge to easier ground.
FA. Ivar Berg 1916

22 Cave Crack Indirect. . . . . S 4a
18m. Start on the right and slant left to join *Cave Crack* above its cave. Continue to the ledge (stance and belay), then follow the groove to the roof and traverse right to escape.

Tintwistle Knarr Quarry

	No star	★	★★	★★★
Mod to S	-	-	-	-
HS to HVS	3	4	3	-
E1 to E3	1	5	3	1
E4 and up	1	2	2	-

A fine but sadly neglected quarry in an impressive setting with a superb outward view towards the wastes of Bleaklow and the proud buttress of Shining Clough lurking in the shadows. The crag has an excellent set of crack climbs and although the walk up tends to put people off, the effort made to get here is usually repaid in full. There are a dozen routes in the shorter left-hand bay but these are not described here. The Central Bay is better, though turf tufts manage to sprout from the most inconvenient of places; please remove any grass you pass in an attempt to keep these great routes clean enough to be climbed. *The Arete* (E2) is especially fine and is worth the walk up alone, as are the classic layback flakes of *The Cornflake* (VS) and the superb finger-wrecking crack of *Kershaw's Krackers* (HVS). The deep groove of *The Old Triangle* (HVS) is also a classic line, well worth doing, though it does take drainage, and next to it the excellent blunt arete of *Sinn Fein* (E3) is only for the really bold.

Approach   Also see map on page 158

There is parking for half a dozen cars on the northern side of the A628 road by the edge of the conifer forest and above the reservoir. A good track (the old quarry road) starts at the gate and weaves up the hill to enter the forest and then continues rightwards to end in front of the Central Bay of the quarry; a steady 20 minutes from the car. Leave nothing of value in the vehicle.

Conditions

The quarry is south-facing and gets all the sun that is going, though it takes quite a bit of drainage from the moor behind. Like nearby Laddow, the grass is gradually taking over the place, choking the cracks, covering the ledges and holding moisture so that over time the whole place becomes slower and slower to dry. With a bit more traffic, the best of the climbs here would be rivals to many of Millstone's most popular outings - helping to spread the load a little. A big hats-off to the anonymous soul who cleaned the ledges above *Cornflake*, and the grooves below them - good effort!

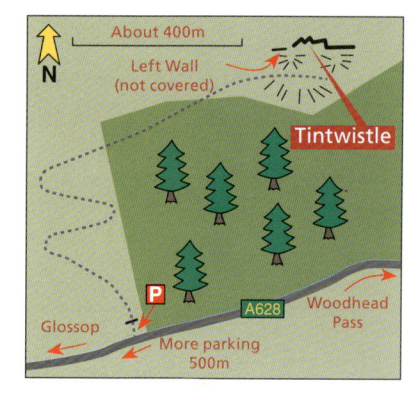

Climbers tackling *The Old Triangle* (HVS) - *page 214* - at Tintwistle. Photo: Philip Ashton

Tintwistle Knarr Quarry — Main Bay

Main Bay

The central section of the quarry is dominated by the prominent feature of *The Arete*, the best route here. Much of the rock is excellent, though the encroaching vegetation is slowly claiming it back.

1 Levl — E2 5b
18m. Climb the slab to its left arete, step back into the centre and finish with increasing apprehension. Neglected, which is a pity. The name is not a misprint, apparently LEVL means smooth.
FA. Mike Simpkins 1962

2 Leprechaun — VS 4c
18m. The groove reached from the left is quite worthwhile but has a crusty finish. Sadly it is rather overgrown at present.
FA. John Gosling 1962

3 Scimitar — HVS 5b
20m. Cut up to the thin curving crack and follow it into and up the groove at its end.
FA. Mike Simpkins 1962

4 Poteen — E1 5b
20m. Stagger up the long right-facing corner/groove. It is worthwhile and proves to be hard work at the overhang.
FA. Mike Simpkins 1962

5 Sinn Fein — E3 5c
22m. Serious and scary. Climb the rib on the left and then the crack on the right to a flaky overlap. Pull over this and step left to a spike where a gripping mantel gains the final slab.
FA. Mike Simpkins 1962

6 The Old Triangle — HVS 5a
24m. Sustained climbing up the long deep groove leads to a big triangular roof. The most popular exit is to teeter right (**4c**) although going left is a harder and more strenuous option (**5a**).
Photo on page 213.
FA. Joe Brown 1951

← - - Descent

Scimitar

The Arete

Main Bay **Tintwistle Knarr Quarry** 215

7 Nil Carborundum Illigitimum E3 5c
22m. The smooth face has good moves but is serious and devious. There may be one peg runner in place. It really needs a direct finish.
FA. Loz Francomb 1979

8 The Arete .... Top 50 E2 5c
22m. The best route here and worth calling in for. Delicate, sustained and elegant moves throughout with enough gear to allow the experience to be enjoyed to the full.
FA. Pete Crew (2 pegs) 1962. FFA. John Allen 1973

The huge grassy and obiously loose groove to the right is Shillelah Groove HVS 5a, the only route in the 1990 guide to get the dreaded 'black spot' - you have been warned!

9 The Little Spillikin E3 6a
22m. Climb thin cracks right of the grassy groove then move out right and climb the shallow groove to a rather unstable exit.
FA. John Gosling 1959. FFA. John Regan 1977

10 O'Grady's Incurable Itch E6 7a
22m. Climb *Little Spillikin* to the traverse then, with gear on the right (wires and RPs), climb the centre of the wall up and left via a hard sequence to better holds. Grade unconfirmed though it is reported as being pretty blank!
FA. Andy Stewart 1999

11 Gobbin Groove .... VS 4c
22m. The delightfully-named long main angle is cleaner than it has been for years (decades even!). Follow it to a finish up the flake on the left at the top.
FA. Mike Simpkins 1962

12 Eireborne E2 5c
22m. Start up Gobbin Groove but follow a ramp out onto the right wall. Climb this to ledges and carefully finish up the sharp arete.
FA. Al Parker 1985 after Keith Ashton had taken a big flier off it.

13 Kershaw's Krackers. E1 5c
22m. The finger-knackering cracks are climbed in three stages with the initial section being the most testing. One of the purest finger-cracks around and excellent (but excruciating) sport.
FA. Barry Kershaw 1958

Tintwistle Knarr Quarry — Main Bay - Right

14 Stiff Little Fingers — E1 5b
22m. The elegant arete is escapable but worth sticking with. Runners can be placed to the left without too much difficulty.
FA. Malc Baxter 1989

15 Cornflake — VS 4c
22m. The long left-hand flake gives great laybacking to its top from where easy ground leads to the cliff top.
FA. Mike Simpkins 1962

16 Soapflake — VS 4c
22m. The right-hand flake is also well worth doing if you enjoy the style of climbing. Again finish up the cleaned ledges.
FA. Mike Simpkins 1962

17 Knobblekerry Corner — VS 4c
22m. The long groove in the angle of the bay is strenuous and sustained, even if you use the bar for support. Climb the wide left-hand crack, then the right-hand one. At its top, swing left with difficulty and escape up ledges.
FA. Joe Brown 1951

18 Nosey Parker — E4 6a
22m. Climb the tough crack in the side-wall (well-protected but exhausting) then swing left to a rest in the main groove. Pull up and right to climb the desperately-thin crack that splits the final short but impending wall.
FA. Al Parker (3 points) 1973. FFA. Steve Bancroft 1980

19 Black Michael — VS 4c
22m. The chimney-crack gives a good struggle up to ledges on the arete. Climb left then right to vegetated ledges then escape from here with care.
FA. Graham West 1958

Right Bay — Tintwistle Knarr Quarry — 217

20 Good Things Come To Those Who Wait — E3 5c
26m. Follows the edge of the steep tower left of *Guns and Drums*. Start to the left of a green wall and climb up and right on pockets, and then the overhanging wall above to a ledge and flake. Go up the left-hand side of the tower (peg) with a spectacular finish rocking right onto the airy arete.
FA. Andy Stewart 1999

21 Guns and Drums — E4 6a
26m. Climb a shallow groove until flakes on the right can be reached; follow these to the break. Climb the blank groove (old peg and Friend in a slot) and the bulge to a crusty finish. *Wall and Groove* makes a better start to the route.
FA. Jim Moran 1983

22 Wall and Groove — HVS 5a
26m. An early attempt on this part of the face, and a good line despite suffering from grass-itis. Climb the steep flake-crack to the break then traverse left to below the base of the shallow open groove. A short pumpy wall gives access to floral climbing in the groove above.
FA. Mike Simpkins 1962

Right Bay
The right-hand section sees even less action than the rest of the quarry - which is saying something! There are some worthwhile climbs here, a couple of which have been given a bit of a spruce up lately. Despite this the routes are probably best enjoyed after a quick abseil to remove the worst of the shrubbery.

23 The Peace Process — E5 6b
26m. Layback up the fin right of *Guns and Drums* to the overhang. Slap up for a ledge and peg runner. Continue with fingery and reachy moves, past another peg as far as the last hold on the blank wall. Escape right to the arete and scramble up steep grass to finish.
FA. Andy Stewart 1999

24 Fenian Wall — E4 6a
12m. The steep and strenuous crack leads via pushy climbing to the break. The wall above is also hard but turns rapidly to easy ground and yet more grass scrambling.
FA. Mike Simpkins 1960s. FFA. Jim Moran 1983

25 Republic Groove — HVS 5a
12m. Climb the acutely overhanging groove that bounds the wall on the right until forced out right. Take the short corner then graze-away to the cliff top.
FA. Mike Simpkins 1962

Hobson Moor Quarry

	No star	★	★★	★★★
Mod to S	3	1	-	-
HS to HVS	5	5	1	2
E1 to E3	2	7	4	1
E4 and up	1	5	4	-

Chris Moor tackling *Gideon* (HVS) - *page 222* - in Hobson Moor Quarry. Photo: Nick Smith

Hobson Moor Quarry 219

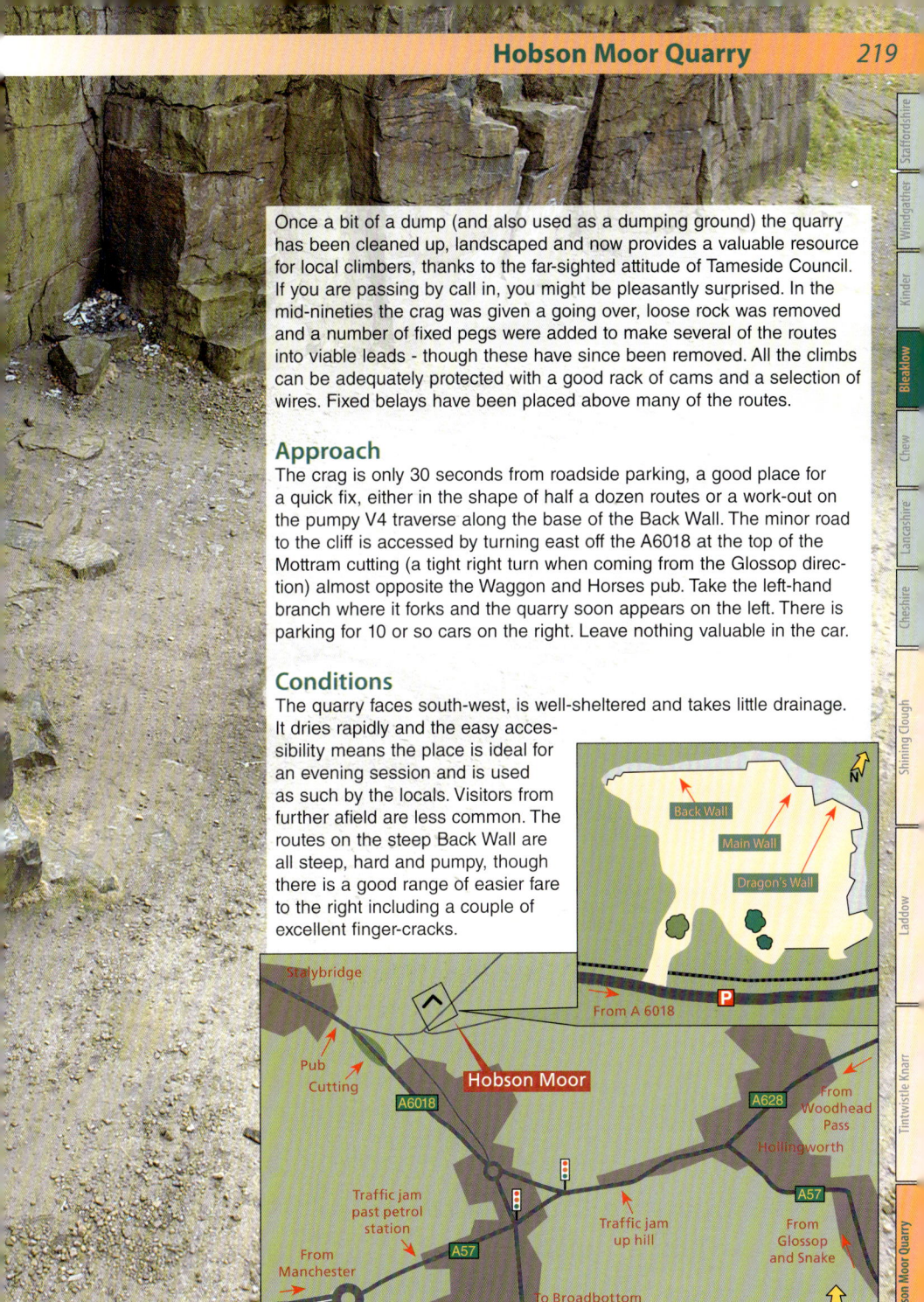

Once a bit of a dump (and also used as a dumping ground) the quarry has been cleaned up, landscaped and now provides a valuable resource for local climbers, thanks to the far-sighted attitude of Tameside Council. If you are passing by call in, you might be pleasantly surprised. In the mid-nineties the crag was given a going over, loose rock was removed and a number of fixed pegs were added to make several of the routes into viable leads - though these have since been removed. All the climbs can be adequately protected with a good rack of cams and a selection of wires. Fixed belays have been placed above many of the routes.

Approach
The crag is only 30 seconds from roadside parking, a good place for a quick fix, either in the shape of half a dozen routes or a work-out on the pumpy V4 traverse along the base of the Back Wall. The minor road to the cliff is accessed by turning east off the A6018 at the top of the Mottram cutting (a tight right turn when coming from the Glossop direction) almost opposite the Waggon and Horses pub. Take the left-hand branch where it forks and the quarry soon appears on the left. There is parking for 10 or so cars on the right. Leave nothing valuable in the car.

Conditions
The quarry faces south-west, is well-sheltered and takes little drainage. It dries rapidly and the easy accessibility means the place is ideal for an evening session and is used as such by the locals. Visitors from further afield are less common. The routes on the steep Back Wall are all steep, hard and pumpy, though there is a good range of easier fare to the right including a couple of excellent finger-cracks.

Hobson Moor Quarry — Back Wall

① Back Wall Traverse V4 (6a)
The most popular route in the quarry! Traverse the Back Wall, starting on the left, all the way to ledges on the right. Well-pumpy and mighty long. Even better, it can be used as the start to girdling the whole quarry - how much time have you got?

② Eastern Touch E4 6a
14m. Climb past a hanging crack to a niche then head left via a hidden crack to a ledge. Climb up past two good pockets and finish through a shallow niche (2 peg runners).
FA. Sid Siddiqui 1992

③ Apres Midi E2 5c
14m. Use a pocket to reach the horizontal, step right then climb leftwards to a groove and finish up this, or its left arete - loose.
FA. Malc Baxter (solo) 1986

④ Wanna Buy a Bolt Kit? E4 6b
16m. The old peg crack is followed until it fades, step left and power up the wall, following the pale streak, to finish through the overlaps.
FA. Nick Plishko 1982

⑤ Heatwave E2 5c
18m. Climb into the open groove and follow it (peg) past the overhang to an awkward exit. Pumpy and with a wild finish.
FA. Al Evans 1989

⑥ Hanging Slab E2 5b
18m. Take the flake to its end then finish direct. The route is low in the grade and has good gear most of the way but the finish feels bold and also a bit crusty.
FA. Malc Baxter (1 peg) 1959. FFA. Loz Francomb 1979

⑦ Crock's Climb E1 5b
18m. Climb steeply to ledges which are followed diagonally rightwards to finish up the groove.
FA. Malc Baxter 1975

⑧ The Heat is On E4 6b
18m. Follow *Fingertip Control* but head up and left to a ledge on *Crock's Climb*. Follow the twin cracks above and finish over a small overhang (peg).
FA. Sid Siddiqui 1992

Descent

Back Wall
An excellent wall but not very popular. It might be because the routes are hard and there is little of quality below E4. The *Back Wall Traverse* sees lots of attention but once you put your head above this chalk-line, you are on your own!

Back Wall   **Hobson Moor Quarry**   221

9 Fingertip Control... E5 6b
18m. Climb the steep wall from left to right by sustained and fingery moves. 3 peg runners protect one of the better routes in the quarry.
FA. Sid Siddiqui 1992

10 Gable End E5 6a
18m. The left-hand of the parallel cracks gives fierce finger-jamming to an easy final groove.
FA. (as Rainstorm) Malc Baxter 1961 FFA. Gabe Regan 1976

11 Hobson's Choice... E5 6b
18m. The right-hand parallel crack is more technical and more sustained than its near neighbour.
FA. Greg Rimmer 1989

12 Great Expectations E3 5c
18m. Climb the leaning groove to the break. Continue up and right then scale the crucial final wall (peg runner). Good honest hard work. The finish is often sandy.
FA. Chris Hardy 1988

Warning - several of these routes have old peg runners - back them up!

13 Monsoon E1 5b
18m. Climb the flake to the large dubious-looking block just above the break, and finish direct up crusty rock.
FA. Al Evans 1989

14 Raindrop E4 6a
18m. The rib/groove and crack lead to the break. A hard move gains a flake (peg) then move right to finish up a groove.
FA. Dougie Hall 1982

15 The Scythe...... E2 5c
18m. Climb *Raindrop* to the ledge then follow the flake as it runs out right to a hard (and grotty) exit.
FA. Dave Knighton 1977

16 Sunshine Super Glue... E3 6a
18m. Climb the middle of the wall past a glued side-pull to a peg runner. Join the right-trending flake on *The Scythe* and pull over an overlap to reach a second peg and a steep finish.
FA. Sid Siddiqui 1992

17 Bring Me Sunshine E1 5b
16m. Climb the wall left of the big groove up flakes to ledges. Step right and climb the exposed arete. Low in the grade but both the rock and the gear leave a bit to be desired!
FA. Harry Venables 1988

Descent

Great Expectations

Hobson Moor Quarry — Main Wall

Main Wall
A less impressive wall than the Back Wall but with more amenable grades including the worthwhile mini-classics of *Parker's Eliminate* and *Crew's Route*.

1 Epitaph Corner . . . . **HS 4b**
14m. The main groove gives a reasonable, well-protected pitch.
FA. Paul Nunn 1960

2 Sunshine Superman . . . **E2 5b**
14m. The wall right of the corner is climbed via a boulder problem up a flake. The upper section is bolder and creaky. A runner can be placed in *Parker's*, lowering the grade a notch.
FA. Phil Booth late 1970s

3 Parker's Eliminate . . . . Top 50 **HVS 5a**
14m. The crack in the centre of the wall cuts through an overlap and is a well-protected gem. The best in the quarry and the equal of Millstone's HVS classics, well almost! A nice first HVS.
FA. Al Parker 1957. FFA. Al Parker 1960

4 Gideon . . . . **HVS 5a**
14m. Balance up the steep arete to reach a short (and narrow!) jamming-crack. Finish up the left-hand side of the final arete.
Photo on page 218.
FA. Paul Nunn 1960

5 Basic Training **E6 7a**
12m. The centre of the wall has a fierce direct start, often avoided by a traverse in from the left. Continue direct passing the large chunk of rust to hard final moves.
FA. Basic Nick Plishko (solo) 1982

6 Gideonite . . . . **HVS 5a**
14m. The large groove leads by oddly technical trickery to a ledge, harder than it looks. Finish up the easy corner behind.
FA. Malc Baxter (2 pegs) 1960 FFA. Jim Campbell 1976

7 Crew's Route . . . . **VS 4c**
12m. The crack gives a good and well-protected pitch. The final overlap can be climbed direct, or bypassed slightly more easily.
FA. Pete Crew 1960

8 Peak Arete **E1 5a**
12m. The arete is followed throughout and is steep and quite precarious. A semi-crucial finger-jam is easily blocked by an indifferent (and rather low) runner, or should you just solo it?
FA. Tom Ellison 1958

9 Steve's Dilemma **E2 6a**
12m. Start just right of the arete and make fingery pocket moves up and rightwards to pass the bulge, where reachy and blind moves reach easier ground. Can be gritty. Finishing up the brittle arete on the right adds a touch of excitement.
FA. Steve Bancroft 1980

10 Evening Ridge . . . . **S 4a**
14m. Climb the groove to a ledge and then the loose flakes to access the right edge a hanging slab. Cross this diagonally leftwards to a ledge and stance. Finish up the corner.
FA. Paul Nunn 1957

11 Midnight Variation . . . . **HS 4a**
12m. From the ledge on the previous route, step right and climb the steep groove throughout, or the narrow wall to its left.
FA. Paul Nunn 1957

Dragon's Wall **Hobson Moor Quarry** 223

12 Dragon's Route....... E2 5c
14m. The thin left-hand crack leads to a break, step left and power up the crusty flake. Strenuous but not too technical.
FA. Loz Francomb 1979

13 Scale the Dragon .. E4 6a
14m. Start right of *Dragon's Route* and crimp to the break then climb powerfully up the shallow groove in the centre of the wall, passing good gear in the break with difficulty. The best route on the wall, but beware the final moves.
FA. Jim Burton (with peg runners) 1992

14 Drizzle....... E2 6a
14m. The groove on the right leads to a break from where technical, strenuous and reachy moves allow the wall to be climbed rapidly. Originally given a pretty hard HVS.
FA. Loz Francomb 1979

15 Drought......... E4 6a
14m. The thin crack left of the groove corner leads to a worrying pull to the horizontal. The move over the overlap is not as blank as it looks, but is still strenuous and the upper wall is easier.
FA. Jim Burton (with peg runners) 1992

16 Foghorn Groove ...... VS 4c
14m. The leaning corner is pleasant if somewhat creaky and is good practice for bigger, looser things! Small wires useful.
FA. Graham West 1959

17 Wind Instrument........ E1 5b
14m. The interesting narrow wall just right on disposable holds.

18 The Harp .... HS 4b
14m. Balance up the wall trending right to a dubious overlap. Pull over this and finish easily. Not too hard or well-travelled, but have your belayer stand aside – just in case!
FA. Al Parker 1957 FFA. Al Parker 1960

Dragon's Wall
The right-hand side of the quarry has some quality routes before the walls diminish to bouldering stature. Once fitted with peg runners, these have been been removed though the climbs remain viable leads with Friends in the various horizontal breaks. There are old bolt and stake belays on the flat rocky ledges above all of these climbs.

19 Pocket Wall .... VDiff
10m. The narrow face has the expected pocket and makes a good warm-up solo, or a well-protected lead for the timid.
FA. Malc Baxter 1956

20 Tighe's Arete E1 5a
12m. The arete is delicate and quite low in the grade. A semi-crucial Friend in the rather shallow slot gets in the way a little, though another out right (and off route?) doesn't!
FA. Trevor Tighe 1968

21 Ledge Way............... HS 4b
12m. Climb the arete but move right to the ledge of the Amphitheatre. A slim groove on the left-hand side of the wall provides an exit.
FA. Paul Nunn 1957

22 Grain of Sand.......... VS 5a
12m. The bulging centre of the wall to the ledge then the face just right of the upper groove. A bit of and eliminate.
FA. Malc Baxter 1959

23 Amphitheatre Climb .... VDiff
10m. A short steep crack leads to the ledge and a final groove.
FA. Al Parker 1957

24 Heather Corner........... VDiff
10m. The final groove of any consequence and the stepped arete directly above it are lacking in heather nowadays.
FA. Malc Baxter 1956

Chew Valley panorama from Alderman.

Upperwood Quarry
Standing Stones
Ravenstones

Den Lane
Diggle
Running Hill Pits
Church Inn
Cross Keys Inn
Uppermill
A670
Upperwood
A635
Holmfirth
Standing Stones
Binn Green picnic site
Alderman
Dovestones
Ravenstones
Greenfield
Bank Lane
Clarence Hotel
Wimberry boulders
Charnel Stones
Oldham Way
Wimberry
Rob's Rocks
Path to Laddow
Wilderness Rocks

Labels on upper photo: Dovestones Edge, Dovestones Quarries, Charnel Stones, Rob's Rocks, Wimberry, Yacht Club car park, Binn Green car park

Chew Valley

It's the early bird .... Wimberry bathed in morning sunshine (5:30 a.m.)

Wimberry

	No star	★	★★	★★★
Mod to S	5	5	1	2
HS to HVS	6	3	6	4
E1 to E3	3	8	7	3
E4 and up	4	7	7	7

Wimberry is the best of the fine set of cliffs in the Chew Valley, the Cinderella of Peak grit, an unsung gem of a crag with a fantastic collection of routes on an impressive series of buttresses in a dramatic setting, and with superb outward views. The down side (there just had to be one) is that the crag faces north and the approach is a bit of a flog. Choose your conditions carefully though and you will be rewarded; here is a superb set of arduous cracks and some thrilling face climbs. The cracks in particular have always had a reputation for being sternly graded - we upgraded several of these last time around and have had few complaints although *Freddie's Finale* appears to be one of those yo-yo routes - now back at HVS! The face climbs include some of the best and hardest in the Peak, though they see a lot less attention then their smaller brethren on Burbage South. It has been said that if the cliff faced south it would be regarded as one of the best gritstone cliffs in the country.

There is some great bouldering at Wimberry on the boulders passed on the approach walk.

Approach   Also see map on page 224

There is extensive parking (Pay and Display - weekends only) below the huge dam that holds back the Dovestone Reservoir. A metalled road leads past the sailing club boathouse then at the bridge across Chew Brook take the path rightwards into the the trees. This passes through the bouldering area and then starts a steady flog up the side of the stream to reach the left-hand side of the cliff in about 30 minutes from the car. The final ascent is a good test of stamina.

Conditions

North facing, the cliff is not a winter venue, as it stays green for much of the rainy season. Despite this it does dry quickly, is well-sheltered from southwesterly winds and forms a great venue on hot summer days, although be wary of the midge factor especially when conditions are calm. Grades here are given for perfect conditions and although the superb roughness of the rock can compensate for the green conditions that are prevalent for much of the year, the grades might feel a little stiff at other times.

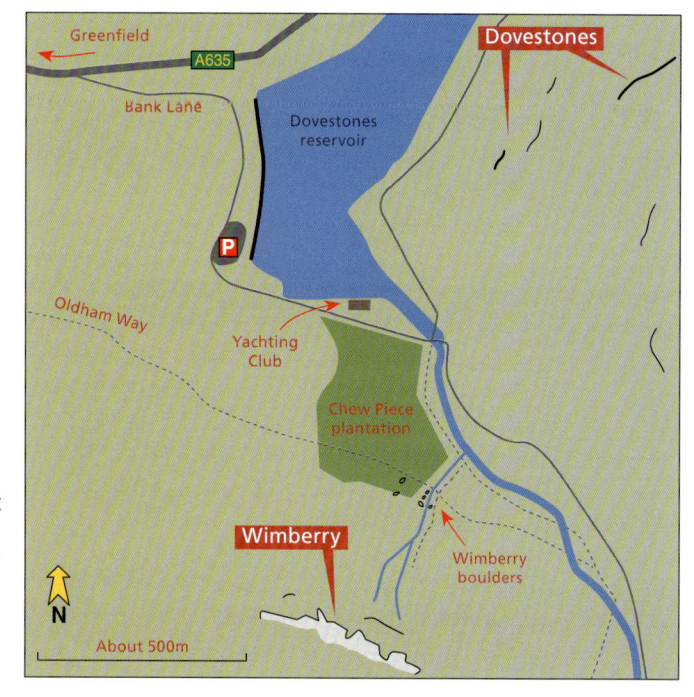

Will Wykes climbing *Blasphemy* (E2) - *page 231* - at Wimberry. Photo: John Coefield

228 Wimberry — Freddie's Finale

1 Thermometer Crack · · · · VS 4c
8m. On the far left is a leaning crack which gives good jamming and laybacking. A good one for steamy summer days.

2 Crack and Slab · · · · · · · · S 4a
8m. From the foot of the chimney, slant left up the slab to enter and climb the groove at its apex. Not very rewarding.

3 Short Crack · · · · · · · · VS 5a
8m. The bulging chimney and narrower crack above gives technical but well-protected bridging.

4 Pinball Wizard · · · · E1 5b
8m. Follow the finger-crack then the middle of the wall above (slightly bold) on small finger holds, trending leftwards. Said by some to be easier than the walk-in!
FA. Steve Bancroft 1972

5 Blind Faith · · · · · · · · E2 5c
8m. The arete has one hard move and then eases with height.
FA. Chris Hardy 1984

6 Eight Metre Corner · · · · · · · Diff
25ft. The deepening angular groove is pleasant enough.

7 Poltergeist · · · · · · · · · · · · · · VS 4b
10m. The arete left of the chimney requires tricky balance moves to reach the hanging crack above (and its chockstones).

8 Blocked Chimney · · · · · · · · VDiff
10m. Climb the chimney to its blockage and an escape left.

9 Arete du Coeur · · · · · · · · · · E4 5c
10m. A bold arete is climbed direct and requires a heart-in-mouth approach. There is some gear but you need know how to find it.
FA. J.Fletcher 1979

10 Ornithologist's Corner · · VS 5a
12m. Great (and avoidable) jamming up the crack above the approach path with a strenuous finale around the overhang.

11 Surprise Arete · · · · HVS 4c
12m. The delicate arete on its right-hand side to the break then move left to finish up the crack. Harder for the short.
FA. Brian Toase 1970

12 One-way Ticket · · · · · · · E2 5b
12m. The direct finish up the arete is bold.

13 Surprise · · · · · · · · · · · · · VS 4b
14m. Climb the flaky crack leftwards then follow the groove to interesting moves past the neb.

14 The Yellow-bellied Gonk · · E4 6a
10m. Climb the bulging arete to a break then pull onto the upper slab with difficulty.
FA. Kevin Thaw 1982

15 Overhanging Chimney · · · · · VDiff
12m. The leaning and narrowing chimney is steep and awkward as far as the thread, then easier above.
FA. Anton Stoop 1910

16 Freddie's Finale · · · Top 50 · HVS 5b
14m. Fist-jamming at its best (not the contradiction in terms non-gritstoner's might imagine). Large gear is a must. Climb through the intimidating overhang to an uncomfortable niche then fist-jam and flail until the crack narrows and easier ground gives you a chance to survey the damage!
FA. Joe Brown, Fred Ashton 1948

Freddie's Finale

The left-hand side of the cliff has a fine selection of jamming cracks and is a good place to get a feel for the crag and the style of climbing. *Freddie's Finale* is one of the classic hand and fist cracks of the Peak.

Hanging Groove **Wimberry** 229

17 Double Take E6 6b
18m. The first of the E-big-numbers. Climb through the first overhang of *Freddie's* then swing right along the break to gain the arete. Slap up this passing the overhang with difficulty. Finish more easily up the superb ramp-in-space. Three ropes (and an RP2) might help just a little.
FA. Dougie Hall 1987

18 Wimberry Overhang ... E6 6c
18m. Leap through the centre of the overhangs (2 ancient peg runners may be in place) to gain the hanging slab and an easier finish up the well-positioned ramp above. The loss of a block and peg runner in 2007 may have made the start harder. The block hit the unfortunate leader on the head and gave him a cracked skull!

19 Space Oddity E5 6c
16m. Starting left of the groove, move up and traverse left on the lip of the overhang to below a thin crack. Climb this (fingery) to the second horizontal then follow the blunt arete above initially on its right and finally on its left. The slab above is easier.
FA. Dougie Hall 1987

20 Space Shuffle E4 6a
22m. Wild and with a lot of shuffling to keep you on your toes! From the second thread in *Hanging Groove* tiptoe out left above the overhangs all the way to the distant arete and a finish up a short hanging ramp on the very edge of the world - wild!
FA. Mike Chapman 1983

21 Hanging Groove .... VS 4c
16m. Climb steeply and strenuously into the well-named feature, pass the chockstones awkwardly and finish more easily up the left-trending ramp. Often green but not unpleasantly so.

22 Hanging Groove Variations . VS 4c
16m. As for the normal route to the ledge then gain the upper groove on the right using a dynamic approach. Follow this to the top in a fine position. There were other variations to the left but these have been absorbed into the hard routes.

23 Order of the Phoenix E8 6c
Climb desperately through the stepped overhangs onto the front of the buttress until things ease in the shallow scoop. A runner in the base of *Coffin Crack* protects the start.
FA. Kevin Thaw 2003. The upper part is The Bad Attitude Brothers (E3 6a) (FA. Steven Delderfield 1990s)

24 Coffin Crack ...... VS 4c
16m. Climb the wide fissure past the coffin-shaped recess. Holds on the right allow some rather frantic laybacking to reach the easier upper crack.

Hanging Groove
The bulging buttress to the right of *Freddie's Finale* has several superb hard routes with steep starts and delicate finishes. Further right are two more of Wimberry's fine wide crack climbs - *Hanging Groove* and *Coffin Crack*.

Wimberry The Trident

❶ Berlin Wall   E6 6c
24m. From the recess on *Coffin Crack* teeter right onto the wall to a pocket. Traverse right again and continue direct in an ever-more committing position to a loose flake in the roof. Traverse right to escape up *The Trident*. Protection includes a (long) hand-placed peg early on and some ancient bolts before things ease.
FA. Nick Plishko 1987

❷ Sectioned   E8 6c
24m. The direct line through the bulge and up the pebbled centre of the wall to the twin pockets common with all the wall's routes. The first ascensionist choose to finish up *Neptunes' Tool's* as he felt this was most fitting. Gear was placed "way right" at the start so as to pull the leader away from the blocks on the terrace!
FA. Kevin Thaw 2004

❸ Neptune's Tool   E6 6c
20m. From the foot of *The Trident* gain and follow the curving flake leftwards out into the middle of the wall (good gear - very hard to place) and climb this trending left again to the edge of the huge overhang and an easier finish. Maybe only 6b for the tall.
FA. Nick Plishko 1986. A 'short' stick was used to place a crucial runner.

❹ Wristcutter's Lullaby   Top 50   E6 6c
22m. Magnificent and high in the grade. Follow *Neptune's Tool* to the centre of the wall then climb straight up the face on pebbles to the roofs. Cross these (a couple of very old bolts can be clipped) finishing leftwards once above the lip. Only 6b for the tall.
FA. (as Desecration)1964. FFA. Nick Plishko 1987

❺ Desecration   E4 6a
28m. An exciting crossing of the face. From the block on *The Trident* climb down and left to a small ledge then follow poor holds delicately all the way to a finish up *Coffin Crack*. Bold and technical, not for faint-hearted seconds.
FA. Jonny Woodward 1982

❻ The Trident   Top 50   E1 5b
20m. Western Grit's tough answer to *The Peapod*; a classic struggle but a classic nonetheless. The narrow central section is an uphill battle especially for those who are large in the chest or short in the arm! The final section gives glorious jamming.
FA. Joe Brown 1948

❼ MaDMAn   E8 6b
20m. The bald blunt and imposing arete to the right of *The Trident* is hard, harrowing and unprotected as far as it goes. If you get that far, move left to finish up *The Trident*. Another desperate outing that is probably unrepeated, the Direct Finish awaits.
FA. Dave Pegg 1990s

The Trident
The smooth wall capped by impressive overhangs is home to some superb hard routes including the mega-classic *Wristcutter's Lullaby*. As ever the cracks between the blank sections providing easier challenges with the *The Trident* and *Bertie's Bugbear* being the pick. Further right is the fine crack of *Blasphemy* and its excellent left-hand finish - *Piety*. *Blue Light's Crack* may not appeal to all but it is a striking line.

The Trident Wimberry 231

8 Cheltenham Gold Cup . . . E5 6c
20m. The left wall of *Bertie's Bugbear* is fiercely technical, especially getting into the shallow groove in the centre of the face. From the top of the groove trend left up easier ground. Often dirty.
FA. Nick Plishko 1985

9 Bertie's Bugbear. . . . . S 4a
18m. The best lower-grade route on the cliff climbs the huge central groove. The crucial bulge is climbed using a highly suspicious looking foothold on the left wall. Excellent stuff.
FA. Anton Stoop 1910

10 Sickbay Shuffle . . . E3 5b
22m. A terrifying crab-wise expedition across the right-hand wall of the big groove. Protection in the gully becomes increasingly useless, then sprint up the final arete. Gibber, gibber.
FA. Nick Plishko 1987

11 Thorn in the Side-wall. . . . E5 6a
18m. The right-hand wall of *Bertie's* leads to the traverse of *Sickbay Shuffle*, then finishing direct. Somehow side-runners will need to be placed en-route though there are some teeny cams to be had too on the line.
FA. Nick Plishko 1987

12 Blasphemy. . . . . Top 50 E2 5c
14m. A superb outing with quality finger-jamming. Gain the sinuous crack from the large block in the corner. Where the crack ends, transfer onto the final slab by a tricky mantelshelf - on the left or right though, which is best? *Photo on page 227.*
FA. Graham West late 1950s. FFA. John Allen 1973

13 Piety. E2 5c
20m. Bold, delicate and superb. Climb the crack of *Blasphemy* until a delicate scoop leads out left to the arete. Step round the exposed corner, move up and immediately step back right onto an easier slab. Watch that rope drag!
FA. Ian Carr 1982

14 Blue Light's Crack. E1 5b
16m. The wide corner is a titanic struggle for most, wedging-away up is the only option, though macho-men with strong arms and little imagination can layback - though they may well end up regretting it as the top approaches. Said by some to make *Freddie's Finale* look like a soft touch and another ancient HVS! **Green Streak, HVS 5a -** For those who haven't had enough make a hand-traverse right to reach the hanging crack - adds half a star.
FA. Don Whillans 1948. FA. (Green Streak) Steve Bancroft 1973

15 The Possessed . . . E7 6b
20m. A desperate direct on *Sacrilege*. Start up a hairline crack (RPs) and gain a broad scoop. Crimp the faint rib on the right to gain the break of *Sacrilege* up which the route finishes.
FA. Dave Pegg 1990

16 Sacrilege. E2 5c
26m. Climb the chimney for 8m to access the imposing crack in the left wall. Plug in a sustained series of solid jams (except when green) to final tricky moves way out left.
FA. Tony Howard 1963. FFA. Martin Berzins 1978

17 Starvation Chimney. . . . S 3c
18m. A (not very) subtle blend of climbing and caving. The compelling narrow rift to a tight exit through the cliff. Speaking as one who emerged trouserless from its clutches the climb is well worth exploring.

Wimberry Route I

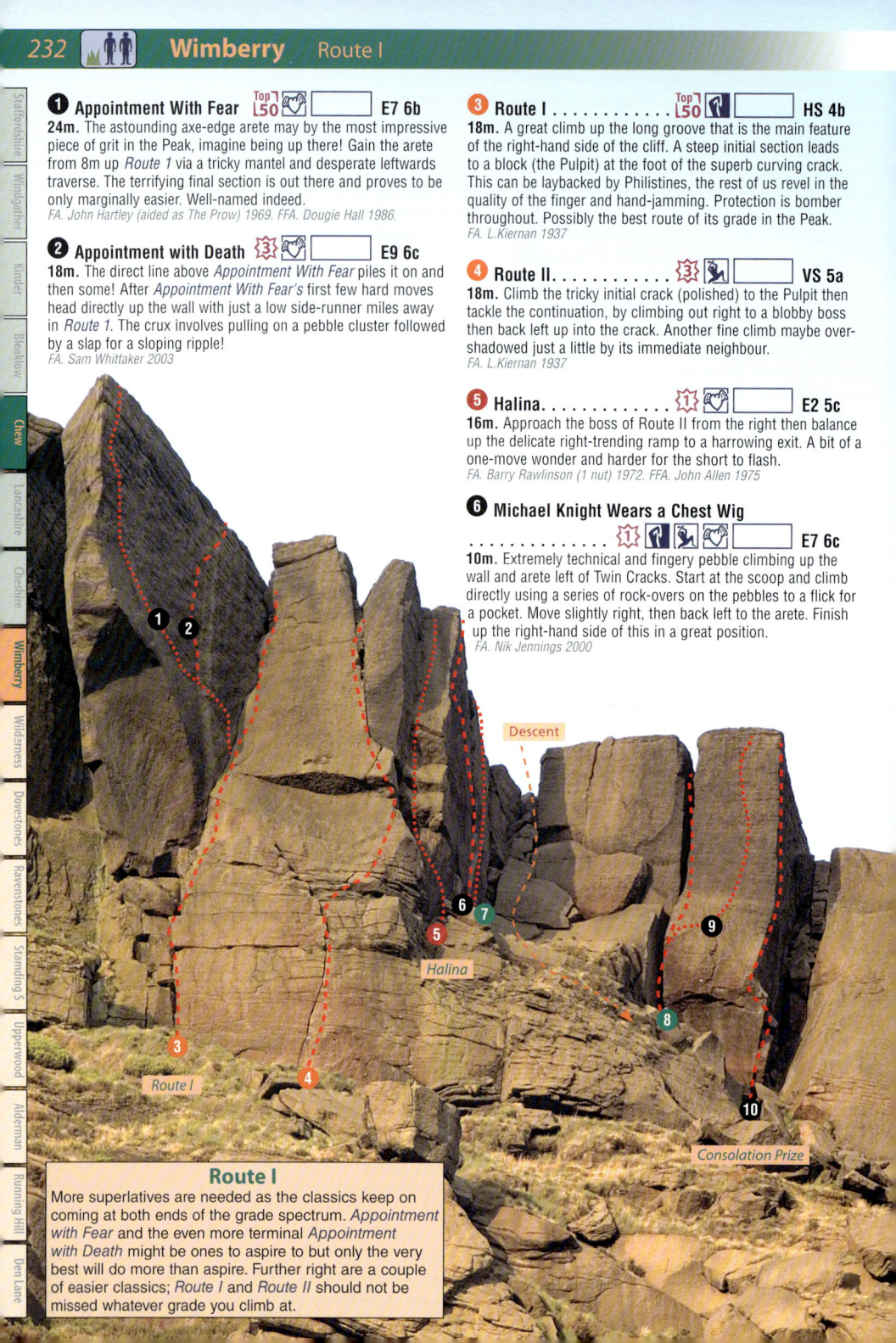

❶ Appointment With Fear — E7 6b
24m. The astounding axe-edge arete may by the most impressive piece of grit in the Peak, imagine being up there! Gain the arete from 8m up *Route 1* via a tricky mantel and desperate leftwards traverse. The terrifying final section is out there and proves to be only marginally easier. Well-named indeed.
FA. John Hartley (aided as The Prow) 1969. FFA. Dougie Hall 1986.

❷ Appointment with Death — E9 6c
18m. The direct line above *Appointment With Fear* piles it on and then some! After *Appointment With Fear's* first few hard moves head directly up the wall with just a low side-runner miles away in *Route 1*. The crux involves pulling on a pebble cluster followed by a slap for a sloping ripple!
FA. Sam Whittaker 2003

❸ Route I — HS 4b
18m. A great climb up the long groove that is the main feature of the right-hand side of the cliff. A steep initial section leads to a block (the Pulpit) at the foot of the superb curving crack. This can be laybacked by Philistines, the rest of us revel in the quality of the finger and hand-jamming. Protection is bomber throughout. Possibly the best route of its grade in the Peak.
FA. L.Kiernan 1937

❹ Route II — VS 5a
18m. Climb the tricky initial crack (polished) to the Pulpit then tackle the continuation, by climbing out right to a blobby boss then back left up into the crack. Another fine climb maybe overshadowed just a little by its immediate neighbour.
FA. L.Kiernan 1937

❺ Halina — E2 5c
16m. Approach the boss of Route II from the right then balance up the delicate right-trending ramp to a harrowing exit. A bit of a one-move wonder and harder for the short to flash.
FA. Barry Rawlinson (1 nut) 1972. FFA. John Allen 1975

❻ Michael Knight Wears a Chest Wig — E7 6c
10m. Extremely technical and fingery pebble climbing up the wall and arete left of Twin Cracks. Start at the scoop and climb directly using a series of rock-overs on the pebbles to a flick for a pocket. Move slightly right, then back left to the arete. Finish up the right-hand side of this in a great position.
FA. Nik Jennings 2000

Route I
More superlatives are needed as the classics keep on coming at both ends of the grade spectrum. *Appointment with Fear* and the even more terminal *Appointment with Death* might be ones to aspire to but only the very best will do more than aspire. Further right are a couple of easier classics; *Route I* and *Route II* should not be missed whatever grade you climb at.

Herringbone Slab **Wimberry** 233

7 Twin Cracks . . . . S 4b
8m. From the terrace, climb the right-hand twin crack. The left one all the way is a slightly longer **HS 4b**.
FA. Anton Stoop 1910

8 Squirmer's Chimney . . . S 4a
12m. Another Wimberry classical rift. Just as tight as *Starvation* and more of a battle as the tussle goes on longer.

9 Chockblock E5 6b
12m. The slab right of *Squirmer's Chimney*, with runners in the flake to the left of *Squirmer's Chimney*, is an inferior - though bold - variation on *Consolation Prize*.
FA. Steven Delderfield 1990s

10 Consolation Prize E5 6a
12m. The **bold** arete by some frantic moves (choose a start) to a poor rest on the left, followed by the even **bolder** though easier and ridiculously exposed upper section. The route may just be E5 for those who spend an age on the psyching/rescue ledge!
FA. Jonny Woodward 1981

11 Slab Gully . . . . VDiff
12m. The narrow gully bounding the left-hand side of the attractive slab.

12 Slab Climb . . . . HS 4a
10m. Pad up the left-hand side of the slab with some apprehension and not much in the way of gear. A pleasant but bold pitch.

Herringbone Slab
The right-hand side of the crag is less spectacular, and less busy, than the rest of the place though it has some worthwhile offerings, including some gripping aretes and is well worth a visit if you have already ticked the more vaunted classics.

13 Herringbone Slab . . HVS 4c
10m. The centre of the slab with a jig right at two thirds-height is pleasant and poorly-protected. Finishing up the right-hand side is bolder again, **E1 5a**.

14 Groove and Chimney . . . . . . Diff
12m. The obviously-named features to the right.

15 Tap Dance E3 5c
8m. Climb the fingery wall to a good horizontal then stretch direct or teeter on the left to reach the top.
FA. Chris Hardy 1986

16 Charm E3 5c
8m. The right-hand line on the slab. Climb to the break (wires) with difficulty then rock over and use a poor pocket to reach the second break and delicate finish up a blind flake. Mild at the grade but memorable enough.
FA. Jonny Woodward 1982

17 The Climb with No Name E5 6a
10m. The steep arete is approached via a groove and a wild finishing layback on its right-hand side.
FA. Johnny Dawes 1984

18 Cooking Crack . . . . HS 4b
8m. Enter the undercut crack awkwardly.

Wimberry — Northern Ballet

1 Sloping Crack ..... HVD
10m. Climb to the crescent-shaped crack and follow it to a steep and exposed finish.

2 Piedra Verde E6 6a
10m. Step from a block onto the steep green wall and climb direct (tenuous) passing the arete and on up the pebbled slab. "Looks like an E5 but climbs like an E6".
FA. Kevin Thaw 2003

3 Wall and Bulge E2 5b
10m. Climb the east-facing wall to the block overhang (poor wires) then scuttle right and finish just left of the arete. Unlikely but excellent.
FA. Malc Baxter 1961

4 Dream of Blackpool Donkeys E3 5c
10m. Finger-traverse right to the arete and climb it with increasing trepidation on its exposed valley face. Nasty landing.
FA. Adrian Garlick 1973

5 Blood, Sweat and Tears E2 5b
8m. Climb directly up the face to the finish of *Wall and Bulge*.
FA. Chris Hardy 1987

6 Appointment Missed E5 6b
10m. Climb through the centre of the roof in between via a stiff pull and some technical moves to get established over the bulge. Climbing the centre of the wall above would be very contrived, so best to finish up either arete above.
FA. Ben Tetler 2004

7 The Twilight Zone E4 5c
10m. Climb the right edge of the arete to a break and the flying rib above to a gripping exit.
FA. Dougie Hall 1987

8 Cranberry Crack ..... VS 5a
10m. Around to the right is this hidden and awkward crack in the upper part of the face. It is reached via an easy groove and proves to be berry-filled no longer.

9 Curving Arete ..... VDiff
8m. The curved arete eases with height.

10 Fisher's Chimney ..... HVD
8m. The widening rift.

11 Kvick Chimney ..... HS 4c
8m. The chimney is entered by moves up its right arete.

12 Village Green E3 6c
8m. The bulging right-hand arete of the buttress is desperate.
FA. Johnny Dawes 1984

13 Cloudberry Wall ..... VS 5b
6m. The centre of the crinkly wall.

14 Cloud Busting E1 6a
6m. Just right balance up the faint rib on small holds.
FA Phil Davies 2000

Not much sun · 30 min · Green · Windy

Northern Ballet **Wimberry** 235

15 Cave Groove .... VS 4b
8m. Bridge past the entrance to the cave then continue up the crack and corner above.
FA. Tony Howard 1961

16 Cave Rib E2 5b
10m. The outside face of the cave system is climbed up the right rib to a ledge (runners on the left) and a bizarre finale.
FA. Steve Bancroft 1974

Below the right-hand side of the cliff is a very large boulder, severely undercut at its left-hand end.

17 A Walk with Whittaker .. E3 6a
10m. The undercut scoop on the left-hand side of the overhang was a "last great problem" and is described as "puzzling and difficult"; it is possibly a major sandbag! Finish in the same place as Northern Ballet.
FA. Steven Fisher 1996

Northern Ballet

A collection of smaller routes set above the attractive (and big) boulder of *Northern Ballet*. The whole area sees little attention though it might be worth a visit if you want to escape the crowds.

18 Northern Ballet E3 5b
16m. An easy slab leads to the right-hand edge of the overhang. Step onto it and pad gingerly all the way out to the (rounded) left arete and a harrowing finish above a big drop - care required.
FA. Johnny Dawes 1984

19 Green but Sure E1 5a
12m. Follow *Northern Ballet* to the slab then climb it on a set of small rounded bumps. Low in the grade but delicate and unprotected, no place for wobbling!
FA. Kevin Thaw 1983

Upper Wilderness Valley

	No star	⭐	⭐⭐	⭐⭐⭐
Mod to S	5	4	3	1
HS to HVS	1	8	3	-
E1 to E3	2	1	1	-
E4 and up	-	2	-	1

Chris Proffitt climbing *Nameless One* (VS) - page 238 - at Rob's Rocks. Photo: Chris Hannah

A interesting set of cliffs in as wild a setting as you might expect from being cut into the moor called Wilderness. The routes on Rob's Rocks are short but the rock is clean and a couple of hours of pleasant sport is available here for climbers operating in the lower grades. The Charnel Stones' routes are generally more serious and (even) less popular. Both cliffs get the afternoon sun. Boulderers might be interested in the huge roof that lies to the west of the main cliff; there appears to be no indication that it has ever been climbed. The nearby Duck Stones are also worth a visit. Rob's Rocks is in a sunny setting and its relatively easy approach makes it a good choice for a short day. It has a better set of lower grade climbs than most cliffs in the area. The classic scramble of *Wilderness Gully East* lies opposite the cliff and is worth a look at too. From its top a right turn leads back along the moor crest to Wimberry and then the parking by the reservoir.

Approach
Also see map on page 224

From the Pay and Display parking by the Dovestones Reservoir follow the tarmaced track past the Yacht Club, over the bridge then fork right up the side of Wilderness Brook, steep initially then easing, Charnel Stones can be seen up and left, Rob's Rocks is hidden up around the next bend both cliffs are reached in about 30 minutes.

Conditions
Despite the altitude, the aspect and clean top mean that Rob's Rocks dry rapidly after rain and is in condition throughout the year whenever the weather is half decent. Charnel Stones takes more drainage due to the steep hillside above but is often cleaner than you might expect.

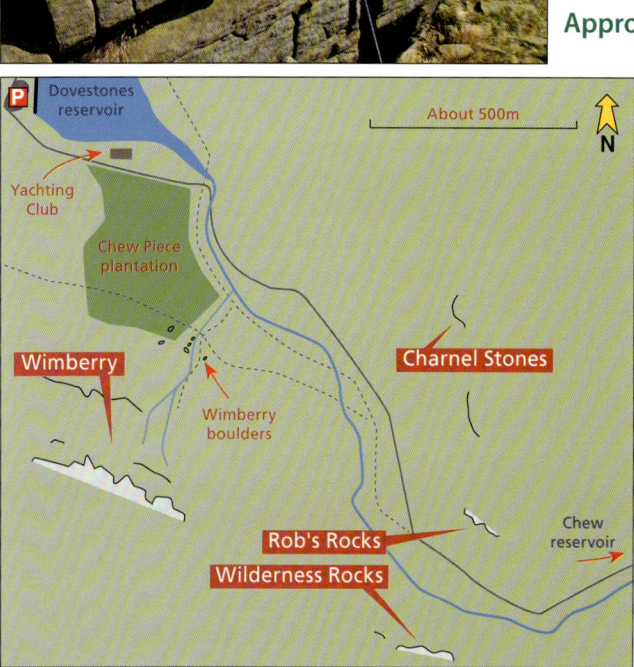

The Charnel Stones — Upper Wilderness

The Charnel Stones
Halfway up the approach road to Rob's Rocks the straggling outcrop of The Charnel Stones can be seen to the left with its attractive central hanging slab. There are several worthwhile climbs here and you will likely be alone. The crag is approached directly up the hillside from the road far below.

1 The Sorcerer's Apprentice — E2 5c
12m. The right-slanting crack/groove is a worthwhile to taxing, especially the final restricted groove.
FA. Adrian Garlik 1969

2 Temptation Crack — VS 4b
22m. The wide crack bounding the left-edge of the slab is more troublesome and less fun that it looks from afar.
FA. Tony Howard 1957. Graham West may have been there before.

3 Mickey Mouse — E5 6a
20m. The hanging arete on its right-hand side is approached via a finger/nut slot from half-way up *Temptation Crack*.
FA. Paul Clark 1994

4 The Wasteland — E4 5c
20m. The right arete of the big slab is a lonely lead. From runners in the corner move out right then balance into ever more trouble. The centre of the slab direct is **Sad, Tired and Old, E5 6b**. The first ascensionist described it as having "five star climbing and zero star independence".
FA. Steve Bancroft 1978. FA. (Sad, Tired,...) Paul Clark 1994

5 The Broomstick — HVS 5a
12m. The steep left-hand crack in the sidewall gives a fine sustained pitch. Well protected, but up-hill.
FA. Tony Howard 1963

6 The Witch's Hat — HVS 5a
12m. The right-hand pair of cracks leads past the spike of the 'Hat' to a steep exit up the leaning groove. Escaping left is easier.
FA. Tony Howard 1963

7 Paul's Perambulation — S 4b
14m. The right-trending groove starting over blocks.
FA. Paul Seddon 1960

8 Paul's Arete — E4 6b
14m. Tackle the arete and face right of *Paul's Perambulation*, joining it at the top of its groove.
FA. Paul Clark 1994

9 The Spog — E2 5c
14m. Climb the slab to the break then use pockets to trend left to a worrying finale on the left arete. Climbing directly up the centre of the slab is **From the Cradle to the Grave, E3 6a**. It features a stretchy final move.
FA. Ian Carr 1982. FA. (From Cradle...) Paul Clark 1994

10 The Tombstone — VS 4c
14m. Follow the previous route to the break then traverse right and finish up the crack.
FA. Tony Jones 1963

238 Upper Wilderness — Rob's Rocks

Rob's Rocks
The routes are spread across the crag following good lines on the separate buttresses. The best of the climbs are on the largest central buttress.

① Snow Crack .... **S 4a**
6m. Drift up the short-lived fissure, it snow push-over!
FA. Jeff Sykes 1961

② Nice Edge .... **HS 4b**
8m. The sharp tilted arete is juggy if diminutive fun.
FA. Paul Seddon 1961

③ Beaky Corner .... **VDiff**
8m. The capped corner to a rightward (or leftward - **S 4a**) exit.

④ Stairway .... **Mod**
8m. The straightforward stepped ramp.

⑤ Stairway Flake Crack .... **HS 4b**
8m. Layback the flake. Pleasant.

⑥ Stairway Arete .... **VS 4a**
8m. The tilted arete has plenty of holds but not much gear.

⑦ Cascade .... **HS 4a**
8m. The centre of the attractive face is short on gear and many of the holds are not the most helpful around, especially at the top.
FA. Tony Howard 1961

⑧ Zacharias .... **VDiff**
8m. The crack right of the arete has a tricky final move.
FA. Tony Howard 1961

⑨ Nameless One .... **VS 4b**
10m. Climb the crack in the west-facing wall to a leftward exit.
Photo on page 236.
FA. Roy (Chubby?) Brown 1950

⑩ Nameless Two .... **HVS 4c**
10m. From the fallen slab, climb the left-hand side of the arete steeply and on poor holds. A little harrowing.
FA. Ian Carr 1985

⑪ Ylnosd Rib .... **HVD**
12m. Pigeon-chested types can squirm the lower crack to ledges and an easier finish. Others will need to start from the right at about the same grade and quality. A fun outing!
FA. J.W.Puttrell 1903

⑫ Letter-box .... **VDiff**
10m. The pleasant slabby face passing a least one useful slot.
FA. J.W.Puttrell 1903

⑬ Cave Crack .... **HS 4c**
10m. The awkward narrowing rift offers a strange affair.

⑭ Cripple's Way .... **VDiff**
10m. Another excellent low-grade route. Finish up the top block for the full effect.

⑮ Owt .... **Mod**
10m. The ribbed-crack and short steep wall above are pleasant.

⑯ Nowt .... **Mod**
10m. The crack just right is okay too.

⑰ Ice Crack .... **VDiff**
8m. The steep groove well to the right gives good bridging with a bold feeling start.

⑱ Digital Orbit **E3 5c**
8m. From a block, make a leap-of-faith to pass the nose.
FA. Paul Moreland 1990

⑲ The Nose .... **VS 5a**
8m. Swing on the right edge of the beak, campus to get established and romp on. Alternatively, approach from the right; **Nosey, HS 4b**.

⑳ Freebird **E2 5c**
8m. The bulge and triangular nose to the hanging arête.
FA. Paul Moreland 1990

㉑ Niche Wall .... **VDiff**
10m. Rightwards into the niche and then up and left to finish.

Wilderness Rocks **Upper Wilderness** 239

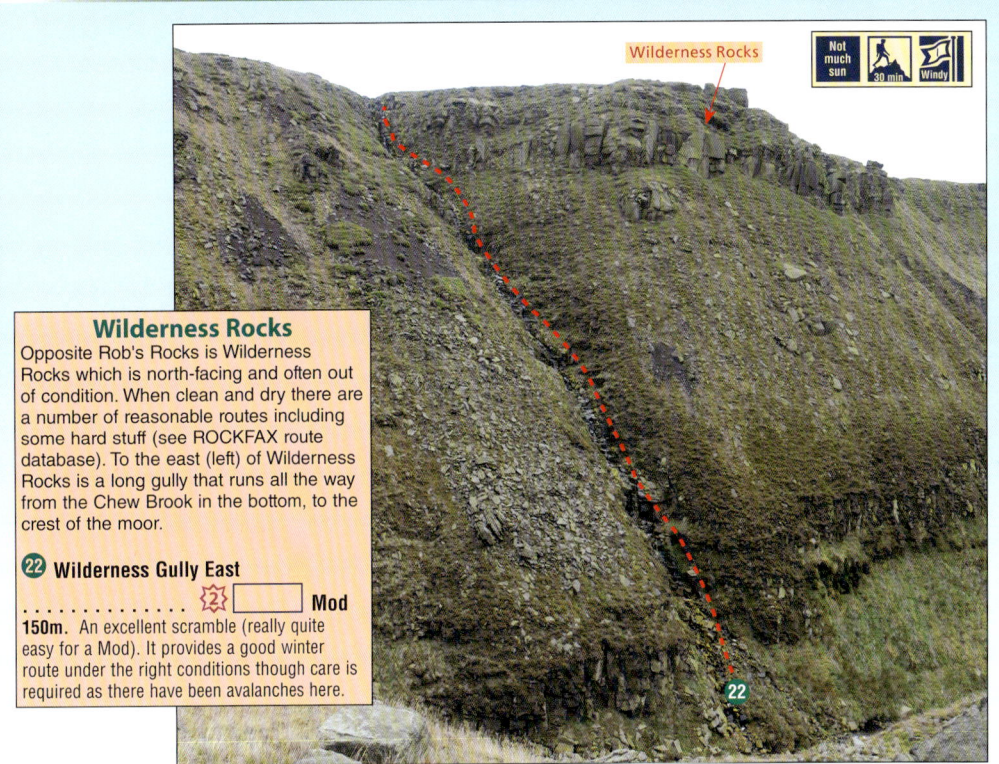

Wilderness Rocks
Opposite Rob's Rocks is Wilderness Rocks which is north-facing and often out of condition. When clean and dry there are a number of reasonable routes including some hard stuff (see ROCKFAX route database). To the east (left) of Wilderness Rocks is a long gully that runs all the way from the Chew Brook in the bottom, to the crest of the moor.

22 Wilderness Gully East
.... ☆ ▢ **Mod**
150m. An excellent scramble (really quite easy for a Mod). It provides a good winter route under the right conditions though care is required as there have been avalanches here.

Descent

Nameless 1

Ylnosd Rib

Cripple's Way

Dovestones Edge

	No star	★1	★2	★3
Mod to S	18	13	3	1
HS to HVS	10	17	4	2
E1 to E3	3	9	1	1
E4 and up	-	2	2	1

Not to be confused with its even more remote namesake in the Eastern Peak, this fine cliff has a good selection of routes and is rarely busy, the flog to get there being the main reason the place stays so quiet. It faces west and north west and is at its best on warm summer evenings when the many lower grade climbs can be enjoyed to the full. Below and to the south west of the main Dovestones Edge are three large rambling quarries on the hillside overlooking the reservoir. All the main lines have been done but the Main Quarry in particular has a habit of falling down big-style. In thirty odd years of climbing in the Peak I have only visited the Main Quarry once, to find the top pitch of our chosen objective missing. We did the route anyway - but I vowed never to return, and never have!

Approach
Also see map on page 224

Park at the Binn Green car park just off the A635, descend to the road, cross over the dam and, either follow the stream to the tunnel then make a steep direct ascent to the cliff via the trackless slope, or do it direct. Alternatively park by the Dovestones Reservoir (page 226), walk round the southern edge of the reservoir, cross the stream and follow main track as it loops round the side of the reservoir. 350m from the bridge, walk up the side of the wall then enter the wood and follow the good track. This passes below the quarries before heading resolutely for the cliff high above.

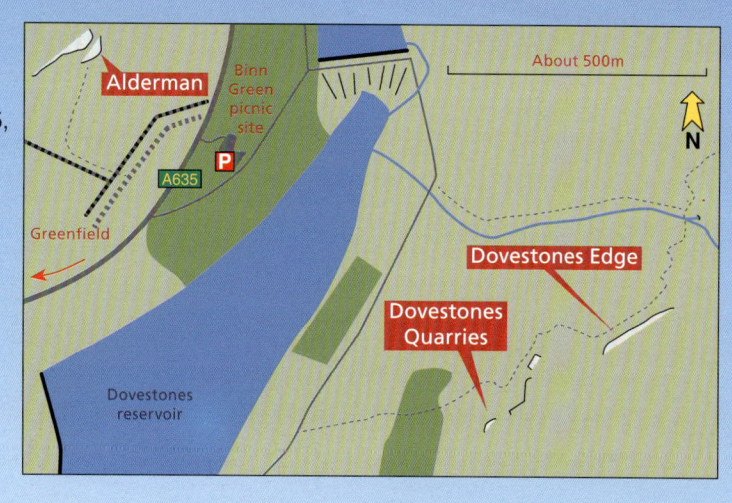

Conditions

A great venue on fine summer evenings when the aspect and position of the cliff can be enjoyed to the full. The cliff dries rapidly after rain and is less green than most hereabouts. On the down-side the left-hand end of the edge can be gritty and the whole crag tends to catch south westerly winds in spectacular fashion.

Jonathan Booth engrossed with *Matchstick Crack* (S) - *page 244* - on Dovestones Edge. Photo: Chris Tan.

Dovestones Edge — Nasal Buttress

Nasal Buttress

The left-hand side of the cliff has a collection of worthwhile easier climbs although the area tends to be green and gritty after wet weather. It is at its best on late summer evenings when the situation can be enjoyed to the full. Some of the rock is a bit crusty and requires careful handling.

1 Route 2 .... HS 4b
16m. Head up the left arete to a ledge then continue up the left-hand side of the pinnacle above.

2 Route 1 .... VS 4b
16m. Climb diagonally left out to the arete and on to reach ledges below the pinnacle. Then climb the fingery centre of its face. This section can be avoided by a start up the arete on the right.

3 Slab and Saddle .... Diff
14m. Climb the slabby face and blunt rib above. The upper part of the projecting buttress on the right can used for an exposed alternative finish for thrill seakers.

4 Stirrup .... S 4a
16m. Climb the slabs straight into the hanging groove then move out right and climb the exposed arete in a fine position.
FA. Tony Howard 1958

5 Double Overhangs .... HVS 5b
14m. The front face of the buttress passing two roofs is effectively a pumpy direct start to *Stirrup*.
FA. Chris Hardy 1982

6 Cooper's Crack .... S 4b
12m. The crack splitting the roof eases once past the overhang - worth seeking out for a couple of nice moves.

7 Sea Route .... VS 4c
12m. Tackle the face then the thin crack that splits the centre of the slab, crossing the major break of *C Climb* at half-height to a worrying finish.
FA. Chris Hardy 1982

8 C Climb .... Diff
14m. Start on the right and climb leftwards to finish up the final two moves of *Cooper's Crack*.

9 Green Crack .... VDiff
12m. The curving groove is a compelling line but not a very edifying experience. It could equally have been called *Gritty Crack* or *Grotty Crack*.

10 Wrinkled Buttress .... VDiff
18m. Climb the lower buttress right then left to a ledge then the upper face on sloping holds, heading back right again.

11 Curving Crack .... VDiff
12m. Climb the slab to reach the deep crack/groove as it bends back right then follow it to the top.

12 Danegeld E1 5b
12m. Steep and worthwhile but with a committing feeling. Climb the face into a scoop then take a crack up the bulging wall. Pull over the left edge of the final overhang or side-step it.
FA. Bill Birch 1986

13 The Tax Collector E2 5c
12m. The right-hand of the wall leads to, and through, the capping roof which makes you pay for all favours received.
FA. Rick Hyde 1990s

14 Knobbly Wall .... HS 4b
12m. The flaky wall to a short crack and awkward finish.

Nasal Buttress — Dovestones Edge

15 The Director's Route — HVD
20m. A long diagonal from the foot of *The Direct Route* to the top left corner of the face involves some nice moves, but it is dirty and there is the odd creaking hold. Exit left under the roof at the end of the wall.

16 The Direct Route — VDiff
12m. Climb the right-hand side of the wall on flakes (some of which are a bit creaky) - care required.

17 The Moocher — VS 4b
12m. Flakes on the right-hand edge of the wall lead to bulges which can be outflanked or climbed direct.
FA. Phil Sneyd 1990s

18 Eyebrow — S 4a
18m. The shady side of the jutting buttress via a short wide crack to a finish on the exposed arete out to the right.

19 Nasal Buttress — HS 4b
16m. The classic of this part of the cliff with a little bit of everything. Climb the steep arete with the nose being passed on the left by delicate moves; good small wires protect. Finish up the superbly-positioned arete.
FA. George Bower early 1920s

20 Eight Hours! — E1 5a
16m. Weave a way up the right-hand face of the buttress until it is possible to escape out onto the left-hand arete.
FA. Chris Hardy 1984

21 The Changeling — HS 4b
16m. The widening-crack is followed past a kink until it is possible to change to the other side of the chimney and finish up the narrow faced. A bit of an oddity.

22 Crack and Chimney — Mod
14m. The widening-rift to an escape over, or under, the chockstone that blocks the chimney.

23 Palpitation — E1 5a
14m. Wander up the narrow buttress passing to the left of the overhang then step out right to a finish on the arete. Not too hard but crusty and a bit of a shocker unless you find all the gear.
FA. Jim Campbell 1973

24 Mother's Pride — E1 5b
14m. The upper half of the rib left of the chimney to a finish over the huge block sitting on the top of the cliff.
FA. Chris Hardy 1980

25 Capstone Chimney — Mod
14m. Climb the rift to the capstone and a subterranean exit.

Dovestones Edge — Maggie

> **Maggie**
> The central section of the cliff consists of a series of fine jutting buttresses with a good selection of routes. The climbs here tend to be cleaner than those to the left since the good bits of rock protrude further from the hillside, taking less drainage and getting more sun.

❶ Kitten Cracks . . . . **S 4b**
10m. Climb the cracks in the right-hand wall of the descent gully to the roof and creep round the right-hand side of this.

❷ Square Chimney . . . . **Diff**
12m. Follow the hanging groove in the left-hand side of the buttress to a platform then take the chimney behind. The cracks just right of the chimney are harder and better (**S 4a**).

❸ Central Tower . . . . **VDiff**
18m. An excellent climb; long and interesting. Ascend the buttress front with a jig right and left through the bulges, then finish slightly right up the well-positioned final slab.

❹ Tower Arete . . . . **VS 4c**
18m. The arete that forms the right-hand edge of the buttress is approached up slabby rock. A pitch of escalating interest.
FA. Rick Gibbon 1986

❺ Left Embrasure . . . . **VS 4b**
16m. The crack rising from the left-hand edge of a shallow recess is pleasant in a graunchy-gritstone kinda-way and less of a battle than appearances might suggest.
FA. Tony Howard 1958

❻ Right Embrasure . . . . **VS 4c**
14m. The right-hand crack is difficult to access and altogether more of a battle although still enjoyable in a strange way.
FA. Barry Kershaw 1958

❼ Matchstick Crack . . . . **S 4a**
10m. The thin crack in the wall, finishing leftwards up the slab.
Photo on page 241.
FA. Tony Jones 1960

❽ Maggie . . . . **HVS 5a**
10m. Take the pleasant square-cut arete on its right-hand side gives a nice pitch, pity about the grubby start.
FA. Tony Jones 1960

❾ Grim Wall . . . . **VS 5a**
10m. Climb the overlap and a crack to its end. Finish up the short face above with difficulty.

❿ Peat Climb . . . . **VDiff**
12m. Trend right to a blocky groove. Included for completeness.

⓫ Noddy's Wall . . . . **VS 4b**
14m. The slim buttress gives a pleasant pitch. Protection is lacking.
FA. John Hadfield (aka Noddy) 1958.

⓬ Swan Crack . . . . **HVD**
14m. From the toe of the arete cross the face rightwards to the ever-popular crack which doesn't normally require a long neck!

⓭ Swan Down . . . . **VS 4c**
10m. From the block climb the wrinkled wall right of the crack.
FA. Graham West 1960

Mammoth Slab Dovestones Edge

⑭ Gnomes' Wall .... VS 4c
14m. Climb the short technical and fingery face to grassy ledges then continue up the buttress above, exiting to the left of the capping snout.
FA. Graham West 1960

⑮ Rib and Wall .... S 4a
16m. Should have called *Groove and Slab*! Climb into and up the groove in the arete to broad ledges. Then traverse right and finish up the centre of the face above.

⑯ Mammoth Slab .... HVS 5a
14m. Not the beast you might expect. Swing over the roof to access the left-hand side of the slab and climb it more easily to the break. Continue up the left-hand side of the buttress above keeping just right of the arete.
FA. Graham West 1960

⑰ Ferdie's Folly E1 5b
14m. The centre of the face is delicate, unprotected and usually green. The upper half is much easier, finish as for *Rib and Wall*.
FA. The first ascent date is not recorded, although it is believed to have been done in the 1940s - good effort!

⑱ Dust Storm. E2 5b
14m. The area's answer to *Chalkstorm* at the Roaches albeit at a lower grade and often dirty. Climb the precarious right side of the slab, initially via a delicate scoop. Step left out of the top of this then make more thin moves to the halfway ledge. Finish direct.
FA. Chris Hardy 1984

⑲ 'K' Climb .... VS 4b
14m. Climb the cracked arete to ledges then the awkward face.

Mammoth Slab
The central section of the cliff has some good routes on a series of fine faces that are generally cleaner than the rock away to the left. *Mammoth Slab* is the best route here but all the others listed are well worth doing.

⑳ Kaytoo. .... VS 4c
14m. Climb onto the block in front of the face then stride left into the thin crack and follow this to ledges. Climb the scoop in the wall behind until an exposed rightward exit is possible, or climb the crack direct - easier.
FA. Barry Kershaw 1958

㉑ Asinine .... HVS 6a
12m. Step right of the block and sketch away up the face to the first decent holds. Finish easily.
FA. Ian Carr 1982

㉒ June Climb .... Diff
14m. Take the fissure in the centre of the face to ledges then amble left, pull onto the slab and exit right below the roof.

㉓ Austin Maxi E2 5c
12m. The delicate face to the right of *June Climb* has technical moves to reach the security of the break and one more tricky sequence to reach easy ground.
FA. Chris Hardy 1982

㉔ June Wall .... VS 5a
12m. Start from the useful tooth and climb the slab by thin moves to ledges. Escape off right or extend things a little up and left. A technical tester from the days of bendy boots.
FA. Graham West 1960

㉕ June Ridge .... S 4a
12m. The right-hand arete of the face is started from the right. Gain a ledge on the front then climb to the terrace and finish leftwards as for *June Wall*.

Dovestones Edge — Answer Crack

1 Rubber-faced Arete — VS 4c
10m. Gurn a way up the thin bending crack in the narrow rib then step right and stretch for better holds and an easier finish.
FA. Malc Baxter 1961

2 Rubber-faced Wall — VDiff
12m. The wide right-slanting crack to ledges and easy ground.

3 December Arete — HVS 5b
12m. Climb the square-cut arete, initially on its left-hand side, with a strenuous start and precarious finish.
FA. Malc Baxter 1961

4 Layback Crack — HS 4b
12m. The classic crack splitting the centre of the buttress eases with height. You can also jam it if you prefer.

5 Friction Addiction — E1 5c
12m. Balance up the slab (clean those boots) to less precarious ground and a sprint up a short crack. Effectively unprotected.
FA. Chris Hardy 1984

6 Slipoff Slab — VS 4c
12m. Balance up the thin crack to the slab which is climbed carefully leftwards on a series of slopers. A Direct Finish is harder.
FA. Barry Kershaw 1958

7 Double Time Crack — HVD
8m. The wide crack on the right-hand side of the slab.

8 Left Chimney — VDiff
12m. More of a groove and a rather grassy one at that!

9 Right Chimney — VDiff
12m. This one is a proper chimney, awkward but worthwhile. Finish up the steep crack above.

10 'Owd on Arete — HS 4b
12m. Get a grip of the arete on its left-hand side, finishing up the left-hand side of the elegant prow above.
FA. Malc Baxter 1961

11 Question Time — E2 5c
12m. Follow the wall, slab and jutting arete to the left of *Answer Crack* to a well-positioned finale.
FA. Rick Gibbon 1990s

12 Answer Crack — Top 50 — HVD
12m. The flake crack is Western Grit's answer to Stanage's *Heaven Crack*, and it's a good effort. Layback to get established and then continue with pleasure. Finish up the wall behind.
FA. Paul Seddon 1960

13 Question Mark — S 4a
12m. Climb the rather awkward crack to its end then move left to get the correct answer. Excellent, though overshadowed by its near-neighbour.
FA. Paul Seddon 1960

Answer Crack **Dovestones Edge** 247

14 Full Stop E1 5a
12m. The wall and right arete are as badly-protected as the grade suggests, though there is only one hard move! Finishing direct is the same grade but manages to feel even bolder.
FA. Steve Bancroft 1973

15 Third Triplet .... Diff
12m. The unremarkable, wide left-hand, fissure.

16 Yellow Crack ..... HVS 5c
12m. The short wall and thin crack lead to easier territory.

17 Second Triplet .... Diff
12m. The narrower central rift of the trio.

18 Loose End .... VS 5a
10m. The thin crack that was pegged in antiquity leads to the steep arete out to the right and a good finish.
FA. Duggy Banes late 1950s. FFA. Paul Seddon 1960

19 First Triplet .... S 4a
10m. Climb the flaky crack through an alcove with difficulty and on up the wall above.

20 Scarface .... VS 4c
10m. The steep groove and curving crack can be dirty and don't see much traffic.

21 Silly Arete .... S 4a
10m. Start up the top groove of the next route then step left onto the pleasantly positioned arete to finish
FA. Jim Heys 1961

22 Tower Ridge .... VDiff
26m. A game of two halves. Start at a lower level and follow a crack and then the blocky ridge to the terrace (belay). Finish up the pleasant crack in the upper tier. The star is for the clean and pleasant upper section.

Answer Crack
A good collection of climbs including a great VDiff in the shape of *Answer Crack* and a whole bevy of other bits and pieces that are worth a minute or two of your time. The rock is clean and fast drying, there is a broad terrace below the climbs and the outward view is great. On the down-side it can get pretty blowy up here.

Dovestones Edge — Hanging Crack

Hanging Crack

The largest buttress on the edge has 'the best jamming-crack on grit,' or so rumour has it - *Hanging Crack* and there is only one way to find out if the hype is true! There are other oddities as well and the place is especially enjoyable in the evening sun - as a high summer only venue though.

23 The Jester .... S 4a
12m. The crack and scoop to a steep juggy exit.
FA. Steve Bancroft 1972

24 Spurt of Spurts E2 5b
20m. An oddity but worth doing if you enjoy being gripped. Follow *The Jester* for 8m then swing rightwards along the break until just left of *Hanging Crack* and finish direct, with difficulty.
FA. Nick Plishko 1983

25 Hymen the Tactless. E5 6c
18m. Trend left to reach the left end of the overhang then monkey right and pull over its centre with great difficulty to reach the easier final wall.
FA. Nick Plishko 1983

26 Hanging Crack E2 5b
16m. A fine jamming-crack; the crag is worth a visit just to do this route. Climb the crack through a host of overhangs.
Photo opposite.
FA. Joe Brown (a little aid) 1957. FFA. Alan McHardy 1967

27 The Gibbet.......... E3 5c
16m. The steep wall is bold (big cams and big balls help) though thankfully things ease with height.
FA. Loz Francomb 1980

28 The Catwalk......... HS 3c
16m. From the gully on the right shuffle left along the highest break to the arete and an easy finish. Technically a cakewalk but exposed and unprotected; a fall would likely prove very serious.
Photo on page 11.
FA. Graham West 1960

29 Strappado E4 6b
10m. The hanging flake is approached from the left and requires plenty of grunt. This is a harder version of its near-namesake at Froggatt which is oddly given E5!
FA. Nick Colton 1981

30 Blank Crack .... S 4b
10m. The crack that runs up the buttress front, passing to the right of the overhang.

31 Long Ridge .... VDiff
28m. Another extended outing. Climb the groove in the lower ridge then scramble to the continuation on the right. Finish up the jutting buttress above.

32 Jam and Jug .... S 4b
12m. Jam the crescent-shaped crack, then follow jugs on the left to exit.
FA. Tony Howard 1958

To the right are a further 10 or so routes, none is of especial merit.

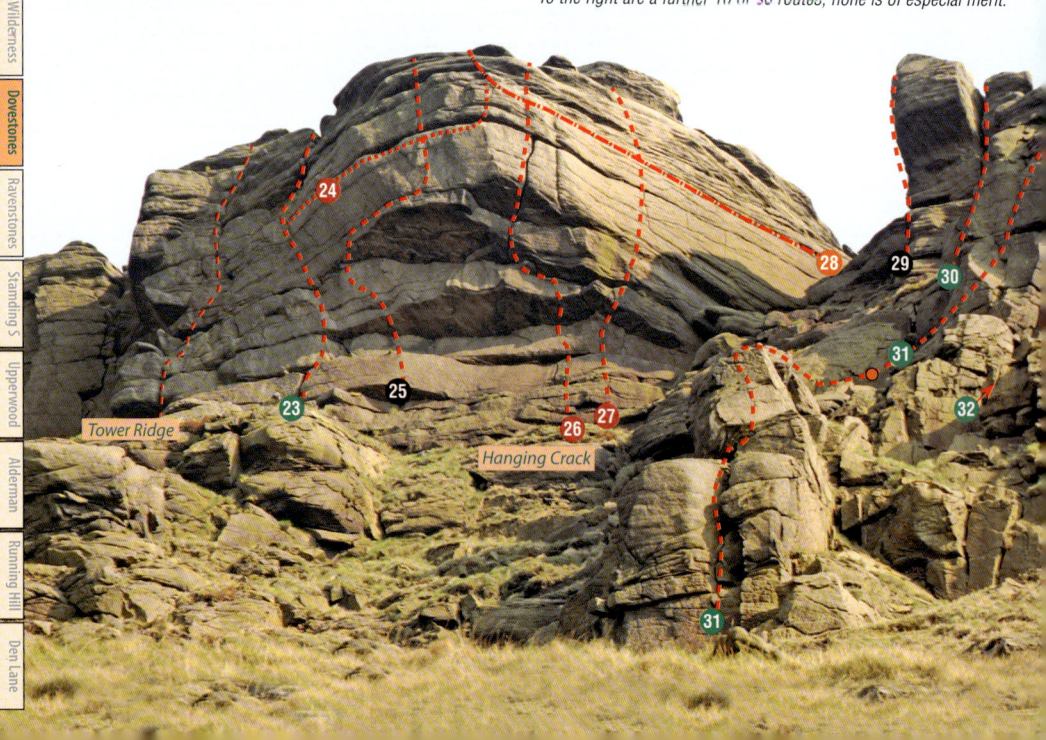

Andrew Sutton doing battle with the magnificent *Hanging Crack* (E2) - *opposite*.
Photo: Chris Tan

Dovestones Quarry — Bob Hope

Bob Hope

The three Dovestones Quarries offer some interesting mountaineering-style routes but really only the Lower Right Quarry has much of interest for more conventional climbers. The seven best routes are described here including the famous finger-crack and Chew classic *Bob Hope*. Scaffold pipes hammered into the peaty slope above the cliff provide belays - always assuming you can find them!

Approach - From the parking by the dam, take the track around the lake and follow the short path that branches diagonally through the trees and up into the quarry.

❶ Ace of Spades — HVS 5a
15m. Similar to *Fox-House Flake* at Burbage but a notch or two harder. Follow the flake-crack all the way.
FA. Joe Brown (as Joe's Layback) 1957

❷ Jet Lag — E5 6b
15m. The slab and wall left of *Tiny Tim*. From low wires climb the slab to a shelf. Step right to a runner in *Tiny Tim*, finish direct.
FA. Kevin Thaw 1990

❸ Tiny Tim — VS 4c
16m. The flake groove leading left from the base of the crack on *Bob Hope* is followed throughout strenuously.
FA. Joe Brown 1957

❹ Bob Hope — Top 50 — E4 6a
15m. Miles better than any other route in the Dovestones Quarries. The finger-crack gives super-sustained finger jamming all the way, well-protected, but with little for your feet. Another classic from the raiding Bancroft. *Photo opposite*.
FFA. Steve Bancroft 1978. Previously aided as *Metamorphose*.

❺ Pedestal Corner — VS 4c
15m. Follow the crack to the right of the fissure of *Bob Hope* to reach the top of a pedestal. Climb the corner above, then move out right to pushy exit.
FA. Graham West early 1960s

❻ Scuttle Buttin' — E7 6c
15m. The impending arete right of *Pedestal Corner* is climbed without side runners. Bold!
FA. Kevin Thaw 1989

❼ Five Day Chimney — E2 5c
15m. The final left-facing corner is gained via a flake. Sustained jamming and awkward corner moves lead to a loose-feeling block. Swing steeply right and up to finish with a flourish.
FA. Bob Whittaker 1977

Twist those fingers - Hugh Cottam on *Bob Hope (E4)* - *opposite.*

Ravenstones

	No star	★	★★	★★★
Mod to S	8	8	2	1
HS to HVS	5	9	6	2
E1 to E3	2	7	5	1
E4 and up	-	2	2	1

A fine austere cliff, north facing in a lofty position looking out over Saddleworth Moors, and the steep slopes running down to Holme Clough and the Greenfield Reservoir. The situation of the cliff and the outlook give a remoter feel that almost any other crag in the Peak, with few signs of human activity from the top of the cliff. The likelihood is that, unless the weather is absolutely perfect, you will have the place to yourself. There is a fine set of climbs here, many following good crack-lines, with more arduous undertakings up the dividing walls and aretes.

The cliff continues westwards for a couple of kilometres and the shorter walls here are home to another hundred or so routes, many of which are worth doing but see little traffic.

Approach   Also see map on page 182

The crag can be reached from the Binn Green picnic/parking area (50 minutes) by dropping down to the reservoir, taking a left turn and walking up the valley until below the left-hand end of the cliff which is reached by a steep ascent. Alternatively use the Standing Stones parking and approach, dropping down to the stream and scrambling up to the left edge of the cliff (30 minutes). The latter is shorter but leaves a harder walk out at the end of the day, no minor consideration if you are here for a full on day!

Conditions

The crag is a harsh task-master in all but perfect conditions, and such conditions are pretty uncommon up here. The climbs are graded for such ideal days, but if you are here when things are damp and greasy, be prepared to lower your sights or get ready for a hard time.

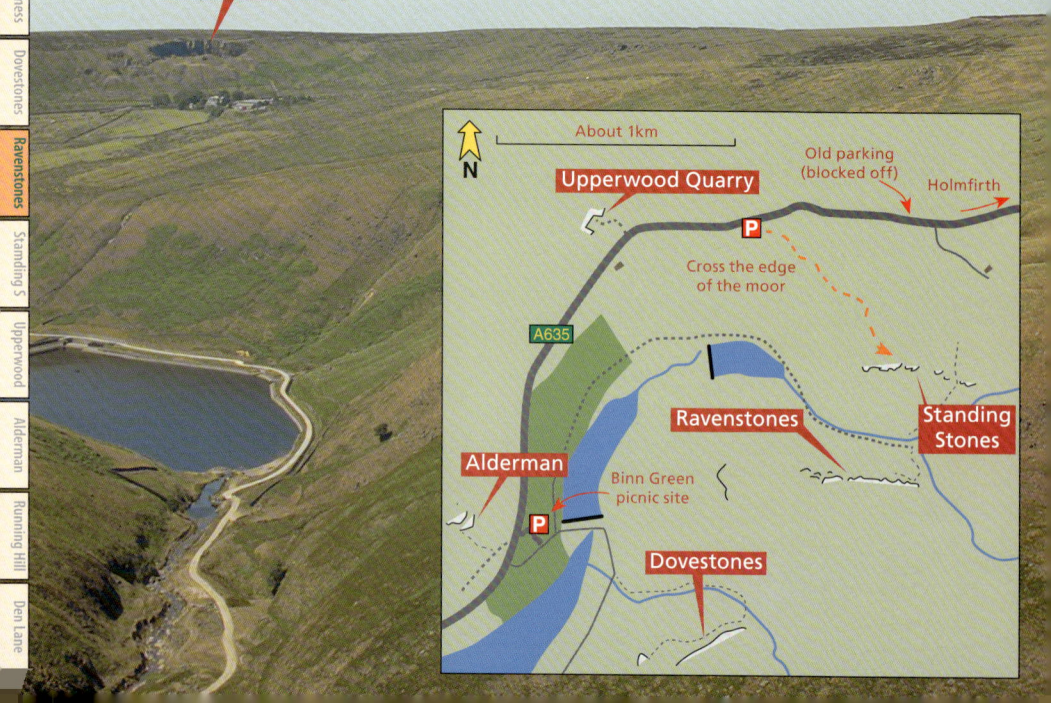

Brain Rossiter cranking up the Ravenstones' classic of *True Grit* (E3) - *page 257*.

Ravenstones — Eastern Slab

1 Strenuosity .... VS 4c
6m. The short steep crack leading to an awkward exit around the huge boulder is not mis-named and sees little attention.

2 Cockney's Traverse .... HS 4b
10m. Climb a short way up *Strenuosity* then follow the sloping ramp rightwards and up until below the overhangs (thread). Hand traverse in the same line to easy ground.

3 Hang-glider E2 5b
12m. Climb straight up to the thread on *Cockney's Traverse*. Then tackle the impressive roof direct, or via the thin crack just to the left. Bold moves and/or flexible holds make the route memorable whichever line you take.
FA. Bob Whittaker 1977

4 Slanter .... VS 4c
10m. Slant up the shallow, leaning groove that sneaks past the right-hand edge of the overhang, to reach easy ground.
FA. Gordon Mason 1977

5 Alpha .... VDiff
8m. The steep and juggy flake-crack on the left-hand side of the front of the buttress is pleasant if somewhat short-lived.

6 Beta .... Diff
10m. The constricted rift gives a bit of a thrash.

7 Grooved Wall .... HS 4b
10m. Balance up the slab leftwards to the ledge on its crest then continue up the crucial steep and technical groove directly above.

8 Eastern Slab .... VDiff
12m. Start up the centre of the well-scratched slab to a ledge then finish easily. Harder variations exist to left and right. A nice lower-grade climb though the lower section is bold.

9 Deep Chimney .... Mod
12m. The deep angular and rather grubby rift.

10 Green Wall .... VS 4b
12m. An ancient classic. Climb the shallow groove in the centre of the buttress, to the right of the chimney, to find a tricky exit on the left. A bold mantelshelf is the traditional way of doing it though there are other (easier!) ways.
FA. Herbert Hartley 1928

11 Boy's Own E1 5b
12m. The square right-hand arete of the buttress is worth doing, giving good open moves, even though it feels rather escapable. The chipped hold at the start is avoidable.
FA. Ray Duffy 1982

12 Nil Desperandum .... S 4a
12m. The classic groove that cleaves the centre of this section of the cliff gives an appealing pitch up a striking line. A leftward escape is traditional though the direct finish is much better.

13 Pulpit Ridge ..... HVS 4c
16m. The bold and imposing arete. Climb onto the Pulpit via a traverse from the right then balance up the exciting edge (low gear) to easier ground. Either of the steep twin diagonal cracks below the ridge can be used as a harder **Direct Start (5a)**.
FA. Arthur Birtwhistle 1938

14 Over the Moors ... E5 6b
16m. Climb the bold and bald wall, directly above the starting crack of *Pulpit Ridge*, trending slightly left (nut in pocket) then back rightwards to the deep break. Escape up the easy crack.
FA. Paul Clark 1990s

15 Black Mountain Collage E7 6b
16m. Climb the initial crack of *Pulpit Ridge* to a break and the first and only runner. Climb straight up for 3m or so with difficulty, then rock onto a sloper (from left or right) and use a thin break to gain the large ledge. Finish direct.
FA. Andy Popp 1990s

Eastern Slab
The left-hand side of the cliff faces north east and so gets the early morning sun; ideal for early risers. Although not as popular as the cliff further right, it has some worthwhile lower-grade climbs of which *Eastern Slab* is the best.

The Drainpipe Ravenstones 255

16 The Drainpipe .... HS 4b
16m. A classic line up the steep and often gritty corner. Good climbing but it is best avoided after (and probably during) wet weather. It can be climbed by secure squirming or rather bolder laybacking. Large gear helps to protect.

17 Guerrilla Action ... E2 5b
16m. From the spout of *The Drainpipe* head out right to the blunt arete and climb it to a deep horizontal break (gear). From here make an airy exit up the final section on sloping holds.
FA. John Smith 1981

18 Unfinished Arete .... VS 4c
20m. Devious but interesting. Slant left to the arete and balance up this to the deep break. Wriggle right along the slot to the short crack (jammed blocks) in the right side of the wall for a finish.
FA. Arthur Birtwhistle 1938

19 Welcome to Greenfield, Gateway to Greenfield
.... E3 6a
16m. Climb the centre of the face to a deep slot. It is normal to have a lie-down here before the pull onto the final wall though the climb is considerably easier if you don't get too embroiled with the break, but it is so tempting!
FA. Mike Chapman 1982

20 Undun Crack .... VS 4c
16m. The thin crack on the right-hand side of the wall, and its wider continuation, are inclined to be green and gritty after rain.

21 Slime Crack .... Diff
16m. The scruffy corner is included because it's there. Belay on the ledge if required then finish up the chimney on the left.

Not much sun | 25 min | Green | Windy

Green Wall

Descent

Pulpit Ridge

Guerrilla Action

The Drainpipe
The central section of the cliff has some worthwhile climbs up a series of impressive corners with *The Drainpipe* and *Nil Desperandum* being aespecially good. The smoother rock in between offers some excellent open aretes and some compelling and bold face climbs that don't see much traffic.

Ravenstones — True Grit

Next is a grassy ledge halfway up the cliff - Muddy Crack Platform. There are three exits from here, the rift on the left Diff, the corner at the back VDiff and the wall to the right S.

① Little Kern Knotts .... S 4a
16m. Climb the crack in the left wall of the buttress passing the recess. Finish up the wall on the right of the final groove.

② Waterloo Climb .... HS 4b
16m. Mount the flake then traverse left to the arete of the buttress and balance up this to the ledge. Choose a finish.

③ The Plonker .... HVS 5b
12m. From the flake climb straight up the centre of the right wall to access the ledge awkwardly. Choose an exit.
FA. Ian Carr 1982

④ Muddy Crack .... VDiff
14m. The crack to the ledge and its continuation at the back.

⑤ No Time to Pose E5 6b
14m. Flash up the steep leaning arete and double overhang above - rapidly! Not well-protected where it matters.
FA. Speedy Dougie Hall 1987

⑥ Napoleon's Direct E2 5c
14m. Follow the slanting groove to the overhang and layback through this with difficulty and usually some grunting.
FA. Bill Wilkinson 1970

⑦ Mark I .... VDiff
12m. Climb the slabby angle in the left-hand edge of the bay then either take the wide crack direct, or the groove on the left with a quick hand-traverse back right to the final ledges.

⑧ Mark II .... VDiff
16m. Climb the crack which delineates the left-hand side of the main bulk of the buttress as it narrows and steepens. The interest is maintained throughout.

⑨ The Derivatives .... HVD
18m. Where *Mark II* begins to feel too pushy, escape right to the arete and then follow the short, exposed and bold slab above.

⑩ Rollup E1 5c
18m. ... if you fancy your chances! Climb right then left through the bulges and into a recess and exit leftwards from this up a crack. Trend right across the exposed and precarious slab above the overhangs to a finish on the flying arete.
FA. Ian Carr 1982

⑪ Rizla .... HVS 5a
22m. Follow *Rollup* to the niche then shuffle right below the roof to a ledge (and a possible stance). Finish up the wide (*Wedgewood*) crack in the back of the corner (**4b**).
FA. Paul Seddon 1961

⑫ Stranger than Friction E3 5c
20m. Access the undercut slab with difficulty and teeter carefully up it and the blunt arete above. Finish up the exposed hanging arete on its left-hand side using a useful thin crack.
FA. John Smith 1981

⑬ Wedgewood Crack .... VS 4c
24m. From the gully, on the right traverse left along the diagonal break to the arete and balance up this (hard for the short) to a possible stance on a good flat ledge. Wedge the wide and wicked *Wedgewood Crack* to finish.
FA. George Bower early 1920s

⑭ Wedgewood Crack Direct .... VS 5a
20m. The thin and awkward left-leaning crack gives an interesting struggle until the ledge below the *Wedgewood Crack* can be reached. Finish up this. "*..has no real attraction save as a gymnastic feat.*" - 1976 Chew Valley guide.

⑮ Wall of China E4 6b
18m. Take the previous climb to the large ledges then head right passing an awkward scoop to reach the exposed arete and climb this boldly to a finish up a crack on the left.
FA. Ian Carr 1987

True Grit **Ravenstones** 257

16 True Grit .... `Top 50` E3 5c
18m. A great outing up the impressive leaning gully wall, low in the grade but exciting and spectacular. Climb the scoop then trend left through the bulges and make long reaches to a deep break (large gear). Continue right of the arete in a fine position. *Photo on page 253.*
FA. John Smith 1981

17 Sniffer Dog E1 5b
14m. Climb the centre of the left-hand wall of the gully, starting on the right and passing a useful crack. The start is steep!
FA. Tony Howard (1 point) 1960s. FFA. John Smith 1981

18 Trinnacle East .... HVS 5a
12m. Climb out onto the north-facing wall to a groove and climb this passing a wobbly flake. *Photo page 24.*

19 The Left Monolith
...... `Top 50` HS 4b
12m. The front face of the monolith is a classic little pitch, well marked and well-travelled. A short-lived but excellent outing. *Photo page 37.*
FA. Herbert Hartley 1928

20 Trinnacle Chimney
...... Mod
10m. The widening rift that splits the towers is a good easy offering and bags a summit or two along the way.

21 The Right Monolith .... HVS 5a
10m. The centre of the right-hand tower is best climbed without deviation, though it is tempting to trend left and use the arete, in which case the grade drops to **VS 4b**.
FA. Herbert Hartley 1928

22 Trinnacle West E1 5b
8m. The leaning south face is climbed via a prominent crack, passing the overhang with difficulty.
FA. Paul Seddon 1963

Descent

True Grit
The right-hand side of the main cliff is composed of two impressive buttresses, divided by a steep grassy gully. On the left are the stacked overhangs of the tall True Grit Buttress and to the right is the free-standing tower of The Trinnacle whose spectacular and photogenic summit can be reached by a short scramble from behind. Almost all the routes here are worth doing. The rock is clean and quick drying and the setting is remote and spectacular - a classic moorland grit experience.

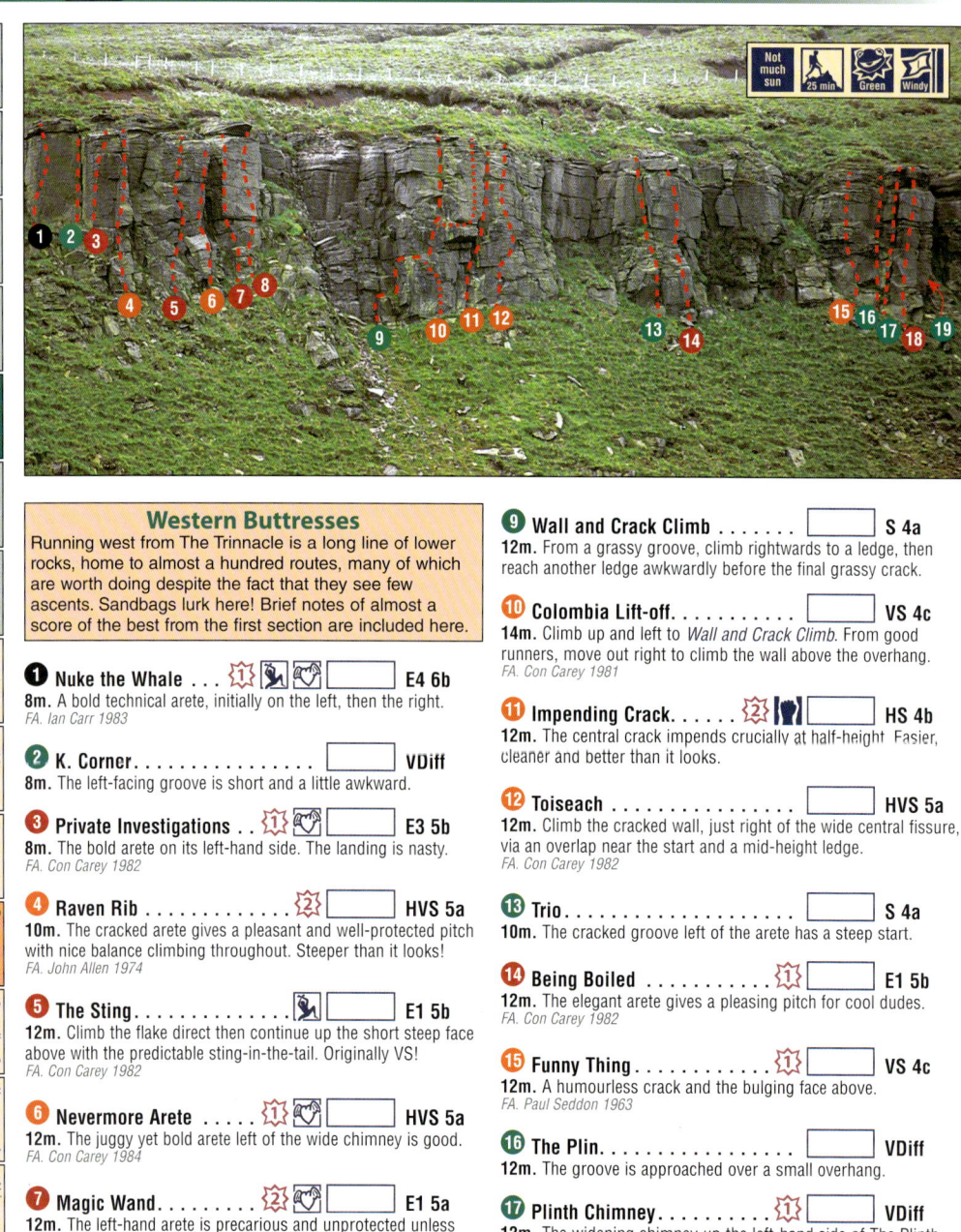

Ravenstones — Western Buttresses

Western Buttresses
Running west from The Trinnacle is a long line of lower rocks, home to almost a hundred routes, many of which are worth doing despite the fact that they see few ascents. Sandbags lurk here! Brief notes of almost a score of the best from the first section are included here.

1 Nuke the Whale **E4 6b**
8m. A bold technical arete, initially on the left, then the right.
FA. Ian Carr 1983

2 K. Corner . . . . **VDiff**
8m. The left-facing groove is short and a little awkward.

3 Private Investigations **E3 5b**
8m. The bold arete on its left-hand side. The landing is nasty.
FA. Con Carey 1982

4 Raven Rib . . . . **HVS 5a**
10m. The cracked arete gives a pleasant and well-protected pitch with nice balance climbing throughout. Steeper than it looks!
FA. John Allen 1974

5 The Sting **E1 5b**
12m. Climb the flake direct then continue up the short steep face above with the predictable sting-in-the-tail. Originally VS!
FA. Con Carey 1982

6 Nevermore Arete . . . . **HVS 5a**
12m. The juggy yet bold arete left of the wide chimney is good.
FA. Con Carey 1984

7 Magic Wand **E1 5a**
12m. The left-hand arete is precarious and unprotected unless you (sensibly!) place side runners in the next climb.
FA. Chris Hardy 1985

8 Abracadabra **E2 5c**
12m. A delicate face climbed centrally with hard, safe moves near the top. Good climbing and much harder for the short.
FA. Con Carey 1982

9 Wall and Crack Climb . . . . **S 4a**
12m. From a grassy groove, climb rightwards to a ledge, then reach another ledge awkwardly before the final grassy crack.

10 Colombia Lift-off . . . . **VS 4c**
14m. Climb up and left to *Wall and Crack Climb*. From good runners, move out right to climb the wall above the overhang.
FA. Con Carey 1981

11 Impending Crack . . . . **HS 4b**
12m. The central crack impends crucially at half-height. Easier, cleaner and better than it looks.

12 Toiseach . . . . **HVS 5a**
12m. Climb the cracked wall, just right of the wide central fissure, via an overlap near the start and a mid-height ledge.
FA. Con Carey 1982

13 Trio . . . . **S 4a**
10m. The cracked groove left of the arete has a steep start.

14 Being Boiled **E1 5b**
12m. The elegant arete gives a pleasing pitch for cool dudes.
FA. Con Carey 1982

15 Funny Thing . . . . **VS 4c**
12m. A humourless crack and the bulging face above.
FA. Paul Seddon 1963

16 The Plin . . . . **VDiff**
12m. The groove is approached over a small overhang.

17 Plinth Chimney . . . . **VDiff**
12m. The widening chimney up the left-hand side of The Plinth.

18 Altered States **E3 5b**
12m. The impressive, poorly-protected front face of The Plinth.
FA. Sid Siddiqui 1982

19 Safety Plin . . . . **S 4a**
12m. The final offering is the narrowing chimney up the right-hand fissure of The Plinth.

Standing Stones

	No star	⭐1	⭐2	⭐3
Mod to S	6	2	1	-
HS to HVS	3	12	2	3
E1 to E3	6	6	5	2
E4 and up	1	3	-	-

An easily reached cliff, from roadside parking near the high point of the A635 Holmfirth to Greenfield road. It is south facing and has a worthy selection of routes though it is inclined to be a little gritty after rain due to the slope directly above the cliff. The chaotic state of the terrain below the cliff reveals that it was formed by a landslip and it has been suggested that Falling Stones might be a better name for the place though the central section of the cliff has stood in its present form for quite a time. The slope above the cliff is not the crisp clean top of the Eastern Edges; care required when setting up belays. Descents can be made round either edge of the cliff - again care required when wearing slick soled boots on steep grassy terrain. The best of the climbs here such as the fine line of *Twin Crack Corner* (VS) the impressive *Fairy Nuff* (VS) the devious *Ocean Wall* (E1) and the pumpy *Fallen Heros* (E1) would be lauded routes were they on the Eastern Edges; here you may have them to yourself.

Approach Also see map on page 224

There is roadside parking about 300m west of the high point of the A635. Park in the large layby on the Standing Stones side of the road. From here head cross country (no path) aiming for a conspicuous small outcrop on the crest of the moor. The top of the crag is a little further on, in the same direction.

Conditions

A splendid cliff, wild and remote feeling, south facing, fifteen minutes from the road - and a downhill approach - what more could you want? The cliff has not been especially popular in the past and the wings in particular are inclined to be grassy - a little more traffic would soon clean up the worst of this. The cliff can give good climbing in winter on calm days, but takes a couple of days to dry after rain. Parts of the crag can be sandy with grit washed down from the moor above after rain.

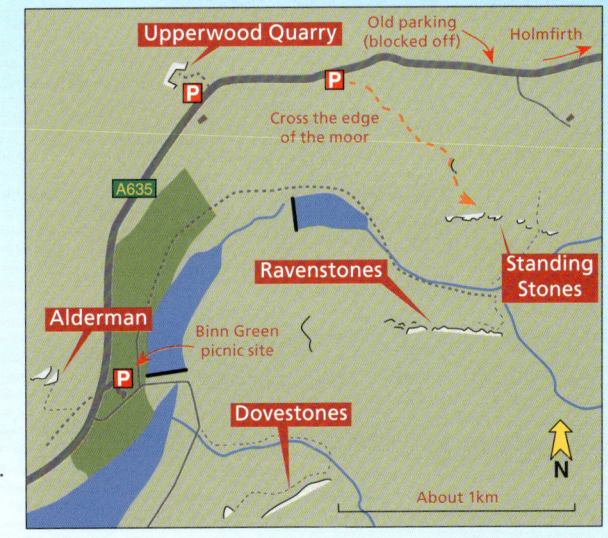

Standing Stones — Smiler's Corner

1. Kathryn's Crack — HVS 5b
22m. Climb the blunt rib to a belay on the terrace (**4c**). Climb to and up the thin crack, then continue up the wall until a leftward exit is possible.
FA. Tony Howard 1960. Originally a pleasant Severe but a rockfall has made it much harder.

2. Echantillon — HVD
14m. A chimney/groove leads to a ledge, step left to a shallower groove leading to a ledge out right. Finish up the wall.
FA. Toni Nicholson 1943

3. Upset — S 4a
14m. A variation to the upper section of *Echantillon* taking the steep groove on its right to the same exit. The start is hard.

4. Greystone Pillar — VS 4c
14m. Follow the crack to an awkward mantel onto the grassy ledge then climb more cracks in the top wall. Finish carefully.
FA. Bob Whittaker 1971

5. It's a Small World — E3 5c
14m. The bold and technical arete is followed throughout.
FA. Gary Gibson 1983

6. Sidewalk — HVS 5b
14m. Devious though with some good climbing. Start up the main groove for 3m then step out left past the arete to a ledge. Take the cracked wall rightwards to a ledge and a direct finish.
FA. Bob Whittaker 1971

7. Smiler's Corner — HS 4b
14m. A great line. The long and interesting groove at the left end of the area of smoother rock. More traffic would help shift some of the grass that is accumulating on the route.
FA. Toni Nicholson 1943

8. Pinocchio — VS 4c
14m. An adventure. A thin crack leads to a good ledge, then climb the slab to the groove and follow it to a crusty rightwards exit.
FA. Tony Howard 1962

9. Digital Dilemma — E3 5c
14m. The thin cracks in the pillar are finger-wreckers. Follow them slightly leftwards (dubious block) to their end then finish out right.
FA. Nadim Siddiqui 1982

Lots of sun · 15 min · Windy

Descent

Smiler's Corner
The left-hand side of the crag has always played second fiddle to the rest of the place. The array of boulders on the slope below suggests it is of recent origin and the amount of grass on the face ensures it sees little attention. A small selection of the better routes is included here for the diligent explorer.
Despite there being some lower grade routes, it is not a good destination for beginners, there is some loose rock, the top-outs are often tricky as is sorting belays on the cliff top.

Mark Binney on *Twin Crack Corner* (VS) - *page 262* - at the Standing Stones.

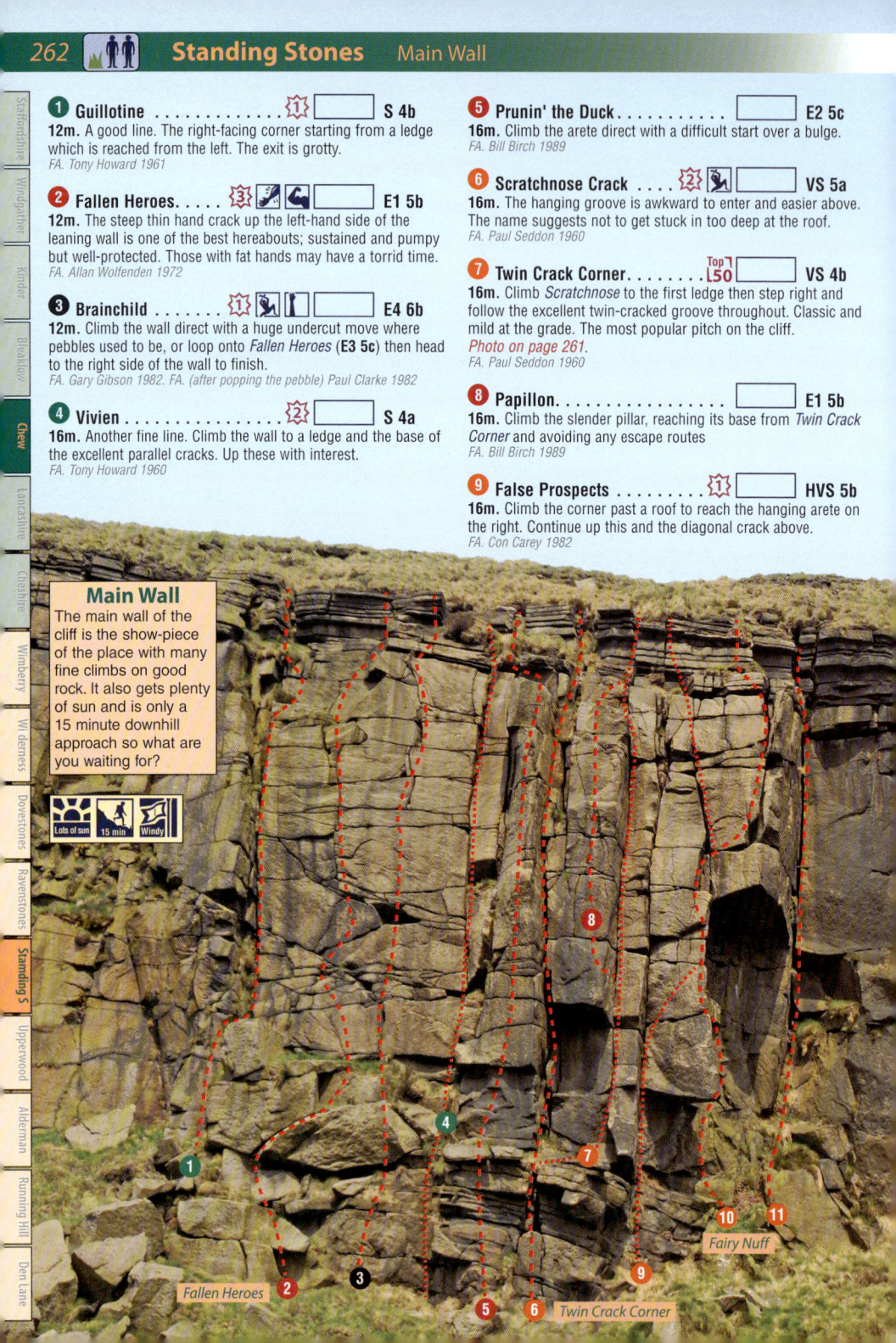

Standing Stones — Main Wall

1 Guillotine .... S 4b
12m. A good line. The right-facing corner starting from a ledge which is reached from the left. The exit is grotty.
FA. Tony Howard 1961

2 Fallen Heroes E1 5b
12m. The steep thin hand crack up the left-hand side of the leaning wall is one of the best hereabouts; sustained and pumpy but well-protected. Those with fat hands may have a torrid time.
FA. Allan Wolfenden 1972

3 Brainchild E4 6b
12m. Climb the wall direct with a huge undercut move where pebbles used to be, or loop onto *Fallen Heroes* (**E3 5c**) then head to the right side of the wall to finish.
FA. Gary Gibson 1982. FA. (after popping the pebble) Paul Clarke 1982

4 Vivien .... S 4a
16m. Another fine line. Climb the wall to a ledge and the base of the excellent parallel cracks. Up these with interest.
FA. Tony Howard 1960

5 Prunin' the Duck E2 5c
16m. Climb the arete direct with a difficult start over a bulge.
FA. Bill Birch 1989

6 Scratchnose Crack .... VS 5a
16m. The hanging groove is awkward to enter and easier above. The name suggests not to get stuck in too deep at the roof.
FA. Paul Seddon 1960

7 Twin Crack Corner .... Top 50 VS 4b
16m. Climb *Scratchnose* to the first ledge then step right and follow the excellent twin-cracked groove throughout. Classic and mild at the grade. The most popular pitch on the cliff.
Photo on page 261.
FA. Paul Seddon 1960

8 Papillon E1 5b
16m. Climb the slender pillar, reaching its base from *Twin Crack Corner* and avoiding any escape routes
FA. Bill Birch 1989

9 False Prospects .... HVS 5b
16m. Climb the corner past a roof to reach the hanging arete on the right. Continue up this and the diagonal crack above.
FA. Con Carey 1982

Main Wall
The main wall of the cliff is the show-piece of the place with many fine climbs on good rock. It also gets plenty of sun and is only a 15 minute downhill approach so what are you waiting for?

Lots of sun | 15 min | Windy

Main Wall — Standing Stones — 263

10 Fairy Nuff .... VS 4c
18m. A real classic, high in the grade and intimidating too. Climb up to the square roof then traverse onto the arete. Follow this before stepping right to finish up the exposed hanging crack.
FA. Paul Seddon 1960

11 Leprechauner........ HVS 5a
16m. The huge groove is a bit of a battle, large gear (the bigger the better) is a good idea. As you might expect, it is often green.
FA. Graham West 1960

12 Kremlin Wall .. E1 5c
14m. The thin crack splitting the fine smooth wall is approached easily and climbed directly with difficulty especially for short, fat-fingered individuals.
FA. Mick Wrigley (2 points) 1969. FFA. John Allen 1973

13 Layback-a-daisical . VS 4b
14m. Follow a groove rightwards to the roof, move left and climb the bold and strenuous crack to a juggy finish out right. Scary!
FA. Tony Howard 1960

14 Obyoyo .... HVS 5b
14m. Climb the wall to the roof then gain the hanging crack on the right by some grim jamming. Once established, finish more easily. Tape might help those with Fairy Liquid hands!
FA. Tony Howard 1961

15 The Trouble with Women is.. E1 5b
14m. Climb directly up the left-hand side of the face.
FA. Chris Hardy 1985

16 Womanless Wall ..... VS 4c
18m. A fine open classic and high in the grade. Climb direct (loose block) or from the right to a huge flake, move up to some big rounded pockets then traverse right to a final steep crack.
FA. Tony Howard 1958

17 Stuck........... E4 6a
12m. Climb the right side of the wall via a blind crack (poor gear) and a couple of small flakes. Finish up the wall above and right.
FA. Gary Gibson 1983

18 Unstuck........... E4 6b
10m. The pebbly wall is climbed desperately to the twin flakes on *Stuck* hoping they and you both stay stuck.
FA. Paul Clark 1990s

19 Diddley Dum Overhang .... HVS 5b
10m. Tackle the tough finger-crack above the niche.
FA. Graham West 1960s

20 Deep Chimney .... VDiff
8m. The short rift on the right.
FA. Graham West 1960s

Standing Stones — Tranquillity

1 Pocked Wall .... VS 4c
10m. Follow the spoor-trail across the face, exiting rightwards.
FA. Tony Howard 1958

2 Touch of Spring ...... HS 4b
10m. The juggy crack to an awkward but well-protected exit.
FA. Tony Jones 1960

3 Yorkshire Longfellow ... E3 5c
10m. The centre of the face to a break (small runners) and a delicate finish up the steep wall above.
FA. Simon Royston 1996

4 Prolapse E2 5c
10m. Start up *Yorkshire Longfellow* but follow lumps, bumps and dimples rightwards to a finish up the arete. Scary climbing.
FA. Gary Gibson 1982

The next two climbs cross both tiers of the crag.

5 Postman's Knock .... S 4a
16m. Follow the arete on the left edge of the lower wall to grotty ledges and its upper continuation via a couple of cracks.
FA. Brian Hodgkinson 1960

6 Pygmy Wall .... HVS 5b
16m. The pocketed wall and tricky layaway moves lead to a shallow groove then ledges. Thin cracks above give the way on.
FA. Bob Whittaker 1977

7 The Ghoul E2 5b
14m. The left-hand of a pair of slanting cracks. Ghoulish indeed.
FA. Bob Whittaker 1977

8 The Slanting Horror .... VS 4c
14m. The right-hand crack is easier (but not that easy) and better, despite its name. Avoiding the left-hand crack is tricky.
FA. Paul Seddon 1960

9 Wits' End E1 5c
14m. Boulder up the lower wall to the horizontal then sprint up the upper section via a series of long reaches and good holds.
FA. Steve Bancroft 1973

10 Tranquillity .... HVS 5a
14m. Mantel onto the niched ledge then climb into and up the steep groove above. Quite high in the grade.
FA. Bill Tweedale 1971

11 Fish-meal and Revenge
.... E5 6a
12m. The centre of the wall on small spaced holds to a gripping slap for the top. A small cam is fairly crucial but difficult to place.
FA. John Smith 1987

12 The Diamond E2 5b
14m. Climb the wall trending right to a bold finish up the blunt arete on slopers.
FA. Paul Cropper 1982

Tranquillity
Two short walls on separate tiers. Although the area looks a bit grotty at first acquaintance there is a collection of worthwhile wall climbs and some testing cracks.

Left Twin and Ocean Wall — Standing Stones

13 Wobbling Corner .... `HVD`
12m. Wobble-a-way up the crack in the west-facing wall to a ledge and short finishing groove.
FA. Tony Howard 1957

14 Piece of Pie .... `HVS 5b`
14m. Climb steeply and swing left to a ledge. Step up then out right round the arete then follow cracks to the terrace. Escape up, or off.
FA. Tony Howard 1964

15 Right of Pie ...... `E3 5c`
14m. Follow the flake to its end then make hard moves to reach and stand on the one really good hold on the pitch. Continue warily up the steep slab to finish. Not well protected.
FA. Paul Cropper 1982

16 Fat Old Sun .... `E1 5b`
12m. Teeter leftwards up the ramp to a thin crack that is tricky to start. The wall above is easier.
FA. Paul Cropper 1982

17 Jiggery Pokery .... `E1 5b`
12m. Climb the ramp and shallow scoop above it to a long reach for a good ledge. Finish up the crack above.
FA. Tony Howard 1964

18 Small c .... `E2 5b`
12m. Climb the right side of the wall using a shallow groove and make a committing long reach for the ledge. Escape off to the left.
FA. Colin Brooks 1977

19 17 Shades .... `HVD`
14m. Climb the chimney and trog left along the ledge system at its top to an escape up a crack just short of the left-hand arete.
FA. Tony Howard 1960

20 The Annoying Little Man `E4 6b`
12m. From left of the large flake climb the face with difficulty.
FA. Steve Delderfield 1993. "Named after an extremely annoying small climbing colleague".

Across the gully to the right is the final decent bit of rock on the cliff, home to several good routes and well worth a visit.

21 Kon-Tiki Korner ...... `VS 4b`
12m. Climb into the groove then where it blanks out make some strenuous layback moves before heading right to finish up the juggy wall and short crack.
FA. Tony Howard 1961

22 The Ocean's Border. `E3 6a`
14m. Climb the roofed-in groove in the arete to its closure then make difficult blind moves up and right past the lip to ledges and a welcome rest. The thin crack in the headwall (**Oceanside**) is the most logical finish.
FA. Gary Gibson 1983. FA. (Oceanside) Paul Cropper 1982

23 Dredger. .... `E2 6a`
14m. The square-cut arete is climbed with difficulty and no gear to ledges at 10m. The *Oceanside* finish is best, though the awkward hanging groove to its right was the original way if you want to be historically correct.
Chris Addy 1977

24 Ocean Wall .... `E1 5b`
16m. Climb the tricky wall to the upper of two ledges then climb out left to the centre of the wall, up a short crack then swing left again to reach the exposed, juggy arete for a well-positioned finale that is great practice for *L'Horla*. Care with rope work required if you want to enjoy the experience to the full.
A lower traverse is **Oceanview, E1 5c**.
FA. Malc Baxter 1960. The first ascent took three days of effort!
FA. (Oceanview) Phil Davies 1992

Left Twin and Ocean Wall
Tucked away on the far right, in a grassy hollow is the excellent venue of *Ocean Wall*, also known as the Right Twin. The Left Twin also has some worthwhile climbs.

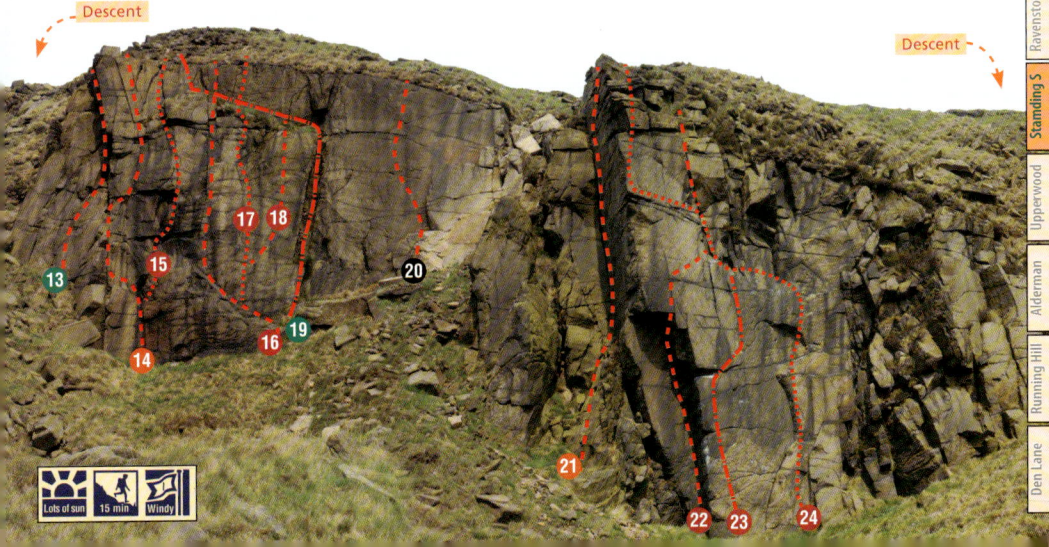

Upperwood Quarry

	No star	★	★★	★★★
Mod to S	-	1	-	-
HS to HVS	4	7	-	-
E1 to E3	4	6	3	-
E4 and up	1	4	1	2

Not the most prepossessing of quarries although the best of the routes are worth calling in for. The place is only a few minutes from the road, and it also gets the morning sun. Following CRoW, the quarry is now on open access land and has a good collection of clean climbs, many of which follow strong lines. Get them done and help keep the place in a decent condition!

Approach   Also see map on page 224

The quarry is situated above the A635 Holmfirth to Greenfield road, which is still known as the 'The Isle of Skye road' after a long-gone pub. There is parking for several cars in a lay-by on opposite side of the road to the farm just downhill from the gated track that leads up into the quarry. The approach takes less than five minutes.

Conditions

With its east-facing aspect the cliff gets the sun until early afternoon, and as such is a good venue for early risers. Some sections of the quarry take drainage (or even spout impressive waterfalls) and are inclined to be sandy after rain, taking several days to come into prime condition. Fortunately several of the buttresses jut forward enough to stay dry, the great classic of *Renaissance* (E4) is especially notable in this respect so you have no excuse for not calling in and getting it done.

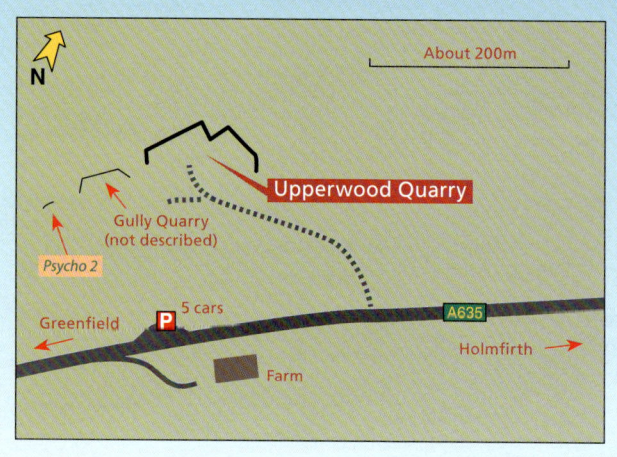

Heap Big Corner — Upperwood Quarry

① Little Running Water — VS 4c
20m. The frequently water-washed parallel cracks on the far left are approached by a tricky bulge and exited rightwards.

② Big Heap — HVS 5b
14m. The steep crack is hardest at the overhangs.
FA. Graham West late 1950s. FFA. Bob Whittaker 1973

③ The Green Meanies — E2 5b
14m. Gain the square arete from *Big Heap*. Proves to be strenuous and then delicate.
FA. Paul Cropper 1980

④ Heap Big Corner — HVS 5a
14m. The angular corner gives a worthwhile route when clean and is much less of the dump than the name suggests.
FA. Graham West late 1950s

⑤ Cochise — HVS 5b
14m. Traverse right from the corner to reach the crack in the wall and power up it. The **Direct Start** is **E'sa**, a dynamic **E3 6a**.

⑥ Blazing Saddles — E4 6a
16m. Climb the wall to the start of the diagonal crack then continue in a direct line by bold, sustained and reachy climbing. A cam in the crusty break is semi-essential.
FA. Allan Barker 2000

⑦ Little Bighorn — E5 6a
20m. The prominent diagonal crack is a bit of a battle. Approach it via the bold and technical wall of *Blazing Saddles* then thug rightwards until a finish can be made up thin cracks on the left.
FA. Tony Howard 1963. FFA. Steve Bancroft 1978

⑧ Tomahawk — E4 6a
16m. The thin once-pegged crack was one of the original routes of the quarry. It is fingery and awkward to protect.
FA. Graham West late 1950s. FFA. Steve Bancroft 1978

Heap Big Corner
The left-hand side of the quarry has some powerful lines and some worthwhile routes. The whole place has been neglected in the past though a little traffic could help keep the place clean.

⑨ Totem Corner — HVS 5a
14m. The angular right-facing groove has recently been cleaned up - get it done before it turns back into a greasy pole.
FA. Tony Howard early 1960s

⑩ Hawkwind — E1 5b
14m. The thin crack just right of the groove is gained from its base. At the top step back into the corner to finish. The gymnastic **Direct Start** makes the route into a worthwhile **E1 5c**.
FA. Brian Cropper 1981. FA. (Direct Start) Allen Barker 2000

⑪ Giteche Manitou — E1 5b
18m. Take either start to *Hawkwind* then move out right to climb the wall and flake trending right to finish.
FA. Paul Cropper 1982

⑫ Cowboys and Indians — E1 5c
24m. Start as for the previous route but continue the traverse all the way out to an exciting finish on the far arete. Thrilling!
FA. Allan Barker 2000

⑬ Play it Safe — E4 6a
16m. Climb to the bulge then continue up curving groove and slab on an array of indifferent pockets. One ancient peg runner.
FA. Loz Francomb 1980

Upperwood Quarry — Renaissance

Renaissance
The main feature of the quarry is the central jutting overhang that catches your attention on entering the place. Originally bolted by Tony Howard in 1969 as **The Walum Olum, A3**, it is now home to three desperate routes including the classic *Renaissance*, arguably the best route in the quarry.

14 Piece of Pipe — HVS 5b
18m. Climb to the diagonal crack and follow it with difficulty to better holds where the crack widens. Finish steeply. High in the grade and often dirty.
FA. Graham West late 1950s. FFA. Jim Campbell 1967

15 Pipe-line — E3 5c
18m. Swarm up the evil narrowing slot (giant cams can be a saviour) until the upper section of *Piece of Pipe* can be gained.
FA. Jim Campbell 1968

16 Waiting for an Alibi — E5 6b
18m. The hairline crack and bold wall are taxing. One poor peg runner and little else to help you along the way.
FA. Dougie Hall 1986

17 Pipe of Peace — VS 4b
18m. Climb across ledgy ground to reach the short-lived crack which was one of the earliest free routes in the quarry.
FA. Tony Howard 1959

18 The Screaming Abdabs — E3 6a
18m. Start from ledges and balance up the bold blunt arete above a worrying drop - hard! One old peg runner just about protects.
FA. Ian Carr 1984

19 Turtle — E1 5b
18m. Climb mixed rock and veg into the open groove (ancient bolt) then follow this to a tricky exit round the capping overhang. The best route of its grade in the quarry and high in the grade.
FA. Bill Birch 1969. FFA. Steve Bancroft 1978

20 Edge Your Bets — E6 6c
18m. The left wall of the great prow with a loop to the right at mid-height to utilise a vital pocket. Micro-cams protect.
FA. P.Kendell 1970. FFA. Dougie Hall 1986

21 Renaissance — E4 6a
20m. Climb *Forked Tongue* then from a highish runner balance and teeter out left to the arete and a bold finish up its left-hand side. The peg on the next route should be avoided if at all possible. Slightly soft rock on the traverse.
FA. Tony Howard (reached by bolting the huge overhang) 1969
FFA. Steve Bancroft 1978. The best of his Chew classics.

22 Give the Dogg a Bone — E5 6b
20m. The technical and fingery right-hand wall of the arete passing stacked (and unclippable) glued pegs. A good climb that had to be done, though its a pity the integrity of *Renaissance* suffered from the placing of the fixed gear.
FA. John Smith 1987

23 Forked Tongue — HVS 5b
16m. The thin cracks are approached easily up grass and are tricky to start but soon ease off. Well-protected by small wires.
FA. Graham West late 1950s. FFA. Gerry Peel 1972

24 Paleface — VS 4c
16m. Scramble to the crack and groove and jam it to a short section of laybacking and an awkward mantelshelf exit.
FA. Paul Seddon 1960

Wampum Wall — Upperwood Quarry 269

25 How .... HVS 5a
16m. The butch groove is approached over cleaned terrain.
FA. Graham West late 1950s

26 Iron Road E2 5c
16m. A good line up the smooth wall right of the groove, generally on better holds than it looks. Cross a block (thread), move out to the arete, step back left then right before finishing direct. Small cams may be found useful.
FA. Bill Birch 1969. FFA. (by a more devious line) Jonny Woodward 1982

27 Renegade .... HVS 5a
16m. The twisting leaning groove, starting from a block (thread) and finishing up the arete on the right.
FA. Graham West late 1950s. FFA. Gerry Peel 1972

28 Wampum Wall .... S 4a
18m. Climb leftwards into the groove and climb it until the arete on the left can be gained for an exposed finish.
FA. Tony Howard 1959

29 Yellow Peril E3 5b
18m. The open tilted groove is like a super version of Curbar's *Peapod*, strenuous precarious and often a bit damp too.
FA. Bill Tweedale (2 points) 1969

30 General Custard E3 6a
18m. The square pillar rising above the grassy ledges is accessed with difficulty then followed centrally.
FA. Chris Hardy 1984

Wampum Wall
The right-hand of the quarry is even more neglected than the rest of the place, but it gets the sun for longer and has some interesting climbs. It is worth a quick visit, ticking all the starred offerings would fill a morning.

31 Adios Amigo E2 5b
20m. Amble up ledges to the huge block then access the face above from its tip. Traverse out to the exposed left arete and finish up this.
FA. Allen Barker 2000

32 Tickled Pink E1 5b
20m. Start ad for *Adios Amigos* to the top of the block but continue up the face above to a crusty exit.
FA. Malc Baxter 1988

A few other indifferent climbs have been done to the right, they are not described here.

The quarry isn't a prime bouldering venue but there is one problem worth seeking out. To the left of the quarries is a 6m bullet-scarred wall.

33 Psycho 2 .... V4 (6b)
Climb the wall centrally. Said by some to be the best route here!
FA. Chris Hardy 1981

Alderman Rocks

	No star	★1	★2	★3
Mod to S	2	3	1	-
HS to HVS	1	2	-	1
E1 to E3	1	2	-	-
E4 and up	-	-	-	-

A mini-peak, the most popular summit in the area and home to a small set of climbs, in a superb setting on good rock. The outward view across the Chew reservoirs and into the heart of the Wilderness Moors is exceptional. The flog from the parking is a bit of a lung-buster (good Alpine training) but only takes a steady 15 minutes and is well worth it. Unusually for grit, the routes in the centre of the cliff are two pitches in length, split at mid-height by a wide ledge, and this gives an extra attraction to the place and is a great spot for an easy intro to multi-pitching. It is possible to link a visit here with a walk over to the monument next to Pots and Pans Quarries (home to a reasonable selection of climbs - not described here) giving the prospect of a neat mountain day out.

Steve Cunnington and Dave Spencer enjoying the classic of the crag, *Great Slab* (VS) - *opposite* - at Alderman.

Approach   Also see map on page 224
There is extensive parking in the Binn Green picnic area directly below the conical hill with the cliff just below its crest. Cross the road and follow the cobbly track leftwards for couple of hundred metres until it descends slightly and meets a wall. Cross the fence on the right carefully and follow the steep track up the side of the wall until it is possible to head rightwards to the base of the cliff at the well-trodden area under *The Great Slab*. More direct approaches are even steeper!

Conditions
The cliff at Alderman faces south east and so is in the sun until mid-afternoon. The rock is clean and takes little drainage and so dries rapidly after rain. On the down-side, it is very exposed to the wind.

Alderman Rocks

1 Edgehog Flavour — E2 5b
8m. A tasty treat up the right-hand side of the rounded pebbly arete on the far left-hand edge of the cliff.
FA. Carl Dawson 1985

2 Pygmy Wall — HS 4b
10m. Climb the slabby wall then trend right to finish by tiptoeing up the very edge of the undercut face. A pleasant little problem.
FA. Tony Howard 1958

3 E Route — S 4a
8m. After a delicate start, the well-scratched slab leads to the wide and easy crack directly above.
FA. Brian Hodgkinson 1958

4 F Route — S 4a
8m. The main groove and wide crack just to its right give an awkward but short-lived struggle.
FA. Brian Hodgkinson 1958

5 Golden Wonder — E1 5b
8m. From a flat block, swing out right to gain the right-hand side of the arete then layback smartly (or jibber) up this. Low in the grade but unprotected and with a pretty poor landing.
FA. Chris Hardy 1982

6 Crispy Crack — HVS 5a
8m. The attractive shallow seam/runnel that crosses the slab diagonally rightwards gives a good little pitch that surprisingly is easier to foot-traverse than to hand-traverse. Variations exist.
FA. Tony Howard 1958

7 Rib and Face — VDiff
1) 10m. Climb the easy-angled rib in the back of the wide groove to a series of ledges then step left to a good stance.
2) 10m. The well-protected crack in the centre of the west-facing continuation wall gives a fine second pitch and is especially neat.
FA. Tony Howard 1958

8 Cleft and Chimney — VDiff
1) 10m. The rather green recessed groove leads without incident to the mid-height terrace and a stance.
2) 10m. The narrow chimney just above is awkward to enter due to its undercut base but then soon eases.
Malc's Flaky Finish - takes the flying flake left of the chimney and has some wild moves at E2 5c.
FA. Brian Hodgkinson mid 1950s
FA. (Flake Finish) Malc Baxter 1960s

9 Great Slab Arete — S 4a
10m. Weave through the bulges (or pull over the lowest one - 4b) to gain and then climb the well-positioned arete on its right-hand side throughout.
FA. Brian Hodgkinson mid 1950s

10 Great Slab — VS 4c
A fine climb though most only do the first pitch. *Photo opposite.*
1) 4c, 10m. The centre of the attractive slab gives good climbing with escalating interest with final tricky moves (good runners in the horizontal break) to reach its crest.
2) 4c, 10m. Move right to the jamming crack in the upper wall and follow this until it widens awkwardly and possible to swing left and mantel into the base of the wide and easy finishing cleft.
A **Direct Finish** above the fist crack is a pumpy **HVS 5a**.
FA. Tony Howard mid 1950s

11 Great Slab Chimney — Diff
10m. The flaky rift to the right of *Great Slab* gives pleasant climbing up a good line. A worthwhile beginners' route
FA. Brian Hodgkinson mid 1950s

12 Great Slab Right — HVS 4c
10m. The right-hand arete of the chimney is delicate and the nose directly above is strenuous. Not well-protected.

13 Pebble Mill — E2 5b
8m. The rather crusty centre of the right-hand slab. Don't pull too hard on those pebbles
FA. Bill Birch 1986

Descents - From the top of the Lower Tier, either descend the blocky gully left of *Rib and Face* or scramble up and left. From the cliff top the easiest descent is down and left to join the route from the Lower Tier.

272 Running Hill Pits

	No star	✪1	✪2	✪3
Mod to S	8	1	-	-
HS to HVS	25	11	-	1
E1 to E3	11	12	5	2
E4 and up	2	3	7	2

Steve Cunnington getting stuck into the Pits' classic of *Plumb Line* (VS) - page 279.

Running Hill Pits 273

The Pits is a smallish set of quarries (8 in all) looking out over the Upper Tame Valley. Although individually quite small there are almost 150 routes here, covering the grade spectrum. Despite their name and the fact that they're rarely busy, their westerly aspect and quality rock make them worth a visit from afar when conditions are right. There are a number of excellent crack climbs here, some fine bold face routes, and some high quality fingery bouldering. Of the quarries, 1 and 2 are the prime venues after a dry spell, and there are some worthwhile routes in 5, 6, and 8. Number 4 (Back Quarry) is worth a visit just to see how neat and tidy the quarrymen can be when they really want to!

Approach   Also see map on page 224

From the centre of Uppermill (when travelling north on the A670) take a right turn by the off-licence and follow the road that climbs steadily uphill, passing a crossroads by Saddleworth Church. Continue uphill passing the Cross Keys to arrive at limited parking at a cross-road (two of the roads - the right-hand and straight on branches - are no more than grass tracks). Follow the deeply incised track ahead uphill for ten minutes to a gate. Number 1 and 2 quarries are here on the right, whilst 8 lies leftwards diagonally down the bank another three minutes away. 7, 6 and 5 are reached by the old track that leads past the entrances to number 8 and the other quarries.

Conditions

The Pits are best avoided if the weather is poor, as the cloud tends to hug the hillside here. Under these conditions the quarries make a dreary venue and the lichen is at its worst. Choose a fine summer's evening and enjoy these holes in the ground when they are filled with glowing golden light and the rock is in prime condition.

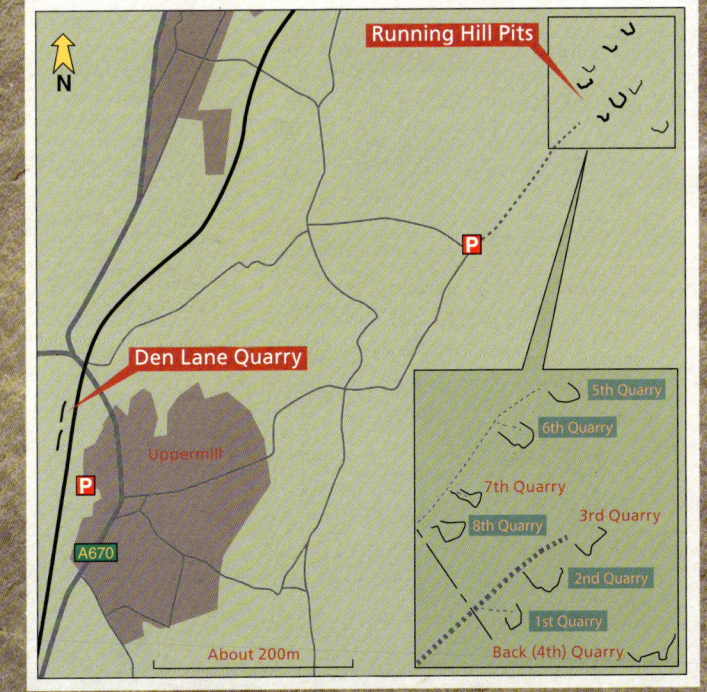

Running Hill Pits — First Quarry

First Quarry

The first quarry reached from the car is tucked away on the right. It has some worthwhile and strenuous crack climbs. The classic pumpy *Calamity Crack* is especially worthwhile, if somewhat arduous in execution.

1 Spider Crack . . . . HVS 5c
8m. The thin crack just right of the left arete of the quarry to a finish up the proper jamming-crack on the right.
FA. Bob Whittaker 1977

2 Nora Batty E1 6a
8m. Attack the thinner, finger-shredding crack leading right out to the arete then back left to the solid jams of *Spider Crack*.
FA. Clive Maybury 1983

3 Acarpous E2 5b
12m. Climb into the recess, pull out right for a breather on the grassy ledge then finish back leftwards up the slanting crack.
FA. Chris Hardy 1987

4 Maquis E1 5b
12m. Take the steep and pumpy jamming-crack to the niche where it joins and finishes more easily as for *Acarpous*.
FA. Bill Tweedale 1966

5 Flush Pipe E1 5c
10m. Climb the tricky arete then make a swift mantel to reach the rest on *Maquis*. Finish direct up the short-lived crusty crack.
FA. Bob Whittaker 1977

6 Gull-wing E2 5c
14m. Start up the wider left-hand crack then swing left on a line of flat holds to access a steep groove. Climb this past the roof and the strength-sapping wall on the right to the top. Hard work.
FA. Paul Braithwaite 1978

7 Mimosa E2 5c
12m. Climb the main right-trending crack strenuously passing a useful hole a short distance from the top. Use the thinner right-hand crack when needed.
FA. Tony Howard (1 point of aid). 1966 FFA. John Smith 1980

8 Calamity Crack E4 6a
14m. Short but action packed. The thin leaning crack is an uphill struggle on thin-hand-jams and fat finger-locks though protection is superb; which way to face is the real conundrum. Most of the old wooden wedges that used to get in the way have now gone. *Photo opposite.*
FA. Tony Howard (aid) 1962. FFA. Steve 'that man again' Bancroft 1972

9 Gargantua E1 5b
14m. Bridge the leaning groove to a niche, pull out of this into another niche and then escape rightwards. Steep, strenuous and high in the grade.

10 Godzilla E3 6a
8m. Start up the groove then layback the right-hand side of the arete until a bit of a pop is need to reach the slab. Exit left.
FA. Chris Hardy 1987

11 Kaptain Klepton E1 5c
8m. Climb a flake to reach the horizontal jams then tackle the blank wall, trending right to finish.
FA. Chris Hardy 1987

12 Mickey Thin E1 5c
8m. Climb to a hanging flake then follow it leftwards to a slim-tips crack. Up this to a mantel and easier finish. Sustained.
FA. Mick Shaw 1974

13 It Only Takes Two to Tango . . E2 5b
8m. Climb out of the left side of the grotty recess to reach a narrow ramp then finish direct via thin cracks. Often wet. The loss of the big block at start may have increased the initial difficulties.
FA. Gary Gibson 1982

14 Tin Man E4 6b
7m. The right-hand side of the undercut wall passing a peg.
FA. John Smith 1989

15 Flue Pipe E1 5c
6m. The hanging crack on the far right is okay, though sadly, escape is too easy an option.
FA. Gordon Mason 1977

Mickey Thin

Jason Pickles finishing off *Calamity Crack* (E4) - *opposite* - Running Hill Pits.
Photo: Ian Parnell

Running Hill Pits — Second Quarry - Spanner Wall

Second Quarry - Spanner Wall

An open aspect and worthwhile routes make this quarry the most popular in the complex. The left-hand wall is the showpiece of the quarry with the clean *Spanner Wall* attracting most attention.

1 Tighten Up Yer Nuts — E4 6a
10m. A fiercely-thin finger-traverse with a particularly hard move to reach the jugs and a sprint finish. Memorable.
FA. Dougie Hall (onsight solo) 1987

2 Iguanodon — E5 6b
10m. Bold and fierce. The blank wall is climbed rightwards by committing moves to better holds where more hard (and even more committing) moves allow access to a shallow groove. Climb this to safety.
FA. Jonny Woodward (onsight solo) 1980

3 Folies Bergeres — HS 4b
12m. The first crack right of the main angle gives a short tussle and is especially awkward at the start.
FA. Bill Tweedale 1966

4 Lolita — HS 4b
12m. A precocious little number up the wall and crack.
FA. Pete Oldham 1966

5 Harvest Moon — E4 6b
12m. Climb into the hanging groove (ancient peg plus newer one over to the right) swing right to a second groove, then make desperate moves to reach good flat holds in the open groove above. Finish up this carefully.
FA. Chris Hardy 1984

6 The Connection — E4 6b
14m. The link-up gives the best way up the wall which is both bold and committing. Replacing the pegs with decent fixed gear might lower the grade a notch or so.
FA. Mike Watson 1987

7 Spanner Wall — E2 5c
14m. Bizarre and excellent. From *Dead Dog Crack* traverse to the spanner (its base is a bit thin, but threading it is better than nothing) then balance up the precarious shallow groove above and right. You need to avoid using the spanner as a hold to claim the full grade! Originally the route stared from *Lolita* - this is harder and more serious. *Photo opposite.*
FA. Dougie Hall 1978

8 Dead Dog Crack — HS 4b
8m. The left-hand of the cracks that form an inverted Y.
FA. Graham West 1962

9 Cave Crack — VS 4b
8m. The right-hand arm of the inverted Y.
FA. Graham West 1962

10 Midsummer — S 4a
8m. The flaky right arete of the wall starting just to the right.
FA. Bob Whittaker 1972

11 Hazy Groove — VDiff
8m. The deep groove stepping right into its extension to finish.
FA. Bob Whittaker 1972

12 The Cracks — S 4a
8m. Climb the cracks to an exit left or right.

13 Breakdown — HVS 5b
8m. The thin crack in the steep slab is pleasantly technical.
FA. Brian Cropper (1 peg) 1974. FFA. Bob Whittaker 1975

Andy Stewart, belayed by Richard Brewster, using of the eponymous spanner as a runner on *Spanner Wall* (E2) - *opposite* - Running Hill Pits. Photo: Chris Hannah

Running Hill Pits — Second Quarry - Scoop de Grace

Second Quarry - Scoop de Grace
The central section has less to offer for the mid-grade climber, but there are three technical gems for the talented including the show-stopping *Scoop de Grace*.

1 Yorick's Crack E6 6c
10m. The thin right-trending mini-seam is superbly desperate. It was only pegged a few times back in t'olden days and so, alas, has maintained its cruel razor-sharp edges. Successful ascents are few and far between.
FA. Dougie Hall 1988

2 Overhanging Chimney ..... VS 4c
10m. The main groove develops from cracks to a wider rift which leads to a rightward exit over the bulge.
FA. F.Farrar (2 pegs) 1972. FFA. Brian Cropper 1974

3 Sagittarius Flake .. E5 6b
10m. The hairline crack leads with great difficulty to a final lunge or massive stretch for the top edge.
FA. Paul Cropper (1 peg) 1978. FFA. Nick Colton 1979

4 Scoop de Grace E5 7a
12m. A stunningly technical wall leads into the precarious scoop which is followed rightwards to easy ground. The tall may find the start only 6c and the short (and don't forget, Dougie was no giant) might consider it impossible although the block to the left may be a help. Scooptastic!
FA. Dougie Hall 1987

5 Phaestus E4 5c
8m. Walk up the ramp leftwards into more harrowing territory and a tough mantel above a big drop. Bold and technical climbers might consider it only **E3 5b**.
FA. Bob Whittaker 1972

6 Windbreaker E2 5b
6m. From the toe of the ramp blast up the centre of the blank slab on a continuously-surprising set of holds.
FA. Bob 'the blaster' Whittaker 1974

7 Cochybondhu E2 5c
6m. The rib on the right-hand side of the slab gives precarious laybacking. Once committed its do or fly!
FA. Bob Whittaker 1974

8 Kneepad .... HVS 5b
6m. The awkward groove is ... er ... awkward, and bit of an ugly beast, but is included for completeness. Knees (and indeed knee pads) might well help.
FA. Bob Whittaker 1974

9 Crosstie .... VS 5a
12m. Mantel onto the tip of the slab with difficulty then trend right until a precarious move gains the V-groove of *Groove-V Baby* and a rightward exit.
FA. Bob Whittaker 1974

10 Pipe Spanner E1 5c
8m. Climb the centre of the slab to a hard sloping exit.
FA. Dougie Hall 1980

11 Pipe Inspector E3 5c
10m. Start as for *Pipe Spanner* but move right then climb direct to a hard exit balancing up into the tiny left-facing groove.
FA. Chris Booth 1985

12 Groove-V Baby .... VS 4c
10m. Follow the groove on the right-hand side of the slab (small wires) as it leads pleasantly to a rightward exit.
FA. Tony Howard 1969

Second Quarry - Plumb Line

The final wall in this quarry lies beyond a grass slope and faces north. It is split by a fine set of cracks, most of which are worth doing when in condition and well worth steering clear of when not!

⓭ Dusty Arete .... **Diff**
12m. The ledgy wall is climbed close to the arete. It has a useful iron bar runner and not too much else in the way of gear.
FA. Pete Oldham 1966

⓮ Midgebite Express **E2 6a**
12m. The arete on its right-hand side.
FA. Kevin Thaw 1989

⓯ William the Conkerer **E1 5b**
12m. Climb the wall 2m right of the grotty groove (**Sardonicous, HVS 5b**). It is often rather green hence its original moniker.
FA. Chris Hardy 1984. Originally called Green Wall.

⓰ Paradise Crack .... **HS 4b**
12m. The first crack in the long north-facing wall is not a patch on its Stanage namesake and is probably a grade harder.
FA. Pete Oldham 1966

⓱ Cameo .... **VS 4c**
12m. The central crack of the trio is a little less of a gem than its Wilton twin though still worth doing when clean.
FA. Bill Tweedale 1966

⓲ Riddler .... **HVS 5a**
12m. The right-hand crack is the pick of the trio. Interest is well-maintained throughout. High in the grade and often green.

⓳ Pantagruel .... **HVS 5a**
12m. The parallel cracks give gruelling jamming that might well leave you panting. Starting up the right and finishing up the left is the easiest combination, and a long reach caps the fun.
FA. Bill Tweedale 1966

⓴ Mangled Digit **E3 6a**
14m. The thin wiggling crack is hard on the fingers and gives reachy moves between sketchy jams. Protection is excellent and the route wouldn't be out of place in Millstone.
FA. Ian Carr 1982

㉑ Plumb Line .... **VS 4c**
14m. An excellent straight jamming crack swallows all the gear you can carry. Quite imposing though there a good jams and the odd flat hold on the walls to easy the narrower sections.
Photo on page 272.
FA. Mick Quinn 1966

㉒ Passport to the Pits **E5 6b**
14m. An eliminate up the wall right of *Plumb Line*.
FA. Dougie Hall 1989

The block chocked rift to the right has never been recorded!

㉓ Liquor, Loose Women and Double Cross
.... **E5 6c**
12m. Direct up the thin balancy wall past a peg.
FA. John Smith 1989

㉔ Sodom **E1 5c**
12m. Boulder up the wall to reach the left-hand crack which gives painful and sustained finger-jamming. It can also be approached from the next climb at a slightly lower grade.
FA. Bill Tweedale (4 pegs) 1966. FFA. Bob Whittaker 1972

㉕ Gomorrah **E1 5b**
12m. The right-hand crack gives good finger jamming on solid lockers with the quality of runners you might hope for. It is easiest of you keep moving.
FA. Ian Lonsdale 1977

㉖ Breakin' for a Bogey **E6 6c**
12m. The thin and fingery wall past a peg.
FA. Kevin Thaw 1989

㉗ Cosmic Enforcer **E2 5c**
6m. From the bank on the right, swing left and climb the short but exposed left-hand side of the arete. A runner up and right is a good idea (hard for the short to place).
FA. Colin Brooks 1983

㉘ Unctious .... **S 4c**
4m. A short wall with a fingery start and a myriad harder variations for those of a bouldering bent.
FA. Ian Lonsdale 1977

280 Running Hill Pits — Fifth Quarry

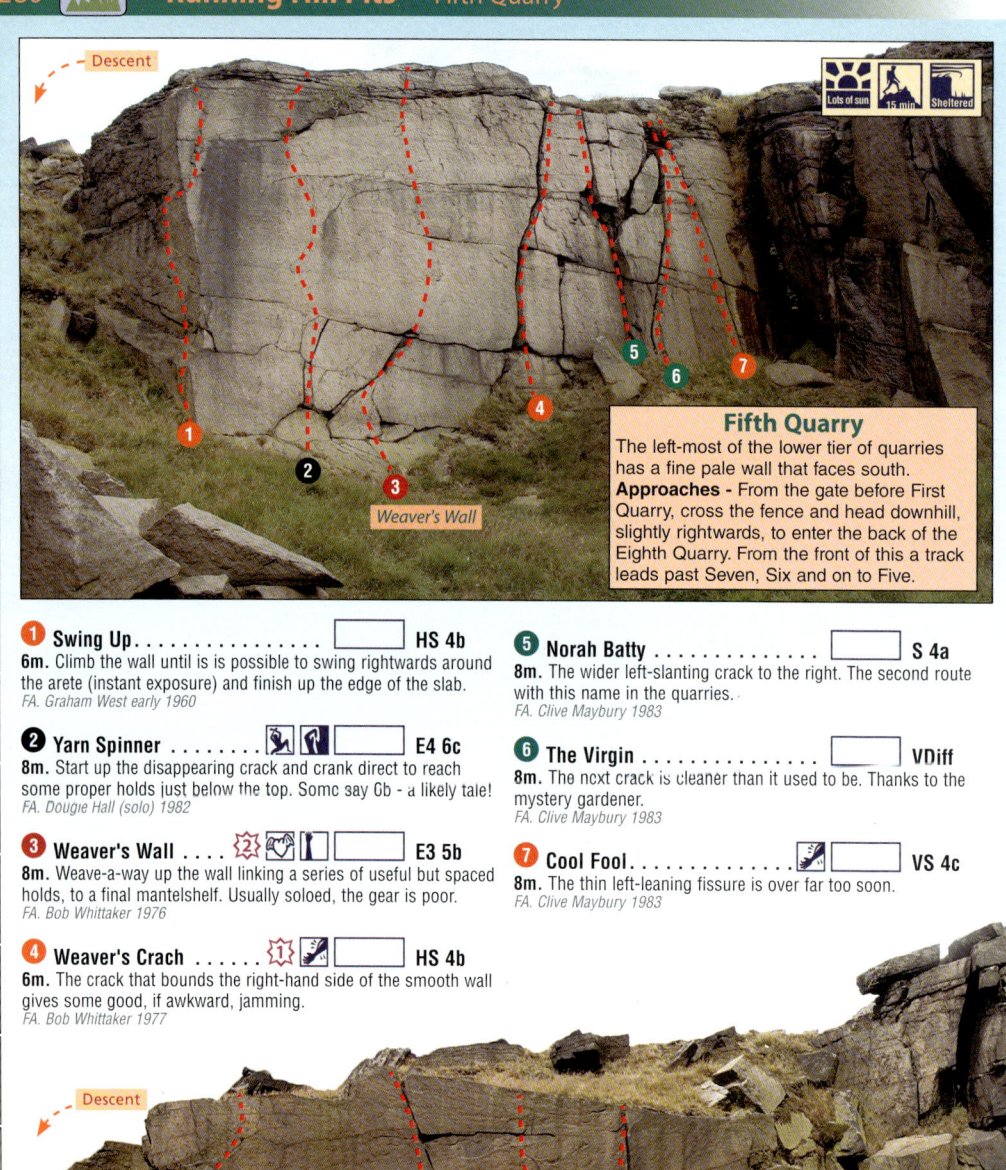

Fifth Quarry
The left-most of the lower tier of quarries has a fine pale wall that faces south.
Approaches - From the gate before First Quarry, cross the fence and head downhill, slightly rightwards, to enter the back of the Eighth Quarry. From the front of this a track leads past Seven, Six and on to Five.

① Swing Up .... HS 4b
6m. Climb the wall until is is possible to swing rightwards around the arete (instant exposure) and finish up the edge of the slab.
FA. Graham West early 1960

② Yarn Spinner E4 6c
8m. Start up the disappearing crack and crank direct to reach some proper holds just below the top. Some say 6b - a likely tale!
FA. Dougie Hall (solo) 1982

③ Weaver's Wall E3 5b
8m. Weave-a-way up the wall linking a series of useful but spaced holds, to a final mantelshelf. Usually soloed, the gear is poor.
FA. Bob Whittaker 1976

④ Weaver's Crach ...... HS 4b
6m. The crack that bounds the right-hand side of the smooth wall gives some good, if awkward, jamming.
FA. Bob Whittaker 1977

⑤ Norah Batty .... S 4a
8m. The wider left-slanting crack to the right. The second route with this name in the quarries.
FA. Clive Maybury 1983

⑥ The Virgin .... VDiff
8m. The next crack is cleaner than it used to be. Thanks to the mystery gardener.
FA. Clive Maybury 1983

⑦ Cool Fool .... VS 4c
8m. The thin left-leaning fissure is over far too soon.
FA. Clive Maybury 1983

Sixth Quarry — Running Hill Pits

Sixth Quarry
The left-hand side of this quarry has a short wall of decent rock that faces south and has a grassy base. Further right, past a tall loose tower is another area of good rock with a small collection of tiny routes.

8 Reachy .... VS 5b
8m. The short problem, with a good landing, on the left.

9 Intro Wall .... HS 4b
8m. The left-hand crack is tricky to exit - stretch for the top.
Photo on page 283.
FA. Tony Howard early 1960s

10 Summary .... HVS 5b
8m. Zigzag up the next crack-line, an awkward little number.
FA. Chris Hardy 1984

11 Seconds .... VS 4c
8m. Jam the crack to its end at the sloping break, then swing left to access the continuation and jam on.
FA. Bob Whittaker 1974

*To the right is a tall and rather shattered looking buttress, home to a solitary route - **Central Chimney E1 5a**, it hasn't proved popular. 10m further to the right is a wall of good rock split by some attractive cracks.*

12 Parallax E3 6a
10m. Climb the left-hand side of the blunt arete. A runner on the right is a good idea and should really be placed on the lead.
FA. Chris Hardy 1987

13 Sticky Fingers E1 5b
10m. The left-hand of a pair of cracks is of an awkward width, offering well-protected exercise. Easier for the small-handed.
FA. Bob Whittaker 1977

14 Widfa .... HVS 5a
10m. The right-hand crack is easier though it widens awkwardly with height. Exit left above the useful chockstone on good jams.
FA. Bob Whittaker 1974

15 Sunstroke V1 (5b)
6m. Climb the arete of the groove throughout, with a tricky initial mantelshelf. The groove can be bouldered direct at 6a.
FA. Bob Whittaker 1974

16 Cosmo Smallpiece V3 (6a)
6m. The narrow wall is eliminatish but worthwhile and the landing is good. A somewhat blinkered approach is best to appreciate it to the full.
FA. Chris Hardy 1985

17 Puffin .... HS 4b
8m. Follow the groove with a useful crack in its left wall to the edge of the hanging slab and pull over the roof to finish.
FA. Bob WHittaker 1974

18 Delicate Wall .... HS 5a
10m. Climb the slab leftwards to the arete and a finish over the roof as for *Puffin* without panting.
FA. Tony Howard early 1960s

19 White Honkey .... VS 5a
10m. Climb the slab then head for the edge of the roof. Above escape or cross easy ground to thin cracks in the final wall.
FA. Bob Whittaker 1977

Running Hill Pits — Eighth Quarry

Eighth Quarry

Good rock with worthwhile mini-routes or bouldering.
Approaches - From the gate just before the First Quarry, cross the fence and head downhill, slightly rightwards, to enter the back of the Eighth Quarry.

1 Firefly .... **HVS 6a**
8m. The the left-hand side of the wall via a crack climbed on tips jams. Short but sweet, keep your nails filed for this one.
FA. Bob Whittaker 1983

2 Duckdoo .... **S 4a**
8m. The wide leaning crack is awkward.
FA. Chris Hardy 1979

3 Axminster .... **HS 4c**
8m. Starting up the cracks to the right is an alternative.

4 A Fist Full of Daggers
.... **E2 6b**
8m. Another searingly thin crack-line giving technical finger jamming of the ouch kind, and a l-o-n-g reach to finish.
FA. Chris Hardy 1987

5 Deliver Us From Evil **E1 5c**
6m. The pair of converging cracks are climbed left then right. There is a hard move between the crack and precious little to stand on.
FA. Gordon Mason 1983

6 Black Watch .... **HVS 5b**
6m. The tricky crack passing a flake with mega-jugs on its crest leads to a monster reach for the top.
FA. Chris Hardy 1980

7 Talliot .... **HVS 5b**
8m. The crack and groove are harder than they appear from below. Finger jam, layaway and tarry not.
FA. Bob Whittaker 1983

8 Eye-catcher .... **HVS 5b**
8m. Climb the right-hand crack in this section of the wall and at its top scoot leftwards to finish above *Black Watch* or, for more of a pump, finish up *Taillot*
FA. Bob Whittaker 1983

9 Repetition **E1 5c**
5m. The thin crack-line has a reachy move.
FA. Bruce Goodwin 1983

10 Fall Guy **E1 5c**
5m. A green crack. Move left at the top to *Repetition*.
FA. Bob Whittaker 1983

11 Chew Grit .... **VS 4b**
5m. Climb the short groove and the slab above. Not very tasty.
FA. Bob Whittaker 1983

12 A Day Too Late .... **V2 (5c)**
Traverse the handrail from the base of *Chew Grit*.
FA. Dave Hinton 1989

13 The Groove **V7**
The steep blank groove. Finish left at the roof.
FA. Kevin Thaw 1991

14 Legacy .... **V0+ (5b)**
The thin crack gets easier with height.
FA. Bob Whittaker 1983

15 Chalkie .... **V0 (5a)**
Climb the short arete right of the corner has nice moves.
FA. Steve Marshall 1980

16 Tomintool .... **V1 (5c)**
The groove just right of the arete is trickier than it looks.
FA. Steve Marshall 1980

17 Auchtermuchty .... **V1 (5c)**
The short wall.

Paul Smith belayed by Alex Jeffrey on the short but sweet *Intro Wall* (HS) - *page 280* - Running Hill Pits. Photo: Paul Smith collection

Den Lane Quarry

	No star	⚀	⚁	⚂
Mod to S	2	-	-	-
HS to HVS	10	5	2	-
E1 to E3	2	1	2	-
E4 and up	1	-	-	-

Den Lane Quarry is situated to the west of the pleasant small town of Upper Mill - birthplace of Troll, the outdoor company. The quarry used to be a bit of a scruffy hole with dumped rubbish and even bits of old cars. In the winter of 2008/9 local climbers gave the place a spruce up and now it is a much pleasanter place. Many of the routes follow strenuous cracks and the rock is of reasonable quality. The best climbing is on the impressive Rake Wall and the loose upper section can be avoided by using the fixed belays at the top of the good climbing. The Long Wall is shorter but has some good strenuous climbs and the potential for some excellent fingery bouldering.

Bolt Belays On Grit - Many of the worthwhile climbs here used to be spoilt by the dangerous unstable and overgrown exits. The addition of a few discrete fixed-bolt-belays below the grot has made the climbing here safer and a little more popular.

Access
Climbing on the right-hand section is not permitted due to being on private land (an industrial estate). The climbs on this section are not covered here.

Approach   Also see map on page 224
When entering Uppermill from the south, take a left turn into the narrow walled lane of Moorgate and follow this as it swings right into Den Lane. About 500m down here there is parking on the left for a couple of cars and further on room for a couple more on the right. A muddy track leads under the railway line and up into the quarry only minutes away - arriving just to the right of the right-hand end of Long Wall. The more impressive Rake Wall is located up the slope to the right.

Conditions
The crag faces east and is well-sheltered from the prevailing winds. It gets the morning sun and can be a pleasant escape from the heat on stuffy summer days. The sheltered nature of the cliff, and the trees that grow in the quarry, make it a potentially midgy venue on humid days. Despite the slopes above the quarry, the faces do not take a lot of drainage and it is usually possible to get something done here even when the weather is poor.

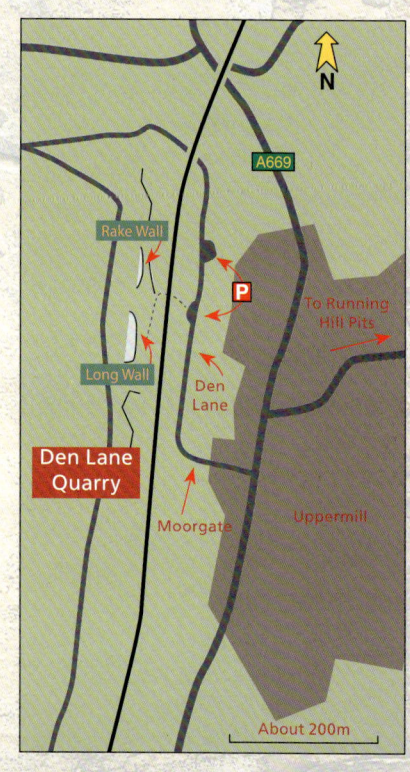

Den Lane Quarry

Jon Winter stepping onto *Three Notch Slab* (VS) - *page 287* - on the Long Wall at Den Lane. Photo: Ian Parnell

Den Lane Quarry — Long Wall

Long Wall
The left-hand section is the well-named Long Wall, which is home to some reasonable short (and not so short) routes, mostly with grotty exits. An abseil descent is normal - care required with the fixed gear.

1 Irish Jig .... VS 4c
8m. The zig-zagging crack to a choice of (dirty) exits. Down and left is the easiest escape
FA. Jeff Sykes 1959

2 Hadrian's Wall E1 5c
8m. From the fallen block pull past the right edge of the cave and use broken flakes to power up to the tree. Hard!
FA. Jim Campbell 1973

3 Ash Tree Direct .... S 4b
6m. Take the crack to above the roof then head left to the tree.
FA. Tony Howard 1958

4 The Ramp .... VS 5b
8m. The fingery wall eases as soon as the ramp is reached.
FA. Mike Pilling mid 60s

5 Cancan .... VS 5a
8m. A good jamming-crack leads to a slanting slab. Escape left up this or tackle the thin crack above to a sea of grot.
FA. Jeff Sykes 1960

6 Elderberry Slab .... VDiff
10m. The diagonal ramp leads left all the way to the tree.
FA. Tony Howard 1957

The next three routes all have poor finishes, best escape right.

7 Calypso Crack .... VS 5a
6m. The sinuous and disjointed crack is tough to start.
FA. Barry Kershaw 1958

8 Quickstep .... VS 5b
6m. Pull over the overlap and climb the crack to tricky moves onto the slab above.
FA. Barry Kershaw 1958

9 Fire-power E1 6b
6m. The thin crack on tips jams and one good locker.
Pass Me That Araldite… Please, E1 6b is the flake just right.
FFA. Steve Bancroft 1984. FA. (Pass Me That Araldite) Ian Carr 1986

10 Jive .... HS 4b
12m. Climb onto a ledge then take the crack as it bends left towards the roof. Escape right round this to an awful exit.
FA. Tony Howard 1959

11 Palais Glide .... VS 4c
14m. Steep and pumpy. Climb the groove to the roof then layback round it. At the second roof move right again to finish. Iron hoop (and nut) belays. Alternate finishes are poorer.
FA. Jeff Sykes 1959

12 Fox-trot .... HVS 5a
14m. Climb straight into the leaning groove, at its top step out left and teeter across to the steep crack above and a sprint finish. Belay as for *Palais Glide*.
FA. Tony Howard 1960. FFA. Roy Brown 1961

13 Mississippi Dip .... VS 4c
14m. Follow the ramp to the groove on *Fox-trot* but pull onto a slab then exit out right to reach a crack. Up this to awkward final moves. Belay as for *Palais Glide*.
FA. Brian Hodgkinson 1959

14 A Stretch Named Desire E5 6b
14m. Climb direct through the traverse of *Long Wall Eliminate*. Slink right at the top to the finish of *Orchestral Crack*.
FA. Kevin Thaw 1988

15 Long Wall Eliminate E3 6a
14m. Climb the groove the tackle the fierce left-slanting crack to join and finish (with luck) up *Mississippi Dip*.
FA. John Allen 1973

16 Orchestral Crack .... HVS 5a
14m. The groove that bounds the wall, steeply, to an awkward exit at an old piece of angle iron. The better belay as for *Three Notch Slab* is down and right.
FA. Jeff Sykes 1960. FFA Bill Tweedale mid 1960s

17 Three Notch Slab .... VS 4c
12m. The classic of the crag - well sort of. Skip onto the ledge then cross the slab rightwards and layback up the arete to a multi-point belay. Abseil/lower off. *Photo on page 285*.
FA. Barry Kershaw 1957

There is some good bouldering on the lower section of the face.

18 Low Level Traverse V3 (6a)
Traverse the low break. The starts of most of the routes are also good problems.

Rake Wall **Den Lane Quarry** 287

The Popple

Rake Wall
The most impressive section of the cliff has some good and strenuous left-leaning crack climbs that lead to The Rake. From here upward progress doesn't add a lot to the climbing experience - best to use the fixed belays. The orange scar of the rock fall on the right, and the small memorial under *The Popple*, point to the fact that care is required when climbing here.

*Left of Rake Wall a couple of lines have been cleaned, they run all the way to the cliff top. On the left is the long groove of **Bivouac Route**, **HVD** and to its right the steeper arete and final spectacular leaning groove of **Tartarus 8**, **VS 4c**. For both routes the descent is 70m to the left.*

19 Noah's Crack . . . .   VS 4b
22m. The leaning groove and tricky layback above leads to easy ground. Move right to the fixed belay.
FA. Barry Kershaw 1959

20 Sunset Crack . . . .   VS 4c
22m. From a large block pull onto a ledge then climb the sharp-edged crack to a leftwards exit under the capping flake.
FA. Tony Howard 1957

21 Tony's Terror . . . .   VS 4b
18m. Climb the steepening groove then exit right to a rest on a hanging slab. Continue up the steep crack to easy ground and the belay. Abseil off.
FA. Tony Howard 1958

22 Midgebite Crack . . . . . .   HVS 5a
16m. Climb the deep groove, left then right, to its apex and pull out right to reach a rest with difficulty. Jam the good crack above more easily, then pass the left-hand side of the large hanging block by more tricky climbing. Pull up to easier ground and then move left to the belay.
FA. Tony Howard 1959

23 The Popple . . . .   HVS 5b
18m. From just right of the memorial, climb the steep jamming crack to a triangular niche then follow the thinner finger-crack (the one to the right with an ancient thread may also be found of use), to reach better holds and one more strenuous pull to easy ground and the belay.
FA. Tony Howard 1959. FFA. Malc Baxter 1962

24 The Drooper. E2 5c
20m. The main angle is bridged to the overhang then power past this (old peg) to reach a jug in the wider crack above. Get established with difficulty then follow the easier crack as it runs leftwards to join *The Popple*. Follow this to the fixed belay.
FA. Barry Roberts (1 peg) 1962. FFA. Jim Campbell 1968
FA. (as Milk Crate Crack) Tony Howard 1958

25 The Wilter E1 5b
24m. The crack running up the left-hand side of the orange scar has some of the best climbing here though it is spoilt by the grubby exit. It has difficult, but well-protected, moves to pass the overhang where wilting arms is a common phenomenon. Above this the difficulties ease. Belay and abseil off.
FA. Tony Howard 1958. FFA. Tony Jones 1963

Nick Galpin climbing the superb *999* (HS) - *page 315* - at Wilton 1. Photo: Nick Verney

Lancashire

Map area:
- Hoghton
- Denham
- Anglezarke
- Cadshaw
- Egerton
- Wilton
- Brownstones

Littleborough Area Map - see page 338

About 5km

Hoghton Quarry

Brian Rossiter aiming to escape the clutches of *Mandarin* (E2) - *opposite*.

A huge lost World of a crag hidden away below the stately home of the same name. There are around 130 routes here but access restrictions over the years have allowed the vegetation free-reign and many great climbs have been lost. Recent negotiations have eased the access a little and tentative steps at regaining the crag have begun. Call in to tick the Big Three E2s here and you will have had a memorable day.

Approach
See also map on page 289

From the tiny village of Hoghton on A675, turn east into Chapel Lane by the Boar's Head pub. After about 600m there is limited parking by the old chapel (don't block any access). A lane leads down to the right, at its end enter a field then cross the railway line (carefully) and scramble up onto the old quarry track. Follow this through a (very) muddy cutting and into the impressive quarry.

Access
BMC and affiliated club members may climb here from the 1st Sunday in June to last Sunday in July inclusive:
8.30 to 5.30 pm (Sun to Thu)
8.30am to 9.00pm (Fri and Sat)

Hoghton Quarry   291

❶ Rhododendron Buttress   `Top 50`   E2 5c
32m. Superb and cleaner than most routes here. Climb the clean-cut crack and groove to the roof. Step left and continue up the wall to a ledge on the left (**4b** - possible stance). Move right then climb the wall to the notch in the roof, layback through this and follow the thin sustained finger-cracks to the top.
FA. John Sumner 1955. Dave Knighton 1976

❷ Cave Route   HS 4b
48m. Devious but engaging, and a true multi-pitch experience. The long traverse on the second pitch might spook nervous seconds. Hop onto the slab then step left and continue as for *Rhododendron Buttress* to the ledge (belay). Traverse round left (some loose rock) then move up until a groove some distance left can be gained. Move up then step left again to a good ledge and stance. The groove at the back of the ledge leads to a higher ledge on the right and a pair of crack that offer a choice of finishes.
FA. Steve Ripley 1950s

❸ Rhododendron Arete   E3 6a
26m. The right arete of the buttress gives a great pitch that is easier than it looks. From the bay on the right, climb the right-hand side of the arete past a roof to an uncomfortable ledge. Move up and right to another ledge then step right and finish boldly up the arete.
FA. Ray Miller 1967. FFA. Dave Knighton 1979

❹ Mandarin   `Top 50`   E2 5c
36m. Magnificent, moody and menacing - accept no substitutes. The soaring groove gives one of the great Grit pitches. The line is impossible to miss and the climbing is exceptionally sustained - you will be impressed! *Photo opposite.*
FFA. John Hamer 1967

❺ Route One   VS 4c
36m. Climb the hand-crack right of the arete then trend left to a good ledge and stance (**4b**). Climb the groove on the right then mantel out right to a position under a square roof. Climb round the left-hand side of this and finish up the corner.
FA. John Hamer 1950s. FFA. John Wareing 1960s

❻ Boadicea   E2 5c
34m. Another cracker up the long thin and sustained crack line running up the wall left of the corner. Carry plenty of small and medium wires.
FA. Phil Paget 1968. FFA. Ron Fawcett 1977

❼ The Wasp   HVS 5a
30m. The long corner is a fine line, though often green and grubby. It gives good bridging when clean.
FA. Geoff Hamridding 1967. FFA. Les Ainsworth 1967

Denham

292

	No star	⭐	⭐⭐	⭐⭐⭐
Mod to S	6	4	-	1
HS to HVS	5	3	1	2
E1 to E3	3	7	3	-
E4 and up	-	3	2	2

Jordan Buys making a late evening sunlit ascent of his own route *Splashback* (E8) - page 297 - at Denham. Photo: Alex Messenger

Denham

Denham is occasionally referred to as the 'Lancashire Lawrencefield', the comparison is quite striking; west-facing gritstone, easy of access, containing a smelly pond, and a good selection of climbs across the grades. Many folks call in here just once to tick the local classic of *Mohammed the Mad Monk of Moorside Home for Mental Misfits* - the longest route name on grit for nearly twenty years until *Clive Coolhead* came along and stole the crown. Having made the effort to get here it is well worth sampling more, especially some of the routes around the pool. These are generally slabby and rather bold, but there are some cracking pitches, almost all of which are well worth the effort. There is also some useful bouldering (slabby and fingery) on the short walls just to the left of the pool and to the right of the base of the groove taken by *Mohammed*.

The rock continues northward from the Pool Area where there are another 50 or so pitches, and although not of the quality of those round the pool there are one or two offerings worth seeking out. At the far end are a series of steep imposing overhangs and to the right of this are some pleasant slabby buttresses, suitable perhaps for beginners and others after a gentle time.

Approach   Also see map on page 232

The M61 motorway is visible from the cliff though access is a little awkward on first acquaintance. It is most easily reached from J3 on the M65. Take the A675 north westwards then turn left and follow signs for Brindel. Drive through the village then take the first left (Holt Lane) which leads round a right-hand bend to the quarry parking on the left. It is also possible to approach the quarry from J8 on the M61. Drive north on the A6 until a right turn onto the B5256 leads towards Brindle and joins the approach described above. There is an extensive parking area 30 seconds from the cliff, right in front of Mohammed. Despite this proximity, the broken glass in the car park suggests it is worth leaving the vehicle empty.

Conditions

West-facing and recessed, the cliff is sheltered and catches the afternoon sun. It dries quickly and, although inclined to be sandy, it is almost always possible to get something done here. Only a few minutes from the motorway, Denham is a good place to grab a few routes if you are passing. As you head home, the weather always improves, here is a chance of salvaging that wet weekend in the Lakes!

Denham Overhang Area

Overhang Area
On the far left of the quarry is a wide wall cut by an impressive band of overhangs. Brief details of the best of the twenty or so climbs here are included. This also covers the slabby walls to the right with their contrasting collection of easier climbs.

1 Main Break . . . . **HS 4a**
14m. On the far left a rib leads to the only gap in the overhangs. Climb the rib and on through the break, step left to climb the slab.
FA. Les Ainsworth 1966

2 Bullworker **E4 6a**
14m. Climbs the old peg route *Toreador*, up the smooth shield of rock. A sustained pitch. A slabby rib leads to the crack.
FA. F.Snalam (aid) 1968. FFA. Dave Cronshaw 1982

3 Screaming Meemies **E3 6a**
14m. Climb the roof at its narrowest point then take the groove and easy ground above.
FA. Roland Foster 1983

4 Quasimodo **E1 5b**
14m. Climb the arete on the left, then finish up the easier groove.
FA. Eric Dearden 1978

5 The Funny Farm . . . . **HS 4b**
10m. Up the groove to the roof, step right and head up the ramp.
FA. Les Ainsworth 1966

6 Step in the Clouds . . . . **S 4b**
10m. Climb the ramp to a ledge. Hop onto the small block in the groove before traversing out right. A start from the right is easier..
FA. Les Ainsworth 1966

Mohammed Buttress — Denham 295

7 The Layback .... VS 4c
10m. The short-lived corner crack. Exit left to easy ground.
FA. Les Ainsworth 1966

8 Cuckoo's Nest .... HVS 5b
8m. Balance up the steep slab past the thin breaks and a useful (nay - essential!) shot-hole.

9 Central Buttress Direct .... VDiff
14m. From the toe of the buttress climb direct via shelves and ledges to a choice of exits.
FA. Les Ainsworth 1966

10 Central Buttress .... Diff
12m. The right-hand side of the buttress leads to a small roof, move out left where ledgy rock leads to the top. Exit right.
FA. Les Ainsworth 1966

11 Lintel .... S 4a
10m. Climb round the left-hand side of the inverted staircase then head rightwards for an easy finish.
FA. Les Ainsworth 1966

12 Intra .... VDiff
12m. Slabby rock and steeper ground lead between the roofs.

13 Extra .... Diff
12m. The right corner of the next shallow bay, finish to the left.
FA. Les Ainsworth 1966

14 Trigular .... Mod
12m. Pleasant ambling up the well drilled centre of the buttress.
FA. Les Ainsworth 1966

15 The Edge .... VDiff
12m. The right arete of the buttress is pleasant enough.

Mohammed Buttress

16 Mohammed the Medieval Melancholic
.... VS 5a
14m. The clean crack left of the arete is approached up ledges and gives a couple of steep moves to easy ground.
FA. Les Ainsworth 1966

17 Mohammed Arete E1 5b
14m. The arete is delicate and the gear sparse where it matters unless you lean over to the right. After an easy start, boldly layback the right-hand side of the arete to terrain where you can breathe again.
FA. Eric Dearden 1986

18 Mohammed the Mad Monk of Moorside Home for Mental Misfits .. VS 4c
16m. Classic. Climb the ledgy left arete then balance right into the beckoning groove. Up this delicately to ledges out right then step right again for a gritty finish. Harder for the very short.
FA. Les Ainsworth 1960s

19 Going For the One E2 5b
20m. Climb to the overlap then use the flakes on the right to reach a traverse leading out left to a rest in the *Monk's Groove*. Move left and climb the crack until a rapid exit to easy ground can be made. The start is bold, the rest somewhat safer.
FA. Tony Brindle 1980

Mohammed Buttress
The buttress facing the car park is home to one of Lancashire's most famous routes up the elegant groove which is also a candidate for the longest route name around; *Mohammed the Mad Monk of Moorside Home for Mental Misfits*. Around this classic are a number of other routes which vary from 'reasonable' to 'minor eliminate' in status but there will probably be some to keep you busy.

296 Denham Concave Wall

20 The Denham Traverse   V9
The low-level traverse of the wall is a long, sustained and excellent. Most only do the section from *Snatch* to *Flick Direct*.

21 Mohammed the Morbid Mogul   S 4a
14m. The flake leads to ledges, move right to the carved letters DC and a step up and left to another ledge. Finish up the steep crack to a shrubby exit.
FA. Les Ainsworth 1966

22 Wall   V2 (5b)
A narrow wall. As an eliminate it can be as hard as **V5**.

23 Timepiece   E1 5a
28m. A wandering oddity though with plenty of good climbing. Climb past the red sandy arse and up the pocketed wall to a ledge. Traverse left along the break all the way to the arete the continue round it to finish up The 'Sad' Monk.
The direct finish is **Private Palpate, E4 6b** (2 peg runners).
FA. Les Ainsworth 1973. FA. (Private Palpate) Andrew Gridley 1980s

24 Little Monkey   V4 (?)
Dyno between the two ledges..

25 Brittle Nerve   E3 6a
16m. The right-slanting break is fiercely technical and a bit snappy; it sees little attention. Originally a peg runner was used.

The slab to the right gives some worthwhile bouldering.

26 Snatch   V11
The impossibly blank slab.
FA. Nik Jennings

27 Pickpocket   V1 (5c)
Climb the wall to the pocket.

28 Pickpocket Direct   V2 (6a)
Direct to the same pocket.

29 Crackpot   V4 (6b)
The thin crack.

30 Crap Pot   V7
Extremely thin wall climbing.

31 Vague Groove   V3 (6a)
Up a very vague groove.

The next routes start past a vegetated section of cliff at the slabby wall just to the left of the pool.

32 Concave Wall   S 4a
18m. Pleasant climbing but somewhat lacking in protection. Climb awkwardly onto the ledge then follow the open groove until an escape up ledges on the right can be made.
FA. John McGonagle 1966

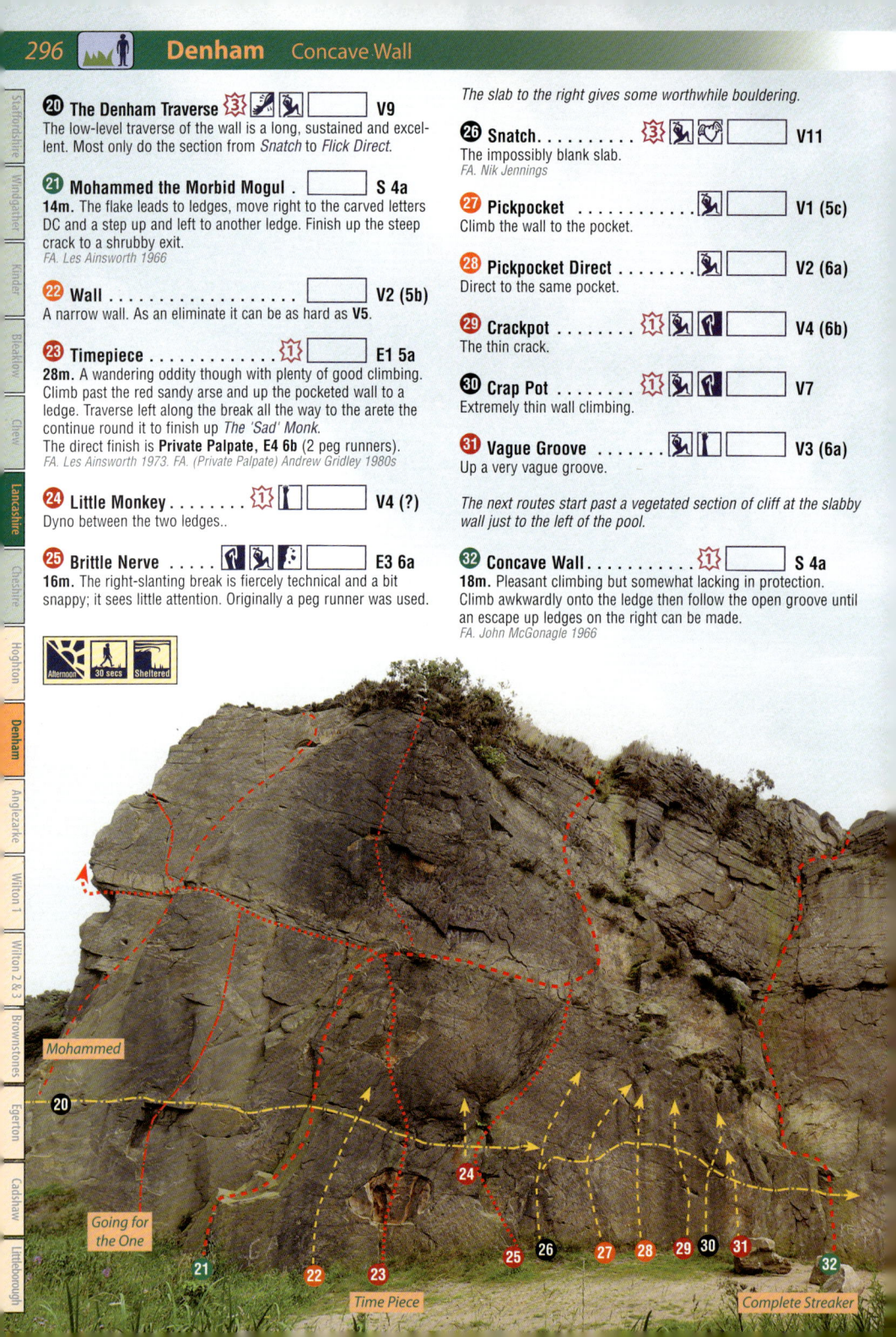

The Pool Denham 297

33 Complete Streaker .... VS 4c
22m. Exciting and a little bold, a fall may reach the waterline! Climb *Concave Wall* then follow the break out right almost to the arete, passing a naughty bolt and some irritating shrubbery on the way. Pull over the roof (old peg) to a good ledge and finish up the exposed rib.
FA. Les Ainsworth 1966

34 Mad Karoo .... HVS 5a
20m. Good climbing but not overly endowed with protection. Climb on the ledge via the groove and then access the flake on the wall behind awkwardly (very hard for the short - at least 5b). Mantel on this then climb straight up to the break and a good runner. Continue leftwards up the pleasant face to the final moves of *Concave Wall*.
FA. Dave Knowles 1969

35 Time E1 5a
20m. A bold number. Climb *Mad Karoo* to the break then head up into the shallow groove using a good pocket to make a spooky reach for the good edge above. From the ledge exit right on jugs.
FA. Dave Cronshaw 1973

36 End of Time E2 5b
20m. Another route with a bold feel. From the mantel on the two previous routes trend right up the steeping wall to the break and a good rest in a shallow cave. Pull left out of this and sprint up the wall above. The route contains an old bolt runner above the roof, but it shouldn't really!
FA. Les Ainsworth (1 peg) 1973. FFA. Les Ainsworth 1977

37 That's All it Takes .. E4 6b
20m. Climb onto a narrow ledge then head up the highly technical face to a crescent-shaped overlap. Pull through the left side of this to rest in the cave. Haul through the centre of the roof of the cave then sprint up the final wall on flatties.
FA. Brian Evans (aid) 1973, Dave Knighton (1 peg) 1977. FFA. Dave Kenyon 1980

38 Undercut Problem .. V8
Powerful climbing over the overlap using an undercut.

39 Flick Direct V5 (6b)
Direct up the arete. An alternative start to *Flick of the Wrist*.

40 Flick of the Wrist E2 6a
20m. Start from a tiny ledge above the waterline (try keeping the ropes dry) and swing left onto the front face at the earliest opportunity. Climb a tough bulge (really ancient bolt runner) to reach the overhang and a junction with *Complete Streaker*. Finish easily.
FA. Dave Knighton 1977

41 Splashback ... E8 6b
20m. Climb up a line of monos to clip a peg and place a small cam. Down climb then walk up the embankment and attack the wall, trending right to another peg. Go right to a porthole (big cam) then contort up the upper wall. *Photo on page 292*.
FA. Jordan Buys 2008

Approach the final two routes by walking round to the other side of the pool and scrambling up onto the ledges.

42 Last Day but One E3 5c
10m. The arete it taken first on the right then on the left. Protection is non-existent though the pond offers the prospect of a softish (and very smelly) landing. High in the grade.
FA. Dave Knighton 1977

43 Splash Arete .... VDiff
16m. A great little outing with an exposed finale. Climb the slab then flop onto a ledge on the left (possible thread belay in the corner to cut down rope drag). Climb the groove to ledges then move out to an exposed finish up the very arete.
FA. Les Ainsworth 1966

Concave Wall and the Pool
The slabby wall left of the pool is home to the best selection of climbs in the quarry, all are worthwhile and most are poorly-protected to a greater or lesser degree. To the right of the pool the well-positioned *Splash Arete* is a good lower grade route.

Anglezarke

	No star	★	★★	★★★
Mod to S	2	1	-	-
HS to HVS	7	12	2	2
E1 to E3	1	3	3	2
E4 and up	-	5	2	4

Nick Galpin in superb afternoon light on *Klondike* (E3) - *page 302* - on the Golden Tower at Anglezarke. Photo: Nick Verney

Anglezarke

One of the more popular venues in the Red Rose County is the extensive quarry of Anglezarke. It is home to a good set of routes across the grade range with some of Lancashire's finest classics standing out from the pack. The easy-angled slabs near the approach are extremely popular with beginners and groups but in reality the better climbing lies deeper into the quarry. A bit of exploration will be rewarded with the dramatic Golden Tower or the steep and unusual routes on the Terror Cotta Wall.

Unfortunately the rock is not best quality millstone grit, but a sandstone with some soft shale bands and other odd crumbly stuff. Only the relatively solid areas have been developed and most of the dangerous rock has gone, although the occasional snappy hold or loose block might still be encountered. Often sand washes down from above, especially on the popular climbs, where the grassy top of the cliff has been eroded. With this being the case, the harder climbs might need a quick brush before your ascent - get your mate to do it if you want to preserve the on-sight.

In recent years much of the base of the quarry has become overgrown, and this has led to standing water and a more humid atmosphere. The place could do with a bit of thinning of the vegetation to open up the walls to the sun and breeze.

Approach   Also see map on page 289

The quarry is most easily reached from the A673, 2km north of Horwich where a right (east) turn by the Millstone Pub leads onto the minor road that runs north then east, around Anglezarke reservoir to parking on the left. The car park is extensive and triple-lobed and is Pay and Display. Also, check the closing time on the barrier, it may be earlier than you really want. A track leads from the upper lobe across a minor road, over a fence and down a series of shelving ledges to arrive in the quarry between Whittaker's Original and Wedge Buttresses. This is directly across from The Golden Tower, which can be seen, jutting above the trees.

A rough path runs around most of the inner edge of the quarry and there are a variety of poorly defined tracks that cut across its centre. The base of the quarry is inclined to be marshy after wet weather; expensive trainers are not the best footwear for swampy jungle bashing.

Conditions

The quarry forms a horseshoe-shape and the walls face in all directions except north. It is sheltered enough to escape the worst of the weather and much of the rock dries quickly after rain. The west-facing walls are especially pleasant in the evening sun and can be enjoyed at almost any time of the year. In humid weather the quarry is unpleasant, the extensive tree cover and standing water promoting insect life, much of it of the biting variety!

Anglezarke — Whittaker's Area

Whittaker's Area
Either side of the descent route into the quarry are two clean walls split by cracks. Unfortunately the easy access of these faces means they have been used by the 'top rope' brigade and are now severely battered - the crisp quarried edges have been worn away and the erosion of the cliff top vegetation means that sand and gravel are forever washing down the faces.

① Side-step .... HS 4b
6m. The left-hand crack to a bulge, side-step this leftwards.
FA. Graham Whittaker 1966

② Alldred's Original .... VDiff
6m. The second crack has tricky initial moves then eases.
FA. Ian Alldred 1966

③ After the Blitz .... VS 4b
6m. Climb the short wall, then up the right-slanting groove.

④ Whittaker's Original ...... HS 4a
6m. The third crack is the pick of the bunch.

⑤ Meanwhile .... S 4a
6m. The right-hand crack in the face is unspectacular.
FA. Graham Whittaker 1966

⑥ Because .... HS 4a
6m. .... it's there. The right arete reached by the short wall below.
FA. Stu Thomas 1968

The next routes are just to the right of the approach scramble.

⑦ Minor .... V1(5c)
6m. The short wall just right of the arete.

⑧ Nightmare .... VS 4b
8m. The inverted Y cracks are pleasant if somewhat polished.

⑨ Elaine .... HVS 5c
8m. A problematical wall which eases with height. Side-runners can be placed on lead to protect.
FA. Mark Liptrot 1983

⑩ Wedge .... HS 4b
8m. The steep and well-protected jamming crack is popular.
FA. Les Ainsworth 1967

⑪ Mark .... VS 4c
8m. The final fissure in the wall continues the theme.
FA. Ian Lonsdale 1977\

Terror Cotta

50m to the right of Whittaker's Area is a steep clean wall.

⑫ Transformation .... VS 4c
14m. The fine thin crack leads to a crusty exit. High in the grade.
FA. Paul Cropper 1978

⑬ Metamorphosis .... VS 4c
16m. Nice wall climbing that would be even better if it stayed clean. Climb the arete to the flake on the left then a ledge. Move right then trend back left to finish.
FA. Graham Whittaker 1968

Terror Cotta Anglezarke 301

19 First Finale E1 5b
18m. Well-protected climbing on pleasing holds, and understandably popular. Climb the crack, passing an overlap early on, to a finish up the final groove (a bit loose) at the left edge of the roof.
FA. Colin Dickinson 1972. FFA. Dave Knighton 1976

20 Third Party ... E3 5c
18m. The line is clear enough, though the moves are less so, and the top overhang is distinctly disposable.
FA. Mark Liptrot 1988

21 Double Trip E2 5c
18m. Technically a touch easier than *Golden Tower*. Climb the slightly-disposable wall (pegs) heading for a rest just left of the notch in the final roof. Finish over this with a flourish. The *Original Finish* out right via the notch is E3.
FA. Bill Cheverst 1971. FFA. Dave Knighton 1977

22 Terror Cotta .... HVS 5a
22m. The classic of the wall, imposing but not too hard! Climb the yellowish groove to a ledge, step out left and climb the wall to the overhangs. Move right through the stacked notches to finish. *Terrorific*, E4 6a - is the bold fingery direct start left of the arete.
FA. Dave Hollows 1971. FA. (Terrorific) Andrew Gridley 1986

23 Cotton Terror E1 5b
18m. From the start of the yellowish groove on *Terror Cotta* move out right to a crack and follow it to a ledge. Climb the wall and its continuation above boldy to a very unstable exit.
FA. Ian Lonsdale 1978

24 Edipol! .... HS 4b
14m. The crack in the wall to the right. Climb the juggy roof and the crack above to ledges. Traverse right to the arete to finish. One of the very first routes in the quarry.
FA. Graham Whittaker 1966

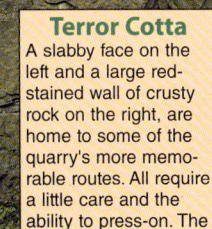

14 Ain't Nothing To It .. E3 6a
14m. Climb the crack on the right to a peg. Swing left and plough up the arete. A direct start is *There's More To This*, E4 6b.
FA. Gary Gibson 1982. FA. (TMTT) Carl Spencer 1997

15 Many Happy Returns ...... HVS 5a
14m. The crack splitting the centre of the north facing side wall.
FA. Arthur Hassall 1974

16 Birthday Crack .... VS 4c
14m. The main angle is a good line but could do with a few more visitors. Exit left at the top to avoid the grot cornice.
FA. Arthur Hassall 1974

17 Zarke .... HVS 5a
20m. Mantelshelf onto a narrow ledge (hard!) then trend left, passing the overlap almost to the corner before heading up to another ledge. Swing back right to access the notch at the top of the wall and finish through this with care.
FA. Les Ainsworth (1 point) 1973. FFA. Ian Lonsdale 1975

18 Fingertip Control. E4 5c
16m. A direct on *Zarke* is bold and reachy. Memorable moves throughout but a possible ground-fall should you muff it unless your belayer is on his toes!
FA. Dave Knighton 1978

Terror Cotta
A slabby face on the left and a large red-stained wall of crusty rock on the right, are home to some of the quarry's more memorable routes. All require a little care and the ability to press-on. The capping roof is loose.

Anglezarke   The Golden Tower

The Golden Tower
The finest of Anglezarke; the best routes in the quarry.
Approach (see map on page 299) - From the base of the approach scramble, paths lead across to the tower.
Abseiling - Please try an avoid abseiling off the Golden Tower since it is causing severe cliff-top erosion.

1 Klondike E3 6a
18m. Fearsome and fingery but sadly often dirty. Layback the once-pegged crack through the bulge. *Photo on page 298.*
FFA. Dave Hollows 1978

2 King of Kings .. E6 6b
20m. Sustained and desperate and worth 7c+! Gain the hairline crack above the right-facing flake and follow it to the midway break. Step right and then back left, before moving up to a flake. Move back right and up. The route may have three peg runners.
FA. Mark Liptrot 1984

3 Please Lock Me Away .. E5 6b
18m. Start as for *King of Kings* but head right up the undercut flake by a tough move. The sustained flake/crack above this leads to a small ledge. Finish up the tricky wall above.
FA. Bernie Bradbury 1983

4 Septic Think Tank E5 6b
18m. The upper wall to the right of *Please Lock Me Away* is bold and hard, keeping just left of the arete throughout. A couple of peg runners (hard to clip) and a good Friend are all fairly critical.
FA. Gary Gibson 1983

5 The Italian Job E6 6b
24m. A direct start to *Septic T.T.* may even improve the original. It is fingery and committing. Climb the arete on its left-hand side to the overlap. Continue up above then head left along a thin crack and steel yourself for the stern upper section.
FA. Tim Lowe 1989

6 The Golden Tower E2 5c
20m. Often regarded as THE Lancashire classic. Start up the crack in the left side of the buttress (awkward 5a) then tackle the fine finger-crack splitting the centre of the upper tower. It is best done in a single pitch. *Photo on page 3.*
FA. Les Ainsworth 1968

7 Gates of Perception. E5 6a
24m. Take the first section of *The Golden Tower* then attack the hairline crack just right of the arete. Excellent sustained climbing.

8 Fool's Gold E2 5b
16m. The wide hanging slot in the right side of the tower is a sod to enter and leads awkwardly to a breather on the ledge. The upper arete is easier but bolder and features a creaky flake. Finish on the right-hand side. Cruely undergraded at HVS in the past.
FFA. Dave Hollows 1969. FA. (2nd pitch as described) Ian Lonsdale 1977

9 Samarkand .... VS 5a
18m. High in the grade and a classic tussle. The deep groove and wide crack give a satisfying struggle with large gear helpful.
FA. John Whittle 1966

10 Glister Wall .... S 4a
10m. The centre of the less-impressive wall to the right of *The Golden Tower* is popular. It sports good holds and runners.
FA. Bev Heslop 1962

11 The Finger .... VS 5a
10m. Climb to the Finger from under its left-hand side, mantel onto the projection then finish up the grim crack behind.
FA. Les Ainsworth 1967

12 Finger Chimney ...... VS 5a
10m. Approach the Finger via the awkward chimney under its right edge. From a standing position the Finger stride right to a ledge and finish direct.
FA. Les Ainsworth 1967

Coal Measures Crag and Grey Wall **Anglezarke** 303

Coal Measures Crag
The most bizarre climbing destination in the quarry and perhaps in the country; a wall of decent quality gritstone capped by a vertical wall of shattered shale! In the 70s the locals undertook the massive effort of quarrying a path along the junction between the strata and fixing a wire cable along its crest. A more recent move was to fix lower-offs along the top of the wall. Sadly the routes have fallen out of favour and see little attention.

Coal Measures Crag

13 New Jerusalem — E4 6a
14m. The thin slanting crack, past a ledge.
FA. Mark Liptrot 1981

14 Shibb — E4 6b
16m. The crack past a niche and finishing up a flake.
FA. Richard Toon 1983

15 The Karma Mechanic — E6 6c
16m. The wall past an assortment of fixed gear.
FA. Paul Pritchard 1986. Bolt added in 2002.

16 Schwartzennegger Mon Amour — E4 6a
16m. Climb the groove and left-hand side of the arete.
FA. Mark Liptrot 1988

17 Gritstone Rain — HVS 5b
18m. The vegetated groove.
FA. Dave Cronshaw 1977

18 Vishnu — HVS 5a
18m. Climb the flake and corner.
FA. Dave Cronshaw 1979

19 The Lean Mean Fighting Machine — E4 6a
18m. The left-leaning crack leads to *Vishnu*.
FFA. Mark Liptrot 1981

Grey Wall
A short wall of good rock on the sunny side of the quarry. The best of the routes are quite good but the unstable slag-heap above the cliff rather spoils the party.
Approach (see map on page 299) - From the base of the approach scramble, vague paths lead around the edge of the pit and right to a short orange cliff above a steep bank.

Grey Wall

20 Sunbeam — VS 4c
16m. Climb the crack up the left-hand side of the pedestal and pull over the juggy roof to finish up a tricky little groove. The finish is horrendous, take care.
FA. Stu Thomas 1967

21 Storm — VS 4c
16m. The original route of the wall. Climb up the flake and crack on the right-hand side of the pedestal to its top. Move left then climb the roof on big holds to the tricky final groove of *Sunbeam*. A more direct finish is **5a**.
FA. Arthur Hassall (1pt aid) 1967

22 Sheppy — E3 6b
16m. Climb the fierce once-pegged crack (pity it wasn't pegged a few more times!) until above the break then trend left for an easier finish.
FA. Arthur Hassall 1967

Wilton 1

	No star	⭐	⭐⭐	⭐⭐⭐
Mod to S	1	1	1	-
HS to HVS	1	10	10	1
E1 to E3	2	1	4	7
E4 and up	3	3	11	5

The Wilton complex of quarries (from 1 through to 4) overlooks Egerton, to the north of Bolton and is reached in minutes from a collection convenient parking places. Wilton 1 is arguably the finest cliff in Lancashire with well over 200 routes, many of which are hard or very hard. Although the thin cracks, with which the place abounds, were originally climbed with aid, the area was never the popular practice-ground that the eastern Peak became. Because of this many of the cracks are in near-pristine condition, making them worthy of the attention of any visiting thin-crack meister. Scattered amongst the hard routes is a reasonable selection of more moderate fare that give the chance to look at the harder routes and imagine - maybe one day! Those who find Wilton 1 a bit intimidating should enjoy Wilton 2 and 3 where the setting and the spread of grades are a little more amenable as is the angle of much of the rock.

Access
Wilton 1 is now owned by the BMC and there are no access issues here.

Approach   Also see map on page 289
There is dedicated parking just down the slope from the Wilton Arms (the Wilting Arms would surely be more appropriate). Steps lead through the bushes in the left-hand corner of this to a wide quarry track that loops right then left to arrive opposite the conspicuous fin of rock that is The Prow. More direct approaches are steeper and save only seconds.

To the left of The Prow the quarry descends into the overgrown depths of The Allotment and to its right the steep walls of The Pit Face. These are home to 60 or so routes, many of which are worth seeking out - see the definitive Lancashire guide. From the approach path minor tracks lead up and right to the White Slabs and Grey Walls, home to many fine climbs and rarely busy.

Conditions
The cliff faces the morning sun and, although in the shade after midday, is sheltered from the prevailing westerly winds. The place is inclined to be green in the winter, or after rain, but if the day turns sour then the sunny delights of Anglezarke or the bouldering of Brownstones are not too far away. The exception to the rule is the west face of The Prow that gets the afternoon sun (until it sets below the quarry rim) and is almost always in climbable condition.

On rare hot summer days the quarry makes an ideal shady retreat.

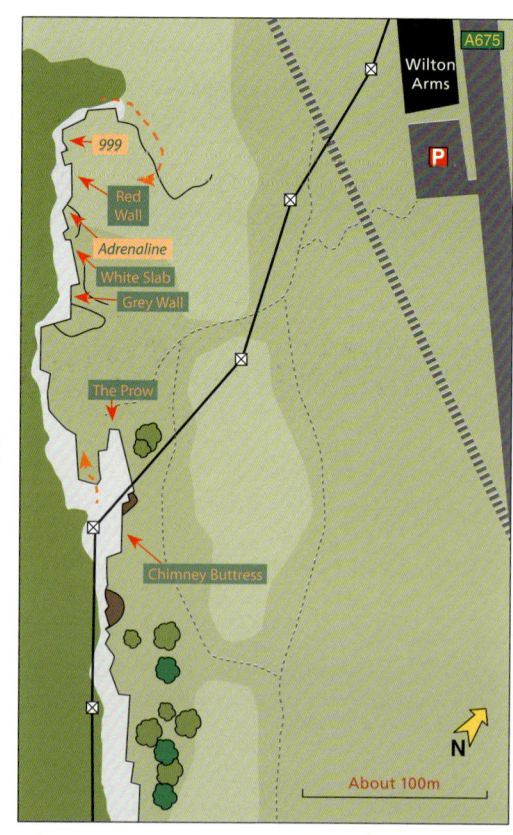

Geoff Mann on the superb and technical *Master Spy Direct* (E4) - *page 314* - at Wilton 1. Photo: Nick Verney

Wilton 1 — Chimney Buttress

Chimney Buttress
This popular piece of rock on the left side of the quarry is split by the shallow cleft of *Wombat Chimney*. All the routes here are steep, pumpy and worth doing; the crack climbs are well-protected, though the gear is often hard-won. In contrast the face climbs tend to be bold and harrowing with gear in the breaks and the odd peg.

❶ Paradox E2 5b
12m. A fine varied pitch up the south-facing side wall, with an interesting start followed by steep finger jamming to a teetering exit. Start up the slanting crack until a short traverse right leads to easy ground. Well-protected where you need it.
FA. Hank Pasquill 1968

❷ Parasite E5 6b
16m. The left arete of the front face is technical and bold. Various old bits of metal provide the protection.
FA. Jerry Peel/Hank Pasquill 1980

❸ Leucocyte Left-hand ... E3 5c
16m. Climb past an iron ring to a good ledge out right then step left and enter the steep hanging crack. Finish more easily.
FA. Ray Evans 1964

Chimney Buttress Wilton 1   307

④ Leucocyte Right-hand . . . . VS 4c
16m. From a ledge on the *Leucocyte Left-hand* climb the groove then the continuation crack past an old peg. Easy ground remains.
FA. Hank Pasquill 1967

⑤ The Hacker E4 6b
16m. Climb the wall past twin overlaps then finish up the bold and technical wall above.
FA. Hank Pasquill 1973

⑥ Central Route E1 5b
16m. A great route which is not as pumpy as it looks but requires sustained effort right to the end. It follows the continuous crack-line past a ledge at 6m. Take care with a couple of rattling holds.
FA. Hank Pasquill 1967

⑦ Max E3 5c
18m. Climb straight up the wall to the overlap (poor rest in a niche) then follow the thin, pumpy crack above. The start is serious; the hard moves near the top can be protected.
FA. Hank Pasquill 1968

⑧ Wombat Chimney E2 5b
18m. The narrow hanging fissure is accessed via a steep crack. Take a rest before the chimney then struggle up it to a dirty but well-protected exit.
FA. Ray Evans 1966

⑨ The Soot Monkey . . E6 6c
18m. Climb the thin wall to a peg then continue right and left boldly to the break. Climb the wall above via a little diversion to the arete of *Wombat*.
FA. Paul Pritchard 1985

⑩ Toxic Bilberrys . E8 7a
18m. Bold, powerful, technical and pushy climbing up the face to the left of *Loopy*. There is a long run-out start and a then a crucial section protected by skyhook runners.
FA. Gareth Parry 1998

⑪ Loopy E4 6a
14m. An intimidating pitch, strenuous then delicate and always bold. Climb cracks to the hanging blocks, pull into the groove on the left then balance up the scooped slab. The direct finish up the groove is harder and safer but less good.
FA. Hank Pasquill 1968 and 1970

⑫ The Corner . . . . VS 4c
14m. The main angle between the buttresses gives a worthwhile pitch that would benefit from a bit more traffic.
FA. Ray Evans 1965

End-on view of the imposing Prow at Wilton 1.

Descent from The Prow (awkward)

308　Wilton 1　The Prow

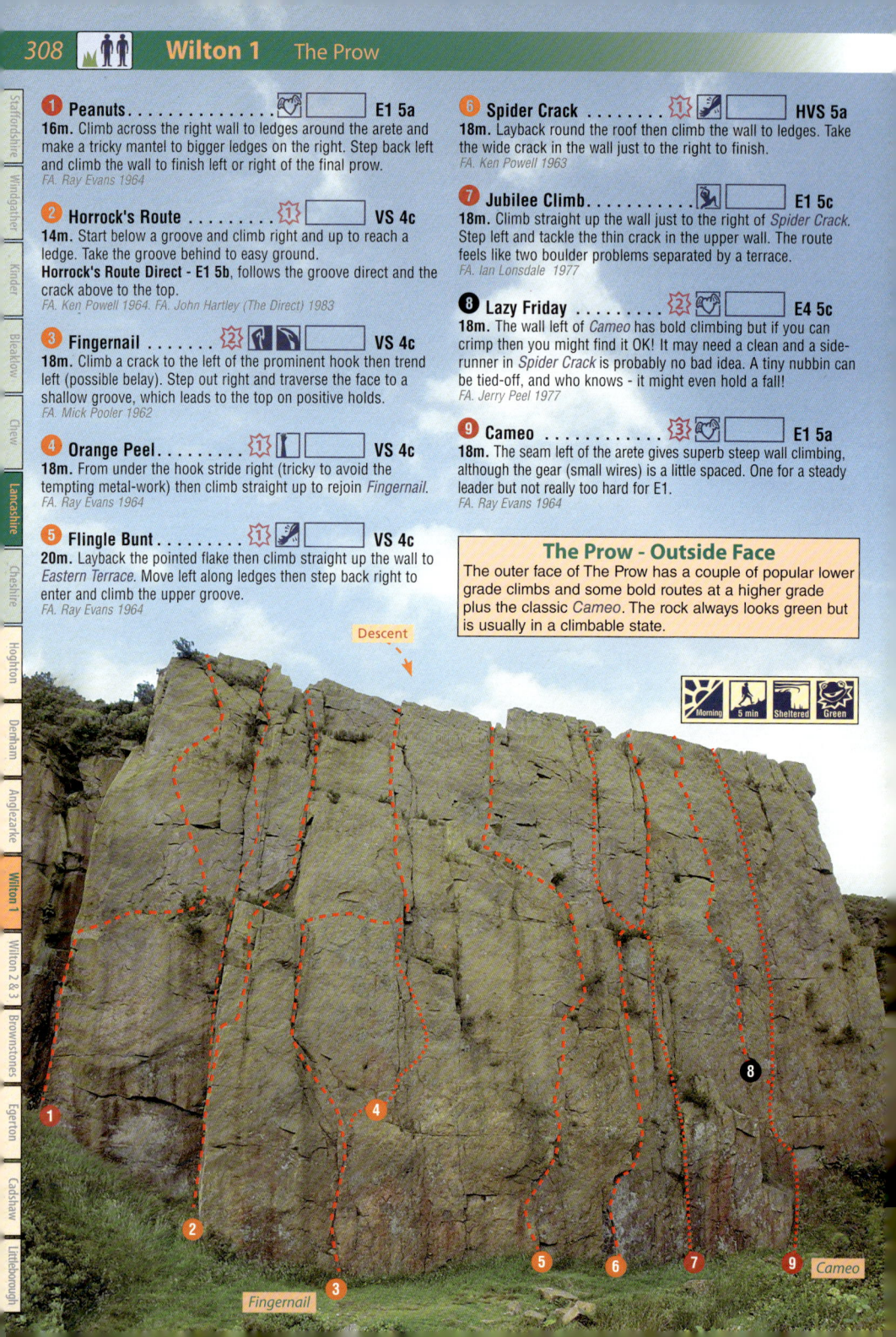

1 Peanuts E1 5a
16m. Climb across the right wall to ledges around the arete and make a tricky mantel to bigger ledges on the right. Step back left and climb the wall to finish left or right of the final prow.
FA. Ray Evans 1964

2 Horrock's Route .... VS 4c
14m. Start below a groove and climb right and up to reach a ledge. Take the groove behind to easy ground.
Horrock's Route Direct - E1 5b, follows the groove direct and the crack above to the top.
FA. Ken Powell 1964. FA. John Hartley (The Direct) 1983

3 Fingernail .... VS 4c
18m. Climb a crack to the left of the prominent hook then trend left (possible belay). Step out right and traverse the face to a shallow groove, which leads to the top on positive holds.
FA. Mick Pooler 1962

4 Orange Peel .... VS 4c
18m. From under the hook stride right (tricky to avoid the tempting metal-work) then climb straight up to rejoin *Fingernail*.
FA. Ray Evans 1964

5 Flingle Bunt .... VS 4c
20m. Layback the pointed flake then climb straight up the wall to *Eastern Terrace*. Move left along ledges then step back right to enter and climb the upper groove.
FA. Ray Evans 1964

6 Spider Crack .... HVS 5a
18m. Layback round the roof then climb the wall to ledges. Take the wide crack in the wall just to the right to finish.
FA. Ken Powell 1963

7 Jubilee Climb E1 5c
18m. Climb straight up the wall just to the right of *Spider Crack*. Step left and tackle the thin crack in the upper wall. The route feels like two boulder problems separated by a terrace.
FA. Ian Lonsdale 1977

8 Lazy Friday E4 5c
18m. The wall left of *Cameo* has bold climbing but if you can crimp then you might find it OK! It may need a clean and a side-runner in *Spider Crack* is probably no bad idea. A tiny nubbin can be tied-off, and who knows - it might even hold a fall!
FA. Jerry Peel 1977

9 Cameo E1 5a
18m. The seam left of the arete gives superb steep wall climbing, although the gear (small wires) is a little spaced. One for a steady leader but not really too hard for E1.
FA. Ray Evans 1964

The Prow - Outside Face
The outer face of The Prow has a couple of popular lower grade climbs and some bold routes at a higher grade plus the classic *Cameo*. The rock always looks green but is usually in a climbable state.

Andy Sinclair not cheating *Cheat* (E3) - *page 310* - at Wilton 1. Photo: Sinclair collection

Wilton 1 — The Prow

The Prow - Inside Face

The sunniest piece of rock in the quarry has a small collection of excellent routes and is the most popular bit of rock here. The routes tend to be strenuous and bold in places, and the rock is exceptionally clean. Belaying on top of The Prow requires a little care (there are various fixed bits of iron work) as does the exposed escape along its crest - all very Culm Coast-ish!

1 Christeena .... VS 5a
14m. Climb the narrow front of the Prow to a ledge. Move up to a good hold on the left arete and use this to swing (low) or teeter (high) round the edge and across into the groove. Climb this pleasantly to the top.
FA. Mick Pooler 1962

2 Christine Arete E4 5c
14m. Bold and fingery climbing up the left-hand arete of the face. No side-runners at this grade. Wires in the upper left-hand crack of *Dawn* knock the grade down to a still scary **E3 5c**.
FA. Hank Pasquill 1967

3 Dawn .... HVS 5b
14m. A steep crack climb which is high in the grade. Jam your way up to a sit-down rest on a sloping ledge. Continue up the draining upper crack past some small wire runners. Following the left-hand crack throughout is E2 5c.
FA. Graham Kilner 1961. FFA. Mick Pooler 1963

4 Innominate E4 6b
14m. A bouldery start (a side-runner brings it down to E3) leads to a break. Follow the upper break to gain the thin crack left of the upper section of *Ann*.
FFA. Hank Pasquill early 1980s

5 Eliminate .... VS 4c
18m. An indirect line but with good climbing. Climb the groove then make a tricky traverse right along the narrow undercut ledges to *Rambling Route*. Finish up its left arete.
FA. Rowland Edwards 1963

6 Ann E1 5b
14m. Two good sections split by a big ledge. Climb the thin once-pegged crack to ledges. Power up the twin cracks in the groove to finish. Ignoring the left-hand crack is a touch harder and also more strenuous.
FA. Les Ainsworth 1967

7 Cheat E3 5b
14m. Steady climbing with a bold feel. Gear in the midway break gives protection that is just about adequate. Climb the reachy lower wall via a thin crack to ledges then attack the upper face by a line of (small) chipped holds. The route is substantially harder for the short. *Photo on page 309.*
FA. Hank Pasquill 1967

The Prow **Wilton 1** 311

8 Rambling Route .... VDiff
14m. Pleasant. Bridge up the chimney to the big sloping ledge then take the jamming crack in the groove above to finish. There are useful holds in the juggy flake that forms the left arete too.
FA. Graham Kilner 1961

9 Bird Chimney .... S 4a
12m. The chimney/groove is normally quitted leftwards where it narrows. The birds have long since flown.
FA. Graham Kilner 1961

10 Flywalk .... VS 4c
12m. Climb strenuously across small ledges to a jammed finger-nipping block. Finish awkwardly through the small roof. **A Direct Start** is V1 (5c).
FA. Graham Kilner 1961

11 Flytrap .... VS 5a
8m. The short-lived groove above the start of *Flywalk* gives a short safe struggle to a shelving rightward exit.
FA. Hank Pasquill late 1960s

12 Veteran Cosmic Rocker E4 6c
6m. The hanging arete on its right-hand side by some seriously powerful pinch-gripping. The left-hand side is a grade or so easier.
FA. Mark Leach 1984

13 Scimitar .... VDiff
6m. The curving crack leads strenuously into the grubby groove.
FA. Graham Kilner 1961

The polished shelving ledges in the back of the bay are **Max's Dilemma, Mod**. *This provides the easiest way down though beginners might be a little fazed. The alternatives are another awkward climb down just over to the right, or the long walk round the northern end of the quarry.*

The vague remains of the painted number 49 at the foot of *Christeena* (VS) on the front of The Prow at Wilton 1. It is currently number 95 in the BMC Guide which shows how pointless writing numbers on the rock is.

Wilton 1 — White Slab

1 Manglewurzle Rib — HVS 5a
26m. Step right into the crack and climb it to the base of the groove (possible stance) then step out right and climb the rib and crack to the top. Currently quite clean without a turnip in sight!
FA. Ray Evans 1964

2 Isle of White — E4 6a
24m. Bold and absorbing - a great route when dry and clean! Climb straight up the face to the horizontal break, fill it with gear then trend slightly rightwards up the wall, passing an overlap with difficulty, to a finish through the blocky overhangs on the right.
FA. Ian Lonsdale 1977. Hank Pasquill (the start) 1978

3 White Slabs Bunt — E3 6a
26m. A devious classic - the name refers to a back flip in aerobatics and is not Cockney rhyming slang! Clipping and passing the second peg is desperate for the short! Climb round the overlap to the main horizontal break, step right then climb straight up the wall into a shallow groove. Finish through the blocky overhanging groove capping the face. Straightening out the loop is *White Lightening* E5 6b.
FA. Hank Pasquill (2 pegs) 1967. FFA. Hank Pasquill 1971

4 Rememberance Corner — VS 4c
22m. What a line, possibly the best in the quarry - pity about the fernage though! Getting it done early in the season is the best bet.
FA. Roland Edwards 1964

5 Sobeit — E3 5c
24m. The first crack in the jutting wall gives a fine outing. Climb the thin crack to a tall slot then pass this to easier rock and an exit leftwards as for *Western Terrace* (the long diagonal ledge system) or move right to the tree lower-off.
FA. Ian Lonsdale 1977

6 Supercrack — E3 5c
24m. A super climb when clean and then the match of anything at Millstone. Well protected and sustained rather than overly technical. Climb the fingery lower wall to the big break then step left and power up the fine continuation crack until respite arrives on the *Western Terrace*. Escape off left or lower-off from the tree.
FA. Ken Powell 1964. FFA. Ian Lonsdale late 1970s

Running across the wall is the stepped ledge of **Western Terrace**, S 4a - it is a poor route. Rising above its right-hand end is Grey Wall with it series of searing finger cracks. These are listed briefly here.

7 Spike — E4 6a
24m. The right trending crack gives good climbing past two pegs and a pair of small recesses to a final taxing sequence near the top.
FFA. Al Pearce 1979

8 Run Wild, Run Free — E6 6b
20m. Climb boldly rightwards to the base of the crack then gallop up it by fierce climbing with an especially pushy central section.
FA. Hank Pasquill 1969. FFA Mark Leach 1985

9 Ego Trip — E5 6b
12m. Up to it? Step right to access the parallel cracks then follow them with escalating difficulty to mid-height and an easier finish.
FA. Ken Powell c 1964. FFA. John Monks 1983

10 K.P. — E6 6b
20m. From the ledges on *Frightful Fred* climb through the blocky slot (you must be nuts!) in the roof then attack the soaring crack.
FA. Hank Pasquill 1969. FFA. Geoff Mann 1978

11 Josser — E5 6a
18m. The last finger-crack is another good one. From *Frightful Fred* climb the shallow groove and crack past a couple of small overhangs to finish direct or, slightly more easily, out left.
FA. Jim Fogg 1969. FFA. Dave Knighton 1978

White Slab

The tallest face in the quarry, and white when it is dry which is fairly infrequently. Under the right conditions *White Slabs Bunt* and *Supercrack* are a couple of classy E3s that are worth the trip from afar - just pick a dry spell.

Grey Wall / Adrenaline **Wilton 1** 313

12 Frightful Fred .... VS 4c
26m. Wandering, though with good and bold climbing. Take the chimney to ledges and a peg belay on the right (8m). Climb up and right then mantelshelf onto a higher ledge by a groove. From a peg gain the higher ledge on the right then continue up and right until an exit leftwards can be made. A right-hand exit is harder.
FA. Ray Evans 1963

13 Adrenaline E4 6a
24m. Despite a poor start the upper groove offers superb unrelenting climbing; just keep pushing on and the holds and runners keep arriving. Protection is good once you reach the crack, though the easy bottom wall and grotty cave are worrying!
FA. Jim Fogg 1969. FFA. Hank Pasquill 1981

14 Chocolate Girl E7 6c
26m. This arduous outing takes the lower of a pair of thin cracks in the pillar right of *Adrenaline*. Climb to the cave then exit right to gain the base of the withering crack. Power up this, sustained, fingery and technical, (four peg runners). A semi-rest is reached in the groove of *Adrenaline*. Finish up this much more easily.
FA. Hank Pasquill 1969. FFA. Gareth Parry 1996

15 Gigantic E8 6c
16m. The right-hand crack was neglected by the aid climbers, leaving it pristine and thin! Climb a flaky crack in the right-hand wall of the groove and a blocky overhang (possible stance out right). Swing around the arete to gain the crack-line and follow it desperately to a final hideous sequence which allows the last couple of moves on *Adrenaline* to be reached - phew!
FA. Ken Powell 1964. FFA. Dave Pegg 1990

Grey Wall / Adrenaline
The tall right-hand end of the Grey Wall rises from behind a heap of grassed-over quarry spoil. All the routes start indifferently but things improve dramatically on the better rock above the mid-height break. Here are as fine a set of hard finger-cracks as you will find anywhere - though the emphasis is on the word 'hard'.

Wilton 1 — Red Wall

① Knuckleduster — HVS 5a
26m. A long climb with some poor rock on pitch 1. Climb a flaky crack left of the arete to an overhang and above this a stance. Balance up the exposed arete on the left then teeter back into the main groove and finish up this (**4c**). The crack and groove to the right offer a tougher though safer option - **The Fist Finish, HVS 5b**.
FA. (pitch 2) Ray Evans 1964. FA. (pitch 1) Ray Evans 1966
FA. (The Fist Finish) Mark Kemball 1982

② Blackout — VS 4c
26m. Another wandering and intimidating classic on which care is required to protect the second adequately. Climb to the top of the pillar then the groove above until its is possible (essential?) to head left to the first of a series of ledges. Move left to a peg belay. Move up and left to more ledges then follow these back right to an exposed and grotty exit.
FA. Dave Brodigan 1963

③ Master Spy — E4 6a
20m. A pumpy Wilton classic, powerful and devious, though with good gear throughout. Rope work can be a little problematical. From *Blackout* climb strenuously to the seagull-shaped roof then compose yourself before launching right along this to a bridged rest at its far end. Just when you thought it was all over you find that the final short crack takes no prisoners.

④ Master Spy Direct — E4 6a
20m. Starting up *Counter Intelligence* and finishing up *Master Spy* gives a superb three star combination. *Photo on page 305*.
FA. Paul Clarke mid 1980s

⑤ Counter Intelligence — E5 6b
18m. Climb the long and sustained crack that falls from the right-hand edge of the seagull-shaped roof to reach a bridged rest on its right. Pull leftwards onto the hanging face then make a daunting and crucial mantel/rock-over way out in space to reach the final thin crack.
FA. John Hartley 1982

⑥ Wipe Out — E2 5b
18m. Another great route at a (slightly) more amenable grade. The next long crack-line gives excellent climbing with sustained and well-protected moves and a more difficult (or at least more pumpy) section to reach the top.
FA. Les Ainsworth 1966

⑦ Black Mamba — E4 6b
16m. A bold outing up the steep face to the right of the continuous crack-line of *Wipe Out*. Climb the wall on good slots to the break (peg) and then a little higher to a bolt. Pass this with difficulty leftwards to reach easier ground in the green groove.
FA. Dave Cronshaw (2 points) 1971. FFA. Dougie Hall 1982

⑧ Shaggy Dog — E4 5c
14m. Bold and serious, and that ain't no lie. Climb the lower section of the soary and horribly wide **Kettle Crack, E2 5c** then launch left at a peg before climbing the intimidating wall; it doesn't ease as rapidly as you might have been hoping for.
FA. Hank Pasquill 1982

Red Wall
A neglected part of the quarry but with some quality rock. As is often the case the best routes tend to be in the higher grades although the intimidating VS classic of *Blackout* is excellent and well worth seeking out.

999 **Wilton 1** 315

9 Knock Out .... VS 4c
16m. Climb awkwardly onto the slab and trend left, passing the metal boomerang to a stance on the arete. Step back right and follow the thin crack just right of the arete and the pleasant groove directly above.
FA. Ray Evans 1966

10 Great Slab .... VS 4c
28m. Wandering but worthwhile. Start under the centre of the slab, mantel awkwardly onto its base and traverse up and left to a stance on the arete (**4b**). Traverse right along the sandy break and climb *999* to a small roof. Head right again to finish up the exposed arete. Care with rope work is needed on this pitch.
FA. Ken Powell 1963. FA. (the finish) Les Ainsworth 1966

11 Virgin's Dilemma ..... HVS 5a
20m. A rare thing indeed, a Wilton slab - what else? High in the grade; thought by some to be better and bolder than *Cameo*. Climb the centre of the lower slab to the sandy break then continue up its centre to enter the shallow open groove splitting the upper face. Follow this by sustained moves.
FA. Hank Pasquill 1967

999
The last section of the cliff has a small selection of worthwhile routes on good rock. They don't see much traffic except for *999*. It is the best lower grade route in the quarry following an excellent natural line, with good protection and (don't tell anyone) is a bit of a soft touch!

12 999 .... Top 50 HS 4b
18m. The long clean groove that bounds the slab gives a fine piece of climbing, sustained and well-protected with a great line.
Photo on page 288.
FA. Ken Powell 1963

13 Left Edge .... HVS 4c
14m. From the grass on the right (reached by a grotty scramble) step left and balance up the fine and poorly-protected arete. Short but well-positioned and worthwhile.
FA. Ray Evans 1964

Descent - - - ➔

Wilton 2 and 3

	No star	⭐	⭐⭐	⭐⭐⭐
Mod to S	15	10	3	-
HS to HVS	6	10	5	1
E1 to E3	3	13	4	5
E4 and up	-	2	1	4

On the crest of the hill above the deep slash of Wilton 1 are three more quarries, numbered from left to right 4, 2 and 3! Number 4 is short, overgrown and unpopular, but both 2 and 3 are well worth a visit and, because of their proximity to each other, a useful day can be spent between the pair of them. The rock is not the most impressive but the routes are more friendly than Wilton 1 and are especially of interest if you operate in the green and orange grade zones. Wilton 2 tends to have the harder routes, offering steep, fingery and challenging climbing whereas, in Wilton 3, there are more routes of an amenable angle and grade. The well-battered areas below the Orange and Rappel Walls are an indication of how popular these places are with supervised groups; be prepared to share the objects of your desire!

Access

Wiltons 2 and 3 are owned by the resident shooting club with agreed times for shooting and climbing. The current agreed times that shooting will take place are Wednesdays, Fridays, Sundays and Boxing Day. Please do not climb on these days, even if there is no shooting when you arrive. Climbing is permitted at other times although the agreed times may change and it is always worth checking the notices in the quarries if you are unsure. A red flag will be flying whenever there is shooting taking place.

Approach   Also see map on page 289

Wilton 2 and 3 (and 4) quarries are set behind Wilton 1 and are most easily reached by driving up the hill - the A675 - past the Wilton Arms and the parking for Wilton 1. After a kilometre or so take the first left turn and continue up the hill to where the quarry tracks can be seen on the right - though the cliffs themselves remain hidden until you are actually inside the quarries. Both quarries are reached by short gated tracks and there is roadside parking on the left opposite the entrances. Leave nothing valuable in the car.

Conditions

The cliffs face north and east and so their right-hand faces are in the sun until early afternoon. They take little drainage and dry rapidly after rain, though many of the climbs tend to be gritty from sand washed down from above. There are belay stakes in place above many of the climbs, checking their solidity before using them is a sensible idea.

Gaz Parry soloing *The S-Groove* (E7) - *page 319* - at Wilton 2. Photo: Ian Parnell

Wilton 2 — Scout Buttress

Scout Buttress

The left-hand side of the cliff has a series of short steep walls with routes that make up in impact what they lack in stature. Many of the climbs tend to be quite fierce for their given grade, but they don't go on too long!

Access - Shooting may take place here on Wednesdays, Fridays and Sundays so please avoid these days EVEN IF THERE IS NO SIGN OF ANY SHOOTERS.

1 Concrete Crack E2 6a
8m. The thin and technical crack is gained from the right. The gear is good, but only if you can stop to place it!
FA. Ian Lonsdale 1982

2 Cement Mix E1 5b
8m. The shallow crusty groove left of the main angle could have done with a bit more cement to hold it together!
FA. Dave Cronshaw 1971

3 Short Corner E1 5c
8m. The groove on the right-hand side of the wall has a stubborn exit (old peg runner).
FFA. Ian lonsdale 1981

4 Start .... Diff
8m. The shot holes-lead to a grassy exit up a corner.
FA. Rowland Edwards 1964

5 Boomerang .... Diff
8m. Climb onto a shelf at 3m then take the slab rightwards and finish through a notch.
FA. Rowland Edwards 1964

6 Shallow Groove ...... HVS 5b
10m. The shallow left-facing groove is worth seeking out, being well-protected, quite technical and pretty steep.
FA. Rowland Edwards 1964

7 Shallow Green E2 5c
10m. Pad rightwards up the slab to a peg, pull rightwards through the small overhang to a welcome jug then finish up the centre of the bold wall above. High in the grade and great when clean.
FA. Nigel Bonnett 1976

8 Shukokia E3 6a
8m. The groove and ensuing thin crack-line give good climbing to a tough exit through the overlap.

9 Kung Fu .... HVS 5a
8m. The crack leads to a deep slot and then a steeper finish.
FA. Rowland Edwards late 1960s

10 The Bod E1 5b
10m. Despite being awkward the shallow left-facing corner-groove is worthwhile.
FA. Hank Pasquill mid 1970s

11 Disappearing Aces E3 6a
10m. Also known as *Ace of Spades*. Despite good climbing the vicious leaning groove sees little attention, hence the herbage!
FA. Terry Waring 1967. FFA. Dennis Gleeson 1982

12 Tweeker E3 5c
12m. Climb the crack of *Throsher* then traverse out left and pull into an awkward groove. Up this to a peg then make crucial moves to pass the centre of the overhang using a wart to gain the final wall and a sprint finish.
FFA. Ian Lonsdale 1978

The S-Groove

Descent

Concrete Crack

Shallow Green

Throsher

S-Groove and The Bee — Wilton 2 — 319

13 Throsher — VS 4c
12m. The crack up the right-hand side of the face is the best VS hereabouts. Nice climbing, fine positions and good protection ensure its continued popularity and 'throshing' should not be necessary. The bore-hole is a cool feature.
FA. Rowland Edwards 1964

14 Ledge and Groove — E1 5b
12m. Climb to the ledge then banzai round the exposed arete and climb the crack and groove.
FA Ray Evans (aid) 1964

15 The Axe Wound — E6 7a
6m. The well-brushed wall on the right of the recess. Only short but savagely technical. Possibly unrepeated since the loss of a foothold!
FA. Gareth Parry 1992

16 The S-Groove — E7 6c
8m. The compelling sinuous groove in the pale wall at a lower level. Originally climbed with side runners at E5 6c; it has now been soloed. Also known as *Against all Odds*. *Photo on page 317.*
FA. Mark Leach (side-runners) 1984. FA. Gareth Parry 1990s

17 Frostbite — E2 5c
7m. Steep climbing up the corner past a low overlap.
FA. Hank Pasquill 1964

Across a grassy descent gully is a slabby looking wall.

18 The Bee — E1 5b
8m. Climb the crack to a ledge then step out left past the overlap and balance up to a horizontal break, runners and an easier finish. Better and much more feasible than it looks, giving nice face climbing, with a bold feel due to the receding runners out right.
FA. Hank Pasquill mid 1970s

19 The Wasp — E3 6a
8m. The balancy right arete throughout. In the upper section a thin crack is useful, leading to a sting in the tail - or not?
FA. John Hartley 1982

20 Laying the Ghost — E2 6b
8m. The thin crack in the left wall is approached from a short way up *Slanting Slab* and climbed tenuously passing a peg runner to a desperate finale.
FFA. John Hartley 1982

21 Slanting Slab — S 4a
8m. The pleasant right-slanting slab is climb right to left then back right to a reach a grassy exit.
FA. Ray Evans 1964

22 Direct — HVS 5a
8m. The leaning groove is best taken at a gallop. Laybacking is the best approach though stopping to place gear can be tricky!
FA. Rowland Edwards 1964

23 Savage Stone — E4 6c
8m. From a couple of moves up the groove of *Direct*, monkey left into the hanging groove and levitate up it using the one decent hold. A vital peg protects. Originally given 7a.
FA. John Hartley 1982

24 Kukri Crack — HVD
8m. The clean-cut crack running right then cutting back left is pleasant at the grade. Protection is good.
FA. Rowland Edwards 1964

25 Three Corner Climb — Mod
10m. The rather grassy three stepped corners can be used as a beginners' route or more usually as a quick way down.

S-Groove and The Bee
The left-hand side of the Main Wall wall has a small selection of short routes on good rock with some surprisingly technical outings. On most occasions you are more than likely to have the routes here to yourself.
Access - Shooting may take place here on Wednesdays, Fridays and Sundays so please avoid these days EVEN IF THERE IS NO SIGN OF ANY SHOOTERS.

Wilton 2 — Wilton Wall

Wilton Wall

The smooth face on the right-hand side of the quarry, and behind the firing range, is the showpiece of the place offering superb fingery routes on impeccable rock. Most of the routes are poorly protected so best arrive with your bold head on, and treat any fixed gear with respect - it has probably been there for years!

Access - Shooting may take place here on Wednesdays, Fridays and Sundays so please avoid these days EVEN IF THERE IS NO SIGN OF ANY SHOOTERS.

1 Deep Groove .... **Diff**
10m. The groove to a ledge and the continuation from here.
FA. Rowland Edwards 1964

2 Meandering Molly .... **VDiff**
10m. From *Deep Groove* access the arete on the right and follow it to ledges. Finish up the short wall behind.
FA. Rowland Edwards 1964

3 Cross Tie .... **S 4a**
10m. Climb the arete until *Meandering Molly* rolls up then step out left to the centre of the face and climb this.
FA. Rowland Edwards 1964

4 Flake Crack .... **S 4a**
10m. The flake-crack right of the grotty corner.
FA. Rowland Edwards 1964

5 Big Dorris **E2 5c**
12m. Interesting climbing which is bold but safe. Towards the centre of the wall is a thin hanging crack, gain this from the left and make some thin crimpy moves to a good rest. The top is delicate and bolder - but easier.
FA. Ian Lonsdale 1977

6 Falling Crack **E2 5b**
14m. Often well-named! The fine fissure cleaving the centre of the face has good gear but is pumpy enough. Gaining the mid-height niche is tricky but interest is well-maintained.
FA. Rowland Edwards 1964. FFA. Hank Pasquill 1974

7 Wilton Wall **E3 6a**
14m. The classic of the quarry. From *Falling Crack*, swing right to the thin seam in the smooth face and climb this with difficulty as it develops into a shallow groove, then to ledges and an easy escape. The **Direct Start** is also **6a** and adds to the pump.
FA. Ken Powell 1964. FFA. Hank Pasquill 1969

8 Pigs on the Wing . **E5 6b**
14m. Great climbing, crimpy, technical and bold. Climb leftwards then direct to jugs and runners. Step right and follow a thin seam to the top. A superb outing but please don't hog it.
FA. John Hartley 1982

9 Pigs Direct **E6 6c**
12m. Steep and intense. Climb *PotW* to the jugs (gear) then head up the wall above by bold, fingery and sustained climbing.
FA. Mark Leach 1985

10 The Swine **E3 6a**
14m. Boulder rightwards up the wall using a pig of a slippy side-pull to good holds. Continue up in the same line past a peg.
FA. Hank Pasquill mid 1970s

11 Iron Orchid **E4 6b**
14m. The square-cut arete of the wall is technical and airy. Climb the arete to a peg, swing right to a second peg below a shallow scoop. Finish up its right arete with increasing trepidation.
FA. John Hartley 1982

12 Saturday Crack .... **HVS 5a**
10m. The butch groove/jamming-crack in the side wall is a change from all the fingery chicanery on the front face.
FA. Rowland Edwards 1964

Scout Buttress — The S-Groove — The Bee — Descent

Wilton Wall **Wilton 2** 321

Wilton 3 — Orange Wall

Descent
Orange Wall
Forked Cracks
Constable's Overhang

① Twin Cracks .... Diff
6m. The twinned cracks just right of the descent gully.
FA. Rowland Edwards 1960

② Sneck .... S 4a
6m. From a ledge, amble up the rib finishing rightwards.

③ Great Chimney .... Mod
8m. The not very great chimney to a leftwards exit.

④ Al's Idea E1 5c
6m. The technical left arete of the wall needs a spotter and a touch of wizardry. Misplaced in the earlier edition.
FA. Al 1984

⑤ Orange Wall .... VS 4c
10m. Climb the centre of the wall rightwards on small flatties; hard for the grade. Other variations exist.
FA. Ken Powell 1963

⑥ Orange Crack .... HS 4b
10m. The awkward right-leaning crack soon eases.
FA. Ken Powell 1963

⑦ Orange Groove .... VDiff
8m. The slanting (and slightly orange) groove is a common introduction to the cliff. It has one tricky jamming move.
FA. Ken Powell 1963

⑧ Monolith Crack .... VS 4c
8m. The tough crack right of the tilted block of the Monolith.
FA. Ken Powell 1963

⑨ Cedric .... S 4a
8m. The right-trending staircase is a popular outing and is tricky to climb with any kind of real style - knees useful!
FA. Les Ainsworth 1967

Descent

Orange Wall and Forked Cracks

The left-hand bay of Wilton 3 contains a popular orange tinged slab split by a series of diagonal cracks. Although few of the climbs are outstanding, it is a good place to up the tick-tally for the day. The cracked slab to the right also has a set of popular lower-grade climbs.

Approach - Either from the lower roadside parking spots or from Wilton 2 via a path to the right of *Wilton Wall*.
Access - Shooting may take place here on Wednesdays, Fridays and Sundays so please avoid these days.

Forked Cracks **Wilton 3**

10 Orange Squash...... E3 6a
9m. The wall via an undercut, a detour out left and the slanting crack on the right.
FA. Ian Lonsdale 1981

11 Orange Corner.......... HVD
8m. The main angle of the bay to an exit on rounded holds. A right-hand start is a similar grade.
FA. Rowland Edwards 1960

12 Oak Leaf Wall .... VS 4b
10m. A direct line up the ledgy wall just right of the angle.
FA. Rowland Edwards 1960

13 Tea Leaf .... VS 4b
10m. From the tip of the earth cone climb the crack and wall into a short finishing groove.

14 Oak Leaf Crack.......... VDiff
10m. The first continuous crack right of the angle is pleasant though it gets a bit grubby towards the top.
FA. Rowland Edwards 1960

15 Forked Cracks .... VS 4c
10m. Climb the right-hand crack of an inverted Y to the junction and continue direct more easily. One of the best routes hereabouts although the upper section can be dusty. The bouldery **Direct Start is 5c.**
FA. Rowland Edwards 1960

16 Parallel Cracks.......... S 4a
12m. The eponymous feature is reached via the rusty hook (runner NOT handhold). Popular and worthwhile.
FA. Ray Cook 1960

17 The Groove .... VDiff
12m. The left-slanting groove above the big rusty hook is awkward to enter and easier above.
FA. Rowland Edwards 1960

18 No Idea .... VS 4b
9m. The arete of the wall.
FA. Geoff Mann 1997

Wilton 3 — Constable's Overhang

Constable's Overhang

Dead ahead when you enter the quarry is the striking hand-fissure of *Central Crack* and to its left the fierce finger-crack that gives the sector its name. There are other good climbs here across a spread of grades.

Access - Shooting may take place here on Wednesdays, Fridays and Sundays so please avoid these days.

Bird Restriction - There is sometimes a restriction due to nesting birds in the area of *Constable's Overhang*. This will be in the spring - see signs at the crag.

❶ Slime Chimney .... HVD
12m. Sustained and awkward, the rift just round the arete is usually misnamed, though if not then stay well away. Exit right at the top.
FA. Rowland Edwards 1960

❷ The Grader E3 5c
14m. The superb thin crack in the left wall of the bay is approached from *Slime Chimney*. It gives sustained jamming and is "much harder than the *Mau Mau*" (which is E4 6a!).

❸ Lightning E3 5c
12m. The steep cracks in the wall lead to a ledge on the right. Swing left and flash up *The Grader* to finish.
FA. Dave Thompson (aid) 1966

❹ Thunder E1 5b
14m. The steep and awkward groove is most difficult above the resting ledge at two-thirds height. More traffic would help.
FA. Rowland Edwards (1 point of aid) 1962

❺ Constable's Overhang .. E5 6b
14m. An arresting little number up the once-pegged crack In the back of the bay. Plod up the lower wall to a rest below the overhang. Once composed attack the slanting, fierce and fingery crack that splits the bulge. High in the grade and one of the hardest around back in the day.
FA. Rowland Edwards 1962. FFA. Hank Pasquill 1973

❻ Nameless Edge .... HVS 5a
14m. The long and sustained groove that runs up the right-hand side of the recess containing *Constable's Overhang* gives a worthwhile pitch when it isn't brim-full of shrubbery.
FA. Nigel Bonnett 1976

❼ Slipshod E1 5a
14m. Climb the right wall of the long corner then make worrying moves around the exposed right arete to gain the easier upper section of *Green Slabs*.
FA. Ray Evans 1963

❽ Green Slabs .... VDiff
14m. Climb the groove as far as a block then follow the rocky steps, and assorted elegant ferns, up past the 'roost' then leftwards to finish on the arete.
FA. Rowland Edwards 1960

❾ Pulley .... S 4a
12m. Climb the groove and exit rightwards to a slab. Continue up the blocky groove until it is possible to escape out left.
FA. Les Ainsworth 1966

❿ Block and Tackle .... VDiff
12m. Tackle the broken blocky groove, passing a ledge just below the top, hopefully without too much trouble. Currently very overgrown.
FA. Ken Powell 1963

⓫ The Arete .... VS 4b
12m. The clean-cut arete is pleasant enough.

Possible restriction in the nesting season in this area in the spring.

Waterfall Wall   Wilton 3   325

12 Central Crack .... Top 50 HVS 5a
12m. The superb jamming-crack is sadly short-lived but near perfection whilst it lasts. The crucial thin lower section (5b for individuals with fat hands) can be passed using small edges on either side of the crack.
FA. Rowland Edwards 1964

13 Crack and Slab Variant .... VDiff
12m. Climb the flake to a good ledge and from its right-hand side continue up cracks to a finish just round the arete.
FA. Rowland Edwards 1960

14 Crack and Slab .... VDiff
12m. A nice beginners' route. Start right of the blunt arete that bounds the wall and climb a crack to the right-hand end of the ledge on the *Variant*. Join it here and finish rightwards.
FA. Rowland Edwards 1960

Across the broken ground to the right is a steep wall split centrally by a crack that finishes around the right-hand side of an overhang - Canine Crucifixion.

15 30 Foot Wall .... HVS 5a
36ft. Climb into the main corner until the angle falls back then trend left and finish up the arete.
FA. Ian Lonsdale early 1980s

16 40 Foot Corner .... VS 4b
12m. The groove with a slabby central section has a heathery exit but is worthwhile all the same.
FA. Rowland Edwards 1960

17 Canine Crucifixion E2 5c
12m. The crack right of the arete gives an entertaining pitch; don't be put off by the flora. Follow the crack to its end to find the finger-jam that gives the route its name, then loop right before heading back left to enter the easy final groove.
FA. Rowland Edwards 1962. FFA. Les Ainsworth 1967

18 Brastium E1 5b
12m. The central crack on the wall takes drainage in winter. At other times it is worth doing providing someone has cleaned it!
FA. Martin Battersby (2 points) 1969

19 Betty's Wall .... HVS 5a
12m. Climb past the annoying heathery ledge then trend left into a slim corner and sprint up this.
FA. Frank Spencer 1964

20 Cabbage Man Meets the Death Egg
.... E3 5c
12m. The continuous crack-line
FA. Paul Pritchard 1998

Waterfall Wall
The wall right of centre is indeed home to a cascade after wetter weather in the winter. After a dry spell it has some worthwhile routes, which are of special interest when some public spirited soul has dug the ferns from the cracks. Removal of the earth on the scruffy ledges would be a substantial but worthwhile undertaking too!
Access - Shooting may take place here on Wednesdays, Fridays and Sundays so please avoid these days.

Descent →

30 Foot Wall

Betty's Wall

326 Wilton 3 — Rappel Wall

Rappel Wall
The last decent rock in the quarry is the attractive light coloured wall behind the shooting gallery. There are several worthwhile lower and middle grade routes here, all or which prove to be better fun than abseiling!
Access - Shooting takes place here on Wednesdays, Fridays and Sundays so please avoid these days.

1 Barbeque .... S 4a
12m. Climb the crack to the ledge and continue in the same line.

2 Rappel Wall .... VDiff
16m. Climb the face leftwards following the zigzagging crack past a useful thread to an exit on the left. A good beginners' route.
FA. Rowland Edwards 1961

3 Peg Free .... VS 4c
14m. A bit of a non-line but pleasant enough moves. Climb the crack just left of the arete until it steepens. Scuttle left and finish up *Rappel Wall* or *Barbecue*.

4 Shivers Arete E1 5b
14m. The striking arete has an technical upper section, it is low in the grade and popular. Starts can be made from either side and a solid cemented peg protects the delightfully technical moves.
FA. Hank Pasquill 1968

5 Canopy .... HVS 5b
14m. Climb the shady right wall of the arete starting on the right and following a thin crack past a small bulge to a sweet finish.
FFA. Mick Pooler 1962

6 Kay .... VS 4c
14m. The deep corner groove gives a rather grubby little pitch which is a pity because it is a cracking line.
FA. Rowland Edwards 1962

7 Crooked Crack .... VS 5a
12m. A seductive line right of the corner is started on the left and has a crucial mantelshelf to pass the mid-height bulge.
FA. Rowland Edwards 1963

8 Mo .... HS 4b
10m. The wall and twinned cracks to a dusty exit.

9 Miney .... VDiff
10m. Head rightwards to the juggy central crack-line.
FA. Mick Pooler 1962

10 Meeny .... VDiff
10m. The widder crack gives short-lived jamming exercise and is a good one to have a first try at the Dark Art.
FA. Mick Pooler 1962

11 Eeny .... VDiff
8m. Approach the final crack by the short wall below.
FA. Mick Pooler 1962

Brownstones

	No star	☆	☆☆	☆☆☆
Mod to S	11	11	2	-
HS to HVS	5	8	2	-
E1 to E3	-	5	-	2
E4 and up	-	-	-	1

Brownstones is a diminutive crag which has one of the longest climbing histories in Lancashire. The reasons are obvious; the crag is seconds from the road, it takes little drainage, faces the afternoon sun, is generally of a height to encourage soloing and the fine-grained gritstone here is pretty good too. There are over 100 named routes/problems in this long-abandoned quarry many of which are of a technical and fingery nature. The crag can be used effectively as a training venue, or simply as a good place to blow away the cobwebs at the end of a day of drudgery. Large sections of the cliff-top are overgrown and/or unstable, making topping out difficult at best and dangerous at worst. Reversing the route is a good way of bringing on the pump or alternatively leap for that crash pad. As is so often the case with an area that is used extensively for bouldering, the grades here may be found to only be an approximation of those used elsewhere in the guide - be prepared for a tough time.

Approach   Also see map on page 289

The crag is situated above Wilton, on the continuation of the road leading up to Wiltons 2 and 3 from the A675. There is roadside parking just uphill (east) from the line of cottages known as New Collier's Row which is 1.5 miles west of the Wilton Quarry complex. From the point where a cinder track cuts diagonally behind the cottages, a muddy track runs straight into the right-hand corner of the quarry, curving rightwards and arriving by the Pool Area. To the left is the Long Back Wall and up the slope beyond this is the popular Ash Pit Slabs area, clearly marked by the easiest angled bit of rock in the quarry.

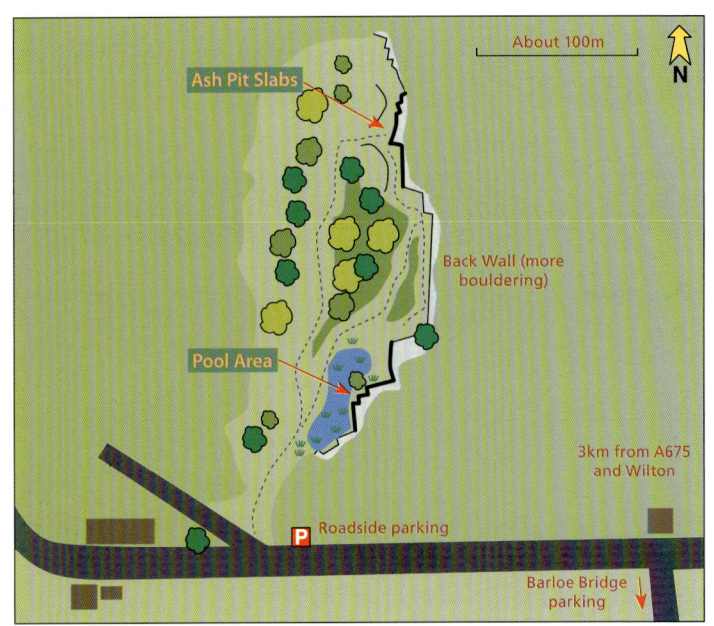

Conditions

The quarry is rapid-drying and faces the evening sun which makes it a delightful place in the right conditions. However it is very well-sheltered and the nearness of the standing water in the Pool Area means it can be a bit torrid here on muggy summer evenings. Also, and not unexpectedly, the mosquito/midge population enjoy a good meal when the weather conditions are right - so don't forget the DEET! The quarry is at its best on crisp afternoons from October through to April, but is popular all the year round.

Brownstones — Ash Pit Slab

1 Unjust V3 (6a)
The blunt arete on the left has (avoidable) chipped holds and is a bit of an eliminate.

2 Corn Mantel V1 (5b)
A mantel to start and then it soon eases.

3 Hopper V0- (4c)
Climb the slab left then back right. A little slippery.

4 Scraper V1 (5b)
From the start of *Degree Crack*, scrape directly up the slab.

5 Degree Crack V0 (5a)
The crack that cuts past the left-hand edge of the overlap.

6 Directissima V2 (5c)
Good technical climbing (faith in friction) through the centre of the narrow overlap halfway up the face. Keep off adjacent routes.

7 Analogue V0- (4c)
The crack through the right-hand edge of the overlap.

8 Fraud V1 (5b)
Start up *Digitation* then use the cheating holds up the slab!

9 Fraudulent Slip V3 (6a)
The same line without the chipped holds is much more taxing.

10 Digitation V2 (5c)
Fingery moves and polished footholds make this one quite hard at the grade. A quality problem from way back when.

11 Ash Pit Slab Direct .... VB (3c)
The thin seam left of the arete leads pleasantly to the upper section of the regular route.

12 Ash Pit Slab .... VDiff
The ledgy right arete of the wall also provides a good way down for the competent. *Photo on page 331.*

13 Ash Pit Traverse V0 (5a)
Popular and polished. The line on the topo is for the footholds, some of which are hidden once you start traversing. Classic. Using the footholds as handholds and keeping your feet off the ground is the **Ash Pit Low Traverse, V3**.

Ash Pit Slab

This is arguably the best bit of the crag; quiet and pleasant although many of the routes have become polished over the years. The bay is a sun-trap and the rock dries quickly, making it a decent winter-bouldering venue.
Approach - From the Pool Area, follow the path round under another steeper wall (The Back Wall) and up a short slope to where things open out again.

Ash Pit Slab **Brownstones** 329

14 Nexus V0- (4c)
The side wall is powerful at the grade. **The Nexus Dyno, V4** links the two good holds on the right with the distant jug. Whereas **The Double Dyno, V4** starts lower and the **Triple Dyno, V5** goes all the way to the top.

15 Wibble V0 (5a)
Wobble up the leaning corner; awkward and unpopular!

16 The Chimney V0- (4c)
The widening crack to the right has a choice of starts.

17 Parabola Direct ... V3 (6a)
Follow the diagonal undercuts left then finish direct.

18 Parabola V1 (5b)
As for *Parabola Direct* to the base of the thin crack then cross the fingery-wall rightwards to the top of *Parr's*.

19 Pigswill V6 (6c)
The wall trending right is a Brownstones' testpiece. The sit-start from undercuts adds about a grade. There are many other eliminates up to **V9**.

20 Parr's Crack V2 (5c)
Amazing for the time (late 1940s) and probably under-graded! A sit-start is **V3**.

21 Hank's Wall ... V7
The wall is unfeasibly narrow and just as technical. Keeping off adjacent routes is tricky; nothing left of *Parr's Crack* is allowed and nothing on *Layback* either. Variations abound including a sit-start (**V8**) and various other eliminates at about **V9**.

22 Layback V1 (5a)
Layback or finger-jam the thin crack - a nice problem.

23 Haskit Left-hand V2 (5c)
The left-hand fork of the Y-crack is popular.

24 Haskit Right-hand V1 (5b)
The right-hand fork is a touch easier and less popular.

25 Dragnet V0 (4b)
The crack passing the edge of a low overlap.

26 Inferno V0- (4c)
Up twin crack and the short wall above.

Pool Area - 100m

330 Brownstones Pool Area

1 Hernia .... VB (4c)
The tiny slab immediately to the right of the edge of the face. Avoiding the big jug on the arete is the norm.

2 Lobotomy V0 (5a)
The slab leads into a short left-trending groove. A bit slippery.

3 Slimer V1 (5b)
Balance up the slippy slab just left of the prominent thin crack.

4 Brownstones Crack .... VDiff
The straight crack in the centre of the slab has a jam or two.

5 Moss Wall .... VB (4c)
The grey wall has variants aplenty and can be as hard as V2 if you choose the wrong set of holds.

6 Verdi Ramp .... VB (4b)
The narrow ramp in the left wall of the main corner.

7 Verdi Corner .... VB (4a)
The green corner to a heathery exit.

8 Verdinand V3 (6a)
The wall just right of the corner is climbed via a shallow groove.

9 Verdigris V3 (6a)
The right side of the wall has a useful hold though the arete is to be avoided otherwise the grade drops a notch or two!

10 Verdi Wall .... VB (4c)
The letter-box and crack a short distance right of the corer

11 Two Step Left-hand V1 (5b)
Trend left up the centre of the short wall from the small ledges at foot of the next route.

12 Two Step .... VB (4b)
Trend right via a trio of useful ledges, with a little flick for the top. Variations are possible including no hands, no use of the top and a directish dyno.

13 Mantelstrug .... Diff
The ledge and face immediately left of the bevels arete.

14 Chockerblock Corner ..... VDiff
Nip up the blocker-chocked coner.

15 Muddy Wall .... VB (4c)
The wall left of the arete starting over an undercut flake.

Afternoon 4 min Sheltered

Descent

Ash Pit Slab - 100m

Brownstone's Crack

Pool Area **Brownstones** 331

16 Muddy Arete V2 (5c)
The blunt arete is nicely technical and not muddy at all.

17 Wet Corner .... VDiff
Strangely, the angular groove is normally dry.

18 Slab Variant.......... VB (4b)
Obvious from the name, and pleasant with a tricky sideways shuffle on polished footholds to gain the arete of the next climb.

19 Watery Arete .... VB (4c)
The arete left of the tide-line on its left-hand side.

20 Wet Foot V0 (5a)
Well named! The wall right of the arete is okay at low tide.

There are a few more V1/V2 problems up the cracks in the wall to the right though these are often inaccessible without a raft - perhaps an inflatable crashpad would do the trick?

21 Pond Traverse ... V3 (5c)
The traverse of the pond is a classic pumpy problem. It is best done right to left if you have any doubts about your stamina although the pros will, of course, reverse it.
It can be extended round the whole section out to *Hernia* at about **V5**.

Jodie Cuff climbing the delightful *Ash Pit Slab* (VDiff) - *page 328* - at Brownstones. Photo: Tristan Peers

Two Step

Muddy Arete

Pool Area
The first section that you arrive at on the approach is the second most popular part of the quarry. It has one pleasant slabby wall and a few, more vertical, walls which lead around over a dank little pool. Bring a towel for muddy boots.

Egerton Quarry

	No star	★	★★	★★★
Mod to S	-	-	-	-
HS to HVS	-	7	2	1
E1 to E3	-	1	3	-
E4 and up	-	-	2	2

Egerton Quarry is an extensive hole in the ground which is close to Wilton Quarries, but nowhere near as popular. Despite being home to nearly 200m routes, much of the quarry is broken and slightly disappointing from a climber's perspective although there are routes dotted all around the edge of the quarry on various decent buttresses. The three spots described here feature the best routes including the fine Wood Buttress, the impressive Red Prow and the aretes and corners around *Cherry Bomb*.

In recent years there have been attempts to clean up sections of the crag and this is an ongoing battle.

Conditions

Red Prow and Wood Buttress are generally north facing which makes them a good retreat on hot days but best avoided after damp weather or when it is cold. *Cherry Bomb* is much sunnier and quicker drying.

Approach   See map on page 289

The quarry is situated near the town of Egerton, only 1.75 km (as the crow flies) from Wilton. From Darwen Road (B6472), just south of the Dunscar Arms, turn east onto Arnold Road. Turn left onto Cox Green Road and follow this as it bends left and starts to rise. Just after a left turn into Rock Terrace is a wide entrance on the right with big gates, leading into parkland. Park sensibly here.

Continue up Cox Green Lane for 160m to a bridge (not obvious from above, but look over the wall) and continue for short distance to a gap on the right. Head through this and down the slope to the floor of the quarry. Turn right and follow the base of the slope to the afore mentioned bridge. Continue left in front of this and down the tree covered slope to the base of the wall. An alternative is to walk down Rock Lane until it bends left, where a track leads rightwards into the trees to an open area, bear right to reach the bridge - 150m from the road. Go under it and turn right to join the other approach.

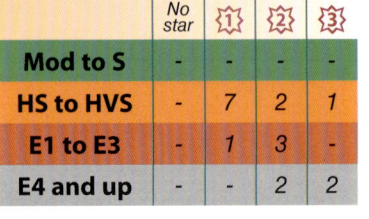

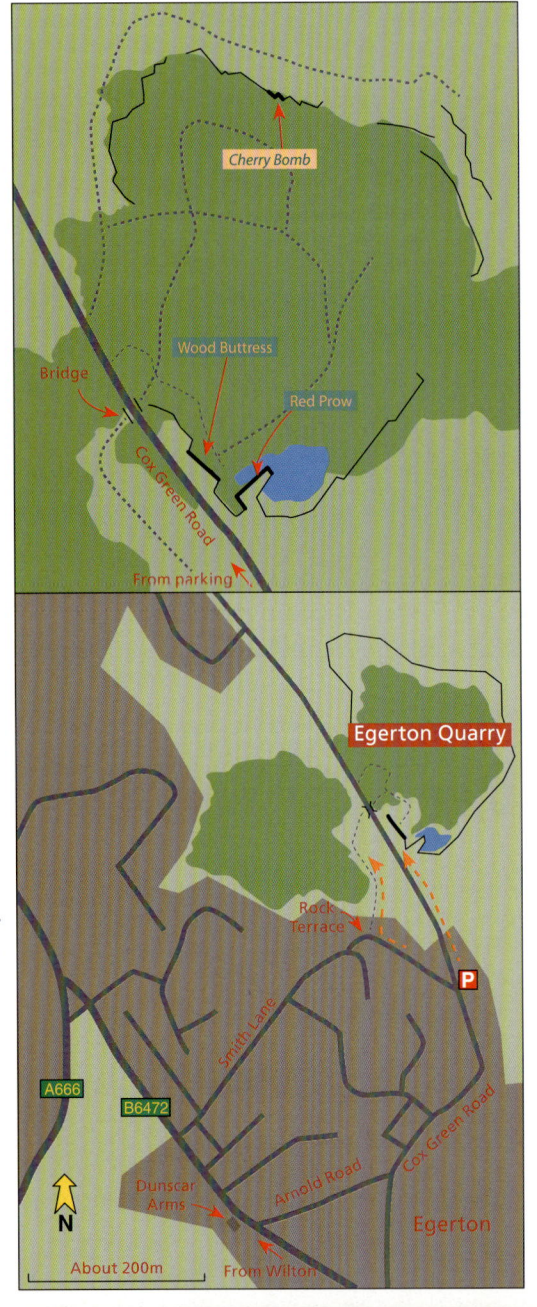

Jordan Buys on *Boomerang* (E8) - *page 334* - at Egerton. Photo: Alex Messenger

Egerton Quarry

Cherry Bomb
The side of the quarry opposite the approach has a sunny wall with some striking aretes and corners.

1 Satin Sapphire E3 5c
14m. Tackle the arete left of *Cherry Bomb* on its left-hand side.
FA. Nick Colton 1978

2 Cherry Bomb .... VS 4c
14m. Climb the corner by tricky bridging. Pull over the roof and finish on the left arete.
FA. Dave Cronshaw 1977

3 Boomerang ... E8 6c
14m. Climb direct up the arete right of *Cherry Bomb* via a dynamic move. No side runners at this grade. *Photo on page 333.*
FA. Jordan Buys 2006

Red Prow
The Red Prow juts out into the stagnant pond, with the tip of the prow known rather hopefully as the Diving Board. There are some good climbs here, though the best are all pretty tough. The Prow protrudes far enough out into the quarry to ensure it gets some afternoon sunshine, at least in its upper parts.

4 The Field of Dreams ... VS 5a
30m. An expedition with comfy bivi-sites along the way. Access the front of the *Diving Board* and climb its right arete (**5a**) to reach *Base Camp*. Tackle the crack in the next riser and follow it round right to an easy groove that leads to *Advanced Base Camp* (**4c**). Tackle the final prow by its right-hand edge and finish airily over the right-hand side of the beak (**4c**). Now where's that flag?
FA. Geoff Hibbert 1996

5 Don't Stop Believing E2 5c
14m. Climb the groove and left-trending crack then make a tricky mantelshelf to reach the horizontal break. A short pumpy wall leads to the easy right-trending break.
FA. Geoff Hibbert 1986

6 Chalk Lightning Crack .. E2 5b
14m. Attack the compelling crack the splits the tower. The hard section is short-lived but quite intense. A huge cam and high-friction jeans might make it nearer **E1 5b**.
FA. Ian Lonsdale 1976

Egerton Quarry 335

❼ Nobody Wept for Alec Trench
.... E5 6a
14m. The right-hand arete is an intimidating outing offering sustain and poorly protected climbing. There may be two, or even three old pegs in place, though these should not be trusted.
FA. Dai Lampard 1982

❽ Ice Cool Acid Test E4 6a
14m. The back (sunny) wall of the Red Prow gives a bold technical pitch. A cam on the right protects the hard moves from the left-hand edge of the initial ledge. Once established press on up the centre of the face.
FA. Dai Lampard 1982

❾ White Out .... HS 4b
14m. The crack bounding the wall on the right gives good jamming to a rather crusty exit.
FA. Nigel Holmes 1975

❿ Vortex E8 6c
14m. Desperate technical wall climbing marked by 2 pegs
FA. Gaz Parry 2002

Wood Buttress
Wood Buttress has some good mid-grade routes in a shady setting making it a good hot weather retreat. The grades and start ratings assume the routes are clean and dry!

⓫ I Shot Jason King .. E5 6a
18m. The bold left arete of the wall eases - eventually.
FA. Mick Johnson early 1980s. Originally it started further right at about E2.

⓬ Ten Minutes before the Worm
.... VS 4c
20m. A mini-adventure. Climb the crack then trend out left to a rest in a niche. Continue up and left again to reach the arete then move back right to exit.
FA. Dave Knighton 1976

⓭ God Save the Queen ... HVS 5a
18m. The first continuous crack leads all the way to a cleaned finish through the gap to the left of the protruding pole.
FA. Dave Knighton 1976

⓮ Gallows Pole .... HVS 5a
18m. The crack-line that drops from the jutting post gives good sustained climbing.
FA. Dave Knighton 1976

⓯ The Disappearing Chip Buttie Traverse
.... E1 5b
30m. A major expedition. Start immediately left the groove that bounds the wall on the right and climb diagonally rightwards passing *Gallows Pole* to reach *God Save the Queen*. Up this for a couple of moves then finger-traverse left to exit beyond the heather cornice.
FA. Geoff Hibbert 1985

⓰ Wednesday Corner .... VS 4b
16m. The long groove gives a good pitch. Exit right.
FA. Dave Knighton 1976

⓱ Insipidity .... VS 4b
16m. The next groove to the right in two sections passing a good ledge at half-height.
FA. Nigel Holmes 1976

⓲ Dickie's Meadow ..... HS 4b
16m. Graze up the final groove in the wall.
FA. Nigel Holmes 1976

Cadshaw Castle Rocks

336

	No star	★	★★	★★★
Mod to S	9	12	2	1
HS to HVS	9	10	2	-
E1 to E3	4	6	2	2
E4 and up	1	4	-	-

A bit of an enigma for Lancashire, a natural outcrop of good quality gritstone in a sunny setting. Not surprising then that the place has long been popular and has become quite polished. Most routes here were first climbed and named by Alan Allsopp in the 1930s.

Approach   See map on page 289

There is limited roadside parking in a lay-by 90m north west of the junction of the A666 (Bolton Road) with the B6391 (Green Arms Road) opposite a wide entrance to a forest track. Cross the road and follow the track as it gently bends left and descends for almost a kilometre (avoid the only sizeable left turn) until the green and grim Cadshaw Quarry on the left. Continue down the track as it loops back right, cross the river and scramble up to the light and airy cliff.

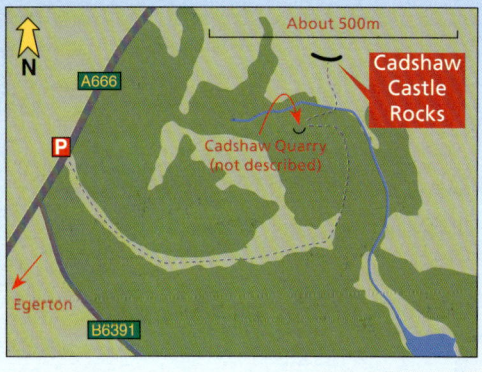

❶ The Bulges. . . . . VDiff
8m. The left arete of the crag.

❷ West Buttress Direct . . . . . . VDiff
8m. The short face just right.

❸ Curving Crack. . . . . VDiff
8m. The crack on the left edge of the buttress.

❹ West Wall . . . . S 4a
8m. The vague groove passing left of the roof.

❺ Split Block Climb . . . . ★ S 4a
9m. The slim hanging groove through the left side of the roof.

❻ Split Block Overhang. . . HVS 5a
8m. The centre of the overhang on sloping holds.

❼ Split Block Crack . . . . ★ HS 4b
10m. ... and the crack to the right of the overhang.

❽ West Slab Direct. . . . . VS 4b
10m. The right side of the slab - direct! Escaping right into the chimney is **VDiff**.

Cadshaw Castle Rocks   337

9 Central Wall .... HS 4b
10m. Excellent. Climb the centre of the buttress passing through the conspicuous shallow notch (the bull's horns) to below the capping roof. Finish left or right over this.

10 Central Crack .... VDiff
10m. The central-ish crack to a rightwards escape from the jaws.

11 Central Chimney .... VDiff
12m. The recessed rift that cuts in behind the buttress.

12 The Slab .... VDiff
12m. Select a way up the slab.

13 Oak Tree Chimney .... VDiff
12m. The blocky rift to you know where!

14 The Mantelshelf .... S 4a
12m. Mantel onto the shiny ledge then skedaddle left of the roof.

15 Overhang Crack .... VDiff
12m. The crack and groove are pleasant.

16 Crack and Wall .... S 4a
12m. The crack rightwards to a polished ledge, finish direct.

17 Column Climb .... Diff
12m. Head up past the conspicuous pillar to a ledge on the right. Finish leftwards up the pleasant face above.

18 East Face Climb .... VDiff
10m. Climb the wall 2m left of the corner to a jutting block and a scruffy finish.

19 Corner Chimney .... Diff
10m. The blocky groove left of the larger buttress.

20 Pagan Wall .... S 4a
10m. The narrow side-wall on slopers.

21 Pagan's Direct .... HVS 5b
12m. Good climbing though the line lacks logic. Monkey over the bulge then move up and hand-traverse the jutting 'coffin' to reach a thin crack in the head-wall.

22 Druid's Direct E3 6a
12m. Mantelshelf fiercely through the overhang to ledge of The Altar, then head over the roof and up the wrinkly wall.

23 Pagan's Progress .... VS 4c
14m. Devious and polished too - not one for damp conditions. From the groove skirt the roof right then left. Move onto the arete and climb into the niche above - the Crow's Nest. Climb the wall above, using the Coffin to get started.

24 Druid's Face E2 5b
12m. Climb direct into the yellow niche, heave past the overhang, move right to a scoop and continue up the wrinkled wall above.
FA. Jim Nightingale 1961

25 Niche Indirect .... HS 4b
12m. Trend left to the niche and back right to the arete.

26 Druid's Corner .... VDiff
12m. Slant right to the niche in the arete and finish on the right.

27 The Staircase .... Mod
12m. The easy slab on the right end of the buttress.

Littleborough Area

These three worthwhile but neglected cliffs sit in fine positions overlooking the town of Littleborough. They are easily reached and can be combined to give a great day's climbing.

	No star	★	★★	★★★
Mod to S	6	3	1	-
HS to HVS	14	11	9	1
E1 to E3	5	8	4	1
E4 and up	1	3	3	1

Summit Quarry

A neglected quarry with a good selection of climbs on the best bit of rock. The quarry gets the afternoon sun and can be a real suntrap on still days. If you enjoy the place there are another 70 or so routes to go at in addition to the ones listed here.

Approach - Leave Littleborough on the A6033 towards Todmorden. On the edge of the town turn right off the main road by the Summit Inn and cross the canal. Turn left and park on the trackside about 50m further on. Walk up the track and cross a stile onto a path. This leads over a marshy section then head right up the hillside into a narrow gorge which leads up to the quarry.

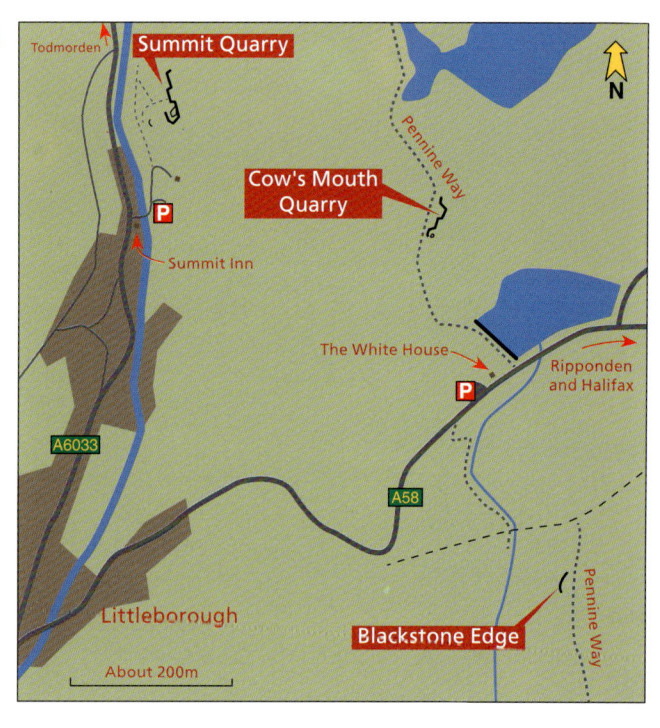

Blackstone Edge

A small outcrop in a fine setting which offers plenty for the middle E-grade climber or a smaller selection of low grade and well-polished ancient classics, but little in the HVS range. The altitude and aspect makes it inclined to be green, although a fine summer's evening here can be exceptionally pleasant. There is bouldering here too, on the blocks scattered below the edge.

Approach - Leave Littleborough on the A58 towards Ripponden and Halifax. Park just before the White House pub which is situated near Blackstone Edge Reservoir, about 3km out of Littleborough. From the parking, walk down the road for 100m to a track on the other side which rises steeply to reach a drainage ditch. Follow this south for 15 minutes to the Roman Road then head up the moor to the crag up and left.

Cow's Mouth Quarry

A remote quarry on the edge of Soyland Moor overlooking Littleborough. The cliff faces south-west, gets the afternoon sun and is slightly recessed, so can be sheltered from the worst of the wind.

Approach - The crag is reached from parking below The White House pub (as for Blackstone Edge). From the parking walk up the hill for 200m and go through the gate on the left (signed Pennine Way). Walk across the dam front then follow the horizontal path to a tiny arched bridge. Cross this to reach the quarry or continue on the main path and jump the narrow canal.

Summit Quarry — Littleborough Area

1 Twixt .... HVS 5a
6m. The square arete that bounds the wall on its left-hand side.
FA. Paul Horan 1967

2 Windy Wall .... HVS 5b
6m. The right-hand side of the arete is tricky and worthwhile.
FA. Clive Morton 1979

3 The Crab .... VS 4c
10m. Nip up the two cracks past a narrowing in the middle section. Finish by favouring the left-hand branch.
FA. Paul Horan 1967

4 Layback Crack .... VS 5a
10m. The compelling (and strenuous) crack leads to crucial moves round the right-hand side of the capping overhang.
FA. Paul Horan 1967

5 Starters .... VDiff
12m. The left-facing groove to a good ledge then finish up the short corner behind. Well-named; the best easy climb here.
FA. Ian Butterworth 1967

6 The Shroud E2 5c
14m. From just right of the arete a layaway leads to a hernia-inducing mantelshelf. Continue into a shallow groove to ledges on the right then head up the final wall. The gear is adequate.
Turin Finish, E2 5c - More exciting. Move left from the groove and climb the arete, initially on the right then on the left.
FA. John Hampson 1971. FA. (Turin Finish) Andrew Eaton 1985

7 Grave's End E1 5b
14m. An adventure, bold, balancy and the best here. Teeter up the shallow right-trending groove, then stride left to small ledges and a runner. Climb awkwardly into and up the scoop above and finish up the wall above. **The Direct Start** just to the left is 5c.
FA. Paul Horan 1967. FA. (Direct Start) Bruce Goodwin 1997

Summit Quarry
A good selection of routes that are generally rather bold but less so than they appear from below; a set of small cams and wires will be found very useful. The quarry extends further right with around 70 or so more routes.

8 Laying-by E3 5c
14m. Start up *Grave's End* but continue up the serious groove with increasing difficulty to its end. Continue direct to the rib above and a wild finish on gradually improving holds.
FA. John Hampson 1985

9 Order .... HS 4a
14m. Climb the corner at the right-hand side of the smooth rock and continue up the groove above join the easy ramp of *Disorder*.
FA. Ian Butterworth 1967

10 Free Spirit E2 5b
14m. A eliminate that seeks out difficulties - and finds them! From *Order* trend right across the wall to *Disorder* then follow the thin crack past the right-hand side of the overhang. A sensible side-runner lowers the grade to **HVS**.
FA. Bob Whittaker 1981

11 Disorder .... HS 4a
14m. The right-hand of a pair of grooves is followed awkwardly as it slants leftwards giving an excellent pitch.
FA. Pete Mustoe 1967

12 Cnig's Direct .... VS 4c
12m. Follow the groove to a crescent-shaped flake and pull over its left-hand edge. Follow the thin crack up the ledgy wall above.
FA. Stu Halliwell 1967

13 Cnig's Underhang ... VS 4b
12m. Follow the crescent-shaped flake out right by underhanded manoeuvres to a finish up a crack on the right.
FA. Stu Halliwell 1967

14 Alexander the Great ... HVS 5b
12m. Climb onto the end of the shelf then continue up a thin crack to and overlap and the final few moves of *Cnig's Underhang*.
FA. Bruce Goodwin 1969

15 Bright Spark .... VS 4b
12m. From the right-hand end of the ledge climb through the inverted V in the roof and up the crack above.
FA. Ron Blunt 1981

Littleborough Area — Blackstone Edge

1 Slim Jim .... VS 5a
8m. The hanging crack that faces the top of the Roman Road.
FA. Paul Horan 1966

2 Manibus et Pedibusque E4 6a
12m. A fierce and scary traverse of the left wall of the chimney.
FA. Paul Horan (with tension) 1967. FFA. Alan McHardy early 1970s

3 Nor Nor' Chimney .... VDiff
12m. Enter the cave recess then do battle with the chimney rising from its left-hand corner.

4 North Cave .... Mod
12m. The easier exit from the cave is rightwards up another chimney. **The Direct Start** is a grovelly **4c** up the steep groove.
FA. John Laycock early 1900s

5 Belly on a Plate .... VS 4c
12m. Delightful! Climb the groove then flop out left onto the ledge. Finish up the well-positioned right arete of the chimney.
FA. C Burridge 1992

6 The Mangler .... VS 5a
12m. The leaning jamming-crack is a bit of a carnivore. Awkward throughout but fun in a perverse kind of way.
FA. Richard McHardy early 1960s

7 Cornflake E2 5c
12m. The flakes in the left wall of *Central Gully* give a pitch of escalating interest and difficult. Protection is adequate but awkward to place and the final moves will wake you up for sure.

8 Central Crack .... VDiff
12m. The left-hand crack in the recess was well-scoured by nailed boots in the past. Start awkwardly then continue by laybacking and jamming. Runners are available in the thin crack just right.
FA. John Laycock early 1900s

9 Central Eliminate .... VS 5a
12m. An uncomfortable eliminate up the ever-narrowing face. Trying to avoid the routes to either side is the real crux!

10 Central Groove .... S 4b
12m. The right-hand groove would be worth more stars if it was a little less inclined to be green.

11 Master Ego E2 5c
12m. Layback the arete to the bulge and sneak round its left-hand side to reach the ledge just above. A long reach from a rounded edge (small wire) gains the top.
FA. Bruce Goodwin 1983

12 Little Miss Id Variations E3 6a
12m. Climb the wall to below the roof then move out right to gain the ledge. Finish right from here with difficulty on sloping holds.

13 Little Miss Id E2 5c
12m. Excellent and surprisingly taxing. Climb the blunt arete with increasing difficulty then make hard and precarious moves up and then left to a good rescue ledge. Finish as for *Master Ego*.
FA. Richard McHardy 1962

Blackstone Edge

This compact buttress is divided by a series of wide chimneys up which many of the easier and more traditional lines go with *Central Crack* being the pick. The other quality routes tend to be on the faces with *Little Miss Id* and her *Variations* probably being the best.

Blackstone Edge Littleborough Area   341

14 Tryche E5 6a
10m. Climb the difficult wall passing a runnerable pocket, then continue up a shallow groove on poor holds to hard final moves. A gripper and easy E5 or hard E4 - you choose!

15 Pots E2 5c
10m. Climb the shallow flakes just left of the chimney to their termination, shuffle left along the break then climb back rightwards to a grasping exit.
FA. Dennis Carr 1977

16 Outside Edge .... VS 4c
10m. Bridge up the outer edge of the chimney by exposed moves with protection to left and right. Harder for the short!
FA. Bruce Goodwin 1994

17 South Chimney .... Diff
12m. An awkward start enters 'the reading room' then select a suitable upward exit towards daylight. The star is for the historical interest as much as the climbing.
FA. John Laycock early 1900s

18 Twin Cracks .... Diff
10m. Climb the chimney using either or both cracks. Well-protected throughout. The right-hand crack direct is **VDiff**.
FA. John Laycock early 1900s

19 Palmistry. E2 5c
10m. Climb the right arete of the chimney/groove to a good ledge. Move over right to finish up the shallow rounded groove.
FA. Bruce Goodwin 1994

20 No Sign of Three...... E2 5c
10m. Climb the right-hand side of the face then move left to a shallow groove and climb the right-hand side of this to ledges. Take the obvious continuation (as for *Palmistry*) to finish. Hard for the grade.
FA. Tony Nichols 1983

21 Swot and Heaty E4 6a
8m. The arete and wall above have reasonable protection.
FA. Ian Dunn 2004

22 Doomidest Hay.... E5 6b
8m. Start below pocket and climb to it (poor gear) then move up and right before heading back left to finish.
FA Nick Dixon 2004

23 Slin and Thippy E4 6a
8m. The belicate and dold wall also has a founded rinish.
FA. Ian Cooksey 1988

24 Pendulum Swing Direct .... HVS 5a
8m. From the foot of the polished crack climb the wall boldly on sloping holds to the base of the wide crack above. Finish up this.
FA. Alan McHardy 1962

25 Pendulum Swing. .... VS 4c
10m. The well-polished crack on the right (better if you avoid the boulder) leads to a tricky traverse back left using a line of tiny holds, provided by the phantom chipper, to reach the final crack.

342 Littleborough Area — Cow's Mouth Quarry

❶ Cornette .... Diff
10m. The awkward blocky groove leads to the juggy arete. Escape off left. A safe first lead.
FA. John Lowthian 1966

❷ Slab Crossing .... VS 4b
20m. Climb the groove then hand-traverse the break rightwards until a ledge can be gained by a mantel. Continue into and up the chimney on the right. Traversing at other levels is possible.
FA. Bob Whittaker 1973

❸ Deadline .... VS 5a
10m. A direct line up the face one metre right of the groove.
FA. Bob Whittaker 1987

❹ Route 1 .... HS 4c
10m. Balance up and right to good holds and runners in the break. Finish up the left-hand groove above to a rounded mantel.
FA. Ian Butterworth 1966

❺ King B E1 5c
10m. Make a bold start up the centre of the slab to the break. Then climb the shallow groove above avoiding *Route 1*.
FA. Bob Whittaker 1981

❻ Route 2 .... HVS 5a
10m. Climb the shallow groove (Rock 1 on the right) then balance left and right to the break and more wires. Finish up the right-hand groove. A traditional VS that was just a bit too bold.
FA. Paul Horan 1966

❼ Slabmaster .... VS 4c
10m. Climb the groove to a ledge then the slotted wall above until it becomes necessary to move left and join *Route 2*.
FA. Bob Whittaker 1981

❽ Route Right .... HS 4b
10m. Trend right from the start of *Slabmaster* until forced off the slab. Finish up the easy chimney; a bit of an anticlimax.
FA. Paul Horan 1966

❾ Jack and Ed's Route E5 6a
10m. Climb the wall left of the arete via a groove to the top.
FA. Jack Geldard, Ed Brown 2000ish

❿ Daytona Wall E5 6a
10m. A bold outing that weaves across the impressive buttress. Since the demise of the ancient bolt runner, it is pretty much unprotected where it matters. Start under the arete and climb up and right through the bulge to a slot, then move right to another. Take a deep breath and finish direct.
FA. Al Evans 1977

⓫ Daytona Wall Direct E5 6b
10m. Climb a faint crack up the lower wall to join the regular route at the bulge. Pull up to the pocket and finish direct.
FA. (Start) Phil Kelly 1984. FA. (Finish) Jerry Peel

⓬ Boldness Through Ignorance E8 6c
10m. From the *Direct* sketch up and right past where a peg used to be to some small finger-pockets and a scary finish.
FA. Gareth Parry (with peg runner) 1991. FA. Jordan Buys (without) 2003

⓭ Overlapper .... HVS 5b
10m. Climb the flaky groove to the bulge then pull left to gain a good pocket, the continuation crack and a sprint finish.
FA. Bob Whittaker 1973

⓮ Lapper E1 5b
10m. Follow the groove throughout then make a pumpy hand-traverse out right to finish.
FA. Bob Whittaker 1981

⓯ Dessers .... VS 4c
10m. The thin crack has an awkward moves to overcome the initial crucial section.
FA. Paul Horan 1967

⓰ Sard .... HVS 5a
8m. After a tricky start head up the fingery wall, or access it from the next route at a more amenable **VS 4c**.
FA. Bob Whittaker 1981

⓱ Seazy .... HS 4c
8m. The thin crack with a triangular niche at three metres. Passing this is tricky though it is steep above.
FA. Stu Halliwell 1966

Cow's Mouth - Left
A pair of contrasting faces, one slabby and pleasant and the other steep and hard, no guesses as to which one is the most popular! Both get the afternoon sun and dry rapidly.

Cow's Mouth Quarry — Littleborough Area — 343

The next climbs are 150m right in the other quarry.

⓲ Groovin' — HS 4b
8m. From a block climb the shallow groove and escape left.
FA. Paul Horan 1967

⓳ The Romeo Error — E1 6a
10m. Sketch up the slab to a mantel, hop onto it (hard) then sneak off left to avoid the cornice. A left-hand start is a grade easier.
FA. Al Evans 1977. FA. (Direct Start) Andrew Unsworth 1984

⓴ Screwy — E2 5c
10m. More thin climbing up the face just right of the unclippable in-situ gear (they look like nails to me). An ancient peg just below the top might help if you have a rope on!
FA. Ras Taylor 1964. FFA. Bob Whittaker 1966

㉑ Groundhog — E1 5b
10m. The face is on small holds to a grubby exit. A side-runner drops the grade a notch. Just keep trying until you get it right!

㉒ Sandy Crack — VS 5a
10m. The crack just left of the chimney/corner is usually clean. No bridging allowed at this grade.
FA. Pete Mustoe 1964

㉓ Curving Chimney — Diff
8m. The rift is 'orrible and desperate too!
FA. Pete Mustoe 1964

㉔ Jumping Jive — E1 5b
8m. Leap for the ledge then finish leftwards.
FA. Bruce Goodwin 1985

㉕ Pavanne — HVS 5a
8m. Crawl on to the ledge then trend right to the top.
FA. Al Evans 1977

㉖ Overhanging Crack — VS 4c
8m. The excellent but short hand-crack has a tricky exit.
FA. Pete Mustoe 1964

㉗ Z Crack — VS 5a
10m. A little classic that thinks its HVS. Well-protected. Finish direct with a long reach or follow the logical line left at real **HVS**.
FA. Pete Mustoe 1964

㉘ The Don — E2 6a
10m. The blank and bold wall right of *Z Crack*.
FA. John Ellis 1980

㉙ Los Endos — HVS 5a
8m. A problem start up the arete leads to easier ground.
FA. Al Evans 1972

㉚ Scree? Pain! — E3 6a
6m. Nasty. Climb the wall, using a slot, to a scary finish.
FA. Bruce Goodwin 1985

㉛ Flupper — VS 5a
6m. Climb the scooped wall until forced right to easier ground.
FA. Bruce Goodwin 1976

㉜ Flipper — S 4b
6m. Polished holds just right of the arete are pleasant.
FA. Pete Mustoe 1964

㉝ Flopper — VS 4c
6m. Use an undercut to reach rounded holds and a quick pull.
FA. John Hampson early 1980s

Cow's Mouth - Right
An interesting set of routes, sheltered from the worst of the wind, though inclined to be green after wet weather. The quarry is the first one reached on the approach.

Cheshire

Hoop-La Buttress beckons through Frodsham's magical woods.

Helsby

A fine two-tiered cliff of New Red Sandstone, overlooking the River Mersey and the M56 motorway. Uninformed climbers often glance up and scorn the place as they speed by on their way to North Wales. Perhaps they should consider taking the time to have a closer look since most will be pleasantly surprised by the compact and clean walls offering some superb routes on great rock. From below, the dark overhangs appear to dominate the view and the fine pink walls tend to blend into the hillside. In reality there is a lot of good climbing here, so next time you are zipping by, call in for an hour, enjoy the fine outward views and do *Grooved Slab*, *Flake Crack* and *Eliminate 1*; the chances are you will be back at Helsby sooner rather than later.

	No star	☆	☆☆	☆☆☆
Mod to S	10	11	-	-
HS to HVS	1	14	6	3
E1 to E3	6	12	9	3
E4 and up	3	15	5	6

Access
There is a seasonal restriction on the buttresses to the east of Classhooks Gully due to nesting birds. No climbing on Upper and Lower Central Buttresses from 1 March to 30 June each year.

Approach   Also see map on page 344
The best approach for most climbers is from junction 14 of the M56. Follow the signs for Helsby village off the motorway and turn left onto the A56 at the first junction. As you arrive in the village fork right. Follow this road for about 2km to a point where there is wide junction with houses on the left and steep wooded slopes on the right. The road on the left here is called Crescent Drive. Park sensibly somewhere on the roadside, there is always plenty of space, then cross the road towards the wood and pick up a path which winds uphill to the crag. This starts off diagonally to the right, then heads back left along a wide track and finally turns up a narrow path through the bushes to arrive at the right-hand end of the cliff; about 5 minutes steep walk from the parking.

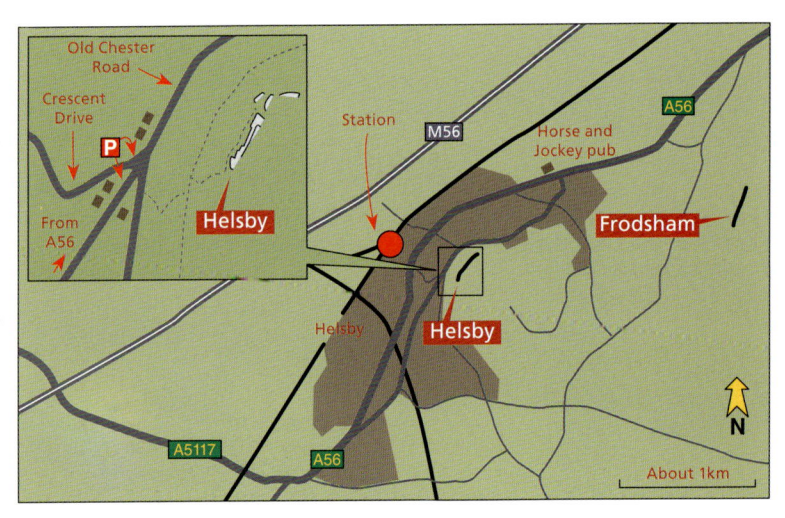

Conditions
Helsby is a crag full of surprises and it is not unknown to arrive here in the middle of winter to find the place bone dry and as clean as a whistle. The western (right-hand) side receives late afternoon sun and the lower sections tend to escape the worst of the greenness. However for the majority of the routes you are better advised to turn up at a warmer time of year preferably after a short dry spell. The eastern side of the crag (not covered here) receives very little sun and only comes into condition rarely. Since the crag is made of sandstone, it is worth keeping away immediately after rain even if the place appears to be dry. Sandstone is porous and once the rock has absorbed rainwater it is prone to snapping suddenly. A badly-timed pull on one of the small flakes could damage a route irreparably and not do a lot for your health! It is worth pointing out that the view from the cliff out across the Stanlow refinery and the Mersey estuary is superb and spectacular sunsets here are common.

Jon Read climbing on the crucial section of *Agag* (VS) - *page 352* - on the Golden Pillar area of Helsby. Photo: Sarah Clough

Helsby Lower Central Buttress

Crack of Doom

Descent

No climbing 1 Mar to 30 Jun due to nesting birds

① Blue Light .... HVS 5b
8m. The left-hand side of the wall, using the arete. Graded for when it is clean which is usually isn't.

② In the Pie E2 6a
10m. An eliminate up the centre of the wall trending left.
FA. David Ranby 1980s

③ Pigeonhole Wall ...... HVS 5a
10m. The slanting groove is entered steeply using the odd holes.
FA. C.W.Marshall 1920s

④ Pigeonhole Arete E1 5c
10m. The blunt rib is steep and worthwhile.

⑤ Crack of Doom .... S 3c
10m. Enter at your peril. Off-width it, facing right, or bridge.

⑥ Whimper E2 5c
10m. The wall just right of the corner past some pockets.

⑦ Wafer Wall E2 5b
10m. Bold with thin moves and some mid-height gear.

⑧ Z Route .... VDiff
18m. A long diagonal along the overlap to a finish above the roof.

⑨ Z Route Direct .... S 4a
12m. Climb direct to the traverse of the previous route and then finish along it.

⑩ Oblique Crack .... VDiff
11m. Climb the diagonal and increasingly grassy crack left of the big roof to meadows.

⑪ Muffin Crack .... HVS 5b
11m. The big roof is split by two prominent cracks. This route tackles the lesser left-hand crack.

⑫ Crumpet Crack E4 6b
11m. The central crack is a classic and crusty struggle but best to lay off the crumpets before you give it a go.
FA. Hugh Banner 1960s

⑬ Hades Crack .... HS 4b
10m. The slashing diagonal line right of the roof is awkward.
FA. C.W.Marshall 1920s

⑭ Two Step Crack .... VDiff
10m. Climb the corner via a step or two, to a grassy exit.

⑮ Honeycomb Wall ...... VS 4c
9m. Follow big but crusty holds up the steep wall.

Descent

Crumpet Crack

Lower Central Buttress
This wall is well-hidden from above but is worth a look, especially if it is blowing a gale since it is reasonably sheltered by the trees. The routes are only short although *Crumpet Crack* will be found long enough for most.
Approach - Scramble easily down a steep path which leaves the base of the main crag below Clashooks Gully.

Upper Central Buttress **Helsby** 349

No climbing 1 Mar to 30 Jun due to nesting birds

Descent - care required

Upper Central Buttress
This fine wall is perched high above the valley at the point where the crag changes angle (the routes further left are both difficult to get to and often very green.) This spot is often very windy and the routes feel much more exposed than their lengths would suggest.

Lower Central Buttress

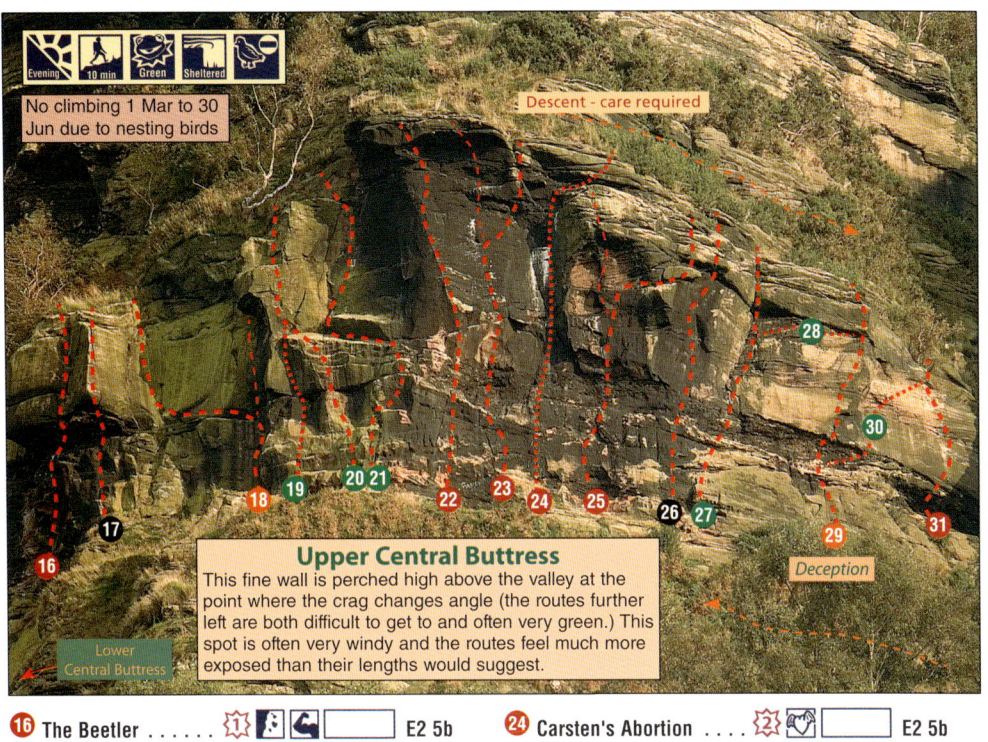

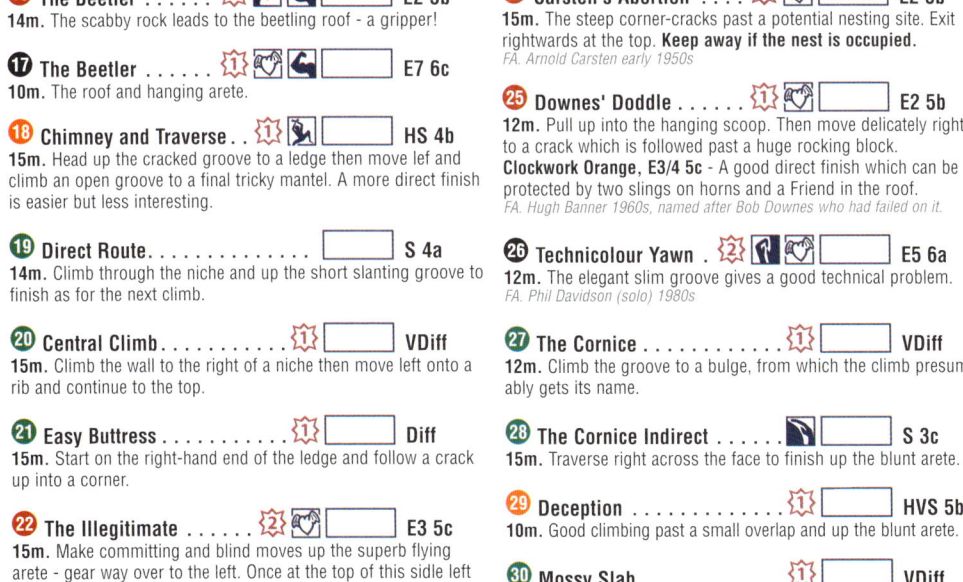

Deception

16 The Beetler — E2 5b
14m. The scabby rock leads to the beetling roof - a gripper!

17 The Beetler — E7 6c
10m. The roof and hanging arete.

18 Chimney and Traverse — HS 4b
15m. Head up the cracked groove to a ledge then move lef and climb an open groove to a final tricky mantel. A more direct finish is easier but less interesting.

19 Direct Route — S 4a
14m. Climb through the niche and up the short slanting groove to finish as for the next climb.

20 Central Climb — VDiff
15m. Climb the wall to the right of a niche then move left onto a rib and continue to the top.

21 Easy Buttress — Diff
15m. Start on the right-hand end of the ledge and follow a crack up into a corner.

22 The Illegitimate — E3 5c
15m. Make committing and blind moves up the superb flying arete - gear way over to the left. Once at the top of this sidle left through the narrowing in the roofs.
FA. Hugh Banner 1960s

23 Carsten's Variant — E2 5b
15m. A scary eliminate up the wall left of the corner.
The **Forceps Finish** over the roof is **E2 5c**.

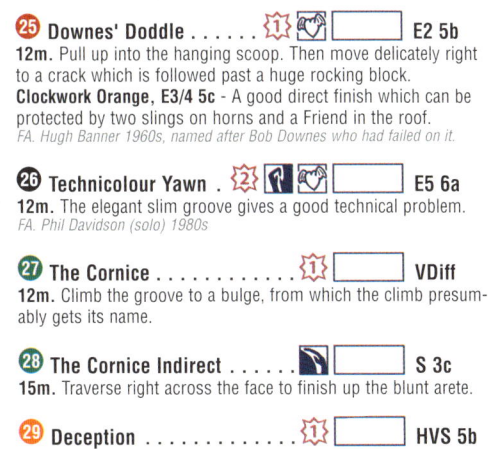

24 Carsten's Abortion — E2 5b
15m. The steep corner-cracks past a potential nesting site. Exit rightwards at the top. **Keep away if the nest is occupied.**
FA. Arnold Carsten early 1950s

25 Downes' Doddle — E2 5b
12m. Pull up into the hanging scoop. Then move delicately right to a crack which is followed past a huge rocking block.
Clockwork Orange, E3/4 5c - A good direct finish which can be protected by two slings on horns and a Friend in the roof.
FA. Hugh Banner 1960s, named after Bob Downes who had failed on it.

26 Technicolour Yawn — E5 6a
12m. The elegant slim groove gives a good technical problem.
FA. Phil Davidson (solo) 1980s

27 The Cornice — VDiff
12m. Climb the groove to a bulge, from which the climb presumably gets its name.

28 The Cornice Indirect — S 3c
15m. Traverse right across the face to finish up the blunt arete.

29 Deception — HVS 5b
10m. Good climbing past a small overlap and up the blunt arete.

30 Mossy Slab — VDiff
12m. Follow the curving flake/groove across the slab which has long been moss-less.

31 Gather No Moss — E3 6b
7m. A short and technical high-ball boulder problem over the roof on the far right.

Helsby The Broadwalk

The Broadwalk
At the tallest part of the cliff a wide ledge runs across the upper section of the crag from the diagonal Clashooks Gully. This ledge is a popular hang-out for local youths but also has a few steep and nasty climbs on compact black rock.

Approach - From the centre of the crag, scramble up Clashooks Gully and double back right onto the ledge.

❶ Hemingway's Wall E3 5c
8m. Start above a boulder in the gully and climb the bulging wall using a rounded shelf. Starting just right is **6a**.

❷ Late-nite Greenhaigh .. E3 6a
8m. Steep moves on horizontal holds up the bulging wall.

❸ The Missing Font ..... NL 5c
8m. An eliminate with thin moves on flakes.

❹ Senile Saunter E1 5b
11m. Start up *West Wall Chimney* and traverse left (exposed) to reach the hanging flake/corner. The steep **Direct Start** is **5c**.

❺ West Wall Chimney.... VDiff
9m. The chimney has a steep start. At the top step left onto the wall for a less-enclosed finish.

❻ Windy Corner........ VDiff
15m. From a short way up *West Wall Chimney*, traverse rightwards in a fine and exposed position. Keep going until you can walk to the top. Mild but wild!

❼ Windy Corner Nose Finish .. HS 4b
9m. Finish up the wall above the traverse on the previous route.

❽ Diopera............. HVS 5a
9m. Climb the edge of the buttress, through a weakness just left of the bigger roofs, often windy.

❾ Eroica .... HVS 5a
9m. The first route through the roofs has some friable holds.

❿ Erotica .... NL 6b
9m. More dodgy rock. Climb the scoop and pockets just right of *Eroica*. Best set a rope up first!

⓫ Coward of the County .. E4 6a
10m. The roofs get bigger and the quality picks up. Make a hard move to gain a good hold on the right. Move back left and finish direct up the steep wall.
FA. Pete Chadwick 1990s

⓬ Spooky E5 6b
10m. Start 4m right of *Coward*. Make a long reach from a small pocket to gain some good holds. Move left and continue up the wall joining *Coward* near the top.

The Broadwalk **Helsby** 351

13 Brandenburg Gate.. E5 6c
10m. The direct start is a serious proposition. Make a big reach from some small pockets to gain a little prow (**V9** to here). Pull up into the parent route above.

14 Brandenburg Wall.. E4 5c
12m. A great route in a spectacular position. Start down and right of the flakes on the upper wall. Climb to the roof (good small cams) then hand-traverse left to below the flakes. Finish up these.

15 Stingray........ E4 6a
10m. A direct finish to *Brandenburg Wall* on small holds.
FA. Mike Collins

16 The Mangler..... E3 6a
10m. A good old-fashioned roof crack which succumbs to a typical struggle. Those with an aversion to jamming can use finger-holds but that misses the point really!
FA. Hugh Banner 1960s

There are two bold routes before Gorilla Wall - **Double Trouble**, E4 5c *and* **Chairman of the Board**, E6 6b.

17 Gorilla Wall........ E3 5c
12m. Start as for *The Mangler* but traverse right along a flake until you can pull over onto the upper wall.
FA. Hugh Banner 1960s

18 Gorilla Wall Direct . E4 5c
10m. The direct start begins at big holds about 2m to the right.

Helsby — Golden Pillar and Morgue Slab

Golden Pillar and Morgue Slab

At the left-hand end of the main section of the face is the long diagonal gash of Clashooks Gully, a useful descent route. To the right of this is a fine pillar and a broad slab, both home to a good selection of climbs across the grades though hard and scary ones out-number easy and safe ones by quite a margin.

1 Cloister Traverse. .... S 4a
30m. The horizontal gash can be gained from Clashooks Gully and followed rightwards until the ground rises gently up to meet you. Not one for a busy day.

2 Chromium Crack. E1 5b
14m. The black, bulging crack in the arete is approached easily and then gives a good pumpy battle with friendly protection.

3 Golden Pillar .... HVS 5b
14m. A fine lead with reasonable but rather fiddly gear. Easy ground up the intial(!) slab leads to bolder moves up and left into a scoop. Follow this with increasing apprehension to the ledge.

4 The Overhanging Crack . VS 4c
14m. Follow the easy chimney into a cave/recess then bridge and ja/layback the steep crack that splits the roof of the cave to reach easy ground and nicely exposed.
FA. Laycock c1910. The hardest route on grit (well sandstone!) at the time.

5 Agag. .... VS 4c
14m. Take *The Overhanging Crack* to the cave then exit rightwards by sustained jamming - or laybacking if you must!. Follow the continuation crack to the terrace. *Photo on page 347.*

To the right is a steep and largely holdless slab hanging above black roof and home to many of Helsby's hardest routes.

6 Cadaver Eyes ..... NL 6b
14m. Climb the rib right of the chimney to the black overhangs and pull through these with difficulty then scale the steep slab above via the green streak and the flutings. Awaits a lead ascent?

7 Magical Charm. E5 6a
14m. Climb the slab left of the diagonal fissure of *Morgue Slab* to the bulges. Stretch through these and make a crucial mantel up the steep slab. Gear under the bulge is your lot!

8 CFK. E4 6a
14m. An excellent route crossing the slab past a prominent undercut. Named after Helsby's Finest son.

9 Morgue Slab E2 5b
14m. A bold classic. Climb slanting cracks to the bulges. Psyche, then pull through these and climb the steep slab rightwards, carefully, to reach easy ground. Beware the sandy exit.

10 Mogadon's Good for You E3 5c
14m. Climb the face right of *Morgue Slab*, past a crucial undercut move, to join its final moves.

11 Necrophiliac E5 6a
14m. A stiff little number. Climb the rounded rib to the bulges, step out right and gain the upper slab with difficulty. Finish direct to the terrace and a tussle with the grass cornice.

Grooved Slab Helsby 353

12 Time Regained — E8 6c

14m. The black, tilted wall is climbed on tiny holds trending left then back right for a sprint finish. A very low, and very thin, thread provides the only protection.
FA. Andy Popp 2001. Formerly the top-rope problem Dog on a String.

13 Beatnik — E5 6a

14m. A classic sandstone test-piece. Climb the short crack then balance up the near vertical slab using the tiny half-moon flake to reach better holds under the overhang. Scuttle left then right to finish up an easy crack. Right-hand Finish is E5 6a.
FA. Jim O'Neill (top-rope) 1960s. FA. Alan Rouse (solo) late 1960s
FA. (Right-hand Finish) Andy Popp 2000s

14 240 Volt Shocker — E5 6c

14m. Trend right up the steep face making strenuous use of the light bulb hold to reach relief at the deep break.
FA. Andy Popp 2000s

15 Twin Scoops — E1 5c

14m. Bold and delicate low down and bolder again higher up. Climb the pair of crescent-shaped grooves to the break then the ever-steepening scoop trending right to finish.
FA. Hugh Banner 1960s

16 The Gangway — VS 4b

24m. Teeter up the crescent-shaped crack then at its top climb the shallow groove leftwards to the the break. Upward progress is problematical so follow the horizontal out left until a crack in a short corner offers a means of escape.

17 Grooved Slab — VS 4a

14m. One of the classics of the crag, although protection could be better. From the grass ledge climb the groove to its end then step left and take the continuation to the terrace and a belay. Nice!

Grooved Slab

A fine slab of sandstone. It has an open aspect and forms a great picnic area making this Helsby's most popular destination. There is a good selection of climbs; *Grooved Slab* is the best lower grade route on the cliff and *Beatnik* is a long-standing test-piece. The outward views are superb, especially as the sun start to go down when a spectacular sunset is almost guaranteed!

18 The Brush Off Direct — E4 6b

14m. Climb the steep slab 2m to the right of *Grooved Slab* to a breather at the break. Step right and finish up the steep upper face using some useful pockets.

19 The Brush Off — E4 5c

14m. Climb past the useful chipped 'R' then trend left up the steep slab to the break and a junction with the *The Direct*. Finish as for this.

20 The Brush Off Direct Finish — E6 6a

14m. Climb *The Brush Off* to the break then step right and sketch up the centre of the bold steep and tenuous wall. The only gear is a wire in a slot on *Jim's Chimney*. Seriously serious! It is possible to avoid the regular route completely, and all the chipped holds, by staying left at the start - 6b (NL).

21 Jim's Chimney — E2 5c

14m. A misnomer if ever there was one. Climb through the shallow oval groove then on up the bulging face above to the ledge. A second pitch above the ledge is 5b.

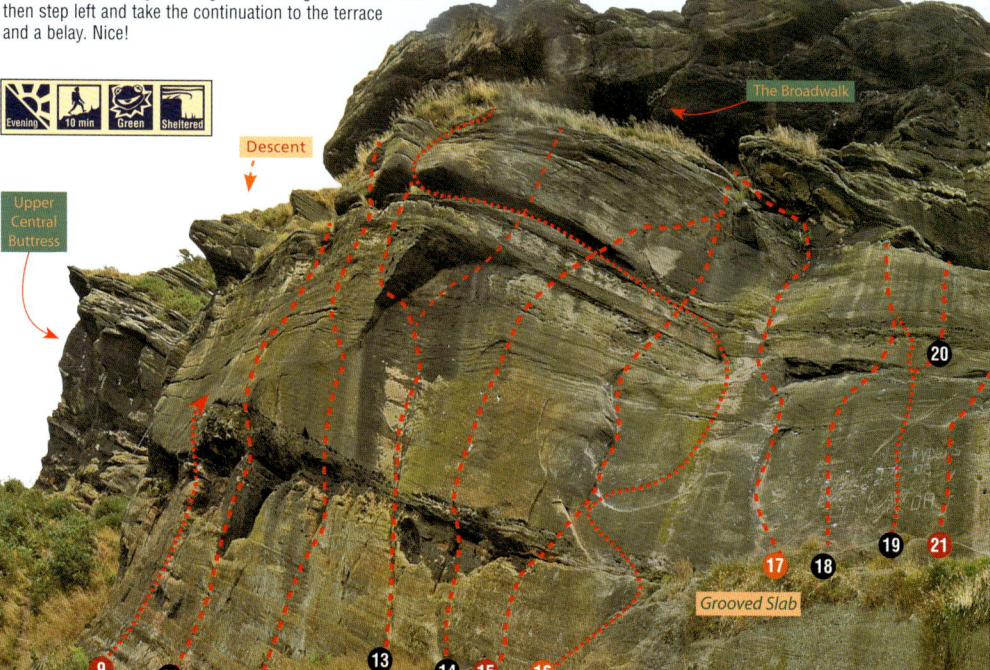

Helsby Wood's Climb

Wood's Climb
Although not the best section of Helsby this is almost certainly the most popular wall due to the abundance of green and orange spot grades. The classics of *Little by Little*, *Wood's Climb* and *Dinnerplate Crack* are the main attractions but most are worthy of attention.

1 Little by Little . . . . VS 4b
14m. A tricky number. Follow the slippery chipped ladder then sidle right into the left-leaning groove which leads to the ledge of Meadow Terrace. *The Notch* provides a logical way to the cliff top at a lower grade or the juggy direct version is worth **VS 4b**.

2 Oyster Slab Super Direct . . . . VS 5a
14m. Climb the slab to the base of the groove of *Little by Little* then continue steeply just to the right of the arete. The start is hard though the interest is maintained.

3 Oyster Slab . . . . S 4a
20m. Not very good though it does see a bit of traffic. Start as for the last route then follow the line of least resistance all the way to *Trojan Crack*.

4 Oyster Slab Direct . . . . VS 4b
14m. Take the centre of the rippled slab to the break in the overhangs. Pull right through this and finish up the face.
FA. Dave Price early 1950s

5 Oyster Slab Route III . . . . VS 5b
14m. A couple of metres left of the grotty groove of *Trojan Crack* climb straight up the slab to the bulges, undercut through these and finish up the slab above. The rather squeezed-in slab right again is climbable at 5c.

6 Trojan Crack . . . . S 4a
14m. The dirty crack is poor.

7 Trojan Nose . . . . S 4a
10m. The blunt nose just right of *Trojan Crack*.

8 The Notch . . . . Diff
10m. Climb the juggy rib to ledges then traverse left and climb steeply to and through the eponymous feature. A well positioned and logical finish to many of the previous routes

9 Waterloo Wall E2 5c
12m. Gain the tiny ledge on the wall right of *Trojan Nose*.

10 Fragile Wall E3 5c
12m. Climb up into the right-facing curving groove and balance carefully up it using the small flakes that are referred to in the name! The left-hand finish is only **E2 5b** but **E2 6a** if you climb it direct from the ground.
FA. Hugh Banner 1960s

11 Jugged Forest E2 5c
12m. The wall just left of the corner past two layaways.

12 Wood's Climb . . . . HVS 5a
12m. The long shallow groove is a fine route. Climb it to the block overhang and exit leftwards under this.
FA. C.W.Marshall 1920s

13 The Unknown Quantity E4 6b
12m. The stretchy and rounded arete bounding the groove.
FA. Andy Popp 1990s

Wood's Climb **Helsby** 355

14 Lipalongago E4 6b
12m. Climb straight up to the overlap and pass it with difficulty making vigorous use of the short diagonal crack

15 Unknown .... NL 6b
12m. Tussle with the next tiny crack in the overlap.

16 Liverpool Lady Boyz E5 6b
14m. Make desperate but short-lived moves up the runnels. Finish over the roof above.
FA. Sven Rowan 2000. Originally the top rope problem of The Runnel.

17 Greenteeth Gully .... Mod
14m. Obvious from the name, it provides one of the easiest outings on the cliff and a suitable way down for the proficient.

18 Greenteeth Crack .... HS 4b
14m. Squirm up the undercut hanging slot with gusto. There is gear in the back but only if you are thin enough to reach it!

19 Dinnerplate Crack .... VS 4c
14m. The left-hand flake on the front face is approached by a bold and tricky start, then gives thrilling juggy climbing. Sadly the dinnerplate was smashed years ago.

Helsby Flake Crack

Flake Crack

The conspicuous fissure of *Flake Crack* is probably Cheshire's most famous route and with good reason, great rock, a cracking line and a long history - just do it! There is other stuff of interest in the area, across the grades.

1 Ho Ho Ho E3 6a
14m. The face between the two cracks.
FA. Mike Collins 1990 (Christmas Day)

2 Twin Caves Crack ..... HS 4b
14m. Climb up the pillar between the two caves then make a steep and contorted 3D pull into the groove.
This gives great juggy climbing.

3 Pathfinder E3 6a
14m. Climb direct over the big bulges and up the blunt flake to join the top section of *Flake Innominate*.
FA. Mark Hounslea 2001

4 Flake Crack .... Top 50 VS 4c
14m. The finest route on the cliff! If you are passing at least call in and tick this one! The upper section is a classic layback although those in the know will jam it. There have been plenty of accidents on it over the years so take care.
FA. Colin Kirkus early 1920s. Climbed on-sight by Menlove Edwards 1931

5 Flake Innominate E2 5c
14m. The small buttress on the left of the final section of *Flake Crack* has a couple of pleasant moves and good positions, although the best climbing is still on the parent route.

6 Foolish Finish E4 5c
16m. Take *Flake Crack* to a point halfway up the layback then crimp along the bubbly break to join *Licentious Jug*.

7 Flake Wall E5 6a
16m. A cracking hard route but with some crumbly holds. Climb the curving flake under the roof (or the wall to its left) until forced into *Flake Crack*. From runners balance out right and boldly climb the centre of the pitted wall. Low in the grade but exciting stuff.

Descent

Flake Crack

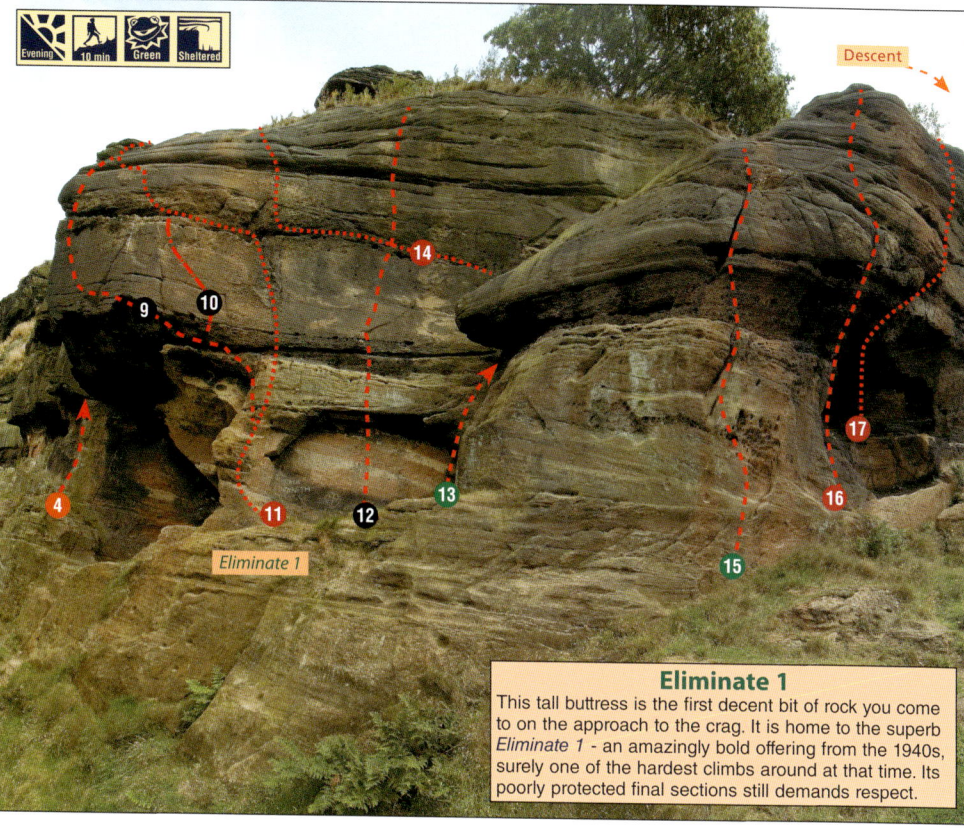

Eliminate 1 **Helsby** 357

Eliminate 1
This tall buttress is the first decent bit of rock you come to on the approach to the crag. It is home to the superb *Eliminate 1* - an amazingly bold offering from the 1940s, surely one of the hardest climbs around at that time. Its poorly protected final sections still demands respect.

8 Licentious Jug — E5 6a
16m. Climb *Flake Crack* to the base of the crack then balance across the right wall and climb the harrowing left-hand side of the arete. Originally done without recourse to *Flake Crack*.

9 Black Hole Arete — E5 6b
16m. Use jugs to reach the lip of the roof then traverse left out to the exposed arete. Make hard moves to an easier finish.
FA. Craig Smith 2006. An old top-rope problem finally gets led.

10 Calcutta Wall — E4 5c
16m. Start up the pillar of *Eliminate 1* but trend left across the bulging wall using the black hole of the route's name.
FA. Hugh Banner 1960s

11 Eliminate 1 — Top 50 — E1 5b
16m. The other great classic of the crag. Climb the pillar and a short pocket-wall to the break and some rounded spike runners. Traverse out left into ever-more exposed terrain then make a tricky move (elusive finger holds) to easy ground. Perhaps only HVS 5a for those used to the vagaries of sandstone.

12 Pratabout — E5 6b
14m. Climb the centre of the wall left of the gully. Pull onto the wall and continue in a direct line to a rounded exit.
FA. Dave Ranby 1980s

13 Easy Chimney — Mod
14m. The deep rift behind the jutting proboscis.

14 The Wendigo — E3 5c
16m. From halfway up *Easy Chimney* make a committing but excellent traverse along the bubbly break all the way out to the spikes on *Eliminate 1*. Finish direct.

15 End Crack — S 4b
10m. The short crack in the bulge is accessed up scoops and leads to a tricky exit.

16 The Umbrella — E2 5c
10m. Climb the pumpy leaning wall to the left of the cave rapidly to reach easy ground.

17 Parapluie — E1 5b
10m. The blocky roof crack out of the cave is hard work. A parachute might be more use than a poncy French umbrella!

Frodsham

	No star	★	★★	★★★
Mod to S	12	13	-	-
HS to HVS	5	11	3	3
E1 to E3	3	9	2	1
E4 and up	1	2	2	-

Frosdsham consists of a small set of west-facing buttresses on the crest of the wooded slopes of Frodsham Hill. The rocks are hidden in a beech forest above the Mersey estuary and are ideal for a short work-out session. The crag receives the afternoon sun and several of the buttresses are steep enough to stay dry in light summer rain. Although relatively diminutive the cliffs are fairly easy to reach from the Liverpool conurbation, or from the M56 if you are Wales-bound. Interestingly, many of the climbing world's luminaries have left their mark here.

The cliff is a very popular bouldering venue and most of the better problems are chalked throughout the year. The climbing is generally steep and juggy; power pays more dividends here than fancy footwork ever will. The routes are almost invariably soloed, though the bigger routes on Cinema Screen and Great Buttress are BOLD. The slightly soft nature of the rock and the steep slope below the cliff all add up to make these particularly serious undertakings.

Approach

To the west of Frodsham (heading towards Helsby) on the A56 and just west of the Netherton Arms, turn left onto the B5393 (Tarvin Road). Drive up the hill for 1.5km to where a narrow farm road branches left and there are buildings on the right. There is limited and narrow (get in close to the hedge) parking here on the right just before the buildings. If this is full (2 or 3 well-parked cars) continue up the road for another couple of hundred metres to more parking on the left. Follow the farm road (try jogging up it!) until it bends right into a big house. Go through the gate on the left then head straight up the steep sandy path towards the crest of the hill. Just before the top, a narrow track leads left to the first - or is it the last - buttress; 10 minutes from the car.

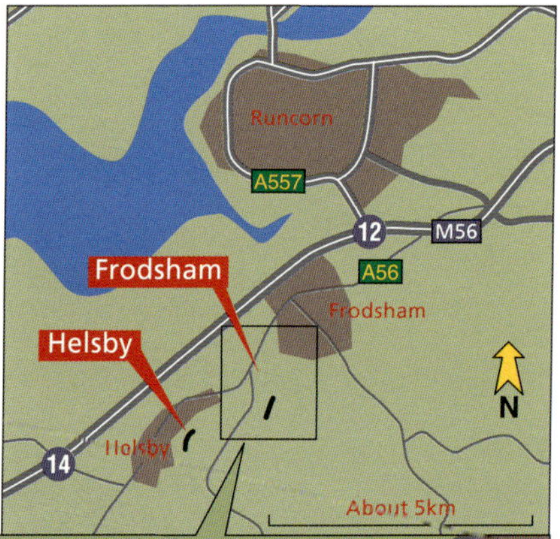

Conditions

The rocks are well-sheltered from the weather because of the extensive tree cover. Some the sections of the cliff capped by overhangs (e.g. Hoopla Buttress) give ever-dry bouldering, though, as with all the sandstone in the area, climbing in damp conditions is not a good idea as the humidity softens the rock. The crag is perhaps at its best on warm spring and autumn evenings when the atmosphere is magical and the foliage doesn't interfere too much with the view.

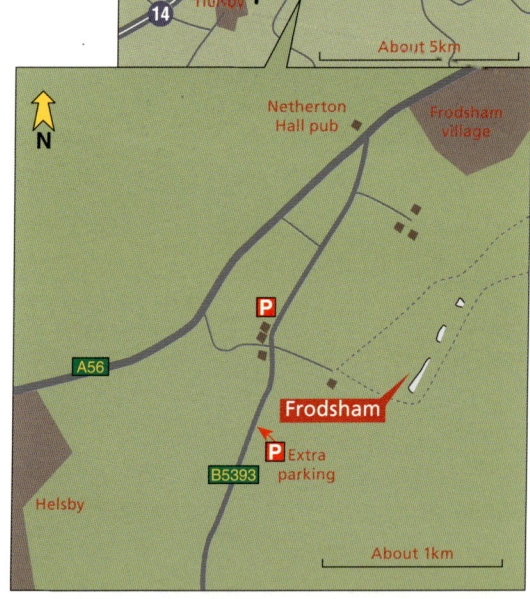

Dan Parkes sneaking through the overhangs on *Superwall* (V1) - *page 362* - Cave Buttress, Frodsham. Photo Graham Parkes

Frodsham Great Wall

St Stephen's Wall
The first routes are on the diminutive beak of St.Stephen's Buttress, 100m beyond the Great Wall.

1 St Stephen's Wall .... VB (4b)
4m. The centre of the north-facing wall starting up a corner.

2 Left Wall V2 (5c)
4m. The wall just left of the arete.

3 Mexican Bob V3 (6a)
4m. The left-hand areto of the front face and roof direct.

4 The Long Lurch V1 (5b)
4m. Climb the middle of the overhang via a l-o-n-g lurch.

5 Rick's Reach V2 (5c)
4m. The right-hand arete of the front face.

6 Right-hand Route V0 (5a)
4m. The blunt rib at the right-hand edge of the face.

7 Big Wall .... VB (4c)
4m. Right of the easy groove is a misnamed wall!

8 Deep Crack .... VB (4b)
4m. The wide and awkward fissure.

9 Twin Cracks .... Diff
4m. The pair of cracks with central block.

Great Wall
The most impressive piece of rock at Frodsham is the Great Wall. Perched high above a steep slope, the routes here are imposing undertakings and are only soloed by the terminally confident. Although bouldering grades have been used in the past E-grades reflect the situation much more realistically. Bring a rope and a rack.

Cinema Screen Wall Frodsham

Great Wall

10 Left Arete E1 5b
12m. The leaning left-hand arete of the impressive face.

11 Tom's Roof E5 6b
12m. The lower wall leads directly to the huge triangular roof that caps the wall. Cross this with conviction - tough at the grade.

12 Unknown E2 5c
12m. Climb the wall passing the right edge of a smaller roof to the big one then do the sensible thing and leg-it out right.

13 Left-hand Route E2 5c
16m. Head up into the hanging groove in the right side of the wall then make a exposed traverse left to outflank the overhangs.

14 Great Wall E2 5c
14m. Follow *Left-hand Route* into the hanging corner but at its top exit rightwards to reach the easier upper wall.

15 Iron Dish Wall E2 5c
14m. The bulging wall right of the big tree is excellent.

16 Frodsham Crack ...... VS 5a
12m. The prominent deep crack on the right gives classic fist jamming - not quite the contradiction that might appear.

17 Unknown Wall E4 6a
12m. The bold and fierce wall just right of *Frodsham Crack*.

Cinema Screen Wall

The Cinema Screen is an imposing and well-named piece of rock which unfortunately doesn't give climbing of the quality that you might expect. The routes are intimidating and a bit crusty. Another piece of rock where Adjectival Grades make more sense than V Grades.

18 Slanting Crack .... Diff
10m. The left-slanting break that bounds the buttress.

19 Slab Route .... VS 5a
10m. Climb the green slab to steep rock then jig left to the slab.

20 Cinema Arete .... VS 4c
10m. The bulging but juggy arete gives a popular pitch.

21 Birch Tree Corner .... S 4a
10m. The left-hand groove of the screen, escape left at the top.

22 Multi-Screen .. E2 6a
10m. The left-hand side of the smooth section of the screen is climbed on brittle holds to a fierce pull and a juggy finish.

23 Central Route E2 5c
10m. The right-hand line on the wall.

24 Cracked Corner .... S 4b
8m. The right-bounding groove of the central screen can be bridged to an escape out right.

25 Arete Route .... V0+ (5b)
8m. Lay-away up the arete on the right side of the face then go!

Frodsham — Cave Buttress

Cave Buttress
To the right of the Cinema Screen, across the slope is Cave Buttress which has better quality rock and routes than its near neighbour. The shortness of the climbs and decent landings also add to their attraction!

1 Corner and Traverse . . . . . . VDiff
6m. A groove in the north-facing wall, exiting up the right arete.

2 Left Wall V0 (5a)
6m. Start right of the arete and spiral left onto the side-wall. Nice.

3 Crew's Arete Left-hand . V2 (5c)
6m. The left-hand arete of the narrow buttress on the left is steep and pumpy.

4 Crew's Arete V1 (5b)
6m. The roof. A classic tussle, easier for the talented and quite high.
FA. Pete Crew 1960s

5 Superdirect V0 (5a)
6m. The right-hand arete to a bulging finish.

6 Superwall V1 (5b)
6m. Take the narrow side-wall directly. Photo on page 359.

7 Leo's Traverse . . . . . V0+ (5a)
10m. Climb into the undercut crack on Ordinary Route then make a gripping traverse out to the right below the big roof.
FA. Leo Dickinson 1960s

8 Ordinary Route . . . . HVD
8m. Climb leftwards into the corner then continue in the same direction to outflank the capping roof.

9 I Was a Teenage Caveman . . V7
8m. The centre of the big roof is approached directly from below and is crossed spookily on a set of rather suspect holds.

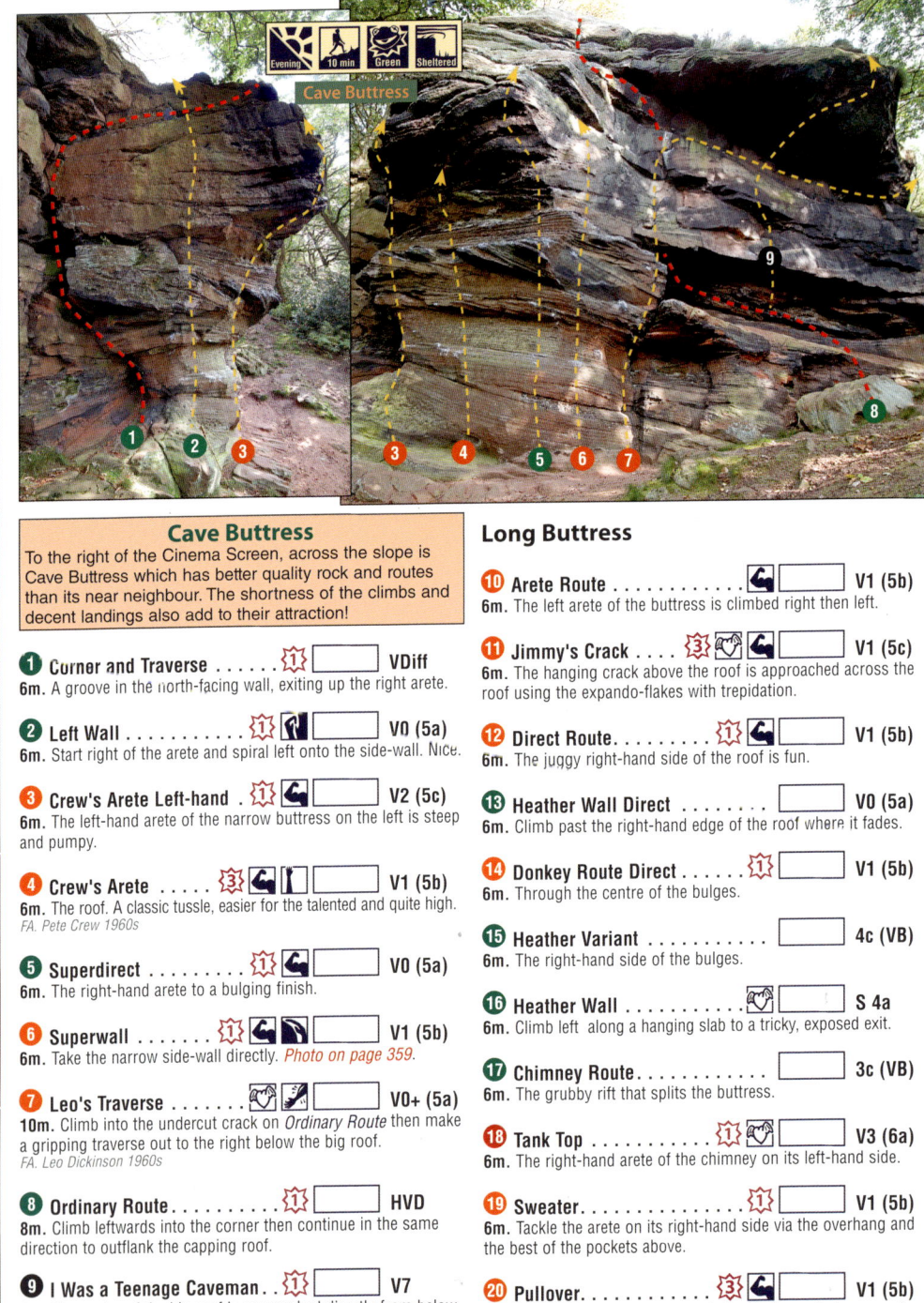

Long Buttress

10 Arete Route V1 (5b)
6m. The left arete of the buttress is climbed right then left.

11 Jimmy's Crack V1 (5c)
6m. The hanging crack above the roof is approached across the roof using the expando-flakes with trepidation.

12 Direct Route V1 (5b)
6m. The juggy right-hand side of the roof is fun.

13 Heather Wall Direct V0 (5a)
6m. Climb past the right-hand edge of the roof where it fades.

14 Donkey Route Direct V1 (5b)
6m. Through the centre of the bulges.

15 Heather Variant . . . . 4c (VB)
6m. The right-hand side of the bulges.

16 Heather Wall . . . . S 4a
6m. Climb left along a hanging slab to a tricky, exposed exit.

17 Chimney Route . . . . 3c (VB)
6m. The grubby rift that splits the buttress.

18 Tank Top V3 (6a)
6m. The right-hand arete of the chimney on its left-hand side.

19 Sweater V1 (5b)
6m. Tackle the arete on its right-hand side via the overhang and the best of the pockets above.

20 Pullover V1 (5b)
6m. The centre of the overhangs is beefy, the wall above much more delicate. Trend left to finish.

Long Buttress Frodsham 363

Long Buttress - left

㉑ Jumper V2 (5c)
6m. The right-hand side of the roof is a bit of an eliminate though the moves are good. A small dyno may be required.

㉒ Thin Crack Superdirect V1 (5b)
6m. An eliminate which gains the thin crack directly and avoids any contamination with the ledge on the right.

㉓ Thin Crack .... 4b (VB)
6m. Using the projecting ledge on the right to access the thin crack is easier and a lot more sensible!

㉔ Left-hand Crack .... VDiff
6m. The short left-hand crack is approached over a bulge.

㉕ Right-hand Crack .... VDiff
6m. The slightly thinner right-hand fissure.

㉖ Flake Route .... VDiff
6m. Pull through the bulges and climb the crack to a tricky exit.

Long Buttress
A short but wide buttress spit centrally by an awkward chimney which breaks an almost continuous line of overhangs and bulges. These provide most of the entertainment here.

Long Buttress - right

364 Frodsham Neb Buttress

1 Wall and Traverse .... VB (3c)
6m. The left-hand wall of the buttress trending left.

2 Intermediate Route .... VB (4b)
6m. The juggy left-hand arete of the front face.

3 Direct Route V0 (5a)
6m. The centre of the front face passing double overhangs.

4 Neb Route V2 (5c)
5m. The right-hand arete of the buttress. Trending left across the face reduces the grade to **5b**.

Neb Buttress
50m left of the popular bouldering of Hoop-La buttress is this short protruding neb of rock, the four problems here are good for a quick workout. Careful, it is not as big as this topo suggests.

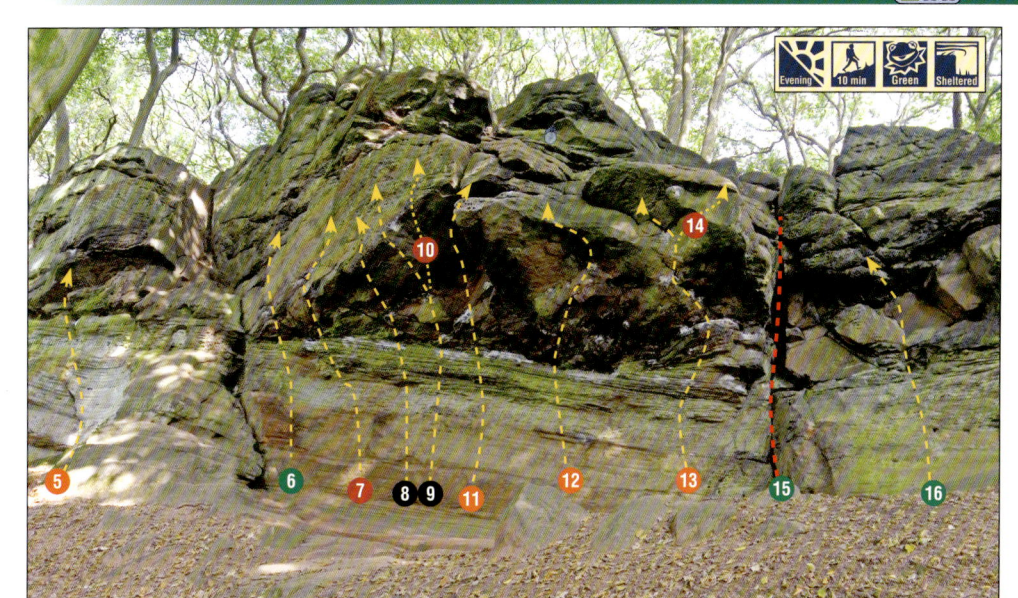

Hoop-La Buttress **Frodsham** 365

Hoop-La Buttress

Hoop-La Buttress is the first piece of rock reached from the parking, a short distance left of where the path reaches the plateau. This jutting buttress gives the best bouldering on the cliff, with countless eliminates. The choicest problems are always well-chalked up. Many of the problems require cunning foot-hooks which can leave you flat on your back if your hands fail. Bring a mat, a friend or both.

5 Pants V1 (5b)
6m. The bulge and flake system in the left-hand buttress are better than the name suggests.

6 The Overhanging Wall ..... VB (4c)
6m. The well-endowed wall just to the left of the overhangs can be climbed by a variety of lines.

7 Colton's Crack V6 (6b)
8m. Approach the thin hanging crack directly below then climb it via a solitary tough move. Neat'n'tough.
FA. Nick Colton 1970s

8 Dave's Roof V7
8m. The desperate bulge right of the crack using poor pockets and slopers. Thought by some (but not many!) to be low in the grade.
FA. Dave Johnson 1990s

9 Mike's Route .. V7
8m. Cross the roof left of the deep crack of *Hoop-La* using a pocket (right-handed) on the lip then finish leftwards with difficulty.
FA. Mike Collins 1990s

10 Pearce's Route V3 (6a)
8m. Follow *Mike's Route* to the pocket on the lip (left-handed) then pull up and right to better holds with a stretch to finish.
FA. Dave Pearce 1960s

11 The Hoop-La V1 (5b)
8m. The crack splitting the centre of the buttress is a classic tussle and forms a good warm-up for the harder roof problems.

12 Boysen's Route.... V2 (5c)
8m. Cross the roof to the right of the crack looping right then left to reach jugs then pull over to easy ground. Somehow manages to be both short AND sustained!
FA. Martin Boysen 1960s

13 Banner's Route.... V2 (5c)
8m. Climb the right-hand side of the overhang heading for the juggy flake on the lip. Loop left to gain easy ground.
FA. Hugh Banner 1950s

14 Tradesman's Entrance .. V3 (6a)
8m. From the juggy flake above all difficulties on *Banner's*, lurch right to locate a finish on slopers to the right of the arete.

15 The Overhanging Crack ...... Diff
6m. The groove to the right of the overhangs provides a descent or a little something for the terminally timid.

16 The Right Wall V0 (5a)
6m. The juggy wall right of the groove is the last (or maybe the first) route on the cliff. Variations exist.

Pex Hill

	No star	★	★★	★★★
Mod to S	4	6	3	-
HS to HVS	4	16	5	-
E1 to E3	11	16	17	5
E4 and up	9	11	10	8

This small hole in the ground holds an important place in the hearts of Merseyside climbers; it has easy access, great rock and is home to a myriad of problems and mini-routes. I lived in Liverpool for a year way back in the 1970s and a short apprenticeship at Pex Hill served me well, the steep and fingery style of the climbing here translating well to Welsh volcanics. Have no doubt, time spent honing finger strength and technique at Pex will be repaid in full. Many of the routes are soloed by the competent (with or without mats) although top-roping is also quite popular here (please don't belay to the railings) despite the fact that the majority of the climbs are less then 10 metres high. The reason is obvious - except for a few exceptions the routes here are effectively unprotected and often very blank with no rest ledges and little prospect of rescue!

Typical highball Pex action. A climber eyeing up the hold on *The Knife* (E5) - *page 368* - at Pex Hill. Photo: Will Hunt

Approach   Also see map on page 344

Pex Hill Country Park is located 15km to the east of the Liverpool conurbation, and is most easily reached from the A5080 as it runs between Widnes and Cronton. Opposite the brick buildings of Widnes 6th Form College are the old cast-iron gateposts that mark the park entrance. Follow the road (speed-bumps) as it loops round to the right then turns left into the parking area by the Visitors Centre. The entrance to the quarry is five minutes downhill walk away from the parking and is sometimes tricky to find on first acquaintance. Take the central track until you hit the railings then follow these leftwards round to the entrance.

Conditions

Over the years the main part of the quarry has gradually filled with trees. These enhance the pleasant nature of the place but reduce the airflow in the quarry and add to the humidity. This appears to be directly responsible for some of the walls being greener than they used to be. Despite this, the quarry dries fast, takes no drainage (well except when NW Water fill it to the brim) and due to it facing in all directions it is usually possible to get something done here in summer or winter.

Climbers are asked not to use wire brushes here as this abrades the sandstone; if you really must, a once-over with a toothbrush should be adequate.

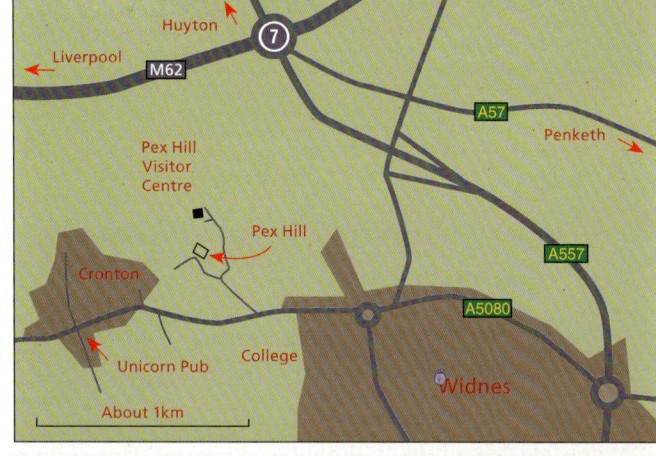

Jack Brunning concentrating hard on *Creeping Jesus* (V8) - *page 373* - at Pex Hill. Photo: Kevin Stephens

Pex Hill — Dateline Wall

Dateline Wall

The recessed bay to the right of the entry has a whole series of hard and bold face climbs plus the classic crack of *Dateline*. The climbs are soloed by the talented, though most are inclined to top-rope them, and leading is possible if you know the tricks. The bay is home to many of the hardest climbs in the quarry, after a dry spell the amount of chalk on them shows how many good climbers there are out there.

❶ The Knife — E5 6a
The arete that forms the edge of the bay was once cutting edge and it remains quite superb. Amigos in the pockets can protect though it is soloed a lot more often than it is led.

❷ Catemytes Crack — E5 6b
The shallow groove in the wall. Can be led with Amigos.

❸ Main Wall — E5 6b
From a little way up *Catemytes*, move right across the wall using pockets to a groove. Climb this to a rightward exit.

❹ Staminade — E6 6b
Climb the hard wall straight into the base of the shallow groove, layback up this then exit to the right. The grade is for leading using the old (off line) bolts for protection. It has been soloed

The wall to the right has become incredibly dirty in the five years since the last guide was produced, sprouting some huge turfy tufts - the lines are listed briefly for completeness.

❺ Lemonade — NL 6b
The dirty wall 3m right of *Staminade*.

❻ Pernod and Black — NL 6b
Another dirty wall climb. Might be good with a brushing.

❼ Rum and Cocaine — NL 6b
2m left of the corner.

❽ One of These Days Direct — E3 6a
Bridge the oft damp angle that bounds the left-hand edge of the back wall. Finish more easily up the parent route. Worth a star when it is clean, sadly an increasingly rare situation.

❾ One of These Days — E3 5c
Climb the right wall of the corner starting at a slot and trending left to enter the groove. Bridge up it - high in the grade.

❿ One of These Days Direct Finish — E4 6a
Follow the regular route then continue up the wall above passing the niche by bridging and undercutting.

DO NOT BELAY TO THE RAILINGS

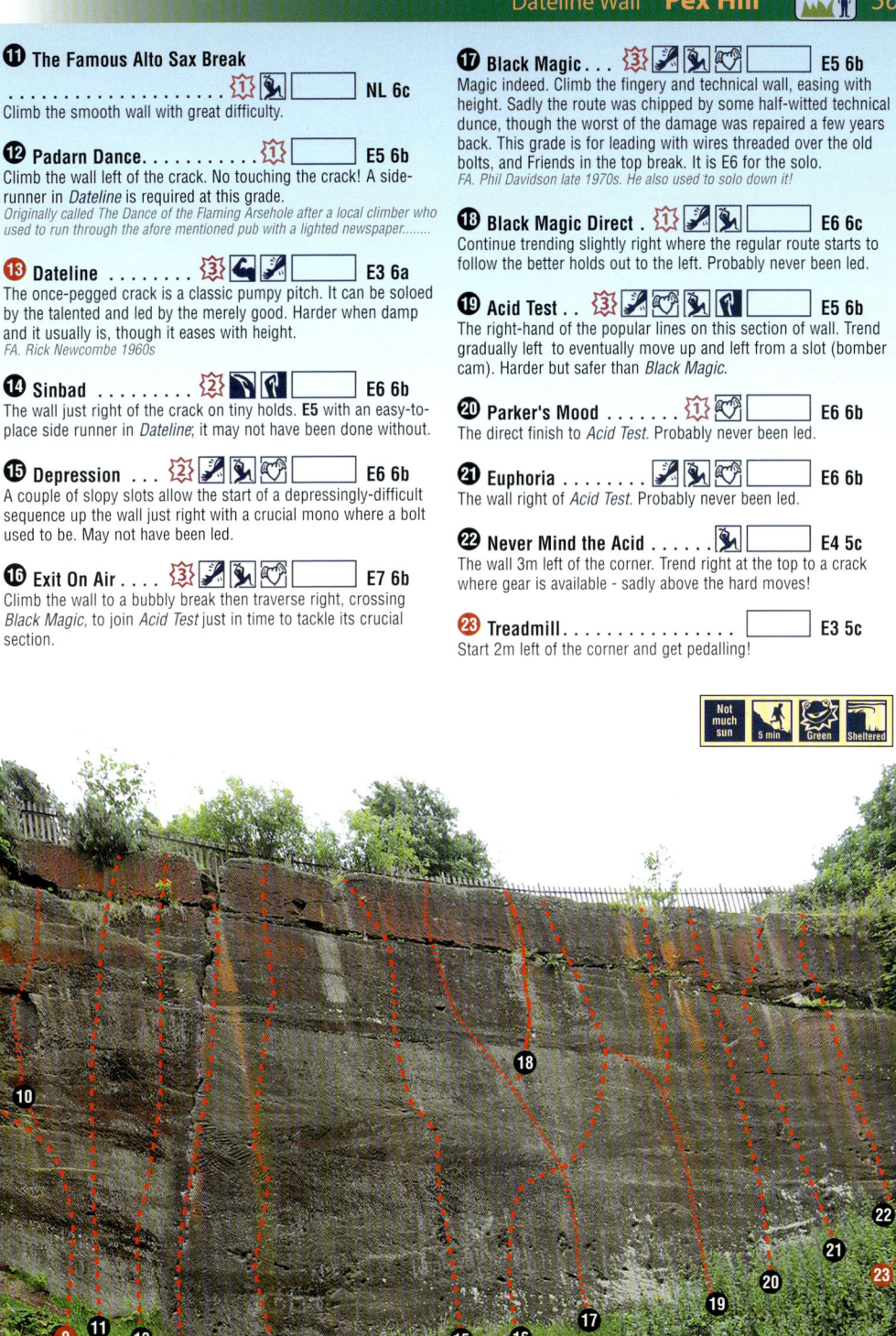

Dateline Wall Pex Hill 369

⑪ The Famous Alto Sax Break .... NL 6c
Climb the smooth wall with great difficulty.

⑫ Padarn Dance.......... E5 6b
Climb the wall left of the crack. No touching the crack! A side-runner in *Dateline* is required at this grade.
Originally called The Dance of the Flaming Arsehole after a local climber who used to run through the afore mentioned pub with a lighted newspaper........

⑬ Dateline E3 6a
The once-pegged crack is a classic pumpy pitch. It can be soloed by the talented and led by the merely good. Harder when damp and it usually is, though it eases with height.
FA. Rick Newcombe 1960s

⑭ Sinbad E6 6b
The wall just right of the crack on tiny holds. **E5** with an easy-to-place side runner in *Dateline*; it may not have been done without.

⑮ Depression ... E6 6b
A couple of slopy slots allow the start of a depressingly-difficult sequence up the wall just right with a crucial mono where a bolt used to be. May not have been led.

⑯ Exit On Air E7 6b
Climb the wall to a bubbly break then traverse right, crossing *Black Magic*, to join *Acid Test* just in time to tackle its crucial section.

⑰ Black Magic... E5 6b
Magic indeed. Climb the fingery and technical wall, easing with height. Sadly the route was chipped by some half-witted technical dunce, though the worst of the damage was repaired a few years back. This grade is for leading with wires threaded over the old bolts, and Friends in the top break. It is E6 for the solo.
FA. Phil Davidson late 1970s. He also used to solo down it!

⑱ Black Magic Direct . E6 6c
Continue trending slightly right where the regular route starts to follow the better holds out to the left. Probably never been led.

⑲ Acid Test .. E5 6b
The right-hand of the popular lines on this section of wall. Trend gradually left to eventually move up and left from a slot (bomber cam). Harder but safer than *Black Magic*.

⑳ Parker's Mood E6 6b
The direct finish to *Acid Test*. Probably never been led.

㉑ Euphoria E6 6b
The wall right of *Acid Test*. Probably never been led.

㉒ Never Mind the Acid E4 5c
The wall 3m left of the corner. Trend right at the top to a crack where gear is available - sadly above the hard moves!

㉓ Treadmill................. E3 5c
Start 2m left of the corner and get pedalling!

370 Pex Hill — Pisa Wall

1 The Widow........... V1 (5b)
The scruffy corner on the left has become overgrown again.

2 Jota................ V3 (6a)
The wall 1.5m right of the corner see little action.

3 Polar Bear......... V5 (6b)
Start 2m right of the corner and reach the deep horizontal slot with difficulty. Finish between the encroaching vegetation.

4 Time Passages..... V4 (6b)
Climb the wall above a rib to the break, swing right and sprint to finish. The **Direct Finish** is 6a and the **Direct Start** 6c.

5 Cyclops............ V1 (5b)
The wall left of the twin slots to a finish by the bee-hive.

6 Two Eyes.......... V0- (5a)
Climb past the sightless sockets. Finish via the bee-hive.

7 Cornea............ V2 (5c)
The wall to the right of the sockets.

8 Willy Simm's Silly Whim V6 (6b)
Climb the tiny blunt arete to the sandy break.

9 Retina............. V1 (5b)
Head left towards the left-hand side of the shrubbery.

10 Nameless......... VB (4c)
Take a direct line into the right-hand side of the hanging gardens.

11 Eliminate........ VB (4b)
The vague groove leads to a leftwards exit.

12 Goliath.......... V2 (5c)
Climb the wall heading for the right-hand side of the beehive and with a crucial stretch for the break.

13 Square Four..... VB (4c)
Balance up to the four neat square-cut holes and then use the left-hand pair to finish. Without the holes is more like 6a and the wall just to the right is a popular **V1**.

14 Greeting........ V1 (5b)
Tricky moves below the break. Avoiding using the right-hand pair of holes is difficult.

15 Handshake...... V1 (5b)
Climb the wall to the useful pinch-grip just below the top.

16 Pisa Wall....... VB (4b)
The short wall into the left edge of the notch at the cliff top.

17 Warm Up....... V0+ (5b)
Warm up on the wall just to the left of *Straight Crack*.

18 Straight Crack.. VB (4b)
The rather battered pseudo-crack is the easiest offering on the wall. Oddly it would probably get 4c on Stanage! It is best to finish direct rather than get suckered into traversing left.

DO NOT BELAY TO THE RAILINGS

Pisa Wall Pex Hill   371

19 Eliminate Wall V2 (5c)
The bulging wall between the two ill-defined cracks is short but manages to be quite pumpy.

20 Mankey Road V2 (5c)
The vague curving right-hand crack is pushy and keeps going.

21 Monkey Grip V1 (5b)
Climb the smooth wall passing a useful hole early on and finishing over a small overhang. Pleasant.

22 Green Streaks V1 (5b)
Twin parallel bogey-lines (or wet streaks!) mark the route.

23 Fingers V2 (5c)
Trend right up the wall to a good break, then really stretch for the gritty break.

24 Bushy Tale V1 (5b)
Climb straight up the wall to another tricky finish.

25 One Move V2 (5c)
The wall below the end of the railings a bit more than a one move wonder though the one finger pocket is fun!

26 Thumb Screw V3 (6a)
Use a bore-hole to start then go.

27 Commando V3 (6a)
2m left of the edge of the wall. Use a sharp slot on the left for the last move to the top. A dyno from the break to the top is superb.

Map features: From parking, About 50m, N, Memorial Corner, The Web, The Rack, The Knife, Dateline, The Jungle, Lady Jane Wall, Pisa Wall

28 Gorilla V2 (5c)
Just left of the edge of the wall; a dyno or static - you choose.

29 Pisa Traverse V4 (5c)
The low-level traverse is the most popular piece of climbing here and sees constant horizontal traffic. From *Gorilla* to *Two Eyes* and back again if you feel like it. The crossing is possible at three different levels. The lowest break is sustained and pumpy with good handholds and poor footholds. The mid height traverse is less sustained but more technical with good footholds, small handholds. The high traverse is technical and a little pumpy too.

Pisa Wall
The most popular section of the quarry with the polish and the chalk to prove it. Turn right at the bottom of the steps and you are there. The 'up' routes are almost all well worth doing, and the top-outs are quite high for boulder problems. The variations on the low-level traverse are also great.

DO NOT BELAY TO THE RAILINGS

Photo labels: Square Four, Handshake, Pseudo-cracks, Descent, Pisa Wall, Behind the tree

Route numbers: 11, 12, 13, 14, 15, 16, 17, 18, 19, 20, 21, 22, 23, 24, 25, 26, 27, 28

Pex Hill — Lady Jane Wall

Lady Jane Wall

The long wall to the left of the entrance has many good routes though a high percentage are hard. The holds on the blanker sections are often so small that they are often invisible unless chalked by previous climbers. There are easier offerings at either end of the wall. Running along the top of the wall are nine bee-hive-shaped niches that aid route identification.

① Too Bold for Steve Boot V1 (5b)
The first offering, just right of the upper arete is a typically deceptive Pex route. Benchmark and harder than it looks!

② Set Square .... VS 4c
The wall with a jig right at half-height to reach the left-hand triangular slot, high in the grade. A direct start is **V2 (5c)**.

③ Tequila Sunrise V3 (6a)
Head straight through the right-hand triangular slot.

④ Harvey Wallbanger V2 (5c)
The wall 1m right on small holds. Requires an udge or a stretch.

⑤ Black Russian V4 (6a)
A direct line 1m right again heading straight to the step at the top of the cliff; interesting and hard to start.

⑥ Lew's Leap V2 (5b)
Climb straight to the first of the niches. A short hop for its base is normal. The right-hand start is **V2 (5c)**. Tricky and a bit fluttery.

⑦ Finger-Ripper V6
An eliminate just right of the first niche. Gnarly in the extreme.

⑧ Bermuda Triangle V5 (6b)
A brilliant problem past the second niche. A hard, reachy start leads right to a rest and then more hard moves. The top out is steady. Soloed barefoot by Bob Drury way back in 1985!

⑨ Cosine Alternative V4 (6b)
A once forgotten counter line to *Bermuda Triangle*. Can be used to gain the upper section of *Bermuda Triangle* for shorties.

⑩ Breakaway V8
Straight up the wall on a series of tiny, tiny holds. Utterly desperate, with steel tendons the minimum requirement. PLEASE go easy on the wire brushing, the holds just don't need it!

⑪ Catalepsy . V7
Reach the third niche by a sustained series of pulls. Very reachy and balancy.

⑫ Monoblock V11
Said to be "The Hardest Route in the World", with holds little bigger than decent-sized atoms - and spaced ones at that!

⑬ Bernie V6
The easiest line on this section of wall! Start right of the old bolts and a bit more like E4 6b if the bolts are actually clipped.

⑭ Termination V7
Make a desperate move to reach the ledge then the large pocket.

⑮ Philharmonic V4 (6b)
Tall climbers can by-pass the hard bit, short ones might want a **V5**.

⑯ Algripper V3 (6a)
The wall is climbed via two good pockets, linking them is hard and a bit higher than you want it to be.

⑰ Jurassic Pork .. V6
A blank wall with a hard move using a pebble. Now clean.

⑱ Lady Jane E1 5c
Climb the right-trending ramp; swing right and follow the pockets to the top passing the left-hand of a pair of niches. Low in the grade (for Pex!) and it can feel like **V1**. A **Direct Start - V3 (5c)**.

⑲ Crossbow E1 5c
Move left into the niche from *Lady Jane*. Recently cleaned.

⑳ Sidestep E1 5c
Climb straight up the the final section of *Lady Jane*.

Lady Jane Wall **Pex Hill** 373

㉑ Twin Scoops Direct.... E1 6a
Climb straight up the wall to the right-hand niche by a balancy mantelshelf and a bit of stretch. Especially reachy for the short.

㉒ Twin Scoops............ HVS 4c
At last an easier offering. Climb the ledgy wall then follow the holds leftwards past *Twin Scoops Direct* to finish up *Lady Jane*. Used as a quick way down by locals.

㉓ Twin Scoops Right-hand E2 5c
Direct above the start of *Twin Scoops*.

㉔ Creeping Jesus....... E1 5b
Climb *Twin Scoops* to the last decent ledge then step right to a good finger-jam (wire) and a sprint finish. Direct start is **V2 (5c)**.
Photo on page 367.

㉕ Kitt's Wall E4 6b
Link the three pockets by hard moves. **V4**.

㉖ The Black Pimp from Marseilles
.... E6 6b
The wall to the left of the low relief blunt rib which is the main feature of this part of the face. **V6**.

㉗ Unicorn E3 5b
Fine climbing straight up the blunt rib to a recess just below the cliff top, exit direct. It used to go left to avoid the prickles.

㉘ Cave Route Right-hand . E6 6b
A hard and bold eliminate via the square pocket. **V6**.

㉙ Ladytron E4 5c
The bold wall between the two blunt ribs to a rounded exit. Named after a Roxy Music track in the early 70s.

㉚ Cardiac Arete E4 6b
Boulder up to the break then from the jug make crucial moves to marginally easier ground. **V5**.

㉛ Hart's Arete ... E4 6b
The bold, blunt arete feels big for its size and is suffering from polish. The grade given is for a lead since there is (spaced) gear. It is **V5** to the break,..... except for locals!

㉜ Zigger Zagger . E2 5b
The stretchy wall has a gripping sloping exit - beware.

㉝ Big Greenie E3 5c
The wall started from *The Hulk* is high but cams protect.

㉞ The Hulk E2 5c
Left of the crack. You won't like it when you are angry!

㉟ Hart's Arete Traverse... V5 (6a)
Start at the crack (*Crack and Up*) and traverse left to *Unicorn*. The higher break is **V3** and the ultra-low level is **V9**.

㊱ Crack and Up E1 5b
The prominent crack gives a good route with solid gear, good holds and a low crux, which might just be 5c!

㊲ Corner and Overhang E2 5b
Start up *Crack and Up* but step right to climb the wall just to its right by sustained moves on reasonably sized holds for once. A *Direct Start* is **V3 (6a)** and well worth doing.

㊳ McArthur Park E3 6a
Climb the pocketed wall (fierce start) past the twin slots.

㊴ Eliminate One E2 5b
The first of four tightly-packed routes.

㊵ The Abort........... E1 5a
A high move on sloping holds feels bold - cams will help.

Pex Hill — The Web

The Web
The walls either side of the long right-angled corner have a fine selection of routes across the grades. The face right of the corner can get quite sunny.

❶ Eliminate Two **E2 5c**
3m left of the corner climb past the edge of the recesses.

❷ One Step **E1 5a**
2m left of the corner through the horizontal slot near the top.

❸ Eliminate Three **E3 5c**
Just left of the corner.

❹ The Web **E1 5b**
Spiderman's fave route. The long corner gives a fine pitch. It can be damp but it is normally possible to bridge past the worst of this. Low in the grade and protection is reasonable.

❺ Pex Wall **E3 6a**
Follow the long, slightly-rising break until it fizzles out. A great work-out. Finish rightwards.

❻ Eliminate Four **E3 5c**
Just right of the corner.

❼ The Witch **E2 5b**
Good holds up the wall 3m right of the corner, past spaced gear to a trickier (and crusty) finish.

❽ Four Jays **E2 5b**
Straight up the wall heading for the small diagonal overlap.

The obvious 'gap' in the wall to right again gives a worthwhile eliminate at 5c, though blinkers might be needed.

❾ The Wizard **E3 5c**
Start at a set of pockets and features gradually easing climbing.

❿ Green Monster **E4 6a**
The wall just left of the in-situ kids!

⓫ Alchemy **E4 6a**
Similar stuff. Don't land on them if you fall off.

⓬ Warlock **E2 5c**
Climb to the break (peg) and continue direct. Excellent.

⓭ Warcry **E5 6b**
A hard and bold wall climb.

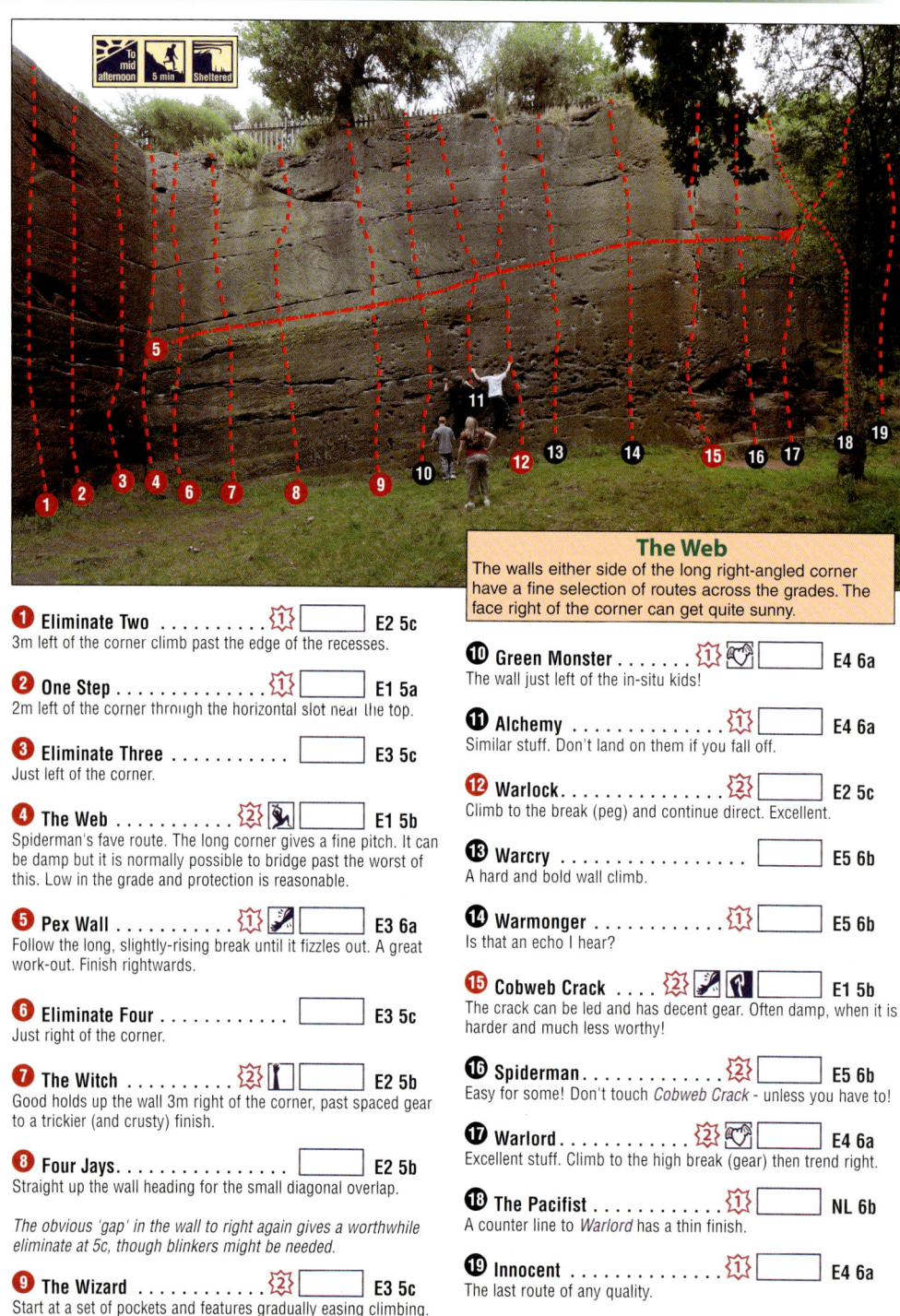

⓮ Warmonger **E5 6b**
Is that an echo I hear?

⓯ Cobweb Crack **E1 5b**
The crack can be led and has decent gear. Often damp, when it is harder and much less worthy!

⓰ Spiderman **E5 6b**
Easy for some! Don't touch *Cobweb Crack* - unless you have to!

⓱ Warlord **E4 6a**
Excellent stuff. Climb to the high break (gear) then trend right.

⓲ The Pacifist . . . . **NL 6b**
A counter line to *Warlord* has a thin finish.

⓳ Innocent **E4 6a**
The last route of any quality.

To the right are more routes but most are overgrown. The prominent arete is **Gaming Club**, *a loose and crumbly* **5a**.

Outlying Areas **Pex Hill** 375

20 Ramble .... VB (4c)
Ramble rightwards to a grubby exit.

21 Short Crack .... VB (4c)
The clue is in the name!

22 Heather Wall V1 (5b)
Trend leftwards up the smoother rock.

23 Bon Ami V0 (5a)
The hole-ridden wall just right.

24 Bon Gre Malgre .... V0+ (5b)
Head up the wall from the end of the ledge - and if you fall ensure to head to the left!

25 Master Race E5 6b
From the pit climb to a scary mantel high up.

26 The Rack E1 5a
A hidden gem which isn't that hard but don't fall off the mantel!

Past some overgrown routes is an open corner with a prominent sharp arete on its left-hand side. The routes here are that awkward height - highball boulder problems or mini-routes - you decide, and be careful!

27 Sweeney Arete V0 (5a)
The arete has a big feel about it despite the green spot!

28 Robbery V1 (5b)
The pocketed wall just right of the arete.

29 Headstone V4 (6a)
A scary and blank wall.

30 Memorial Wall .... VB (4b)
Wander left then right up the wall via good pockets.

31 Tombstone V0 (5a)
The wall just left of the corner.

32 Memorial Corner .... VB (4b)
The corner is a good line but is often wet.

33 Hunter's Walk V2 (5c)
The wall to a scary sloping top-out.

34 St Paul V2 (5c)
Gain a big pocket and finish either left or right.

Outlying Areas
Many of the walls opposite the quarry entrance are short and overgrown. In amongst them are one or two good sections worth seeking out if you want to escape the crowds. There are a few easier routes scattered around here too. A couple of sections are listed left to right.

Route Index

Grade	Route	Photo	Page
HVD	17 Shades.		265
VDiff	1st Holiday		206
* E5	240 Volt Shocker		353
Mod	2nd Holiday		206
HVS	30 Foot Wall		325
E2	39th Step		50
* VS	40 Foot Corner		325
HVS	45 Degrees		181
* HS	999	288	315
Diff	A Chimney		206
S	A Crack		206
* V2	A Day Too Late		282
*** E6	A Fist Full of Crystals		69
* E2	A Fist Full of Daggers		282
* E6	A Flabby Crack		96
* E6	A Little Peculiar		76
* HVS	A.M. Anaestheti		56
HS	A.P. Chimney		140
E5	A Stretch Named Desire.		286
E4	A Walk with Whittaker		235
S	Abdomen		110
* E1	Abort, The.		373
** E2	Abracadabra		258
E2	Acarpous		274
* HVS	Ace of Spades.		250
* E4	Acid Drop		52
* E5	Acid Test		369
* HVS	Ackit		68
* E4	Act of Faith		176
* S	Adam's Apple		176
** E2	Adios Amigo		269
*** E4	Adrenaline.		313
VS	After the Blitz		300
* VS	Agag	347	352
*** E6	Against the Grain		74
* S	Aged Crack		133
E3	Ain't Nothing To It.		301
E1	Al's Idea.		322
** E1	Alcatraz		108
* E4	Alchemy.		374
* HVS	Alcove Crack		146
* HVS	Alexander the Great.		339
* V3	Algripper		372
* HVS	All-star's Wall		124
VDiff	Allred's Original		300
* S	Alpha Arete		50
* VDiff	Alpha (Ravenstones)		254
* VDiff	Alpha (Skyline)		50
* S	Alpine Sports		156
* E3	Altered States		258
E4	Amaranth		78
* VDiff	Amphitheatre Climb.		223
* S	Amphitheatre Crack		105
* HS	Amphitheatre Face Climb		185
** E4	Anaconda		98
** E3	Anaconda Breakout		98
V0-	Analogue		328
* VDiff	Ancient		98
** E4	Andromeda		159
* E1	Ann		310
* E4	Annoying Little Man, The		265
*** HVD	Answer Crack		246
V6	Ant Lives		68
* E3	Anthrax		96
*** E5	Antithesis		90
* E5	Apache Dawn		66
* HVS	Apostles' Wall.		176
*** E3	Appaloosa Sunset.	58	60
E5	Appointment Missed		234
*** E9	Appointment with Death		232
** E7	Appointment With Fear		232
E2	Apres Midi		220
* VS	Aqua		84
** E3	Arabia.		158
** VDiff	Arete and Crack		112
E4	Arete du Coeur		228
* V0+	Arete Route (Frodsham)		361
V1	Arete Route (also Frodsham)		362
* VS	Arete, The (Brownstones)		324
** HS	Arete, The (Castle Naze)		138
** VDiff	Arete, The (Hen Cloud)		98
** E2	Arete, The (New Mills Tor)		146
* S	Arete, The (Ramshaw)		106
*** E2	Arete, The (Tintwistle)		215
** VDiff	Arete Wall (Hen Cloud)		98
* E6	Arete Wall (Ramshaw)		114
* E6	Aretenaphobia.		103
*** E6	Art Nouveau.		49
* E6	Artifact		200
* HS	Artillery Chimney		161
** E3	Ascent of Man.		66
* E3	Ascent of Woman.		66
* VDiff	Ash Pit Slab	331	328
* VB	Ash Pit Slab Direct		328
* V0	Ash Pit Traverse.		328
S	Ash Tree Direct		286
** HVD	Ashop Climb		170
* HS	Ashop Corner Climb		170
** E2	Ashop Crack		170
* HVS	Asinine		245
** E1	Asparagus.		159
E3	Aspirant, The		66
* VS	Assegai		112
* E5	Assembled Techniques		106
** S	Atherton Brothers.		195
E1	Atone		182
* E1	Atrocity Exhibition, The		181
** VS	Atropine.		143
V1	Auchtermuchty.		282
E2	Austin Maxi		245
* E1	Avatar		154
* VS	Ave		195
* E6	Axe Wound, The		319
HS	Axminster.		282
*** E7	B4, XS.		98
* E1	Babbacombe Lee		90
* HVS	Bachelor's Buttress		86
* E1	Bachelor's Climb		101
*** HVS	Bachelor's Left-hand	100	101
** V4	Back Wall Traverse		220
* E4	Bad Joke		95
* Diff	Bad Poynt.		54
E2	Bad Sneakers		54
* HS	Bags That		157
* HVS	Baldstones Arete		124
* HVS	Baldstones Face.		124
** V7	Baldstones Traverse.		124
S	Banjo Crack.		174
* V2	Banner's Route		365
* VDiff	Bantam Crack		96
* VDiff	Barbara		172
* S	Barbeque		326
* E4	Bareback Rider	67	66
* HVS	Bareleg Wall.		124
*** E6	Barriers in Time.		68
* E1	Basic Arete		146
* E6	Basic Training.		222
VDiff	Bastion Corner		45
* VS	Battery Crack		77
* VS	Battle of the Bulge		108
* E1	Be Calmed		115
VDiff	Beaky Corner		238
E2	Beast, The.		186
* E5	Beatnik		353
* E3	Beautiful Losers.		163
* HS	Because.		300
* HVD	Beckermet Slab		83
* E3	Bed of Nails.		90
* E1	Bee, The.		319
* E2	Beetler, The		349
* E1	Being Boiled.		258
* VS	Belladonna		143
* VS	Belly on a Plate		340
* VS	Bender, The.		61
* VDiff	Bending Crack		154
* HVS	Bengal Buttress		70
* E6	Berlin Wall		230
** V5	Bermuda Triangle		372
* V6	Bernie.		372
* E1	Bertie Meets Flash Gordon.		165
* S	Bertie's Bugbear		231
Diff	Beta		254
* E5	Bethan		157
* E3	Better End, The		97
* HVS	Betty's Wall		325
*** E2	Big Brother		172
** E2	Big Dorris		320
* HS	Big Flake, The.		61
* E3	Big Greenie		373
* HVS	Big Heap		267
S	Big Richard		116
* VS	Big Traverse, The		172
VB	Big Wall.		360
* E3	Big Wall, The		200
* E4	Bionic's Wall	145	149
* S	Birch Tree Corner		361
* S	Bird Chimney		311
* HVS	Birthday Climb		142
* VS	Birthday Crack		301
* S	Bitching.		98
*** S	Black and Tans		87
* E6	Black Eyed Dog		96
* E5	Black Hole Arete		357
* E5	Black Magic		369
* E6	Black Magic Direct		369
VS	Black Mamba		314
* E7	Black Michael		216
* E7	Black Mountain Collage.		254
* VS	Black Pig		54
* E6	Black Pimp from Marseilles, The		373
* V4	Black Russian		372
* E1	Black Seven.		164
* S	Black Slab.		130
* S	Black Velvet.		87
HVS	Black Watch.		282
* VDiff	Blackbank Crack		124
* VS	Blackout.		314
* S	Blank Crack		248
** E2	Blasphemy	227	231
* E4	Blazing Saddles		267
* E2	Blind Faith.		228
* VDiff	Block and Tackle		324
* E5	Blockbuster.		111
* VDiff	Blocked Chimney		228
* E4	Blood Blisters.		95
** E2	Blood, Sweat and Tears		234
*** E6	Bloodrush.		196
** E6	Bloodspeed		75
* E5	Bloodstone		75
* E1	Bloody Thirteenth, The		187
S	Bloody/Block Cracks		138
* HVS	Blue Light.		348
* E1	Blue Light's Crack.		231
*** E2	Boadicea		291
* E1	Bob Hope	251	250
* E1	Bod, The.		318
* E4	Body Popp		106
* Diff	Boken Groove.		107
* E8	Boldness Through Ignorance		342
* VS	Bollard Edge		45
V0	Bon Ami.		375
V0+	Bon Gre Malgre		375
* E7	Book at Bedtime		159
* E4	Boom Bip		114
** E8	Boomerang (Egerton)	333	334
* VDiff	Boomerang (Ramshaw)		112
Diff	Boomerang (Wilton 2)		318
V8	Boozy Traverse, The.		69
*** E4	Borstal Breakout		98
HS	Boulevard Traverse		182
* VDiff	Bow Buttress		99
HVD	Bow Crack		138
E1	Bow Wall		175
* VS	Bowrosin		112
E1	Boy's Own		254
* HVS	Boysen's Delight		59
* V2	Boysen's Route		365
* E1	Brain Drain		161
** E1	Brainchild		262
*** E4	Brandenburg Wall.		351
NL	Brandenburg Wall Direct		351
* E1	Brastium		325
** V8	Breakaway		372
HVS	Breakdown		276
Mod	Breakfast Corner		50
* VDiff	Breakfast Problem		50
* E6	Breakin' for a Bogey		279
V0-	Bridget		122
* VS	Bright Bastard		339
* E1	Bring Me Sunshine		221
S	Bristly Chimney		156
** E1	Britt's Cleavage		171
E3	Brittle Nerve.		296
VDiff	Broken Chimney		164
* Diff	Broken Groove		133
* HS	Broken Slab		84
** HVS	Broomstick, The		237
** E1	Brother's Eliminate		172
** E2	Brown's Crack		110
* VDiff	Brownstones Crack		330
* VS	Bruno Flake		56
* E6	Brush Off Direct Finish, The.		353
** E6	Brush Off Direct, The		353
** E4	Brush Off, The		353
* E1	Brutality		161
* VS	Bulger, The		76
* VDiff	Bulges, The		336
S	Bulging Arete		132
* E4	Bullworker		294
* E1	Bulwark		94
* VS	Burnham Crack		44
* V1	Bushy Tale		371
* HVS	Buster the Cat.		96
* Mod	Buttress Two Gully		133
Diff	C Climb		242
* E3	Cabbage Man Meets the Death Egg.		325
* NL	Cadaver Eyes		352
*** E4	Caesarean.		97
*** E4	Calamity Crack	275	274
* HVS	Calcutta Buttress		91
* HS	Calcutta Crack.		91
* E4	Calcutta Wall		357
* VS	Calypso Crack.		286
* VDiff	Camelian Crack		111
* VS	Cameo		279
* E1	Cameo (Wilton 1).		308
* VDiff	Campus Chimney		174
* VS	Cancan		286
** HVS	Candle Buttress		180
*** E3	Candle in the Wind		175
* S	Candy Man		122
* E2	Canine Crucifixion.		325
* VS	Cannon, The		108
* S	Cannonball Crack		70
* HVS	Canopy		326
* HS	Capitol Climb		83
* S	Capstone Chimney (Back Forest)		45
* Mod	Capstone Chimney (Dovestone)		243
* HVD	Captain Lethargy		81
* V6	Captain Quark.		123
** HVS	Captain Zep.		202
** E4	Cardiac Arete		373
*** E5	Caricature.		101
* E3	Carrion		77
** E4	Carsten's Abortion		349
* E2	Carsten's Variant		349
** HS	Cascade.		238

Route Index 377

Grade	Route	Photo	Page
* E2	Cassandra		169
*** V7	Catalepsy		372
*** E5	Catastrophe Internationale		66
* E5	Catemytes Crack		368
** E7	Catharsis		97
HS	Catwalk, The	11	248
** VS	Cave Arete		210
** E1	Cave Arete Indirect		211
S	Cave Crack Indirect		211
*** HVS	Cave Crack (Laddow)		211
* VS	Cave Crack (Running Hill)		276
* HS	Cave Crack (Wilderness)		238
VS	Cave Groove		235
S	Cave Gully		161
HVS	Cave Rib (Kinder South)		161
E2	Cave Rib (Wimberley)		235
** HS	Cave Route		291
* E6	Cave Route Right-hand		373
E6	Cedez le Passage		112
* S	Cedri		322
* HVS	Ceiling Zero		117
* E1	Cement Mix		318
Diff	Central Buttress		295
* VDiff	Central Buttress Direct		295
VDiff	Central Chimney (Cadshaw)		337
VS	Central Chimney Direct		188
* Diff	Central Chimney (Kinder Downfall)		188
VS	Central Climb Direct		98
* VDiff	Central Climb (Helsby)		349
VS	Central Climb (Hen Cloud)		98
** VS	Central Crack (Blackstone)		340
* VS	Central Crack (Castle Naze)		337
*** HVS	Central Crack (Wilton 3)		325
* VS	Central Eliminate		340
* S	Central Groove		340
* HS	Central Route (Back Forest)		45
** E2	Central Route (Frodsham)		361
* VS	Central Route (Kinder South)		159
* VS	Central Route (Roaches Upper)		89
* HVS	Central Route (Shining Clough)		202
** E1	Central Route (Wilton 1)		307
VDiff	Central Tower (Castle Naze)		143
* VDiff	Central Tower (Dovestones)		244
* HS	Central Wall		337
* HVD	Centre		133
* S	Centre Route		131
** E2	Chalk Lightning Crack		335
V0	Chalkie		282
* E3	Chalkstorm		80
*** E4	Chameleon		103
HS	Changeling, The		243
** E2	Charlie's Overhang		120
* E3	Charm		233
*** E3	Cheat	309	310
* VS	Cheek		133
* E6	Cheesemonger, The		162
* E5	Cheltenham Gold Cup		231
* VS	Cherry Bomb		334
VS	Chew Grit		282
** E7	Chiaroscuro		101
S	Chicane		56
* E1	Chicken		94
HVD	Chicken Run		82
* VDiff	Chimney and Crack		130
* VDiff	Chimney and Slab Variations		159
* HS	Chimney and Traverse		349
VB	Chimney Route		362
V0-	Chimney, The		329
E5	Chockblock		233
VDiff	Chockerblock Corner		330
* VDiff	Chockstone Chimney (Kinder Downfall)		185
** VS	Chockstone Chimney (Kinder South)		160
* VS	Chockstone Chimney (Ramshaw)		108
* Diff	Chockstone Chimney (Windgather)	128	131
Diff	Chockstone Corner		59
HVD	Chockstone Crack		97
** E7	Chocolate Girl		313
* E1	Choka		78
* VS	Christeena		310
** E4	Christine Arete		310
** E1	Chromium Crack		352
* E3	Cinema Arete		361
* E3	Circuit Breaker		80
VDiff	Cistern Groove		197
VDiff	Cleft and Chimney		271
* V7	Clever Skin		125
* E5	Climb with No Name, The		233
** E7	Clippity Clop, Clippity Clop		111
* E5	Clive Coolheed		76
S	Cloister Traverse		352
VS	Clotted Cream		146
E1	Cloud Busting		234
VS	Cloudberry Wall		234
** E4	Cloudbusting		60
* E5	Club Class		157
* VS	Cnig's Direct		339
* VS	Cnig's Underhang		339
* E1	Cobweb Crack		374
HVS	Cochise		267
* E2	Cochybondru		278
* HS	Cockney's Traverse		254

** VS	Coffin Crack		229
* E1	Cold Sweat		103
** E4	Colly Wobble		110
VS	Colombia Lift-off		258
* V6	Colton's Crack		365
* Diff	Column Climb		337
* S	Combs Climb		141
*** E3	Comedian		100
HVS	Comedian Direct, The		111
* VS	Comedian, The		111
** E2	Commander Energy	Cover	81
* V3	Commando		371
* VS	Communist Crack		63
* VDiff	Communist Route		168
** VS	Complete Streaker		297
* S	Concave Wall		296
** E2	Concrete Crack		318
* VS	Condor Chimney		56
VDiff	Condor Slab		56
** E4	Connection, The		276
** E5	Consolation Prize		233
*** E5	Constable's Overhang		324
* VS	Contrary Mary		84
HS	Cooking Crack		233
** E6	Cool Fool (Hen Cloud)		100
VS	Cool Fool (Running Hill Pits)		280
* S	Cooper's Crack		242
*** E3	Corinthian		100
HS	Corinthians, The		176
V1	Corn Mantel		328
* V2	Cornea		370
* E2	Corner and Overhang		373
* VDiff	Corner and Traverse		362
Diff	Corner Chimney		337
* S	Corner Crack (Ramshaw)		108
* VDiff	Corner Crack (Windgather)		133
* VS	Corner, The		307
* Mod	Corner, The (also Windgather)		132
Mod	Corner, The (Windgather)		131
* Diff	Cornette		342
** E2	Cornflake (Blackstone)		340
* VS	Cornflake (Tintwistle)		216
S	Cornice Indirect, The		349
* VDiff	Cornice, The		349
* V4	Cosine Alternative		372
* E2	Cosmic Enforcer		279
* V3	Cosmo Smallpiece		281
* E1	Cotton Terror		301
* E1	Count Dracula		175
** E5	Counter Intelligence		314
* E5	Counterstroke of Equity		48
* E4	Coward of the County		350
* E1	Cowboys and Indians		267
* HVS	Crab Crack		175
* VS	Crab, The		339
* S	Crab Walk		110
VS	Crab Walk Direct		110
* HVS	Crabbie's Crack		61
* HVS	Crabbies Left-hand		61
* V3	Crack and Arete		120
* Mod	Crack and Chimney		243
* HS	Crack and Corner		90
* VDiff	Crack and Slab (Wilton 1)		325
* VDiff	Crack and Slab (Wilton 3)		325
S	Crack and Slab (Wimberley)		228
* E1	Crack and Up		373
* S	Crack and Wall		337
* S	Crack of Doom		348
* E1	Crack of Gloom		71
* VS	Crack, The		142
* VDiff	Cracked Arete (Ramshaw)		114
* HVD	Cracked Arete (Skyline)		56
* S	Cracked Corner (Frodsham)		361
* HS	Cracked Corner (New Mills Tor)		148
* Diff	Cracked Gully		114
* V4	Crackpot		296
S	Cracks, The		276
* VS	Cranberry Crack		234
* VS	Crank, The		107
* V7	Crap Pot		296
* E4	Creep, Leap, Creep, Creep		112
* E1	Creeping Jesus	367	373
* VS	Creme Eggs		154
** V1	Crew's Arete		362
** V2	Crew's Arete Left-hand		362
* E1	Crew's Route		222
** E2	Crimson Wall		164
* VDiff	Cripple's Way		238
* HVS	Crippler, The		116
* HVS	Crispy Crack		271
* E1	Crock's Climb		220
* VS	Crooked Crack		326
* VS	Crooked Overhang		185
* S	Cross Tie		320
* E1	Crossbow		372
VS	Crosstie		278
*** E4	Crumpet Crack		348
* E5	Crystal Grazer		69
* E1	Crystal Tipps		114
HVS	Cuckoo's Nest		295
* HVS	Curfew		117
HVD	Curver		117
VDiff	Curving Arete		234

Diff	Curving Chimney		343
VDiff	Curving Crack (Cadshaw)		336
VDiff	Curving Crack (Dovestones)		242
S	Curving Crack (Kinder Downfall)		181
V1	Cyclops		370
* HVS	Daddy Crack		174
** HS	Damascus Crack		84
VS	Dan's Dare		113
* E1	Danegeld		242
*** E7	Dangerous Crocodile Snogging		111
E3	Dari's Bedroom Pursuits		154
* E7	Dark Side of the Moon, The		180
HS	Darkness		114
* E3	Dateline		369
* V7	Dave's Roof		365
HVS	Dawn		310
HVS	Dawn Piper		84
* S	Days Gone By		50
** E3	Days of Future Passed		66
*** E5	Daytona Wall		342
** E5	Daytona Wall Direct		342
* VS	Dead Chimney		177
** HS	Dead Dog Crack		276
* VS	Deadline		342
*** E4	Death Knell		78
** E4	Deborah		177
* HVS	December Arete		246
* HVS	Deception (Helsby)		349
HVS	Deception (New Mills Tor)		149
V1	Deception to Original Route		149
HVD	Deep Chimney (Castle Naze)		142
* Mod	Deep Chimney (Ravenstones)		254
VDiff	Deep Chimney (Standing Stones)		263
VDiff	Deep Crack (Castle Naze)		142
VB	Deep Crack (Frodsham)		360
Diff	Deep Groove		320
* E1	Definitive Gaze		50
* V0	Degree Crack		328
* VS	Delectable Deviation, The		115
* VS	Delicate Wall		281
* E1	Deliver Us From Evil		282
*** HVS	Delstree		97
VS	Demon Wall		82
*** V9	Denham Traverse, The		296
* VS	Dependence Arete		169
VS	Dependence Wall		169
* VDiff	Depot Chimney		175
* E6	Depression		369
** HVD	Derivatives, The		256
* E4	Desecration		230
VS	Dessers		342
** E7	Destination Earth		70
HVD	Deviation		169
VS	Devoted		50
* E1	Dewsbury's Route		155
* E2	Diamond Arete		160
E2	Diamond, The		264
* HVS	Diamond Wednesday		87
* HS	Dickie's Meadow		335
HVS	Diddley Dum Overhang		263
E3	Digital Dilemma		260
E3	Digital Orbit		238
* V2	Digitation		328
** V6	Dignity of Labour, The		68
* VS	Dinnerplate Crack		355
* E2	Diopera		350
HVS	Direct		319
* V0	Direct Route (also Frodsham)		364
* V1	Direct Route (Frodsham)		362
S	Direct Route (Helsby)		349
VDiff	Direct Route, The		243
* V2	Directissima		328
* VS	Director		132
HVD	Director's Route, The		243
Diff	Dirtier Groove		202
Diff	Dirty Groove		202
S	Dirty Trick		172
* E3	Disappearing Aces		318
* E1	Disappearing Chip Buttie Traverse, The		335
* HS	Disorder		339
E7	Do the Rocksteady		162
* E1	Domino Wall		183
E2	Don, The		343
* HVS	Don's Crack		110
* HVS	Don't Look Back		188
* E2	Don't Stop Believing		334
V1	Donkey Route Direct		362
* E5	Doomiest Hay		341
* E1	Dorothy's Dilemma		70
* Diff	Double Crack		138
* E1	Double Overhang		44
HVS	Double Overhangs		242
* E6	Double Take		229
HVD	Double Time Crack		246
* E2	Double Trip		301
VS	Doubloon		168
** E8	Doug		69
E2	Dour Power		157
* E2	Downes' Doddle		349
** Mod	Downfall Climb		187
** HVS	Downfall Groove		187
** VDiff	Downfall South Corner		187
V0	Dragnet		329

Route Index

	Grade	Route	Photo	Page
*	E2	Dragon's Route		223
***	HS	Drainpipe, The		255
	E3	Dream Fighter		106
*	E3	Dream of Blackpool Donkeys		234
*	E2	Dredger		265
	E7	Driven Bow, The		98
**	E2	Drizzle		223
**	E2	Drooper, The		287
	E4	Drop Acid		52
	E4	Drought		223
*	VDiff	Druid's Corner		337
*	E3	Druid's Direct		337
*	E2	Druid's Face		337
	S	Duckdoo		282
	E1	Dud Chimney		186
**	VS	Dunsinane		173
*	E2	Dust Storm		245
*	Diff	Dusty Arete		279
	S	E Route		271
*	E1	Earth Plumbit		162
	VDiff	East Face Climb		337
*	E2	East Rib	203	195
*	E5	East Rib Direct		195
*	E2	Easter Bunny	205	206
**	E2	Easter Ridge		206
	HVS	Eastern Arete		181
*	S	Eastern Crack		181
	HVS	Eastern Promise		181
*	VDiff	Eastern Slab		254
*	Diff	Eastern Touch		220
	Diff	Easy Buttress		349
	Mod	Easy Chimney		357
	Diff	Easy Corner		138
	Diff	Easy Crack		138
	HVD	Easy Gully Wall		90
	V0	Easy Slab		121
	VB	Easy Slab Right-hand		121
	HVD	Echantillon		260
*	E4	Eclipsed Peach		60
***	E5	Edale Bobby		164
*	VS	Edale Flyer		165
	VDiff	Edge, The		295
***	E6	Edge Your Bets		268
*	E2	Edgehog Flavour		271
	HS	Edipol!		301
*	VS	Editor's Note		134
	VDiff	Eeny		326
	S	Egg Bowl, The		202
**	E5	Ego Trip		312
*	E1	Eight Hours!		243
*	Diff	Eight Metre Corner		228
	E2	Eireborne		215
	HVS	Elaine		300
*	E1	Elastic Arm		60
*	E2	Elastic Limit		111
	VDiff	Elderberry Slab		286
	E2	Electric Chair		95
*	E3	Electric Circus		147
*	E3	Electric Savage		113
***	E2	Elegy		76
**	V0	Elephant's Ear		125
*	V4	Elephant's Eye		125
***	E1	Eliminate 1 (Helsby)		357
	E3	Eliminate Four		374
*	E2	Eliminate One (Pex Hill)		373
*	VB	Eliminate (Pex Hill)		370
	E3	Eliminate Three		374
*	E2	Eliminate Two		374
*	V2	Eliminate Wall		371
*	VS	Eliminate (Wilton 1)		310
*	VS	Embarkation Parade		184
**	HVS	En Rappel		97
***	E1	Encouragement		98
	S	End Crack		357
**	E2	End of Time		297
*	VS	End Wall		181
*	E3	English Towns		112
**	E2	Enigma Variation		52
**	HVS	Ensemble Exit, The		183
***	E5	Entropy's Jaw		49
*	HS	Epitaph Corner		222
	HVS	Eroica		350
	NL	Erotica		350
	E1	Escape		116
	S	Esgee Crack		181
*	E2	Eugene's Axe		74
	E6	Euphoria		369
***	VS	Eureka		170
*	HVS	Eve		176
	S	Evening Ridge		222
***	E7	Exit On Air		369
*	VS	Exodus		174
*	VS	Extinguisher Chimney		180
	Diff	Extra		295
*	HVS	Eye of Japetus		45
	HVS	Eye-catcher		282
*	S	Eyebrow		243
	S	F Route		271
	HVD	Face Route 1		134
	Diff	Face Route 2		134
***	VS	Fairy Nuff		263
	E1	Fall Guy		282
***	E1	Fallen Heroes		262
***	E2	Falling Crack		320
*	HVS	False Prospects		262
	NL	Famous Alto Sax Break, The		369
**	E5	Fashion Statement		157
	E3	Fast Hands		177
*	E4	Fast Piping		100
	Mod	Fat Man's Chimney		142
*	E1	Fat Old Sun		265
	E4	Fenian Wall		217
*	E1	Ferdie's Folly		245
**	S	Fern Crack		82
*	VS	Field of Dreams, The		334
*	V5	Fielder's Corner		125
	V1	Fielder's Indirect		125
*	V9	Fielder's Wall		125
	HVS	Fifth Horseman, The		138
**	E8	Final Destination		81
	E2	Final Frontier		184
***	E3	Final Judgement		182
*	E2	Finger Chimney		302
*	V4	Finger of Fate	62	62
*	VS	Finger, The		302
*	V6	Finger-Ripper		372
*	VS	Fingernail		308
*	V2	Fingers		371
***	E4	Fingertip Control (Anglezarke)		301
*	E5	Fingertip Control (Hobson Moor)		221
	E1	Fire-power		286
*	HVS	Firefly		282
***	E1	First Finale		301
*	S	First Triplet		247
*	VDiff	First's Arete		134
*	E5	Fish-meal and Revenge		264
	HVD	Fisher's Chimney		234
*	E2	Five Day Chimney		250
	E1	Five o'clock Shadows		156
	HS	Five Ten		185
*	Diff	Fixation		169
	VS	Flake and Chimney		156
*	Diff	Flake Chimney		78
	VS	Flake Crack (Castle Naze)		139
***	VS	Flake Crack (Helsby)		356
	S	Flake Crack (Shining Clough)		200
*	S	Flake Crack (Wilton 2)		320
	VDiff	Flake Groove		200
	Mod	Flake Gully		114
*	E2	Flake Innominate		356
*	VDiff	Flake Route		363
	VS	Flake, The		148
**	E5	Flake Wall		356
*	VS	Flaky Wall Direct	104	114
	VS	Flaky Wall Indirect		114
*	E1	Flaky Wall Super Direct		114
***	VS	Flash Wall		164
*	HS	Fledgling's Climb		77
*	V5	Flick Direct		297
*	E2	Flick of the Wrist		297
	S	Flimney		78
*	VS	Flingle Bunt		308
	S	Flipper		343
	VS	Flopper		343
**	E2	Flower Power Arete		61
	E1	Flue Pipe		274
	S	Flupper		343
	E1	Flush Pipe		274
*	VS	Flytrap		311
***	VS	Flywalk		311
*	S	Flywalk, The		140
*	VS	Foghorn Groove		223
	HS	Folies Bergeres		276
*	E2	Fool's Gold		302
	E4	Foolish Finish		356
***	E2	Foord's Folly		117
*	VDiff	Footprint		132
	S	Footstool Left		141
	HVD	Footstool Right		141
*	E4	Force Nine		115
*	E3	Foreigner		182
*	VS	Forked Cracks		323
	HVS	Forked Tongue		268
*	Diff	Forking Chimney		124
	E3	Formative Years		50
	E2	Four Jays		374
*	E2	Fox, The		122
*	HVS	Fox-trot		286
*	E3	Fragile Wall		354
*	V1	Fraud		328
*	V3	Fraudulent Slip		328
*	E5	Frayed Nerve		100
	VS	Fred's Cafe		69
**	HVS	Freddie's Finale		228
	E3	Free Fall		201
*	E2	Free Spirit		339
	E2	Freebird		238
**	E1	Friction Addiction		246
*	E1	Frightful Fred		313
	VS	Frodsham Crack		361
*	E2	Frostbite		319
*	E1	Full Stop		247
	HS	Funnel, The		181
	HS	Funny Farm, The		294
*	VS	Funny Thing		258
**	E5	Gable End		221
*	E1	Galileo		199
**	E2	Gallows		95
**	HVS	Gallows Pole		335
	S	Ganderhole Crack		125
	VS	Gangway, The		353
*	VDiff	Gaping Void, The		44
	S	Garden Wall		209
**	E1	Gargantua		274
***	E5	Gates of Perception		302
	E3	Gather No Moss		349
	E3	Gather Ye Gritbudds		154
	E3	General Custard		269
	VS	Genetix		91
	E3	Geordie Girl		61
	E2	Ghoul, The		264
	E3	Gibbet, The		248
*	VS	Gideon	218	222
	HVS	Gideonite		222
*	E8	Gigantic		313
*	E5	Gilted		88
*	E1	Giteche Manitou, The		267
*	E5	Give the Dogg a Bone		268
	VDiff	Glass Back		60
*	S	Glister Wall		302
	E4	Glock Over		174
	E2	Glorious Twelfth, The		186
	VS	Glory Boys		182
	VS	Gnomes' Wall		245
	VS	Gobbin Groove		215
*	HVS	God Save the Queen		335
	E3	Godzilla		274
*	E2	Going For the One		295
	E4	Gold Rush		124
**	HVS	Golden Pillar		352
***	E1	Golden Tower, The	3	302
*	E2	Golden Wonder		271
*	HVS	Goldsitch Crack		124
	V2	Goliath		370
*	VS	Gomorrah (Kinder Downfall)		188
**	E1	Gomorrah (Running Hill Pits)		279
*	E3	Good Things Come To Those Who Wait		217
	V2	Gorilla		371
*	E3	Gorilla Wall		351
*	E4	Gorilla Wall Direct		351
***	E3	Grader, The		324
*	E1	Graffiti		70
	VS	Grain of Sand		223
*	E3	Grape Escape		195
	HS	Grasper		45
	Diff	Grassy Chimney		158
**	E5	Grave's End		339
***	S	Great Chimney (Hen Cloud)	102	103
*	VS	Great Chimney Left-hand		183
	HS	Great Chimney, The		183
	Mod	Great Chimney (Wilton 2)		322
**	E3	Great Expectations		221
	S	Great Scene Baby		116
*	VS	Great Slab		315
***	VS	Great Slab (Alderman)	270	271
*	S	Great Slab Arete		271
*	Diff	Great Slab Chimney		271
	S	Great Slab (Kinder Downfall)		188
	HVS	Great Slab Right		271
***	E2	Great Wall		361
**	HVS	Great Zawn, The		107
*	E1	Green but Sure		235
	S	Green Corner (Hen Cloud)		95
	S	Green Corner (Ramshaw)		113
*	S	Green Crack (Castle Naze)		143
	VDiff	Green Crack (Dovestones)		242
*	VS	Green Crack (Ramshaw)		106
	E3	Green Crack (Shining Clough)		195
**	S	Green Crack (Windgather)		130
	E2	Green Meanies, The		267
*	E4	Green Monster		374
*	VDiff	Green Shaker		45
*	S	Green Slab		130
	VDiff	Green Slabs		324
*	V1	Green Streaks		371
**	VS	Green Wall		254
	VS	Greenfinger		162
*	HS	Greenteeth Crack		355
*	Mod	Greenteeth Gully		355
*	V1	Greeting		370
*	VS	Gremlin Groove		200
	HVS	Gremlin Wall		200
*	E4	Grey Slayer, The		177
*	VS	Greystone Pillar		260
	E1	Grilled Fingers		91
*	E5	Grim Reaper, The		147
	S	Grim Wall		244
*	V3	Grinding Sloper, The		121
*	HVS	Gritstone Rain		303
	Mod	Groove		135
	Diff	Groove and Chimney		233
*	V7	Groove, The (Running Hill Pits)		282
**	VDiff	Groove, The (Wilton 3)		323
	VS	Groove-V Baby		278
*	E5	Grooved Slab		353
**	VS	Grooved Wall		254
	HS	Groovin'		343

Route Index 379

Grade	Route	Photo	Page
HS	Groovy Baby		116
* E1	Groundhog		343
* E4	Growth Centre		173
* VS	Grunter		161
S	Guano Gully		75
** E2	Guerrilla Action		255
* S	Guillotine		262
* E2	Gull-wing		274
HVS	Gully Wall (Ramshaw)		113
VS	Gully Wall (Roaches Upper)		91
*** E2	Gumshoe		108
** E4	Guns and Drums		217
* E4	Gypfast		86
* E4	Hacker, The		307
* HS	Hades Crack		348
E1	Hadrian's Wall		286
* E3	Half a Friend/High Life		160
** E2	Halina		232
* E5	Hallelujah Chorus		149
* E4	Hallow to our Men		50
* E4	Hand of the Medici		154
* E2	Handrail		112
* E4	Handrail Direct		112
* V1	Handshake		370
* E2	Hang-glider		254
* HVS	Hanging Around		87
*** E2	Hanging Crack	249	248
** VS	Hanging Groove		229
** VS	Hanging Groove Variations		229
** E2	Hanging Slab		220
S	Hangman's Crack		90
*** V5	Hank's Wall		329
* E2	Hard Times		187
* E3	Harlequin		175
* HS	Harp, The		223
** E4	Hart's Arete		373
* V5	Hart's Arete Traverse		373
** E2	Hartley's Route		155
* HVS	Harvest		187
** E4	Harvest Moon		276
** V2	Harvey Wallbanger		372
* V2	Haskit Left-hand		329
V1	Haskit Right-hand		329
E1	Hawkwind		267
*** E1	Hawkwing		77
* E1	Haze		148
* VDiff	Hazel Barn		120
* S	Hazel Barrow Crack		120
V4	Hazel Groove		120
VDiff	Hazy Groove		276
E1	Headless Horseman		77
V4	Headstone		375
* HVS	Heap Big Corner		267
* E4	Heat is On, The		220
Diff	Heather Buttress		131
VDiff	Heather Corner		223
HVD	Heather Face		132
* S	Heather Slab		83
VB	Heather Variant		362
V0	Heather Wall Direct		362
S	Heather Wall (Frodsham)		362
* V1	Heather Wall (Pex Hill)		375
* E2	Heatwave		220
** E2	Heavy Duty		149
* VS	Hedgehog Crack		100
* V3	Hem Line		110
** E3	Hemingway's Wall		350
*** HVS	Hen Cloud Eliminate		100
* E3	Herford's Girdle Traverse		138
*** HVS	Herford's Route		155
* VB	Hernia		330
** HVS	Herringbone Slab		233
** Diff	High Buttress Arete		132
* HVS	High Tensile Crack		96
* HS	Hiker's Chimney		160
* S	Hiker's Crack		160
HVD	Hiker's Gully Left		161
S	Hiker's Gully Right		161
VDiff	Hippo		122
* VS	Hitch Hiker		161
E1	Hitching a Ride		160
E3	Ho Ho Ho		356
** E5	Hobson's Choice		221
Diff	Holly Tree Niche		45
* S	Holly Tree Niche Left		45
* VS	Hollybush Crack		87
* E1	Holme Moss		200
* E4	Honcho		148
VDiff	Honest Jonny		106
* VS	Honeycomb Wall		348
HVD	Honeymoon Route		177
** V1	Hoop-La, The		365
V0-	Hopper		328
* VS	Horrock's Route		308
* HS	Hot Flush Crack		164
* HVS	How		269
E2	Hulk, The		373
** E1	Humdinger		86
*** E3	Hunky Dory		80
* E3	Hunter, The		186
* V2	Hunter's Walk		375
** E5	Hymen the Tactless		248
* HVS	Hypothesis		70
** E5	I Shot Jason King		335
* V7	I Was a Teenage Caveman		362
* E4	Icarus Allsorts		61
** E4	Ice Cool Acid Test		335
VDiff	Ice Crack		238
E2	Icebreaker		138
** HVS	Icon		195
** E5	Iguanodon		276
** E3	Illegitimate, The		349
* HS	Impending Crack		258
** E2	Imposition		114
* E2	In the Pie		348
VS	Inbetweenie, The		148
VS	Incognito		124
** E2	Independence Crack		187
VS	Indianapolis Slab		158
*** V8	Inertia Reel		68
*** V12	Inertia Reel Traverse		68
V0-	Inferno		329
* E4	Innocent		374
* E4	Innominate		310
* VS	Insipidity		335
** VB	Intermediate Route (Frodsham)		364
* HS	Intermediate Route (Kinder Downfall)		181
* E1	Intestate		172
VDiff	Intra		295
*** HS	Intro Wall	283	281
*** Diff	Inverted Staircase		82
* VS	Irish Jig		286
** E2	Iron Dish Wall		361
* Diff	Iron Horse Crack		114
*** E4	Iron Orchid		320
* E2	Iron Road		269
** E4	Isle of White		312
** E2	It Only Takes Two to Tango		274
* E3	It's a Small World		260
*** E6	Italian Job, The		302
* V2	Itchy Fingers		122
* V4	Itchy Groove		122
*** E1	Ivory Tower, The	150	161
** E5	Jack and Ed's Route		343
E1	Jacob's Bladder		154
S	Jam and Jug		248
HS	Jeffcoat's Buttress		86
** VDiff	Jeffcoat's Chimney		86
* VS	Jelly Baby Slab		172
* VS	Jelly Roll		90
*** HVS	Jester Cracks		175
* S	Jester, The		248
* E5	Jet Lag		250
* E1	Jiggery Pokery		265
* E2	Jim's Chimney		353
S	Jimmy Carter		62
*** V1	Jimmy's Crack		362
HS	Jive		286
* E3	Joe's Hanging Crack		68
VS	John		177
E5	Johnny's Indirect Rear Entry		125
VS	Jolsen Finish, The		180
** E5	Josser		312
V3	Jota		370
* E5	Juan Cur		108
E1	Jubilee Climb		308
E2	Jugged Forest		354
* V2	Jumper		363
E1	Jumping Jive		343
* Diff	June Climb		245
* S	June Ridge		245
VS	June Wall		245
** V6	Jurassic Pork		372
E6	Just for Today		68
* E5	Just in Time		96
VS	'K' Climb		245
VDiff	K. Corner		258
** E6	K.P.		312
* E7	K.P. Nuts		66
** S	K2		98
* E1	Kaptain Klepton		274
* HVD	Karabiner Chimney		52
Diff	Karabiner Cracks		52
* HVS	Karabiner Slab		52
** E6	Karma Mechani, The		303
* HVS	Kathryn's Crack		260
* VS	Kay		326
* VS	Kaytoo		245
** VS	Keep Arete	126	141
* HVS	Keep Buttress		140
* S	Keep Corner		141
S	Keep Face		45
HS	Keeper, The		45
* E1	Kelly's Direct		89
* S	Kelly's Shelf		89
HS	Kelvin's Corner		164
VDiff	Kensington High Street		157
VS	Kensington Left Crack		156
VDiff	Kensington Right Crack		156
* E1	Kershaw's Krackers		215
** VS	Kestrel Crack	18	77
* HVS	KGB		62
** E4	Kicking Bird		75
* E1	Kindergarten		157
* E1	King B		342
* S	King Harold		117
*** E6	King of Kings		302
** E1	King of the Swingers		149
** E4	Kinsman		172
** E4	Kitt's Wall		373
S	Kitten Cracks		244
** E3	Klondike	298	302
HS	Knapp Hand		174
HVS	Kneepad		278
*** E5	Knife, The		368
* VS	Knobblekerry Corner		216
* HS	Knobbly Wall		242
** VS	Knock Out		315
** HVS	Knuckleduster		314
** VS	Kon-Tiki Korner		265
** E1	Kremlin Wall		263
* HVD	Kukri Crack		319
* HVS	Kung Fu		318
* HS	Kvick Chimney		234
* S	Ladies' Day		201
* HVS	Ladies' Day Direct		201
* E1	Lady Jane		372
** E4	Ladytron		373
** HVS	Lager Lout		202
** E6	Laguna Sunrise		60
* E1	Lapper		342
* E3	Last Day but One		297
* E2	Last Fling, The		185
* HS	Late Night Final		83
** E3	Late-nite Greenhaigh		350
VDiff	Layback		141
* V1	Layback		329
*** E4	Layback Crack (Dovestones)		246
S	Layback Crack (Kinder South)		154
** E3	Layback Crack (Summit Quarry)		339
* VS	Layback, The		295
* VS	Layback-a-daisical		263
* E2	Laying the Ghost		319
* E3	Laying-by		339
* E4	Lazy Friday		308
* E4	Leaf Buttress		208
* HS	Leaf Crack		208
** E4	Lean Mean Fighting Machine, The		303
* E4	Leather Joy Boys		120
* E1	Ledge and Groove		319
** E6	Ledge Shufflers, The		183
* HS	Ledge Way		223
* HVS	Ledgeway		140
* Diff	Leeds Crack		106
* HS	Leeds Slab		106
E1	Left Arete (Frodsham)		361
* V2	Left Arete (Newstones)		121
VDiff	Left Chimney		246
* HVS	Left Edge		315
* VS	Left Embrasure		244
* Diff	Left Fork Chimney		184
*** HS	Left Monolith, The	37	257
S	Left Route		202
Mod	Left Triplet Corner		135
* VS	Left Twin Chimney (Kinder Downfall)		182
Diff	Left Twin Chimney (Laddow)		209
* HS	Left Twin Crack (Hen Cloud)		103
HS	Left Twin Crack (The Skyline)		55
* V0	Left Wall (also Frodsham)		362
V2	Left Wall (Frodsham)		360
S	Left-hand Block Crack		59
* VDiff	Left-hand Crack		363
** E2	Left-hand Route (Frodsham)		361
** S	Left-hand Route (Roaches Upper)		90
* Diff	Leg Stump		133
VS	Leg Up		134
* HVS	Legacy (Kinder North)		172
V0+	Legacy (Running Hill Pits)		282
* E3	Legends of Lost Leaders		62
NL	Lemonade		368
VDiff	Lenin		62
V0+	Leo's Traverse		362
VS	Leprechaun		214
* HVS	Leprechauner		263
* E3	Les Dawson Show, The		173
* VS	Letter Box Cracks		55
Mod	Letter Box Gully		55
* VDiff	Letter-box		238
* E3	Leucocyte Left-hand		306
* VS	Leucocyte Right-hand		306
* E5	Levitation		97
* E2	Levl		214
* V2	Lew's Leap		372
* HVS	Libra		84
* E4	Licence to Lust		72
* E4	Licence to Run		72
* E5	Licentious Jug		357
VDiff	Lighthouse		55
* E3	Lightning		324
* HVS	Lightning Crack		68
S	Lintel		295
* E4	Lipalongago		355
* E2	Liquid Skin		159
* E5	Liquor, Loose Women and Double Cross		279
E5	Little Bighorn		267
* E1	Little Boy Blue		172
* VS	Little by Little		354

Route Index

Grade	Route	Photo	Page
Mod	Little Chimney		77
** S	Little Crowberry		208
HVS	Little Flake, The		61
* HS	Little Giraffe Man		117
S	Little Kern Knotts		256
* E2	Little Miss Id		340
* E3	Little Miss Id Variations		340
* V4	Little Monkey		296
E1	Little Nasty		113
VS	Little Pillar		140
VDiff	Little Pinnacle Climb		94
* HVS	Little Red Pig		195
* VS	Little Running Water		267
* E3	Little Spillikin, The		215
V2	Little Traverse		120
* E4	Live Bait		83
** E5	Liverpool Lady Boyz		355
* VS	Loaf and Cheese		106
VS	Loan Arranger		163
* V0	Lobotomy		330
* VS	Lobster Crack		175
** E5	Loculus Lie		89
** E7	Logical Progression		78
HS	Lolita		276
* E1	Long and Short, The		98
* S	Long Chimney Ridge		208
VDiff	Long Climb (Castle Naze)		143
*** S	Long Climb (Laddow)	211	208
* V1	Long Lurch, The		360
VDiff	Long Ridge		248
* E3	Long Wall Eliminate		286
* HVS	Looking for Today		50
*** E4	Loopy		307
* VS	Loose End		247
HVS	Los Endos		343
* E1	Louie Groove		106
* V6	Low Girdle, The		149
V3	Low Level Traverse		286
* S	Lucas Chimney		77
* E1	Luke		177
HVS	Lum, The		96
S	Lung Cancer		56
HS	M.G. Route		181
VDiff	Machine Gun		174
* HVS	Mad Karoo		297
** E8	MaDMAn		230
* HVS	Maggie		244
** S	Magic Roundabout		115
* HVS	Magic Roundabout Direct		115
* E1	Magic Roundabout Super Direct		115
** E1	Magic Wand		258
* E5	Magical Charm		352
* HS	Main Break		294
S	Main Corner		140
* VS	Main Crack		97
* E5	Main Wall		368
* VDiff	Main Wall Climb		202
* HVS	Mammoth Slab		245
*** E2	Mandarin	290	291
* S	Mandarin's Arete		168
* E5	Mandrake, The		95
* E5	Mandrill		95
*** E3	Mangled Digit		279
* VS	Mangler, The (Blackstone)		340
* E3	Mangler, The (Helsby)		351
* HVS	Manglewurzle Rib		312
* E4	Manibus et Pedibusque		340
* V2	Mankey Road		371
* Diff	Mantelshelf Route		59
* VS	Mantelshelf Slab		52
* S	Mantelshelf, The		337
Diff	Mantelstrug		330
*** E1	Mantis		50
HVD	Mantrap		116
* HVS	Many Happy Returns		301
* E1	Maquis		274
* VS	Mark (Anglezarke)		300
* VDiff	Mark I		256
* VDiff	Mark II		256
HS	Mark (Kinder North)		177
* VS	Mark's Slab		176
* V1	Martin's Traverse	6	120
V2	Marxist Undertones		63
* E1	Masochism	109	107
E2	Master Ego		340
* E5	Master of Puppets		94
*** E6	Master of Reality		94
E5	Master Race		375
*** E4	Master Spy		314
* E4	Master Spy Direct	305	314
* S	Matchstick Crack	241	244
* E2	Mather Crack		147
** HVS	Matinee	73	72
* HVS	Matthew		176
*** HVD	Maud's Garden		83
* S	Max		307
* E3	Maximum Hype		108
* E3	McArthur Park		373
* HVS	Meander Arete		169
* VDiff	Meander (Five Clouds)		59
** HS	Meander (Kinder North)		169
E1	Meander Variation		59
VDiff	Meandering Molly		320
* S	Meanwhile		300
* S	Medicine, The		131
* VDiff	Meeny		326
* HVS	Melaleucion		50
VB	Memorial Corner		375
* VB	Memorial Wall		375
*** E7	Mentalist's Cupboard, The		154
* V3	Mermaid's Ridge, The		182
* VS	Metamorphosis		300
V3	Mexican Bob		360
* E7	Michael Knight Wears a Chest Wig		232
* E5	Mickey Mouse		237
* E1	Mickey Thin		274
* Diff	Middle and Leg		133
* VDiff	Middle Buttress Arete		131
* Diff	Middle Chimney		159
S	Middle Triplet Crack		135
HS	Middleton Groove		201
VS	Middleton's Motion		54
* HVS	Midgebite Crack		287
E2	Midgebite Express		279
HS	Midnight Variation		222
S	Midsummer		276
* V7	Mike's Route		365
* Diff	Mild Thing		49
* V8	Milky Buttons		59
E2	Mimosa		274
*** HVS	Mincer, The		75
* E7	Mindbridge		94
VDiff	Miney		326
VDiff	Minipin Crack		124
* V1	Minor		300
* E5	Mirror, Mirror		59
NL	Missing Font, The		350
** S	Mississippi Crack		131
VS	Mississippi Dip		286
* E2	Mistral		91
*** VS	Misty Wall		168
* HS	Mo		326
* VS	Modern		98
*** E3	Modern Times		210
* E3	Mogadon's Good for You		352
* E1	Mohammed Arete		295
*** VS	Mohammed the Mad Monk		295
*** VS	Mohammed the Medieval Melancholic		295
S	Mohammed the Morbid Mogul		296
*** VS	Moneylender's Crack		163
* V1	Monkey Grip		371
*** E6	Monkey Madness		175
*** VS	Monkey Magi		181
* VS	Monkey Puzzle		195
** V11	Monoblock		372
* VS	Monolith Crack		322
E1	Monsoon		221
* E4	Monty		112
VS	Moocher, The		243
* E1	Moonshine		120
*** E2	Morgue Slab		352
VS	Morridge Top		124
* S	Morrison's Route		155
* HVS	Mortgage Wall		163
VB	Moss Wall		330
* VDiff	Mossy Slab		349
E1	Mother's Pride		243
* E1	Motherless Children		173
E2	Mousey's Mistake		76
HVS	Mr Creosote		44
* HVS	Muddy Arete		331
VDiff	Muddy Crack		256
* VB	Muddy Wall		330
* HVS	Muffin Crack		348
* E2	Multi-Screen		361
* E1	Mummy Crack		174
S	Muscle Crack		138
*** V10	Mushin'		68
S	Mustard		45
** E2	Mustard Walls		174
* E6	Myxi		96
* E1	Naaden		197
* V9	Nadin's Secret Finger		62
* HVS	Nagger's Delight		197
* VB	Nameless		370
* HVS	Nameless Edge		324
* VS	Nameless One	236	238
* HVS	Nameless Two		238
* E1	Napoleon's Direct		256
* HS	Nasal Buttress		243
* E5	National Acrobat		106
* HS	Nationalist Route		168
* E6	Natural Born Chillers		177
E5	Nature Trail		48
VDiff	Navy Cut		56
* V2	Neb Route		364
* E6	Necrophilia		352
* E6	Neptune's Tool		230
E4	Never Mind the Acid		369
* E3	Never, Never Land		113
* HVS	Nevermore Arete		258
* E6	New Fi'nial		89
* E4	New Jerusalem		303
Diff	Newstones Chimney		120
** V0-	Nexus		329
* HS	Nice Edge		238
* VS	Niche Arete		140
* HS	Niche Indirect		337
** S	Niche, The		140
* VDiff	Niche Wall		238
* E4	Night of Lust		117
* E4	Nightflight		158
* VS	Nightmare		300
* E3	Nil Carborundum Illigitimum		215
** S	Nil Desperandum		254
S	Nimrod		201
* S	Nithin, The		139
VS	No Idea		323
S	No Name		140
** E2	No Sign of Three		341
* S	No So Central Route		45
*** E5	No Time to Pose		256
* VS	Noah's Crack		287
Diff	Noah's Pair		176
*** E5	Nobody Wept for Alec Trench		335
* VS	Noddy's Wall		244
VDiff	Nor Nor' Chimney		340
* E1	Nora Batty (Running Hill Pits)		274
S	Norah Batty (also Running Hill Pits)		280
* S	North Buttress Arete		130
* VS	North Buttress Arete Direct		130
Mod	North Cave		340
* VDiff	North Climb		210
* VS	North Tier Climb		186
* HS	North Wall		210
* E5	Northern Ballet		235
* E6	Northern Comfort		72
* HVD	Nose Direct		132
* HS	Nose, The (Castle Naze)		139
* VS	Nose, The (Wilderness)		238
* E1	Nosepicker		56
* E4	Nosey Parker		216
* Diff	Notch, The (Helsby)		354
* VS	Notch, The (Hen Cloud)		94
* HVS	November Cracks		94
* Mod	Nowt		238
*** VS	Nozag		142
* E4	Nuke the Whale		258
* HVS	Nursery Arete		139
* HS	Nutmeg		121
* V2	Nutmeg Groove		121
* E1	Nutted by Reality		94
E6	O'Grady's Incurable Itch		215
* VDiff	Oak Leaf Crack		323
* VS	Oak Leaf Wall		323
* VDiff	Oak Tree Chimney		337
* E3	Oak Tree Wall		147
* VDiff	Oblique Crack		348
*** E8	Obsession Fatale		81
* HVS	Obyoyo		263
*** E1	Ocean Wall		265
* E3	Ocean's Border, The		265
* VDiff	Ogden		54
* HS	Ogden Arete		54
* VDiff	Ogden Recess		54
* E3	Old Fogey		117
*** E5	Old Fogey Direct		117
* HVS	Old Triangle, The	213	214
* E1	Olympus Explorer		158
Diff	Omelette Crack		202
* HVD	Omicron Buttress		206
* E3	Once in a Blue Moon		180
* V2	One Move		371
* E3	One of These Days		368
E3	One of These Days Direct		368
* E4	One of These Days Direct Finish		368
* E1	One Step		374
* E2	One-way Ticket		228
* VS	Orang Arete		195
* HVD	Orange Corner		323
* HS	Orange Crack		322
* VDiff	Orange Groove		322
* VS	Orange Peel		308
E3	Orange Squash		323
* VS	Orange Wall		322
* HVS	Orchestral Crack		286
* HS	Order		339
* E8	Order of the Phoenix		229
* HVD	Ordinary Route (Frodsham)		362
* Mod	Ordinary Route (Shining Clough)		200
* E2	Orgasmo		170
* S	Original Route		201
*** E2	Original Route (Bladstones)		124
* VDiff	Original Route (New Mills Tor)		148
E1	Orm and Cheep		140
* VS	Ornithologist's Corner		228
** E6	Ou est le Spit?		91
* VS	Our Doorstep		154
* E1	Outdoor Pursuits Cooperative, The		63
Diff	Outlook		154
* VS	Outside Edge		341
* E5	Over the Moors		254
* VDiff	Overhang Crack		337
VDiff	Overhanging Arete		134
* VS	Overhanging Chimney (Run Hill Pits)		278
* VDiff	Overhanging Chimney (Wimberry)		228
* VDiff	Overhanging Chockstone Crack		138

Route Index 381

Grade	Route	Photo	Page
** VS	Overhanging Crack		343
Diff	Overhanging Crack, The (Frodsham)		365
* VS	Overhanging Crack, The (Helsby)		352
* VB	Overhanging Wall, The		365
** HVS	Overlapper		342
S	Overlapping Wall		135
HS	Overlooked Groove, The		148
* HVD	Oversite		54
* HS	'Owd on Arete		246
* Mod	Owt		238
S	Oyster Slab		354
* VS	Oyster Slab Direct		354
* VS	Oyster Slab Route III		354
* VS	Oyster Slab Super Direct		354
* NL	Pacifist, The		374
* E5	Padarn Dance		369
S	Pagan Wall		337
** HVS	Pagan's Direct		337
* VS	Pagan's Progress		337
*** E6	Painted Rumour		88
* VS	Palais Glide		286
VS	Paleface		268
* E2	Palmistry		341
* E1	Palpitation		243
E1	Pan Crack		176
* HVS	Pantagruel		279
* V1	Pants		365
E1	Papillon		262
* V1	Parabola		329
* V3	Parabola Direct		329
HS	Paradise Crack		279
** E2	Paradox		306
E3	Parallax		281
** S	Parallel Cracks		323
* E6	Parallel Lines		101
*** E7	Paralogism	85	90
* E1	Parapluie		357
* E5	Parasite		306
** HVS	Parker's Eliminate		222
* E6	Parker's Mood		369
* HVS	Parliamentary Climb		177
** V2	Parr's Crack		329
E5	Passport to the Pits		279
E1	Pat's Parched		111
* E3	Pathfinder		356
* E4	Paul's Arete		237
* S	Paul's Perambulation		237
* HVS	Pavanne		343
* E5	Peace Process, The		217
* E1	Peak Arete		222
E1	Peanuts		308
VS	Pear Chimney		156
* V3	Pearce's Route		365
VDiff	Peat Climb		244
E2	Pebble Mill		271
* HVS	Pebbledash		74
* Diff	Pedestal Climb		181
* VS	Pedestal Corner		250
*** HVD	Pedestal Route		88
* S	Pedestal Wall		162
VS	Peg Free		326
* E1	Pegasus Left-hand		184
* E1	Pegasus Right-hand		184
* VS	Pencil Slim		154
VS	Pendulum Swing		341
HVS	Pendulum Swing Direct		341
S	Penniless Crack		174
** VDiff	Perambulator Parade		124
** VDiff	Perched Block Arete		54
* Diff	Perched Flake		115
NL	Pernod and Black		368
* V3	Persistence		60
HVS	Perverted Staircase		82
* E6	Peter and the Wolf		100
* E3	Pex Wall		374
* E4	Phaestus		278
*** HVD	Phallic Crack		108
E3	Phantom		201
V4	Philharmoni		372
*** V3	Phoenix Climb	193	195
* HVS	Piano Stool		141
V1	Pickpocket		296
V2	Pickpocket Direct		296
*** E2	Piece of Mind		81
* HVS	Piece of Pie		265
* HVS	Piece of Pipe		268
S	Pieces of Eight		168
* E6	Piedra Verde		234
* E2	Piety		231
VS	Pigeon Corner		188
* E1	Pigeonhole Arete		348
* HVS	Pigeonhole Wall		348
* VS	Piggy and the Duke		157
* VS	Piggy's Crack		146
** E6	Pigs Direct		320
* E5	Pigs on the Wing		320
*** V6	Pigswill		329
* HVS	Pile Driver		116
* HS	Pilgrim's Progress		140
** HS	Pillar Ridge		206
* E1	Pinball Wizard		228
* VS	Pincer		75
E1	Pinch, The		97
* E4	Pindles Numb		69
VDiff	Pinnacle Arete (Castle Naze)		138
* VS	Pinnacle Arete (Skyline)		52
VDiff	Pinnacle Crack (Castle Naze)		138
VS	Pinnacle Crack (Shining Clough)		201
Diff	Pinnacle Crack (Skyline)		52
* HVS	Pinnacle Face (Hen Cloud)		103
* VS	Pinnacle Face (Shining Clough)		201
Diff	Pinnacle Gully		161
* HVS	Pinnacle Rib		103
VS	Pinocchio		260
* VS	Pint of Beer		202
E3	Pipe Inspector		278
VS	Pipe of Peace		268
* E1	Pipe Spanner		278
* E3	Pipe-line		268
* VS	Pisa		199
* HVS	Pisa Direct		199
*** HVS	Pisa Super Direct	199	199
** V4	Pisa Traverse		371
* VB	Pisa Wall		370
VS	Piston Groove		95
HVS	Pitoned Crack		140
E4	Plankton		142
E1	Plastic Saddle		199
* E4	Play it Safe		267
HVS	Playground Twist		159
** E5	Please Lock Me Away		302
VDiff	Plin, The		258
* VDiff	Plinth Chimney		258
* HVS	Plonker, The		256
* VS	Plumb Line	272	279
HVD	Plumber's Passage		162
** E4	Plumbertime		160
* HVS	Poacher's Crack		187
* VS	Pocked Wall		264
E1	Pocket Battle		157
* VDiff	Pocket Wall (Hobson Moor)		223
* VS	Pocket Wall (Kinder Downfall)	189	188
HS	Pocket Wall (Ramshaw)		117
E1	Pod Crack		140
* E2	Poise, The		148
* HVS	Poisonous Python		70
* V5	Polar Bear		370
* VS	Poltergeist		228
*** V3	Pond Traverse		331
** HVS	Popple, The		287
HVS	Porky's Wall		146
* S	Port Crack		115
** S	Portcullis Crack		45
* HVS	Portfolio		131
** E7	Possessed, The		231
S	Postman's Knock		264
* E2	Pot Belly		173
* E1	Poteen		214
E2	Pots		341
E2	Powerplay		195
*** E5	Pratabout		357
* HVS	Praying Mantle		120
* HVS	Prelude to Space		48
* E2	Press on Regardless		98
* E1	Press, The		117
E4	Primadonna		143
* HVS	Priscilla		208
* HVS	Priscilla Ridge		208
* E1	Private Display		59
* E3	Private Investigations		258
* E3	Privilege and Pleasure		157
* V2	Problem 1		100
E1	Proboscid, The		116
* Diff	Professor's Chimney		183
* VDiff	Professor's Chimney Direct		183
* E2	Prolapse		264
VDiff	Promontory Groove		161
* HVS	Prostration		110
* VDiff	Prow Corner		80
* HVD	Prow Corner Twin Cracks		80
** VDiff	Prow Cracks		80
* HVD	Prow Cracks Variations		80
E2	Prunin' the Duck		262
* HVD	Pseudo Crack		45
* V4	Psycho 2		269
* E4	Puffed Up		122
HS	Puffin		281
VS	Pug		96
* E1	Pullet		95
S	Pulley		324
* V1	Pullover		362
Diff	Pulpit Chimney		176
** HVS	Pulpit Ridge		254
* E3	Pumping Irony		182
* E3	Punch		78
* E1	Punter, The		161
* HS	Pygmy Wall (Alderman)		271
HVS	Pygmy Wall (Standing Stones)		264
E1	Quasimodo		294
** S	Question Mark		246
* E2	Question Time		246
* VS	Quickstep		286
*** E1	Rack, The		375
* E1	Raggald's Wall		183
* E4	Raid, The		97
** VS	Rainbow Crack		103
* Diff	Rainbow, The		202
* E4	Raindrop		221
S	Ralph's Mantelshelves		55
VB	Ramble		375
** VDiff	Rambling Route		311
* VS	Ramp, The		286
*** E4	Ramshaw Crack		113
** VDiff	Rappel Wall		326
** HVS	Raven Rib		258
* Diff	Raven Rock Gully		71
* VS	Raven Rock Gully Left-hand		71
*** E7	Ray's Roof	118	124
* S	Razor Crack		173
VS	Reachy		281
HVD	Recess Chimney		96
* E2	Recoil Rib		165
* E3	Redemption of a Grit Pegging Antichrist		149
HS	Rejoyce		165
VS	Remembrance Corner		312
* E4	Renaissance		268
** HVS	Renegade		269
E1	Repetition		282
HVS	Republic Groove		217
* HVS	Requiem for Tired Fingers		45
* HS	Reset Portion of Galley 37		84
* V1	Retina		370
** VS	Reunion Crack	92	97
* E3	Rhododendron Arete		291
** E2	Rhododendron Buttress		291
* HVS	Rhodren		78
* VS	Rhynose		122
* VDiff	Rib and Face		271
Mod	Rib and Slab		133
* S	Rib and Wall		245
** S	Rib Chimney		101
* VS	Rib Crack		101
HVD	Rib Right-hand, The		130
Diff	Rib, The (Roaches Upper)		91
* Diff	Rib, The (Windgather)		130
S	Rib Wall		91
V2	Rick's Reach		360
VS	Rickshaw Ridge		168
* HVS	Riddler		279
V2	Right Arete		121
* VDiff	Right Chimney		246
VS	Right Embrasure		244
* S	Right Fork Chimney		184
* HVS	Right Monolith, The		257
* E3	Right of Pie		265
VS	Right Route Right		89
*** VDiff	Right Route (Roaches Upper)		89
VDiff	Right Route (Shing Clough)		202
S	Right Triplet Crack		135
** HVS	Right Twin Chimney (Kinder Downfall)		182
HVD	Right Twin Chimney (Laddow)		209
* VS	Right Twin Crack		103
V0	Right Wall, The		365
S	Right-hand Block Crack		59
VDiff	Right-hand Crack (Castle Naze)		138
* VDiff	Right-hand Crack (Frodsham)		363
V0	Right-hand Route (Frodsham)		360
* HS	Right-hand Route (Roaches Upper)		90
** S	Right-hand Route (Skyline)		50
*** V3	Ripple		120
* HVS	Rippler, The		108
* HVS	Rizla		256
* Diff	Roaches Ridge, The		81
* V1	Robbery		375
** E2	Robert		162
* E2	Robot		162
VS	Rock Bottom		154
HVS	Rock Reptile		181
* E2	Rock Trivia		107
HVD	Rocking Stone Gully		81
VDiff	Rocking Stone Ridge		45
* VS	Rodeo		185
* E6	Roller Coaster		114
* E1	Rollup		256
* HVS	Roman Candle		59
* E2	Roman Nose		59
* VS	Roman Roads		170
* E1	Romeo Error, The		343
* VS	Roof Climb		98
* HVD	Rooster		82
* HVS	Roscoe's Wall		90
S	Rosehip		122
* VS	Rotunda Buttress		86
Mod	Rotunda Gully		86
VDiff	Round Chimney		173
* E1	Round Table		90
* E1	Round Up		168
** HS	Route 1 (Cows Mouth)		342
* VS	Route 1 (Dovestones)		242
* VDiff	Route 1 (Laddow)		206
* VS	Route 1 (Windgather)		135
* VS	Route 1.5		134
** HVS	Route 2 (Cows Mouth)		342
* VS	Route 2 (Dovestones)		242
HVD	Route 2 (Laddow)		206
* VS	Route 2 (Windgather)		134
VDiff	Route 3		206

Route Index

Grade	Route	Photo	Page
S	Route 4		206
*** HS	Route I (Wimberley)		232
*** VS	Route II (Wimberley)		232
E1	Route Minus One		206
** VS	Route One		291
HS	Route Right		342
VS	Rubber Crack		114
VS	Rubber-faced Arete		246
VDiff	Rubber-faced Wall		246
HVS	Rubberneck		60
** E2	Ruby Tuesday		87
NL	Rum and Cocaine		368
*** E6	Run Wild, Run Free		312
* HS	Runner Route		84
V7	S & M		120
* E7	S-Groove, The	317	319
* E2	Sacrilege		231
*** E1	Safety Net	57	55
* S	Safety Plin		258
* E5	Sagittarius Flake		278
* VS	Samarkand		302
E4	Sampson		201
*** E3	San Melas	51, 7	50
E1	Sandman, The		146
* E4	Sands of Time		60
VS	Sandy Crack		343
HVS	Sard		342
** E3	Satin Sapphire		334
HVS	Saturday Crack		320
* E4	Satyr		196
VDiff	Saucer, The		45
* E4	Saucius Digitalis		196
*** HVS	Saul's Crack		86
* E5	Sauria		103
* E1	Savage Breast, The		173
* E4	Savage Stone		319
** E4	Scale the Dragon		223
E2	Scalped Flat Top		161
VS	Scarface		247
* HS	Scarlet Wall		90
* E3	Schoolies		71
* E4	Schwartzennegger Mon Amour		303
** HVS	Scimitar (Tintwistle)		214
VDiff	Scimitar (Wilton 1)		311
*** E5	Scoop de Grace		278
* HVS	Scoop Direct		141
*** HVS	Scoop Face	136	141
* E1	Scoop Face Direct		141
* E1	Scoop Wall		141
E3	Scooped Surprise		114
V1	Scraper		328
* HS	Scratch Crack		122
* VS	Scratchor, The		174
* VS	Scratchnose Crack		262
* E3	Screaming Abdabs, The		268
* E3	Screaming Meemies		294
E3	Scree? Pain!		343
* E2	Screwy		343
* E6	Script for a Tier		49
** E7	Scuttle Buttin'		250
* E2	Scythe, The		221
* VS	Sea Route		242
HS	Seazy		342
Diff	Second Triplet		247
* HVS	Second's Advance		100
HVS	Second's Retreat		100
VS	Seconds		281
* E4	Secrets of Dance		74
*** E8	Sectioned		230
* E1	Senile Saunter		350
VDiff	Sennapod		50
VDiff	Sennapod Crack		50
** E5	Septic Think Tank		302
* VS	Set Square		372
* E4	Seven Deadly Skins		177
* E4	Shaggy Dog		314
** E2	Shallow Green		318
* HVS	Shallow Groove		318
VDiff	Shandy		202
*** V0	Shark's Fin		117
* VDiff	Sheltered Crack		138
* E3	Sheppy		303
* E4	Shibb		303
** E7	Shining Path, The		59
*** E1	Shivers Arete		326
S	Short Chimney (Kinder South)		156
Diff	Short Chimney (Newstones)		120
E1	Short Corner		318
VB	Short Crack (Pex Hill)		375
* VS	Short Crack (Wimberley)		228
V1	Short Wall		120
** E1	Shortcomings		55
* HVS	Shotgun Grooves		187
** E2	Shroud, The		339
* E3	Shukokia		318
* E3	Sickbay Shuffle		231
HVD	Side Face		134
HS	Side-step		300
* E1	Sidestep		372
* HVS	Sidewalk		260
E5	Sidewinder		343
* HS	Sifta's Quid		81
S	Sifta's Quid Inside Route		81
E1	Sign of the Times		91
S	Silly Arete		247
** E4	Simpkins' Overhang		82
** E6	Sinbad		369
S	Singer Corner		181
** E3	Sinn Fein		214
* S	Siren's Rock		208
** E6	Sketching Wildly		110
** E8	Skin and Wishbones		89
* E2	Skytrain		52
** S	Slab and Arete		52
Diff	Slab and Saddle		242
** HS	Slab Climb		233
* VS	Slab Crossing		342
VDiff	Slab Gully		233
* VS	Slab Route		361
* VDiff	Slab, The		337
VB	Slab Variant		331
VS	Slabmaster		342
* HVP	Slant Start, The		131
* VS	Slanter		254
HVD	Slanting Crack (Castle Naze)		138
Diff	Slanting Crack (Frodsham)		361
* VS	Slanting Horror, The		264
* S	Slanting Slab		319
** HS	Slice, The		174
S	Sliding Chimney		172
* VS	Slim Jim		340
* HVD	Slime Chimney		324
Diff	Slime Crack		255
* V1	Slimer		330
** E1	Slimline		100
E4	Slin and Thippy		341
* VS	Slipoff Slab		246
* HVS	Slippery Jim		66
* E1	Slipshod		324
HVS	Slipstreams		94
** HVD	Sloping Crack		234
** S	Sloth, The		89
** E1	Slowhand		94
* VS	Sly Corner		123
V0	Sly Direct		123
* HVS	Sly Mantelshelf, The		123
** V4	Sly Stallone		122
* V1	Sly Super Direct		123
* E2	Small		265
HVS	Small Buttress		98
S	Small Wall		131
** E3	Smear Test	79	75
* HS	Smiler's Corner		260
* VS	Smun		59
* VS	Snake, The		122
*** V11	Snatch		296
* S	Sneck		322
* E1	Sneeze		107
* E1	Sniffer Dog		257
* VS	Snooker Route		164
VS	Snorter		161
S	Snow Crack		238
VDiff	Snow + Rock		157
* VS	Soapflake		216
** E3	Sobeit		312
S	Socialist's Arete		168
VDiff	Sodom (Kinder Downfall)		188
* E1	Sodom (Running Hill Pits)		279
* E1	Solid Geometry	12	99
HVS	Solstice		196
E2	Some Product		196
E2	Something Better Change		70
** E7	Sons of the Desert		158
* E6	Soot Monkey, The		307
* E3	Sorcerer, The		96
* E2	Sorcerer's Apprentice, The		237
E1	South Buttress Arete Direct		135
* Mod	South Buttress Crack		135
* Diff	South Chimney		341
* VDiff	South Wall		181
** VDiff	Southern Arete		206
* E5	Space Oddity		229
* E4	Space Probe		101
* E4	Space Shuffle		229
* E4	Spacerunner		172
** E2	Spanner Wall	277	276
* VS	Spare Rib		54
HVS	Spectrum		54
* HVS	Spider Crack (Running Hill Pits)		274
* HVS	Spider Crack (Wilton 1)		308
* E5	Spiderman		374
E4	Spike		312
** Diff	Spike Chimney		180
* E1	Spin-up		185
*** VDiff	Splash Arete		297
** E8	Splashback	292	297
* S	Split Block Climb		336
* HS	Split Block Direct		336
HVS	Split Block Overhang		336
E1	Split Personality		52
** E2	Spog, The		237
* E5	Spooky		350
* E2	Spurt of Spurts		248
Diff	Square Chimney (Dovestones)		244
Mod	Square Chimney (Kinder Downfall)		185
Diff	Square Chimney (Skyline)		55
VDiff	Square Cut		164
* V2	Square Cut Face		121
* VB	Square Four		370
* HVD	Squashed Finger		133
E4	Squatter's Rights/Blue Jade		172
*** S	Squirrrer's Chimney		233
* V2	St Paul		375
VB	St Stephen's Wall		360
** VS	Stable Cracks		199
VDiff	Stag Party		201
* HVD	Staircase (Castle Naze)		141
** Mod	Staircase (Laddow)		206
Mod	Staircase, The (Cadshaw)		337
Mod	Staircase, The (Windgather)		130
HS	Stairway Arete		238
** HS	Stairway Flake Crack		238
* S	Stalin		62
* V6	Stallone Arete		122
*** E6	Staminade		368
* E2	Stampede		168
* E1	Starboard Crack		115
Diff	Start		318
** VDiff	Starters		339
* S	Starvation Chimney		231
HVS	Steamboat		165
* E1	Steamer, The		165
* HVS	Steeple, The		146
* S	Step in the Clouds		294
E2	Steve's Dilemma		222
* E1	Sticky Fingers		281
* E1	Stiff Little Fingers		216
** E5	Stigmata		154
E1	Sting, The		258
*** E3	Stingray		351
* S	Stirrup		242
* V3	Stokes' Line		100
* E5	Stone Loach, The		96
* HVS	Stonewall Crack		147
* VS	Storm		303
Mod	Straight Chimney		209
Diff	Straight Crack (Kinder South)		154
S	Straight Crack (Laddow)		209
* VB	Straight Crack (Pex Hill)		370
* HS	Straight Crack (Roaxhes Lower)		78
* E4	Strain Station		55
** E3	Stranger than Friction		256
E1	Stranglehold		59
* E4	Strappado		248
* VS	Strenuosity		254
* VS	Struggle		133
* E4	Stuck		263
* HS	Studio		140
* S	Subsidiary Chimney		195
* VS	Substance		55
* HVS	Summary		281
* E4	Sumo Cellulite		81
* VS	Sunbeam		303
** E6	Sunday at Chapel		68
* E2	Sunset Crack		287
** E3	Sunshine Super Glue		221
* E2	Sunshine Superman		222
* V1	Sunstroke		281
*** E3	Supercrack		312
* V0	Superdirect		362
** V1	Superwall	359	362
* VS	Surprise		228
* HVS	Surprise Arete		228
* E2	Suture		156
* E4	Swan Bank		74
* HVD	Swan Crack		244
* VS	Swan Down		244
*** E3	Swan, The		74
* V1	Sweater		362
* V0	Sweeney Arete		375
** E3	Swine, The		320
* HS	Swing Up		280
* VS	Swinger		71
* VS	Swinger, The		117
* E4	Swot and Heaty		341
** E5	T' Big Surrey		165
E2	T'rival Traverse		107
E2	Tall Stories		159
* VS	Taller Overhang		131
** HVS	Talliot		282
* HVS	Tally Not		108
* V3	Tank Top		362
* E3	Tap Dance		233
* E1	Tax Collector, The		242
* VS	Tea Leaf		323
* S	Tealeaf Crack		84
** HS	Technical Slab		88
NL	Technicolour Yawn		349
** E1	Teck Crack		68
* V4	Teck Crack Direct		68
* V9	Teck Crack Super Direct		68
* VS	Temptation Crack		237
* VS	Ten Minutes before the Worm		335
* V3	Tequila Sunrise		372
V7	Termination		372
*** HVS	Terror Cotta		301

Route Index 383

Grade	Route	Photo	Page
* E3	Terrorist, The		168
* E4	That's All it Takes		297
* VS	Thermometer Crack		228
*** E5	Thin Air		81
* HS	Thin Crack (Back Forest)		45
* VB	Thin Crack (Frodsham)		363
* V1	Thin Crack Superdirect		363
VS	Thin Cracks		138
*** E6	Thing on a Spring		74
* E2	Third Degree Burn		84
* E3	Third Party		301
* Diff	Third Triplet		247
* E3	This Poison		100
* HVD	Thompson's Buttress Route 1		103
HVD	Thompson's Buttress Route 2		103
E5	Thorn in the Side-wall		231
Mod	Three Corner Climb		319
* E1	Three Flakes of Man		161
** VS	Three Notch Slab	285	286
* VS	Throsher		319
* VS	Thrug		54
V3	Thumb Screw		371
* E1	Thunder		324
* E1	Tickled Pink		269
* VS	Tier's End		110
*** E5	Tierdrop		110
** E1	Tighe's Arete		223
* E4	Tighten Up Yer Nuts		276
* E3	Tim Benzadrino		61
* E1	Time		297
* E2	Time Out		115
* V4	Time Passages		370
* E7	Time Regained		353
** HVD	Time to be Had		56
* E1	Timepiece		296
* E4	Tin Man		274
* HS	Tin Tin Wall		172
* VS	Tiny Tim		250
* V10	Tit Grip		110
* VS	Toadstool Crack		200
* VS	Tobacco Road		56
* VDiff	Toe Nail		132
* HVS	Toe Rail		45
* HVS	Toiseach		258
** E5	Tom's Roof		361
* E4	Tomahawk		267
* V0	Tombstone		375
* VS	Tombstone, The		237
* V1	Tomintool		282
* E1	Tony's Terror		287
* V1	Too Bold for Steve Boot		372
** E2	Topaz	53	55
E4	Torture		108
* HVS	Toss up		185
* HVS	Totem Corner		267
* HS	Touch of Spring		264
* VS	Tower Arete (Dovestones)		244
* HVS	Tower Arete (Laddow)		210
* Diff	Tower Chimney		54
* HVS	Tower Eliminate		54
** VS	Tower Face (Laddow)	190	209
* E2	Tower Face (Skyline)		54
* E3	Tower of Bizarre Delights, The		83
* VDiff	Tower Ridge		247
E8	Toxic Bilberrys		307
*** E5	Track of the Cat		48
V3	Tradesman's Entrance		365
* HS	Traditional		133
* VS	Tramline Cracks		175
* HVS	Tranquillity		264
* VS	Transformation (Anglezarke)		300
* HVS	Transformation (New Mills Tor)		147
** E4	Traveller in Time		106
* HVD	Traverse and Crack		154
E3	Treadmill		369
VDiff	Tree Chimney		103
E4	Trepidation		122
* HVS	Trial Balance		171
* HS	Tricouni Crack		114
** E1	Trident, The		230
* Mod	Trigular		295
* Mod	Trinnacle Chimney		257
** HVS	Trinnacle East	24	257
* E1	Trinnacle West		257
S	Trio		258
* VDiff	Trio Chimney		55
* VS	Trio Wall		188
* E1	Triple Point		49
* VS	Trivial Pursuits		154
* HVS	Trivial Traverse		107
** E1	Trojan		169
S	Trojan Crack		354
* S	Trojan Nose		354
*	Trouble with Women is..., The		263
** E3	True Grit	253	257
* HVS	Trungel Crack		199
** E5	Tryche		341
* HVS	Tum Tum		173
VDiff	Tuppence Ha'penny		206
** E1	Turtle		268
* E3	Tweeker		318
** E3	Tweeter and the Monkey Man		174
** E4	Twilight Zone, The		234
* HS	Twin Caves Crack		356
*** VS	Twin Crack Corner	261	262
Diff	Twin Cracks (Blackstone)		341
Diff	Twin Cracks (Fordsham)		360
Diff	Twin Cracks (Wilton 3)		322
* S	Twin Cracks (Wimberry)		233
* E1	Twin Scoops Direct		373
* E1	Twin Scoops (Helsby)		353
* HVS	Twin Scoops (Pex Hill)		373
E2	Twin Scoops Right-hand		373
S	Twin Thin		45
*** HVS	Twisted Smile		175
* HVD	Twister		171
* HVS	Twixt		339
* V0-	Two Eyes		370
* VB	Two Step		330
VDiff	Two Step Crack		348
V1	Two Step Left-hand		330
S	Two Twist Chimney		174
HVD	Two-step, The		142
Diff	Typists' Chimney		199
E3	Ugly Bloke, The		143
** E8	Ultimate Sculpture		107
* E2	Ultra Direct, The		114
* E2	Umbrella, The		357
VS	Un-natural Act		149
S	Unctious		279
* V8	Undercut Problem		297
VS	Undun Crack		255
* VS	Unfinished Arete		255
** E3	Unicorn		373
HS	Unicorn Cracks		199
* V3	Unjust		328
* E2	Unknown (Froldsham)		361
NL	Unknown (Helsby)		355
E4	Unknown Quantity, The		354
E4	Unknown Wall		361
* E1	Unstuck		263
*** HS	Untouchable, The		108
*** HS	Upper Tor Wall	4	160
S	Upset		260
VS	Ure		170
HS	Usurer		163
S	V-Corner		138
V3	Vague Groove		296
* VS	Valhalla Crack		201
** VS	Valkyrie	42	72
* HVS	Valkyrie Direct		72
* E3	Valley of Ultravixens		123
* E4	Valve, The		83
S	Vanishing Groove		195
* V3	Varicose		121
* V3	Varicose Traverse		121
* VB	Verdi Corner		330
* VB	Verdi Ramp		330
* VB	Verdi Wall		330
* V3	Verdigris		330
* V3	Verdinand		330
E4	Veteran Cosmic Rocker		311
*** S	Via Dolorosa		71
*** S	Via Principia		195
* HVS	Viaduct Crack		148
* E2	Viaduct Wall		148
VDiff	Vice, The		202
* VS	Victory		95
* E3	Village Green		234
* E2	Violent Outburst		156
VDiff	Virgin, The		280
* HVS	Virgin's Dilemma		315
* HVS	Vishnu		303
** S	Vivien		262
* HVS	Vixen, The		123
** E8	Vortex		335
** E2	Wafer Wall		348
* E5	Waiting for an Alibi		268
V2	Wall		296
** E2	Wall and Bulge		234
S	Wall and Crack Climb		258
* S	Wall and Groove (Ramshaw)		106
* HVS	Wall and Groove (Tintwistle)		217
* V3	Wall and Mono		121
* VB	Wall and Traverse		364
* HVD	Wall Climb		131
* E4	Wall of China		256
* HVS	Wallaby Direct		83
* HS	Wallaby Wall		50
** E2	Walleroo		83
* S	Wampum Wall		269
E4	Wanna Buy a Bolt Kit?		220
* E1	War Wound		90
E5	Warcry		374
* E2	Warlock		374
E4	Warlord		374
* V0+	Warm Up		370
* E5	Warmonger		374
* HVS	Wasp, The (Hoghton Quarry)		291
E3	Wasp, The (Wilton 2)		319
** E4	Wasteland, The		237
HS	Watercourse		112
HS	Waterloo Climb		256
E2	Waterloo Wall		354
VB	Watery Arete		331
* HS	Weaver's Crach		280
** E3	Weaver's Wall		280
** E1	Web, The		374
* HS	Wedge		300
*** VS	Wedgewood Crack		256
* VS	Wedgewood Crack Direct		256
* VS	Wednesday Corner		335
** E3	Welcome to Greenfield, Gateway		255
* E3	Well Suited		154
* VDiff	Wellingtons		107
** E3	Wendigo, The		357
VDiff	West Buttress Direct		336
* HVS	West Ridge		201
VS	West Slab Direct		336
S	West Wall		336
* VDiff	West Wall Chimney		350
* S	West Wall Route 1		201
* VS	West's Wallaby		83
VDiff	Wet Corner		331
V0	Wet Foot		331
* HVS	Wheeze		56
* VS	Whilly's Whopper		108
E2	Whimper		348
VS	White Honkey		281
* HS	White Out		335
*** E3	White Slabs Bunt		312
* HS	Whittaker's Original		300
** V10	Who Needs Ready Brek?		60
V0	Wibble		329
*** E5	Wick Slip		112
* E4	Wicked Uncle Ernie		108
* HVS	Widfa		281
* V1	Widow, The		370
** HVS	Wild Thing		49
* Mod	Wilderness Gully East		239
E1	William the Conkerer		279
** E4	Willow Farm		48
* V6	Willy Simm's Silly Whim		370
** E1	Wilter, The		287
*** E3	Wilton Wall		320
* E6	Wimberry Overhang		229
E1	Wind Instrument		223
** VS	Wind Wall		169
* HS	Windbreaker		278
* VDiff	Windy Corner		350
* HS	Windy Corner Nose Finish		350
** E5	Windy Miller		159
* HVS	Windy Wall		339
** E4	Wine Gums		108
** E4	Wings of Unreason	33, 46	48
E1	Winter in Combat		59
* E2	Winter's Block		154
* E2	Wipe Out		314
** E2	Wire Brush Slab		174
* VS	Wisecrack		70
* Diff	Witch, The (Newstones)		122
** E2	Witch, The (Pex Hill)		374
* HVS	Witch's Hat, The		237
** E1	Wits' End		264
* E3	Wizard, The		374
HVD	Wobbling Corner		265
S	Woe is Me		175
*** VS	Womanless Wall		263
** E2	Wombat		83
** E2	Wombat Chimney		307
*** HVS	Wood's Climb		354
V5	Wraparound Arete		120
* HS	Wriggler, The		112
* VDiff	Wrinkled Buttress		242
*** E6	Wristcutter's Lullaby		230
* HS	Yankee Jam		62
E4	Yarn Spinner		280
* E2	Yellow Brick Road		180
* HVS	Yellow Crack		247
E3	Yellow Peril		269
* E4	Yellow-bellied Gonk, The		228
** E2	Yerth	197	197
*** HVD	Yinosd Rib		238
** HVD	Yong		70
* S	Yong Arete		70
** E6	Yorick's Crack		278
E3	Yorkshire Longfellow		264
* E4	Young Turks		162
* VS	Z Crack		343
* VDiff	Z Route		348
S	Z Route Direct		348
VDiff	Zacharias		238
** HVS	Zarke		301
* E5	Zebra		177
* VDiff	Zig-a-Zag-a		142
*** VS	Zig-zag		185
* S	Zig-zag Crack		185
** E2	Zigger Zagger		373
* Diff	Zigzag		132
* HS	Zigzag Crack		142
* E2	Zyphyr		169

General Index and Map

Lancashire Map . 288	
Anglezarke	298
Blackstone Edge	340
Brownstones	327
Cadshaw Castle	336
Cow's Mouth Quarry	342
Denham	292
Egerton	332
Hoghton Quarry	290
Littleborough Area	338
Summit Quarry	339
Wilton 1	304
Wilton 2	316
Wilton 3	322

Chew Valley Map . . . 224	
Alderman	270
Den Lane	284
Dovestones Edge	240
Ravenstones	252
Running Hill Pits	272
Standing Stones	259
Upper Wilderness Valley	236
Upperwood Quarry	266
Wimberry	226

Bleaklow Map 191	
Hobson Moor Quarry	218
Laddow	204
Shining Clough	192
Tintwistle Knarr	212

Cheshire Map 344	
Frodsham	358
Helsby	346
Pex Hill	366

Kinder Map 151	
Kinder Downfall	178
Kinder North	166
Kinder South	152

Windgather Area Map . . 126	
Castle Naze	136
New Mills Tor	144
Windgather	128

Staffordshire Map 42	
Back Forest	44
Baldstones	124
Five Clouds	58
Hen Cloud	92
Newstones	118
Ramshaw	104
Roaches	64
Roaches Lower	66
Roaches Skyline	46
Roaches Upper	82

Access	8
Accommodation	19
Acknowledgments	10
Advertiser Directory	12
Area Table	38
BMC	9, 16
Bouldering	6
Bouldering Grades	28
British Trad Grade	28
Climbing Shops	20
Climbing Walls	22
Contents	3
Crag Symbols	Cover flap
Ethics	26
Gear	26
Grade Colour Codes	28
Graded List	32
Grades	28
Groups	26
Introduction	4
Logistics	14
Map Key	Cover flap
Mountain Rescue	16
Online Route Database	6
Other Guidebooks	30
Pubs	20
ROCKFAX Books	Cover flap
ROCKFAX Web Site	6
Route Index	376
Route Symbols	Cover flap
Symbol Key	Cover flap
Top Roping	26
Topo Key	Cover flap
Tourist Information Offices	16